BREAKOUT FROM
JUNO

FIRST CANADIAN ARMY
AND THE NORMANDY CAMPAIGN,
JULY 4–AUGUST 21, 1944

MARK ZUEHLKE

BREAKOUT FROM JUNO

Douglas & McIntyre

D&M PUBLISHERS INC.

Vancouver/Toronto/Berkeley

Douglas & McIntyre
An imprint of D&M Publishers Inc.
2323 Quebec Street, Suite 201
Vancouver BC Canada V5T 4S7
www.douglas-mcintyre.com

Cataloguing data available from Library and Archives Canada
ISBN 978-1-55365-325-7 (cloth)
ISBN 978-1-77100-067-3 (pbk.)
ISBN 978-1-55365-972-3 (ebook)

Editing by Kathy Vanderlinden
Copyediting by Ann-Marie Metten
Cover photograph by Lt. Ken Bell, Canada. Dept. of National Defence,
Library and Archives Canada, 1967-052 NPC, PA-132727
Typeset by Naomi MacDougall
Maps by C. Stuart Daniel/Starshell Maps
Map 8 based on sketch by Lt. Ken Gartley in "Battle Accounts Algonquins,
6–12 August," 145.2A1013(D1), DHH, DND, and base map Potigny, 2nd ed.,
scale 1:25,000, 1944 Mar. (France 1:25,000; sheet no. 40/14 S.W.)
(GSGS: 4347), grid ref 1449
Photos used with permission from Library and Archives Canada
Printed and bound in Canada by Friesens
Distributed in the U.S. by Publishers Group West

We gratefully acknowledge the financial support of the Canada Council
for the Arts, the British Columbia Arts Council, the Province of British Columbia
through the Book Publishing Tax Credit, and the Government of Canada
through the Canada Book Fund for our publishing activities.

And so I have decided the time has come to have a real "show down" on the eastern flank.

—*General Bernard Law Montgomery, July 14, 1944*

Forward, men! We've got to keep going!

—*Major Philip Griffin, Black Watch Regiment of Canada, July 25, 1944*

It was just a job to do because I realized that they were out to get me. If I didn't stop them, well, I guess that's the basics, isn't it, of war? You get the other guy before he gets you...I was never a killer or any-thing, never wished to kill anyone, but I know I did.

—*Private Albert Clare Huffman, Argyll and Sutherland Highlanders*

[CONTENTS]

THE MONTHS OF July and August 1944 saw the greatest cata-
clysm of combat on the western European front during all of
World War II. More than 2.5 million Americans, Britons, Canadians,
Poles, and Germans locked in unrelenting battle within the narrow
confines of a small part of Normandy. Here in the blood-soaked
farm fields, *bocage,* woods, towns, and cities, soldiers fought with a
desperate fury. Both sides knew the war was being decided in this
conflict. When it ended, the Allies advanced towards victory, while
the Germans could only delay that inevitability for as long as
possible.

Yet these two months—generally considered the crux of the Normandy Campaign—have always languished in the shadows of World
War II history, eclipsed by that longest of days, June 6, 1944. D-Day,
the great all-or-nothing gamble of the amphibious invasion of Normandy, is without doubt the climactic event of the western Allies'
war on Germany. Had the Canadians failed at Juno Beach, or the
British at Gold and Sword, or the Americans at Utah and Omaha,
World War II may have had a different outcome. And so, perhaps
rightfully, it is the invasion that captures the popular imagination.

Despite the violence of the fight to gain the sand and stave off the
hard counterattacks that followed from June 7 to 12, the long series
of offensive operations in July and August were more costly.

Throughout attempts to break free of the beaches and surge into the French heartland, victory was never assured and proved repeatedly elusive—each Canadian win often reversed by a grim and bloody defeat.

Perhaps that is why this campaign is seldom accorded its unique and rightful place. *Breakout from Juno* is the first major account of First Canadian Army's operations over the course of these two months. Generally, this part of the army's story has been encompassed in accounts running from June 6 to the closing of the Falaise Gap on August 21. A few writers have focused only on one or two specific army operations—Operation Totalize, for example. The result is that much of the scope and significance of the fighting during those forty-eight days has been abbreviated, diminished, and, finally, lost.

One of the most daunting tasks in telling this story was managing the wealth of historical information available. The Canadian Army generated masses of reports, after-actions accounts, and interviews with officers and the occasional other rank to build a record of events. Failures, such as the disastrous July 25 Black Watch attack at Verrières Ridge, were extensively analyzed to determine what went wrong, how such a debacle could be prevented in future, and who, if anyone, was ultimately to blame. All of this information has greatly informed this book.

But historical records are not enough to bring history to life. For that I turned, once again, to the voices of the veterans. With so few still living and able to discuss their experiences, this book depends more on accounts hunted down in archives and a host of other sources. As before, the task is then to blend official accounts with the personal story. The battlefield is a place of chaos. Often exhausted and disoriented when they were young men fighting for their lives in a foreign land, old soldiers struggled to place a certain incident into the mosaic of an extended campaign. Many times it was access to extensive historical records that enabled a veteran's unique experience of a few brief moments to be situated in time and place. These personal stories also informed and, in some cases, corrected the "official" accounts.

The Canadian Battle Series recognizes and honours the experiences and sacrifices of our soldiers during a time when a generation was called upon to step forward in the cause of world freedom. World War II was, as Studs Terkel has written, "the last good war."[1] But it was also a time when many young soldiers from all parts of our sprawling nation went into combat one day after another with only the scantest hope that they and their friends would live to see loved ones and home again.

ACKNOWLEDGEMENTS

RESEARCHING THIS BOOK, as is true for each Canadian Battle Series volume, is not a singular exercise. Many people contribute enthusiastically with their knowledge, time, and memories. Veteran Charles Goodman and I exchanged a series of e-mails and telephone calls discussing some little-documented periods of the South Saskatchewan Regiment's experiences. It was fortunate he was there and could shed light on those events. Other veterans sent correspondence or provided interviews. Everyone is listed in the bibliography.

Over the years, Ken MacLeod has gathered a large collection of audio and video interviews with veterans. These include luminary figures, such as Major General George Kitching, but also many soldiers of lower ranks. Ken has graciously shared the entire collection.

In France, we were fortunate to stay at the Priory in Gouvix (a beautiful old mansion spared destruction when Bomber Command was unable to locate the village due to low cloud and smoke from nearby bomb strikes). Host David Brewer was always able to help with directions to and from various battle sites. The Juno Beach Centre hosted a book signing that was well received.

Back at home, I was able to call upon two other friends in Normandy to answer questions that arose while I was writing. Paul Woodadge, a D-Day historian and tour guide, helped me sort out the

terrain of Bourguébus and Verrières Ridges and offered other helpful advice. Philippe Guérin also brought to bear his considerable
knowledge of the campaign, including tracking down the name of
the French Resistance guide who was killed while helping the
Regina Rifles patrol into Vaucelles on July 18.

Once again my Dutch colleague, Johan van Doorn, was a great
help with assembling the massive spreadsheets required to identify
every relevant document at Library and Archives Canada in Ottawa
that related to the campaign. Many would have been missed without
his fine organizational mind. It was a pleasure for us to link up with
him and Anneke in Normandy for a few short hours.

At Library and Archives Canada itself, Paul Marsden also helped
with accessing files, and the staff in the records room were always
supportive and willing to ensure that someone from far away was
not unnecessarily delayed in doing so. It was a similar story at the
Directorate of History and Heritage, Department of National
Defence. Carol Reid at the Canadian War Museum's archives scoured
the collection and provided a good number of interviews with veterans and other material. Staff at Special Collections, University of
Victoria, were also very helpful with ensuring that I was able to get
digital copies of every interview I sought.

Research and writing of this book was greatly assisted by a British Columbia Arts Council grant.

I remain indebted to Scott McIntyre at D&M Publishers Inc. for
his unfailing support of the Canadian Battle Series. These are difficult days in the publishing industry, both in Canada and worldwide.
Yet Scott remains committed to ensuring that the entire series continues to be available to readers. Kathy Vanderlinden was once again
welcome company through the editing process, always a tough job.
C. Stuart Daniel of Starshell Maps again stepped forward to provide
those so necessary maps. Agent Carolyn Swayze continues to help
keep this writing career on course with a steady hand to the financial
and business detail tiller.

In the inanimate realm, thanks to Serena, the U.K. voice of Gar-
min GPS, for its sometimes extraordinary ability to keep us on course
along the many narrow byways and lanes of the Normandy

countryside. When in doubt, there's always another roundabout to circle around until you're sure.

Back in the animate realm, I sincerely and gratefully thank my partner, Frances Backhouse, for sharing with me this journey across the vast landscape of a nation's history of war and also down those Norman byways and lanes. We have stood on a lot of battlefields together over the years, and I hope we continue to do so for many years to come.

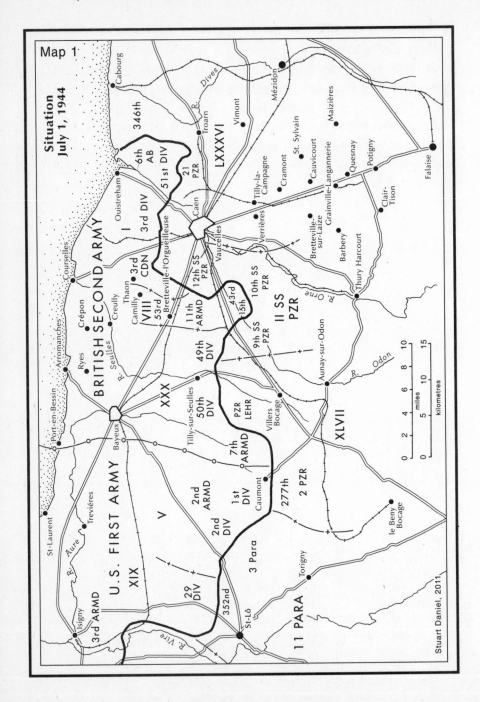

Map 1

Situation
July 1, 1944

Stuart Daniel, 2011

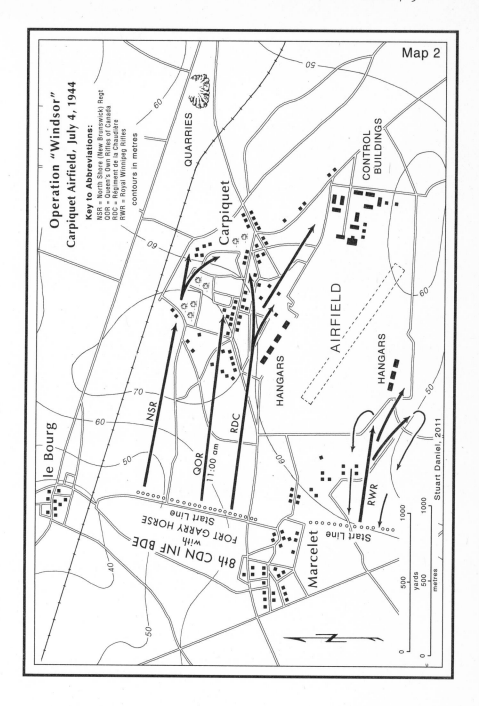

Map 2

Operation "Windsor"
Carpiquet Airfield, July 4, 1944

Key to Abbreviations:

NSR = North Shore (New Brunswick) Regt
QOR = Queen's Own Rifles of Canada
RDC = Régiment de la Chaudière
RWR = Royal Winnipeg Rifles

contours in metres

QUARRIES

Carpiquet

CONTROL
BUILDINGS

AIRFIELD

HANGARS

HANGARS

NSR

QOR

RDC

11:00 am

RWR

le Bourg

8th CDN INF BDE
with
FORT GARRY HORSE
Start Line

Start Line

Marcelet

Stuart Daniel, 2011

1000

1000

500

yards

500

metres

0

0

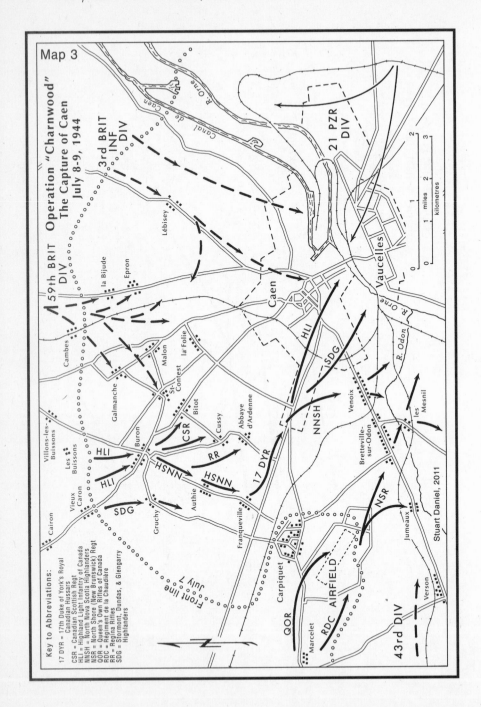

Map 3

Operation "Charnwood"
The Capture of Caen
July 8-9, 1944

59th BRIT DIV

3rd BRIT INF DIV

21 PZR DIV

Canal de Caen
R. Orne

Lébisey

la Bijude
Epron

Cambes

Caen

Vaucelles

R. Orne

Villons-les-Buissons

Les Buissons

Vieux Caron

Cairon

Galmanche

Malon
St. Contest
la Folie

Bitot
Cussy
Abbaye d'Ardenne

Buron

CSR

RR

R. Odon

les Mesnil

Venoix

Bretteville-sur-Odon

SDG

NNSH

17 DYR

HLI

HLI

HSNN

HSNN

Authie

Gruchy

SDG

Franqueville

NSR

Jumeaux

43rd DIV

Verson

QOR

Carpiquet

RDC AIRFIELD

Marcelet

Front line July 7

Stuart Daniel, 2011

Key to Abbreviations:

17 DYR = 17th Duke of York's Royal
            Canadian Hussars
CSR = Canadian Scottish Regt
HLI = Highland Light Infantry of Canada
NNSH = North Nova Scotia Highlanders
NSR = North Shore (New Brunswick) Regt
QOR = Queen's Own Rifles of Canada
RDC = Regiment de la Chaudière
RR = Regina Rifles
SDG = Stormont, Dundas, & Glengarry
            Highlanders

miles
kilometres

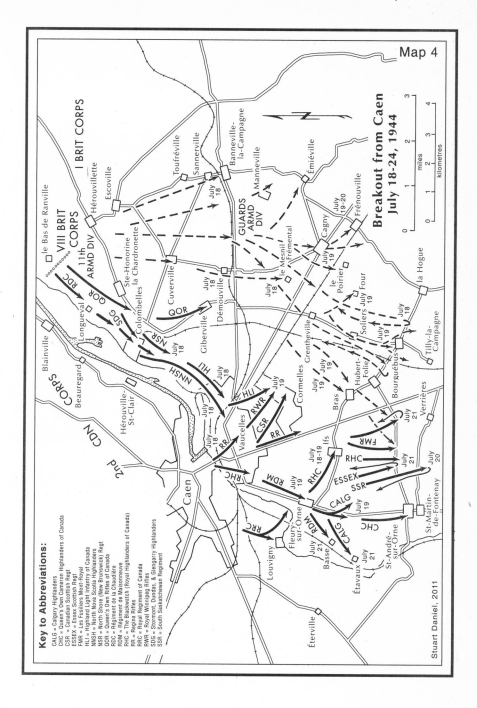

Map 4

Breakout from Caen
July 18-24, 1944

Key to Abbreviations:

CALG = Calgary Highlanders
CHC = Queen's Own Cameron Highlanders of Canada
CSR = Canadian Scottish Regt
ESSEX = Essex Scottish Regt
FMR = Les Fusiliers Mont-Royal
HLI = Highland Light Infantry of Canada
NNSH = North Nova Scotia Highlanders
NSR = North Shore (New Brunswick) Regt
QOR = Queen's Own Rifles of Canada
RDC = Régiment de la Chaudière
RDM = Régiment de Maisonneuve
RHC = The Blackwatch (Royal Highlanders of Canada)
RR = Regina Rifles
RRC = Royal Regiment of Canada
RWR = Royal Winnipeg Rifles
SDG = Stormont, Dundas, & Glengarry Highlanders
SSR = South Saskatchewan Regiment

Stuart Daniel, 2011

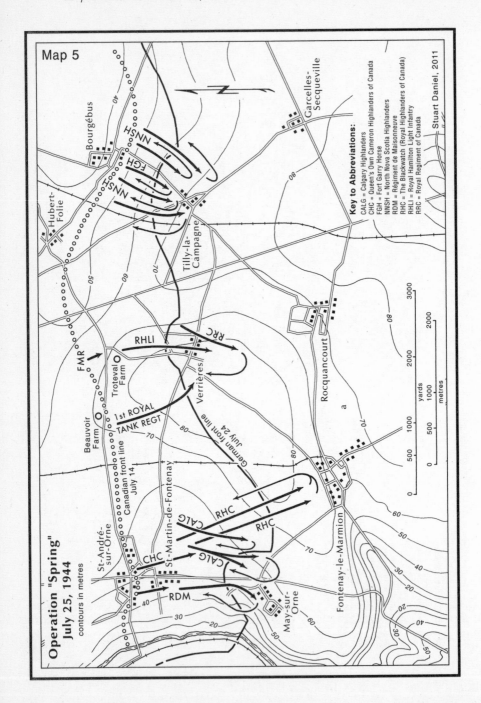

Map 5

Operation "Spring"
July 25, 1944
contours in metres

Key to Abbreviations:

CALG = Calgary Highlanders
CHC = Queen's Own Cameron Highlanders of Canada
FGH = Fort Garry Horse
NNSH = North Nova Scotia Highlanders
RDM = Régiment de Maisonneuve
RHC = The Blackwatch (Royal Highlanders of Canada)
RHLI = Royal Hamilton Light Infantry
RRC = Royal Regiment of Canada

Stuart Daniel, 2011

Bourgébus

Hubert-Folie

Garcelles-Secqueville

Tilly-la-Campagne

HSNN
FGH
NNSH

RHLI
RRC

FMR
Troteval Farm

Verrières

1st ROYAL
TANK REGT

Beauvoir Farm

German front line
July 24

Canadian front line
July 14

Rocquancourt

CALG
RHC
RHC

CHC

St-André-sur-Orne

St-Martin-de-Fontenay

CALG

RDM

May-sur-Orne

Fontenay-le-Marmion

yards
metres

3000

2000

2000

1000

1000

500

500

0

0

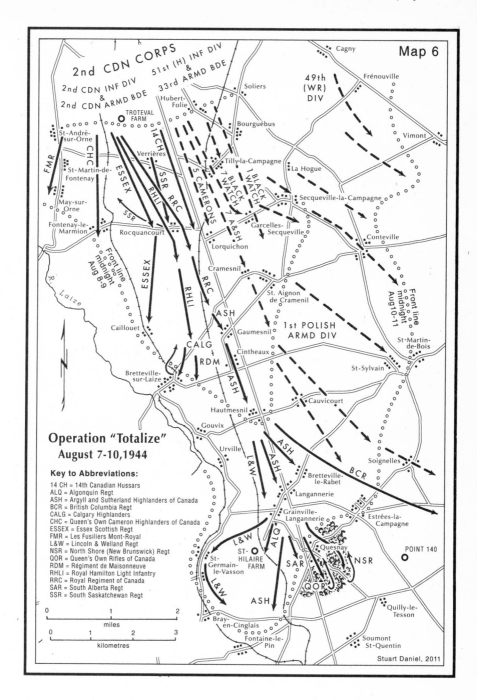

Map 6

Operation "Totalize"
August 7-10, 1944

Key to Abbreviations:

14 CH = 14th Canadian Hussars
ALQ = Algonquin Regt
ASH = Argyll and Sutherland Highlanders of Canada
BCR = British Columbia Regt
CALG = Calgary Highlanders
CHC = Queen's Own Cameron Highlanders of Canada
ESSEX = Essex Scottish Regt
FMR = Les Fusiliers Mont-Royal
L&W = Lincoln & Welland Regt
NSR = North Shore (New Brunswick) Regt
QOR = Queen's Own Rifles of Canada
RDM = Régiment de Maisonneuve
RHLI = Royal Hamilton Light Infantry
RRC = Royal Regiment of Canada
SAR = South Alberta Regt
SSR = South Saskatchewan Regt

Stuart Daniel, 2011

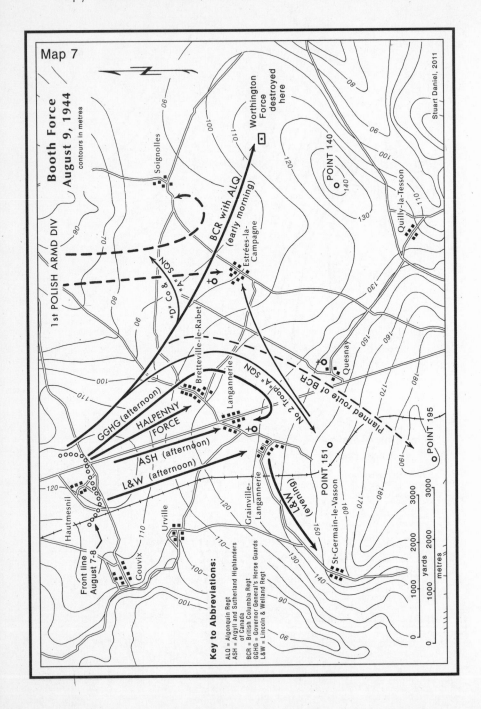

Map 7

Booth Force
August 9, 1944
contours in metres

Stuart Daniel, 2011

1st POLISH ARMD DIV

Soignolles

Worthington
Force
destroyed
here

POINT 140

Quilly-la-Tesson

BCR with ALQ
(early morning)

Estrées-la-
Campagne

"D" Co & "A" SQN

Bretteville-le-Rabet

Quesnay

Langannerie

No. 2 Troop/"A" SQN

Planned route of BCR

POINT 195

GGHG (afternoon)

HALPENNY
FORCE

ASH (afternoon)

L&W (afternoon)

POINT 151

POINT 195

Hautmesnil

Urville

Grainville-
Langannerie

L&W
(evening)

St-Germain-le-Vasson

Front line
August 7-8

Gouvix

Key to Abbreviations:

ALQ = Algonquin Regt
ASH = Argyll and Sutherland Highlanders
     of Canada
BCR = British Columbia Regt
GGHG = Governor General's Horse Guards
L&W = Lincoln & Welland Regt

1000   yards   3000
1000   metres   3000

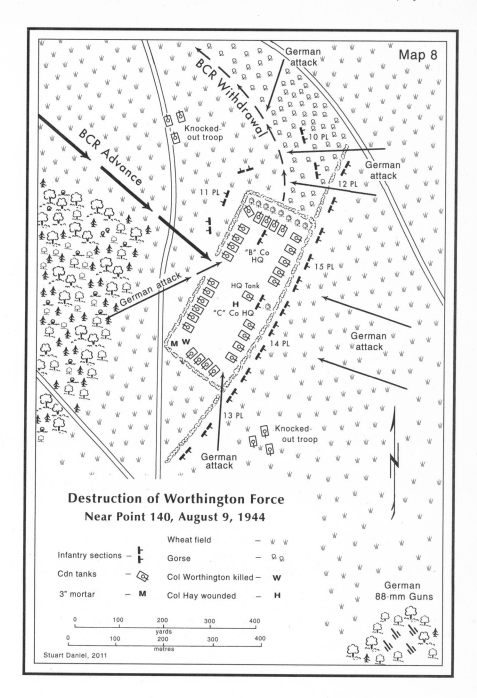

Map 8

German attack

BCR Withdrawal

Knocked-out troop

BCR Advance

10 PL

German attack

12 PL

11 PL

German attack

"B" Co HQ

15 PL

HQ Tank

H
"C" Co HQ

14 PL

M W

13 PL

Knocked-out troop

German attack

German 88-mm Guns

Destruction of Worthington Force
Near Point 140, August 9, 1944

Infantry sections —	Wheat field —		
Cdn tanks —	Gorse —		
3" mortar — M	Col Worthington killed — W		
	Col Hay wounded — H		

0 100 200 300 400
yards
0 100 200 300 400
metres

Stuart Daniel, 2011

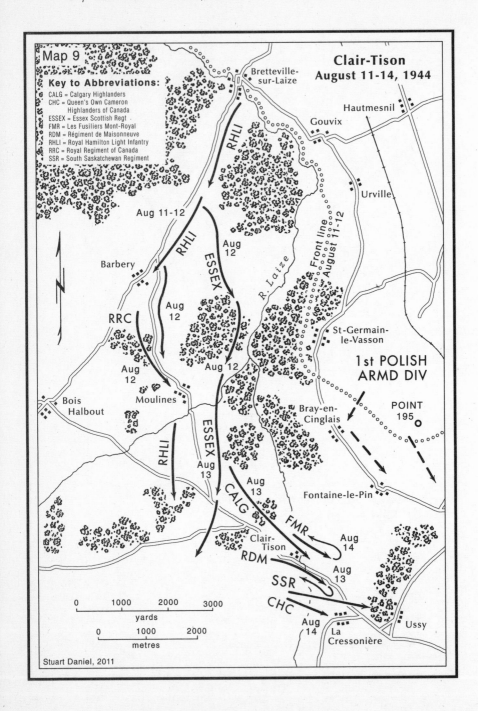

Map 9

Key to Abbreviations:
CALG = Calgary Highlanders
CHC = Queen's Own Cameron
    Highlanders of Canada
ESSEX = Essex Scottish Regt
FMR = Les Fusiliers Mont-Royal
RDM = Régiment de Maisonneuve
RHLI = Royal Hamilton Light Infantry
RRC = Royal Regiment of Canada
SSR = South Saskatchewan Regiment

Clair-Tison
August 11-14, 1944

Bretteville-
sur-Laize

Hautmesnil

Gouvix

Urville

RHLI

Aug 11-12

RHLI

Aug
12

ESSEX

Barbery

R. Laize

Front line
August 11-12

RRC

Aug
12

St-Germain-
le-Vasson

Aug
12

Aug 12

1st POLISH
ARMD DIV

Aug
12

Moulines

Bois
Halbout

Bray-en-
Cinglais

POINT
195

RHLI

ESSEX

Aug
13

Aug
13

CALG

FMR

Fontaine-le-Pin

Clair-
Tison

Aug
14

RDM

Aug
13

SSR

CHC

Aug
14

La
Cressonière

Ussy

0   1000   2000   3000
yards

0   1000   2000
metres

Stuart Daniel, 2011

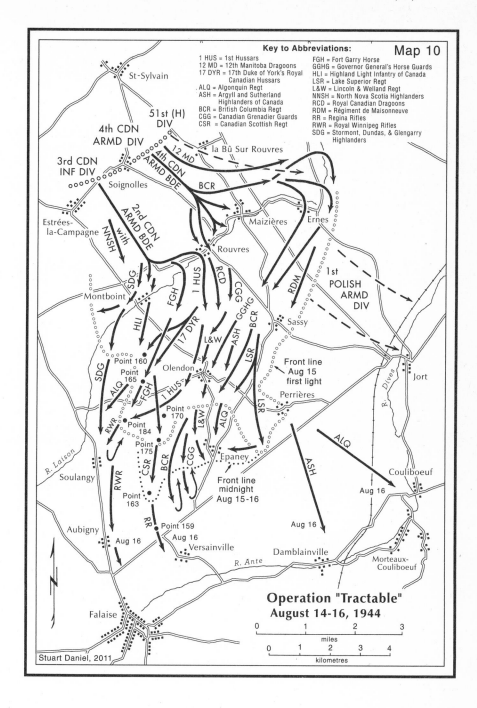

Key to Abbreviations:

1 HUS = 1st Hussars
12 MD = 12th Manitoba Dragoons
17 DYR = 17th Duke of York's Royal Canadian Hussars
ALQ = Algonquin Regt
ASH = Argyll and Sutherland Highlanders of Canada
BCR = British Columbia Regt
CGG = Canadian Grenadier Guards
CSR = Canadian Scottish Regt

FGH = Fort Garry Horse
GGHG = Governor General's Horse Guards
HLI = Highland Light Infantry of Canada
LSR = Lake Superior Regt
L&W = Lincoln & Welland Regt
NNSH = North Nova Scotia Highlanders
RCD = Royal Canadian Dragoons
RDM = Régiment de Maisonneuve
RR = Regina Rifles
RWR = Royal Winnipeg Rifles
SDG = Stormont, Dundas, & Glengarry Highlanders

Map 10

Operation "Tractable"
August 14-16, 1944

Stuart Daniel, 2011

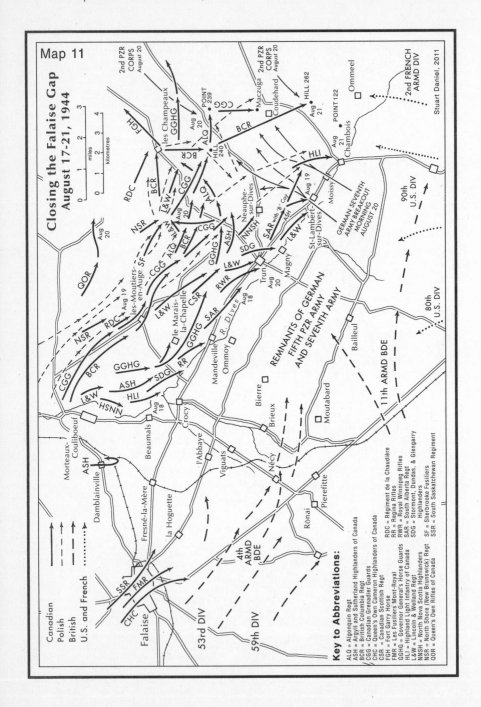

Map 11

Closing the Falaise Gap
August 17-21, 1944

Stuart Daniel, 2011

Canadian
Polish
British
U.S. and French

Key to Abbreviations:

ALQ = Algonquin Regt
ASH = Argyll and Sutherland Highlanders of Canada
BCR = British Columbia Regt
CGG = Canadian Grenadier Guards
CHC = Queen's Own Cameron Highlanders of Canada
CSR = Canadian Scottish Regt
FGH = Fort Garry Horse
FMR = Les Fusiliers Mont-Royal
GGHG = Governor General's Horse Guards
HLI = Highland Light Infantry of Canada
L&W = Lincoln & Welland Regt
NNSH = North Nova Scotia Highlanders
NSR = North Shore (New Brunswick) Regt
QOR = Queen's Own Rifles of Canada

RDC = Régiment de la Chaudière
RR = Regina Rifles
RWR = Royal Winnipeg Rifles
SAR = South Alberta Regt
SDG = Stormont, Dundas, & Glengarry Highlanders
SF = Sherbrooke Fusiliers
SSR = South Saskatchewan Regiment

A Formidable Array

MAJOR LOCHART "LOCHIE" Fulton scanned a killing ground. Morning sunlight graced golden wheat fields between the Royal Winnipeg Rifles' start line and three large hangars on the southern edge of Carpiquet airfield. Arrayed in a tidy west-to-east row, the hangars were the regiment's objective. Fulton had no eye for the beauty of the day. He saw only a mile of open ground, absent any cover. The waist-high wheat—uncut this summer because of war—offered no concealment. The long, wide, flat ridge that was Hill 112 stood just to the east. German artillery observers up there waited to zero in field guns and mortars the moment his men moved into the open. West of the airfield, the tower of the Abbaye d'Ardenne provided another perch from which fire could be directed against them.[1] Fulton was helpless to prevent this fire. He could only lead 'D' Company into the wheat, where the dying would once again begin.

Since Fulton had scrambled out of a landing craft onto the sand of Juno Beach that morning of June 6, 1944, there had been so much dying. By day's end the Canadians had been six miles inland at a cost of 340 dead and another 574 wounded from a total force of 14,500 men.

The Canadian advance had been the deepest achieved by Allied forces on D-Day. But it still left them four miles short of their final objective—Carpiquet airfield. The next day a few got within a mile before a fierce German counterattack threw them back. A bloody six-day battle had ensued. The fate of the invasion hung in the balance, as three German panzer divisions tried to drive the Canadians back into the sea. Had they succeeded, the two British beaches on either flank of Juno—Gold and Sword—would have easily been rolled up. Then the American beaches to the west could be eliminated at the Germans' leisure. Holding Juno cost the Canadians 196 officer and 2,635 other rank casualties. Of these, 72 officers and 945 other ranks died. The casualties left the Canadians incapable of further offensive action until this summer day of July 3.

After the brilliant success of the landings and days spent fending off counterattacks, the Allied invasion had stalled. Caen, a city of about 54,000, had been the main British D-Day objective. Despite repeated assaults through June, it still remained in German hands. The Americans had fared only marginally better. After quickly linking their Utah and Omaha beachheads, the American drive inland mired in the nightmare maze of hedgerows *(bocage)* that bordered every Norman farm field and roadside. It took them until June 17 to isolate the Cotentin Peninsula in Brittany, a vital first step in what was to have been a quick dash to secure the major port of Cherbourg. Another nine days had passed before the city was reached, and three more were required before the German defences were completely quelled. The Allies had hoped to seize an intact port through which to move the majority of their supplies and men. Instead, they won a port that been systematically rendered useless by demolitions.

Now dependent on bringing all their supplies across the beaches, the Allies faced a supply crisis. Adding to their woes was the damage the ingenious artificial harbours—"Mulberries"—had suffered during a four-day storm that had begun on June 19. The storm destroyed the American Mulberry at Omaha Beach and severely damaged the one at Arromanches-les-Bains, which served the British and Canadians. Hundreds of landing craft had also been wrecked.

At the end of June, 861,838 Allied troops were crammed into a beachhead bursting at the seams with men, vehicles, and supplies.[2] Adding to the congestion were nine British and Canadian Spitfire squadrons from 2nd Tactical Air Force and six American P-47 Thunderbolt squadrons operating from ad hoc landing strips.[3]

Supreme Headquarters Allied Expeditionary Force (SHAEF) demanded a breakout. Its staff officers grew increasingly critical of the overall ground commander, General Bernard Law Montgomery, for failing to deliver one—particularly on the British front facing Caen. Montgomery, however, was a victim of a plan that had worked too well.

With its key crossings over the Orne River, Caen was like a cork bottling up the British-Canadian force. A series of roads radiated from Caen into the French interior. Paris lay just 149 miles distant. Possessing Caen would threaten the capital. Yet winning Caen itself was not enough. To gain sufficient elbow room for manoeuvre, the surrounding countryside must also be taken—especially the ground to the southeast, where Carpiquet airfield stood.

Caen's strategic importance was obvious, so the Germans had committed their strongest divisions to its defence. By month's end fully seven and a half of eight panzer divisions in Normandy faced the British and Canadian troops. A smaller number of infantry divisions, some of poor quality, were deployed against the Americans.

Montgomery was not unhappy about this. His "broad policy," as he explained on June 30, "has always been to draw the main enemy forces into the battle on our eastern flank [around Caen], to fight them there, so that our affairs on the western flank could proceed the easier . . . By forcing the enemy to place the bulk of his strength in front of the Second [British] Army, we have made easier the acquisition of territory on the western flank. Our policy has been so successful that the Second Army is now opposed by a formidable array of German Panzer Divisions."[4]

Ultra, the top-secret agency reading German encrypted wireless traffic, regularly updated Montgomery on the movement of German armoured units. As the Germans fed the powerful 11 SS Panzer Corps into Normandy, he saw its divisions drawing towards Caen. His strategy to present the Americans with a weakened defensive crust they could punch through and then launch a broad armoured sweep into the French interior appeared to be working.[5]

To keep the Germans fixated on Caen required an aggressive offence. Repeatedly throughout June, Montgomery had chipped away in search of a hole through which Second British Army could gain the city. Operation Epsom on June 25 had been the most ambitious effort. About sixty thousand men from British VIII Corps had advanced on a four-mile front west of Carpiquet across the Odon River and onto the facing high ground. This was an attempt to encircle Caen from the southwest. Hill 112, northeast of Évrecy, had been the key initial objective. Once this broad, flat prominence fell, the British could advance to the south of the city and cross the Orne River.[6]

Epsom had died on Hill 112 after fierce fighting. The British failed to win and hold more than a sliver of it. For weeks the Germans and British sparred on its heights. Never were the British able to possess the vital parts that would afford them observation of the southern plain outside Caen where the Germans mustered, rested, and resupplied. Yet the Germans, from the parts of Hill 112 they held, enjoyed excellent observation over the British and Canadian positions.[7]

With Epsom's failure, Montgomery turned to the Canadians on the left flank of Hill 112. They could broaden the front next to VIII Corps and win a starting point for a direct assault on Caen from the west. Operation Windsor would seize Carpiquet airfield and Carpiquet village immediately north of it. Neither the Allies nor the Germans contested the airport out of interest in its landing fields. There were three strategic reasons justifying a fight for possession of the airport and village. First, the airport stood on high ground that allowed the Germans a clear view of any movement in the VIII Corps area. Montgomery was teeing up another assault on Hill 112—Operation Jupiter—and he wanted to prevent the Germans from being able to see the 43rd (Wessex) Division begin to form for this attack.[8] Second, the airport would give Second Army good observation into Caen and provide a platform from which to advance towards the city. Finally, the Germans could ill afford to accept its loss. If they were pushed out of the airport and village, they would surely try to regain both. The Canadians could chew these up, leaving the Germans with insufficient reserves to either effectively oppose a following attack on Caen or pinch out the salient across the Odon River that the British had won during Epsom and hoped to expand with Jupiter.

On June 30, 3rd Canadian Infantry Division and 2nd Canadian Armoured Brigade were Canada's only fighting formations in Normandy. These were the same that had landed on D-Day. Plans to bring all of First Canadian Army ashore by June 23 had gone badly awry due to the severe storms and German counterattacks bottling up the beachhead. On June 22, Montgomery cautioned Lieutenant General Harry Crerar—who had established his army tactical headquarters staff at Amblie, close to Montgomery's headquarters at Cruelly—that his army might not be completely landed until mid-July. Before that date there would be room for at most a single corps. II Canadian Corps, Montgomery said, would serve under British Second Army command until such time as there was room for Crerar and the rest of First Canadian Army to be phased into operations. That was unlikely to occur before Caen fell.[9]

While Crerar appreciated the problem, he chafed at being unable to establish his entire army headquarters at Amblie. Montgomery, however, bluntly refused. "I am not going to have Canadian Army HQ over here with all its Army troops until we really have enough room," he told Crerar on June 26.

But lack of elbow room was not his real reason for denying Crerar operational command while placing Lieutenant General Guy Simonds, who commanded II Corps, under Second Army. For several years Simonds had been Montgomery's protégé, and he was confident the younger man could competently lead II Corps in battle. Not so Crerar. The fifty-five-year-old Canadian general had got on Montgomery's wrong side during a brief term of service as I Canadian Corps commander in Italy. Montgomery and Crerar were polar opposites, both in manner and command style.

A casual dresser, who preferred precise, often verbally delivered orders, Montgomery was a shameless self-promoter. Crerar's laboriously written orders and reports were legendary. The British found them a source of great amusement. Crerar always dressed formally, easily became defensive at any perception of insult to Canadian national pride, and was noticeably shy and retiring. Montgomery confessed that because of his "grave fears that Harry Crerar will not be good...I am keeping him out of the party as long as I can."[10]

This was why on July 4 the Canadians lined up in front of Carpiquet airfield for Operation Windsor were four battle-weary regiments of 3rd Canadian Infantry Division and one regiment of 2nd Canadian Armoured Brigade. They were the only troops on the ground.

PART ONE

BATTLE FOR CAEN

Little Short of Hell

BOTH CARPIQUET AIRFIELD and village were held by the 12th ss (Hitlerjugend) Panzer Division, which had proven a tenacious and ruthless foe during the June 7–12 fighting. All ss divisions were fierce and fanatical, but the 12th ss was uniquely comprised almost entirely of teenaged soldiers commanded by older, veteran officers and NCOs. The youths had been indoctrinated to believe they were Aryan "supermen."[1] The 12th ss was commanded by the extremely capable, thirty-three-year-old Standartenführer Kurt Meyer.

Its thick stone-walled buildings bordered by the Caen-Bayeux railway to the north and the airport to the south, Carpiquet was a typical Norman farm village. On the other side of the railway was a series of iron quarries. To the east and west were grain fields.

In front of the village, fifty panzer grenadiers from 26th Regiment hid in trenches and bomb shelters. Another 150 of Meyer's men were mostly sheltered in thick concrete bunkers.

The June fighting had scythed through Meyer's infantry strength. Lacking reinforcements, his only hope was to break the Canadian attack with heavy weapons. The troops in front of Carpiquet were intended to lure the Canadians into a series of minefields and then suck them into the village by executing a rapid withdrawal. All available artillery and mortar units had the village zeroed in. Chief among these was an 88-millimetre battery next to Saint-Germain, a village to the east. Five Panzer Mark IV tanks lay in ambush position inside the southern hangars.[2] A dozen-strong company of Panther Mark V tanks nearby could also be brought into play. Meyer had several unique 50-kilogram rockets filled with either explosives or flammable oil.[3]

Meyer never doubted his young soldiers would fight like lions. They had done so during the attacks on the beaches—and events during those days left many fearful for their lives should any decide to surrender. During that fighting, 156 Canadian prisoners had been brutally murdered by the 12th SS.[4]

Although most execution sites, such as the Abbaye d'Ardenne, remained behind German lines, enough bodies had been recovered for the atrocity to be known. Without orders being issued, it was understood among the Canadians that they should show "little mercy in subduing the German defenders" of Carpiquet.[5]

Brigadier Ken Blackader knew his 8th Canadian Infantry Brigade would aim "at the heart" of the 12th SS and "the fanatical youth of this division" would fiercely defend it.[6] A forty-six-year-old World War I veteran, who had won a Military Cross during that war, Blackader had a rock-solid reputation for competent leadership and personal courage.[7] Quickly realizing his three battalions were insufficient to win both airport and village, he acquired 7th Brigade's Royal Winnipeg Rifles as reinforcement. Two Fort Garry Horse tank squadrons would help the North Shore (New Brunswick) Regiment and Régiment de la Chaudière gain the village, while a third supported the Winnipeg advance on the hangars. Once these two objectives were taken, the Queen's Own Rifles would clear the control and administration buildings on the airfield's northern edge. A squadron each of the 79th British Armoured Division's specialized tanks, known as "funnies," were also on hand. One squadron mounted Petards—short-barrelled guns that fired a heavy charge intended to destroy concrete bunkers. The Flail squadron's tanks were fitted with rotating drums to which long chains were attached that slapped mines into harmlessly detonating. The third was a Crocodile squadron, its tanks equipped with flame-throwers.

A lavish artillery plan included every gun within range—428 from one heavy, eight medium, and twelve field regiments. There were also six 16-inch guns of battleship HMS *Rodney,* two 15-inch guns of monitor HMS *Roberts,* and nine 6-inch guns of cruiser HMS *Belfast.* A total of 30,250 shells would provide a creeping barrage for the troops to advance behind while also concentrating on specified strongpoints. The entire complement of the Cameron Highlanders of Ottawa (MG) 4.2-inch mortars and Vickers medium machine guns were ranged on village and airfield. Two squadrons of tank-busting Typhoon fighter-bombers were also available.[8]

In the North Shore's perimeter on the night of July 3–4, four men huddled in a slit trench. Lieutenant Chester MacRae was upset when Lieutenant Hector "Hec" MacQuarrie and Company Sergeant Major Joe Murray both confessed to premonitions that they were sure to die in the fight. Neither McRae nor Lance Corporal Wes McDavid could offer meaningful reassurance, because it was clearly going to be a rough attack.[9]

At 0300 hours, the North Shores, Chauds, and Queen's Own moved to starting positions in front of La Villeneuve, while the Winnipegs formed up outside Marcelet. To avoid being seen, the men lay down in the wheat fields. Major Lochie Fulton walked over to greet Major Alex Christian, whose Fort Garry Horse 'B' Squadron had just rumbled up.[10] Intelligence staff reported that the airport was "a very strong defensive position" with many "concrete strong points, barbed wire, communication trenches, gun positions of all types and even extensive underground tank hangars and tunnels... Also many infantry trenches with machine guns and mortars and anti-personnel and tank minefields."[11] Yet, because 8th Brigade's main thrust was directed towards Carpiquet and the control complex on the northern side of the airport, the tanks supporting the Winnipegs were not accompanying the infantry. They would instead remain on the edge of Marcelet to serve as an armoured reserve that could be sent towards Carpiquet if required. Christian's Shermans would fire their 75-millimetre guns over the advancing infantry's heads—scant help on a battlefield boiling with blinding smoke and dust raised by the massive artillery bombardment.[12]

AT 0500 HOURS, North Shores' Major Clint Gammon, commanding 'D' Company, looked over his shoulder in amazement as "the
whole horizon in a semi-circle behind us became a blaze when the
artillery opened up."[13] Major J.E. "Ernie" Anderson at the head of 'A'
Company thought the barrage "awe-inspiring." One minute he was
"in a quiet and peaceful countryside with dawn just breaking; the
next, the ground...was shaking from the bursts of shells."[14] When
the great naval guns on *Roberts* and *Rodney* joined in, the noise rose
"to a crescendo."[15] Anderson's men were on the battalion's right,
Gammon's on its left. They were to secure the first half of the village,
and the two following would clear the rest. Gammon had two platoons out front, the third hanging in reserve. As the advance was not
to begin until ten minutes into the bombardment, Gammon decided
he had time to check on the rear platoon. He had covered just fifty
yards when the start line exploded with shell bursts. Through burning and smoking wheat, Gammon ran back to the company front
and discovered that "a lot of my men were dead or wounded."

German artillery and mortar units had deliberately struck at this
moment to catch the Canadians on their start lines. Increased wireless traffic the day before had warned Meyer that a Canadian strike
was imminent, and past experience led him to expect a dawn attack.
So he arranged a coinciding fire plan. Perfectly timed, it had devastating results.

The bombardment and counter-fire came as Meyer was scram-
bling over the rubble of destroyed airfield buildings. A salvo of
50-millimetre rockets flashed overhead, "leaving their long, fiery
trails behind them." Dashing into the concrete bunker of the infantry
battalion's headquarters, Meyer was unable to hear Sturmbannführer
Bernard Krause's report. There "were crashes and shrieks all around
us. We crowded together in the bunker entrance. The bunker shook
as the...rounds from the battleships exploded nearby...The naval
rounds spun entire hangars into the air. The village could not be identified...Thick clouds of smoke lay to the west."[16]

German casualties were heavy. "Many...survivors had to dig
themselves and their weapons out of the rubble," the 12th ss historian
recorded.[17] Every building in Carpiquet and at the airport was either

destroyed or damaged. While most exterior walls of the stone houses in the village withstood the shellfire, their roofs were torn open.

Lying in the dew-drenched wheat field had left Rifleman Alex Kuppers of Fulton's 'D' Company soaking wet. He was watching the fall of the incoming shells. Kuppers poked the guy beside him. "I think we should move—either right, left or back," Kuppers shouted. "The way these are coming, the next one's going to be here." The soldier refused. Kuppers scrambled back about four yards to where a sunken road afforded some shelter. Then the signal to advance sounded. When Kuppers reached his previous spot, he saw that "the shell had landed right beside [the other soldier] and the only thing missing was that half his foot was gone. Blood was running from his eyes."[18]

As the Winnipegs crossed the start line, Fulton thought the artillery was falling short, "but then I realized we were under German barrage, which had been waiting for us. Their locations made it possible to direct their fire with deadly accuracy. Casualties were immediate, and in the waist-high wheat, the stretcher-bearers had difficulty finding the wounded and in giving first aid. Jeeps usually used to evacuate casualties to the regimental aid post (RAP) could not be used because, as soon as a vehicle appeared on the airfield, it was knocked out by the German guns.

"We kept moving ahead but soon all the Platoon officers were hit. The last one to go was [Lieutenant] Jack Mitchell. He came over to…say that he was hit in the arm and would go back to the RAP to get fixed up and would be right back. Jack was a stout-hearted individual, but his wounds were more severe than he realized, and his war was over."[19]

'A' Company led the Winnipeg advance in arrowhead formation with Lieutenant Richard Moglove's No. 9 Platoon at the front and the other two platoons behind and out on opposite sides. Rifleman Arthur Davey was on No. 9 Platoon's point. Davey was packing bolt cutters, his task to cut a hole through the eight-foot perimeter fence. To his relief, the artillery had ripped the fence asunder. The platoon dashed through great gaping holes and Davey threw the cutters aside.

"Davey, get up on the tarmac and dig me a slit trench for OP [Observation Post] purposes," Moglove yelled.

"Why me?" Davey replied.

"Because you have the pick." True enough. It was slung across Davey's back. "I crawled up and took one swing with the pick when a sniper shot ricocheted between me and the handle of the pick. I moved out of there fast," leaving the pick "stuck in the tarmac."[20]

ALL THREE BATTALIONS were taking heavy casualties. Private Abraham Feldman, a young wireless operator assigned to Major Hugues Lapointe of the Chauds' 'A' Company, weighed 122 pounds and stood just five feet, five inches tall. The No. 18 set weighed 35 pounds, his rifle 11 pounds. Feldman figured he carried at least 70 pounds of equipment.

Walking out from the start line in reserve position behind the two leading companies, 'A' Company was "clobbered." Feldman saw Carpiquet "inundated with bombs, shells and bullets. You just had to keep going. It's hard to describe. You'd move, advance two feet at a time, drop down, get up again and bingo you hear the 88s. It was a slow advance with men dropping like flies."[21]

To indicate the location of a wounded man, the nearest soldier would drive the man's rifle bayonet into the ground so the butt was visible above the wheat. The rifle markers also helped prevent tanks and Bren carriers from running over the fallen.[22] On the extreme left flank, the North Shore's carrier platoon rumbled along in their Bren carriers next to the railroad. Their commander, Captain J.A. Currie, thought the "dust and smoke made it like a night attack...and during the clear spots, we could see men going forward, but had no idea so many had been hit. Padre [R. Miles] Hickey was right among them, giving the last rites and so was Doc [John Aubry] Patterson with his medical kit. No other unit had a pair to match them."[23]

Hickey had waded into the midst of 'B' Company, shredded even as it advanced towards the start line. "Everywhere men lay dead or dying," Hickey wrote. "I anointed about thirty right there."[24]

'A' Company's Major Anderson thought the "advance through the grain field was little short of hell." He kept his bearings in the boiling smoke by taking constant compass readings. Behind him, one platoon wandered off at a right angle to the line of advance. Lieutenant Darrel Barker had been mortally wounded, and, unable to see the rest of the company, the platoon drifted out of sight into the smoke before Anderson could bring it back on course.

Many of the fifty 12th ss soldiers deployed in the field west of Carpiquet had been killed or so badly dazed by the shelling that they meekly surrendered when overrun. But a few remained defiant. Their fire added to the casualty toll. "I am sure at some time during the attack," Anderson recalled, "every man felt he could not go on. Men were being killed or wounded on all sides and the advance seemed pointless, as well as hopeless. I never realized until the attack on Carpiquet how far discipline, pride of unit, and above all, pride in oneself and family can carry a man, even when each step forward meant possible death."[25]

'B' Company's Lieutenant Charles Richardson had only twenty of the thirty-five men in his platoon left. Lieutenant Paul McCann's platoon was on his right. Both men were using compasses. When the smoke lifted momentarily, Richardson saw that McCann's men were now to his left. He had no idea how that had happened. His men emerged from the smoke in an extended line and suddenly faced a field that had been burned to stubble by artillery fire. Charging forward, they wiped out a slit trench defended by five Germans. Richardson saw a pinwheeling stick grenade land in front of him. "I felt a hot stinging in my right side and left hand, then thought it didn't matter too much." Suddenly alone, Richardson took on the German position single-handedly and killed its defenders. His batman and two runners had all been seriously wounded by the grenade.

"My side started to bother me badly and my left hand was peppered with shrapnel. I had a long cigarette case in the inside pocket of my battledress and a towel wrapped around my waist. In order to look at my side, which was throbbing, I unbuttoned my tunic and the towel was full of shrapnel. I reached for a cigarette and found the case bent almost double by a large piece of shrapnel. I felt I was not hit too badly but out of nowhere appeared our beloved colonel and I quickly had orders to get back to the first aid post—which marked the finish of my first month in action."[26]

Two Fort Garry Horse squadrons were riding right on the heels of the North Shores and Chauds. One Sherman rolled up and spun in a full turn that buried Sturmmann Karl-Heinz Wambach to the chest in the sandy soil of his slit trench. He was trying to free himself when a voice yelled, "ss bastard, hands up!" Two North Shores dragged him free and tied his hands. One then punched him in the face. He was taken to the rear, urged along by rifle butt blows, and tied to a fence post for some hours in an area subjected to frequent shelling by German 88-millimetre guns.[27]

Wambach's complaints about his treatment led the North Shore's historian to comment that "given the way Canadians felt about the 12th ss, he got off lucky." During its advance across the field, the North Shores took thirty-five prisoners and killed an equal number.[28]

At 0625 hours, almost ninety minutes after the attack began, the North Shores reached the shelter of a stone wall in front of Carpiquet and reported being on their first objective. The Chauds signalled brigade a few minutes later that they had men on the village edge and among the nearby hangars.[29] Carpiquet was still being heavily shelled, forcing a twenty-minute pause. More casualties resulted when shells burst in the tree canopy next to the Canadian positions. When the artillery ceased firing, both battalions plunged into the village. Most of the small garrison actually deployed within either surrendered, were already dead, or quickly fled. The North Shores sent back twenty more prisoners.[30] In the Chaudière sector, a handful of hard-core 12th ss in the hangar complex were burned out of concrete pillboxes by Crocodiles.[31] At 1056, the Chauds reported their grip on the hangars secure.[32]

Surprisingly, there were French civilians still living in the badly damaged village. Some, who emerged from bomb shelters and basements, had been wounded, and most seemed to be "in a state of severe shock," Lieutenant MacRae wrote. "One old couple passed me going to the rear with their few possessions in a wheelbarrow. They looked too dazed to know what was going on." While most of the civilians immediately fled towards the Canadian lines, a few were driven back into hiding when the Germans slammed Carpiquet with heavy and continuous mortar and artillery fire.

Private Feldman manned his wireless in a concrete bunker the Chauds were using as a battalion headquarters. Lieutenant Colonel Paul Mathieu, Major Lapointe, the battalion padre, and Feldman felt pretty secure there until "we heard this big noise and knew it was coming close. I was facing one way and the shell...hit the HQ in another place. I was in the 'dead zone' or I'd have been killed by the concussion...I was knocked flat into the bunker and the officers looked at me and thought I'd died...I had landed on my set and that really prevented me from getting hurt, but the set was damaged. We got it going again and it was a miracle."[33]

TO THE SOUTH, as Fulton's 'D' Company had closed on the first of the three hangars, it began taking heavy small-arms fire in addition to being shelled and mortared. All three platoons were shredded. Fulton was the only officer still standing. "We made a final rush and got into the hangar, taking over the extensive network of deep weapon pits and trenches developed by the Germans to guard the hangars. It was then that the heaviest bombardment I experienced throughout the whole war was brought down upon us. If it hadn't been for the excellent German trench system, I believe none of us would of survived."

Fulton radioed Lieutenant Colonel John Meldram. His company held the hangar but was too weak to go any farther, Fulton reported. However, he believed it could repel the likely counterattack.[34] 'A' Company had been forced to ground a hundred yards short of the hangars. Meldram decided to feed 'B' Company through to the hangar held by Fulton. He also requested that 8th Brigade release some of 'B' Squadron's tanks to accompany it.[35]

Blackader reluctantly agreed to release one troop along with four Crocodiles. 'B' Squadron was Blackader's only armoured reserve, and he intended to have it support the follow-on assault by the Queen's Own Rifles to clear the control and administration buildings in the northeast corner of the airfield. Because the Winnipegs had failed to clear the hangars and remove the German threat to the Queen's Own from that flank, Blackader had delayed this phase. He also ordered the Queen's Own to form up inside Carpiquet for the launch of their attack.[36]

'B' Company met the same murderous hail of German shells the two leading companies had endured. Only about half the men reached the hangar Fulton held. Captain Jack Hale had been wounded. Fulton combined the survivors with his own.[37] But the Winnipegs were still unable to clear the Germans out of the concrete pillboxes and trench systems defending the other hangars. The Crocodiles, the Winnipeg war diarist wrote, "proved useless."[38] As for the Fort Garry troop, its four Shermans met deadly fire from hidden anti-tank guns. Lieutenant Arthur Edwin Rogers and Sergeant Alastair James Innes-Ker were both mortally wounded when their tanks burst into flames. The demise of those two tanks prompted the remaining two to flee.[39]

Wireless contact between battalion headquarters and the forward companies was so erratic that Meldram ordered Fulton to come back for a briefing. "I had no desire to make my way back across the airfield again, a target for the German guns; mine not to reason why, however." As Fulton ran back, he spotted Rifleman Leonard Miller calmly lying in a slit trench and reading a pocket-sized New Testament.[40] Meldram ordered the lead companies pulled back to a small, sparse wood a few hundred yards ahead of the original start line. Artillery would then plaster the hangars, and a new attack would go in with 'B' Squadron alongside.[41] As Fulton passed Miller's slit trench on his return run, he saw the man had been killed by a mortar round.[42]

At 1600 hours, the new attack went in behind another bombardment. Rifleman Edward Patey, a Bren gunner in 'C' Company, had just started forward when mortar and machine-gun fire tore into his platoon. Three men went down. He recognized one as a man in his mid-thirties everyone had nicknamed "Pops." The man lay "writhing on the ground, his whole stomach ripped with bullets." Patey "was hit by a mortar piece in the eye and upper chest and...left deaf for a couple of days."[43]

'B' Company's Sergeant Major Charles Belton suffered a chest wound. "I can remember when we were kids, we watched an Indian-cowboy movie and someone got shot and hit the ground and was dead. When I looked down and saw this blood spurting out of my chest, I thought I'd better lie down, so I did. I was fortunate. The shrapnel came through a book I had in my upper right breast pocket.

Otherwise I would probably have had that shot go right through me. But the book stopped the shrapnel, although it took two pieces of cardboard and that book into the wound and that infected it and made it worse."

As Belton started crawling to the rear, a German sniper in a nearby tree shot him in the leg. One of his men gunned the sniper down. Belton was evacuated to a field hospital. "There were so many of us in that tent that stretchers were only about [six] inches apart, just enough room for the nurses to walk in between...just row, and row, and row of us on these stretchers. I lay so long on this stretcher that my back pain was far worse than the wounds. I finally got back to England on a barge."[44]

While the infantry had gone straight for the hangars, the Shermans had executed a "sweeping attack" to get around the left flank of the Germans inside. Within minutes the tankers found their planned charge slowed to a crawl by thick bands of barbed wire and other obstacles, as well as anti-tank fire coming from in and around the hangars. Major Christian also reported the squadron was taking heavy fire from Panthers on the high ground behind the village of Verson to his right. The British were to have taken this ground but were stalled inside Verson.

'B' Squadron was completely out of contact with the infantry, which, having regained the first hangar, were again stuck there. Christian manoeuvred the squadron towards the hangars but found his tanks caught in a vise between a force of Mark iv and Panther tanks near Verson and other tanks at the hangars. A fierce shootout ensued. Soon burning tanks littered the airfield. 'B' Squadron had gone into the attack fifteen strong. When the tank battle broke off, nine remained operational.[45]

The battle clearly stalemated, Meldram told Blackader at 1725 hours that "it would be impossible to hold on without increased [support]. Blackader had nothing more to send. When a mixed force of tanks and infantry approached the airfield from the east, artillery managed to scatter it. But the Germans only "dispersed and rallied" the moment the guns ceased firing. Blackader ordered the Winnipegs back to Marcelet. As the infantry withdrew, the surviving tanks joined them. At Marcelet the Winnipegs dug in. Blackader ordered his battalions to reorganize where they were.[46]

"What had we accomplished?" Fulton wondered. "Possibly the Germans recognized our intention to take Carpiquet and that we would be back. But at what a cost!"[47]

BLACKADER ORDERED THE Queen's Own to join his other battalions holding Carpiquet. To reach the village meant running the gauntlet of artillery and mortar fire through the wheat field. En route, 'B' Company's Rifleman Alex Gordon was wounded and left behind. Rifleman J.P. Moore rolled up in his Bren carrier just as the men in Gordon's platoon realized he was missing. They warned Moore that "the fire was so heavy that anyone in the wheat field would be killed." Moore gave the carrier full throttle, drove like mad into the wheat field, grabbed up Gordon and threw him in the carrier, and brought him to safety.[48]

As the battalion closed on Carpiquet, one carrier platoon section, operating as foot infantry, sought shelter beside a concrete bunker. Suddenly, a German inside it opened up with a Schmeisser, and Rifleman Art Reid was shot dead.[49] The entire battalion went to ground and called for tanks and Crocodiles to destroy the position.

When the armour arrived, the Crocodiles blasted "with flame the walls about the entrances, which were set in a wide trench on the south side. This treatment merely blackened the [heavy] concrete walls and appeared to have no effect upon the enemy within. Nor were the tanks able to damage the structure," Major Steve Lett, the battalion's second-in-command, wrote.[50]

Corporal Tom McKenzie noticed six ventilation shafts poking out of the bunker's roof and dropped a Mills grenade down one of the pipes. When nothing happened, he realized the pipe was virtually the same diameter as the grenade and this prevented the firing pin from releasing. Flipping the pins free and then dropping the grenades down the pipe worked, but the explosions still failed to convince the Germans inside to surrender.

Because the Germans had killed Reid, McKenzie was getting "madder than hell." So he stole a carrier's four-gallon jerry can, emptied the gas down the pipe, and dropped a phosphorous grenade down after. A lot of smoke boiled out of the ventilation duct and there were some satisfying secondary explosions, but still no Germans appeared.[51]

While McKenzie had been taking on the bunker, the battalion's pioneers had unsuccessfully tried to blow the roof open with a 25-pound demolition charge. "Others tried to blow the steel doors set within the entrances, but here the approach was covered by fire from a sliding panel in the wall through which weapons could be pointed. Several men were killed in this attempt."[52]

McKenzie took the problem to an engineering officer, Lieutenant John L. Yeats from 16th Field Company, RCE, which was supporting 8th Brigade. When he explained the problem, Yeats showed him a shaped explosive 10-pound charge he had slung on his back. When detonated, this type of charge focused on a wall rather than dissipating the blast in all directions. With McKenzie providing covering fire, Yeats wriggled up to the bunker door, set the charge, lit its fuse, and then both men scrambled for cover. This time the explosion had the desired effect.[53]

A German soldier "emerged from the outer door, announcing himself as spokesman for the remainder, who were afraid to come out, and asking permission to surrender." Eleven 12th SS troops warily emerged. Several said they had been "told that Canadians take no PW. Consequently they [were] reluctant to surrender, preferring to fight to the last." The youths admitted "a great hatred for our arty, which is far superior to their own, and never gives them rest."

Inside the bunker, Lett found the corpses of an officer and sixteen other men, who had been killed by the grenades, burning gasoline, and detonation of the shaped charge.[54] Having cleared the bunker, the Queen's Own continued into Carpiquet. "Jutting into enemy territory at the tip of the newly-won salient, the village was open to hostile fire from three sides and the three battalions, huddled with their tank squadrons and other supporting arms under the shelter of battered walls, were now being severely shelled and mortared."[55]

Winning Carpiquet had exacted a dreadful toll. The North Shores lost more men than on any other day of the war—132, of which 46 were killed. The Chauds had 57 casualties, 16 killed. The Queen's

Own suffered 4 killed and 22 wounded. In its failed assault on the southern hangars, the Winnipegs lost more men than during the D-Day landings or when they were overrun at Putot-en-Bessin on June 7–8. Forty of its 132 casualties proved fatal. The Fort Garry Horse lost 8 men killed and 20 wounded—most from 'B' Squadron—while 16th Field Company, RCE, had 10 casualties, of which 3 were fatal.[56]

North Shore's medical officer, John Patterson, and Padre Hickey opened an RAP in a German dugout within the village because "there wasn't a building left standing, even the trees were smashed to splinters." Wounded poured in, and the medical teams worked frantically to stabilize people before evacuating them rearward to casualty clearing stations and field hospitals. When Major Blake Oulton was carried in on a stretcher with a bullet in his leg, Hickey said he was a "lucky dog" to have received such a "lovely wound" that would take him out of this hellhole. As dusk fell, Hickey and Major G.E. Lockwood led a burying party during a short lull in the German shelling. You "could fancy how the wheat field had been just like any of our wheat fields back home," Hickey wrote. But "now the wheat was just trampled into the earth; the ground was torn with shell holes and everywhere you could see the pale upturned faces of the dead. That night alone we buried forty—Carpiquet was the graveyard of the regiment."[57]

A Murderous Beating

DESPITE THE VERY limited success of Operation Windsor on July 4, the Canadian gains forced the German command in Normandy to recognize that it was only a matter of time before Caen was lost. Panzer Group West's General der Panzertruppen Leo Freiherr Geyr von Schweppenburg—responsible for the panzer units in western Europe—had started advocating on June 30 for an immediate withdrawal from all of Caen north of the Orne and concession of the ground on either side of the Epsom salient. These moves would straighten the German line, enabling the creation of an armoured reserve that could then act as a fire brigade to stem an imminent Allied breakthrough wherever one threatened to occur.[1]

Army Group B commander Generalfeldmarschall Erwin Rommel—charged with defending the northwest coast from Holland to the Loire—agreed. So, too, did Rommel's immediate superior, Commander in Chief, West Generalfeldmarschall Gerd von Rundstedt. The latter recommended the realignment to Oberkommando der Wehrmacht (OKW) in Berlin and requested a free hand in disposing forces as required without first seeking Hitler's approval. The response from Berlin was an immediate phone call from Generalfeldmarschall Wilhelm Keitel, Hitler's chief of staff. Keitel implied that the crisis was von Rundstedt's fault. Von Rundstedt snapped back: "If you think you can do better, you had better come down here and lead this filth yourself." Keitel pleaded, "What shall we do?" Calmly, von Rundstedt replied, "What shall you do? Make peace, you idiots! What else can you do?"[2]

Infuriated, Hitler immediately replaced both von Schweppen-burg and von Rundstedt. General der Panzertruppen Hans Eberbach succeeded the former and Generalfeldmarschall Günther von Kluge the latter. Hitler warned both men that Caen must be held to the end. Eberbach and von Kluge were optimistic. They considered Rommel's pessimism "defeatist."[3]

But the situation at Carpiquet was troubling. Surely the Canadian purpose was to establish a base for a drive on Caen from the west. To prevent the Canadians strengthening and expanding on their gains, an immediate attack was ordered for the early morning hours of July 5.[4] Because of the 12th ss Division's depleted state, a 1st ss Pan-zer-Grenadier Regiment battalion from 1st ss Panzer Division, Leibstandarte Adolph Hitler (LAH), would carry out the attack with support from several Panther tanks.[5]

With the Germans holding the ground on three sides of Carpi-quet, the Canadians knew they were certain to be attacked at any time. Despite having all three 8th Brigade battalions in the village, their total manpower was low because of the severe losses suffered the day before. Most companies were at half strength or less. 'A' and 'B' Squadrons of the Fort Garry Horse added their weight to Carpi-quet's defences, but the latter squadron had been reduced to just nine tanks.[6] There were also three troops from the 3rd Canadian Anti-Tank Regiment. Two 105th Battery troops were equipped with 6-pound anti-tank guns, while its 'L' Troop fielded M-10 self-propelled guns.[7] Also deployed in Carpiquet were two platoons from the Cameron Highlanders of Ottawa (MG). 'B' Company's No. 6 Pla-toon had set its heavy machine guns in the village's southeast corner, while No. 7 Platoon deployed in the northeast corner. 'D' Company's No. 14 Platoon settled into "what was left" of an orchard on the west flank. Equipped with 4.2-inch mortars, this Cameron unit could range from here to anywhere along Carpiquet's perimeter.[8] Under cover of darkness, the defenders strung barbed wire and sowed mines in front of their positions.

Throughout their preparations the Canadians were harried by intense artillery and mortar fire. Nebelwerfers—the multi-barrelled rocket projectors nicknamed "Moaning Minnies" because their 50-millimetre rounds shrieked during flight—fired incessantly. Rocket strikes collapsed building after building with a mighty roar. The North Shore's Sergeant Fulton Noye emerged shaken but physically unscathed when three buildings were destroyed around him.[9]

Just before nightfall on July 4, 22nd Canadian Field Ambulance's Medical Officer Douglas Oatway replaced the wounded doctor who had been serving Le Régiment de la Chaudière. The battalion's RAP was in a small courtyard next to the bunker where Lieutenant Colonel Paul Mathieu was headquartered. Oatway had just met his French-Canadian medical staff when the shelling increased. At midnight, the battalion's ambulance jeep evacuated its first load of wounded and never returned. Oatway and Mathieu concluded the crew had found running the gauntlet of German shelling on the road from Carpiquet to Marcelet too dangerous. This left Oatway with no choice but to "leave our seriously wounded on stretchers in the courtyard for the rest of the night."[10]

AT 0130 HOURS, the German counterattack was signalled by a sudden increase in the already intense rate of shelling, followed by a flight of 50-kilogram rockets filled with flammable fuel, which set Carpiquet alight. Flames providing illumination, the 1st SS battalion descended from the heights towards the village. The 1st SS were crack soldiers and fanatical Nazis, who adhered to a collective ethos that "glorified fighting for fighting's sake."[11]

With ten tanks in support, the SS troops lunged towards Carpiquet only to see the lead company savaged by an artillery concentration that might have been friendly German fire or a scheduled Canadian defensive fire task. Whatever its source, the concentration inflicted so many casualties that another company had to advance to the head of the attack.

As the battalion gained the raised railway, the Cameron Highlanders No. 7 Platoon let loose with its machine guns, and No. 14 Platoon's mortars weighed in. Earlier, the North Shore's commander,

Lieutenant Colonel Donald Buell, had ordered the other forces in Carpiquet to hold fire until the Germans were right on top of their defences. As the fires in the village died away, the Germans' "only reference points were the enemy muzzle flashes," one ss veteran later wrote. "We had to move forward precisely into that!"[12] Their numbers decreasing rapidly, the troops descended from the railway into low fields overlooked by the village. It was about 0330 hours.[13]

Lieutenant Paul McCann thought Buell's plan was working wonders. As "Jerry advanced over the hill and across the valley we waited and...sucked wave after wave...into the hollow where the withering cross-fire of the Camerons cut off any hope of escape. There was only one way to go once in the valley and with all respect to Jerry he never faltered. By the time our signal was given they were right on our doorstep, so out went our grenades followed by a withering small arms fire that saw barrels of Bren guns get white hot before the show was over. There were no casualties among my men but Jerry took a murderous beating and very few of their attacking force got back to their line."[14]

At 0530 hours, the Germans tried again, sending tanks and infantry towards the village from the quarries to the east. This attack was quickly broken when artillery knocked out two tanks and caused the rest to veer away into "hull down positions." Renewed efforts at 0610 and 0650 were equally shattered by artillery.[15]

At 0725 hours, the Germans attempted a thrust against the point where Le Régiment de la Chaudière's 'A' Company held the edge of the village close to the airport administration buildings. With at least six Panthers leading, the Germans overran one platoon and the company's anti-tank section. While some Germans paused to round up prisoners, most descended on the North Shore's 'C' Company and the Cameron's No. 6 Platoon.[16]

'C' Company was the battalion's weakest, fielding only forty-one men and two officers, Major Ralph Daughney and Lieutenant Chester MacRae. Dodging through enemy fire, MacRae urged his men to keep pouring out a stream of fire, until an exploding tank round knocked him unconscious.[17] On 'C' Company's flank, No. 6 Platoon could no longer rake its entire front with machine-gun fire for fear of hitting the Chauds, who had been taken prisoner.[18]

At this critical moment, two M-10s came to the rescue. One dealt a killing blow to a Panther with a single round, while the other slammed a second tank with six rapidly delivered shots. This largesse of ammunition use was chided by 3rd Anti-Tank Regiment's historian. "One round would have done," he wrote, "because, when the tank was later examined, all six hits were found to be within the circumference of a dinner plate." With the loss of these tanks, this last German attack crumbled.[19]

As the Germans pulled back, a tank herding some Chauds in front of it passed No. 6 Platoon's position. The tank commander shouted at the Camerons to surrender. The platoon's commander had other plans. Earlier he had sent some of his men to take over a nearby abandoned Chaud 6-pound anti-tank gun. The lieutenant now signalled the men to open fire. When the first shell hit the turret, one section of machine guns started hammering the tank. The other section began raking German infantry trying to crawl to safety through the cover of a wheat field. "At the same time Corporal R.A. Henderson crawled forward with the PIAT [Projector Infantry Anti-Tank launcher] and succeeded in putting a bomb into the tank and the crew of five bailed out and came forward with their hands up." The infantry fled, leaving the vehicles abandoned.[20]

This ended 1st SS Panzer Division's efforts to regain Carpiquet. The Germans withdrew to the area of the quarries.[21] But there was no safety there. Minutes later, Typhoon fighter bombers struck and left fifteen tanks burning. The infantry battalion had 115 men killed, wounded, or missing. Already desperately short of armour, the 1st SS suffered the heavy loss of twenty tanks. For its part, the 12th SS reported 155 of its men either dead, wounded, or missing after the fight for Carpiquet.[22]

When Eberbach advised Rommel of the failed effort, the latter said, "One ought to try getting out of the bridgehead [Caen and its defensive perimeter] without being fleeced too much." He expected British and Canadian divisions to assault the city at any moment. Rommel knew it was time to withdraw his forces west of the Orne before they became inextricably entangled in a battle for Caen that would achieve nothing.[23]

UNABLE TO RETAKE Carpiquet, the Germans returned to slathering it with artillery. The Chaud's regimental historian declared the village "a literal hell. The fire of the mortars, the rockets, and the enemy artillery never ceased for an instant."[24]

Private Alex Greer, a stretcher-bearer in the Queen's Own Rifles, thought Carpiquet "was a terrible battle. Everyone possible was below ground in a trench." Whenever the stretcher-bearers heard someone cry out in pain, they had to go out and find the man. "We were losing so many [stretcher-bearers]... It could be quite nerve-racking. I was with a fellow at Carpiquet who was to be my partner. When night fell, everyone went below ground. He and I were in a slit trench, and he went bananas. I was wrestling with him, yelling, when the shelling eased and we took him away. He was able to come back after a period at rest camp. The people suffering from battle fatigue were not cowards, I assure you... After a while, the casualties all looked the same... arms and legs off. I found the people who were wounded the least, made the most fuss."

Greer never forgot the image of "a tank captain who had both legs blown off and when I found him, he was sitting beside his tank, quietly smoking a cigarette." A corporal and sergeant working in the RAP were both evacuated with battle fatigue because of the horrors they witnessed as dozens of casualties were brought in for triage. The medical officer asked Greer to take over their duties. Seeing a chance to escape the front lines, Greer said, "If you let me... work... with you from here on in, I'll come." The doctor agreed. Greer remained in the RAP for the rest of the war.[25]

When Lieutenant MacRae had regained consciousness after the last German counterattack, he was disheartened to learn that the premonitions of his two friends that they would die in Carpiquet had been prescient. Company Sergeant Major Joe Murray had died during the assault on the village. Lieutenant Hector McQuarrie died in the subsequent siege, as did Lance Corporal Wes McDavid, the third man in the trench the night of their fateful conversation. MacRae was the only survivor.[26]

Any open movement in Carpiquet drew fire. North Shore's Major G.E. Lockwood was standing with Captain Willard Parker at the town's main intersection late on the afternoon of July 5 when medium artillery plastered the area. "[Parker] and I took off on a dead run through the back gardens of a row of houses, with the shells carefully following behind us with what appeared to be a deliberate attempt to make us increase our speed. Of course it was just a general shelling of the town. Finally we could run no more and dropped into a shallow ditch where we lay looking at each other. A shell dropped further up the ditch and he received hits in both legs while I was untouched. That was my third near miss."[27]

Dug into their strongholds on the airfield, the Germans were practically on Carpiquet's doorstep. Captain H.S. MacDonald's platoon was just three hundred yards from a group of 12th ss. "The town is a mass of rubble and animals are decaying in nearby fields," he wrote in a letter home. "There is a permanent stench everywhere you go. The morning was fairly quiet, just shelling. Only one hit on our house, though a rocket shell got four men in one trench." In the afternoon, MacDonald checked the company perimeter and was nearly crushed when a wall tumbled down after being hit by a shell. He and his runner then dodged through machine-gun fire across an open farmyard. When MacDonald joined one platoon, he helped free a man who had been entirely buried by erupting dirt and concrete that had blanketed his slit trench. Three men went "windy" and one entirely nuts. "Got two of them pacified, using strenuous methods. Was caught by shells in one trench, and two men were praying fervently while shells hit the wall and exploded just behind us." Days "seemed years long and all the time the ear-cracking bedlam of shells, mortars, machine guns and bombs. There were flies and more flies. We couldn't take our clothes off and only shaved once in three days."[28]

On July 6, 8th Brigade's Brigadier Ken Blackader told the Queen's Own Rifles that their attack on the airfield was cancelled. Instead, they were "to hang on in...present positions for two more nights and one day. Then there will be a big attack on our left flank by 3 [British Division] and 7 [and] 9 [Canadian Infantry Brigades.]"[29] This news buoyed the spirits of those in Carpiquet. They also found solace in thinking that holding Carpiquet must have contributed to making this advance on Caen possible. Operation Windsor had failed to achieve its original intentions, but some good had come of it.

ON JULY 5, hoping to capitalize on the capture of Carpiquet village, 1 British Corps's commander, Lieutenant General John Crocker, set in motion a new operation, code-named Charnwood.[30] Its purpose was to capture the old medieval heart of Caen, which lay to the northwest of the Orne, and secure crossings just west of where the Canal de Caen merged into the Orne River. Across the river from the city centre was the large suburb of Vaucelles—distinguishable from Caen only by the fact that its architecture was more modern. A small, narrow, and heavily industrialized island separated river and canal northward to the sea. East of the island lay the factory town of Colombelles with a sprawling steelworks on the southern outskirts. Crocker intended to close in a semicircle on Caen with three infantry divisions. The 3rd Canadian Division (lacking its 8th Brigade still in Carpiquet) would be on the right, the just-arrived 59th (Staffordshire) Division in the centre, and the 3rd British Division on the left. The two British divisions would descend in a tight grouping from the north, while the Canadians—advancing on a broader front—struck from the northwest.[31]

Operation Charnwood would entail four phases yielding a four-thousand-yard advance. In the first phase, the British would capture the villages of Galmanche, La Bijude, and Lébisey Wood. The Canadians would then carry Buron, Gruchy, Château de Saint-Louet, and Authie, with 59th Division on the left flank taking Saint Contest and Epron. In phase three, the Canadians would push through Cussy-les-Forges to the Abbaye d'Ardenne.[32] Finally, all three divisions would advance to a "line running through the villages of Franqueville and Ardenne and onward north of Caen to a point about a mile north" of city centre. These final objectives were designated "objectives for exploitation," because Crocker knew they were likely unattainable.[33]

The villages set as objectives all stood on the only remaining high ground before Caen. Their loss would force the Germans to pull back to their next defensive line—a series of ridges south of the city. If not for Hitler's intransigence, Rommel would have already done this.[34] Instead, the 16th Luftwaffe Field Division supported by twenty tanks of a 21st Panzer Division battalion would face the British onslaught, while the 12th ss met the Canadians and the portion of 59th Division attacking La Bijude and Galmanche.[35]

Transferred from the Netherlands to Normandy, the Luftwaffe division had relieved 21st Panzer Division on July 5. Formerly a garrison unit, it had never seen combat. Its troops were well equipped with supporting artillery, anti-tank guns, and 7.62-centimetre anti-aircraft guns usable in a ground support role.[36] Eberbach considered it "numerically strong," possessed of a good commander, and better trained than most such Luftwaffe formations.[37]

Despite their losses, the four 12th ss battalions poised to meet the advance could be counted on to offer their typical fanatical resistance.[38] The Germans had established a strong defensive line of "mutually supporting positions based on what were by now virtually tank-proof villages."[39]

To shatter this defensive crust, the British and Canadian divisions would be lavishly supported by artillery. Each division's inherent field regiments were supplemented by the heavy guns of 3rd and 4th Army Groups, Royal Artillery, and the field regiments of the Guards Armoured and 51st divisions—altogether 656 guns. The battleship *Rodney,* monitor *Roberts,* and the two cruisers, *Belfast* and *Emerald,* would be on hand.[40]

Charnwood would also mark the first Allied attempt to support a ground attack with heavy bombers. The decision to assign RAF's Bomber Command and the U.S. 9th Air Force to support the offensive came at the insistence of General Bernard Montgomery. Bombers, he wrote, could "destroy enemy defensive positions and artillery, and...cut off the enemy's forward troops from their lines of supply in the rear."[41]

Allied Expeditionary Air Force staff, recognizing the potential hazard of bombing friendly forces, established a six-thousand-yard buffer zone. The area targeted encompassed the northern part of Caen and surrounding open countryside. This four-thousand-yard by fifteen-hundred-yard rectangle was nicely captured within four topographical map squares. Lying outside the bomb area, however, were all the fortified villages. These were too close to the Allied lines. In fact, the designated area was largely devoid of German forces, because they were crowded up close to the front in expectation of the forthcoming offensive.[42] Although it was recognized that the bombing would fail to harm the German forward defences, it was believed that "the supply routes through the medieval streets of Caen could be blocked, the soldiers manning the outer defences deprived of food, their vehicles of petrol, and their guns of ammunition, and they would lack direction in battle from their command through the disruption of their communications."[43]

Timing of the bombing operation was badly flawed. Instead of occurring shortly before the attack, which might have dazed and disorganized the Germans, the bombers were inexplicably scheduled to attack between 2150 hours and 2230 hours on July 7. Charnwood was not to begin until 0420 hours the next morning. This left the Germans six hours to recover from what arguably would be a new horror they had never before experienced. As one commentator later observed, "there was little point in RAF Bomber Command delivering such a heavy blow—and then giving the enemy time to get over it."[44]

Bomb loads were also problematic. Ideally, delayed-action fuses, allowing the bombs to bury themselves deeply before exploding, would be used because this amplified the destructive force. But such bombs created large craters that would hamper the Allied forward advance. Most of the bombs were consequently fitted with instantaneous fuses that detonated on contact—meaning smaller craters but also less "destructive effect upon the enemy's defence works."[45]

DESPITE STRATEGIC BOMBERS and extensive artillery, Charnwood's success depended on the infantry and tankers. Jockeying their divisions to adapt to what promised to be a rapidly changing battlefield would require highly competent commanders. Yet at this crucial juncture, both Crocker and his superior, Second Army's Lieutenant General Miles Dempsey, had lost faith in 3rd Canadian Division's Major General Rod Keller. Dempsey thought the Royal Winnipeg attack on Carpiquet airfield had not been "well handled."[46] Carpiquet, Dempsey told Montgomery on July 7, "proved...quite conclusively that [Keller] is not fit to command a Division...Had it been a British Division I would recommend strongly that he be removed from command at once." Crocker more than agreed. On July 5, while the battle was still unfolding, he wrote Dempsey that the "limited success of this operation" resulted from "a lack of control and leadership from the top."[47]

The two British generals conceded that 3rd Division had done well on D-Day but had since become "jumpy and excitable." Crocker argued that this "was a reflection of the state of its commander [who was not] standing up to the strain and showed signs of fatigue and nervousness (one might almost say fright) which were patent for all to see." The division no longer showed "anything approaching its original offensive enthusiasm." Dempsey concurred. "It will never be a good division so long as Major-General Keller commands."

In his note to Dempsey, Crocker allowed that Keller "has the appearance of having lived pretty well."[48] This referred to Keller's reputed heavy drinking. At forty-three, Keller's round face was perpetually ruby red. Rumour had it he drank a bottle of whisky a day. Yet Keller never seemed to be drunk. Before promoting Keller to command of 3rd Division on September 8, 1942, Lieutenant General Harry Crerar had confronted him about the rumoured drinking. Keller had assured him it was never overindulgent. Crerar took him at his word.

Until recently, Crerar had considered the tall man with a ramrod-straight bearing one of Canada's most promising officers. He had even confided to Montgomery that Keller would be the next Canadian up for a corps command, probably that of 1 Canadian Corps in Italy. On July 7, Montgomery repeated this assertion to the Chief of Imperial General Staff, General Sir Alan Brooke, with the admonition that the "idea is quite absurd." Montgomery added that he was "not too happy about the Canadians. Keller has proven himself to be quite unfit to command a division; he is unable to get the best out of his soldiers—who are grand chaps."[49]

For his part, Crerar was now also anxious about Keller and thought his removal might prove necessary. But he was wary of the British tendency to unfairly criticize Canadian commanders. It was difficult to know whether Operation Windsor's difficulties arose from lack of divisional leadership or not. At no time had Brigadier Blackader sought additional support. When he had requested a fourth battalion to attack on the southern part of the airfield, Keller had immediately provided one. With the division maintaining a large swath of front line and already preparing for Operation Charnwood, Keller had been left with no real reserves. So, Crerar thought, it was hard to see how Keller could be directly responsible for Windsor's shortcomings. These were likely due more to stiff German resistance than to lack of Canadian skill or vigour.

[3]

Hopeless Situation

EXCEPT FOR THE senior commanders, the Canadians were unaware of the controversy swirling around 3rd Division's recent performance. On the evening of July 7, their attention was riveted on 467 heavy bombers unleashing a rain of destruction upon Caen. Bomber Command committed 283 Lancasters, 164 Halifaxes, and 20 Mosquito pathfinders from Nos. 1, 4, 6, and 8 Bomber Groups. Within forty minutes, 6,000 bombs totalling 2,276 tons of explosives were dropped.[1]

"As far as you could see forward and far as you could see back," Canadian Scottish Regiment's Captain Harvey Bailey recalled, "you could see big Lancaster airplanes. When they finished the bombing...the dust from the city was just something. It was a terrible bombing."[2]

Fellow Can Scot Lieutenant J. Duncan Lorimer saw the bomb-bay doors open and sticks of bombs fall. "The whole sky was red. The planes were silhouetted in red." The ferocity of the explosions seemed unimaginable.[3]

When 3rd Division solicited an opinion on the effectiveness of the bombing, a battalion officer in Carpiquet signalled: "Everything to our front seems to be in flames." The Highland Light Infantry's intelligence officer gushed: "This stuff going over now has really had an effect upon the lads on the ground. It has improved their morale five hundred per cent."[4]

The Allies unanimously declared the bombing a great success at little cost. Bomber Command reported only one Lancaster from No. 166 Squadron shot down over enemy lines. Two other Lancasters and a Mosquito crashed inside Allied territory.[5]

In Caen, the bombing continued a nightmare of destruction begun on June 6, when the city had been subjected to heavy air bombardment and naval fire to disrupt German movement towards the invasion beaches. Although air-dropped leaflets had warned of the attack, only a few hundred of its sixty thousand residents had fled before the bombers arrived. For the next forty-eight hours, the bombing and shelling had been relentless. Eight hundred civilians died; thousands were injured. Much of Caen dated back to the eleventh century. William the Conqueror had bestowed two abbeys here and, as one Canadian Army report put it, "this treasure house of the Romanesque had survived through a congenial academic, administrative, and commercial existence as the chief town of the Calvados...But it was also a hub from which many spokes of road, rail and waterway ran out in every direction."[6]

After the June 6–7 bombings, about fifteen thousand people found refuge in the underground medieval stone quarries south of the city. They were still hiding there when the bombers returned on July 7. Another fifteen thousand were scattered throughout the ruined city. Three thousand sheltered in the Abbaye aux Hommes, the Bon Sauveur convent and hospital, and Saint-Étienne church. Conditions everywhere were terrible.

The July 7 raid razed the city's university, and at least two smaller civilian shelters were destroyed. About 350 people died. The civilian death toll due to Allied bombing and shelling from D-Day to its liberation would ultimately number 1,150.[7]

With the city reduced, in General der Panzertruppen Hans Eberbach's words, to "a pile of debris...it could only be passed through with difficulties."[8] Neither the 16th Luftwaffe or 12th ss troops received either rations or fresh ammunition during the morning of July 8.[9] Still, the overall effect was considered negligible. The 12th ss reported only two Mark iv tanks destroyed and several others "turned over and covered with rubble and dirt. They could be righted and made ready for action again."[10] Personnel losses were estimated to number less than twenty men.[11] Visiting his front-line troops, Standartenführer Kurt Meyer was surprised how little their morale had suffered. "The troops hated the fighter-bomber attacks far more than the mass bombardment of those cumbersome juggernauts."[12]

Clearly the bombing presaged an attack, so Meyer braced his men to meet it. Headquartered in Abbaye d'Ardenne, the 25th Panzer-Grenadier Regiment held a two-mile-wide front from La Bijude to Franqueville. The 2nd Battalion of 26th Regiment concentrated at Saint-Germain-la-Blanche-Herbe, a village on Caen's western outskirts next to the Caen-Bayeux highway running between Carpiquet and Franqueville. Their role was to block any Canadian breakthrough towards the city. Inside Caen, 26th Regiment's 3rd Battalion hunkered in the northwest corner. After Carpiquet, this regiment's 1st Battalion had been withdrawn to a rest area south of Caen. The division's reconnaissance battalion and one battalion of artillery were also in this reserve area. Holding Meyer's left flank was the attached 1st ss Panzer-Grenadier Regiment from 1st ss Panzer Division. It held a three-mile front from Franqueville, past Carpiquet and the airfield, to Éterville.

With thirty-two Mark IVs and twenty-eight Panthers, the 12th ss were strong in armour. Nine Mark IVs lay in ambush around Buron and Gruchy. Five others held the eastern edge of Carpiquet airfield. Eleven Panthers were stationed between Bretteville-sur-Odon and Éterville. The remaining seventeen Panthers and eighteen Mark IVs were in reserve near the Abbaye d'Ardenne or in Caen's western outskirts. Clustered about were various artillery and anti-tank guns, including an 88-millimetre gun battery in Cussy.[13]

Meyer still felt "anxious misgivings." The forthcoming battle could not be won; the situation was "hopeless." His troops could only fight until wiped out or allowed to withdraw. Meyer hoped he would be allowed to quit while some of his men still lived.[14]

THE BRITISH DIVISIONS on the left were to begin Charnwood with the Canadians joining the second phase, scheduled to start July 8 at 0730 hours with 9th Brigade advancing about a mile from Vieux

Cairon to Gruchy and Buron. From here the brigade's North Nova Scotia Highlanders would push on to Authie and Franqueville, a mile southward. In Charnwood's third phase, 7th Brigade would capture Cussy to the southwest and the ancient Abbaye d'Ardenne. The division would then be halfway to Caen and ready for a full-court push by all three brigades to shove the Germans out of the city and away from the Orne's western bank.[15]

In support of the infantry would be 2nd Canadian Armoured Brigade and the division's field artillery. A good number of Flails, Crocodiles, and Petards from 79th British Armoured Division were also available.

If Keller suffered from nerves, he displayed no signs of this on July 7. In the late afternoon, he discussed the map dispositions of 9th Brigade's Stormont, Dundas and Glengarry Highlanders (Glens) with Lieutenant Colonel G.H. Christiansen at the regiment's Vieux Cairon headquarters. Then he went forward to where both Companies 'A' and 'B' were on their start lines in order to look "over the ground ahead." Many a divisional commander would never go this far forward, particularly as the area was being intermittently shelled.[16]

The Germans hoped to disrupt the Allied preparations with harassing fire, but it was largely ineffective. By this time, 3rd Division was well seasoned. Everyone knew what had to be done. "Each [infantryman] carried at least sixty rounds of ammunition; spare Bren-gun magazines were filled and distributed, No. 36 grenades cleaned and primed, the 3-inch mortar bombs stacked, wireless sets checked, maps issued, and other preparations made as the officers briefed their NCOs and men on the plan of attack." Tankers spent the evening loading the "ninety shell racks inside their tanks with armour-piercing and high-explosive shells."[17] Gunners sweated in the July heat to unload ammunition from trucks and stack it near the guns. For the first twenty-four hours of Charnwood, each field artillery regiment's gun crew shifted 27,000 pounds of shells.[18]

At 2300 hours, the 656 guns fired heavy concentrations at all fifteen villages within the German outer defensive ring and identified enemy gun positions.[19] The 12th Field Regiment threw out a feverish rate of fire throughout the night. Like all 3rd Division's field regiments, shortly before the invasion, the 12th had exchanged its

25-pounders for 105-millimetre self-propelled M-7s. Nicknamed "Priests," these guns provided the Canadians with greater mobility than the towed 25-pounders. One drawback was that every shell in a gun's 27,000-pound allotment "had to be lifted from the ground up some seven feet." It was backbreaking work.[20] During the night leading up to the barrage that would support the attack, 12th Field fired several missions directed by an air observation officer circling the battlefield. They also ranged in on six "Uncle" targets (all divisional artillery firing as one), and one "Victor" concentration (all corps artillery firing).[21] At 0420 hours, all guns assigned to support Charnwood opened up and "fired continuously during the day."[22]

ON THE RECEIVING end, Kurt Meyer thought the artillery "of unimaginable intensity." His headquarters in a cellar under the ancient Abbaye aux Dames, northeast of Caen, was shaken by explosions. Plaster and dust showered on the candle-illuminated map table. Over the din, Meyer heard the drone of countless fighter-bombers attacking. Wireless traffic indicated 12th SS units being heavily engaged by 59th Infantry Division's assault towards Galmanche and La Bijude.[23]

The 16th Luftwaffe was terrifically hurt. For two hours, 250 medium bombers of the U.S. 9th Air Force had blanketed its positions with pattern bombs. Losses were so heavy that 3rd British Division swept through to Lébisey almost unopposed. In the centre of the British attack, the 59th Division faced tougher going.

At 0730 hours, Lieutenant General John Crocker signalled 3rd Canadian Infantry Division to head for Buron and Gruchy.[24] For weeks the Canadians had monitored the German preparations. Highland Light Infantry (HLI) observers had carefully mapped the anti-tank ditch that the 12th SS engineers had dug on an east-to-west line for eight hundred yards across the front of Buron. This ditch was connected to an extensive network of trenches and covered bunkers, behind which were thick minefields. A scattered system of dugout fighting positions encircled the village. In the cover of an orchard south of Buron were numerous dugouts sheltering artillery and machine guns. Hidden from view in the village were known to be some tanks.[25]

The battalion advanced with Captain Vincent E. Stark's 'B' Company aimed at the left side of Buron and Major Harry Anderson's 'D' Company aimed at the orchard. En route they would clear the anti-tank ditch. 'C' Company would then go head-on into the village with 'A' Company passing through to the south. This company's job was to establish the start line for the North Nova Scotia Highlanders' assault on Authie.[26] Lieutenant Colonel Franklin McCallum Griffiths tucked his command group behind 'A' Company.

'A' Squadron of the Sherbrooke Fusiliers, under command of Major Sydney Valpy Radley-Walters, was in support. Because of earlier casualties, his squadron fielded only three troops of four tanks instead of four troops. He had the regular complement of three Shermans in the headquarters troop and a troop of five British Flails under command.[27] No. 1 Troop would accompany 'D' Company and No. 2 Troop 'B' Company, while No. 4 Troop and the headquarters troop formed a reserve.[28]

The moment the creeping barrage had begun, the Germans retaliated by shelling and mortaring the start line. There was no cover. The Canadians advanced through an open, level grain field that stretched about three-quarters of a mile to the anti-tank ditch. Corporal Frank Weitzel in 'D' Company's No. 18 Platoon was hit in the leg as they set out. But Weitzel's section was leading the company through to the orchard, and the big twenty-three-year-old farmer from Tavistock, Ontario, refused to leave his men.[29]

Lieutenant Douglas Barrie of 'D' Company's No. 16 Platoon was stunned by the cacophony. The explosions were deafening. There was the stench of cordite and of richly fertilized soil being thrown high into the air. Smoke and drifting dirt obscured the sun. He advanced into a false night, vision reduced so only one or two men nearby were visible. The whereabouts of the rest of his platoon was a mystery.[30]

No. 1 Troop's tanks mired in a minefield that ripped the tracks off three of the Shermans. An 88-millimetre gun firing from 7,500 yards to the southwest quickly knocked out the disabled tanks. Flails churned into the field to beat a pathway so that the fourth tank could escape. It hooked up with the headquarters troop, but

'D' Company had now lost its tank support. Radley-Walters ordered No. 4 Troop to fill the void.[31]

A German came out of the grain in a rush at Sergeant James Peter Kelly of 'B' Company's No. 12 Platoon, but started to run away when he saw a raised Lee-Enfield. Kelly calmly shot the German in the back of the head at twenty yards. Mindful of the 12th ss murders of Canadians, Kelly was "pretty mad." There would not be many prisoners this day. Later, Kelly returned to the corpse and took a Luger pistol and Iron Cross that the soldier, only eighteen years old, had won on the Russian front.[32]

Major Ray Hodgins of 'C' Company thought the advance was like something out of the Great War. He and his men plodded across open ground. The artillery crashed down. They paused to wait for the forward companies to root out some enemy and then trudged forward again as the advance resumed. He tried to keep the men spread out in order to lessen casualties from a single bomb or shell. A lot of men were still falling. Shell bursts cratered the field, "and earth and shrapnel flew in every direction. The smell of battle for the first time is terrible with the smell of burned cordite...Cattle were roaming around, sometimes hit by shells. Vehicles were burning and the smell gave you a very funny feeling the first time. After that, it became commonplace. There were also people in the burned out tanks."[33]

Private Michael B. Borodaiko of 'B' Company's No. 10 Platoon was a tough case, given to independent action. Closing on the anti-tank ditch, the company was fired on by one machine gun after another. As each of the guns opened up, Borodaiko charged with Bren gun firing from the hip and killed the enemy gun crew. "We were very bitter," he said after. "Some of us had seen the North Novas being taken POW into some bushes [on June 7]—then gunfire.

"Then [Captain] Vince Stark was shot in the back by a German hiding in [the ditch]. So there was no mercy after that. In battle, it's kill or be killed." Past the ditch, the platoon found cover in a sunken road leading into the village. Borodaiko's loader announced he could see Buron clearly through some bushes, so the Bren gunner took his place. Emptying the magazine, Borodaiko called for another. When no magazine was passed forward, he turned to discover the other man had taken "a bullet through the head, lying in my old position."

Single-handedly, Borodaiko had cleared six machine-gun positions despite fire that was "so thick...other members of his section were pinned down," read his Military Medal citation. "Yet he continued on and cleared the way for them, miraculously escaping injury himself."[34]

When Lieutenant Charles Donaldson Campbell, the battalion's intelligence officer, reached the anti-tank ditch, it struck him that it looked "like a World War One trench with systems of bays and shelter areas. It was hard hand to hand fighting with the 12th SS Panzer-Grenadiers—bayonet, knife and bare fist. They were all young lads, big and strapping. In their wallets we later found that most of them had pictures of themselves in various uniforms from kids on up. They had been told that the Canadians would take no prisoners so they never seemed to quit. They were tough. One Nazi had an arm blown off by his own hand grenade tossed back at him. He reeled for a moment then picked up another grenade and threw it with his remaining hand.

"We lost about half of the two assault rifle companies in the first two hours." The anti-tank ditch measured fifteen feet wide by twelve feet deep and was lined with machine guns within and behind. The moment the HLI finished clearing the ditch, they were lashed by artillery and mortar fire that caused more casualties.[35]

As Hodgins's 'C' Company reached the spot where Vince Stark had been wounded, Hodgins saw that his friend was badly hurt. The two were so close they had been nicknamed "the Gold Dust Twins." "I injected morphine, saw he was almost gone and put a tag on that he'd been given morphine. He knew me and called me by name...and I called a Stretcher Bearer because I knew he was so badly hurt. Then I had to go on." The twenty-nine-year-old officer soon died.[36]

WHEN THE HLI attacked Buron, the Glens had likewise advanced towards Gruchy. The Canadian artillery-support fire going out towards the Germans struck their war diarist as "unbelievable.

Nothing like it has ever been heard. The dust raised now is so great as to obscure the sun." 'A' and 'B' Companies led with the other two in trail and the Sherbrooke's 'B' Squadron in support.

Initially spared German counter-battery fire, the leading companies were caught in the open by mortars and medium artillery at 0749 hours. They were swallowed inside a cloud of smoke.[37]

It quickly became evident that Gruchy was not as strongly held as Buron. Despite heavy machine-gun fire and the shelling, the Glens were only finally "stopped by heavy machine-gun fire just outside the town." At that decisive moment, however, the Glens were unexpectedly reinforced by Bren carriers of the 17th Duke of York's Royal Canadian Hussars. Because of lack of depth in the beachhead, only two of this regiment's reconnaissance squadrons had so far been put ashore. For Charnwood, 'B' Squadron's sixteen carriers had been tasked with "mopping up" German resistance pockets bypassed by the assaulting regiments. Seeing the Glens blocked in front of Gruchy, Lieutenant Don Ayer decided to act. "Without hesitation, he charged right through them, in real old cavalry style, right into the middle of an enemy Company position. With grenades and Bren guns...firing at point-blank range, they drove the enemy from his dug-outs, killing dozens, wounding others, and capturing 25 or 30 prisoners. This act of extreme gallantry on the part of all ranks allowed [the Glens] to advance into Gruchy." Sergeant Bob McDougall and Trooper Doug Turner were killed, while Ayer and another man were only slightly wounded.[38]

Ayer's charge freed 'B' Squadron to eliminate machine-gun positions on the left-hand side of the village. Closing on Gruchy, 'B' Squadron tried to pass two troops around the southern outskirts, while No. 3 Troop pushed in head on. The two troops moving past Gruchy were immediately fired on from the Château de Saint-Louet farther to the south, and two tanks in No. 2 Troop were knocked out. The remaining two Shermans moved to the orchard on the southern edge of Buron to help 'A' Squadron, which was locked in a fight there. Despite losing one tank to 88-millimetre fire from a concealed position, No. 1 Troop remained on the southern edge of Gruchy. Here it attacked a small-calibre anti-tank gun. Opening their hatches, the tank commanders wiped out the crew by throwing grenades into their position. A Panzerfaust round penetrated one Sherman but failed to seriously damage it. Several minutes later, this tank engaged and knocked out a Panther attempting to enter Gruchy.[39]

Inside Gruchy, the Glens were caught up in a fierce street fight beginning at 0820. The shootout lasted only fifteen minutes, but when it ended, all of 'B' Company's officers except Major Neil Gemmel were dead or wounded. Also dead were 'A' Company's Major Frank Lester Fisher and Company Sergeant Major George Dickson.[40] The two men had been killed by a single shell.[41]

The moment the firefight ended, the surviving panzer grenadiers in Gruchy attempted to flee southward. No. 1 Troop cut many of them down with its machine guns. When some survivors sought refuge in weapon pits hidden in the grain field between Gruchy and the château, the tankers closed up and killed them with machine-gun fire.[42]

Inside the town, No. 3 Troop had also met stiff opposition. One tank was knocked out when a panzer grenadier attached a magnetic bomb to its side. The ensuing explosion killed the gunner and loader-operator. Then an anti-tank gun brewed up two tanks. The lone survivor was later destroyed by an 88-millimetre firing from near Buron. 'B' Squadron could only support the Glens in their subsequent advance on the château with its headquarters troop and the three surviving No. 1 Troop tanks.[43]

Despite subduing Gruchy, the Glens were too disorganized to immediately take on the château. Christiansen was having difficulty reorganizing his men in the midst of German shellfire still pounding the town. He advised Brigadier J.C. "Ben" Cunningham that "it is evidently [going to be] a long slogging match to get anywhere today." He asked brigade headquarters to direct artillery onto Authie because "the enemy is lively in that direction." No sooner had Christiansen sent this message than his battalion headquarters back at Vieux Cairon was shelled. The battalion's second-in-command, Major A.M. Hamilton, was wounded. Christiansen requested even more counter-battery fire because Gruchy was being saturated. Cunningham replied that brigade needed the Glens to "spot the direction." By 0900 hours, the shelling of battalion headquarters had tapered off, but Gruchy remained under heavy fire.

Finally, at 0950, Christiansen reported the Glens ready to attack the château. Cunningham told him to wait so this advance could coincide with the North Nova move on Authie. This plan was badly delayed by the HLI still being locked in a struggle for control of Buron. Until the village fell, the North Novas lacked a start line.[44]

THE HLI'S DELAY in clearing Buron was not due to lack of effort. While they had been fighting through to its outskirts, the German garrison within had been steadily growing. From the north, the 25th Panzer-Grenadier Regiment's company at Galmanche had retreated to Buron to escape the British attack there. Part of the company in Gruchy had also successfully reached Buron. Consequently, by the time the HLI gained the town, it faced all that remained of 25th Regiment's 3rd Battalion. These panzer grenadiers were amply supported by mortars and machine guns, tanks, and most of the 12th SS artillery. Although the HLI was not outnumbered, the Germans possessed a superior weight of supportive weapons. They also fought from well-prepared defensive positions that gave them a significant edge.[45]

Both leading HLI companies had been shredded in gaining the outskirts, and 'A' Squadron had lost half of its fourteen tanks. Those Shermans remaining could not find a route into the village, so they "browsed about the slit trenches immediately in front of Buron, shooting up anything and everything."[46]

The HLI's 'D' Company had been pounded at the anti-tank ditch and then left dozens of dead and wounded strewn on the ground between it and the orchard beside the village. On the edge of the orchard, Sergeant August Paul Herchenratter quickly dressed Corporal Frank Weitzel's leg wound. But when he tried to get Weitzel to go back, the man brushed off the wound. Both men had played a large part in getting the company to its current position. Together or alone, they had overrun many machine-gun and rifle positions. Now, before them, the orchard teemed with more Germans.

Herchenratter gathered the nineteen men that were all that remained of two platoons and attacked some dugouts next to the stone wall that encircled most of Buron. Seeing a German in one dugout, he was unable to get an angle for a rifle shot. After he threw in two grenades, both of which failed to explode, the German rested a potato-masher stick grenade on the dugout's ledge. Herchentratter took a bead on the grenade, and when the man popped up to throw it, shot him dead. The sergeant received a Distinguished Conduct Medal for his heroism this day.

Weitzel, meanwhile, had led a section-strong charge through the orchard. When only three other men were still standing, he told Private William Spencer to go back for reinforcements. Then he led the other two men forward. Lieutenant G.E. Lowe witnessed Weitzel "going down the orchard with his Bren gun on his hip and two riflemen beside him, then only one, then nobody but himself. The trenches were thick and well filled...Weitzel cleaned them all out but the last one." Plunging into the last dugout, Weitzel disappeared. The following morning his corpse was found in the body-filled dugout. He had been riddled with bullets. Weitzel was unsuccessfully nominated by the regiment for a Victoria Cross.[47]

Once the orchard was cleared, the remnants of 'D' Company worked into Buron. A straggling affair, its well-spaced houses had been reduced to rubble and the intervening gardens and orchards reduced to thickets of shell craters. On the northern flank, 'B' Company was unable to get into Buron at all because of the heavy defences. The company needed tanks, but the nearby Sherbrookes were milling about in front of a wide stretch of ground they thought concealed an anti-tank minefield. Lieutenant Colonel Griffiths knew the east side of the road leading into Buron was mine free, but his signallers were unable to raise the tankers. Lieutenant Campbell, the intelligence officer, finally dashed across the bullet-swept ground to the tanks. On the back of a Sherman was a button infantry could push to signal the crew commander to open his turret for a talk. Campbell told Radley-Walters how they could get forward, then dodged back to the battalion command group, only to see the tanks still stalled. He made another "broken field zig-zag dash to the Squadron co's tank," his Military Cross citation read. This time he was successful in getting his message across.

When the tanks followed his instructions, they were able to engage the German defenders. "Grenades, mortars and small arms

fire hadn't budged the group of seventeen- and eighteen-year-old Hitler Youths," Campbell later wrote. "Twice the tanks overran the slit
trenches and the Germans just lay down to avoid being crushed,
then rose up again to fight. It wasn't until the tanks ran right up to
the trenches and fired right down on them that they were wiped out.
All this time they must have known they didn't have a chance. The
group had two officers. One was twenty-one and the other
twenty-three."[48]

After establishing his tactical headquarters in a large dugout
designed to shelter vehicles, Griffiths compensated for the battalion's depleted state by instructing both 'A' and 'D' Companies to
attack from the orchard while 'C' Company would assist 'B' Company on the opposite flank.[49] Ten men were standing in a cluster to
hear these instructions when a shell struck a nearby tree, and jagged
pieces of steel and wood sprayed the dugout.[50]

One of the signallers landed with his head on Griffiths's shoulder. Blood ran from the dead signaller's eyes and nose. Griffiths
realized he would have been killed had this man's body not absorbed
most of the shrapnel. As it was, the lieutenant colonel had a chunk
in his ankle.

Major Ray Hodgins regained consciousness lying on his side. On
the other side of the dugout he saw Lieutenant Clarence Sparks dead
with a cigarette hanging out of his mouth. Hodgins had shrapnel in
his buttocks, "which is the best place you can get hit."[51] All three signallers were dead. Griffiths, Hodgins, Major Dave Durward, who
commanded 'A' Company, and four other ranks were wounded. Only
Lieutenant Campbell was unscathed. Hodgins and Durward both
refused evacuation until they were able to reorganize their
companies.

Campbell arranged for Griffiths's Bren carrier to come forward to
evacuate the battalion commander. His carrier driver, Private A.P.
Ableson, had been evacuating wounded from the grain field and the
anti-tank ditch when the call came for him to fetch Griffiths.
Manoeuvring over "extremely rough ground" under intense shellfire,
Ableson reached the dugout. Loading Griffiths and the wounded
other ranks aboard, Ableson had just set off when a shell knocked

Griffiths overboard and disabled the carrier. Despite his own shrapnel wound, Ableson retrieved a nearby abandoned carrier, single-handedly transferred Griffiths and the other four wounded to it, and then drove through heavy fire to safety.[52]

'D' Company, by now, numbered just twenty men commanded by a single officer, Major Harry Anderson. Thirty men in 'B' Company were led by Lieutenant J. Chantler. The wounded Hodgins was the sole officer in 'C' Company. He had fifty men. 'A' Company was the only one that remained fairly intact.

Prior to every engagement, a nucleus of officers, non-commissioned officers, and some other ranks were selected to be Left Out of Battle (LOB) to provide a core group around which the battalion could be rebuilt if it were destroyed in combat. This group came forward to join their comrades.[53]

So reinforced, the HLI fought its way into Buron. At 1010 hours, Major G.A.M. Edwards—the battalion's second-in-command and now leader—reported they controlled Buron's centre. "But amongst the rubble small parties of enemy clung on desperately and fought throughout the day—the last of them were not uprooted until the next morning."[54] Headquarters company commander Major F.A. Sparks—whose younger brother had been killed when the shell hit the command group—was shocked when German artillery began showering shells on Buron even while the HLI was still fighting to eliminate these pockets of resistance. Then he realized that the panzer grenadiers were so dug in they were protected, while his men were dangerously exposed.[55] Clearing these fanatics was all the HLI remained capable of, and Edwards "appreciated that it would be impossible for him to send his men out across the fire-swept open ground to the south with any hope of success."[56]

This meant the HLI was incapable of securing the North Novas' start line. It fell to the surviving tanks of 'A' Squadron under Major Radley-Walters to advance into the open and gain the higher ground south of Buron. Fortunately, the tankers had been joined by two troops of British 17-pounder M-10 tank destroyers from 245th Anti-Tank Battery. Just as the Shermans and M-10s advanced from Buron, German Panthers counterattacked from the high ground that was their objective. In a fierce melee, the M-10s destroyed thirteen Panthers at a cost of six of their own, while 'A' Squadron was reduced to just four Shermans.[57] One M-10 picked off nine Panthers as each trundled from behind a stone wall into its sights. When the M-10 ran out of ammunition, it was knocked out by another Panther.[58] Fourteen of twenty-three German tanks were knocked out.[59] When the fighting ended, Radley-Walters led the surviving four Shermans onto the high ground. They were soon joined by two machine-gun platoons from the Cameron Highlanders of Ottawa (MG). "Thus precariously established," as an official army report later stated, "the position held firm. An uneasy situation had been set right. The advance could be resumed."[60]

The HLI suffered its bloodiest losses of the war—262 casualties, of which 62 were fatal.[61] 'A' Squadron lost eleven tanks, but seven were repairable. Three tankers died and five were wounded.[62]

[4]

Day of Revenge

FOR HOURS, MAJOR General Rod Keller had been anxiously urging 9th Brigade's Brigadier Ben Cunningham to get the Canadian advance moving towards Authie and Château de Saint-Louet.[1] But the delay in capturing Buron had made such an advance impossible. Finally realizing that "a fresh start must be made," Keller rescheduled the advance to 1430 and arranged for supporting artillery for that time.[2]

To the Canadian left, meanwhile, the inexperienced 59th British Infantry Division had fought its way through to Épron, only to be thrown out by a 12th ss counterattack. The 59th's attack stalled in front of this village and neighbouring Saint Contest.[3] Left of 59th Division, the veteran 3rd British Infantry Division had slashed through the 16th Field Division, which had virtually ceased to exist by mid-afternoon of July 8. All battalion commanders and 75 per cent of its infantry were killed or wounded in the earlier bombing or following fighting. Lébisey fell, and Hill 64, which overlooked Caen, was taken by late afternoon. The road was open for the British push into Caen.[4]

Not so for the Canadians. Here chaos reigned. Expecting to pass through Buron for Authie at 0830 hours, the North Nova Scotia Highlanders had followed close behind the Highland Light Infantry.[5] This was to be a "day of revenge for the North Novas," their regimental historian declared, "and every man was filled with grim resolve." They sought to avenge the June murder of thirty-seven North Novas and Sherbrooke Fusiliers at Authie.[6]

Instead, with the HLI stymied in Buron, the North Novas had to hole up for hours in the anti-tank ditch under continuous shelling. Many men were killed or wounded during the long wait.[7] Only at 1045 was Lieutenant Colonel Charles Petch able to move the battalion to the orchard south of Buron, which would be their start line. The men dug in under a rain of mortar fire and the shells of an 88-millimetre gun battery firing from Saint Contest, which remained in German hands.[8]

As the North Novas entered the orchard, 'A' Company's Major Errol Stewart Gray became their first officer casualty. Captain L.J. "Lou" Sutherland took over. Then shrapnel severed the right arm of 'D' Company's Major C.F. Kennedy. Arm hanging by "a small shred of skin," he ordered Private Adrian Gaudet to slice it off with a knife. Kennedy continued command for two hours before handing over to Captain Stephen Stanley Bird and walking unaided to the RAP. Bird and four others were mortally wounded by a shell a few minutes after Kennedy left. Battalion's support company commander Captain Cecil Matson took over 'D' Company.[9]

At 1430 hours, the order finally came for the advance. As the North Novas went in behind a creeping barrage, they saw 'C' Company of the Stormont, Dundas and Glengarry Highlanders advancing to the right from Gruchy towards the Château de Saint-Louet.[10] The five remaining tanks of the Sherbrook Fusiliers' 'B' Squadron supported the Glens, and only five tanks of 'C' Squadron accompanied the North Novas. The rest of this squadron remained behind to help 'A' Squadron quell resistance at Buron.[11]

The North Novas came upon a trench system in front of Authie, but the tankers ripped down the length of one after another with their machine guns. As the Shermans tackled each length of trench, those Germans not killed immediately surrendered. As 'D' Company's point platoon reached a trench, machine-gun fire killed one of the section leaders and wounded the other two. Lieutenant Everett Sutherland cut down four Germans with a Sten-gun burst. As

'D' Company dived into the narrow trenches, a melee broke out with men throwing grenades and wielding bayonet-fixed rifles. One North Nova single-handedly killed six of seven Germans in a trench and then took the survivor's surrender. When the panzer grenadier raised his arms, he was holding a stick grenade in one hand and trying to set off the fuse with the other. Three North Novas riddled him with Sten-gun bursts.

The two company commanders, Matson and Sutherland, "seemed to have charmed lives. They led rush after rush until the entire system of enemy trenches...had been cleared." Pushing on, the battalion found itself entering the trench system in which it had been overrun on June 7. "There were rusted rifles and broken Stens and respirators, even North Nova tams with the badges still on them." These trenches were on the edge of Authie, which proved only lightly defended. Not realizing some North Novas had already entered the village, the Shermans opened fire to cover their advance. A shell struck the side of a building just as Captain Sutherland looked out its door. Sutherland was killed, and his signaller, Private D.W. Ferguson, was blinded by the blast.[12]

Authie was reported taken at 1530 hours, but it would be hours before the last panzer grenadiers would be either killed or taken prisoner.[13] At the head of 'A' Company's leading platoon, Lieutenant R.G. MacDougall had an eye shot out. Company Sergeant Major F.J. Paynter took over the platoon and led it through the right side of Authie in a rush that cleared the Germans from that part of the village.[14] On the opposite flank, Lieutenant Donald Columba Mackinnon and six other men were killed by the last machine-gun position in Authie.[15]

RIGHT OF AUTHIE, Lieutenant Donald Stewart's No. 15 Platoon had led the Glens of 'C' Company in the attack on Château de Saint-Louet. In arrowhead formation, No. 15 Platoon was point with No. 13 Platoon to the right and No. 14 Platoon the left. Major Archie MacDonald's command group was immediately behind Stewart's men. Hugging a creeping barrage, the company advanced to within three hundred yards of the château before taking cover in a series of abandoned German slit trenches in the grain field, to allow time for the artillery to work over the mostly destroyed buildings. As MacDonald stood in the trench telling his platoon leaders what their next moves should be, a German grenade exploded and he was mortally wounded.[16]

No. 14 Platoon's Lieutenant J. McKinnell took over and led the company into the château grounds. After taking thirty prisoners, the men started digging in, while German artillery began falling. Sergeant Harry Wilson was struck in the eye by a shard of shrapnel that cleanly excised his eyeball. He refused to be evacuated until his men promised to search for the missing orb. As Wilson turned to go, one man grumbled, "Jesus, I don't know how you expect us to do it!" In their fight for Gruchy and the château, the Glens lost thirty men.[17]

As 9th Brigade's fight for its objectives had moved into the afternoon, the North Shore (New Brunswick) Regiment still in Carpiquet village had reported a steady stream of 12th ss panzer grenadiers "withdrawing southwards in disorder." Pursued by artillery, many were seen to be struck down. The North Shores also believed the mile of country separating Carpiquet and the château was no longer strongly held.[18]

When the North Novas sent a 'C' Company patrol to Franqueville, this proved to be the case. Only some stragglers were encountered, and they immediately surrendered. 'C' Company quickly advanced on and began digging in among the ruined buildings of the village.[19] There was a moment of surprise when they discovered a wrecked Sherbrooke Sherman tank in the ruins. Then someone realized it was left over from the tank regiment's June 7 advance. Franqueville had been the farthest point inland from Juno Beach that the Canadians reached that day before being driven back by German counterattacks.[20] The North Novas felt fortunate to have escaped another fight for Franqueville. Authie had already cost them more than a hundred casualties.

Seizing Franqueville concluded 9th Brigade's phase of Operation Charnwood. The way was now open for 7th Brigade to take the Abbaye d'Ardenne and village of Cussy. Although the Abbaye was now a working farm, its medieval buildings included a large Gothic church with a small circular tower built into each front corner. High stone walls surrounded the complex, and access was limited to a few narrow portals. It was surrounded on all sides by grain fields.

The Abbaye had regularly served as Standartenführer Kurt Meyer's headquarters since June 7, specifically because the church's left tower provided an unrestricted view across open country all the way to Juno Beach. Presenting a large and obvious target, the church had by July 8 been badly damaged by artillery and bombs, its soaring roof shot away. Both towers were in rough shape, but they still served as observation platforms. Meyer's actual headquarters was not in the church. It was in a cellar under a sturdy building adjacent to a small orchard in the middle of the complex.

By afternoon the Abbaye confirmed Meyer's fears as to how July 8 would develop. Dead Hitler Youth were scattered about, and the little orchard "looked like an inferno." In the cellar headquarters, the ceiling shivered under the shells despite its being deep underground and buttressed by massive arches. Climbing to the top of the battered tower, Meyer watched Authie, the Château de Saint-Louet, and Franqueville fall. Obviously the Abbaye and Cussy were next. Meyer warned the commanders responsible for both that it was imperative they hold until nightfall in order to screen the division's withdrawal into Caen's outskirts. He then requested his immediate superior, I ss Panzer Corps Obergruppenführer Josef "Sepp" Dietrich, to permit the 12th ss to withdraw east of the Orne at nightfall. Hitler had ordered Caen held to the last man, Dietrich replied.

Meyer decided to prepare a withdrawal across the river anyway. The heavy weapons would go first. Then the rest of the 12th ss would begin to slip away. But until night fell, the Abbaye and Cussy must be held.[21]

ALSO PLANNING MOVES from a church tower were two officers from 7th Brigade's Regina Rifles. Captain Gordon Brown and Major C.S.T. "Stu" Tubb had ascended a rickety ladder inside the tower of a church in Rots to study the battalion's line of advance on the Abbaye. It was a sobering sight. "The area was flat, open, and devoid of cover where an attacking force would easily be seen. What is more, the defenders had the advantage of dug in defences and clear fields of fire."[22]

Brown, who commanded 'D' Company, took in the massive stone Abbaye surrounded by high walls. "We were looking at what seemed to be an impregnable fortress. My God, I didn't want to do this attack." Lieutenant Colonel Foster Matheson's plan called for 'B' Company, under Major Eric Syme, to advance from Authie to some curious small mounds about four hundred yards out in the field. These were believed to be fortifications, likely held by forty to fifty Germans. Once secured, Brown's company and Tubb's 'C' Company would advance past and then cross the remaining seven to eight hundred yards to the Abbaye.[23] Captain Bill Grayson temporarily commanded 'A' Company, which had been so badly shot up on D-Day that Matheson hoped to keep it out of this fight.

A squadron of tanks from the 1st Hussars, a section of 6th Field Company engineers, and guns of 12th Field Regiment would be in support.[24] Brown thought the Hussars would be of little help. There were too many places where German 88-millimetre guns could be hidden. Once the Hussars saw this, they would likely baulk at advancing. If they didn't, the Shermans would end up on the losing end of a turkey shoot. Brown figured the Reginas would have to fight this one alone.[25]

Given the terrain they faced, nobody in 7th Brigade was keen on their phase of Operation Charnwood. Not only did the Canadian Scottish face the same kind of open ground as the Reginas, but they noted with concern how it gradually rose from the start lines to Cussy and the Abbaye. This meant they would constantly be under German observation and fire from higher ground. A map overlay with expected and known defensive positions pencilled in had been helpfully provided by divisional intelligence staff. Lieutenant N.T. Park of 'B' Company's No. 10 Platoon duly placed the overlay on his map and saw "so much red on the map that it was difficult to trace [my] platoon's route on it."

The Can Scots had waited out 9th Brigade's operations in the grounds of a large estate east of Cairon. Its ten-foot stone wall provided some protection from the German shelling, but the battalion still suffered casualties during the increasingly protracted wait. Despite 9th Brigade's advance being far behind schedule,

Lieutenant Colonel Fred Cabeldu received orders at 1030 hours to move to the attack assembly area—an open field midway between Buron and Gruchy that was exposed to fire from the Germans still defending Authie and their objective of Cussy.

No explanation was given as to why they must go to such an exposed position for an attack not scheduled to begin until 1400 hours. Cabeldu looked at the open wheat fields the battalion must cross and the similar field in which they were to loiter. There was no cover anywhere. The Can Scots would have to dig slit trenches, likely under fire. Casualties were inevitable.

A single gate provided an exit from the estate onto the southeast-running road from Cairon to Vieux-Cairon. The Can Scots were to use the road to reach the assembly area. Knowing Canadians were inside the estate, the Germans regularly shelled the road in front of the gate. When the battalion burst out of the gate, Cabeldu led the men away from the road and in a wide circling manoeuvre to the left of Vieux-Cairon. This brought them into lower ground that was less visible to the German artillery observers. 'A' and 'C' Companies led.[26] En route, 'C' Company's No. 13 and No. 15 Platoons encountered dugouts hidden in a wheat field that were still held by panzer grenadiers unwittingly bypassed by 9th Brigade. Some of these youths were scared stiff and immediately surrendered. But others wanted a fight. At the head of No. 15 Platoon, Lieutenant Geoffrey Corry suffered a tremendous blow to the head. "I found myself on the ground staring at my steel helmet with a bullet hole through the rim, which had cut my chin strap and nicked my temple. I got to my feet, burning with fury that anyone should have the audacity to fire at me and began to clear the area." The Can Scots rooted out thirty prisoners. "My blood was up and, if time had permitted, I would have gleefully shot the lot."[27]

At the assembly area, Cabeldu's fears were realized. Shells rained down as the men dug frantically. Ahead, 9th Brigade's battalions were still heavily engaged. There would be no 7th Brigade advance until the highland brigade won its fight. Gunfire was still steadily ringing out from Authie as 1400 hours came and went. A wireless signal pushed the attack back to 1730 hours, and the Can Scots were told to start closing on their start line, the road running between Buron and Authie. Cabeldu "could visualize many casualties while waiting close to the start-line for our zero hour. I therefore asked the Brigadier for permission to remain where we were, assuring him that we would make a forced march to the start-line and hit it at the appointed zero hour." Brigadier Harry Foster agreed.[28]

Cabeldu was not just worried about the delays caused by 9th Brigade's slow progress. He was equally concerned about the British 59th Infantry Division's failure to clear the village of Bitot, which directly overlooked Cussy. The British had signalled that they were so badly held up that Bitot would not be attacked until the next day.[29] Cabeldu expected his exposed flank to come under heavy fire from Bitot during the advance on Cussy.

WHILE CABELDU HAD held the Can Scots as far back as possible, the Regina Rifles had paced along a short distance behind the Stormont, Dundas and Glengarry Highlanders 9th Brigade's advance. The battalion was woefully understrength. Instead of eight hundred men, it numbered less than five hundred.[30] Matheson had wanted the Reginas positioned to directly attack the Abbaye the moment 7th Brigade gave the signal. But that had left the battalion out in the open ground, digging in repeatedly to escape heavy artillery and mortar fire. 'B' Company suffered five casualties by mid-day and 'C' Company, nine.[31]

Captain Brown's 'D' Company hunkered beside a large hedgerow from which his men could watch the North Novas' advance on Authie. Several Sherbrooke tanks were sheltering in a nearby gully that provided hull-down protection. Only the turrets were exposed so the main gun could be fired. One Sherman was hit in the turret by several anti-tank rounds, and its crew bailed out. Suddenly, the crewless tank reversed on its own. The Sherman "wandering backwards," struck Brown as "a ridiculous sight," even as his men scrambled to get out of its way before one track slid into a ditch and the engine stalled.

Spotting a German Panther approaching the hedgerow, Brown ran to a nearby British M-10 tank destroyer and tried unsuccessfully to get the crew commander's attention. Finally he hugged the armoured hull, "hoping it would soon fire." Instead, the steely-nerved gunners waited until the Panther was about seventy yards distant before opening up with their 17-pounder. "When it fired I was stunned by the noise and the jolt as the gun recoiled and the chassis seemed to rise right off the ground. The German tank burst into flames."

A few minutes later, three Bren carriers arrived. Matheson, Tubb, and Syme were aboard, and the lieutenant colonel told Brown to climb onto one. They were going into Authie—now reportedly taken—for a reconnaissance. En route, the carriers took a wrong turn into a field west of the village, where the North Novas were still duelling with a strong force of 12th ss troopers. A bullet to the head killed Matheson's driver. The officers dived into the tall wheat beside the road, while the carrier crews turned around under fire. Panzer grenadiers were chucking grenades, and one exploded at Syme's and Brown's feet. Both men were shaken but otherwise unharmed. Suddenly, the carriers started rolling, and the officers scrambled to get aboard. Brown chucked himself flat "on top of some boxes which read clearly, 'High Explosives.'" These contained ammunition for the 3-inch mortars, and Brown shivered as "bullets bounced off the rear of the carrier."

Authie also proved still bitterly contested. The officers took to a ditch occupied by some North Novas. "Where are the forward lines?" one asked. "Right here. Be our guests," a North Nova snapped back.

From the ditch, the officers could see nothing but the "stone walls of battered buildings in the village." It was 1700 hours, and the Reginas were to attack in just thirty minutes. Already, supporting artillery was saturating the Abbaye with shells. The explosions were so loud Brown could barely hear Matheson. Finally, the lieutenant colonel yelled: "The companies are on their way to join us and our tank support will be here soon. We must launch our attack without delay or lose the benefit of the barrage."

Realizing their companies were unlikely to find them, the officers moved into the field behind Authie. They spread out and lay down in the open, so the approaching troops would see them and be able to rally on their respective commander.[32] Several 1st Hussar's 'A' Squadron Shermans moved close to where Brown lay in order to gain a line of fire on the Abbaye. No sooner did they stop rolling than a hidden 88-millimetre gun opened up. Three Shermans were quickly knocked out, including that of squadron commander Major W.D. "Dud" Brooks. Trooper Raymond Patterson was killed, and three other men wounded.[33] Brooks and his crew would likely have died had it not been for the extra tracks welded onto the front of their Sherman, which lessened the penetrating impact of the armour-piercing shell.[34] Brown saw a lot of machine-gun fire coming towards the tanks from the mounds midway between Authie and the Abbaye. Clearly, that position was heavily defended. Syme's 'B' Company faced a tough fight.

When the three companies of Reginas arrived, their commanders had a difficult time organizing them in the midst of intense enemy shelling. The men in Brown's 'D' Company were reeling, many wiping tears from their eyes. Moving towards the start line, Company Sergeant Major Jimmy Jacobs had been killed by shellfire.[35] As the battalion was starting to advance, a Sherman rolled up with Lieutenant E.J. Hooper, a 12th Field Regiment forward observation officer (FOO), aboard.[36] The barrage had come and gone, but he promised to direct more artillery on the mounds and the Abbaye. Hooper hid his tank behind the last building in Authie that faced the Abbaye. As Brown had predicted, the tankers refused to advance into open fields covered by at least one 88-millimetre gun waiting to pick them off.

Left of the Reginas, meanwhile, the Can Scots had fulfilled Lieutenant Colonel Cabeldu's promise to Brigadier Harry Foster. After a forced march, they went right over the start line on schedule at 1730 hours. On their flanks, Gruchy, Buron, and Saint Contest were all still embattled. The 12th ss firmly held Bitot, which left the battalion exposed to flanking fire from the left. But there was no question of waiting for any of this to be cleared up. The Can Scots and Reginas were going to attack, and because the Reginas were still getting organized behind Authie, this would not be a coordinated assault. Each battalion would instead fight its own isolated battle.

5

A Terrible Dream

YPICALLY, THE GERMANS began to heavily shell the ground directly behind the creeping barrage as 'A' and 'C' Companies led the Canadian Scottish advance on Cussy. 'A' Company vectored towards a strongpoint surrounded by hedges midway between the start line and village. Its No. 7 Platoon headed for the 88-millimetre gun position with No. 8 Platoon close behind. 'A' Company's plan called for the Highland Light Infantry in Buron to provide fire support with their Bren guns, mortars, and anything else within range. The Can Scots' 'C' Company would also help as much as it could while advancing alongside. On 'C' Company's opposite flank was 'C' Squadron of the 1st Hussars under Major D'Arcy Marks.[1]

This was No. 7 Platoon's Lieutenant Duncan Lorimer's first battle. He was anxious, particularly because his year-younger brother, George, was a sergeant in No. 8 Platoon. He worried that two of his parents' four sons might be dead by nightfall. As the platoon had started forward, he had been further discomfited when a stretcher-bearer suddenly started crying. "Don't make me go on. Send me back. I can't go," he pled. Lorimer ordered him to the rear and hurried the rest of his platoon in the opposite direction.

Despite the terrific rain of mortar rounds, No. 7 Platoon suffered not a single casualty in gaining the strongpoint. With the supporting barrage and the mortar bomb explosions, the noise was deafening. Glancing over his shoulder, Lorimer saw Major Bill Matthews knocked down by an explosion. He was relieved when Matthews bounced back on his feet and resumed walking. The major had only been nicked in the side by a sliver of shrapnel.[2]

To his right, Lorimer spotted a large, twenty-foot-high cross with a Christ figure attached. "Amidst all the shelling, the smoke, the dust, the noise," it struck him as strangely out of place. He was amazed that the cross remained unscathed. Why was there a cross in an open field, he wondered. A second later smoke roiled, and the cross was lost from view.[3]

As the platoon advanced, the mortar fire was joined by that of Nebelwerfers, machine guns, anti-tank guns, and artillery. Can Scots started falling. "The ground shuddered and shook with the pounding of exploding shells and bombs. Men were covered with dirt, grimed with dust and some dazed and knocked over by blast as the ss troops poured their fire into the open fields over which the... Scottish advanced. It was the most intense and concentrated fire the men had ever experienced."[4]

Shells detonated all around Lorimer, but he remained untouched. He suddenly believed himself immune, unable to be hit. Seeing Sergeant John Crawley leading the platoon's headquarters section, Lorimer formed an O with thumb and forefinger to signal all was okay. Grinning broadly, Crawley returned the gesture.[5]

Because of the smoke, 'A' Company could no longer see 'C' Company to its right. None of the planned support fire was happening, because the smoke had blinded everyone. When the company was less than 250 yards from the strongpoint, Matthews ordered everyone to lie down and wait for the artillery to lift. Suddenly, the shelling moved forward, and "clearly before us across the fields" the men saw torn hedges that marked the strongpoint. Somebody shouted, "Come on, Scottish," and the platoons "surged forward." The men saw muzzle flashes in the hedge, tracers streaked towards them, bullets snickered past. They returned fire from the hip, sprinting forward.[6]

Lorimer spotted the 88-millimetre and a series of weapon pits right of it that were his objective. Plunging through the hedge, the platoon found the pits had been abandoned seconds before. A terrific explosion caught Lorimer from behind as he came through the hedge. His rifle went flying. Thrown off his feet, he landed face first. His back and legs burned as if on fire. He tried standing, but his legs were useless. Lorimer feared he had been paralyzed. Dragging himself through the hedge, he lay on his stomach. Shells exploded all around and shrapnel sang over his head. Lorimer told a man to let Sergeant Crawley know he had the platoon. Looking at his watch, he saw it was 1757 hours.[7]

Each officer carried a morphine vial to use on casualties. Lorimer gave himself a shot, but it did nothing for the pain. Private Alexander Lamb lay nearby with a leg wound. Lamb tossed a pack of cigarettes to the lieutenant. Despite being a non-smoker, Lorimer lit one. "Never realized before how just having that cigarette in your mouth and drawing on it, plus maybe the morphine, quieted you down," he later said.[8] Lorimer's wound was sufficiently grave that his war was over.

'A' Company, meanwhile, broke into the strongpoint. Damaged by the shelling, the 88-millimetre gun crew abandoned it after blowing it up with an explosive charge. Seeing the Can Scots pouring in with bayonets fixed, the 12th ss toughs fled in terror. Despite repeatedly being knocked down by explosions, Company Sergeant Major John Stanley Grimmond dashed about, keeping the men focused on the job. A desultory attempt by the panzer grenadiers to regroup behind the far hedgerow collapsed when Nos. 7 and 8 Platoons charged them. The surviving Germans ran through the wheat for Cussy.[9]

Just as 'A' Company began sorting itself out inside the strongpoint, the sound of multiple tanks with engines roaring and tracks screaming was heard. Lorimer's first thought was, "Oh good, our tanks are here." Then he realized a German Panther was bearing down on him. He dragged himself into the cover of the hedge, but Lamb was in the open and unable to move. The tank ground over the spot where Lorimer had been lying and then rolled right over Lamb, a track crushing one of his feet.[10]

Three Panthers barged into the midst of 'A' Company, and men scattered every which way. Lance Corporal George Kawiuk stood his ground, grabbing a PIAT dropped by its wounded operator. He fired a bomb that broke the track on the tank that had run over Lamb's leg. When the Panther lurched towards him, Kawiuk dived into a trench, and it rolled harmlessly overhead. Kawiuk then popped up and blasted it from behind with a second bomb, which penetrated the hull, set it afire, and killed the crew.[11] The rapid loss of one Panther convinced the other two tank crews to return "home right smartly."[12] Kawiuk received a Military Medal for his courage. It was now about 1800 hours. To the right, there was still no sign of the Reginas moving against the Abbaye.

ALTHOUGH THE CAN Scots were unable to see them, the Reginas had managed to advance not too far behind schedule from Authie towards the Abbaye. But they had lost the artillery barrage and the tanks were not venturing into the open fields, so the Reginas walked forward entirely exposed and unsupported.[13]

Major Eric Syme's 'B' Company headed for the mounds in the middle ground. They walked directly towards machine guns burning off bursts from the mounds. Snipers were also shooting from Authie. Artillery, mortar, and anti-tank fire came from all points of the compass. Men were falling fast when Syme suddenly collapsed from shell shock. He was evacuated.[14] Captain John Treleaven immediately took over.[15]

The company advanced with Nos. 10 and 12 Platoons forward and No. 11 Platoon behind. The platoons moved in bounds, one section covering the others. Slow going, but the manoeuvre gave the illusion of advancing with some supporting fire on hand. A scattered line of fallen men marked their course across the field. Thirty minutes gaining the mounds, and then they fell without a fight—the Germans had fled as the first Reginas arrived. The men started digging in as mortars soaked the mounds with bombs, and machine guns and two tanks at the Abbaye raked their position with fire. "Dig deep," Treleaven told the men. Their job was done. A hundred men had gone forward, and sixty-one had been killed or wounded. Several of the injured refused evacuation.[16]

Passing by the shattered company, Major Stu Tubb saw that the Abbaye, "surrounded by a high stone wall and a cluster of farm buildings, stood out prominently on the flat plain and open fields in the late afternoon sun, and it commanded all approaches to it." With no artillery available, Tubb had asked the Regina's company mortar section to hit the Abbaye with high-explosive, only to be told they were out of those rounds. Smoke was all they could offer.[17] This supporting fire began just as Tubb's 'C' Company moved into the open beyond the mounds with No. 13 and No. 14 Platoons leading. No. 15 Platoon followed out on one flank so its men could offer fire support to the other platoons.[18]

The smoke screened the company until it was five hundred yards from the Abbaye. Then a breeze swept it away, and Tubb and his men found themselves "completely naked to view... Rifle and automatic small arms fire came at us through the slits in the protecting stone wall and walls of the Abbaye buildings, thickened up by support from [two] dug-in tanks slightly off to the right front...13 Platoon got onto a field of buried mines, adding to the general turmoil." Tubb left his company headquarters section and ran to help extricate the platoon from the field. "I was hit in the leg by a machine-gun burst and sat down abruptly. It felt as though someone had hit me a mighty wallop with the broadside of a shovel."

Led by second-in-command Captain Lyle White, his headquarters section ran to Tubb. "Just as he got ten or twelve feet away, he was hit in the chest by an MG burst, dying instantly. The rest were unhurt." "Jack, it looks like you'll have to take over the rest of the way," Tubb told Company Sergeant Major Jack Adams. As Adams started to stand up, "he was literally bowled over, head over heels, with a hit in the shoulder. Someone came back to report two Platoon commanders killed, the third wounded and all section leaders out of action, with a few survivors fighting on the Abbaye threshold."[19]

As Tubb was loaded onto a salvaged door serving as a stretcher, he ordered the company back to the mounds. 'C' Company was finished. Twenty-one men fit to fight made it back to the mounds. Fifteen of these crawled to Authie and returned with stretchers to undertake the slow, deadly job of rescuing the wounded from a field in which the company had suffered eighty-five casualties—twenty-two fatal.[20]

Captain Gordon Brown's 'D' Company had also been pinned down when the smokescreen dissipated. Brown saw the tanks, saw an MG-42 firing from a pillbox at one corner of the stone wall, and saw another shooting from the top of the church. To prevent his signallers—marked by the long and distinctive whip antennae of their wireless sets—from being killed, Brown had left them in Authie under control of his second-in-command, Captain Hector "Hec" Jones. He was reduced to sending a runner back to Jones, who then transmitted messages to battalion headquarters.

"As the struggle went on it was almost like a terrible dream," Brown recalled. "The occasional man fell wounded or dying and was treated by his buddies." Lieutenant Jack Mooney's No. 16 Platoon and No. 18 Platoon, commanded by Lieutenant Dick Roberts, led 'D' Company's advance with Lieutenant Al Law's No. 17 Platoon in trail. Brown's headquarters section was at the back. Everyone was "crawling, running and diving into the high grass to escape death. We lost track of time and space. The Abbaye appeared from time to time through the haze of smoke, looming ominous and still spitting gunfire of all kinds." At 2100 hours, a runner reported that Mooney and his platoon had gone left around the Abbaye walls to get behind the main German defences, and disappeared. Brown ordered the other two platoons to attack frontally.

Brown went in search of No. 16 Platoon's thirty men. After blundering upon a Can Scot platoon concealed in a depression by scrubby bushes—its men all either dead or wounded—Brown realized the futility of this effort and raced through machine-gun fire to rejoin the other two platoons. He arrived just as the men started a long dash for the Abbaye wall. Sixty "young men running like hell and firing as we went. I found myself in the middle of the group...Grenades were thrown into slit trenches and some bodies were blown out. Our losses were light although a handful of soldiers were hit."

Lieutenant Law and his platoon passed through a gate on the left, while Brown and Roberts took the other platoon to the right alongside the outer wall. It was about 2200 hours. Still enough light for the men to orient themselves, since the Allies used double daylight savings time whereby the clock was advanced two hours instead of the normal one. Brown glanced through a large hole and spotted a tank turning its turret slowly towards him. He pointed it out to Roberts. The two men dived out of its line of fire, but soon realized its main gun must have been disabled and the tank could no longer move. Judging the machine gun harmless, as long as everyone kept out of its firing line, Brown decided to leave it alone. He ordered Law to pull back, and the two platoons started digging in alongside the outside wall. Brown expected the Germans to start shelling the interior of the Abbaye grounds at any moment.[21]

Mooney's No. 16 Platoon was still missing. But in fact it was alive and well after going a quarter-mile left of the Abbaye and spotting an 88-millimetre gun battery in a dugout position. When Mooney and his men charged, one gun fired an armour-piercing round directly at the lieutenant that "ploughed a furrow between his legs." Although badly shaken, he led the platoon in wiping out the battery crews. The platoon then returned to the Abbaye and entered the complex via an opening in the northeast wall.

As the men picked their way warily through the grounds closest to the wall, they came upon the abandoned 25th Panzer Grenadier Regiment headquarters. Ignoring the cellar, Mooney entered the main part of the building and soon came upon Obersturmbannführer Karl-Heinz Milius's bedroom. The bed was nicely made up with crisp, clean white sheets. A bowl of fruit and bottle of wine stood on a bedside table. Mooney then withdrew and gathered his men. They continued through the grounds to the northwest gate and exited to rejoin the rest of 'D' Company.[22]

The 12th ss started shelling the Abbaye at midnight, the fire directed by an observer still inside the complex. Brown was happy to let any 12th ss in the compound stay until daybreak. That would give the Reginas time to reorganize and then systematically clear the Abbaye grounds.[23]

ABOUT THE TIME the Reginas had started towards the Abbaye, the Can Scots' 'B' and 'C' Companies had passed to the right of the strongpoint taken by their 'A' Company and headed for Cussy. 'B' Company immediately shook out to the right of 'C' Company and both advanced in line, with Lieutenant Colonel Cabeldu's head-quarters section behind. Cabeldu walked briskly, his wireless men and the battalion's intelligence officer, Lieutenant T.A. Burge, at his shoulder. Cabeldu was always close to the front in an attack. This, one company commander felt, left the men with a "feeling that with Fred Cabeldu at the helm we were being *looked* at; that he was in a position to *see* at all times and, if we were in a jam, help would be on its way if it was physically possible."[24]

Right of the Can Scots, the 1st Hussars in 'C' Squadron became locked in a duel with the 88-millimetre battery in Cussy. They also engaged Panthers in the village and others firing from the heights near Bitot. Without a single loss, 'C' Squadron wreaked havoc on the gun battery and eliminated two Panthers.[25]

Although the tank support was welcome, the Can Scots still suf-fered heavy losses in the advance. Just beyond the strongpoint, 'B' Company was struck by fire from all sides. To escape the shots directed at it, the platoon on the right side of the road dashed to the other side. This left the company bunched up and subject to even more-withering fire. Realizing their only chance was to gain the vil-lage, 'B' Company forgot about finding cover and picked up its pace.[26]

Major Desmond Crofton's 'C' Company was also caught in the "terrific crossfire from...Bitot" and the Abbaye. Twenty men fell dur-ing the advance.[27] At the head of No. 15 Platoon, Lieutenant Geoffrey Corry realized it was "no good ducking" the fire. Better to keep mov-ing. Knocked flat by a mortar round, he stumbled to his feet and carried on. Like someone trying to escape the buffeting of rain car-ried on a strong wind, the men were all drifting to the right to distance themselves from the fire coming out of Bitot. Corry was try-ing to get his platoon back on line when Cussy emerged from the smoke. "My god, it's a walled village," he hissed.

There was so much smoke and flying dirt, Corry was unable to see any Can Scots beyond those of his platoon. "Can't take the whole village with one platoon," he thought. Then someone ordered a charge. "Up the Scottish!" Corry bellowed. The platoon ran shouting to the wall, found a gap, and slipped through. Coming out into a small orchard, Corry turned and realized he had only a single section of the platoon with him. No idea where the rest of his men were. The orchard was hemmed in by walls on all sides. Corry spotted a German on the other side of one wall and fired his Sten gun. Chips flew off the wall, but the man ducked clear. A terrific blow tore Corry's leg out from under him. Struggling to his feet, he hobbled to the shelter of a wall. All alone now, everyone else vanished.

A mighty blast deafened him. He stared right at a Panther tank only yards away. Slithering off on his stomach, Corry took shelter behind the rubble of a destroyed wall. When he poked his head up, a bullet punched another hole in his helmet. Two Germans were shooting at him from twenty yards away. Twice lucky. Corry figured the third bullet hitting his helmet would surely pierce his brain. He decided to play dead. But what would he do if they rushed him? Corry took stock. Having lost the Sten gun, he had a single grenade and his pistol. Rising slightly on his side, he chucked the grenade overhand at the Germans. Had no idea if the explosion hurt them or not. Pistol at the ready, he waited.

All through the village the sounds of battle raged. In the midst of this mayhem it struck Corry as ironic that "in this considerable orchard there were three soldiers all lying flat on their bellies waiting for someone to make the first move." Suddenly there was a shout, and Sergeant Tom Carney and some other men stood over the German position. A Bren gun chattered. Carney walked over. The village was taken, he said, and hefted Corry over his shoulder. Carney carried him to Crofton's company headquarters, where wounded were being collected for evacuation.[28]

Cussy had fallen in about twenty minutes. The ferocity of the Can Scot attack broke the 12th ss troops, who were mostly anti-tank crews rather than panzer grenadiers. About seventy-five fled before the Canadians reached the village. They left two 88-millimetre guns, two heavy howitzers, a smaller anti-aircraft gun, and numerous machine guns. Some twenty snipers remained active. The Can Scots lost more men as they hunted them down one by one. Two Panthers were also knocked out by 'C' Company's PIAT men. As darkness fell, the familiar chorus started up as the Germans subjected Cussy to intense artillery, mortar, and Moaning Minnie fire for two and a half hours.

At one point, several German tanks growled to within three hundred yards of Cussy. Instead of attacking, however, they fired their machine guns into the village and then retired. Crofton thought the tanks were trying to cover the escape of any Germans who might remain in the village. But none escaped. During the night, 'C' Company rounded up thirty prisoners. They counted about forty German dead. Two German veterans of North Africa and the Eastern Front said they thought "it was a miracle how we advanced so close to our barrage, leaving them no time to man their weapons. When our men let out blood curdling yells their men broke and ran and they could not hold them. They stated they would rather meet four Russians than one Canadian."[29]

The July 8 attack on Cussy cost the Canadian Scottish two officers killed and another five wounded. There were thirty-two other rank fatalities, sixty-three wounded, and two missing.[30] Corry was evacuated to the beach, where the bullet was removed at a field hospital. After thirty-five days in Normandy, his war was over.[31]

FOR THE REGINAS, the night of July 8–9 was extremely tense. Only one company, Captain Brown's, had managed to gain the outside wall of the Abbaye. As he had left the wireless set at Authie, Brown and Lieutenant Jack Mooney returned there to contact battalion headquarters. En route they were caught in a terrific mortar bombardment. Throwing themselves to the ground, they lay with arms over their heads as eighty or more rounds detonated around them. Covered in dirt but otherwise unhurt, they carried on. A few minutes later the two came upon the stretcher party carrying Major Tubb on a door. Brown saw his friend's leg was "badly mangled...but he seemed unconcerned about himself. All he could talk about was his men, so many of whom had fallen." Tubb would lose the leg.[32]

In Authie, Brown tried unsuccessfully to raise Lieutenant Colonel Matheson on the wireless. Learning that battalion headquarters had moved to a nearby field, he told Mooney and Captain Hec Jones to take the wireless sets to the Abbaye while he reported to Matheson.[33]

Brown found Matheson in the battalion's headquarters van. Matheson looked "wan and drawn in the dim light inside the vehicle." Brown thought of how Matheson "had served so courageously throughout the first month, only to have many friends killed or wounded. At 40, he was 'old' for infantry warfare." Matheson had written 'D' Company off entirely until Brown appeared and explained that the Abbaye was in his hands. But he wanted 'A' Company sent to strengthen the Regina's hold. When Matheson asked how the company could find the Abbaye in the pitch-black night, Brown took him outside and pointed to "the fires still burning brightly in and near the Abbaye. It stood out like a beacon."

Matheson agreed to release 'A' Company on condition that Brown guided it forward. Brown and Captain Bill Grayson got the men moving. At the Abbaye, they dug in alongside 'D' Company. Most of 'A' Company's men were green troops. Grayson told Brown that, although dug in, his men were scattered "helter skelter." Many were unwittingly pointing their guns at each other rather than outwards. Suddenly, at 0300 hours, the German guns that had been unceasingly battering the Abbaye fell silent. An eerie quiet settled in.[34]

The battalion's losses were staggering. Eleven officers and 205 other ranks became casualties on July 8. Of these, 36 were fatal. Another man was missing. It was the worst fighting the Reginas had seen since D-Day itself. Those two days alone accounted for so many casualties that few of the men who had landed on Juno Beach remained.[35]

THE 12TH SS had ceased fire because they were withdrawing to the east side of the Orne. At 2100 hours, Rommel had approved Eberbach's request to immediately withdraw all heavy weapons from Caen. All artillery, heavy mortars, Nebelwerfers, and tanks were to be gone before daybreak. A strong infantry force, supported by engineers, would remain and hold for as long as possible. This plan was meant to buy time to form a new line stretching from behind Hill 64 to the north of Caen to the northern outskirts of Saint-Germain-la-Blanche-Herbe, just east of Carpiquet. Rommel realized this front could not be held for long. When it was broken, the Germans would then withdraw to a stronger position running through Caen along the eastern bank of the Orne to Bretteville-sur-Odon, immediately south of Carpiquet airfield. The intention was to maintain a toehold in Caen for as long as possible.[36]

Kurt Meyer had ordered the shelling of the Abbaye to gain the 25th Panzer-Grenadier Regiment "some breathing space."[37] When the Canadians failed to follow, which he had feared they would, he relaxed a little. The 12th ss was battered, but not broken. At about 0300 hours on July 9, he ordered the division to fall back across the Orne. The 26th Panzer-Grenadier Regiment's 3rd Battalion would serve as a rear guard—delaying the advance into Caen for as long as they could. Meyer realized that, with the Abbaye and Cussy lost, holding any ground west of the Orne River would be possible for only a short time.[38]

As July 8 closed, Lieutenant General John Crocker concluded that Caen west of the Orne was his for the taking. Because its combat initiation had been harsh, the 59th Division's tasks were limited to completing clearance of the fortified villages in its sector. The Canadian and 3rd British Divisions would respectively pinch out the 59th and then push into the city from the west and north. They would join hands in the centre of Caen at a point where several bridges crossed the Orne.[39]

On the Canadian front, 9th Brigade would attack Caen from Cussy and the Abbaye, while an armoured-car column would try reaching the bridges inside the city ahead of the infantry, in an attempt to secure a crossing before the Germans blew them all. Meanwhile, 8th Brigade would break out to the west from Carpiquet, take the airfield, and, if possible, press on to the Odon.[40]

After a hurried Orders Group of 9th Brigade's battalion commanders at 0300 hours, the Stormont, Dundas and Glengarry Highlander war diarist wrote skeptically: "The Corps Commander, Lieutenant General Crocker claimed that the enemy had fled that region."[41]

6

Most Successful Operation

AT DAWN ON July 9, Captain Gordon Brown led 'D' and 'A' Companies of the Regina Rifles into the Abbaye d'Ardenne. Resistance was confined to a few snipers, who were not all eliminated until mid-afternoon. Dead and wounded panzer grenadiers were scattered throughout the complex.

At the former German headquarters, Brown found "a large military telephone exchange against a wall outside...but the operator was dead in the midst of the wreckage." Brown took over the place for his company headquarters. Then he and 'A' Company's Captain Bill Grayson walked over to a field northeast of the Abbaye, where Lieutenant Colonel Foster Matheson had established the battalion headquarters. Matheson looked less worn than he had the night before.

As Brown and Grayson were returning to the Abbaye, it was rocked by a salvo from German artillery near Carpiquet airfield. Lieutenant Al Law of 'D' Company—the first man inside the Abbaye the night before—was badly wounded. His runner lay dead.

'D' Company's second-in-command, Captain Hec Jones, had found a basement where the German headquarters staff had stored a huge collection of wines. Jones led Brown to the room with the tidily made-up bed Lieutenant Jack Mooney had discovered the previous night. While Jones popped a cork from a bottle of champagne, Brown removed his boots. Then he drank a glass of champagne, crawled under the bedcovers, and fell asleep.

A mere hour later, a runner shook Brown awake. Top brass had shown up, the man warned. He led Brown to where a British general with several staff officers in tow stood staring out a glassless window towards Caen.[1] Brown had no idea the general was 1 British Corps commander Lieutenant General John Crocker.[2] Nonplussed, Brown looked about for Matheson to appear. Unshaven, covered in the filth of battle, Brown realized he was on his own. The general took one look, sniffed, and then snorted, "Are you in command here?"

Brown said he was and suggested that it would be good if "such distinguished visitors" stepped away from the window. He was keenly aware that a few snipers still lurked. Instead, the man glared out the window and pointed. "Look, man, look! There lies Caen like a plum to be plucked."

Brown agreed that Caen was definitely there, a "massive pile of rubble as far as the eye could see."

"Yes," the general thundered, "it's there for the taking. Good God, man, exploit success. Get your troops together and seize it."

Brown responded "with a stream of less than respectful language. I made it clear that our battalion had just captured this place after losing almost half of our 500 infantry soldiers killed or wounded." While his company had been lucky and lost only twenty-five, 'B' and 'C' Companies were decimated. "Further," Brown exclaimed, "our Colonel tells me when to attack Caen or any other place. I just don't on my own decide to take on the German army." Harrumphing and snorting, the general led his coterie back to a cluster of armoured cars and demanded directions to Brigadier Harry Foster's headquarters. After the vehicles left, Brown returned to the bedroom, drank more champagne, and caught another hour of dreamless sleep. This time when he was roused, it was to find Matheson had set up shop in the Abbaye.

Brown found Matheson standing at a large map, explaining to the other officers what the Reginas were to do next. The lieutenant colonel bowed at the waist and said, "Major Brown, I believe."

Smiling, Brown looked at the three pips of a captain on his shoulder. "I don't see a crown there yet, sir."

"You will," Matheson grinned. He then explained that 7th Brigade would follow 9th Brigade's advance into Caen. The Reginas needed to be ready by mid-afternoon.[3]

WHILE THE REGINAS were making ready at the Abbaye, 8th Brigade had attacked Carpiquet airfield at 1000 hours. The Queen's Own Rifles struck out of Carpiquet village for the airfield control-tower complex, and Le Régiment de la Chaudière advanced from Marcelet towards the hangars on the southern edge. As the Queen's Own's 'D' Company started out, it was struck by several shells that fell short from the supporting barrage. Several men were killed or wounded. One of the men killed was Lieutenant John Denison Dickson, who had just celebrated his twenty-second birthday the day before.[4]

Both regiments met very little resistance and were on their objectives within thirty minutes. The Chauds, however, found the hangar area so heavily sown with mines that it was mid-afternoon before they could report the area truly secure.[5]

Brigadier Ken Blackader was encouraged to think that the Germans had pulled back beyond the Odon River. South of the airfield, the ground sloped into a shallow valley, and Bretteville-sur-Odon stood adjacent to the river. Seizing the village would anchor 3rd Canadian Division's right flank alongside that of the British 43rd Infantry Division, which was advancing on Verson. Blackader ordered the North Shore (New Brunswick) Regiment to take the village.[6] Because the ground was so open, Lieutenant Colonel Donald Buell decided to keep everyone well dispersed. 'A' and 'C' Companies would lead, with 'B' and 'D' Companies following loosely behind. He sent the carrier platoon to show itself on the edge of the valley to the left, hoping this would divert German attention from the spot where the attack was going in. At 1525 hours, placing his headquarters' carrier between the two forward companies, Buell ordered the men forward.[7]

The moment the carrier platoon showed itself, the Germans fired on it with heavy artillery. Seeing no signs of movement in the village below, Lieutenant Bob Currie signalled Buell that "Jerry was gone on the run."[8] When the main force came over the crest and began their descent, they were ranged on by mortars and 88-millimetre and 105-millimetre guns. By the "time the two reserve [companies] had started down the slope the shelling had reached a terrific pitch and it could be seen that 'B' and 'D' [Companies] were suffering casualties."[9]

Buell jumped from his command carrier and ran over to steady some men who were wavering. No sooner had he left the vehicle than a shell knocked it out. Captain Harold Arseneau, the second-in-command, and the others aboard dragged the wireless sets free and jumped into a large shell crater. Looking back at the wrecked carrier, Buell smiled and started walking into the valley. Arseneau sent one signaller with the portable wireless to catch up, while he stayed in the crater with the larger wireless set, which was too heavy to carry.[10]

By sprinting forward during momentary lulls and throwing themselves to the ground when shells exploded nearby, the leading companies descended rapidly into the valley and broke into the village at 1630 hours. Forty-five minutes later, they reported Bretteville secure and that they were digging in under intense artillery fire and bracing for a possible counterattack. Inside Bretteville, the North Shores had met "very light" resistance. The "enemy had evidently moved out in a great hurry."[11]

Having endured endless shelling for four days in Carpiquet, the North Shores were subjected to what seemed even heavier artillery and mortar bombardment in this new village. Lieutenant Currie set up in a small house, until one of his men got twitchy and insisted they move to slit trenches. They had just finished digging in when "a direct hit blasted the whole interior of the place we had been in. A slit trench was as safe a place as a man could find in those towns."

Captain Robert Robichaud thought the fact "that we had moved out of Carpiquet seemed to give renewed energy to the unit; the Carpiquet we [left] behind was a dreary place indeed as by this time all the trees were completely denuded of their leaves, and stood like soldiers on guard where so many gallant men had fallen."[12]

WHILE 8TH BRIGADE had been seizing the airport and Bretteville-sur-Odon, 9th Brigade had thrusted towards Caen. The Stormont, Dundas and Glengarry Highlanders led the advance with a column consisting of its 'C' and 'D' Companies, four 3-inch mortars loaded on carriers, two sections of carriers, four 6-pounder anti-tank guns, and two sections of pioneers. Advancing from Château de Saint-Louet, the column was to pass through Franqueville and gain the Caen-Bayeux highway. It would then move through Saint-Germaine-la-Blanche-Herbe and into the city. Although running along a prominent ridge visible to German forces within the city and to the southeast, the highway offered the most direct route. All intelligence reports stressed that there would be next to no resistance and speed was imperative.[13]

Everything was rushed. Lieutenant Colonel G.H. Christiansen briefed his company commanders at 0500 hours and said they must be ready to move by 0730 hours. The "remainder of details," he told them, would "be tied up later." Even as the men bolted breakfast, organized their fighting kits, and headed towards the start line, Brigadier Ben Cunningham hectored Christiansen to hurry. The brigadier, Lieutenant Reg Dixon wrote in the war diary, "is most anxious that we push on...He is being pushed from higher formations. We work as urgently as possible, but we are very tired." The 0730 start time passed, the Glens still shaking off a stupor from the past day's combat and overall weariness from being on the front lines since June 6. At 0900, Christiansen signalled Cunningham that the column would not be ready until 0930 hours. Cunningham retorted that they were "to start at once." Reluctantly, Christiansen ordered the Glens forward.[14]

Heading out, the column was joined by two tank squadrons of the Sherbrooke Fusiliers Regiment. Between them 'A' and 'B' Squadrons fielded thirty-four Shermans, and the tankers counted each Glen company as numbering only fifty-one men.[15]

As this weightier column lumbered forth, a second, nimbler one comprised of armoured cars from the British Inns of Court armoured reconnaissance regiment and 'B' Squadron of the 17th Duke of York's Royal Canadian Hussars had gathered.[16] Not tied to the highway, the armoured cars darted down narrow farm lanes and tracks in a race for Caen.

Confined to the highway, the main column advanced warily. After two miles absent resistance, Christiansen ordered the column "to proceed at the best possible speed, only deploying if fired on." Christiansen noted that the Sherbrooke tankers kept pace on the left.[17]

Captain Don Scott, the battalion's support company commander, provided direct liaison with the tankers. It was unappreciated duty because he rode in one of the leading tanks. Wireless linked Scott with Christiansen. Theoretically, this allowed tankers and infantry to work together. In reality, Scott's wireless proved useless. But the tankers had started moving, and bailing out was not an option. Like most infantrymen, Scott hated the Sherman's close confines.

As the tanks crossed the start line, Scott saw Brigadier Cunningham "waving the tanks on." Scott grabbed a headset and announced he was in the tank. Cunningham said excitedly, "It's you, Don. God, keep those tanks going. There's nothing between you and Caen."[18]

The brigadier's words were not prophetic, as just in front of Saint-Germain, the advance ran afoul of a "belt of mines...across the road." Then, when the pioneers came up to lift them, they were fired on from nearby buildings. At the same time, several tanks were disabled by mines. The rest stopped, but started firing on the houses.

With Scott's wireless not working, Christiansen could not coordinate his infantry with the tank actions. The moment the tanks stopped firing, he sent a platoon into the houses. They "found only dead and wounded Germans."[19]

'B' Squadron started advancing, but without Scott's tank. A mine had blown a track, and thirty seconds later a shell struck close by. The crew commander told everyone to bail out. Leaving the tankers, Scott ran to rejoin the infantry. Behind him, the tank exploded.[20] Ranging from about two thousand yards, a German Tiger tank's 88-millimetre had destroyed Scott's Sherman and knocked out two more 'B' Squadron tanks. Seeing this, 'A' Squadron fired smoke shells to blind the Tiger and advanced a troop on either side of the road.[21]

With the tanks screened by smoke, the Tiger then turned on the infantry column, firing high-explosive that sent the men scattering off carriers for the cover of ditches.[22] At 1245 the fire abated, and Christiansen ordered his other two infantry companies forward to join the advance.[23]

The Glens bumped continuing sporadic opposition as they entered Caen's outskirts. Each time, the tanks shot up the buildings the Germans were in, and the advance rapidly recommenced. Soon the column pushed into Caen proper and, at 1330 hours, Christiansen reported being "in the centre of town." The tanks eliminated each small pocket of resistance. During these short, sharp engagements, the Glens were surprised by civilians emerging "out of cellars at the first lull, bringing roses and wine to the troops. The roses were gratefully accepted, but the drinking of wine during the action had been strictly forbidden and no soldier broke that rule," Christiansen later claimed.

The destruction in the city increased with every yard gained. Soon the streets were so clogged with rubble the tanks could go no farther. The two leading infantry companies, advancing along parallel streets, repeatedly had to scale hills of debris created by collapsed buildings. At 1440 hours, they reached the Orne and spread out between an old stone bridge on their left and a railway bridge on the right. Both had been blown, so gaining a crossing was impossible.

Within his occupation area, Christiansen was dismayed to find a large hospital—Hôpital du Bon Sauveur—containing "about 4,000 patients, far in excess of its normal capacity, most of them victims of the bombing of Caen."[24]

The Glens declared themselves the first Canadians into Caen, but they competed for that honour with 'A' Squadron of the 17th Duke of York's—particularly with the Humber armoured car crew of Lieutenant A.E. Doig, Trooper K. Johnson, and Trooper L. Mathew.[25] The army's official historian hedged his bets on the real winner by declaring that the armoured cars "had been little if at all in advance of the infantry."[26] Doig had gained the river by weaving along various streets and alleys that were not hopelessly clogged by collapsed buildings or downed power lines. At the river he thought they might have won a bridge intact, only to find it blocked by rubble and covered by German machine-gun positions on the opposite shore. The rest of 'A' Squadron soon caught up and spread into defensive positions, from where they enjoyed shooting up retreating German forces that came within range. When infantry arrived, the armoured cars withdrew.[27]

Caen "was a painful spectacle." Only the "island of refuge" around the great Abbaye-aux-Hommes and the hospital had been spared destruction. This area lay within the sector the Glens controlled. It turned out the French Resistance had managed to warn the British not to shell this area, to avoid killing the thousands who had taken refuge there.[28]

The Glens were welcomed as liberators. Roses and wine provided "a heartfelt welcome. It makes us feel proud to have had a small part in the relief of these, and other people," Lieutenant Dixon wrote.[29] More importantly, only eight Glens had died this day.[30] But as they dug in alongside the river, unerringly accurate artillery and mortar fire started falling. The battle for Caen was not yet done.

BY NIGHTFALL ON July 9, all of 9th Brigade and two 7th Brigade battalions had moved into Caen. Although the other battalions entering the city suffered few casualties getting there, their positions along the river were subject to mortar and sniper fire. They were also beset by the usual calamities and accidents that occur when everyone carries a gun he is quick to use. Captain Gordon Brown's 'D' Company led the Regina Rifles from the Abbaye d'Ardenne to Caen. Moving through the city's outskirts, their attention was drawn to a large property surrounded by a stout fence with a locked gate. Not wanting to pass by a potential enemy fortress, Brown ordered a man to shoot the lock off. "The bullet broke and the larger part entered my neck, struck a vertebra just behind the throat and...remains there to this day," he later wrote. This mishap hospitalized Brown for ten days.[31] He was one of three Reginas wounded that day.[32]

The Canadians were repeatedly finding civilians hiding in unexpected places. When Canadian Scottish Regiment's Lieutenant Tom Butters and one of his men happened on a Frenchman harvesting vegetables from a Saint-Germain garden, the farmer led them to a deep mine shaft. Access was via a steel ladder anchored to one wall. Candlelight illuminated the bottom of the shaft. Butters saw that the shaft was sheltering a large number of women and children. Shouldering his bag of vegetables, the man prepared to climb down the ladder. Hoping to find some food to contribute, Butters patted his pockets, only to come up with a cigarette pack. He handed this to the man, who accepted it with much gratitude.[33]

Along the banks of the Orne, 9th Brigade had tied in with soldiers of the 3rd British Infantry Division. West of the city, meanwhile, an 8th Brigade patrol out of Bretteville-sur-Odon had linked up along the Odon with 43rd British Infantry Division. Because 8th Brigade faced in a southeasterly direction away from Caen, British Second Army headquarters decided to place it temporarily under 43rd Division's command.[34]

The advance into Caen closed Operation Charnwood. With the objective won, Canadian divisional staff declared Charnwood "most successful... Again the [division] had risen magnificently to the occasion in spite of being a trifle war weary after thirty-five days steady front line fighting and no easy victories." But the cost was high—1,194 casualties of which 330 were fatal. The 9th Brigade bore the brunt with 616 battle casualties.[35] The division's total losses in the two-day period exceeded those of the D-Day assault. The 2nd Canadian Armoured Brigade fared far better, just two officers and eleven men killed, three officers and thirty-eight wounded.[36]

Despite being personally exhausted from not having slept for forty-eight hours, Brigadier Ben Cunningham wrote a message to 9th Brigade's troops before going to bed on the night of July 9.[37] "The determination, skill and bravery displayed by you in your battles for Buron, Gruchy, Authie, Saint-Louet, Franqueville and finally Caen is deserving of and is receiving the highest praise. You, one and all, may feel proud of the individual part you have contributed. The spirit of the 9th Canadian Infantry Brigade once more displayed itself. The result of the battle may be considered by each one of you as a personal victory; it was by your efforts the battle in our sector was won. You have proved by your actions that there are no better troops than yourselves. Of this you have never had a doubt; now it has been demonstrated to the world."[38]

But in fact 9th Brigade was unwittingly embroiled in a controversy over its performance in Charnwood. 1 British Corps's Lieutenant General John Crocker felt Cunningham had been overly cautious, frittering away opportunities for rapid advances.[39] Agreeing, Major General Rod Keller asked Lieutenant General Harry Crerar on the evening of July 9 to fire Cunningham. The brigadier,

Keller said, had repeatedly failed to "get-on," while hesitating to commit reserves quickly. Cunningham's "lack of drive" had cost the brigade heavily on July 8 at Authie and delayed its arrival in Caen.

Still dealing with the earlier criticism of Keller himself made by Crocker, Second Army commander Lieutenant General Myles Dempsey, and Montgomery, Crerar was exasperated. He told Keller to present Lieutenant General Guy Simonds with a full written complaint.[40]

Crocker, meanwhile, was even more loudly demanding Keller's head. Crerar knew the allegations against both Canadians must be addressed. But he decided to let Simonds resolve them. Crerar cautioned Simonds that Crocker's way of working with Keller might not have "brought out the best in the latter." He added that until Simonds was convinced that Keller's judgment was sound, he could not "give weight to [Keller's] views concerning his own immediate subordinate."[41] Simonds was to deal with these matters by July 13.[42]

CRERAR ALSO REMAINED on shaky ground, as Montgomery continued to impede First Canadian Army's full deployment. Whenever Crerar sought a firm date, Montgomery was evasive. In a note to the Chief of Imperial General Staff, General Sir Alan Brooke, Montgomery reiterated that Crerar was "a bad judge of men...and does not know what a good soldier should be. When I hand over a sector to Crerar I will certainly teach him his stuff, and I shall give him tasks within his capabilities. And I shall watch over him carefully. I have a great personal affection for him, but this must not...lead me into doing unsound things."[43]

Instead, Montgomery assigned both 11 Canadian Corps and 1 British Corps—eventually to be consigned to First Canadian Army command—to Dempsey's Second British Army. This gave Dempsey responsibility for five full corps instead of the normal army maximum complement of three. Montgomery's insistence that the bridgehead remained too constricted to permit deployment of another army headquarters increasingly strained credulity.[44]

Saddling Dempsey with responsibility for five corps was not really an undue hardship, because Montgomery expected the corps commanders to operate independently during battle—turning to army command more for logistical support than operational guidance. Regarding the Canadians, Montgomery thought Simonds "far better than Crerar" and "the equal of any British Corps Commander." He also had faith in Crocker. So there was no reason to let Crerar into the game.[45]

Brooke, however, had acquaintance with Crerar and trusted his generalship. Isolating Crerar for much longer would not do, Brooke wrote Montgomery, because Canada's government "will *insist* that Canadian forces should be commanded by Canadians...For that reason, I want you to make the best possible use of Crerar, he must be retained in Command of the Canadian Army, and must be given his Canadians under his command at the earliest convenient moment. You can keep his Army small & give him the less important role, and you will have to teach him."

Brooke's note forced Montgomery to abandon the hope of getting rid of Crerar entirely. But as all the Canadians in Normandy were at the moment coming under command of II Canadian Corps, national honour should be assuaged by having Simonds at its head. Now was not the time, he reiterated, to let First Canadian Army become operational.[46] Montgomery conceded to having Crerar exert "executive" command over the Canadians. This position played to Crerar's strengths as an administrator. Crerar was strict on discipline, something he thought had slipped badly in the 3rd Division ranks. He ordered Simonds and Keller to exert a firmer grip. He fretted over the increased rates of venereal disease and battle exhaustion cases, suspecting that many of the latter were fraudulent. The cure for all these ills, he told Simonds, was strict discipline. Suspected cases of faked exhaustion were to be thoroughly investigated and the guilty men harshly punished to warn others not to try seeking "this way out."[47]

As for Crerar, even as he put his mind to competently performing the limited role Montgomery allowed him, he was seething with barely hidden outrage. Montgomery's treatment, he believed, reflected the "Englishman's traditional belief in the superiority of the Englishman." No "Canadian, or American, or other 'national' [commander], unless possessing quite phenomenal qualities, is ever rated as high as the equivalent Britisher."

Montgomery, of course, believed that Simonds possessed those "phenomenal qualities," while Crerar was written off as "a most awfully nice chap" but one who was "very prosy and stodgy, and...very definitely not a commander."[48]

Simonds had commanded 1st Canadian Infantry Division under Montgomery through the Sicily invasion. By the time that campaign ended, Montgomery had developed "the highest opinion of Simonds...Briefly my views are that Simonds is a first class soldier. After a period with an armoured division," he had written in late 1943, "he will be suitable for a corps. He will be a very valuable officer in the Canadian Forces as [there is] no one else with his experience."[49]

7

Little Excuse for It

AT FORTY-ONE, LIEUTENANT General Guy Simonds had enjoyed a spectacular rise through the course of the war to date. By January 1944, he had been promoted from the rank of major to that of major general. That month, he took over II Canadian Corps and gained a lieutenant generalcy. Tall and lean with grey-blue eyes that fixed others with unnerving steadiness, jet-black hair that had a little wave at the temple, and a precisely trimmed moustache, Simonds looked exactly the way a senior army officer should. Like Montgomery, his words were always clipped and to the point. Born in England but raised in Victoria, Simonds retained or emulated many British mannerisms. Time spent at British staff college had further cemented his anglophilia. As had his adulation of Montgomery. Although inclined more towards proper dress than Montgomery, he still affected Eighth Army's careless manner and favoured the armoured service black beret. Also like his mentor, Simonds was supremely certain of his innate ability, sharply critical of others, and egotistic. Unlike Montgomery, however, Simonds had little ability to inspire common soldiers. He was too cold, too withdrawn, and too arrogant. Even with fellow officers he was distant, reserved, and all too often condescending.

What Simonds looked for in subordinates was competency and obedience. Upon arriving at II Canadian Corps, he had announced to its officers: "There are some of you in whom I have not much confidence. I will see you all individually the next day and tell you why." Many top corps staff officers were summarily dismissed. So, too, were the commanders of 2nd Infantry Division and 4th Armoured Division.[1] Only 3rd Division's Major General Rod Keller remained standing. Persuaded by Crerar, Simonds agreed that Charles Foulkes would have 2nd Division and selected a personal favourite, George Kitching, to lead the armoured division.

Simonds had a reputation as the Canadian Army's most gifted strategist and tactician. He had authored several influential military journal articles addressing the future of warfare in a modern setting, where armour would play a decisive role. Once at the helm of 11 Canadian Corps, Simonds began "educating" his formation commanders by distributing writings on subjects such as operational policy, attack strategy, efficiency of command, removing ineffective officers, recommending others for promotion, and even his view of "essential" leadership qualities. On the latter subject, he offered three legal-sized pages of observation and advice in single-spaced type. Among specifics covered were what he identified as moral qualities—character, loyalty, self-confidence, and a sense of duty. Mental qualities, such as knowledge, judgement, initiative, and alertness, were equally necessary. So, too, were the physical qualities of fitness, skill at arms, and youth. Of the latter, Simonds wrote, "A man is never too young for a job, but he may well be too old, for age reduces speed of mental and physical reaction." Age was often cited as sufficient justification for his relieving an officer. Simonds also expressed his thoughts on the common soldier. "If well trained, directed and led," he wrote, "the Canadian soldier is unsurpassed by any in the world. Coupled with a rugged courage, ready adaptability, initiative and amenability to sound discipline, the average standard of intelligence of our soldiers is very high indeed. If properly directed in battle, this intelligence is a great asset, for it makes troops very quick to take advantage of the breaks on the battlefield. But if indifferently directed or led, this same intelligence becomes a great disadvantage, for Canadian soldiers are quick to detect a badly planned or organized operation or wavering and indecision in leadership, and their confidence is more easily shaken than is the case with a more stolid soldiery. They will go into the attack with great dash and courage and a badly planned operation may result in failure with heavy casualties and a loss of confidence requiring a long time to recover. The responsibility which falls to those who undertake to lead Canadian troops in battle is not a light one."[2]

AT 1500 HOURS on July 11, "1 year and 1 day since [1 Canadian Infantry Division] under Gen. Simonds went ashore in Sicily," he assumed command of those Canadian Army units operating in Normandy. 11 Canadian Corps chief of staff Brigadier Elliot Rodger scrawled this notation in his personal diary.[3] He later added: "Never have I worked with such a precise and clear and far seeing mind, he was always working to a plan with a clear cut objective which he took care to let us know in simple and direct terms...He reduced problems in a flash to basic facts and variables, picked out those that mattered, ignored those that were side issues and made up his mind and got on with it."[4]

Simonds immediately set about learning what plans Montgomery had for the next stage of operations and the Canadian role. 11 Canadian Corps took 3rd Infantry Division, standing guard in Caen, under command. It also controlled 2nd Infantry Division, which had deployed into the crowded beachhead only on July 9.[5] Arrival of 4th Armoured Division would be delayed until there was more shoulder room. The delay in bringing in the armoured division added credence to Montgomery's argument that Crerar and his army headquarters need not yet become fully operational. But Montgomery was running out of time. The Chief of the Imperial Staff, General Sir Alan Brooke, had set a July 23 deadline for Crerar to be given command of the Canadians and 1 British Corps.

For now, however, he could keep Crerar isolated. When Montgomery met with his army commanders on July 10, Crerar was notably not invited. Yet this was an important meeting—one called to discuss the future of Allied operations in Normandy. The mood among the assembled generals was glum. While Caen had finally fallen, there was no hope that an immediate breakout from the beachhead would follow. American General Omar Bradley's divisions remained mired in marshy countryside, segmented into checkerboard squares by rows of thick *bocage*. Bradley confessed that the attempted U.S. First Army breakout had failed. He feared a Great War–style stalemate could develop in Normandy.[6]

Even after winning Caen, the Allies remained "roped off" from the open ground of the French interior. A Twenty-First Army Group intelligence report warned that the Germans would continue to "resist any attempt to break out of his cordon," for the most defensible ground lay immediately east of the city. Keeping the Allies penned in, however, also required the Germans to keep their armoured divisions in the front lines. While doing so had prevented any major Allied armoured thrust, it was inflicting upon the German panzer divisions unsustainable rates of loss. Every time the Germans tried to withdraw armoured divisions from the front for rebuilding, they were forced to return in order to stem a renewed Allied advance. Montgomery's dilemma was how to break this impasse.[7]

Montgomery, Bradley, and General Myles Dempsey had each come to this meeting with ideas. Earlier, Montgomery's chief planner, Brigadier Charles Richardson, had gloomily reported on the present situation. In the British sector, eight divisions held a front 77,500 yards wide. Their numerical superiority in manpower was just two to one, but in tanks they had a four-to-one advantage. The Americans were stretched across a 108,000-yard front with a comparative manpower ratio of three to one and a significant eight-to-one tank superiority. This positive imbalance in armoured strength would not hold indefinitely. It was the result of continued suspicion on the part of Hitler and his most senior generals that the Allies planned a second invasion on the coast of Calais. Eventually, the Germans must realize that the Allies had committed everything to Normandy. They would then send the divisions being held at Pas de Calais to Normandy, and the Allies would lose much of their numerical advantage.

Richardson recommended a major British armoured thrust in the Caen sector. "Our tank superiority is sufficient to enable us to take big risks provided a plan can be formulated to use tank superiority on ground of our own choosing," he advised. A "thrust towards Falaise provides an opportunity to use tanks en masse and hence to assert our great superiority in numbers. The enemy is fully alive to this, but unless we are prepared to fight him with our tanks it seems that no further progress on the British sector is likely for many weeks to come."[8]

Richardson's plan was at odds with Montgomery's original strategy, whereby the British role was to tie down German armoured divisions while the Americans broke out into the French interior. But clearly the Americans were unable to do so. Just before the meeting, he had confided to Dempsey, "I'm afraid Brad is barely off his start-line. It'll take him two or three weeks to organize enough strength to break out. You'll have to continue your holding battle on the left."[9] Bradley confirmed Montgomery's assumption. He did not expect a breakout attempt to be possible until July 20.

After Bradley left, Dempsey and Montgomery turned to considering the British sector. Dempsey was unhappy with the holding-action role, which forced him to keep engaging the Germans with his infantry divisions. Even now, 43rd British Infantry Division on the Odon River front was launching Operation Jupiter—aimed at capturing Hill 112, Éterville, and Maltôt. As the two men talked, a fierce battle raged on the hill and around Maltôt with the 9th and 10th ss Panzer Divisions having raced to the scene to stem the British advance.

Already it was clear the operation would have limited success beyond, of course, forcing the German armoured divisions into another fight. But 43rd Division was suffering heavy casualties for little ground won.[10] The British and Canadians could not sustain their current attrition rates.

Even before Operation Charnwood the army had suffered 28,000 casualties—nearly 4,000 of them Canadian. The infantry divisions would inevitably cease to be effective fighting units. As one Canadian analysis put it, "There was every prospect of an increasingly heavy toll. The country in which Second Army was now fighting was ideal defensive country. The British and Canadian forces were doing the attacking; the Germans had the advantage of being the defenders."

Second Army had, however, reached its peak in strength. It had three operational armoured divisions that "were quite fresh and practically untouched. Another, 4th Canadian Armoured Division, was expected to arrive before the end of the month." There were also eight armoured brigades with a combined strength of a thousand tanks.[11] This was why Richardson and Dempsey both advocated "an armoured assault of great dash and violence through the bridgehead across the Orne below Caen into the wide and promising tank country to the south."

Such bold action, Dempsey argued, would still tie the German armour in front of Second Army. But it would also break through to Falaise, a vital German supply and communication node. Montgomery worried that an offensive "into the open and heavily defended country to the south" would be "fraught with crippling possibilities of congestion and delay from the very outset." However, he agreed that such a bold strike would achieve "complete tactical surprise." The Germans would surely never consider that "such a blow" would come on this flank, where movement was constrained by the "double obstacle of ship-canal and river, the narrowness of our lodgement, and [the Germans'] excellent observation from the high ground overlooking the Orne's lower reaches." Montgomery weighed the odds and approved Operation Goodwood to begin on July 17.[12]

ARMY GROUP B commander Generalfeldmarschall Erwin Rommel had hoped to escape Caen without "being fleeced too much." Instead, two divisions had been badly mauled. By the time the 12th ss Panzer Division crossed the Orne, it had become "a badly depleted force."[13] Between June 7 and July 9, the division had suffered between 3,000 and 3,300 casualties. From a strength of ninety-six Mark IVs and a precisely equal number of Panthers, fifty of the former had been lost and forty-eight of the latter.[14] Most of its anti-tank guns had also been destroyed.

Standartenführer Kurt Meyer estimated that among the frontline troops in 12th ss Division, 20 per cent of his young soldiers were dead and another 40 per cent had either been wounded or taken prisoner. On July 11, the division was relieved by 1st ss Panzer

Division and withdrew to Vimoutiers, about thirty-five miles south-east of Caen, to rebuild.[15]

Giving up the west bank of the Orne enabled the Germans to shorten their front while setting up behind a water obstacle, either the Orne or the Odon River. To the south and southeast of Caen, Rommel was able to replace some panzer formations with infantry. He started this process on July 10 by relieving the 9th ss Panzer Division with the 277th Infantry Division, but had to feed some of the armour units back to the front in order to stem the 43rd British Infantry Division's advance against Hill 112 and Maltôt.

Although 1st ss Panzer Division had taken over from the 12th ss, this formation also needed relief and was duly replaced by 272nd Infantry Division. More slowly, 271st Infantry Division enabled 10th ss Panzer Division to withdraw. Although withdrawn from the front, these divisions remained close by in case they were needed to meet an offensive. Intelligence estimates placed some seventy infantry battalions and just 250 tanks in front of the Americans, while British Second Army was squared off on a shorter frontage against fifty-five infantry battalions and at least 650 tanks.

Still, British Second Army held the initiative. The Germans, concluded one intelligence report, could only try to "slow down our advance wherever we look like pushing on. It means [a] heavy expenditure of valuable equipment and manpower."[16]

As the Germans struggled to find troops and equipment sufficient to contain the beachhead, British Second Army deployed more divisions into its front lines. Among these was 2nd Canadian Infantry Division, which began relieving 3rd Division's 8th Brigade on the line running southwest from Caen to the eastern slope of Hill 112 on July 10.

The division's field regiments deployed about Buron and Authie on the night of July 10–11. Bombardier Ken Hossack of 4th Field Regiment found the night move very different from the practice runs conducted in England. "No lights are allowed, the roads are dusty and visibility poor; large...vehicles loom up on us out of the darkness...Our advance party leads us into the selected field and the guns are pointed at the front. As...daylight comes most of us feel that this is our initiation to the battlefield. The air has held a strange, new and obnoxious stench and morning's light reveals the cause. Dead and decaying men are everywhere—Canadians... Germans—and in addition dead cattle and horses, wrecked tanks, jeeps, and other vehicles."[17]

The artillerymen were assigned the grim task of burying the decaying corpses strewn about inside their gun lines. The Germans were interred first without ceremony. Burying the Canadians had to wait until a padre arrived to not only offer a short service for the dead but also recover an identity disc from each soldier and mark his temporary resting place on a map. This would enable their eventual recovery and movement to a permanent cemetery. To the right of 4th Field Regiment's position a battery of medium artillery kept firing throughout the day. But in the regiment's gun lines, noted Captain George Blackburn, there were "only the sounds of picks and shovels as the gunners dig shallow holes under the burning July sun to receive the stinking corruption that once were men."[18]

At 1700 hours that afternoon, the regiment hitched its guns back to the tractors and headed "through smashed villages and littered roads into a wheat field beyond the shell-ventilated hangars of Carpiquet airfield," Hossack scribbled in his diary.[19] Nobody was happy with the position southwest of the airfield assigned by 2nd Division's chief artillery officer, Brigadier R.H. "Holly" Keefler. "It was obvious to officers with maps and to gunners without maps that this natural amphitheatre faced the high, enemy-held territory across the Orne River and that, if they could see enemy ground, then the enemy must be able to see them. But nevertheless not one, no matter how long he looked with apprehension at the unforgettable water tower standing like a big mushroom across the Orne, realized what was to come. And even when it did come, it was accepted by everyone as what war must be like. Hell was to be expected," Blackburn later wrote.[20]

While the inexperienced gunners stoically dug in, one veteran artilleryman was horrified by the scene. Major James Douglas Baird of 3rd Division's 13th Field Regiment stood on a hill overlooking Carpiquet airfield. "I just stood there and almost cried." Since the first day of the invasion, Baird had found fifteen separate gun positions for his regiment. Despite the ground often being dangerously level or apparently overlooked by Germans, Baird had worked with maps and visual reconnaissance to find gun sites "that occurred between the contour lines." His success led to the nickname "Back Slope Baird."

Now he watched 4th Field Regiment's gunners dig their 25-pounders into pits, camouflage them with nets, set up ammunition storage areas, and move vehicles out into the open. "No excuse for it," he muttered. "Any officer that deployed artillery on a forward slope should be shot."[21]

Digging in the guns and carving out slit trenches for personal shelter was almost complete and darkness was closing when a single German shell landed near 'B' Troop. Blackburn felt a growing unease. The solitary round struck him as intended to confirm the range for a German battery. To the southeast, the ground sloped gently almost four miles to the Orne. Just over the river was high ground marked on the maps as enemy territory. The tall concrete water tower next to the village of Fleury-sur-Orne, the one he had noted earlier, provided a dream observation post for an artilleryman. To the south stood Hill 112, over which British and German troops were still fighting. Perhaps, Blackburn thought, the situation was not as dire as it seemed. Other officers concurred. For no one could "bring himself to believe the brass would place in jeopardy all seventy-two guns of the division by deploying them in full view of the enemy."[22] Blackburn rejected the notion that Keefler or 11 Canadian Corps's senior artillery officer, Brigadier Bruce Matthews, were "madmen." More likely the guns were being deployed at the airfield because concealed positions that stood in range of the front line were in short supply due to the "awesome accumulation of guns in the bridgehead."[23] On every side of their position, other guns and tanks were arrayed. Just 4,000 yards ahead was the front line— shockingly close for artillery with a normal maximum range of 12,500 yards or up to 13,400 yards when firing a supercharge round.

The night passed quietly, but a few minutes after sunrise 'A' Troop came under heavy mortar and shellfire. At 0713 hours, 4th Field Regiment fired its first shells against a suspected German concentration point. The regiment suffered its first casualty when a signaller in one of the forward observation posts was wounded. Then, precisely at 0945 hours, a terrific shower of mortar and artillery fire descended and "all ranks experienced for the first time the nerve-wracking sensations of lying in holes in the ground, hearing the air ripped around them and feeling the ground shake under them as enemy shells smashed in one after another until it seemed that they would never stop. And when it seemed every hole in the regimental area must have been hit except 'this one,' it was suddenly quiet—so quiet that the buzz of flies was noticeable. Then the damage was assessed. Number One gun, you all right?...Number Two?...How miraculous it seemed that no one nor equipment had been hit. It was generally agreed then and there that slit trenches were definitely the answer, but that these were not quite deep enough."[24]

In the late morning of July 11, 5th Field Regiment deployed in front of the 4th Field "under shellfire" that continued "most of the day, causing two casualties."[25] The 6th Field Regiment was fortunate to arrive after dark at 0100 hours on July 12.[26]

ALSO ON THE night of July 11–12, the battalions of 4th Canadian Infantry Brigade took over the villages of Éterville and Verson. The Royal Regiment of Canada moved to Éterville, and the Royal Hamilton Light Infantry to Verson, while the Essex Scottish lay back in a reserve position. Confused by the French countryside, the Royals became badly disorganized. "Somehow the battalion's vehicle column became mixed up on the narrow road with the marching troops; the head of the vehicle column halted at Éterville in the darkness...For a mile or more back towards Verson, Canadian vehicles were lined up nose to tail on the road, and the quiet of the night was made hideous with the noise of racing motors, clashing gears, and grinding trucks. It was a sobering introduction to battle, and proved that, in spite of the excellent and lengthy training in England, the Regiment still had much to learn," observed its historian.

As dawn broke, the infantry soon realized why their British counterparts, who had been holding this section of line, had seemed so keen to depart. German artillery and mortars opened up with a drenching bombardment across the entire battalion perimeter. Snipers weighed in with rifles and light machine guns. For "the next five days," the shelling and sniping "continued with never more than a five-or-ten-minute respite. This was a baptism of fire with a vengeance."

Éterville was a salient in British Second Army's line that jutted into German-held territory with Hill 112 looming nearby. The tiny village anchored the battalion's left flank. A grey stone château, surrounded by gardens and hedges, stood in the centre. The company on the far right had dug into a savaged orchard. "Shattered equipment littered the ground everywhere, and a burned-out Panther tank still protruded half-way through a hole in the garden wall. About 50 unburied British and German dead still lay scattered throughout the area—fresh evidence, if it were needed, of the dangers of moving during daylight. Worse still, the tactical layout of company localities was unsound, since small parties of the enemy were still occupying positions within the battalion lines. As the sun climbed higher...the stench of the unburied dead was breath-taking."[27]

At Verson, the Royal Hamilton Light Infantry's experience was much the same. Even as the men moved into their positions, heavy mortar and 88-millimetre artillery fire started falling. Two men were killed and five wounded just moments before everyone got underground at 0500 hours. The battalion was in an open wheat field and orchard on the side of a hill where the Germans occupied the reverse slope.[28]

A short distance to the northeast, the last of 2nd Division's artillery regiments had moved in close to the southern edge of Carpiquet airfield. The 6th Field Regiment gunners had dug fiercely through the early morning darkness and beat the clock by having the guns ready by 0400 hours, just ahead of sunrise. Within two hours, thirty-four-year-old Gunner Percy Charles Lincoln was killed. He may have been the first 2nd Division soldier to die in Normandy.

July 12 and the ensuing five days were nightmarish for the division's gunners and 4th Brigade's infantry. German shelling never relented. Just behind the 6th Field's guns was a T-junction where the road running south to Verson branched off the one going west from Carpiquet to Saint-Manvieu. The junction was so heavily and constantly shelled it was dubbed "Hellfire Corner." Although the intersection was considered the most dangerous spot in their area, nowhere was really safe, because the Germans could see everything, whereas the Canadians were unable to make out any enemy gun or infantry positions.[29]

So relentless was the shelling that by July 14 every man was staggering with exhaustion. Lieutenant Colonel Denis Whitaker's pioneer platoon came up with a solution that gave the Riley commander a safe place to bed down. With grenades they blasted out a hole just large and deep enough to fit in a camp cot and constructed a roof from a sheet of galvanized iron, which was then camouflaged with a thick covering of dirt. Whitaker slipped into this coffin-like hide just shortly before midnight. He had just let out a satisfied sigh when there was a terrific crash, and a shell chopped a hole in the roof and exploded in Whitaker's face. Knocked unconscious, he awoke at a casualty clearing centre. The doctor treating him said shrapnel gashes to his face had been stitched, but his eyes were bandaged tight and he was being evacuated to England. Whitaker had been a star quarterback with the Hamilton Tigers. At twenty-nine, he was one of the Canadian Army's youngest, but also most seasoned, battalion commanders. He had been with the Rileys on the blood-soaked beach at Dieppe, winning a Distinguished Service Order. Now he faced possible blindness, which would end his military career and any future in professional sports. Fortunately, after three weeks in an English hospital, Whitaker recovered his sight. But he did not return to the Rileys and their command until September.[30]

Equipment, "clothing, compo food rations, mail-box, tires, tarpaulins riddled by shrapnel—everybody is tired, it is all too noisy and too new to sleep—snipers in area—dust from passing trucks brings shell fire," wrote 4th Field Regiment's Gunner Ken Hossack in his diary of 'A' Troop's experiences. "Two 'B' Troop guns receive direct hits—[Ronald John] Hooper killed—Coughlin hurt in motorbike accident—dud lands beside James Beatty—Caen [actually, Vaucelles suburb] is bombed at daylight; church steeples fall—wagon lines being shelled—heat and jitters bring out itchy hives—heavy firing—good weather—Moaning Minnies continually falling, generally on the infantry ahead of us—OP crews going through HELL; must be changed every 48 hours. 'Is every day like this?' 'When do we sleep?' Ambulances race to front, return slowly—horses and cows wander aimlessly about; they don't react as shells explode near them—no wonder, they're deaf. Bill Walden nicked by bullet as strafing plane attacks command post. [Sergeant Major] Tommy Mann's shoulder scratched and helmet dented as shell explodes nearby—other troops being hit—fire started in ammo pile. We develop great respect for the very fast German 88-mm. shells." The whole experience, Hossack declared, was "better noted than storied."[31]

PART TWO

THE RIDGES

8

Offensive Spirit

LIEUTENANT GENERAL GUY Simonds had two primary tasks. First, he had to prepare 11 Canadian Corps for its forthcoming role in the breakout southwards from Caen. Second, he needed to integrate 3rd Canadian Infantry Division back into the corps.

As part of the latter task he must decide the fates of Major General Rod Keller and Brigadier Ben Cunningham. On July 13, Simonds summoned Keller to his headquarters at a château about three miles northwest of Caen. Keller came expecting to talk about Cunningham, and Simonds dealt with that matter first. Simonds said he was unwilling to fire Cunningham before personally assessing the brigadier's competence.[1]

Then Simonds slapped the adverse reports on Keller on the desk before him. After reading them Keller was clearly upset, but his response caught Simonds off guard. Keller, he wrote, "indicated...he did not feel that his health was good enough to stand the heavy strain and asked that he be medically boarded as he felt that he would be found to be unfit." Instead, Simonds asked him to think it over for a day before making such an irreversible request.

Keller did so and then expressed a desire to retain his command. During the intervening twenty-four hours, Simonds had toured 3rd Division and been struck by its apparent low morale. Removing

Keller would likely only worsen the situation. Keller would have ten days with Simonds looking hard over his shoulder. If he disappointed, Keller would be gone.[2]

Simonds tackled the morale issue by calling all 3rd Division and 2nd Armoured Brigade unit commanders together on July 16. "My view is that we will have the war 'in the bag' this summer or at least in a matter of weeks if we pursue the advantage we now hold," he said. "I cannot stress too highly what effect this all-out effort will have on the enemy and its advantages to us...If the war drags out, normal wastage will ensue and casualties will mount up. On the other hand, by making use of an all-out effort our casualties may be initially high, but in the long run they will be less. I think that it is safe to compare the enemy in his present situation to a boxer who is groggy on his feet, and needs but the knockout blow to finish him off.

"You must always remember that if you rest, so does the enemy; and the final outcome takes considerably longer. You must therefore call on your troops for this all-out effort...We can't fight the Boche without incurring casualties and every soldier must know this." If an operation was ended because 50 per cent of the troops became casualties "then I have achieved nothing but a waste of lives; if I continue, and incur a further 20% casualties and bring the operation to a successful conclusion, then the operation is worthwhile." Such figures, he said, were obviously grossly exaggerated.

Both 3rd Division and 2nd Armoured Brigade needed to show more battle stamina. "A 'flash in the pan' formation is useless. It has to be good to the end. This will only be the case if the commander down to the platoon commander" ensured his troops were physically and mentally fit and showed good morale. Going "easy" on men appearing prone to battle exhaustion was a grievous error.

Morale hinged on discipline, and Simonds demanded no relaxing of the stern British Army approach. "If you explain to the Canadian soldier what is required of him and give him a good reason for it he will produce the goods every single time and do it twice as well as any other individual...Every effort must be made to ensure that the discipline and deportment of our troops is kept up to the highest standard."

When "things are bad," Simonds concluded, "the reins should be kept tight. Don't do nothing. Commence smartening up, holding parades, etc. Discipline...should always be at its highest. It must always be borne in mind that troops are inclined to get morbid after hard fighting." Saluting was essential. Its absence was "an indication of a lack of morale and the fighting spirit...My experience is that troops like saluting if it is done properly and the custom is properly explained to them. I lay stress on what seem to be little things. Little things are important in battle. In battle men risk lives. You can't get them to do the big things if they are not made to do the little things."[3]

AS SIMONDS LECTURED, 3rd Division had been withdrawing from the front along the Orne in Caen. The infantry battalions had been promised a rest and chance to absorb reinforcements. Their "rest" areas, however, turned out to still be close to the front or on a portion of it considered quiet. The Canadian Scottish Regiment's experience was typical. It moved to La Folie, having three men killed and nine wounded in the process, only to still be within German mortar and artillery range.[4]

The division's new location was adjacent to 3rd British Division and included responsibility for holding a sector of the industrial "island" between the Canal de Caen and the Orne. So close were the Germans to the Canadian forward positions that neither side could bring artillery or mortars to bear. Can Scot's Captain Harvey Bailey considered this "weird situation" unlike anything he had witnessed before. Snipers traded shots across the Orne, firing at the slightest movement. At night, Bailey sent men fluent in German to eavesdrop on German conversations across the river.[5] Rations and water could only be brought onto the island at night, manhandled across a "shaky bridge" that was routinely raked by enemy machine guns.[6]

Bailey was dismayed by the reinforcements the Can Scots were receiving. "Have you ever fired a rifle?" he asked one group. They shook their heads. "You don't even know whether it will shoot or how to shoot it do you?" Bailey accused one man awkwardly holding a Lee-Enfield. "No, sir, I don't."

"Ever thrown a hand grenade?" Another negative head shake. "Used a PIAT?" "No, but once a sergeant shot one for us to see," the man answered.

"This is just pitiful. To send up people like that. These poor fellows, just haven't been trained to be soldiers at all," Bailey told his company sergeant major. Rumours were flying that a big operation was coming. There was no time to lead these men through the basic training they were lacking.[7]

If many reinforcements were unready for battle due to lack of training, an equally worrisome problem was that—despite Simonds demanding it not be—morale among the veterans was at a dangerous ebb. More than a month at the front, "and having gone through three major battles in thirty days and losing about half the battalion through casualties in the process, was beginning to tell on the nerves of all ranks," the Can Scot regimental historian recorded. "The situation in Caen, although static, was generally miserable. The city, with French and German dead beneath the ruins and rubble, exuded an all-pervading smell of death. To this mixture of desolation, smell and dirt, was added continual harassing artillery and mortar fire during the day and night by an enemy who continued to have good observation of the city and its approaches." At night the Luftwaffe routinely bombed the Allied lines. "This shelling and bombing caused a constant trickle of casualties. Men were hit as they ate or slept or went from one place to another. Reinforcements coming to the battalion were sometimes killed or wounded before they ever reached the company to which they were posted. The 'old timers' were cut down also in one and twos every day. The initials 'PBC' (Psychiatric Battle Casualty) appearing under a man's name on the casualty list, if not common, was no longer unique."[8]

On July 17, the Can Scots pulled out of La Folie to an area safe enough to bring in the mobile baths and an issue of clean uniforms.[9]

OPERATION GOODWOOD HAD come together rapidly. As a preliminary step, the two British corps on either side of the Canadians had launched advances on July 15. Despite more than 3,500 casualties in two days of fighting, little ground was won. But the Germans were forced to keep 1st ss, 10th ss, and 2nd Panzer Divisions in the line and to recommit 9th ss Panzer Division on the Odon River front. So intense was the fighting on the Odon that the Germans pegged it as the probable point where the next true British breakout attempt would be made. In fact, this was precisely opposite to where Goodwood would fall. Instead, three British armoured divisions would "attack in an unexpected quarter from the shallow and congested bridgehead east of the Orne." Attacking here, the British hoped, would catch the Germans off guard because this was where their defences were strongest and they enjoyed an excellent "advantage of ground observation and fields of fire."

Goodwood was a complicated affair. To prevent the Germans from realizing an attack was coming, none of the three divisions' tanks were allowed to cross to the west bank of the Orne until after nightfall on July 17. Only three bridges between Ranville and the sea were available, so the divisions would have to proceed in single file to the west bank and then go into the attack one behind the other— hardly the hammer blow Second British Army's Lieutenant General Myles Dempsey had hoped to deliver, but the only course of action possible in such constricted ground.

Lack of bridges would also limit artillery support. Together the British and Canadian artillery formations possessed twice as many guns as the Germans did. But most of the artillery was positioned west of the river and the Canal de Caen. Only after the armoured divisions cleared the bridges could guns be sent across. This meant that, as the tanks rolled southward, they would be rapidly moving beyond the range of the supporting artillery.

To offset this handicap, the plan was to unleash "the largest force of both tactical aircraft and strategic bombers...ever employed in direct support of ground forces in a single action." More than 4,500 Allied aircraft would support Goodwood. Just after dawn on July 18, Bomber Command would strike German defences on either flank of the line of advance. On the left flank, a series of fortified villages would be destroyed and then overrun by 3rd British Infantry Division. To the right, the sprawling steelworks at Colombelles would be smashed. Heavy cratering was permitted in the flank target areas, so they would be struck by 500- and 1,000-pound bombs, fitted with delayed-action fuses, which would bury themselves into the ground and then detonate when the fuse ignited. But Cagny, a fortified village directly in the path of the advance, would be saturated with instantaneous-detonation fused bombs to avoid cratering that might hinder tank movement.

Four other German concentration points on both the flanks and in front of the advance would be targeted by heavy bombers of U.S. 8th Air Force. Medium bombers from U.S. 9th Air Force would also drench German forward positions with a mix of 500-pound and 260-pound fragmentation bombs. Villages would receive the heavier bombs, while the lighter ordnance was dropped on targets in the open countryside. Also supporting Goodwood would be all fighter bombers of 83 Group, RAF, and six wings of 84 Group. Their targets included a long list of pre-selected gun positions, strongpoints, and defensive works, as well as bridges over the Dives and Orne Rivers that could be used by the Germans to advance reinforcements. Each armoured brigade involved in the offensive had air personnel attached who were able to direct fighter-bombers onto specific targets.[10]

The bombers were indispensible, but throughout July 17 low fog and dense cloud kept Allied aircraft grounded.[11] If the predicted overnight clearing was not forthcoming, one army analyst wrote, "the entire project would have to be called off." Everything now wound up like a "powerful spring" would have to be "uncoiled without a sign being given to the enemy that anything untoward had been taking place."[12]

At the mercy of the weather, Dempsey could only pray the skies would clear and keep Goodwood moving along its complicated path. This included the pivotal role given to 11 Canadian Corps of advancing behind the armoured divisions to establish a "very firm bridgehead south of Caen." The Canadian role, dubbed Operation Atlantic, was to secure the rear and right flank of the advance by the three armoured divisions of British VIII Corps. To do so, the Canadians must capture Caen's sprawling Vaucelles suburb, the smaller industrial suburb Giberville to the east, and the steelworks and Colombelles to its north. By the end of July 18, Canadian engineers were to have bridges over the Orne within Caen. The Canadian line that Dempsey required by day's end was to curve from Cormelles on the left, through Fleury-sur-Orne in the centre, and terminate at Éterville on the right. Dempsey considered the bridges a particularly "vital part of the whole operation." While the Canadians were winning these objectives, the British armoured divisions would have advanced four to five miles southward to the localities of Hubert-Folie, Verrières, and Garcelles-Secqueville. If the Canadians failed in their tasks, Dempsey planned to order the tanks to halt on this line.[13]

Operation Atlantic would rest largely on the shoulders of 3rd Division's 8th and 9th Brigades. Caen's streets remained so clogged with rubble that it was impossible to position the division for attacks directly across the river into Colombelles and Vaucelles. Instead, the two brigades were to cross to the east side of the river on the bridge next to Ranville. At 2300 hours on July 17, London Bridge would be opened to 8th Brigade. This brigade would then launch its attack from in front of Ranville at 0745 hours. In the ensuing hour, 9th Brigade would cross the bridge. Thereafter it would revert to VIII Corps control.

Once 8th Brigade captured Colombelles and the steelworks, 9th Brigade would pass through to clear Vaucelles. The division's 7th Brigade would remain on the west bank of the Orne. Its job would be to conduct a limited amphibious assault to establish a bridgehead capable of protecting the division's engineers as they erected the required bridges. Two squadrons of tanks from 2nd Armoured Brigade's 1st Hussars would support the division. Artillery support would come from its three field regiments, 19th Canadian Field Regiment, and two Canadian medium-gun regiments.[14]

While 3rd Division carried out the main task, 2nd Division would advance its 4th Brigade west of Caen to clear Louvigny. The brigade would then attempt to cross the Orne. The division's 5th Brigade, meanwhile, would cross the Orne between Caen and Vaucelles and advance on a southerly line across 4th Brigade's front to gain the high ground at Saint-André-sur-Orne.[15]

DESPITE BRITISH SECOND Army's elaborate attempts to deceive the Germans, Luftwaffe photo reconnaissance flights on July 15 had detected a buildup under way east of the Orne and even greater activity on the river's west bank near the Ranville bridges. "The enemy command," a signal that day predicted, "plans from about 17 July onwards, the start of an operation across the Orne towards the southeast."[16]

Allied intelligence, meanwhile, was largely in the dark regarding the strength of the divisions against which Goodwood must fall. In the absence of good information, Dempsey's planners placed their bets on being able to deliver a devastating blow against a thin German defensive crust and then range freely into an undefended rear in the finest cavalry tradition. For staff officers who had spent more than a month measuring gains in yards won only at heavy cost, this was a pleasing image. It was, however, entirely false. In reality, the Germans had constructed a defence in depth that stretched back seven and a half miles from their front lines.

Dempsey's staff calculated that they were fielding 1,000 tanks against just 230 panzers—a four-to-one superiority. In fact, the Germans had 377 tanks and self-propelled guns. General der Panzertruppen Hans Eberbach had separated 150 of the tanks into two armoured "wedges." Stationed well back, they would be committed when he felt the time was ripe for a decisive counterattack.[17]

German defences anchored on the village of Bourguébus, which stood on a commanding ridge three miles south of the city. The British armour must pierce five separate defensive lines to win. Each line was well defended by infantry from 16th Luftwaffe, 272nd and 346th Divisions. Spread across the anticipated line of advance were seventy-eight 88-millimetre guns, twelve heavy flak guns, 194 pieces of field artillery, and 272 six-barrelled Nebelwerfers. Eberbach hoped to draw the British tanks into a killing ground in front of Bourguébus Ridge, which ran from east to west directly across VIII Corps's path and had an average height of 165 feet. From this commanding ground, his deadly 88-millimetre guns would outrange the guns of the British tanks by at least 1,500 yards.

Back of this ridge, another defensive zone had been created by transforming villages and farmhouses into strongpoints surrounded by aprons of barbed wire and minefields. These were manned by six 1st ss Panzer Division infantry battalions. And behind this line lurked the two armoured wedges. Those tanks and self-propelled guns not forming part of the wedges were scattered throughout the German defences, mostly in dugouts that increased the protective density of their armour.[18]

One handicap that left the Germans reeling was the grievous loss of Generalfeldmarschall Erwin Rommel. Anticipating that an offensive was imminent, Rommel had set out by staff car from his headquarters on the Seine to personally inspect the defences around Caen. It was a journey of almost two hundred miles. Although the coastal region about Caen was fogged in, inland skies were mostly clear. Just outside the village of Sainte-Foy-de-Montgommerie, two Spitfires from 412 RCAF Squadron flying off a landing strip at Bény-sur-Mer spotted the car travelling on a main road flanked by trees. Flight Lieutenant Charles Fox began firing three hundred yards off.[19] Bullets chewed into the car, the driver lost control, and it overturned. The driver and Rommel, both badly injured, were thrown clear.

That evening, the German doctor treating his injuries reported that Rommel had suffered a fractured skull, severe brain concussion, and an injured eye. He estimated that recovery would require three months of close medical attendance and another three months of convalescence. In the interim, Commander in Chief, West General-feldmarschall Günther von Kluge took over Rommel's position as Army Group B commander while retaining his other post. Kluge's dual role would be confirmed by Hitler on July 19.[20] (Rommel, being implicated in the July 20 failed assassination attempt on Hitler, opted to commit suicide by taking poison on October 14, rather than be arrested and face likely public execution.)

AT 0100 HOURS on July 18, 3rd Division's 8th Brigade finished crossing London Bridge. As it moved off, 11th British Armoured Division took its place. The Canadians walked to the south of Ranville and faced Colombelles.

It was a warm night, a moonless sky brilliant with stars. Over Britain the weather was similarly fine, and the great bomber armada took off on schedule.[21] Shortly before 0500 hours, 4th Field

Regiment's Captain George Blackburn heard the faint drone of air-craft approaching. The sound grew in intensity until he was "enveloped in the throbbing roar of a huge flock of bombers lumber-ing in from the coast." Then these "great four-engined machines, flying in from the northwest at a moderate height, [were] plainly vis-ible in all detail to the troops on the ground."[22]

A total of 1,023 Lancaster and Halifax bombers, guided by Path-finders dropping red flares over the targets, rolled in "seemingly endless succession across a brilliant sky" to drop more than five thousand tons of explosives. Much of this ordnance slammed down on Colombelles, the steelworks, and Vaucelles.[23] At first, German anti-aircraft fire rose to greet the bombers. This was soon mostly quelled when hundreds of Canadian and British guns unleashed a pre-planned thirty-seven-minute "Apple Pie" fire program against the anti-aircraft guns.[24]

There were so many bombs exploding with such force that the ground Blackburn stood upon, fully five miles from the target, shook jarringly. Clouds of smoke and dust rolled hundreds of feet into the air over Colombelles and Vaucelles. Just before all view of the smoke-stacks and remaining church steeples was obscured, Blackburn saw one spire topple. He also saw one Liberator go down in flames and another trailing smoke as it turned homeward.[25] Only six bombers were lost.

As soon as Bomber Command's squadrons were clear, more than three hundred American medium bombers scattered thousands of fragmentation bombs from the start line for the three armoured divisions to Cagny. As these planes departed, another six hundred Liberators arrived to bomb targets to the south and east of the battleground.

The Germans were given no pause to recover. As soon as the last bombers left, more than eight hundred guns from fifteen field, thir-teen medium, three heavy, and two heavy anti-aircraft artillery regiments unleashed a ninety-minute bombardment that led up to the 0745 start of Goodwood and Atlantic. The HMS *Roberts* and two cruisers, HMS *Enterprise* and HMS *Mauritius*, also joined in.[26]

Eberbach was astonished by the "hailstorm" of shells and bombs. That hail, he quickly concluded, "had simply swept away not only the remaining half of [16 Luftwaffe Field Division], but also the elements of [21st Panzer Division] which had been assigned to the second position in its rear. The local reserves had been annihilated or shattered, the guns smashed before they even fired a shot.

"In addition the telephone communication lines had been cut. The radio stations of the intermediate command staffs insofar as they had not been damaged, had been put out of commission by dust and concussion. The observation posts, even insofar as they were not situated in the sector under attack, saw for hours nothing but a screen of smoke, dirt and flames. Thus the batteries which were left intact did not know where to fire. And if they fired all the same, then enemy fighter bombers immediately dived...and silenced them with machine-gun fire and bombs."[27] Eberbach estimated that the Allied bombardment had created a six-kilometre-square swath of annihilation.

He could only hope that sufficient German forces survived to stall the advance. Believing a breakthrough all but unavoidable, Eberbach launched his two armoured wedges towards a converging point at Hubert-Folie. Here there was a strong position of 88-millimetre guns that could help break the enemy advance. The two wedges would go forward at noon.[28]

Eberbach's conclusion—matched by British Second Army assumptions—that "nothing could live under the bombardment" proved false. While the destruction was tremendous, the number of Germans who survived in the forward positions was almost unimaginable. The 503rd Heavy Panzer Battalion's No. 3 Company, for example, had only four Tigers destroyed—one of the fifty-seven-ton behemoths was actually flipped upside down. But the others survived, though buried in dirt. This had to be cleared before they could move. Although hurt, the company was soon ready to fight. All but one of the armoured-assault-gun batteries escaped unscathed. In Colombelles, a panzer-grenadier battalion stood ready to meet 8th Brigade.[29]

9

Expensive Victories

AT 0745 HOURS, 8th Canadian Infantry Brigade advanced on Colombelles. Le Régiment de la Chaudière was immediately right of the Orne, the Queen's Own Rifles to its left, and the North Shore (New Brunswick) Regiment close in reserve. Each lead battalion was trailed by a squadron of 1st Hussars—'C' Squadron with the Chauds, 'B' Squadron with the Queen's Own. At 0842 hours, they crossed the start line behind a two-thousand-yard-wide barrage.

At first they met only "stunned and shaken troops" from [16th Field Division] eager to surrender. Then the Chauds came under fire from a large, walled château.[1] Although this sprawling two-storey, seventeenth-century building had been badly damaged, it still provided a strong defensive position.

Major F. L'Espérance's 'B' Company, just fifty men strong, ground to a halt facing the château, while Captain J.G.A. Beaudry's 'C' Company entered a maze of shattered factory complexes to the left, only to become enmeshed in such a fierce firefight that battalion commander Lieutenant Colonel Paul Mathieu ordered it reinforced by 'A' and 'D' Companies. This left L'Espérance's men to take the château. Colombelles was a chaotic ruin. Many tall foundry chimneys, surrounded by huge rubble piles, stabbed the sky. Eighty per cent of the town had been destroyed. By 1040 hours, the Chauds were stalemated.[2]

The Queen's Own, meanwhile, had been swarmed by 16th Division troops surrendering from shattered factories on the eastern outskirts. Captain Dick Medland's 'A' Company and 'B' Company under Captain Jack Mills became so engaged in disarming prisoners that they lost the barrage meant to screen them to Giberville. Several 'A' Company men were hit by sniper fire from the heart of Colombelles. Medland was planning to clear this opposition when he realized that Mills had already led his company towards Giberville. The two men were best friends. Their families lived a block apart in Toronto, and Medland's older brother had married Mills's sister. He was not going to leave Mills out there alone.

Sending the prisoners back unescorted, Medland rallied his platoons, and 'A' Company headed for Giberville. As they started forward, Medland pointed at Lieutenant Gerry Rayner's map case and said, "For God's sake get rid of that." He had meant to warn the other two lieutenants as well. Carrying a map case identified them to snipers as officers. Although Medland had seen combat before, this was his debut in company command. He was determined to get it right. Moving quickly through slag heaps, Medland's men paused only to strip weapons off surrendering Germans.

Just in front of an open field eight hundred yards from the village, Medland caught up to Mills. Right of the field was a raised railway, to the left a road linking Giberville to Colombelles. 'B' Company waited next to the road with some tanks idling behind. The plan called for this group to provide fire support while 'A' Company dashed into the village. Once Medland's men were in the village, the two companies in reserve would come up along the other side of the road and make for a rail station to the south.

Medland had to get moving, but the raised railway was worrisome. He considered whether to send No. 9 Platoon across the railway to cover his left flank.[3] 'A' Company, about fifty strong, could ill spare the men. Still, he sent one section over the embankment.

GIBERVILLE WAS NOTHING special—smashed-up outbuildings and farmhouses grouped around a small village square with farms spread from this hub like wheel spokes. Most of the fields were covered in tall grain, heads almost formed and ready for harvest. Hay and turnips grew in other fields.[4]

Medland started forward. It was ominously quiet.[5] As the leading troops reached the village, "the air became alive with the rat-a-tat of machine guns and the crash of mortars." Men fell. All three lieutenants, Gerry Rayner, Jim McNeeley, and Ken MacLeod, died. Rayner and MacLeod had both enlisted as riflemen and earned battlefield commissions.[6]

Across the road, 'C' and 'D' Companies were heading for the rail station seven hundred yards past the village. 'C' Company's Bren carrier clattered along the road loaded with spare ammunition, the No. 18 wireless set, and an artillery FOO with his wireless gear. Suddenly, a mine went off under the driver. Flung forty feet into the air, Rifleman Charles Pettit slammed hard onto the road next to the carrier.

"Stay still, don't move till we get you out," Major Allen Nickson told Pettit.

"No, I'm dead," he gasped, and died. Nickson was stunned. Pettit had been the company's driver forever.

With the road mined, the supporting Hussars refused to keep going, particularly when a hidden 88-millimetre gun started firing. The FOO said he was unable to angle artillery onto the suspected gun position.

Nickson and 'D' Company's Major R.A. Cottrill decided to switch over to 'A' Company's line of advance. The men dodged across the road and ran for the village. German dead and wounded lay scattered in 'A' Company's wake. Nickson saw one German with a grenade. When the soldier pulled the pin, Nickson froze, waiting to see where he threw it. The German hugged the grenade to his chest and blew himself up.

From the railway embankment, meanwhile, Company Sergeant Major Charlie Martin of 'A' Company shouted that Germans were coming up on the other side. Medland and an artillery FOO dashed over. Dozens of men in field grey uniforms were running forward in short bounds, dropping, and then repeating the manoeuvre. Medland figured they numbered three hundred.

The foo registered the range with a single round and called for his regiment's guns to all fire five rounds each. Two minutes later, Medland heard the whistle of shells. Explosions sent clots of earth and body parts flying. After another volley, several white flags appeared through the smoke and the only movement Medland saw was that of Germans fleeing.

Martin, meanwhile, had run forward to lead two 'A' Company platoons through the village to the rail station.[7] As this group came out of the south side of the village, they faced another raised rail bed and came under fire from machine guns dug in behind its cover. Martin could see more infantry massing behind the railway embankment. To give Medland and the foo room to engage this opposition, Martin ordered his men back to a line parallel with the village. Thirty-nine-year-old Rifleman Harry Henry Hawkins and three men volunteered to cover the withdrawal. Only when their ammunition was gone did the four start back. Hawkins was struck by a machine-gun burst and killed. Although artillery quickly broke the German attack, Hawkins's death served to remind the regiment's other D-Day veterans that their numbers were dwindling. Three out of four had been either killed or wounded and evacuated.[8]

While 'A' Company had fought off these counterattacks, 'C' and 'D' Companies had entered the village to give it a methodical clearing. Men chucked grenades through doors and windows and then raced in with rifles, Sten and Bren guns blazing.[9] Nickson's men were soon almost out of ammunition. They used captured Schmeisser submachine guns and punched holes in walls with Panzerfaust shoulder-launched anti-tank rockets. As they came out of the village and headed for the rail station, 'C' Company came face to face with "hundreds of Germans…just dropping their arms at their feet." Their officers lined them up in three orderly parade-ground-style rows.[10]

Lieutenant J.A.C. Auld, commanding 'C' Company's No. 13 Platoon, was dumbstruck that these Germans were surrendering without a fight. The Queen's Own were few and, almost out of ammunition, conducting "a colossal bluff. The whole of 'C' Company could have been wiped out but their persistence convinced the enemy that the situation was hopeless." In contrast to the Canadians, the Germans were "well-equipped with masses of weapons and ammunition." And yet one officer told Auld, "I surrender, sir, because I have no ammunition." Auld looked at the bounty of German guns and munitions and decided against skewering the man's pride by pointing to it.[11]

Back in Giberville, Medland and the other company commanders determined that, in addition to the three lieutenants from 'A' Company, thirteen other ranks had died. Sixty-eight other ranks had been wounded. But the Queen's Own estimated two hundred Germans killed and six hundred captured.[12] Medland felt he had passed the test of company command, making the right decisions. Had he not, more men would have died.[13]

IN COLOMBELLES, THE Chaudière had remained deadlocked through the morning, delaying the planned North Shore (New Brunswick) Regiment pass through to the large steelworks to the south. The North Shores bumped into the rear elements of the Chauds, and "a scene of indescribable congestion followed."[14] Brigadier Ken Blackader tried to get 8th Brigade back on track by ordering the North Shores to pass to the east of the Chauds. Lieutenant Colonel Donald Buell was in the midst of extracting his battalion from the jam behind the château when 9th Brigade's Stormont, Dundas and Glengarry Highlanders—expecting to go forward to Vaucelles—arrived to add even further confusion.[15]

At noon, Major General Rod Keller, nagged by Lieutenant General Simonds to keep on schedule or risk dangerously exposing the British armour's right flank, arranged a fighter-bomber attack on the château. The bombs, however, struck the sun-hardened ground with such force they bounced high into the air and pinwheeled right over the building.[16]

Exasperated by this sight, Buell went back to brigade in the North Shore's headquarters carrier. Blackader and Buell agreed that the North Shores should move well to the east of where the Chauds were mired and go directly for the steelworks. The Glens from 9th Brigade would push past the Chauds when opportunity presented and carry the rest of the town.[17]

received a Military Cross. His injuries were sufficiently severe that he was evacuated to Canada.[34] Also wounded in Vaucelles was Captain Bill Grayson, who had led one of 'A' Company's platoons ashore on June 6.[35]

By nightfall on July 18, 3rd Division had largely achieved its assigned tasks for Operation Atlantic's opening day. Despite major delays in seizing Colombelles, the decision to shift the Reginas across the river to win the southwestern portion of Vaucelles rescued the situation. During the night, 9th Brigade—ordered by Major General Keeler to carry out its tasks despite the darkness—moved the North Nova Scotia Highlanders into the northern part of Vaucelles. The Highland Light Infantry soon followed.

Opposition in this part of Vaucelles was confined to snipers and the harassment of light artillery and mortar fire. The men's biggest problem had proven to be getting through the giant steelworks. Unable to find straightforward routes for the vehicles, the infantry marched on alone. The North Novas' carrier platoon was still winding through the steelworks when a mine exploded and flipped the lead vehicle onto its back. Lieutenant Glen Leland Gammel and Sergeant Carl Rector were killed. The driver, Private B. Irving, was caught under the carrier and badly burned, while Private Joe Staples lost both feet.[36]

The Highland Light Infantry also had difficulty circumnavigating the steelworks. Its temporary commander, Major G.E.M. Edwards—having taken over after Lieutenant Colonel Frank Griffiths had been wounded in Buron—was injured by a sniper. Despite these setbacks, the HLI and Novas were established in the north part of Vaucelles by the early morning hours of July 19.[37]

10

Greenhorners

OUTHWEST OF CAEN, 2nd Canadian Infantry Division's Major
General Charles Foulkes had lingered through the morning
of July 18 and into the mid-afternoon consulting brigade commanders, confirming plans with corps staff, and attending a meeting at
43rd British Infantry Division regarding its proposed attack on
Maltôt. As 2nd Division's war diarist noted, this attack "had been
previously discussed" by staff of both divisions.[1]

Lieutenant General Harry Crerar had once described Foulkes as
possessing "exceptional ability; sound tactical knowledge; a great
capacity for quick, sound decision; energy and driving power." But
on the eve of his first battle, he seemed hesitant and uncertain. At
forty-one, Foulkes was a contemporary of Guy Simonds. Both Royal
Military College graduates and Permanent Force officers, they
started the war as majors and enjoyed subsequent rapid promotion.
Similarities ended there. Foulkes was a Crerar favourite, who
advanced through staff positions to brigadier.

Pudgy and dour of expression, Foulkes seemed to many senior
officers the army's most unapproachable general. Brigadier Harry
Foster considered him "mean and narrow," possessed of a "hard-
shelled Baptist mind" and a "sneering supercilious attitude toward
anyone his own rank or below." At the same time, he had a reputation for "groveling to everybody" senior. Foulkes was a consummate

politician, instinctively striking the right balance of servility and self-confidence required to impress. This nature, however, garnered lukewarm personnel assessments, such as one concluding: "Sound and competent…Should make a good commander though possibly not a very sympathetic one."[2]

It was this somewhat enigmatic figure who spent from 1130 to 1300 extensively reviewing with Brigadier Sherwood Lett 4th Brigade's one-battalion attack on Louvigny, a village west of the Orne and south of Caen. The brigadier worried that the supporting artillery plan might prove inadequate if the attack was delayed till after dark—a circumstance ever more probable as the day trailed away. Currently, artillery would be limited to what FOOs with the regiment directed against observed targets. This would hardly work at night. Foulkes assured him all would be well. Lett asked for two hours' notice to allow for moving the Royal Regiment of Canada from its current front line position to the start line.

Foulkes left for the 43rd Division meeting. Returning to his headquarters in the mid-afternoon, he issued Lett's movement order. The Royals' acting commander, Major Jack Anderson, got it to the start line at about 1800 hours. Three companies were to attack in line. 'D' Company would lead, followed by 'A' Company and then 'B' Company. 'C' Company stationed itself on high ground to the west to provide a firm base. The line of advance was across a wheat field and then through an orchard surrounded by a high stone wall. Having gained Louvigny, 'A' and 'B' Companies would clear the village while 'D' Company passed to their left to seize a château and then a small wood. All 2nd Division's artillery was available for support. Both Toronto Scottish (MG) Regiment's heavy-machine-gun and mortar companies were on hand. A Fort Garry Horse tank squadron stood beside 'C' Company.[3]

Once again 2nd Division's inexperience became quickly apparent. Start-line reconnaissance had been limited to studying maps and aerial photographs. None had shown the few houses backed by a twelve-foot wall that blocked their line of advance. It took twenty minutes for the three infantry companies to climb over this obstruction, so the advance got going late at 1920 hours. As 'A' Company moved into the tall wheat close behind 'D' Company, it came under inaccurate fire, but Major Tom Whitley was unable to situate its source. Nobody was hit, and the company soon reached the orchard wall. Having blown holes in it with a PIAT, 'D' Company had already passed through and gained the orchard. But when Whitley looked through one of the holes, he saw that the lead company was stalled in the trees just beyond—leaving insufficient room to crowd his men in as well. Intending to get Major Jim Fairhead moving, Whitley ducked through the gap, discovered the other company commander dead on the ground, and learned that the company's only other officer, Lieutenant Eric James Chellew, had also been killed. All the sergeants were casualties as well. Most had been hit during the advance to the orchard, while the remainder fell to the mortar and artillery fire zeroing in with increasing accuracy and intensity.

Whitley realized that he either got 'D' Company moving or the Royals would take a pasting. Suddenly, Sergeant Oliver Clifford Tryon, from the battalion's 3-inch mortar section, was at Whitley's shoulder. He had gone forward with 'D' Company to act as a fire controller for the mortars. Tryon assured Whitley he could get the company organized. Whitley slipped back through the hole and instructed his platoon commanders to bring 'A' Company forward by themselves. He was going to stay with 'D' Company to keep it "pressing on."

Despite Whitley and Tryon's best efforts, by the time they got 'D' Company to the other side of the orchard, it was clear the men left were not up to seizing the château and woods. So he told Tryon to just establish a blocking position on the southwest edge of the château grounds. The other two companies would clear the village.[4]

Tryon decided that even this task would expose 'D' Company to machine-gun and mortar fire coming from Louvigny and the château, so he led the men in a bold charge across the open ground to the cover of the woods. The move was executed so rapidly the Germans had no time to react. Tryon's actions garnered a Military Medal.[5]

From the outset, the No. 18 wireless sets the companies carried had ceased functioning. "Worse than useless," Whitley raged, "for people wasted time tinkering with them." Unable to call in supporting fire or even contact 'B' Company's Captain D.S. Beatty, who was just 150 yards distant, Whitley sent a runner to fetch him. As Whitley and Beatty were agreeing to jointly attack the village, the latter was hit and wounded. Beatty was evacuated, and a lieutenant took over 'B' Company.

Meanwhile, Lieutenant Len Gage of 'A' Company's No. 8 Platoon had decided on his "own hook" to advance from near the château to the village. By the time Whitley led the rest of the force into Louvigny, Gage's men had gained the village centre.

Civilians warned that a strong German force held the other half of the village. Whitley also knew that the western half, although cleared by Gage's men, had not been thoroughly searched. Having never been trained in night fighting in built-up areas, Whitley withdrew to the orchard. The Royals would return at daybreak.[6]

It was midnight, and the attacking companies had been out of contact with battalion headquarters for almost five hours. Major Anderson had tried re-establishing contact with his companies by sending Sergeant James Corbett forward in a carrier, but en route it hit a mine, killing the driver and wounding Corbett. Despite severe pain and concussion, Corbett staggered into Louvigny, failed to find any Royals, and finally returned to headquarters with a German prisoner. Corbett received a Military Medal for his valour.[7]

Equally in the dark about what was happening, Brigadier Lett and his intelligence officer, Lieutenant William Lloyd Paterson, drove to Anderson's headquarters. With little learned, they were heading back when a mortar round struck their jeep. Paterson was killed, and Lett, who had been wounded at Dieppe, suffered a debilitating wound. Brigade command passed temporarily to Lieutenant Colonel Charles "Bud" Drury of 4th Field Regiment.

ALTHOUGH FAILING TO take any objectives, the Royal Regiment's gains sufficiently secured 5th Brigade's right flank to permit its advance on Fleury-sur-Orne from Vaucelles. While 3rd Division held much of the suburb, the southern portion remained contested. This meant 5th Brigade would have to win the ground from which it would then advance. The Black Watch was to cross first at 2215 hours. Because of double daylight savings time, it would still be light.

As nobody knew where 3rd Division's battalions were, no artillery was permitted.

'B' Company, with thirty-six carrier platoon personnel acting as paddlers, formed the assault force.[8] The crossing would be made in eighteen-man assault boats and on a Kapok bridge. This was to be constructed by linking together shoulder-width steel sections, which rested on floats. Infantry would then cross in single file.

'D' Company was to provide covering fire. 'B' Company's start line lay eight hundred yards from the water, open ground between. Major Alan Stevenson's men, burdened by the bulky canvas assault boats and Kapok bridging gear, were halfway to the river when the major realized 'D' Company had failed to arrive. Fifty yards from the river, machine guns started firing from the high ground on the other bank. Stevenson fell wounded, and Lieutenant Robert Eliot Austin was mortally injured.

All boats, save one, were shredded. Corporal John James Watson's party launched the surviving boat and paddled across under intense fire. As they clambered ashore, all were either killed or mortally wounded. Watson died of his wounds on July 22.[9] 'B' Company went to ground, waiting for nightfall.

Once it was dark, Lieutenant T.K. Dorrance swam out and assembled the Kapok bridge almost single-handedly. After 'B' Company crossed in line without incident, the rest of the battalion followed. The Germans having withdrawn, the Black Watch quickly advanced to the southern edge of Vaucelles. The river crossing attempt had cost them thirty-six casualties.[10]

During the night, the Black Watch linked up with the Regina Rifles in Vaucelles, allowing engineers to begin bridging the river. By the early hours of July 19, two bridges were under way. The 29th Field Company worked on a 150-foot standalone Bailey bridge, while 31st Field Company incorporated the undamaged pier of a blown bridge into its construction. One fifty-foot span extended from the west bank to the pier, and then an eighty-foot section gained the opposite shore.

At 0902 hours, 29th Field Company's bridge opened. Then at 1130 hours, the more robust 31st Field Company span, capable of carrying heavy vehicles, was ready. While the bridging had been under way, 30th Field Company—using hand tools and explosives—carved a route through rubble to the southern edge of Vaucelles. "To clear it entailed cutting away the remains of a demolished railway bridge, burrowing under another dropped at one end, and dealing with three miles of craters, traps, barricades and rubble." The first traffic over the stronger bridge consisted of bulldozers that improved the road and rendered it capable of being used by vehicles at 1330 hours.[11]

By this time, the Royals had easily taken Louvigny and the château at dawn. Fifty-five prisoners were rounded up. Despite the easy end, Louvigny cost the Royals 111 casualties, 34 fatal.[12]

Major Tom Whitley believed most of the losses resulted from the incident in the orchard when 'D' Company had frozen after losing its leadership. It seemed men were unable to tell whether small-arms fire was "close to them or not. They must know their crack and thump," he said later, "so that they can tell whether the fire is falling fifty yards or five feet away from their heads. They now come into battle assuming that every round they hear passes just above the napes of their necks. They believe their enemies are crack shots who will bring them certain death. Hence they are paralyzed or go to ground."[13]

BY LATE MORNING on July 19, Lieutenant General Simonds believed his corps ready for Operation Atlantic's second phase. At 1100 hours, he announced that 3rd Division would concentrate on reorganizing while consolidating its grip on Colombelles and Vaucelles. The 7th Brigade would, however, attack and clear the industrial suburb of Cormelles southeast of Vaucelles.

Simonds declared the highway running from Caen to Falaise as the boundary between his two divisions, with 3rd Division to keep left of it and 2nd Division to the right. The latter division's 5th Brigade was now to advance from Vaucelles to Fleury-son-Orne and the high ground through to Hill 67, which lay a short distance beyond. One battalion would then go left to secure Ifs. At the same time, 6th Brigade would advance from Hill 67, due south to Saint-André-sur-Orne.[14]

How 11 Canadian Corps operations coordinated with the bold armoured breakout of Operation Goodwood was no longer clear. Throughout July 18, the three armoured divisions had advanced at great cost in tanks disabled or destroyed. The 11th Armoured Division alone counted 126 tanks, virtually half its strength, out of action by nightfall.[15] On the left flank, the Guards Armoured Division had lost sixty tanks in their battle christening.[16] Yet at 1620 hours, General Bernard Montgomery had signalled General Sir Alan Brooke, "Complete success...bombing decisive...spectacle terrific...ordered recce regiments to crossing between Mezidon and Falaise...difficult to see what the enemy can do...few tanks met so far." Appended was a long list of villages and towns taken, several of which remained firmly in the German grip.[17]

By the time Simonds issued his orders on July 19, great expectations for Operation Goodwood had been abandoned. Although VIII British Corps continued battering away, it was clear there would be no breakout. Instead, at 1035 hours, Lieutenant General Richard N. O'Connor and his three divisional commanders agreed on a series of set-piece attacks starting at 1600 hours against villages that were to have fallen the day before. Bras was 11th Armoured's target, Bourgébus 7th Armoured's. The Guards Armoured would reorganize around Cagny.[18]

Well before this, Simonds launched the Canadians on their tasks. A report that the Germans had withdrawn from Cormelles and that 29th British Armoured Brigade had tanks in orchards immediately to the south prompted Simonds to order 3rd Division's 9th Brigade to make a grab from the eastern flank of Vaucelles, rather than waiting for 7th Brigade to get organized.[19]

The Highland Light Infantry's 'B' and 'C' Companies, accompanied by the mortar, carrier, and anti-tank platoons, headed towards Cormelles a little after noon. Caught in a rain of mortar and shellfire, the force was repeatedly driven to cover. When it was discovered that some of the fire was coming from Canadian artillery, the advance was held up until these guns were stopped. At 1647 hours, the Highlanders reported they were in Cormelles and meeting only snipers.[20]

Cormelles was a big town, so the HLI were unaware that

Lieutenant Lorenzo Bergeron and his Regina Rifles scouts had arrived at noon. Bergeron and his men encountered a large, happy group of civilians "who laid out an excellent meal for them, also bottles of wine in celebration of liberation from the Hun." The platoon remained in Cormelles until after dark, when the Royal Winnipeg Rifles arrived to relieve them. At no time did the scouts and the HLI meet. Bergeron returned to the Regina headquarters with seven prisoners, two German motorcycles, and a couple of bottles of cognac.[21]

FOR 2ND DIVISION's 5th Brigade, July 19 was its combat debut. Le Régiment de Maisonneuve (Maisies) led off with an advance from Vaucelles adjacent to Route 162. Fleury-sur-Orne was three miles distant. 'A' Company under Major Alexandre Dugas led on the left with Major Léon Brosseau's 'D' Company out front on the right. Behind them, 'C' was on the left and 'B' Company the right. Fleury was clearly visible, standing on a hill's summit. The plan was simple: leading companies would follow a creeping barrage to the edge of the village. Then the reserve companies would pass through and clear it.[22] 'B' Squadron of the Sherbrooke Fusiliers was accompanying the infantry. A 2nd Canadian Anti-Tank Regiment troop would come forward once the village was secure and help repel any counterattack. Because it was unclear whether the Royal Regiment had driven all German forces away from the west bank of the Orne River, which Route 162 followed closely, a Toronto Scottish heavy machine-gun platoon was positioned to screen that flank.

At 1300 hours, the two leading companies advanced to the start line, misread its location, and went on another three hundred yards. This placed them precisely where the first salvo of the creeping barrage was to fall. The mortar platoon commander, Captain Achille Louis Orieux, was up with the lead companies in order to situate his mortars to cover the advance. Before anyone realized the deadly error, the barrage started. Both companies were smothered with shells. Terrific carnage ensued. Brosseau was killed while trying to get his men under cover. Orieux fell dying.[23] Eleven other men died, thirty-seven were wounded, and twenty-seven were evacuated as battle-exhaustion cases.[24]

Realizing that his two lead companies had been shattered, Lieutenant Colonel H.L. Bisaillon immediately ordered 'C' and 'B' Companies to take the lead. The company commanders had their men run until they caught up to the barrage, which the gunners—oblivious to what had happened—were continuing as scheduled. Dugas, meanwhile, managed to restore 'A' Company to order and it fell in behind.

The advance was virtually unopposed. By 1630 hours, Fleury was secure, and the battalion had established an all-round defence.[25] Despite the tragedy, the Maisies had proven their ability to recover quickly and continue their mission. Although the Maisies had gained Fleury, they had taken longer than originally planned. This had left the Calgary Highlanders waiting on their own start line, sweating in the intense mid-afternoon heat with no source of shade. Finally, at 1715 hours, their advance began. Their first battle, they had decided it appropriate to go forward to the skirl of their three pipers. The Calgaries passed through Fleury and headed for their objective—Hill 67—fifteen hundred yards off. Lieutenant Colonel Donald MacLauchlan advanced his men in the standard box pattern with two companies forward, two back, his headquarters in the middle, and the support company at the rear. The pipers skirled away as the battalion marched through "a hail of terrific" mortar and artillery fire.[26]

Advancing across open fields, they heard machine-gun and rifle bullets swishing through the waist-high wheat. The Sherbrooke squadron in support opened fire with its machine guns and 75-millimetre guns, zeroing in on any muzzle flash or stream of tracers marking an enemy position. As the Highlanders went up the hill, they saw German infantry "scurrying out of the wheat fields." At 1800 hours, Hill 67 was theirs.

Thirty minutes later, they were still digging in when the Germans counterattacked. Captain S.J. "Sandy" Pearson was with 'C' Company on the forward slope and "could see them across the valley," tanks and infantry, coming fast.[27] Supported by the Sherbrooke tanks, the company held its ground, despite taking heavy casualties. 'B' Company, on its right, caught the attacking Germans with flanking fire. As casualties mounted in 'C' Company, two platoons from 'D' Company reinforced it.

To one side of the hilltop position, a small patrol from 'C' Company had been caught in the open.[28] Lieutenant Vernon Francis Kilpatrick saw three German tanks closing in for the kill. Grabbing a PIAT and some rounds, Kilpatrick moved fifty yards to the front of his men, as if to shield them from the tanks. Two Panthers and a Mark IV presented difficult targets for a PIAT, but Kilpatrick managed to immobilize the Panthers and his final round blew the turret off the Mark IV. Moments later the twenty-two-year-old, who had begun the war as a private, was killed by a sniper round. Soon after Kilpatrick knocked out the tanks, the counterattack crumbled.[29]

Holding Hill 67 had cost three officers and eighty-nine other ranks wounded, one officer and three other ranks killed, and two men missing. "It can be safely said now," the Calgary war diarist wrote, "that for 'green horners' in real live battle, we have proven our worth."

While the Calgary Highlanders had advanced on and then held Hill 67, the Black Watch had also moved through Fleury eastward to Ifs. Encountering several groups of Germans probing towards Hill 67 from the east, the Black Watch sent them running. By midnight, the battalion had taken the village but was being harried by snipers and subjected to the inevitable heavy shelling.[30]

When one shell set the Regimental Aid Post on fire, Sergeant William Francis Clements organized stretcher-bearer parties and made sure all the wounded were safely evacuated despite the flames and smoke boiling around him. His selfless heroism garnered a Military Medal.[31]

AS JULY 19 closed, General Myles Dempsey decided Goodwood was finished. Montgomery was in damage-control mode, claiming the offensive's objective had really only been to enlarge the Orne bridgehead and keep German armoured divisions fixed there.[32] Such a reversal in twenty-four hours from his signal to Brook was hard to credit and contradicted statements he and his staff had made to attached war correspondents. "All the high hopes were not realized," Canadian Press correspondent Ross Munro wrote, "for the tanks had not been able to shake loose through the open country leading to Falaise, twenty miles south of Caen."[33] Twenty-First Army Group's Brigadier Charles Richardson bemoaned the fact that Goodwood "had been a tremendous flop."[34]

Dempsey set about securing what had been won. He made 1 British Corps responsible for the left flank and reinforced it with 49th British Infantry Division and 33rd Armoured Brigade from XXX Corps on the western flank. The flagging VIII Corps must finish taking Bourguébus and hold until relieved by 11 Canadian Corps, which would have to broaden its front substantially. The Canadians would take over "Bras and Hubert-Folie and be responsible for all the country westwards to the Orne, establishing a forward division to the west of Bourguébus on the Verrières ridge. West of the Orne XII Corps would conform with 11 Canadian Corps's operations, working forward from Hill 112 to Maltôt...while further west XXX Corps was also to work forward." This realignment would strengthen Second Army's hold on what it had won and continue to divert German attention from the American front.[35]

VIII Corps had lost 271 tanks. Though many were retrievable, repairing them and replacing those destroyed would take time. The armoured divisions had suffered thousands of men killed and wounded—the numbers were still being tallied. More, undoubtedly, would result from the remaining fighting, which would fall upon 7th Armoured Division's shoulders.[36] The other two divisions were being pulled out immediately, 3rd Canadian Infantry Division relieving 11th Armoured Division. Simonds announced his intention to carry out that relief on July 20. More importantly, however, 2nd Division must advance southward and establish itself on the "Verrières feature."[37]

Although intelligence regarding German defences on Bourguébus Ridge and the higher Verrières Ridge was vague, Foulkes told Simonds that "the enemy forward appeared to be softening up." As late as 1800 hours, Simonds was considering "a real push that night."[38] He ordered the Queen's Own Cameron Highlanders to move from Carpiquet to the western outskirts of Caen at 1500 hours "with the object of preparing a night attack." Arriving in this concentration area at 1630, the battalion immediately moved through to Fleury-sur-Orne, its forming-up position. The Camerons were still marching when informed at 2000 hours that "the plans had been changed and the...decision was that the attack must go in the following day."[39]

Simonds and his staff had realized belatedly during the evening that 6th Brigade and the Sherbrooke Fusiliers could not possibly move that night from positions on the west side of the Orne to the start lines. There was also the need to reorganize 2nd Division, so that it would be in a position to capitalize on the breakthrough Simonds expected to win in the morning.[40] If Bourguébus and Ver-rières Ridges fell, and he took for granted they would, 4th Brigade would advance to Bruyères Château next to the village of Lorguichon. This was about two miles south from Verrières along the Caen-Falaise highway.[41]

Accordingly, 2nd Division's 4th Brigade was pulled from positions west of the Orne around Louvigny and replaced by 43rd Division's 4th Brigade. The British would protect the Canadian right flank during the forthcoming advance.[42]

As darkness fell, 6th Brigade's three battalions learned they would carry out the forthcoming attack. The Camerons were on the march. South Saskatchewan Regiment started walking towards the Caen bridges at 0200 hours.[43] For some reason, Les Fusiliers Mont-Royal was only ordered to move at 0415 hours. The men were quickly mustered and set marching with the expectation that they would receive breakfast at the forming-up position.[44] The Sherbrooke Fusiliers also spent a busy night getting across the Orne. There was no bridge for the tankers, so each Sherman was loaded onto a raft and winched across the river by engineers. Although this only took five minutes per tank, the night was well advanced by the time all were across.[45]

In Operation Atlantic's planning there had been provision for the Canadians possibly seizing Bourguébus Ridge, so Simonds reworked this. It had been anticipated that 11th Armoured Division's tanks would have gained most of the ridge and so "there would not be very heavy opposition." Now the British tanks were mostly gone. There-fore, Simonds decided he needed more infantry. Each brigade normally advanced two battalions while keeping the third in reserve. As the front was so broad, Simonds decided to deploy the entire brigade forward and bring in a battalion from 4th Brigade to form the reserve. This task went to the Essex Scottish.[46]

Learning of their assignment at 0200 hours, the Essex Scottish had to hand off their current area to the British and did not start marching until 0445.[47] It took until 1130 hours to reach their forming-up position, which was thirty minutes before the original start time for the attack. In the words of one official army historian, the men "had little sleep, a poor breakfast, and less lunch."[48]

All 6th Brigade battalions and the two Sherbrooke squadrons that were to support the attack reached forming-up positions at about the same time as the Essex. Everyone was tired, most hungry. It was a hot, muggy day. Low cloud and haze meant limited air support. None of this concerned Simonds. At 1000 hours, 6th Brigade's Brigadier Hugh Young attended a divisional Orders Group (O Group). Simonds offered the "presumption...that the opposition on our front was not great and that quick offensive action should break through the enemy screen."[49]

There would be the usual plethora of artillery, a creeping barrage to precede each battalion, and timed concentrations against suspected German positions. In addition to all Canadian divisional artillery regiments, 2nd Army Group, Royal Canadian Artillery, and 8th Army Group, Royal Artillery would add their medium and heavy artillery regiments.[50] Despite the fact that 6th Brigade would advance on a front four thousand yards wide, except for the creeping barrages, the only large timed concentration consisted of a single three-minute "Murder" barrage on Saint-André-sur-Orne. Smaller concentrations "were [to be] fired on other targets across...2nd Division's front."[51]

The 6th brigade objectives were between one and two miles distant. On the right, the Camerons need go only a mile to gain the twin villages of Saint-André-sur-Orne and Saint-Martin-de-Fontenay. These villages marked the most westerly flank of Bourguébus Ridge. Left of the Camerons, South Saskatchewan Regiment would ascend the long slope of Bourguébus Ridge and continue advancing southward up the eighty-foot-higher Verrières Ridge to look down upon Fontenay-le-Marmion beyond. On the far left, Les Fusiliers Mont-Royal would first seize two large farms—Beauvoir and Troteval—and then carry on to Verrières village on the eastern flank of its name-sake ridge.[52]

The Sherbrooke's 'C' Squadron would support the Fusiliers and 'A' Squadron the Camerons. No armoured support went to the Sasks. They were dependent on their own anti-tank guns and those of a 2nd Anti-Tank Regiment troop. All three attacking battalions and the Essex Scottish had a troop from this anti-tank regiment. The Sherbrooke's 'B' Squadron would stand ready to go wherever it was most needed. Two other troops from the anti-tank regiment were also in reserve. Additional fire support would come from the Toronto Scottish Regiment's heavy mortars and machine guns. Once all first objectives were won, the Essex Scottish would pass through the cen-tre and establish a defensive line extending across the heights from Verrières to Saint-André.

Having reached the forming-up positions barely on time, all four battalions were forced to dig in to avoid German shells and mortar rounds. Then the attack was pushed back to 1500 hours, for two rea-sons. Simonds still hoped the clouds would lift and allow air support. There had also been an unexpected development on 2nd Division's left flank.

Tanks from 7th Armoured Division had succeeded in occupying Bourguébus at first light. Except for a single Tiger tank, the village had been abandoned. Emboldened, the 4th County of London Yeo-manry advanced tanks onto the crest of Bourguébus Ridge and west to Beauvoir Farm. Circling the buildings, the tankers decided to punch south to Verrières. Although driven off by strong opposition at noon, they were still on the ridge and where the Canadian artillery was to fall. Time was required for the tankers to get clear. Nobody considered altering the artillery program to enable the tanks to hold Beauvoir Farm until the Fusiliers relieved them. Instead, they pulled back to the east side of the Caen-Falaise highway near Bras.[53]

From vantages on the ridges, the Germans watched Canadian preparations and brought in reinforcements. Saint-André was defended by the 272nd Infantry Division, formed out of shattered Russian-front formations on December 12, 1943. It had arrived in Normandy with just under thirteen thousand men on July 13. By July 20, it had suffered losses of 40–50 per cent. But the survivors were seasoned and determined fighters.[54] Facing the Sasks and Fusiliers was a still tougher foe—2nd ss Panzer-Grenadier Battalion and two companies of 1st ss Panzer Division's reconnaissance battalion. Lurking nearby were two companies of the division's 2nd ss Panzer Battalion, a company of self-propelled guns, and elements of 1st ss Panzer-Grenadier Regiment.[55] The Germans had about seventy tanks in close proximity.

At 1500 hours, the artillery began firing, while several squadrons of Typhoon fighter-bombers briefly appeared overhead. The Canadians stepped out behind the creeping barrage and into the waist-high wheat. They advanced towards tragedy.

11

We Need Help

U NLIKE THE SOUTH Saskatchewans and Fusiliers Mont-Royal ascending the long slopes up the ridges, the Queen's Own Camerons descended towards Saint-André-sur-Orne and Saint-Martin-de-Fontenay. Saint-André's small cluster of buildings stood west of the main road and slightly north of Saint-Martin on the road's east side. Immediately south of Saint-Martin was a mine complex with buildings surrounding the main shaft's tall lift tower. Maps incorrectly had identified this complex as some kind of factory. The Canadians were unaware of the network of iron mines running through the area south of Caen.

The Camerons passed through a gap east of Hill 67 and the slopes of Verrières Ridge. They were deployed in T-formation— 'A' Company out front on the right, 'B' Company on the left, and 'C' Company following. 'D' Company was farther back. The Sherbrooke Fusiliers' 'A' Squadron, under Major Sydney Radley-Walters, would provide fire support from alongside Hill 67.[1]

Lieutenant Colonel Norman Ross's tactical headquarters was tight behind the leading companies. He was walking with the battalion adjutant, a wireless signaller, and a 6th Field Regiment FOO team. The battalion's White scout car followed a few yards back with the headquarters' company commander, battalion intelligence officer, two signallers, and a driver aboard. The large wireless in the scout car provided Ross's lifeline to 6th Brigade.[2]

Communications were immediately damped when the leaden sky opened with heavy rain. The Camerons were five hundred yards out, moving through a wheat field adjacent to the road from Hill 67 to Saint-André when a hidden anti-tank gun destroyed the scout car. Headquarters commander Captain Howard Grundy and intelligence officer Lieutenant James Edward Maloney were killed. The scout car's loss severed the link to brigade.[3]

Across the Orne, the ground was supposed to have been secured by 43rd British Infantry Division. But it was clearly in German hands. Besides the anti-tank gun, machine guns opened up on 'A' Company.[4] The 6th Field Regiment's FOO, Captain Robert Lucy, had contact with his regiment. He called in fire that silenced the machine guns. Lucy also shelled Saint-André to quell fire from there. Unmindful that the wireless set's long antenna marked him and his signaller for snipers, Lucy kept feeding targets back throughout the advance. Even when a mortar dropped well-aimed rounds just feet away, Lucy kept working the guns. His unceasing efforts, which Ross figured enabled the advance to continue, resulted in a Military Cross.[5] "We had tremendous support from the guns. We just asked for gunfire and we got it," Ross said.[6]

As they closed on the villages, machine-gun and mortar fire from the western flank of Verrières Ridge thickened. Snipers were also taking a toll. Moving through the wheat fields, 'B' Company presented an easy target. Blinded by the rain, the Camerons could only keep walking. When 'B' Company gained the outskirts of Saint-Martin, they reported "no live enemy...due to their hasty withdrawal." 'B' Company quickly pushed on and soon looked out upon the mine complex. 'A' Company, meanwhile, had cleared a large orchard on Saint-André's west flank, and Ross pushed 'C' Company in between to clean out this village. The moment the Camerons entered Saint-André, they came under heavy mortar and artillery fire.[7]

Ross used a network of German trenches in the orchard for a battalion headquarters. As some prisoners marched by, Ross liberated a huge pair of binoculars from a passing officer. Rumour held that

German optics were superior, a fact confirmed the moment he looked through the lenses.

After touring the Cameron position, Ross decided the battalion front was too wide. He was particularly uneasy because German tanks were rolling along the ridge to the east and between his battalion and the Saskatchewan Rifles.[8] Drawing 'B' Company back from Saint-Martin, Ross concentrated his defences around Saint-André and the orchard. The move was just finished when the Camerons were subjected to a series of counterattacks—mostly falling on 'B' Company. "Everyone was thoroughly miserable, although still keen for more fighting," 'B' Company's Captain H.R. McGill later wrote.[9]

Next to Hill 67, Radley-Walters and 'A' Squadron had supported the Camerons with main-gun fire. Spotting two German Panthers silhouetted on the ridge's horizon about five hundred yards distant, his headquarters troop opened fire. One Panther brewed and the other was immobilized.[10]

Ross's anxiety kept growing. The Camerons were out in a two-mile-deep salient. As the battalion's support company had joined the rifle companies, Ross was now in contact with 6th Brigade via a Bren carrier's wireless. But information from Brigadier Hugh Young's staff was contradictory and confused. While they said all was well, when Ross peered through the rain with his fine new binoculars he saw Saskatchewan Regiment soldiers clinging to Verrières Ridge "by the skin of their teeth." The Essex Scottish behind appeared surrounded by German tanks and infantry. Through the fury of the rainstorm, Ross was not sure he was interpreting the situation correctly. But he never doubted that the brigade's attack against the ridge had gone badly and the Camerons were hanging in the wind.[11]

WHEN THE SOUTH Saskatchewan Regiment's Major Reg Matthews had explained the brigade plan, there had been a general sense of disbelief. Matthews had shared his company commander's concern. So had Lieutenant Colonel Fred Clift, sent the day before to temporarily take over 4th Infantry Brigade. Clift had tried to stay with the battalion until the attack was done. "I need tanks," he told Brigadier

Young. "I won't put men across there unless you give me tank support." Clift pointed out the advance up the long slope and the probability that, either before or after the objective was taken, the Germans would counterattack with a combined infantry-armour force.

Young promised tanks and ordered Clift to the 4th Brigade posting. But by the time the Sasks formed up in front of the village of Ifs, Matthews had been advised there would be no tanks.[12] Major John Edmondson and Major Len Dickin declared the plan crazy. Matthews testily replied that the Shermans supporting the Camerons and Fusiliers Mont-Royal on their flanks would come to the rescue if needed. The two officers countered that the Sasks would be under enemy observation from at least two positions to the right. These were Point 88, the highest spot on Verrières Ridge, and the infamous Hill 112 across the Orne River. A Dieppe survivor, Edmondson finally demanded, "Is this action a must?" It was a divisional order, Matthews replied, and likely one coming from corps.[13] During the divisional briefing, Matthews added, the German tank threat had been dismissed. Between the squadrons supporting the flanking battalions and the anti-tank guns, they were covered. Once the objective was gained, the battalion's 6-pounders and the attached 17-pounders of 2nd Anti-Tank Regiment would rush forward to protect the infantry. Although a counterattack was to be expected, Matthews had been assured it would be infantry. Edmondson and Dickin were out of arguments.[14]

Of 6th Brigade's battalions, the advance by the Sasks was deepest—three miles from the start line to the ridge's main crest, between Saint-Martin-de-Fontenay and Verrières village. From their objective, the battalion would look down upon Saint-Martin to the west and Fontenay-le-Marmion to the south. The 4th Brigade's Essex Scottish Regiment would advance behind the Sasks to the road running from Saint-André past Beauvoir and Troteval Farms to Hubert-Folie. This would put the Essex where they could shift quickly to support whichever leading regiment most needed help.[15]

The Sasks advanced with 'A' Company under Major Robert Wells left and Major Dickin's 'D' Company right. In standard box formation, Major Edmondson's 'B' Company trailed Dickin's men while Captain Charles Doyle's 'C' Company followed 'A' Company. Matthews had his tactical headquarters behind the two leading companies with a carrier hauling its wireless sets. Once on the objective, Matthews would quickly bring up the support company with its mortar platoon and anti-tank guns.[16]

Keeping close to the barrage, the two leading companies had advanced about two thousand yards when 'D' Company came under fire from an infantry platoon supported by several 75-millimetre guns. The Germans were spread out and concealed in the wheat. 'D' Company broke into sections to eliminate these strongpoints. In the tall wheat, a section had to practically stumble on a German strongpoint to engage. Two Germans in a fighting pit, four feet square by one and a half feet deep, their tactic was for one to pop up to locate the nearest Canadians. When he ducked down, he would direct his light machine-gun partner where to fire through the wheat. It was almost impossible to situate the source of this fire unless one got lucky and noticed the spotter.

Neither side enjoying good fields of fire, fighting at each strongpoint was usually hand to hand or at close quarters. When Dickin's men located a German dugout, they chucked in phosphorous and fragmentation grenades. Mostly, however, the strongpoint was only revealed when the Canadians happened upon it. Then it was the Sten gun, a man spraying the two Germans with a full magazine. "We killed more Jerries with Stens that day than with any other weapon," Dickin recounted.

In the midst of this running fight, a corporal with Dickin squeezed the Sten's trigger just as a German fired a rifle at him. Both triggers clicked harmlessly—the Sten out of ammunition, the rifle jamming. The corporal reversed the Sten and smashed the German over the head. He then seized the enemy rifle, worked the jammed round clear, rammed a fresh bullet home, and shot the dazed German dead.

Dickin's company kept moving up the slope, overrunning one strongpoint after another. But the fighting had caused 'D' Company to lose the barrage, and Dickin figured at least a company of

Germans was trying to fight his men to a standstill. "The whole advance to the objective was a series of small actions—section commanders sending men forward with rifles, Stens, or Brens, to wipe out a slit trench." Grenades were running short.[17]

Lieutenant A. Frederickson at the front of No. 18 Platoon spotted two Germans and killed both with rifle shots before a machine-gun burst cut him down. Sergeant P.T. Maule was just behind Frederickson with two men on either side of him. The machine-gun burst dropped the others but left Maule standing alone and unscathed. He summoned stretcher-bearers to evacuate the five wounded men.

Having lost twenty men and two platoon commanders, Dickin ran back to Matthews and asked that Edmondson's 'B' Company take over the lead. Matthews said, "John, can you take over? You know where to go?" Edmondson nodded. "Yes, that's alright."

"Just move through him and that crossroad and go up onto the high ground," Matthews added.[18] Edmondson led 'B' Company to the front.[19] To the left, 'A' Company was meeting stiffening resistance from machine-gun positions hidden in manure piles and haystacks. Snipers hunted through the tall wheat.[20]

'A' Company kept going despite the opposition, and Edmondson slipped his reserve platoon left so that his company was tied in alongside. The Germans started shelling directly behind the barrage. Germans were trying to surrender. Edmondson would yell at them to drop their weapons and point them towards the Canadian rear. Stopping would lose the barrage, and he had too few men to send back guards. After directing the occupants of one trench rearward, Edmondson glanced over his shoulder in time to see an ss soldier aiming a rifle his way. Then Lieutenant Bob Pulley appeared behind the man and shot him dead with a pistol. Edmondson realized the lieutenant had just saved his life.[21]

Shortly after the advance began it had started drizzling, but at 1600 hours this turned to a downpour. All wireless communication was immediately lost.[22]

The Sasks pushed on through increasingly stubborn infantry resistance. 'A' Company reached its objective on Verrières Ridge at 1725 hours. They were in an open field. Stretching from Verrières to their position was a dense row of tall trees not marked on the maps.

MG-42 machine guns dug into this tree line started raking the exposed ground. Major Wells pulled back two hundred yards into the cover of a wheat field.[23]

Edmondson's 'B' Company was to the right in an open pea field that offered no cover and was on the forward slope overlooking Fontenay-le-Marmion. Eight hundred yards west stood Point 88, the highest spot on Verrières Ridge. The major considered capturing it, but the attack plan had not allowed for this. Edmondson told the men to dig in.

Unable to see 'A' Company, Edmondson set out to find Wells. He had gone about twenty-five yards when someone yelled, "Get yourself out and dig fast!" Edmondson turned and saw the company sergeant major heading towards the rear with a wounded man. "Sergeant Major, where the hell are you going?" Edmondson yelled. The man lifted an arm dripping blood down the forearm. Edmondson waved the two onward.[24]

German artillery was inflicting casualties. Edmondson counted between one and two dozen of his men going back with shrapnel wounds. Close behind 'B' Company, Dickin's 'D' Company was digging in. The ground the battalion was on was flat, the only cover the tall wheat. But the wheat also blocked the view. Edmondson was unable to see either 'A' or 'C' Companies on his left.[25]

Looking up, Dickin saw a lot of Germans moving about on Point 88. He pointed them out to an artillery FOO. The man was just beginning to direct fire on the hill when German tanks suddenly popped up inside 'B' Company's area and began "shooting all hell out of everything in their path."[26] It was 1750 hours.

LEFT OF THE Sasks, Les Fusiliers Mont-Royal had won the two farms next to the Saint-André–Hubert-Folie road. Lieutenant Colonel J.G. "Guy" Gauvreau had advanced 'B' Company on the right towards Beauvoir Farm and 'C' Company left to Troteval Farm. Once these were taken, 'D' Company would seize Verrières village. 'A' Company was in reserve.[27]

Notice of the attack had come so late that the Fusiliers had marched to the forming-up position without breakfast and lacking time for lunch. So it was a hungry group of men who advanced at

1500 hours. Still, Captain A. Britton Smith—a 4th Field Regiment FOO attached to 'C' Company—thought the men were in good spirits.

Advancing behind the creeping barrage, they were fired on by German snipers and machine-gun positions hidden in stooks of cut grain scattered across freshly harvested fields. Captain Fernand Mosseau's 'C' Company two-inch mortar section retaliated by setting several stooks alight with phosphorous bombs. Facing the prospect of burning to death, the Germans started surrendering.[28]

Two cobbled-together tank troops from the Sherbrooke's 'C' Squadron were in support. One had a full complement of three Shermans with 75-millimetre guns and a Firefly mounting a 17-pounder. The other had just three 75-millimetre Shermans. These represented all of 'C' Squadron's operational tanks.[29]

At 1630 hours, the Fusiliers gained the two farms, and a fierce close-quarters struggle ensued. Having secured Beauvoir Farm, 'B' Company's Major J.P.C. Gauthier advanced his men to the southern slope of the ridge. 'C' Company, meanwhile, dug in right inside Troteval Farm. Lieutenant Colonel Gauvreau and 'D' Company's Major Jacques "Jimmy" Dextraze walked through Beauvoir Farm to talk with Gauthier. Suddenly, a "terrific concentration of mortar and gun fire opened up on the whole [battalion] front, especially around Beauvoir Farm," Gauvreau wrote later. Gauvreau told Dextraze to push his company on to Verrières as planned. He then tracked down 'A' Company, finding it "pinned...to the ground," and advanced it to a position right of 'B' Company.[30]

The tankers were also hard hit. Lieutenant William James Charters was killed by a mortar round striking his turret. With only three tanks, the troop advanced in support of 'D' Company, but as it crossed the Saint-André–Hubert-Folie road, a 75-millimetre anti-tank gun hit the troop commander's tank with two rounds. The first was deflected by tracks welded onto the turret, but the second smashed the drive shaft and immobilized the Sherman. The crew bailed out safely.

Sergeant Martin Lefebvre and the other tank commander started backing up. A round pierced Lefebvre's tank, killing him and Trooper Arthur Jelly. The German anti-tank gun continued hammering these two knocked-out Shermans until they brewed. Corporal A.T.P Connell, commanding the third tank, disengaged. He could barely see through the driving rain. Within an orchard next to the farm and alongside the other troop's remaining two tanks, Connell "took up a position of observation." At 1700 hours, three Panthers approached from Verrières. When they were five hundred yards from the orchard, Sergeant H. Fowlis in the Firefly knocked two out. The third Panther fled.[31]

Rain was jamming Gauvreau's wireless communications, and he was completely out of touch with 'B' and 'C' Companies. He had ordered the battalion support company and his headquarters forward to Beauvoir Farm, but this formation was stopped by fire four hundred yards to the north. When the gunfire lulled, Gauvreau jumped into a jeep and roared back to his headquarters company to use the more powerful wireless set there. Establishing contact with Dextraze, who was making no progress towards Verrières and taking heavy losses, Gauvreau ordered him back to a position left of 'B' Company.

Gauvreau's only link to 'B' Company was via runners, who crawled through the grain to bring him news. They reported a desperate need for ammunition and grenades. Gauvreau loaded a small convoy of Bren carriers with ammunition, food, wireless sets, and other equipment. After only a short advance, several carriers were knocked out and "the project had to be abandoned." German infantry and tanks were visible in the ground between his and 'B' Company's area.[32]

Some relief reached 'C' Company at Troteval, the company sergeant major managing to get a jeep load through from rear echelon under the covering rain. On board were two canisters filled with stew and coffee, kept warm by insulating hay. There were also cases of .303 ammunition, 2-inch mortar bombs, and No. 36 grenades. Gunner Captain Smith noted the Fusiliers went for the ammunition first. Tearing cases open, men grabbed handfuls of bullets and filled Bren magazines. When these were all loaded, they pulled out khaki bandoliers containing five-round clips for the Lee-Enfields. After stuffing web kit pockets full, remaining bandoliers were slung around necks to be close at hand. Only when everyone was rearmed did attention turn to food. "Good discipline," Smith thought.[33]

By 1900 hours, both forward companies had lost half their strength either killed or wounded. An 88-millimetre gun started shooting at any movement between 'C' Company and Gauvreau's support group north of the farms, ending his ability to communicate with it by runner. He also learned the FOO, Captain Gordon Hunter, who had been with 'B' Company, was dead. That left Smith, isolated with 'C' Company, to direct the artillery. Then, at 1920 hours, there were so many Germans between Gauvreau's position and the two farms that runners could no longer operate.[34] Gauvreau could only hope that the Fusiliers could hang on through a long, deadly night.[35]

AT 1750 HOURS, Major John Edmondson heard men shout, "Tanks!" As he spun around, four panzers charged into the left rear of 'B' Company. They were firing high-explosive shells and raking his men with machine guns. Nobody had managed to dig more than a few inches into the ground, so they were completely exposed in the pea field.[36]

One tank rumbled into the midst of No. 12 Platoon, grinding men under its tracks while shooting at others. Edmondson shouted for the platoon's PIAT man to fire. But the assistant, who had charge of the bomb fuses, was dead. As Edmondson turned to order the platoon sergeant to move his men towards the cover of a wheat field, the man was struck by a tank shell "and disappeared in front of me." The men were running into the tall wheat of their own accord. A tank turret swung menacingly, its barrel aimed directly at Edmondson. He started running, looking over his shoulder, seeing machine-gun tracers honing in. A running dive carried him into the grain. Edmondson rolled left, stopped, rolled right. Bullets ripped the ground where he had been.[37]

Edmondson saw German artillery flashing across the Orne River, and seconds later shells exploded all around. He started crawling and dashing through the wheat, organizing the remnants of 'B' Company. The Bren gunners had all been cut down covering the company's withdrawal. No. 12 Platoon's PIAT was gone. Lieutenant

Bob Pulley and Lieutenant Cas Treleaven were deploying their PIAT teams. One of the teams knocked out a tank with two bombs. Another tank was hit, but whether it was immobilized was uncertain. Edmondson and his second-in-command, Captain Johnny Gates, told men to head north and get behind 'D' Company. Gates kept yelling into the wireless handset that they needed artillery, any bloody thing, but there was only static.

The tanks were slashing the wheat with machine guns and growling around in circles to crush men or flush them into the open. Lieutenant Treleaven fell wounded. He would lay for an hour no less than twenty-five feet from one tank before managing to crawl away unseen. As the rest of the company moved back, Pulley stayed behind to provide cover. His body would not be discovered until early August.

Edmondson and Gates had fragments of the company headquarters section and No. 12 Platoon with them. The other two platoons were also moving back in some semblance of order. Everyone crawled through the saturated wheat, their uniforms sodden. When Edmondson and Gates reached 'D' Company's position, they found it had already pulled back. There were a few wounded men lying about, obviously overlooked in the withdrawal.[38] "We stop here," Edmondson told Gates. "Hold everybody who comes back. Start digging in. Create as much cover as you can." Edmondson left to report to battalion headquarters.

Chaos had reigned as the tanks punched in, and the shelling had risen to a fierce crescendo. When Major Len Dickin had seen the tanks boring into Edmondson's company, he immediately thought of the battalion's supporting anti-tank guns. They were just coming into position behind the two rear infantry companies. The crews of two 17-pounders from 2nd Anti-Tank Regiment's 'K' Troop were still unhooking the guns when tanks destroyed them. The other gun crews managed to get their 17-pounder or 6-pounder guns deployed but were stuck in the open with no cover. Five tanks closed in for the kill. The anti-tank gunners never stood a chance.

Dickin ordered his PIAT men to engage. Because of the tall wheat, the men could not fire from the normal prone position. So the teams tried firing while standing up. Exposed, both PIAT gunners were quickly cut down. Dickin started moving his men back, planning to take them behind the Saint-André–Hubert-Folie road. They could dig in behind the Essex Scottish and bolster that battalion's defensive line. Dickin headed towards the rear, intent on contacting the Essex battalion commander and explaining his intentions.[39]

Edmondson, meanwhile, had just about reached where the Sasks' headquarters company should be when the signals officer, Lieutenant B.A. Smith, charged up. "Where the hell are you going?" Edmondson demanded. "I'm getting out of here," Smith replied. "The headquarters has been knocked out. The Colonel has been killed. They knocked out the carrier and the company that was here has been ordered to withdraw."[40] More calmly, Smith explained that artillery fire had killed Major Reg Matthews and intelligence officer Lieutenant Doug Pedlow. They had been killed minutes after sending a message to 6th Brigade at 1750 that stated: "We are being attacked by tanks. We need help from the tank counterattack coming from the south." There had been no response from brigade.[41]

The wireless link to brigade had been lost with the command carrier, so Edmondson decided to go to Ifs and ask Brigadier Young for reinforcement. If he gave the Sasks tanks, the unfolding debacle might be reversed. When Edmondson reached the narrow road cutting across the ridge from Saint-Martin-de-Fontenay to Verrières, he happened on a battalion carrier. Edmondson hitched a ride to Ifs. As the carrier descended the ridge, Edmondson noticed many "small figures far down the slope in front of the Saint-André crossroads stand up and converge for a moment as if to consult and then double to the rear." Edmondson realized these were Essex Scottish officers. As planned, the battalion had advanced to the Saint-André–Hubert-Folie road to support 6th Brigade's collapsing attack. Edmondson thought the Essex "were in a precarious position and had to seek cover from the intense enemy fire."[42]

THE ESSEX SCOTTISH had advanced at 1727 hours, just twenty-three minutes before Major Matthews reported the tank attack. By the time the battalion reached the crossroads it was 1820 hours, and the

Sasks were being slaughtered ahead in plain sight. Lieutenant Colonel Bruce Macdonald had barely ordered his companies to start digging in when Major Dickin arrived and told him the Sasks were falling back behind his position.[43] Dickin then left for Ifs. Like Edmondson, he was determined to get brigade to send some support.[44]

The Essex had advanced through intense German machine-gun, mortar, and artillery fire. Many men were lost. When the first men were struck, their friends tended to rush to help. But 'A' Company's Major H.W.P. Thomson ordered them to keep going and leave the wounded to the stretcher-bearers. Minutes later, Thomson fell wounded. Lieutenant Tom Martin took over. By the time 'A' Company reached the crossroads, most of its platoon sections had lost half their strength killed or wounded. 'B' Company, also leading, had fared no better.

Their objective was littered with dead and wounded from the South Saskatchewans. The two companies were immediately subjected to fire from German tanks. 'B' Company's Major D.W. McIntyre consulted with Lieutenant Martin, and the two men agreed they should withdraw to the forming-up position east of Ifs. Otherwise, they faced elimination. Neither officer was in communication with battalion headquarters. As Martin returned to 'A' Company, he was badly wounded in both legs. After ordering the men back to the forming-up position, he bled to death.

Having lost all their officers and most non-commissioned officers, 'A' Company crawled back through the wheat. Nobody provided direction. The men just went their own way. Corporal John Cross and his brother Ken, a private, stuck together. One would rise up to track the German tanks. When a tank rotated its turret away from them, he would shout for the other brother to move. Then they would alternate the process. All around, other men were being killed or wounded. Only a remnant of the company managed to escape.[45]

'B' Company's withdrawal was better organized and was intercepted by Lieutenant Colonel Macdonald when it reached the two reserve companies. McIntyre had already sent thirty of his men to help the wounded get back to the forming-up position, but

Macdonald told him to dig the rest of the company in behind 'D' Company's position.[46] The situation was dire, what was left of the battalion being counterattacked by an estimated two companies of infantry and up to thirteen tanks.[47]

Withdrawing in concert with 'A' and 'B' Companies of the Essex were many South Saskatchewans. Captain George Lane had watched in dismay as the men streamed past where he had set up the 3-inch mortars behind the Essex reserve companies. There seemed to be countless walking wounded. Several carriers rumbled past over-loaded with men suffering immobilizing wounds. The unwounded passed in small groups. Sometimes these were under command of a sergeant or corporal. Often they were just a collection of dispirited privates.[48]

At brigade headquarters, Major Edmondson went straight to Brig-adier Young. Matthews was dead, communications cut, the Sasks had withdrawn, and the area they vacated could now be saturated with artillery that would catch the Germans in the open, he said. "Take it easy, young man," Young said. "You're excited. Take it easy." Edmondson denied being excited. If they got tanks and artillery, the Sasks could "save the battlefield."

Dickin arrived and reiterated Edmondson's report, offering the same suggestions. Young interrupted. "Who's senior here?" Edmondson said, "Guess I am by two weeks." Young told him to "go back and rally your battalion and hold them solid. We'll do what we can." Realizing arguing was useless, Edmondson headed back. Dickin stayed on, urging Young to commit more tanks, to call in artillery, but the brigadier finally dismissed him.[49]

Edmondson found the battalion gathering at the forming-up position. He got sergeants to sort men into their respective compa-nies and get them dug in. At 2030 hours, Edmondson counted one sergeant and thirteen men from 'B' Company remaining. As night fell, men were still trickling in.

By 0800 hours the following morning, 'B' Company's numbers had risen to Edmondson, Lieutenant Treleaven, and twenty-seven men—out of ninety-five who had gone into the attack.[50] The final toll for the Saskatchewans was thirteen officers and 209 other ranks killed, wounded, or missing. In addition to the battalion's acting commander, two company commanders were dead.[51] 'K' Troop of the 2nd Anti-Tank Regiment reported losing all four 17-pounders, seven men killed, and several others missing.[52]

Out front of the Saskatchewan position, the Essex Scottish still held just north of the Saint-André–Hubert-Folie road. Lieutenant Colonel Macdonald moved through the perimeter at 2000 hours and talked to every man. He told them they "must hold...at all cost. Some were shaken a bit by the [Sasks] and 'A' and 'B' Coy withdrawals, but seemed reassured and steadied by my visit."

Macdonald then went back and organized the men at the forming-up position. He found about fifty men who were not walking wounded and marched them to brigade headquarters to get refitted with missing kit and ammunition. Told there was nothing for them, Macdonald decided the men might as well stay in the rear, get some rest and food, and be ready to return to the line in the morning.

After he left, Young showed up. He sent to division for the necessary ammunition and equipment. At 0400 hours, Young ordered these men forward. Lieutenant A. McCrimmon, who had been LOB, had already rounded up about fourteen men an hour earlier and led them back to the crossroads. McCrimmon assumed command of 'A' Company. Dawn was fast approaching, and the Essex fully expected a counterattack they were ill prepared to repel.[53]

Not a Pleasant Picture

A T 0130 HOURS on July 21, Major General Chris Foulkes told Brigadier Elliot Rodger at 11 Canadian Corps that "things were sticky and confused" on 6th Brigade's front. While the rest of the battalions had been "repulsed" back to the Saint-André–Hubert-Folie road, the Queen's Own Camerons "were okay."[1]

Earlier, Foulkes had apprised Lieutenant General Guy Simonds that 6th Brigade was in trouble. At 1800 hours on July 20, Simonds had accordingly ordered 5th Brigade's Black Watch placed at Brigadier Hugh Young's disposal and all of 2nd Armoured Brigade under 2nd Division's command. Young was free to use the 1st Hussars to protect his left flank and redeploy all the Sherbrooke Fusiliers to reinforce the Camerons.

The entire Canadian front, Simonds warned, was in "danger of caving in entirely," clear back to Vaucelles.[2] During the night of July 20–21, the only good news was the absence of counterattacks against the Essex Scottish. But the heavy rain filled slit trenches and made the "task of keeping weapons in working order...almost impossible. The men worked continuously on their MGS, even tearing off their shirts for rags in a futile attempt to keep them in order," the Essex war diarist recorded.[3]

On Les Fusiliers Mont-Royal's front the night had also brought a lull, the Germans only probing Troteval and Beauvoir Farms with small infantry patrols. Although easily driven off, the Germans cap-tured a few men from 'C' Company at Troteval Farm.[4]

Night brought no relief for the Camerons, as eight Panthers struck 'D' Company on the southern edge of Saint-André just before dusk. When the supporting 2nd Anti-Tank Regiment troop attempted to move three guns to meet the attack, all were knocked out. With the Panthers focused on the anti-tank guns, 'D' Compa-ny's PIAT team crept in close and knocked two out. Despite this success, the tanks and accompanying infantry soon threatened to overrun the company.[5] Lieutenant Colonel Norman Ross ordered it back five hundred yards to a position next to 'B' Company on the edge of the orchard. This meant surrendering most of Saint-André, but Ross felt the Camerons were too weak to hold the entire village and orchard both.[6]

Although the tanks withdrew, German infantry continued counter-attacking 'A' and 'C' Companies through the rest of the night. In the pitch black, with rain cloaking their stealthy approach, the Germans were only detected when they were inside close-quarter fighting distance.

At about 0230 hours, two German vehicles rolled blithely through Saint-André in the direction of Fleury-sur-Orne. The carrier platoon's PIAT team punched both vehicles with bombs that killed their crews. The lead vehicle proved to be a half-track marked with a red cross but loaded with ammunition.[7] Despite the half-track's load, which contravened the Geneva Convention, Ross ordered the Red Cross markings covered over to avoid allegations of wrongdoing by the Camerons.[8] A dreary dawn found the Camerons and Germans exchanging desultory small-arms fire.[9]

ALL THREE 6TH Brigade battalions were facing strong German forces by the early morning of July 21. Les Fusiliers Mont-Royal's 'B' Company at Beauvoir Farm was completely surrounded and out of contact with Lieutenant Colonel Guy Gauvreau. From Troteval Farm, Major Fernand Mosseau and 4th Field Regiment's FOO, Captain A. Britton Smith, could see Beauvoir. But they were unable to offer any assistance.

Shortly after first light, artillery and mortar fire drenched both farms. Then ss panzer grenadiers charged in. At Troteval, 'C' Company easily repulsed the assault. 'B' Company, however, ran out of ammunition and was overrun. Smith and Mosseau watched helplessly as the survivors were taken prisoner.[10]

About the same time Beauvoir Farm fell, several German tanks opened fire on the two Essex Scottish companies astride the Saint-André–Hubert-Folie road. As the morning wore on, tank and infantry attacks on 'C' and 'D' Companies intensified. The situation was badly confused. Lieutenant Colonel Bruce Macdonald was unable to calculate his actual strength because of the disorganized state of the survivors from 'A' and 'B' Companies. Some of these men were intermixed with the other two companies, while others apparently still remained at the forming-up position despite orders for them to come forward at dawn. At 0930 hours, Macdonald left to gather these men and urge Brigadier Hugh Young to send armoured support.

Macdonald was consequently gone when the Germans managed to cut off 'C' Company, 'D' Company's No. 17 Platoon, and battalion headquarters from the rest of the Essex force. Helpless against the tanks, men from both groups began withdrawing while others surrendered. Lieutenant L.R. Morgan and most of No. 17 Platoon put down their arms. Battalion headquarters scattered. Lieutenant K. Jeanneret, the signals officer, spent hours crawling through the high wheat. Intelligence officer Lieutenant W.C. Wilson and most of the headquarters staff were captured.[11] By 1100 hours, fugitives from the crossroads began trickling in to where Young had ordered Macdonald to have the 'A' and 'B' Company remnants form a new line in front of Ifs.[12]

Around noon, uncertain about the Essex dispositions and seeing German tanks less than a mile from Ifs, Young feared losing the village itself and ordered the Black Watch to advance and establish a defensive line on Point 61, a thousand yards south of Ifs. He also placed two squadrons of the 1st Hussars on the edge of the village. Not sure if there were still Essex Scottish on the Saint-André–Hubert-Folie road, Young set the Black Watch advance for 1800 hours. This would allow time to ascertain if any men remained there who would be caught in the supporting artillery barrage and send a warning for them to withdraw.[13]

WHILE YOUNG WAS fixated on rescuing the centre of his line, the Camerons and Fusiliers clung to their positions with little support. At 0900 hours, the Camerons spotted tanks on the heights both to the east and south of Saint-André. German infantry then crossed the Orne River and attempted to infiltrate 'A' Company's lines. Captain Bob Lucy, 6th Field Regiment's FOO, broke this effort with artillery, and many of the Germans chose to surrender rather than attempt a river crossing under shellfire. Throughout the day, the Germans repeatedly pounded the Camerons with mortar fire followed by an infantry assault.[14]

In the mid-morning, the German tanks on the hills struck in unison from both directions. Major Sydney Radley-Walters had fifteen 'A' Squadron tanks of the Sherbrooke Fusiliers on Hill 67 overlooking the Cameron position. He saw the tanks about six hundred yards off, but through the rain was unable to identify them as friend or foe. The rain had also cut the effective range of his wireless so drastically he could barely communicate with his own tanks. Finally, peering through binoculars, Radley-Walters made out the distinctive low turret profile of Panthers—six in one group, eight the other, and separated by about three hundred yards. 'A' Squadron opened fire and the Germans replied. For the next hour, the two sides traded shots. One Sherman was knocked out, but the Germans appeared unscathed.

To break the impasse, Radley-Walters decided to go on the offensive. He ordered smoke shells fired to screen a move by the two Shermans of No. 1 Troop to the orchard north of Saint-André. Once among the trees, this troop fired smoke to cover an advance by seven tanks led by Radley-Walters past the northeastern edge of the village. When the smokescreen thinned momentarily, one tank was knocked out crossing the main road through Saint-André. The rest, however, reached a position from where they could engage the Germans from three sides. "With the battle raging in ['A' Squadron's] favour," the shootout continued until 1430 hours, when Radley-Walters counted eight Panthers knocked out in exchange for five Sherbrooke tanks. But where he had positioned six tanks on the northeastern flank of Saint-André, the situation "was becoming perilous." Two Shermans had been knocked out, the turrets of two more were jammed, and the crew commander in another had been killed. German infantry were attacking with Panzerfausts from just twenty-five yards distant.

Firing more smoke shells to cover his movement, Radley-Walters led three tanks to the rescue. As they closed in, the German infantry fled, and the surviving Panthers withdrew. At 1800 hours, a troop of tanks from 'B' Squadron arrived to relieve 'A' Squadron, which had just six operational tanks remaining.[15]

'A' Squadron's intervention had prevented the Germans from using their tanks to support their infantry in overrunning the Camerons. But in two days' fighting, the Camerons had suffered eighty-one casualties, twenty-nine fatal.[16]

THERE WERE NO tanks supporting the Fusiliers of 'C' Company still clinging to Troteval Farm in the late afternoon of July 21. Nor was there any prospect of reinforcement. Lieutenant Colonel Guy Gauvreau had too few men in the two companies dug in to the north of Beauvoir and Troteval Farms to possibly break through to Troteval. The only thing keeping 'C' Company alive was the artillery called down by the FOO, Captain Smith. Major Mousseau and he agreed that unless soon reinforced, the company was doomed.

None of Mousseau's wireless sets worked, but Smith's Nos. 18 and 19 sets functioned. He had 4th Field Regiment rout him through to 6th Brigade and begged for "an additional company of infantry or even better, the reserve battalion." The farm could be held, the day saved. No help was offered. Smith felt as if nobody at brigade "appreciated the importance of reinforcing 'C' Company's success."

They had already repelled four counterattacks. The company was down to just seventeen men, twelve of them, including Mousseau, wounded. Breaking out with so many injured was impossible. Ammunition was disappearing, all PIAT bombs already gone.

As the fifth attack came in, Smith cut down many ss panzer grenadiers with artillery, but others just kept coming, forming up behind and alongside German tanks that looked to Smith like Tigers. Mousseau and Smith decided to play their last card. 'C' Company was dug into deep slit trenches. The Germans were in the open. Smith ordered artillery on top of Troteval Farm. Shrapnel and blast scythed through the German infantry, while the Fusiliers remained safe in their holes. When the shells lifted, through the slowly dissipating smoke Smith saw the ground blanketed with dead and wounded panzer grenadiers. But the Tigers still prowled unharmed through the farm. Mousseau told Smith the Fusiliers either surrendered or died needlessly.

Smith agreed, but said he was going to make a break for it with the artillery carrier. Bombardier Chris May jumped behind the controls, only to discover the rain had shorted out the engine. May opened the engine compartment and started trying to fix the problem. Smith considered escaping by crawling through the tall grain. Rolling his binoculars inside a raincoat, Smith buried the bundle in the mud of a slit trench to lighten his load. Smith expected to be back. He would recover the binoculars then.

Suddenly, the engine started. Smith and signaller Bombardier John Clark hopped on, and May stepped on the accelerator. Smith had called down a final artillery concentration to cover the escape attempt, and the carrier plunged through the exploding shells. Apparently not deigning to fire the massive 88-millimetre main gun at such an insignificant target, the Tigers raked it with co-axial machine guns. White powder flew all around. Smith's first thought was phosphorous, a horrible image of burning to death. Bits of meat and flesh seemed to be spattering everywhere. Then the carrier was hurtling down the slope, the farm well behind.

Smith saw that a large tin of powdered hardtack was riddled with bullet holes. The contents had been the white powder. A PIAT ammunition box welded to the carrier's front, which had been loaded with tins of bully beef and stew, had also been ruptured and its contents had "splattered gruesomely over everything." The carrier's armoured sides were chipped by countless bullet strikes.

When the carrier reached Gauvreau's position, Smith advised him of 'C' Company's surrender.[17] Gauvreau walked among the remaining Fusiliers dug in on the slope four hundred yards north of Beauvoir Farm. They stayed here no matter what, he said. This was the base from which the farms would be retaken. The Fusiliers had suffered traumatic losses in men and leaders, but they knew their performance had shown "bravery and determination."[18] Gauvreau had earned a Distinguished Service Order, gunner Smith a Military Cross.

THE BLACK WATCH attacked at 1800 hours, behind a creeping barrage and with the tank support that could have prevented the South Saskatchewan and Essex Scottish disasters. The Sherbrooke's 'B' Squadron was on one flank, 'A' Squadron of the 1st Hussars the other.

Private W.T. Booth and two other Black Watch intelligence section members assigned to establish an observation post on the objective walked alongside one of the tanks. Every few seconds its 75-millimetre gun boomed, the noise making it impossible for Booth to hear the incoming German shells that were being dropped behind the barrage. But he could see its effects, particularly when Lance Corporal Roderick Hudson was "thrown into the air by a mortar bomb" and killed. "Yet the entire attack, which didn't last long, had an air of unreality, as if it were a movie I was watching. When we had taken the hill, this feeling vanished in the shock of seeing Canadian dead, the Essex Scottish, lying on the ground. Seeing Hudson fall did not have the effect on me of seeing [the] sleeve patch of the Second Division on the uniforms of those killed."[19]

When the infantry came under intense mortar and machine-gun fire, the 1st Hussars dashed forward to help their "little friends" and moved directly in the line of fire of several anti-tank guns. Lieutenant "Alabama" Correy's tank brewed, and he and Trooper J.A. Brown suffered severe burns. Then Lieutenant Aisbitt's Sherman was knocked out. Everyone escaped unharmed, but while taking cover, Trooper R.A. Wallwin was wounded by a mortar shell. Lieutenant C.A. Mills lost his tank, while that commanded by Sergeant Inglis had its hull split open by two high-explosive strikes. Having lost an eye, Sergeant Payne continued to command his tank until the squadron withdrew.[20]

The Black Watch advance made such good progress that the battalion pushed past Point 61 and to the crossroads where the Essex Scottish had broken.[21] The successful operation placed the Black Watch to the right of the Fusiliers facing Beauvoir Farm and straightened 6th Brigade's front with three battalions astride or close to the Saint-André–Hubert-Folie road.

Stabilizing this line effectively closed Operation Atlantic. Both 3rd and 2nd Divisions had suffered heavy losses over four days, but the latter division's casualties were shocking. For its part, 3rd Division counted 386 casualties, 89 fatal. For 2nd Division the price was 1,149 with 254 men dead. Hardest hit had been the Essex Scottish and South Saskatchewans. The Essex Scottish reported 244 casualties, of which 37 were dead.[22] Included in the Essex figure were 102 men taken prisoner.[23] No casualty totals for Les Fusiliers Mont-Royal were recorded. Given the loss of two companies, it is probable that this French-Canadian unit suffered comparable casualties.

WHAT HAD BEEN achieved? A greater lodgement on the east side of the Orne that left more room to prepare another offensive without being so tightly constricted around Caen, one Canadian analysis offered. That and the continuation of tying down German armoured divisions in front of British Second Army. Three full Panzer divisions—1st ss, 12th ss, and 21st—along with battle groups of 2nd and 9th ss Panzer Divisions, were fixed here. From the Canadian view, the report added, Atlantic had "prepared the way for the operations to be mounted by First [Canadian] Army, which would [now drive] the enemy out of the country between Caen and Falaise."[24]

Simonds had bet wrongly that Operation Goodwood would cripple the Germans in front of 11 Canadian Corps and a breakout would be easily attained. Instead, the Germans had deftly blocked 2nd Division's assault and mauled four infantry regiments. July 20 had been a disaster for 6th Brigade. Although subsequent reports claiming that the South Saskatchewan and Essex Scottish Regiments had fled in disorder were false, their losses were such that both would require major rebuilding before they could fight again.

The Saskatchewan attack had been conceptually flawed. Simonds and Young both erred in assuming tanks supporting the battalions on the flanks would be able to also protect the Sasks in the centre. As Major Radley-Walters later told the Sasks' Major John Edmonson, his 'A' Squadron near Hill 67 had neither line of sight to the centre nor any instruction to support the battalion there. "We never fired a round in support of you," he said.[25] The tanks on the left were few in number and mostly knocked out early in the fight for Beauvoir and Troteval Farms.

In February 1944, Simonds had emphasized in a II Corps operational policy statement that success in an attack hinged on defeating the inevitable counterattacks after an objective was won. Meeting these counterattacks had to "form part of the original plan of attack."[26] But the Sasks, the Fusiliers, and then the Essex Scottish were given no opportunity to prepare to repel the armour-infantry counterattacks. The Fusiliers were inadequately supported by seven tanks from 'C' Squadron, which were greatly outnumbered. And except for anti-tank guns, knocked out before they had time to bring their weapons into action, the Saskatchewan and Essex regiments were not equipped to fight tanks. Their fate was sealed the moment the Panzers broke into their midst.

Not that Simonds, Major General Charles Foulkes, or Brigadier Young were prepared to accept any blame. On July 22, Foulkes took Edmondson aside.[27] "Who gave you the authority to withdraw? Why didn't you stay and dig in on your objective? Why have you lost all of your automatic weapons and other equipment?" were some of the questions Foulkes threw at the Saskatchewan major.

Keeping calm, Edmondson replied that the battalion had been caught in the open field objective by an immediate tank counter-attack that rolled right over it. Nobody had time to dig in. The men with automatic weapons were killed. There was no communications, no tank support, no artillery support, and the anti-tank guns were knocked out immediately. Edmondson considered his remaining duty was to save lives, so he ordered the withdrawal.

Foulkes offered no response but ordered a Court of Enquiry in the Field to investigate the loss of weapons by both the Saskatchewan and the Essex Scottish regiments.[28] It was held on August 2.

Evidence presented by the few surviving Saskatchewan officers painted a compelling picture of a battalion torn asunder but wherein isolated elements fell back in stages with hope of reaching a position that could be held.

After extensive testimony by officers of both regiments, the court exonerated the Essex of any neglect and concluded that the "excessive loss of stores" by the Sasks "was largely due to the manner in which the withdrawal was carried out." The court added, however, that the losses were at least partly due to the tank counterattack. While refusing to speculate on whether the Saskatchewan withdrawal had been premature, the court emphasized that there was "no armour support for the infantry."[29]

The court's exoneration of the Essex Scottish came too late to save Macdonald. He was relieved on July 22.[30] A respected Windsor lawyer, Macdonald had ten years' experience as a militia officer with the Essex before the war. He had led a company at Dieppe and then became the battalion's second-in-command. In May 1943, Macdonald took over command. His promotion had been welcomed by the Essex intelligence officer, Lieutenant Fred Tilston, who commented effusively in the war diary on Macdonald's qualifications, experience, and knowledge of training.[31]

On July 22, Tilston was still maintaining the war diary and could not bear to mention Macdonald's relief. Perhaps he hoped it was a temporary measure. But he unhesitatingly expressed his feelings about the debacle. "It is not a pleasant picture to realize that so many of the [battalion] have been lost, especially when the action was not successful and many of the casualties could have been avoided by better planning and the observance of the procedure that our [training] had led us to believe would be followed before going into battle. All the rules of man management were either violated or ignored, by the sudden move ordered after midnight, the loss of sleep by all ranks, a poor breakfast and little or no noon meal before battle, and the general or detailed picture and plan, if known, was not given to the junior officers or troops."[32]

Macdonald made a concerted, ultimately doomed effort to rescue his reputation and that of the regiment he loved. But Young stood behind the criticisms set out in a blistering report that accused

Macdonald of failing to control his men and losing their confidence. Young also alleged that Macdonald had displayed such nervousness that he appeared to have suffered a breakdown. Generally, he had demonstrated unsuitability for command.

When every man in the regiment signed a petition supporting Macdonald, it was ignored. Before he left them, many assured Macdonald of their belief in him and declared he was being "unjustly punished."[33] But Young had found someone to blame. Without that, questions might have been raised that exposed his own poor handling of the attack. The brigade war diary asserted that upon receiving the second appeal from the Sasks for tank support, Young had ordered the reserve Sherbrooke squadron and a troop from 'A' Squadron to their aid.[34] There is no record anywhere else of this order—not in the Sherbrooke war diary, their after-action report on Operation Atlantic, or in the brigade operational logs. The brigade war diary blamed all the losses on German mortar and artillery fire. Never was it noted that the Saskatchewan and Essex regiments were overwhelmed by tanks or that the Fusiliers suffered almost the same fate.

Young's assertions were accepted without comment by Foulkes and Simonds. But then the 6th Brigade assault plan had come from them. So Macdonald made a convenient scapegoat for all.

RECRIMINATIONS REGARDING ATLANTIC and Goodwood echoed throughout the Allied command chain. So much had been expected, yet the result disappointed all. SHAEF Supreme Commander General Dwight D. Eisenhower and many of his senior officers felt Montgomery had failed them. "A few days ago, when armored divisions of Second Army, assisted by a tremendous air attack, broke through the enemy's forward lines, I was extremely hopeful and optimistic. I thought that at last we had him and were going to roll him up. That did not come about," Eisenhower wrote Montgomery.

Despite British manpower shortages, Eisenhower demanded that Second Army continue winning more ground on the Allied eastern flank. "Eventually the American ground strength will necessarily be much greater than the British. But while we have equality in size we must go forward shoulder to shoulder with honors and sacrifices equally shared." Eisenhower was clearly implying that the British-Canadian forces were "not pulling their weight."[35]

Plans were already afoot for a renewed attack, wherein 11 Canadian Corps took centre stage. As Operation Atlantic had reached its sad climax, Simonds and Second Army's Lieutenant General Myles Dempsey were discussing Operation Spring—aimed at ensuring that the Germans continued to concentrate their armoured divisions on Second Army's front.

While Goodwood and Atlantic had failed their purposes, they had left the Germans certain that the greatest threat of an Allied breakout was here. But the Americans were poised to begin the real Allied breakout—Operation Cobra—at Saint-Lô. Like Goodwood, Cobra was to be preceded by a massive aerial bombardment. The rains that had transformed Verrières Ridge into a quagmire had also grounded the Allied bombers. When the skies cleared, which was not predicted to occur for several more days, Cobra would proceed.

While the rain continued, however, it was necessary to keep the Germans engaged. Thus Operation Spring—not a breakout attempt but instead "a holding attack." And to give 11 Canadian Corps more punch, Dempsey gave Simonds 7th Armoured and the Guards Armoured divisions. There would be three phases. In phase one, 2nd and 3rd Canadian Infantry Divisions, supported by 2nd Canadian Armoured Brigade, would seize a line along the crest of Verrières Ridge running from May-sur-Orne through Verrières to Tilly-la-Campagne. This involved an advance of about a mile across a four-mile-wide front. If this attack succeeded, phase two would commence, in which 7th Armoured Division would charge over the ridge to gain the commanding heights of Point 122 near Cramesnil. This feature, also known as Cramesnil Spur, was about three miles beyond the phase one objectives. Also during phase two, 3rd Canadian Division would advance a further mile. If all went well, phase three would see the British armour push south along the Caen-Falaise highway to Cintheaux or even farther. This was the broad outline that Dempsey gave Simonds on July 22, but the specifics of Operation Spring were his to arrange.[36]

Spring was to launch on July 25, and before then 11 Canadian Corps must first secure the start lines from which the operation would begin. On the western flank, the Camerons were still hanging on to Saint-André. Complicating matters was the fact that Etavaux, a village east of the Orne, remained in German hands. This village was behind the Camerons and roughly adjacent to Hill 67. The Germans were reinforcing the Etavaux garrison by passing troops and supplies across the Orne from Maltôt.

Before Simonds met with Dempsey on July 22, he ordered the Germans thrown out of Etavaux by 5th Brigade's Le Régiment de Maisonneuve. At the same time, a 43rd British Infantry Division battalion would seize Maltôt. Because the German hold on Etavaux depended on possession of Maltôt, the British assault was of primary importance. During his O Group, Lieutenant Colonel H.L. Bisaillon said the Maisies were not expected to hold the village. They would instead pull out of Etavaux just before the British shelled Maltôt.

Because his 'A' and 'B' Companies had been badly mauled in the earlier assault on Fleury-sur-Orne, Bisaillon used only his other two companies—'D' Company, under Major Gérard Vallières, and Major Jacques Ostiguy's 'C' Company. Their line of advance was on either side of a railroad track that crossed the Orne by bridge just south of Etavaux. The Maisies attacked at 1300 hours behind an artillery barrage.[37]

When the barrage lifted, the Maisies were met by heavy machine-gun fire from a network of trenches in front of the village. Major Vallières was killed, and the attack stalled. That was when Sergeant Benoit Lacourse, commanding 'C' Company's No. 15 Platoon, charged the machine guns with four men. In quick succession, the little party wiped out three machine-gun posts with grenades.[38]

The rest of 'C' Company, however, failed to follow Lacourse's group. Seeing his troops going to ground, Major Ostiguy filled a haversack with grenades and rushed the machine-gun line alone. After knocking out four positions, Ostiguy was out of grenades and under fire from a fifth machine gun. Snatching up a rifle, Ostiguy dashed forward and shot the crew dead. Between them, Lacourse and Ostiguy shattered the German resistance.[39] 'C' Company pushed into the village and then withdrew as scheduled at 1500 hours. The sergeant was awarded a Distinguished Conduct Medal and the major a Distinguished Service Order. After dark, the Maisies returned and secured the village, gathering about a hundred prisoners in the process.[40]

Opposition in Etavaux had been badly underestimated, and the attack cost the Maisies ten dead, forty-eight wounded, and another fifty evacuated with battle exhaustion. Combined with the Fleury-sur-Orne losses, the battalion was down about two hundred men, who could not be immediately replaced with French-speaking reinforcements. This put the Maisies temporarily out of the fight.[41]

Southeast of Etavaux, the Camerons had spent another hard day repelling counterattacks from "unfriendly neighbours, strongly posted in St. Martin-de-Fontenay...The casualties from shelling mounted steadily and our troops faced the added discouragement of having to exist for long hours in muddy slit trenches, without food or sleep. But the Camerons held firm and beat off every attack," stated one report.[42]

The unfriendly neighbours in Saint-Martin were infantry, but the Germans persisted in throwing armour against the Camerons as well. Fortunately, Major Radley-Walters and his Sherbrooke's 'A' Squadron kept a watchful eye over Saint-André. Counting only six Shermans, 'A' Squadron squared off against about fourteen Panzers at 1000 hours. After a rapid hour of exchanging fire, five of the German tanks were burning and the rest withdrew. Then, at 1600 hours, the Germans returned but kept outside of 'A' Squadron's range. Radley-Walters managed to get 'B' Squadron to send him a Firefly Sherman with the 17-pounder gun. At 1800 hours, he was guiding this tank into a firing position when several Panzers appeared just a hundred yards distant. Somehow they had managed to navigate through dense woods and the ruins of buildings to close on the Canadians. A quick exchange of fire followed that left two Panzers burning, but also one Sherman. The Germans broke off the engagement.[43]

One thing that allowed the Camerons to hold on was the liberal medium artillery support directed against the Germans in

Saint-Martin. In the afternoon, Lieutenant Colonel Norman Ross went back to brigade headquarters in Ifs to ensure that Brigadier Hugh Young kept these guns on call. Young told Ross to be careful with it, because his FOO, Captain Bob Lucy, was dropping shells very close to the Camerons. "The lads are quite happy," Ross replied. "Nobody's upset about this." With the artillery support, the Camerons felt they could hold Saint-André indefinitely.

Ross was in his jeep en route to Saint-André when an 88-millimetre shell exploded, and he found himself lying on the ground. The smashed jeep stood neatly parked on the verge with the driver dead behind the wheel. One of Ross's legs gushed blood. He hefted it up on the bumper and tried to remember the first-aid training he had taken in Winnipeg before going overseas. "Where the hell were the damned pressure points to stop the bleeding in the lower part of the leg? Blood was spurting all over. I didn't know how to stop the stuff." He was lying there cursing, certain he would die because of a simple failure of memory, when a jeep full of Camerons arrived. They had been searching for their overdue commander. Ross would live, but his war was over.[44]

A Bren gunner and his loader are deployed in a ditch during the July 4, 1944, 8th Canadian Infantry Brigade attack on Carpiquet. Ken Bell photo. LAC PA-131417.

top · A Sherman tank stands next to burnt-out hangars on the southern end of Carpiquet airfield. Possession of author.

bottom · Surrendering Germans emerge from a machine-gun position near Gruchy on July 9. Harold G. Aikman photo. LAC PA-151169.

top right · The Cameron Highlanders of Ottawa (MG) Vickers machine-gunners inflicted heavy casualties on SS troops in their counterattack against Carpiquet on July 4. Donald I. Grant photo. LAC PA-138359.

bottom right · Canadian troops use Luftwaffe bunkers as quarters at Carpiquet airfield. Note the men cooking in the field kitchen. Possession of author.

A Canadian patrol moves cautiously along a battered street in Caen on July 10.
Harold G. Aikman photo. LAC PA-116510.

top · Regina Rifle Regiment infantrymen and a despatch rider (in long jacket) engage in house-clearing operations in Caen on July 10. Ken Bell photo. LAC PA-132727.

bottom · A platoon of Canadian troops leapfrog through one of the countless small villages that had to be taken in the advance south from Caen to Falaise. Possession of author.

top left · A soldier stands amid the ruins of the still-burning factories of Colombelles on July 19. Harold G. Aikman photo. LAC PA-131396.

bottom left · Stretcher-bearers from the Cameron Highlanders of Ottawa treat a wounded soldier during the fighting around Caen on July 15. Possession of author.

above · Heavily laden Private R. Pankaski waits for the barrage to clear near Ifs before joining the advance on July 25. Canadian soldiers quickly disposed of the small folding regulation shovel in favour of regular shovels and picks that, despite their extra weight, enabled them to dig slit trenches quickly. Ken Bell photo. LAC PA-163403.

top · Just after dawn on July 25, infantry advance on Verrières Ridge as part of Operation Spring. Ken Bell photo. LAC PA-131378.

bottom · Self-propelled tanks like these were used to counterattack the Royal Hamilton Light Infantry at Verrières. Possession of author.

Desperate Move in the Dark

BEFORE OPERATION SPRING could be launched, 11 Canadian Corps had to control the necessary start lines. In 2nd Canadian Infantry Division's sector, this entailed the Saint-André–Hubert-Folie road passing by Beauvoir and Troteval Farms and a road south of Saint-André-sur-Orne. On July 23, Simonds ordered 6th Brigade's Brigadier Hugh Young to evict the Germans from these starting points by no later than midnight of July 24–25. Young duly directed the Queen's Own Cameron Highlanders to gain control of the twin villages of Saint-André and Saint-Martin-de-Fontenay while Les Fusiliers Mont-Royal took the farms.[1]

Because of the rain, little photo-reconnaissance intelligence existed on the German defences. Simonds fully appreciated that the Goodwood and Atlantic plans had failed to take into account the extent to which the terrain south of Caen favoured the Germans. The Caen-Falaise highway, one analysis began, ran for thirteen miles "without a curve or bend, and...was flanked by fields of tall wheat." It passed "villages built well back in the surrounding farmland, and climb[ed] steadily from near sea-level to a height of nearly 600 feet." The Germans held the crest of the ridge that extended from May-sur-Orne "across the smooth hump of Verrières [Ridge] through Tilly-la-Campagne." Behind this covering position, the main German forces were believed to be "disposed...from Fontenay-le-Marmion through Rocquancourt to Garcelles-Secqueville." But the real strength of the German position lay "in the spur immediately behind this line, for just west of Cramesnil the road rises to a point over 250 feet higher than Bourguébus. From this series of increasingly lofty elevations the enemy could see as far back as the Canadian gun-positions in the vicinity of Faubourg [de Vaucelles.] Thus all movement in that long perspective could be observed and was likely to bring about immediate and violent reaction from the enemy's guns, mortars and machineguns."

In front of 2nd Division, the "ground was particularly hazardous... The way up along the road through Fleury-sur-Orne and Saint-Martin-de-Fontenay was largely dominated by the high ground west of the river," particularly from Hill 112, "and the ridge running south-west from Verrières." It was at Verrières Ridge that the attack's first phase would be directed. And the infantry would have no alternative but to climb "these exposed and enfiladed slopes" in the face of enemy fire. "Attacking these positions again would inevitably be costly, for as experience had shown, the Germans could be counted upon to resist any penetration with the utmost vigour."[2]

Another feature working to German advantage and unappreciated by Canadian intelligence staff were the mines south of Caen. Two iron mines—one immediately south of Saint-Martin and another on the southern outskirts of May-sur-Orne—had been reported by French civilians on July 23. The lift tower of the first stood over a twelve-hundred-foot-deep shaft. A network of tunnels spidered out from this shaft, and via one of these, Germans defending the twin villages were able to move freely without being seen or fired upon. A system of large vents that fed air into the tunnel served equally well as points through which the Germans could come and go.

The May-sur-Orne shaft was the hub for an even more extensive tunnel network running to an opening on the edge of the Orne River and also through Fontenay-le-Marmion to Rocquancourt. 11 Canadian Corps intelligence officers concluded that the "enemy is probably making use of this as a storage place or part of a defensive system." That the various mine-shaft openings and air vents were used to move troops between May-sur-Orne, Fontenay-le-Marmion, and Rocquancourt was so ill appreciated that existence of the tunnels was not passed down from 2nd Division headquarters to 5th Brigade.[3]

Arrayed in front of 11 Canadian Corps was a formidable force. On the left, 1st ss Panzer Division held the ground from Cagny west to Verrières. This division had been bulked up with the remnants of 16th Field Division's infantry and artillery.[4] From Verrières to Saint-André, 272nd Infantry Division was in place. Its troops were of uneven quality, sometimes fighting tenaciously while at other times prone to surrender. To stiffen the 272nd's backbone, a tank battalion and panzer grenadier battalion from both 2nd Panzer Division and 9th ss Panzer Division had been added to this sector. A 10th ss Panzer Division reconnaissance battalion was also at hand. The rest of 9th ss Panzer Division stood in close reserve northwest of Bretteville-sur-Laize, and 2nd Panzer Division's main body was farther back at Tournebu.[5] These two divisions had been facing xxx British Corps to the west but had just been shifted to face the Canadian front, because the Germans were certain it was here that the next offensive would be launched. The newly arrived 116th Panzer Division stood in reserve near Saint-Sylvain, about seven miles south of the Canadian left flank.[6]

Canadian intelligence had no reliable information on the strength of these divisions. Later investigations, however, determined that on July 24, the Germans had approximately 8,850 men before them. This was approximately half the total strength that these formations normally fielded. At their disposal were 5,900 rifles, 1,910 machine guns, 57 mortars, 54 Panzerfausts, 48 20-millimetre anti-aircraft guns, 113 75-millimetre guns, 18 105-millimetre guns, and 3 150-millimetre guns. They also fielded a mixture of 72 Mark iv and Mark v tanks, with some 20 Tigers lurking near Verrières. Added to this strength were the artillery, mortars, and tanks that could bear from Hill 112 west of the Orne River.[7]

Equally mysterious was the German main resistance line's location. General opinion placed it well south of the crest of Verrières Ridge. The Germans on the ridge were considered a delaying force intended to slow any advance towards the higher ground adjacent to

Bretteville-sur-Laize. Aerial photographs showing construction of defensive positions under way in this area led to the belief that the main resistance line was situated here.[8]

As unobserved movement in the Canadian sector was impossible, Simonds decided that "any major attack had to be done in darkness." Because of 2nd Division's combat inexperience, he wanted to allow them as much time for forming up as possible while leaving sufficient time for Verrières Ridge to be won before daylight. "These conditions," he wrote, "left very little latitude in the choice of 'H' hour."[9]

The attack was set for 0330 hours. To prevent troops from blundering blindly across the battleground, anti-aircraft searchlights would bounce beams off the clouds. Nicknamed "Monty's Moonlight," this technique not only lit the way but supposedly blinded the German defenders.

Simonds thought creeping barrages wasted ammunition, alerted the enemy, revealed the start line, and drew accurate counter fire onto the advancing troops. Instead of relying on a barrage, nine field, nine medium, and two heavy artillery regiments would carry out a fire program on July 24 from 1800 hours to midnight against seven selected targets. Then, for sixty minutes before the attack, a series of timed concentrations would be fired.[10] Operation Spring would proceed no matter the weather conditions, so air support was not assured and Simonds confined it to medium bombers targeting the woods east of Garcelles—once at 2120 hours on July 24 and then again at 0730 the following morning.

Despite its limited intentions as a holding exercise, Operation Spring was still an ambitious enterprise. Yet its success depended on just three Canadian infantry battalions bringing off a night assault—the North Nova Scotia Highlanders, the Queen's Own Cameron Highlanders, and Les Fusiliers Mont-Royal. In this first phase, 3rd Division's North Novas would assault from Bourguébus to Tilly-la-Campagne. Once that village fell, the Highland Light Infantry would pass through with a supporting squadron of Fort Garry Horse to Garcelles-Secqueville.

On the Canadian right flank, 2nd Division would advance 5th Brigade's Calgary Highlanders from Saint-André to take May-sur-Orne.

Their start line was to be won before midnight by the Camerons. At the same time, 4th Brigade's Royal Hamilton Light Infantry would pass through Troteval Farm—to be secured earlier by the Fusiliers—to seize the village of Verrières. At 0550 hours, 5th Brigade's Black Watch would advance on Fontenay-le-Marmion, while 4th Brigade's Royal Regiment of Canada passed through Verrières to capture Rocquancourt.[11]

SIMONDS BRIEFED HIS senior officers during the early afternoon of July 23.[12] Although having no role in the operation, 4th Canadian Armoured Division's Major General George Kitching attended. Kitching saw that both Major General Charles Foulkes and Major General Rod Keller were "concerned at what lay ahead." Earlier, Simonds had confided to Kitching his growing misgivings about both men.[13] Foulkes's handling of 2nd Division during Operation Atlantic had led Simonds to suspect he "did not have the right qualities to command."[14]

A meticulous planner, Simonds had so tightly scripted Operation Spring that Foulkes and Keller were reduced to stage managers for their divisions. Both aware that they skated on thin ice, neither offered suggestions nor raised any concerns.

Foulkes could well have questioned his division's ability to fulfill its role. Two of nine battalions—the South Saskatchewan and Essex Scottish Regiments—were incapable of offensive action. Les Fusiliers Mont-Royal was on the brink of incapacity, and the attack on Troteval Farm would likely tip it over the edge. Le Régiment de Maisonneuve was so reduced by casualties that Foulkes had placed it in divisional reserve. The Queen's Own Cameron Highlanders were just hanging on at Saint-André, and securing the start line for 5th Brigade's advance could exceed its capabilities. That left just four battalions, of which two—the Calgary Highlanders and Black Watch—had been heavily engaged during the past couple of days and so were well below regular strength.

Brigadier Bill Megill, the 5th Brigade commander, was dismayed. The operation seemed to have been planned without consulting a contour map or conducting any detailed ground reconnaissance. Megill saw little hope of success in assaulting Verrières Ridge from the north and west flanks, where the troops would be under observation from three sides.

Megill was a Permanent Force officer, who had held a variety of staff positions before assuming command of the Algonquin Regiment in June 1943. The following February, he had been promoted to head 5th Brigade.[15] The thirty-seven-year-old was a solid soldier, not easily rattled.

His concerns, however, grew as preparations continued through July 24. When he sent a couple of headquarters staff officers to establish a tactical headquarters in Saint-André, they picked a suitable-looking house, opened the front door, and heard voices speaking German. Discreetly exiting, they reported to Megill. He decided to inspect the situation personally. With Lieutenant Colonel Norman Ross wounded, Major John Muncie commanded the Camerons. Muncie confessed that his battalion was still fighting for control of Saint-André and had no presence in Saint-Martin at all. Although trying to clear the start line for the Calgaries, the Camerons were under constant tank, mortar, and artillery fire, while finding Germans immediately infiltrating back into any areas they cleared. Muncie thought the Camerons would prevail, but Megill was doubtful.

At 1600 hours, the Camerons cobbled together a composite force to secure the start line by merging 'B' and 'D' Companies, which gained a strength equivalent to two normal platoons. Major R.H. Lane commanded. 'A' Company's Lieutenant D. Rogers led one platoon, Lieutenant Stanley Anthony Chopp the other. The moment the force crossed the highway, it came under heavy fire.

By 2300 hours, a fierce fight was on in Saint-Martin. Small-arms fire wounded Lane in the neck and shoulders. Then Chopp was killed.

The Camerons were to have secured the 5th Brigade start line by midnight. But it was 0100 hours when the attack stalled entirely. Major E.P. Thompson and two lieutenants rushed to the scene with seventy-five men drawn from the carrier section, scout platoon, a few men of 'B' Company, and two sections of 'C' Company. Soon the Camerons gained Saint-Martin's southern outskirts and started digging in, with the iron mine to their front. Then Captain J.E.E.

McManus reported that the Black Watch was to occupy this forward position and they should withdraw to the church in the village centre. The Camerons duly pulled back into a series of deep slit trenches recently abandoned by the Germans.[16] McManus's information was faulty. No provision for a hand-off to the Black Watch existed, so the start line for the Calgary Highlanders remained in German hands.

WELL LEFT OF Saint-Martin, Les Fusiliers Mont-Royal had started gearing up in the late afternoon to attack Beauvoir and Troteval Farms. The Germans were firmly ensconced at Troteval. But because the Fusiliers were dug in just four hundred yards from Beauvoir, they had prevented the enemy from establishing a tight hold on this farm. A small force comprised of 'A' Company and a carrier section platoon was tasked to secure Beauvoir. Lieutenant Colonel Guy Gauvreau expected the farm to fall quickly.[17]

Troteval was a harder nut. The farm was surrounded by a high wall with an orchard in the southern half and gardens the north. The farmhouse and adjacent courtyard were in the centre but backed against the eastern side of the enclosure. Wheat fields stretched in every direction. Earlier patrols had identified its garrison as consisting of two infantry platoons supported by six tanks. The Germans had circled the farm with a hastily laid necklace of anti-personnel and anti-tank mines thrown on the ground and concealed with loose piles of hay. At night they would be difficult to spot. This was especially true for the carrier crews and supporting tankers of the Sherbrooke Fusiliers' 'B' Squadron.

The Fusiliers were hard pressed to assemble enough men for the new assault. To hold their position north of Beauvoir it had been necessary to put "cooks and drivers...in the trenches."

As neither of the two surviving companies numbered more than fifty men, Gauvreau told Major Jacques Dextraze to cherry-pick seventy-five men from anywhere in the battalion. Dextraze organized these into three twenty-five-man platoons. To compensate for lack of numbers, he equipped the company with eighteen Bren guns rather than the normal nine. Each platoon also had two PIAT teams. All section leaders carried a Sten gun. Only those acting as loaders for the Bren and PIAT gunners carried rifles. To help the gunners steady themselves when firing from the hip or while running, the Brens were fitted with shoulder slings.

Dextraze planned to hit fast and light. The men carried only their weapons, skeleton web gear, a ground sheet with a tin of bully beef and hardtack rolled inside, two Type 36 grenades, and fifteen Bren magazines.

The tank squadron would cover the flanks as Dextraze led the men towards the farm. They would go in behind a creeping barrage fired by one field and one medium regiment. Offering closer fire support was a Cameron Highlanders of Ottawa 4.2-inch mortar platoon. The battalion's 3-inch mortars covered the approaches from Verrières village. Going into the attack with Dextraze was Captain A. Britton Smith, the 4th Field Regiment FOO who had narrowly escaped Troteval on July 21.[18]

Ready to advance behind the Fusiliers was the Royal Hamilton Light Infantry scout platoon. Once the Fusiliers took the farm, its task was to mark with white tape the boundary of the start line. This would enable the infantry companies to precisely situate themselves in the dark.[19]

Dextraze formed his men in a wheat field one thousand yards north of the farm. When the two forward platoons gained Troteval, they would encircle it from opposite directions. The reserve platoon would then push in at the northwest corner, while the forward platoons provided covering fire from the flanks.

At 2000 hours, Dextraze signalled his men forward. They "moved very close, only seventy-five yards from our barrage, taking the chance, in this case luckily, that no one would be hit. My appreciation was that there were so many men in the farm that if my force of seventy-five had been 300 yards behind the barrage, the force...would have had time to reorganize in such strength as to prevent us from seizing and holding the farm," Dextraze later said.

The Fusiliers covered eighty yards a minute. As they came up on the farm at 0215, they met fire from machine guns dug in at the corners of the walled compound, and several men fell. German infantry scattered about in the fields also opened up with ineffective rifle fire.

Dextraze realized the majority of the enemy had withdrawn into the fields to avoid the artillery barrage. Because the advance was so quick, the Fusiliers had gained the farm before they could return. The Bren gunners sprayed long bursts into the fields. This seemed to panic the Germans, causing many to flee. Some ran away without helmets or weapons. "Jerry is no good at night," Dextraze noted.

Artillery had blown holes in the walls and most buildings, so the Fusiliers easily entered the compound. They encountered snipers firing from trees in the orchard, some of whom had tied themselves into the branches. The Fusiliers closed in and shot them—their bodies were left dangling.

Although the German tanks attempted a stand in the dark, they were vulnerable to the PIAT gunners.[20] One man on the hunt was Private Amedee Joseph Philippe Thibault. As the tanks came in, Thibault opened fire with a PIAT. Although his accurate fire failed to knock out any Panzers, the rapidity of shots striking their armoured skins convinced the tankers to withdraw. Thibault was awarded a Military Medal.[21]

Adding to the PIAT bombs hammering the German tanks was Corporal Paul Lebrun. The senior non-commissioned officer in his platoon, Lebrun had taken over command when its officer was killed. He led the platoon in clearing out the machine-gun positions at the corners of the wall before taking personal control of a PIAT and going at the tanks. His Military Medal citation declared that Lebrun's "actions throughout the night were fine examples of bravery, coolness, and leadership."[22]

Although FOO Captain Smith had accompanied the Fusiliers, he never made it to the farm. Riding in the artillery Bren carrier, Smith recognized the trench in which he had buried his binoculars on July 21. When he directed his driver, Bombardier Christopher May, towards it, the carrier struck a mine. May was killed and Smith was blown out of the vehicle. Smith turned a complete somersault before slamming down in the tall wheat. The flash of the explosion immediately attracted the fire of four machine guns, which raked the wrecked carrier and nearby grain. Smith's two signallers were unhurt. Despite realizing that one of his legs was badly broken,

Smith crawled quickly along with the signallers to get about fifty yards away from the machine gun's line of fire.

One of the signallers gave Smith a shot of morphine and then used a rifle for a splint. Smith asked if his leg was truly broken. "Between the ankle and knee, shards of bone are sticking through the skin," the man answered. Smith was also bleeding from several wounds, particularly one from a bullet that had pierced the muscle in his upper back during the crawl to safety. Several field dressings were required to staunch all the blood flowing from his body. Eventually, a field ambulance evacuated Smith.[23]

Once the Fusiliers finished clearing the farm, Dextraze abandoned it for German trenches fifty yards distant. He had too few men to defend Troteval against a counterattack. At 0200 hours, he received orders to withdraw north of the farm because it was to be shelled in an attempt to drive off the German tanks still sniffing around. Four had taken up position southwest of the farm and another two were stationed to the southeast. Dextraze ordered his men to hunker in the trenches. He figured they were safer there than moving in the open. The fire rolled harmlessly past the Fusiliers and out to where the German tanks were. Although the fire drove off the tanks, Dextraze did not think any were damaged. At 0300 hours, he received orders to fall back on Gauvreau's position. The Royal Hamilton Light Infantry were expected to take over the farm, and their scouts were already laying tape there. Dextraze left thinking the clearing of the start line for the Rileys well completed.[24]

When Dextraze returned to the battalion area, intelligence officer Maurice Gravel observed he had "very few men left."[25] Since July 20, the Fusiliers counted seventeen officers and 128 other ranks either killed or wounded.

THREE CANADIAN BATTALIONS moved towards start lines in the hour before the assault was to begin at 0330 hours. It was a clear, moonless night. The rains of the past few days had ceased, leaving the ground muddy underfoot. A warm breeze carried the raw scent of rotting flesh down from the ridges. Strewn across its gentle slopes, the corpses of those killed during Operation Atlantic lay where they had fallen. Hundreds of dead cattle and other livestock had also been caught in the murderous artillery that had drenched this disputed landscape.

At Troteval Farm, the Royal Hamilton Light Infantry's Lieutenant Hugh Hinton and his six scouts worked under fire from mortars and tanks to tape the start line. They crawled through waist-high wheat. The engine noise of the lurking Panzers and loud talking of the tankers covered any sounds they made. Taping was time consuming. Two scouts would crawl in opposite directions until they were about twenty yards apart. Then they stopped, listened. If there were no signs either man had been detected, Hinton came forward and reeled the tape from one to the other. Then the man to the east would join them and the little party would repeat the process, working steadily westward. They were almost at the western edge when a Panzer's shadowy bulk appeared. A moment later, the tank started spraying the field with its machine gun. That was it for further taping. Hinton led his scouts back to guide the companies forward and warn Lieutenant Colonel John "Rocky" Rockingham that the start line was not secure.[26]

This news hardly surprised the thirty-three-year-old Rockingham, who had only returned to the battalion on July 18 from a staff college course in England. As Lieutenant Colonel Denis Whitaker had been wounded four days earlier, Rockingham was leading the Rileys.[27] Rockingham was being groomed for brigade command. He was a tough, pragmatic, clear-thinking soldier. Leaving the Fusiliers to secure the start line barely an hour before the attack had struck Rockingham as "a bit risky." Now the Rileys would have to fight just to get in place for the attack. His attack plan called for an advance with three companies forward—'B' in the centre, 'A' to the right, and 'D' plus No. 15 Platoon from 'C' to the left. The rest of 'C' Company was to be in reserve, with the carrier platoon providing flank protection and the mortar platoon laying down covering fire. Rockingham passed word for Captain Robert Gordon Hunter's 'C' Company to move out front and secure the start line.

"Stomachs turned and flesh tightened in the forward companies as they saw the reserve pass through their ranks in the dark of night.

It was a disconcerting sight for a battalion inexperienced in battle and the final confirmation that something had gone wrong," the regiment's historian observed. So that 'C' Company could do its work, Rockingham received permission to delay the assault for thirty minutes. The Rileys would go for Verrières at 0400 hours.[28]

Hunter led his two rifle platoons and headquarters section to the wheat field next to Troteval Farm. There were tanks on both the western and eastern sides of the field, but Hunter considered those to the east the greater threat. He sent two PIAT teams crawling through the wheat to engage them. When the PIAT teams opened fire, they scored two direct hits. Although neither knocked out a tank, the Panzers withdrew to higher ground southwest of the farm. From here they blazed away with machine guns, but it was clear they were firing blind.

Having seen off the tanks, Hunter sent patrols into the farm to clear it of snipers. They reported the farm vacated. No sooner had the patrols returned when the rest of the battalion arrived and went straight into their attack.[29]

Sending Hinton's scouts in behind the Fusiliers had yielded the unintended result of alerting the Rileys to the necessity of winning their start line. Having done so, they now attacked in a well-organized formation. Neither the Calgary Highlanders to their right nor the North Nova Scotia Highlanders out to the left were as fortunate.

THE CALGARIES HAD formed up at 0130 hours "under terrific mortar and shell fire...and to add to the almost demoralizing sound of all this noise, the Hun sent a number of planes over and bombed and strafed surrounding points. Great fires were seen burning in...Vaucelles and our own guns beat out a blood-curdling rhythm," the battalion war diarist wrote. Lieutenant Colonel Donald MacLauchlan was fatigued and edgy. Like Rockingham, he doubted the start line was secure despite assurances by the Camerons that "all was well."

MacLauchlan had intended to advance two companies forward from the start line on the Saint-André–Hubert-Folie road, immediately east of Saint-André. Major John Campbell's 'A' Company was to be on the left and Major Cyril Nixon's 'B' Company the right. As the Calgaries marched from Hill 67, MacLauchlan decided on the fly to put 'C' Company up front as well and advance it straight down the road running from Saint-André into May-sur-Orne. 'A' and 'B' Companies would move through open country to bypass Saint-Martin to the east, while 'C' Company would brush past its outskirts to the west.

As word was passed through the battalion, MacLauchlan learned that 'D' Company's Captain Del Harrison and his headquarters section had become lost. Captain Sandy Pearson took over the company, which now formed the battalion's only reserve. Harrison's going missing, the Calgary's intelligence officer noted, caused MacLauchlan "great worry" and confusion. There was "no question," he later wrote, "but that 10 years were added to his life during these first hours of the attack."[30]

At 0330 hours, the Calgaries crossed the start line and headed for May, about fourteen hundred yards distant. They had two hours to reach and clear the village before dawn. This timing was critical, for at dawn (approximately 0530 hours) the Black Watch would advance on Fontenay-le-Marmion. That advance was to begin from a start line behind a road running northeast from May.[31]

The three leading companies immediately came under heavy machine-gun fire, the greatest volume hitting 'A' and 'B' Companies originating from an orchard next to a church on the southeast edge of Saint-Martin. 'C' Company, meanwhile, found itself fired at from behind by Germans in Saint-André. With a dawning horror, the Calgaries realized that the Camerons had totally failed to clear the start line and they were exposed to fire from all sides.[32]

ON THE FAR left flank of 11 Canadian Corps, the North Nova Scotia Highlanders had blundered through the darkness and managed to form up on their start line at 0230 hours. "It had been a desperate move in the dark," the regiment's historian wrote. "There was much confusion and it was difficult to find the way." Adding to the confusion, the battalion was bombed by the Luftwaffe. Several men were wounded, including Captain Bob Graves of 'C' Company. The companies became badly disorganized as men sought cover from the bombs. Still, they were in place ahead of time and found the start line fully secured.[33]

From the start line in front of Bourguébus, Lieutenant Colonel Charles Petch planned to advance three companies forward. They would guide on a rough track running to the objective of Tilly-la-Campagne. 'D' and 'B' Companies would be east of the track and 'C' Company west of it. Their way was to be illuminated by search-lights.[34] Petch had argued against the night attack and had no faith in Monty's Moonlight. His concerns had been brushed aside. It was "insisted that the searchlights would be excellent and the artificial moonlight all that was desired."

Ten minutes before 0330 hours, the artillery smashed the small woods to the south and east of Tilly. Then, as the Novas crossed the start line, the guns shifted to the German trenches in front of the village. The advance of about a thousand yards would take twenty minutes. Just before the Novas reached the edge of the village, the artillery would swing onto an orchard immediately northeast of Tilly and also box the village itself. The Novas went into the attack blind. Not a single searchlight beam stabbed the night. Only the flash of exploding shells lit their way.[35]

[14]

Violence of Battle

A S THE THREE battalions crossed their start lines, it became obvious that the German main line of resistance anchored on Verrières Ridge. Canadian and British intelligence had badly
miscalculated, and every battalion paid the price. Although not
required to fight for its starting point, the North Nova Scotia Highlanders advanced into ground devoid of cover and were immediately
zeroed in on by German artillery. 'D' Company's Lieutenant Don
MacLellan fell wounded. Fearing this platoon might waver, Major
Cecil Matson rushed to lead its men forward. Shrinking from the
shells, the troops drifted into an ever-widening line.

Right of 'D' Company, Major A.J. Wilson's 'B' Company had covered about five hundred yards and was probably two-thirds of the way
to the village without having drawn any fire. Wilson's men were
spreading out too far; the left-flank platoon drifting in that direction
to maintain contact with 'D' company, while the right platoon dog-
gedly stuck by the road. Suspecting the Germans were sucking the
Novas into a box, Wilson decided to concentrate the company alongside the road. He sent Captain Jock Grieve to bring the reserve
platoon forward, so they would have maximum firepower available
when things went to hell. Sending his runner to ensure the platoon
next to the road kept its alignment, Wilson set off to bring the left
platoon back on line. With a signaller trotting along behind with the

wireless, Wilson moved through the darkness without encountering any of his men. Although the searchlights had finally come on, in the cloudless night their beams shot straight up and did little more than cast a dim glow upon the open ground over which the North Novas were advancing. Realizing he was likely behind his platoon, Wilson was just turning about when he saw a German trench system thirty yards away. Shadows rose up and bullets riddled the signaller. A slug hit Wilson in the stomach and he collapsed.

To the front of where Wilson had fallen, 'B' and 'D' Companies approached a trench system that cut across their path. Suddenly, a long row of panzer grenadiers rose up and "shot and shouted and threw grenades like wild men." The night exploded into bedlam. Machine guns fired from every angle. Germans were hidden in hay-stacks. There was a long tin-roofed barn alongside the road, next to an orchard, that concealed a row of machine guns. The orchard itself hid numerous German positions. Several dug-in tanks blasted away with main guns and machine guns, firing blind along marked lanes.

The Novas went for the nearest enemy "with bomb and butt and bayonet in one of the wildest melees ever staged." Matson fell dead. Captain Daniel John Nicholson took command of 'D' Company. The wireless was out, leaving Nicholson with no way to call battalion for reinforcements. 'B' Company's set was with the dead signaller lying next to the wounded Wilson. Then Nicholson was killed. All of 'D' Company's officers were out of action. 'B' Company was similarly cut up. The men from each became badly intermixed. Men fought alone, in pairs, in little groups.

'B' Company's Sergeant S.S. Hughes was the last platoon leader among the two companies to still control his men. Hughes led No. 12 Platoon towards a dug-in tank, but his PIAT man was shot down. Hughes snatched up the weapon. The platoon fought through a maze of trenches until they were in range, and then Hughes knocked the tank out with a bomb. Suddenly, panzer grenadiers swarmed the platoon. Hughes was "bowled over by a burst of wooden bullets," and the PIAT flew into the darkness. Fortunately, none of the wooden slugs splintered as they were designed to do, so Hughes was only winded rather than pierced by multiple slivers. The

7-millimetre wooden slug was an ammunition type ss troops occasionally favoured.

As Hughes struggled to regain his breath, his men fought at point-blank range. The moment they finished eliminating this group, however, the surviving platoon members came under fire from another German tank. Hughes and his men hugged the ground, machine-gun rounds whipping through the grain around them. At a brief pause, Hughes ordered the platoon to crawl back to Bourguébus. 'B' and 'D' Companies were finished. They could only try to escape.

Major Wilson had heard the two companies fighting and dying. Two Germans walked over from the trench. When Wilson indicated his wound, they seemed surprised he was still alive. The nearest man aimed a machine-pistol and squeezed the trigger, but it jammed with a harsh clack. That gave Wilson time to draw his pistol. He shot both men dead. Another German stood in the trench and Wilson shot him down. When another popped up with a rifle, Wilson killed him, too. Then he started crawling through the wheat towards the start line.

Lieutenant Colonel Charles Petch had told Major J.A. MacDonald that his 'C' Company was to follow 'D' Company into Tilly and clear the southern portion. MacDonald had been given a map reference indicating where he would hold 'C' Company until the signal for its advance through 'D' Company was given. Reaching the designated spot, he ordered his men to dig in.

Then the shootout across the road broke out and voices started yelling, "Surrender, Canada." A German officer, well back from the fighting, started screaming such a rapid stream of orders that he sounded crazed. Apparently the men he commanded understood his ravings, for suddenly 'C' Company was lashed with fire. Most of it was coming from the same long tin-roofed barn that 'B' Company had faced. MacDonald realized the barn was heavily fortified. Using the wireless, MacDonald asked Petch what was happening.[1]

Petch had no idea. There was no wireless link to 'B' or 'D' Companies. White and green signal flares had been spotted, which 'D' Company was to have fired once it entered Tilly.[2] He instructed

MacDonald to send a patrol to determine what was happening with the other companies. MacDonald thought it poor tactics to send a patrol anywhere, so he decided to carry out the reconnaissance alone.

MacDonald circled north to get around the barn. Just as he crossed the road, 'A' Company's Major A.W. Jefferson appeared. The reserve company had come up against the barn and been shredded. The survivors were scattered in shell craters, hanging on grimly before the fort. "Where the hell are the other companies?" Jefferson asked. MacDonald said he was off to find out. An ominous lull had settled over the battlefield. MacDonald crept into the orchard. Slit trenches full of dead Germans were everywhere. Enemy stretcher-bearers were carrying out wounded. They ignored MacDonald. He saw no North Novas. Then a shot rang out, and a bullet ripped apart the muscle in one of his arms. MacDonald ran back to his company and told them to hold where they were. Losing blood rapidly, Mac-Donald was carried to the rear.

Jefferson was also trying to figure out the situation. It seemed 'C' Company was the only unit still fighting. His 'A' Company was scattered. Jefferson had only the headquarters section with him. That consisted of second-in-command Captain James Patrick McNeil, three signallers, and a stretcher-bearer. As Jefferson moved towards 'C' Company, snipers and machine guns zeroed in. McNeil was hit and the wireless set destroyed. The stretcher-bearer died trying to reach McNeil. Caught in the open, McNeil was digging at the ground with his hands when a sniper round killed him. Realizing he and the signallers would never reach 'C' Company alive, Jefferson made for the start line.[3]

Petch's only forward contact was a 'C' Company signaller hiding in a shell hole with three other men. They were north of the village, he said, cut off and unable to see any other North Novas.

Dawn brought no clarity. All Petch knew was that the battalion had met disaster. The RAP was clogged with wounded. Petch's reserve consisted of the support company. He decided to send two Bren carrier sections and a troop from 3rd Anti-Tank Regiment's 94th Battery to the companies. The Anti-Tank Battery was equipped with M-10 self-propelled guns.

The little force dashed forth. One carrier section went straight up the road and into Tilly. There followed a great roar of gunfire and the section was "swallowed up," as the battalion war diarist put it. An anti-tank gun fired on the fortified barn, only to be knocked out by a hidden German gun. Having failed to contact any North Novas, the small force returned to the start line.[4]

At 0614 hours, Petch asked Brigadier Ben Cunningham to release the Fort Garry Horse's 'B' Squadron waiting to accompany the planned Highland Light Infantry advance through Tilly to Garcelles-Secqueville. Realizing that advance was moot while Tilly remained in German hands, Cunningham agreed. Major Alex Christian rolled his sixteen Shermans out and ran directly into a counterattack by 1st ss Panzer Division's 7th Panzer Company. Having hooked around Tilly in an attempt to encircle any North Novas in the town, the Panthers caught Christian's tanks in the open and demolished them. In a matter of minutes, eleven tanks were knocked out or in flames. Christian withdrew.[5]

The 'C' Company signaller reported to Petch that he could see "at least five enemy tanks with self-propelled guns...around the village and [these] were shooting our men...with machineguns if they so much as moved." With 9th Brigade offering no support that would "hold us in our position...the order was given by the battalion commander for those who were able to, to withdraw...Quite a large number were able to do so," the war diarist recorded.[6] The majority of these, however, came back on their own initiative, the remaining signaller unable to pass the news to more than a handful of men.

It would be several days before casualties were fully tabulated. The final tally was 139, of which 61 were killed, 46 wounded, and 32 taken prisoner.[7] So many men died because many of the wounded perished either where they fell or trying to crawl unaided to safety. Since landing on D-Day, the North Novas had lost about 850 men, slightly more than their allotted normal strength.[8]

While the debacle had still been in play, orders had been issued for the Stormont, Dundas and Glengarry Highlanders to advance with another tank squadron to assist the Novas in taking Tilly. But then divisional headquarters ruled that no more "tanks could be

202 / BREAKOUT FROM JUNO

committed as the remainder of the Regiment [Fort Garry Horse] might have been required...in other important operations."[9]

The Glens responded with dismay to the alert at 1125 hours for an immediate advance on Tilly from Hubert-Folie. "This is indeed a mental blow and is felt by all ranks," intelligence officer Lieutenant Reg Dixon observed. "We need a rest and refit, having been in the line since D-Day. The last rest was spent travelling and preparing for the exercise following. The men and officers are looking worn out and are very weary for the most part. This is especially a disappointment as even Jerry with his reported lack of divisions and manpower has withdrawn divisions for a refit and rest."[10]

After the alert, Lieutenant Colonel G.H. Christiansen went to Petch's headquarters. Brigadier Cunningham was already there. Petch had just refused to attack Tilly with the remnants of his battalion. Christiansen said he too would not send the Glens into an obviously doomed assault. Cunningham returned to his tactical headquarters and notified Major General Rod Keller that 9th Brigade would not further reinforce failure. Having just been instructed by Simonds to hold Tilly so that the second phase of Spring could begin, Keller warned Cunningham that he would be sacked if the brigade did not advance. "I understand that, sir," Cunningham replied while refusing to budge.[11]

AS THE DISASTER at Tilly-la-Campagne played out, the Royal Hamilton Light Infantry had advanced on Verrières village. Three companies led with 'C' Company in reserve. Because of the thirty-minute delay resulting from the need to clear the start line, the barrage supporting the Rileys had come and gone.

'A' Company's objective was the right side of Verrières. Major Jack Halladay, a Dieppe veteran, had two platoons out front. This part of Verrières was more farm than village. There were several large barns with surrounding orchards and farmhouses. A dense hedgerow blocked the line of advance, and as the company closed on it, four machine guns within started firing. Another machine gun opened up from the grain field to the right. Caught in the open, the men fell in rapidly mounting numbers. Within seconds, Halladay was the only officer standing. All platoon sergeants and section leaders had been cut down. Yet 'A' Company kept going, privates leading their comrades forward. "They got into the hedgerows and cleared the enemy out of there," Halladay said after. "They killed about ten and took ten additional prisoners. This was just before dawn."[12]

On the opposite flank, 'D' Company was also lashed by machine guns in the hedge and from a grain field to its left. Lieutenant Henry Percy Beasley was killed. All the non-commissioned officers fell dead or wounded.[13] The company went to ground. Rockingham, his signaller in tow, raced to lend a hand. Major George Stinson "put his head up to show me where he was being held up from and his bloody head disappeared."[14]

In the gathering light, Rockingham realized the machine guns in the grain field were actually mounted on tanks. If they rolled into the battalion's left flank it would be a slaughter. By this time, in the battalion centre, 'B' Company was well ahead. Major J.L. "Johnny" Firth had lost few men because the other two companies absorbed the flanking fire. As 'B' Company gained the hedge, which lay about three hundred yards from Verrières, a "costly and cruel" hand-to-hand fight ensued. Firth was wounded. Intelligence reports had led the Rileys to believe the ground past the hedge would be open through to the village, but as 'B' Company broke free, it looked straight at another. Four successive hedges had to be stormed in turn. Then, as the regiment's historian wrote, there came the "headlong plunge past dung heaps and cow byres to close with the enemy. There was fighting from one stone cottage with its weathered roof to another, the painful decision of crossing a lane. Then the fruit trees to the right and left, the dusty road, and finally the southern slope that was all part of Verrières, a village that had stood in tranquility for centuries and was now ruptured and half destroyed by the violence of battle."[15]

Lieutenant Ernest T. Harshman, commanding No. 12 Platoon, had his leg fractured by a bullet during the first hedge fight. Harshman crawled to Verrières and helped settle his remaining men into defensive positions before agreeing to be evacuated. He was awarded a Military Cross.[16]

With Firth and Harshman down, No. 10 Platoon's Lieutenant Hugh Harrison had led the fight for Verrières. Harrison ran continuously between platoons to direct the actions of each during "extremely heavy house fighting." When the fight was won, Harrison got 'B' Company digging in. Everyone expected a counterattack. A Military Cross was his.[17]

While 'B' Company had fought for Verrières, Halladay had been forced by casualties at the main hedge to pause and reorganize 'A' Company. No. 9 Platoon counted only seven men. He broke it into two small sections under corporals and sent these to clear slit trenches dug in next to a hedge bordering the road that passed the village. The other two platoons went for the farm buildings. The few Germans there proved to be men who had fled the fight in the hedge and again took to their heels as the Rileys approached.[18]

On the left flank, Rockingham was still personally leading 'D' Company in its fight by the first hedge. Only one company officer, Lieutenant J.T. Clark, still stood and even he was wounded. Rockingham called up the carrier platoon and engaged the tanks with artillery to cover their advance. Shellfire having no visible effect, the tankers quickly knocked out several carriers and sent the others retreating to Troteval. Rockingham shifted the artillery onto the hedge to get rid of the machine-gun positions and called 2nd Anti-Tank Regiment's 'B' Troop to deploy its 17-pounder guns at Troteval Farm and engage the tanks. After the anti-tank troop knocked out four tanks, the rest withdrew.[19]

With the tanks gone, Rockingham pulled the rifle companies into Verrières and established an all-round defence, as the Germans could counterattack from any direction. The original plan called for a squadron from 7th British Armoured Division's Royal Tank Regiment and the battalion's support company to reinforce the infantry in Verrières, but this column ran into a minefield on the road. Several vehicles were knocked out, and only a narrow passageway remained open. Rockingham demanded that jeeps and carriers come through first to evacuate his seriously wounded. Then he called up the battalion's anti-tank guns. He put two on the southern edge of Verrières and three each on the eastern and western flanks.[20]

Twenty minutes later, the counterattack began. "Nine tanks

roared and clattered through the long wheat toward the ridge, filling the air with splinters of steel from their machineguns."[21] The two guns facing the southern slope were knocked out, as was one on the flanks. When the tanks tried pushing into the village, the Rileys met them with PIATs. All the German tanks were Mark IVs, far more vulnerable to PIAT bombs than were Panthers or Tigers.

The tanks were blasting buildings with 75-millimetre guns and tearing up the open ground with machine guns. That was when Rockingham saw the "most extraordinary thing happen."[22] Private Ray Meloche of 'B' Company's No. 10 Platoon crossed thirty yards of bullet-swept ground to gain a trench next to two tanks. His first round knocked one out, but then he was struck by a burst of fire. Despite being badly wounded, Meloche continued to reload and fire the awkward PIAT until the second tank withdrew. Meloche received a Military Medal for bravery.[23] When another PIAT team disabled a Mark IV, the counterattack crumbled. It was 0750 hours. Rockingham reported that the Rileys owned Verrières. The way was open for Operation Spring's second phase to begin on this front, with the Royal Regiment of Canada and 'C' Squadron of the 1st Hussars advancing from the ridge crest down the slope to Rocquancourt.

THE ROYAL REGIMENT's advance was to coincide with that of the Black Watch, but the Calgary Highlanders had fallen into disarray from the outset of their attempt to secure the required start line by May-sur-Orne. When 'A' and 'B' Companies had swung past Saint-Martin-de-Fontenay on the right and headed into the open country with the mine works immediately to their left, they had come under machine-gun fire from the church on the southern edge of the town. This slowed their advance so much that they fell far behind the creeping barrage. When 'A' Company was also fired on from a nearby orchard, Major John Campbell decided to swing out to the east along the slope leading up to Verrières Ridge. His men stepped directly into an "area infested with German slit trenches and dug outs." Campbell opted to drive past these in order to regain the barrage. This left enemy machine-gun positions and snipers behind the company and on either flank.[24]

Four hundred yards from May, Campbell had to halt to avoid

running into the falling shells. One gun kept firing short, each shell causing casualties. The FOO with Campbell was unable to get this gun to quit shooting.[25] Campbell's wireless contact with battalion was erratic, and he had lost sight of 'B' Company. He was considering the company's next move when a sniper bullet deflected off his revolver and lodged in a thigh muscle. In the confused next moments, a wireless signal went out with the false claim that 'A' Company was on its objective inside May.[26]

'B' Company had fallen well behind 'A' Company because Major Cyril Nixon had paused to send a platoon to clear the orchard on the southern edge of Saint-Martin. Gaining the sunken road that ran from Saint-Martin to Verrières, the company was raked by Germans in the hedges on either side. To escape this fire, Nixon led a platoon through the southern hedge. As Nixon stumbled out the other side, he was killed. Two men who tried to reach Nixon joined him in death.

The company broke up. Company Sergeant Major Ralph Wilson and one group went to ground, while Lieutenant John David Moffat led his platoon towards May. Dawn was breaking as Moffat's men entered the village and met three Tiger tanks and two self-propelled guns. The German armour started shooting. Moffat prudently pulled out to the east of the mine and dug in.[27]

At every turn the Calgaries came under fire from areas previously cleared or considered undefended. They had no idea the Germans were infiltrating back and forth via the mine shafts. 'C' Company, under Major Sherwin Robinson, tried following the road that ran from Saint-Martin past the mine to May. The area was built up, and Monty's Moonlight cast the buildings into shadow while illuminating the road. The men were thus silhouetted but unable to see into the surrounding gloom.[28] When machine guns started firing from the flanks and front, Robinson led a hasty retreat to the cover of some buildings on the edge of Saint-André.

The Calgary reserve company, still missing commander Captain Del Harrison and his headquarters section, had tried following 'B' Company to the east of the mine. Coming under fire from the orchard, Lieutenant Sandy Pierce—commanding in Harrison's absence—took a platoon over to silence the position once and for all.

"I was trying to keep people organized and keep them moving," he said. "If you ever stop in that situation you're dead." Pierce was shot through both legs. Lieutenant E.A. Michon took over. Turning away from the orchard, he led the men south, only to be fired upon by three tanks. After evading this fire, Michon was totally disoriented. Encountering a road, Michon hoped it led to May. After following it for awhile, Michon spotted buildings to the north and led his men to them. As 'D' Company dug in, Michon was certain he had reached May. In reality, the company was on the southern edge of Saint-André.

Amid this confusion, Lieutenant Colonel Donald MacLauchlan had taken the erroneous 'A' Company report at face value and ordered his signals platoon to run a telephone line through to May as a preparatory step in establishing the battalion tactical headquarters there. Sergeant Alvin H. Palfenier and two men drove towards May in a jeep with a reel of telephone line winding out in their wake. Soon they entered the northern outskirts of May. It was a small village that trailed along either side of the N162 highway—some red-tile-roofed farmhouses, a small commercial district, a little church, and thick stone walls surrounding courtyards. Leaving the signallers to guard the line, Palfenier drove to the church and stopped in the centre of the road with the engine running. If there were snipers about, that should draw their attention. Nothing happened. So Palfenier drove back to battalion headquarters and reported May "absolutely devoid" of Germans.

Not long after Palfenier's departure, the battalion's support company commander, Captain Mark Tennant, walked into May to determine likely positions for the anti-tank guns. Unarmed, Tennant strolled through the village without seeing either a German or Calgary soldier. Tennant left May with no idea that many of the buildings concealed Germans who had silently watched him pass through.

Back at Saint-André, 'D' Company's Lieutenant E.A. Michon had become entangled in an awkward confrontation with a major from the Black Watch. Major Philip Griffin had appeared and urged him to take 'D' Company and clear the mine. Realizing that if the mine

208 / BREAKOUT FROM JUNO

was where Griffin indicated, then he was in the wrong village, Michon agreed to the attempt. But he no sooner led his men forward then they were driven back by machine-gun fire from a spot where several knocked-out German tanks stood near the mine. Griffin then told Michon he wanted him to go to the Black Watch's start line and find out whether the Calgaries held it or not. Michon, tiring of being ordered about by someone outside his command, said he needed to talk with his battalion commander first. When he did so, Michon was ordered to "try and get forward to the objective."[29]

Michon was about to set off when Captain Del Harrison wandered in and resumed command. As he led the men towards May, they were met by withering mortar and shellfire. Heavy casualties ensued. Michon was among the wounded. Harrison gave up. That was it for the Calgary effort against May.[30] The Black Watch not only had no secure start line, the ground between Saint-André and May remained in dispute.

15

A Stone Wall

N THE EARLY morning of July 25, despite Operation Spring's bru-
tal first phase setbacks, Lieutenant General Guy Simonds ordered
the second phase begun. Signals reaching 11 Canadian Corps headquarters were fragmentary, leaving Simonds confused. He
understood that the North Nova Scotia Highlanders, supported
by the Fort Garry Horse, were renewing efforts to take Tilly-la-
Campagne. The Royal Hamilton Light Infantry had secured Verrières, while the Calgary Highlanders had either won May-sur-Orne or
were in strength nearby. From his headquarters in Vaucelles, Operation Spring still seemed viable.

The only accurate information in all that was that the Rileys held
Verrières. No effort was under way against Tilly.[1] After moving the
Highland Light Infantry to a start line at Hubert-Folie, Brigadier
Ben Cunningham ordered no further action.[2] The battalion's regimental historian observed that the mauling suffered by the North
Nova Scotia Highlanders "showed that we were up against a heavily
defended enemy line and resulted in the cancellation of the [battal-
ion's] part in the operation."[3] Cunningham's refusal of a direct order
from Major General Rod Keller abruptly closed 3rd Division's part
in Operation Spring.

At 2nd Division, Major General Charles Foulkes faced no dissent
from brigadiers. With Verrières in hand, developments on

4th Brigade's front looked promising. The brigade also had a new brigadier as of that morning—J.E. "Eddy" Ganong. Previously 4th Armoured Division's general staff officer, Ganong had only just arrived in France. When he took over from Lieutenant Colonel Fred Clift, the South Saskatchewan Regiment commander returned to the urgent task of rebuilding his shattered battalion.[4]

While the situation on 4th Brigade's front appeared in hand, Foulkes decided 5th Brigade needed a personal prod. He walked into Brigadier Bill Megill's headquarters and growled that Simonds "was furious at the lack of progress by Megill's brigade and had sent him forward to get it moving."[5] Despite the fact that the Calgary Highlanders had neither won May-sur-Orne nor the Black Watch's start line, Megill started phase two rolling.

The Black Watch had met problems the moment they withdrew from their position astride the Saint-André–Hubert-Folie road in front of Ifs. At 0330 hours, as they began marching towards Saint-André, the battalion was sporadically fired on by mortars and machine guns stationed on Verrières Ridge. A dozen men were wounded.

Their destination was next to the church on the southern edge of Saint-Martin-de-Fontenay, where they were to be joined by the 1st Hussars' 'B' Squadron. The tanks were to shield the battalion's left flank. According to the plan, the Black Watch would march from the church to their start line adjacent to a quarry alongside a road running northeastward out of May-sur-Orne. They would then go straight from May to Fontenay-le-Marmion at 0530 hours. A complex artillery fire plan with fixed timings was in place.[6]

Believing Saint-Martin secure, Lieutenant Colonel Stuart Cantlie got a rude awakening when the battalion came under intense fire from the village. Moving "in the old snake formation" with 'D' Company at the head, Cantlie ordered Captain John Kemp to clear Saint-Martin. Kemp quickly reported that 'D' Company was meeting stiff resistance. Cantlie decided he had no option but to commit all his rifle companies to winning the village.[7]

"Along the east edge of the town there were high walls and hedges surrounding orchards," the carrier platoon's Captain E. R. "Ronnie" Bennett said later. "Next to these were three or four knocked-out

Panther tanks. The Huns had weapon slits outside the walls and hedges and dug-outs and scurry-holes inside. The posts were almost all MG posts and had to be taken out one at a time. This had to be done when it was pitch black and...the artificial moonlight...did not improve close-in fighting to any degree. We were fighting in the shadows against a good many Huns—probably about a company in strength...Everyone realized that we were losing valuable time."[8]

In the midst of the fight, Cantlie, 'B' Company's Major Eric Motzfeldt, and Captain Kemp huddled by a hedge outside Saint-Martin. Suddenly, a machine gun ripped off a long burst. Cantlie fell dying, Motzfeldt—the battalion's senior company commander—was severely wounded. It was about 0500 hours.

Command devolved to 'A' Company's Major Philip Griffin. The twenty-six-year-old had been a McGill University Macdonald College post-graduate student when the war broke out. Like most 2nd Division company commanders, he had seen little combat and had no battalion command experience.

However, Griffin stepped quickly into his new role. Captain Bennett described him later as "a brilliant officer of absolutely outstanding courage and ability. His takeover in this strained and ticklish situation was superb."[9] The battalion was still a mile from May-sur-Orne with the attack time fast approaching. Griffin convened an O Group next to the Saint-Martin church.[10]

He was relieved to learn that 'B' Squadron was deployed in a nearby orchard on the southeast edge of Saint-André. The 1st Hussars had lost one of fifteen Shermans to an anti-tank mine and had arrived ninety minutes late. Major Walter Harris had expected the Black Watch to have already gone into their attack so was pleased to see they were still at Saint-Martin. It was worrisome, though, that the Calgaries reportedly did not control May-sur-Orne.[11]

Griffin told the assembled officers the attack could not proceed at dawn, which meant the already started artillery program was wasted. He and the battalion's FOO, 5th Field Regiment's Captain G.D. Powis, needed to develop a new fire plan. Griffin also wanted to find out precisely how much of Saint-André the Cameron Highlanders controlled and whether the Calgaries actually held May and his start line.

"There was no uncertainty whatever in his actions," Bennett observed. "He foresaw only a delay, which would at the outside be two hours, while he re-arranged timings and obtained essential information. The plan for the attack would be the same as...previously planned." In the meantime, he ordered the rifle companies to the edge of Saint-André and next to a road running east to Verrières. This would expose them less to fire from the ridge. "So complete was his control and so well trained the battalion that this was done at once and in incredibly good order." In the fighting for Saint-Martin, only ten to fifteen men had been hit, so Bennett considered the Black Watch in good shape.[12] The artillery program was set for 0930 hours, concentrated on the same targets as before.

During this delay, Griffin was incessantly peppered with messages from Brigadier Megill. "Push on now," Megill signalled at 0647 hours, "speed essential." At 0715 hours, just before Griffin held a second O Group in Saint-André, Megill ordered the Black Watch "to go ahead."[13]

Megill was reacting to events on Verrières Ridge. At 0800, 4th Brigade intended to advance the Royal Regiment of Canada through to Rocquancourt. The "prospect of the thrust forward over and down the farther slope of Verrières Ridge...appeared bright," one army observer noted. But the Royals "would be imperiled if swift action was not taken to secure the flanks. Here may be found the real reason for the peremptory orders which reached the Black Watch to press on to Fontenay-le-Marmion."[14]

But Griffin was unable to do so immediately. He had already set the attack for 0930 hours and needed the intervening time to determine what was happening at May-sur-Orne. Major Harris of 'B' Squadron, suspecting the Calgaries had failed to secure the start line, had independently sent a tank troop to investigate. Harris was unaware that Griffin had also sent a patrol towards May.[15]

EQUALLY PRESSURED BY Brigadier Ganong, who was responding to Simonds snapping at everyone's heels, the Royals' Lieutenant Colonel John "Jock" Anderson made two quick decisions at 0800 hours. Having waited on the Black Watch, his artillery support program had come and gone. Anderson decided against arranging another. Instead, the 4th Field Regiment FOO would just direct fire on targets as they arose. Second, instead of passing through Verrières according to plan, the Royals would bypass it on the left flank to avoid getting entangled in the fighting still under way there.

Anderson advanced the Royals with 'C' Company on the right, 'B' Company the left, and the other two companies following. As the companies passed Verrières, the battalion's mortar platoon raced to a gravel pit next to the Caen-Falaise highway on the left. They were just deploying the mortars when some SS panzer grenadiers attacked their position. A short, sharp engagement ensued with the platoon firing Bren guns and mortars at close range, until the Germans were driven off.[16]

'C' Squadron of the 1st Hussars was also left of the Royals with nineteen tanks. Approaching the crest of Verrières Ridge, its second-in-command, Captain Brandy Conron, spotted eight Panthers. "Recognizing the rounded turret lids, he laid a fire plan whereby each troop engaged specific tanks. Then he opened up the barrage with his own tank knocking out and brewing a Panther in the centre. In just a few seconds all…the enemy tanks were 'kaput' and most of them blazing merrily."[17]

How vulnerable Shermans were to being hit by the Panther's long 75-millimetre gun was evidenced when the single Hussar tank struck "burst into flames…The hatch flew open, emitting clouds of black smoke, and those of the crew who could do so threw themselves out. One man came out backwards, catching his knees on the edge of the hatch, and hung there for a moment, blazing like a torch, before he fell to the ground on his head. The burning trooper actually set the wheat field afire, and the stretcher-bearers, who rushed forward, had to put out these flames as well as those that covered the body of the man. Soon there were burning tanks and vehicles throughout the entire area of advance."[18]

Once the Hussars crossed the ridgeline, the balance tipped against them. A mine crippled Lieutenant Roy Kenny's Sherman. Then a Ferdinand tank destroyer opened fire. The Ferdinand was a modified Tiger with a heavily up-armoured, boxy turret mounting an 88-millimetre gun. Lieutenant Valdi Bjarnason already knew his troop was in trouble before this monster appeared. "There was no cover, and the Germans had the advantage of the higher ground and they could manoeuvre behind the crest. It was one hell of a fight, and the fire from the tank guns on both sides was absolutely ferocious. I remember firing at the Ferdinand...and seeing the armour-piercing rounds just bounce off, but I did get two...Panthers, and I saw them both burn. One of the most awful moments was when one of our own airplanes came in and knocked out one of our Shermans."[19]

The Ferdinand smashed three tanks in Lieutenant Bruce Caw's troop, including that commanded by Sergeant "Doc" Doherty. He and Trooper George Hamilton died.[20]

'C' Squadron's commander, Major D'Arcy Marks, led the surviving tanks into a field surrounded by a hedge that screened it from the Ferdinand and Panthers left of the Hussars. Marks had just jumped out of his tank to look through the hedge when several self-propelled guns and tanks opened fire from the opposite flank. Captain Brandy Conron started shouting for everyone to reverse off the ridge crest, but before any tanks moved, an armour-piercing round punched through Marks's tank and killed Trooper John Monteith and Sergeant Bill Easton. Trooper Hector Lamont and Corporal Fred Baker also died as seven Shermans were knocked out in a matter of minutes.

Just five tanks escaped from the crest to the protective northern slope. Conron's tank had been holed three times by armour-piercing rounds. Then a mine ripped off half a track. It lurched to safety and became a regimental showpiece for a few days—"one of the most badly battered Shermans ever to disgorge a crew alive." The squadron had lost fourteen tanks and suffered twenty-seven casualties. By 1100 hours, it was out of action.[21]

The Royals had crossed the crest of Verrières Ridge at the same time as the Hussars and started descending the long, gentle slope towards Rocquancourt—about a mile distant. The sky was clear. Across the wide horizon, Typhoons swooped down from a circling cab rank to rocket or dive-bomb German tanks and positions.

As the Royals came off the ridgeline, they were "struck by a hurricane of fire" from dug-in tanks and self-propelled guns.[22] Mortars and machine guns ripped into the badly exposed infantry.[23] In the wide-open field, there was nowhere to hide.

Realizing it was suicide to continue, 'B' Company's Major J.F. Law ordered his men to dig in along the crest about two hundred yards south of Verrières. Major K.G. Singleton's 'C' Company pressed on a few hundred yards farther under "murderous enemy fire...until [it was] almost annihilated." Suddenly, ss panzer grenadiers burst out of the grain, and those of 'C' Company not already killed or wounded were taken prisoner, Singleton among them. Only eighteen escaped.

At 1000 hours, when Anderson reported the situation, a 4th Brigade staff officer ordered him to "get on at all costs." He directed 'B' Company to advance, but Law failed to comply. Anderson then told Major E.J.H. Ryall to pass 'D' Company through Law's position. It was a fruitless effort, the company immediately driven back by fierce fire. Ryall was among the wounded. Reporting the situation "very sticky," Anderson had 'D' Company dig in to the left of 'B' Company. Despite repeated orders from 4th Brigade headquarters, the Royals refused to budge. Adding to their woes, a Typhoon accidentally rocketed the two forward companies and Law was wounded.[24]

Verrières stood out, as one observer put it, "like a sore thumb." Within the village, the Rileys were digging in. To their left, the Royals were in place. Everyone knew the Germans were not going to let them stay without a fight.[25]

MEANWHILE, WEST OF Verrières village, Major Philip Griffin had spent much of the early morning hours waiting for scouts to report back on the situation at May-sur-Orne. Hurrying, the scout platoon's Lieutenant L.R. Duffield, Sergeant B.F.A. Benson, and another man had gone straight down the middle of the road from Saint-Martin into May without seeing any sign of life. As they passed the church, an MG42 dug in at the corner of a house opened fire. Deciding they were too few to tangle with the machine gun, Duffield decided they should withdraw. Even if the only German presence in the village consisted of the machine-gun crew, they could rip into the Black Watch's right flank during the attack and cause serious harm. It was 0845 hours, just forty-five minutes from the new attack time, when Duffield reported to Griffin. The major ordered Sergeant Benson and six scouts to neutralize the machine gun.[26]

As Duffield's party had been probing May, a troop of 'B' Squadron Shermans had gained the village's outskirts. They encountered 'C' Company of the Calgaries hunkered in a hollow. The company's wireless sets were knocked out, and they were "badly cut up and in need of stretcher bearers [and] ammunition," Major Harris reported. When the troop entered the village, an anti-tank gun knocked out one tank. The troop withdrew and Harris ordered it to support any Calgary attempt to clear the village.

This left ten tanks to accompany the Black Watch. Harris led this group along a series of narrow, sunken roads towards the mine. His intention was to move into the gap between May and the forward slope of Verrières Ridge to screen the Black Watch's right flank, although this was directly contrary to the original plan whereby the tanks would screen their left flank. Harris realized this but felt the Germans in May posed the greater threat. He also understood that tanks from the 7th British Armoured Division should about this time be advancing towards Garcelles-Secqueville and Rocquancourt. If they were, the left flank should be secured by their presence.[27]

About the time Harris and 'B' Squadron started moving, Brigadier Megill arrived at Saint-Martin. Standing on the verandah of a house looking towards May, Griffin calmly explained his plan.[28] Instead of moving to the start line at May, he had established a new line by the mine. The Black Watch would advance on a compass bearing aimed directly at Fontenay-le-Marmion. Megill looked at the open ground Griffin proposed crossing. Wheat fields and patches of rough ground devoid of cover stretched up a long slope that rose some hundred feet over a thousand-yard distance to the crest. No doubt at all that the 272nd Infantry Division waited on the ridge line.[29] A "dicey proposition," Megill thought, and suggested that Griffin secure May first. Griffin said he had patrols in May and the village did not appear to be held on "a continuous basis." When the

Black Watch advanced, he felt, the pressure on the Calgaries would be relieved and they could "fill in behind, on into May-sur-Orne."[30] Megill knew one thing. Simonds and Foulkes were impatient. "An attack had to be made and it was made," he wrote later. "Once started, everyone was determined that there would be no drawing back."[31]

Megill left, and Griffin led the Black Watch towards the forming-up position, a cabbage field next to the mine. The battalion was dogged during the move by heavy artillery and mortar fire. In the resulting confusion, Captain Powis, the 5th Field Regiment's FOO, lost contact with Griffin. Attempts to raise Griffin on the wireless proved fruitless. Griffin had in fact lost all wireless communication when the jeep carrying his set had been knocked out by shellfire.[32]

The Black Watch attacked in box formation, with 'A' Company on the left and 'C' Company the right. 'D' Company was behind 'C' Company and 'B' Company behind 'A' Company. Griffin's battalion headquarters was in the centre behind the two reserve companies. Captain John Taylor commanded 'C' Company. There is no record of who led 'A' Company, which had been Griffin's command. Officers were so short that Sergeant Victor Leonard Foam had 'B' Company. Captain John Kemp headed 'D' Company.[33] About three hundred men started up the long slope at 0930 hours.[34]

Private A.R. Williams was in 'D' Company's No. 16 Platoon. The men "walked forward across the open field 'spread out' in 'battle formation.'" Williams "knew...a frontal attack of this sort across open ground was unsound tactics, but the unit had been ordered to push on and was determined to do so."[35]

Sergeant Benson, having been unable to reach the machine gun in May, watched helplessly from a ditch outside the village. "As they started up [towards] the crest of the hill," he observed, "German mortar fire came down on them and they were under heavy fire for an hour. Jerry had Panther and Tiger tanks dug in on the crest of the hill...Our battalion was pinned down by this fire until our Shermans came forward and diverted the attention of the tanks from our infantry."[36]

"Dug-in tanks, 88-millimetre guns, mortars, rocket projectors, machine guns, and other small arms opened up on the advancing companies," one army report stated. "The enemy's strength in this area, hitherto in great part concealed, was now fully unmasked. His weapons were skillfully sited and well dug in."[37]

Harris and the tanks had arrived five minutes after the Black Watch advanced. He saw the infantry already far ahead. Whether the British tanks were out on the left flank was unclear. The Hussars advanced into the open, but Shermans started being knocked out "as soon as they exposed themselves to anti-tank fire directed from the ridge and the east corner of May."[38]

Such a storm of shellfire rained on the infantry that none could say afterwards whether the planned artillery support occurred. In fact, the gunners were firing extra concentrations—dropping shells as close to the Black Watch as they could without hitting them. A smokescreen was also fired onto the left flank to blind the Germans there.[39]

As the Black Watch closed on the crest, Griffin appeared at their front. "Forward, men! We've got to keep going!" he shouted.[40] Private M. Montreuil heard Captain Kemp shout "that it was murderous to continue." Griffin replied that "the orders were to attack and...the battalion would therefore carry on."[41]

Private Williams found it "difficult to maintain direction, on account of the heavy fire which made men tend to 'dodge' and therefore change direction."

So many officers and non-commissioned officers were killed or wounded that Williams thought nobody was in control. Men were just going forward. Although twice wounded, Williams was one of these.[42] Only about sixty reached the crest. Those watching the attack from the bottom of the slope saw this tiny, scattered force cross over the crest of the ridge and disappear.[43]

It was about 1020 hours. Six of 'B' Squadron's ten tanks had been knocked out. A sniper had wounded Major Harris. He handed command to Captain J.W. "Jake" Powell. There was no possibility that the surviving tanks could reach the Black Watch or offer any further fire support.[44]

It hardly mattered. Those who passed over the crest of Verrières Ridge stood little chance. Private Williams saw 88-millimetre guns firing side on at them. There were machine guns firing from concrete blockhouses and enemy positions camouflaged in haystacks on all sides.[45]

Private T. Murphy saw six Tiger tanks hidden in haystacks as he dodged over the crest. His group of men were "overwhelmed very shortly afterwards."

To Private E.T. McCann there was no question of withdrawal. "We had the feeling that the enemy was behind us as well as to the front and two sides. The fire that was coming from the rear may have come from a mine shaft that we had passed earlier."[46]

Captain John Taylor was wounded short of the crest. Sergeant Foam was dead. Griffin sent a wounded officer back with the simple message, "Don't send reinforcements—we have too many men trapped here now."[47] At about 1400 hours, a scout appeared at the battalion's rear headquarters saying he had been sent by Griffin. It had taken the scout an hour to descend the shell-torn slope. He reported that Griffin "had decided it would be necessary to withdraw...and had organized a covering party to do so."[48] Disengaging proved impossible. Finally, Griffin—wounded himself—ordered "every man to make his way back as best he could."[49]

Everyone was wounded. Men headed back over the crest and down the slope in any way possible. Griffin was killed—not at the head of his men, charging towards the enemy, as would eventually be enshrined in the myths that emerged in the months and years following the battalion's destruction. The most credible account determined he was "killed by a mine while walking back after being wounded."

Private Williams hid in the wheat, watching Germans overrun the area. When it was dark, he crawled towards the Canadian lines but eventually happened into a German position and was captured.[50] Captain Kemp was also taken prisoner. No more than fifteen men escaped.

On July 25, the Black Watch lost 307 men. Five officers and 118 other ranks died, 101 were wounded, and 83 were captured. Of the last, 21 had been wounded.[51] Only six officers and 326 other ranks remained. That night, the battalion withdrew to Fleury-sur-Orne to begin rebuilding.[52] Excepting the battalions involved in the Dieppe raid, no single regiment in the war suffered such heavy casualties in a single day.[53]

THE GERMANS, MEANWHILE, took the offensive with 9th ss Panzer Division ordered to regain Verrières village and restore the integrity of the main line of resistance along the ridge.[54] At 1700 hours, Lieutenant Colonel Rocky Rockingham watched tanks roll into his positions with infantry close on their heels. The mixed force of Panthers and Tigers rolled over the trenches. From a slit trench in 'B' Company's sector, Rockingham saw a "huge tank was right on top of me." Rockingham ordered a PIAT man to fire a bomb "right up through its belly. The bomb punched a very small hole in the armour." The crew bailed and was taken prisoner.[55]

At least eight other tanks remained inside the village, and Major Hugh Arrell was "scared to death." At this propitious moment, a British tank squadron commander made a surreal appearance. "He wore a soft hat, corduroy trousers and suede shoes; he carried a cane of brass and burnished wood; a well-worn pair of binoculars hung from his neck and he seemed quite oblivious to the shelling...We didn't know whether we should get out of our slits to greet him or not." After being guided to an observation point on the roof of a building under German fire, he calmly surveyed the scene. "It's a bit sticky, isn't it?" he said.

The 1st Royal Tank Regiment squadron plunged into the thick of the village fight with crew commanders all exposed from the waist up in their turret hatches. "What do you want us to shoot at, matey?" one yelled to Sergeant Gordie Booker. Rileys pointed out targets all around them, and the tankers blazed away so accurately with main guns and machine guns that the counterattack quickly collapsed.[56] At 1750 hours, as the battle had been raging in Verrières, the 9th ss commander leading the counterattack had warned, "Whoever crosses this ridge is a dead man!"[57]

The Rileys stood firm inside Verrières. During the long fight, the battalion suffered fifty men killed and 126 wounded.[58] "Not one of our men is in enemy hands and none are known to be missing," the regiment's war diarist recorded.[59] It was, the army's historian recorded later, "a proud declaration...confirmed by post-war study." The Rileys, he added, "may well remember Verrières."[60]

STILL DETERMINED TO keep Operation Spring rolling, Simonds pressured Foulkes to secure May-sur-Orne no matter the cost. Clearly, the Calgaries were in no shape to finish the job, and Foulkes was down to one battalion still capable of fighting. In the late afternoon he visited the headquarters of both Brigadier Megill and Brigadier Hugh Young. Both cautioned that operations in the Saint-André and Saint-Martin area were going poorly. Despite this, Foulkes ordered Le Régiment de Maisonneuve "to restore the situation and capture May-sur-Orne."[61] Dutifully, the French Canadians went forward at 1900 hours.[62]

As the forward companies crossed the start line at Saint-André, they came under heavy fire. "They were fired on from the rear, as the enemy, evidently jumping up like rabbits from the air shafts leading to the underground tunnels, hammered them from all directions. Not only were the Germans difficult to spot, but out in the fields between the villages the Canadians could be seen and fired on from the left, from the front, even on the right from across the Orne River." Accepting that the attack was doomed, Megill ordered the Maisies back to Saint-André.[63] Twelve men were dead and another forty wounded.[64]

Foulkes, meanwhile, had convened a meeting of brigadiers at his headquarters in Fleury-sur-Orne. During the evening, he said, Brigadier Young's 6th Brigade would resume the offensive on 5th Brigade's front by attacking May. At his headquarters, Young studied his maps. The more he looked at the plan, "the more he felt that it would be unlikely to achieve success with the intensity of mortars and artillery which the enemy could bring down on the area of the objective." At 2000 hours, Young informed Foulkes that the operation was ill advised and he was prepared to tell Simonds this. Offering no argument, Foulkes went to see Simonds alone.[65]

Having already learned that 2nd Division was not launching the night attack, Simonds was in a rage. Foulkes recalled telling him, "I had no intention to continue the battle as I had nothing left to fight with."[66] With 3rd Division's 9th Brigade already in revolt, Simonds could only suspend Operation Spring.[67]

With the exception again of Dieppe, July 25 was the most costly single day of the war for Canada. Painstaking research later placed the total casualties at about 1,500, of which approximately 450 were fatal. And, as the army's official historian put it, 11 Canadian Corps "had struck a stone wall."[68]

16

Simple Plans

EXCEPT FOR 4TH Infantry Brigade at Verrières, by dawn on July 26 the Germans had re-established their main line of resistance along Verrières Ridge. The night before, 9th ss Panzer Division regained control of the church at Saint-Martin-de-Fontenay. In tenacious fighting, Le Régiment de Maisonneuve clung to most of the village, while the Queen's Own Cameron Highlanders successfully defended Saint-André-sur-Orne.[1] An intelligence report summarized the facing opposition. "Some of the best equipped and most efficient of his ss Panzer Units now dominate the battlefield from the high ground on our front." The report closed with the wry observation: "The events of the past forty-eight hours may perhaps mitigate any concern as to the whereabouts of the 'flower of the German Army in the west.'"[2]

Operation Spring had been a bloody defeat. Yet Lieutenant General Guy Simonds accepted neither responsibility himself nor explanation from others. May-sur-Orne, Verrières, and Tilly-la-Campagne "could and should have been taken and held without heavy casualties." That May and Tilly were not won "and that we suffered what were, in my opinion, excessive casualties was due to a series of mistakes and errors of judgement in minor tactics," he wrote. "It seems that nothing but the actual experience of battle will forcibly imprint on men's minds the great importance of certain tactical measures, no matter how often they have been reiterated in training." Start lines had not been secured, troops had failed to closely follow barrages, and ground had not been thoroughly searched and mopped up.

Simonds conceded that German strength had rendered breaking through to Cintheaux impossible. He claimed to have recognized this by the forenoon and "made the decision not to launch the two British armoured divisions" but to "reinforce the success" of the Rileys with 7th Armoured Division tanks.

Simonds concluded his analysis by declining to examine the Black Watch attack, as this was "a most distasteful task [requiring] criticism of some, who, whatever mistakes they made, made them in good faith and paid the supreme sacrifice."[3] This disingenuous stance deflected criticism away from himself and his insistence that the Black Watch carry out the doomed attack and that he was still demanding more until Major General Charles Foulkes openly disobeyed him by declaring 2nd Division incapable of further fighting.

Simonds was not prepared to sack Foulkes for this defiance, but 3rd Division's 9th Brigade was subjected to a court of enquiry convened on July 29. Brigadier Ben Cunningham and his intelligence officer, Captain G.E. Franklin, testified. Curiously, Stormont, Dundas and Glengarry Highlanders' Lieutenant Colonel G.H. Christiansen was appointed a member of the court. Two days later, Christiansen explained to his battalion's officers "his policy in regard to his reporting to higher authority of the efficiency and battle worthiness of the battalion. [He] is emphatic he would not tolerate a court of enquiry [into] this unit not being able to take its objective, [which was due to the] failure of higher command to appreciate the battle worthiness of [the] unit. If [the] unit is not fit to fight, he will definitely tell them so," Lieutenant Reg Dixon summarized.[4]

Following the proceedings, Simonds relieved Lieutenant Colonel Charles Petch of his command of the North Nova Scotia Highlanders. "The Commanding Officer left the Battalion this evening," wrote its war diarist, "a loss which will be greatly felt throughout the whole unit."[5] Two days later, Brigadier Ben Cunningham was dismissed and sent to Kingston to run a staff course.[6] On August 4,

Christiansen also "announced that he had been relieved of command. The news spread quickly throughout the unit and all ranks from all companies assembled around the C.O. of their own volition and audibly expressed their regret at his leaving the regiment. The C.O. expressed his reluctance to part company from men whom he held in such high regard, and then left with a warm send-off."[7]

Christiansen's relief came less than twenty-four hours after he wrote to Major General Rod Keller stating his loss of confidence in "leadership and command that kept every unit...in action continuously in spite of severe casualties, and culminated in the launching of several worn-out and disorganized men...into the attack on Tilly La Campagne on 25 Jul 44." He unequivocally declared that he would have refused to send the Glens forward and would unhesitatingly do so again. Keller recommended that Christiansen be repatriated with recommendation for "no further employment" by the army. Simonds agreed that he was "unfitted to lead Canadian Troops with determination" because of his "impression that battles can be fought on a 'limited liability basis.'"[8]

Seeking some justification for Operation Spring, Simonds could only offer the well-hewn refrain that its primary intention had been to hold German armour in front of Caen, despite the hopes he had earlier held for a limited breakout.[9] Given that the Americans had launched Operation Cobra—their full-out assault against German Seventh Army at Saint-Lô—on the same day, Canadian Army analysts heavily emphasized the fact that nine enemy armoured divisions had remained tied down.

Stalemated for weeks in the *bocage* country, the Americans had unleashed a hundred-mile-long bomber stream that obliterated 3,200 Germans inside a 7,000-by-2,500-yard rectangle held by the Panzer Lehr Division, the 257th Infantry, 5th Parachute Division's 5th Regiment, and elements of 2nd ss Panzer Division. Panzer Lehr was virtually annihilated, most of its remaining forty-five tanks thrown pinwheeling into the air. All command posts were vapourized. The division suffered at least 70 per cent casualties.[10] Plunging into the lunar landscape created by the bombing, the Americans put into play Montgomery's overarching strategy. Once the Americans romped

226 / BREAKOUT FROM JUNO

into the guts of France, Montgomery believed, there would be little the Germans could throw in their way. The British Second Army and First Canadian Army could then punch down the Caen-Falaise highway. Either the Germans must flee behind the Seine River or risk encirclement and complete destruction.

It was true that the Germans had continued to believe, even for two days after Operation Cobra started, that the main thrust was still to come on the Caen front. Not until July 27 was the full extent of the American breakout recognized and 116th and 2nd Panzer Divisions sent to meet it. The only two German armoured divisions close to full strength, they represented a significant force. But as they had to move at night to avoid the Allied fighter-bombers, days would be required for their redeployment.

AS OPERATION SPRING had been nearing its launch, General Montgomery had finally agreed that Lieutenant General Harry Crerar's First Canadian Army would become operational on July 23. Crerar's army until Spring concluded consisted of 1 British Corps and its British 3rd, 49th, and 51st Infantry Divisions, plus 6th Airborne Division. Included in the Airborne's ranks was 1st Canadian Parachute Battalion. Having jumped into Normandy on the night of June 5–6, the paratroops had spent most of June and all July holding the Allied eastern flank from the coast near Ouistreham inland to Ranville. From July 23 to the battalion's transfer back to England on September 7 was the only period when Canadian paratroops were connected to First Canadian Army, although they would never serve alongside any other Canadian units.

Sergeant Dan Hartigan recalled this time when neither the facing Germans nor the paratroops were under orders to win ground. They were instead focused on pinning each other in place by engaging in constant fighting. "Casualty lists piling up. Short, wicked encounters between fortified positions and minefields, killing and maiming the soldiers of both sides. Shallow patrols into thick enemy lines...the unit lost numerous men, killed and wounded, to the whims of the so-called 'static battle.'"[11]

Montgomery had given 1 Corps precise marching orders that left Crerar in a steward role. Montgomery had decided that an advance should be made to seize the heights overlooking Ouistreham. This would enable Caen's port facilities to be opened.[12]

Having received Montgomery's instructions on July 22, Crerar duly set about generating paper that included a detailed operational and tactical directive. The following day, he presented this to Lieutenant General John Crocker. In addition to explaining the operation, the long document offered an analysis of German armoured tactics as displayed in June and other commentary drawn from an address Crerar had earlier delivered to his army's senior staff and officers. Crerar helpfully provided Crocker with multiple copies for distribution throughout the corps.[13]

Crerar was "astonished" when Crocker dismissed the directive and said the operation was "not on." In his stern and humourless manner, Crocker told Crerar that freeing Ouistreham from German observation accomplished nothing. There were too many other observation points on the heights east of the Dives. All that would be achieved would be five or six hundred casualties the British could ill afford.[14] If Crerar insisted on the advance, Crocker was "not prepared, personally, to be responsible for carrying it out."

Crerar turned to Montgomery. Crocker, either for personal reasons or "because of the fact that I am a Canadian...resented being placed under my command," Crerar argued. Further, he showed "no tact, nor desire to understand my views." Crocker was "temperamentally unsuited" to serve under a Canadian. Crerar suggested he be exchanged for another British corps commander.

Montgomery vetoed exchanging Crocker but agreed to chat with the "somewhat difficult" officer on July 25. Crerar could then discuss the "tactical problem" with Crocker later that day "with the air cleared and good prospects of mutual understanding." Montgomery told Crocker to "quit bickering" and be "a loyal subordinate." He cautioned Crerar against interfering with Crocker's handling of his corps. Crocker was "a very experienced fighting commander" who needed to be led rather than "driven." Crerar should also "cut down paper in the field" and deal verbally with his corps commanders while actively soliciting their views.[15]

In a July 26 letter to the Chief of Imperial General Staff, General Sir Alan Brooke, Montgomery wrote: "Harry Crerar has started off his career as an Army [Commander] by thoroughly upsetting everyone; he had a row with Crocker the first day, and asked me to remove Crocker. I have spent two days trying to restore peace; investigating the quarrel, and so on. As always, there are faults on both sides. But the basic cause was Harry; I fear he thinks he is a great soldier, and he was determined to show it the very moment he took over command at 1200 hours 23 July. He made his first mistake at 1205 hrs; and his second after lunch. I have had each of them to see me—separately of course. I have told Harry in quite clear terms that in my opinion the basic fault lies with him, in this quarrel. I have seen Crocker, and told him he must play 100% ... I now hope I can get on with fighting the Germans—instead of stopping the Generals fighting amongst themselves."[16]

Montgomery's intervention worked. On July 27, Crocker dutifully presented a plan that modestly sought to push the Germans back sufficiently to enable use of Caen's port facilities. It would involve two British divisions and be launched on August 8.

This limited operation accorded with Montgomery's new intentions for the Caen front. With the American breakout fully under way, Montgomery decided that "any large scale operations ... in [the Caen] area are definitely unlikely to succeed." German attempts to draw armoured divisions away from this front had been frustrated, Montgomery counting six panzer and ss divisions still blocking the road to Falaise.[17]

All these divisions were east of the village of Noyers, none faced the British sector west of here. British Second Army would therefore regroup and attack with at least six divisions from the area of Caumont-l'Éventé. VIII British Corps would pull up stakes from east of Caen and move in beside XXX Corps. This would place all of Second Army west of the Orne. II Canadian Corps would come under First Canadian Army command, and Crerar would be responsible for the entire front east of the river.

By July 30, Montgomery had reconfigured Twenty-First Army Group by stripping divisions from I British Corps to strengthen Second British Army. This left First Canadian Army with two corps comprising one airborne, three infantry, and one armoured division;

supported by two commando brigades, three armoured brigades, and three army groups of artillery. Opposing them were three German armoured divisions and a heavy tank battalion, three infantry divisions, and two Nebelwerfer brigades. In reserve, the Germans had another armoured division and heavy tank battalion. West of the Orne, the line was held by the British XII, XXX, and VIII Corps. Together, these fielded five infantry and three armoured divisions. They also had four armoured brigades and three army groups of artillery. Opposing the British were four infantry divisions, one armoured division, one heavy tank battalion, a Panther anti-tank battalion, and a Nebelwerfer brigade with two fresh infantry divisions and another armoured division en route.

The realignment by Montgomery left First Canadian Army facing twice as many armoured divisions as before, but about a third fewer infantry divisions. West of the Orne, infantry ratios were close to equal, but the British had three times the armour. Montgomery also enjoyed overwhelming artillery and air superiority.[18]

Strengthening British Second Army came at the price of gutting I Corps. Crocker was left with just 6th Airborne and 49th Infantry Divisions. Although this doomed the planned operation towards the Dives River, Montgomery accepted its cancellation.[19] The realignment created a robust Second Army that should easily knife through the facing Germans.

Operation Bluecoat was to begin on July 30. Characteristically, Montgomery failed to appreciate the disadvantageous country where XXX and VIII Corps were to attack—*bocage* at its worst, broken by a "succession of pronounced ridges [that] ran across the axis of advance." This included Mont Pinçon, which at twelve hundred feet was Normandy's highest point. "Streams, many of which were tank obstacles, ran in all directions. Numerous deep wooded valleys, small fields surrounded by thick hedgerows, and scarcity of good...roads were features of the terrain to be crossed," one army analysis stated. "It will be evident...that movement in such country is bound to be difficult and slow, hampering the bringing up [of] reserves, preventing the cross-country movement of anything except men on their feet or Churchill tanks, and hindering supply and replacement."[20]

Nevertheless, Montgomery urged Lieutenant General Myles Dempsey on July 28 to press the attack "with utmost vigour and all caution thrown to the winds." He was to "step on [the] gas."[21] For First Canadian Army, meanwhile, no "large scale effort was immediately required," Montgomery said, but Crerar needed to keep the Germans east of the Orne "nervous and pinned down."[22]

EVEN AS MONTGOMERY reduced First Canadian Army's strength, he advised Crerar "to be prepared to strike towards Falaise." Having anticipated this, Simonds had already concluded that to succeed, II Canadian Corps would require two additional divisions—one infantry and one armoured—and full air support for forty-eight hours. He still had only two divisions, 2nd Canadian Infantry Division holding the line from the Orne River to Verrières village and 3rd Canadian Infantry Division east of the Caen-Falaise highway to Tilly-la-Campagne and La Hogue. These heavily fortified villages were held by 1st SS Panzer Division.[23]

Simonds considered Tilly's capture "a necessary preliminary to an offensive" towards Falaise, and ordered it taken on the night of July 30.[24] But first, 2nd Division's Essex Scottish Regiment would capture a farm and adjacent orchard that stood on a high point next to the Caen-Falaise highway to the northwest of Tilly. Major T.E. "Si" Steele's 'D' Company with one 'C' Company platoon was to carry out the attack. Both 4th and 5th Field Regiments would provide a covering barrage. A troop of British tanks, an anti-tank gun troop, and the Bren guns of the Essex carrier platoon would also assist.

At 1655 hours, the tankers blasted the large, ruined main farmhouse for five minutes. Then the Essex advanced behind the barrage at 1708 hours.[25] Lieutenant Walter Pope's No. 16 Platoon headed for a machine gun on the northern flank, while Sergeant Russ Burdick's No. 17 Platoon advanced against one on the opposite side of the orchard. 'C' Company's No. 15 Platoon laid down covering fire while No. 18 Platoon advanced close behind Burdick's men. After crossing three hundred yards of open ground, No. 16 Platoon was driven to ground when Pope fell wounded. On the right, Burdick's men eliminated two machine-gun positions. This enabled No. 18 Platoon to pass through and clear the rest of the orchard. When Burdick was killed, Steele reorganized the company and personally led it towards the farm.

The panzer grenadiers offered desperate resistance. Canadians and Germans fought with bayonets and rifle butts. Steele saw a recent reinforcement deflect a bayonet thrust and ram his own blade into the German before suddenly being struck down by a bullet through the heart. Then suddenly the surviving panzer grenadiers fled. Thirteen Essex were dead and another nineteen wounded. Fourteen dead Germans were counted and another eight had been captured.[26]

Why the position had been so hotly defended was soon clear. The high ground provided superior observation in every direction for up to five miles. More importantly, the large ruined building proved not to be a farmhouse but rather a waterworks with an adjacent reservoir containing about thirty thousand litres, which supplied Tilly.[27]

The Essex operation was a welcome success. There had been little recent good news. On 2nd Division's western flank, attempts to win ground had been consistently frustrated. Although Le Régiment de Maisonneuve had managed to hang on to most of Saint-Martin, it had lost control of the church in the southeast corner. A small field separated the church from the mine complex. The lift tower over the mine shaft provided excellent observation, as did the battered church steeple. Brigadier Hugh Young and Major General Charles Foulkes decided they must regain control of the church. Then they could think about winning the mine.

Two companies attacked on the night of July 28–29. Major Jacques Ostiguy's 'C' Company secured a crossroad to cover 'A' Company's assault on the church, only to see Captain A. Angers and his forty-five men stopped cold by machine-gun fire. Angers was ordered to try again the following night. This time, the "reduced company" resorted to stealth and infiltrated two sections into the church. An immediate counterattack threatened to overwhelm the French Canadians, and they fought a running gun battle to regain friendly lines. On July 30, the Maisies were relieved by Les Fusiliers Mont-Royal.[28]

The relief was part of a major corps reorganization. On July 26, 3rd Division's senior medical officer had warned Major General Keller that this formation's front line troops were completely exhausted after seven weeks of continuous fighting. With weariness "greatly impairing their efficiency as fighting soldiers," he urged that the division be granted a well-deserved rest.[29]

Normally, Simonds would have baulked at any accommodation of perceived weakness, but passing 3rd Division into reserve meshed with his plans. Accordingly, the division was relieved by the newly arrived 4th Canadian Armoured Division. Simonds planned to gradually allow this division to get "the feel of things" by sending its battalions into small-scale operations.[30]

The hand-off was carried out on the night of July 30–31. Because 4th Division would require time to get sorted out on the front line, Simonds decided that 5th Brigade's Calgary Highlanders should carry Tilly the following night. At the same time, Les Fusiliers Mont-Royal would take the church at Saint-Martin.

Army intelligence later learned that the past two nights' attacks had greatly worried the Germans. To regain the initiative, they attempted to dislodge the Royal Hamilton Light Infantry from Verrières by unleashing an experimental weapon. At 0845 hours, a heavy smokescreen smothered the village. Everyone could hear the grinding of tracks and braced for another attack by Panthers or Tigers. Suddenly, through the smoke appeared a dozen "miniature radio-controlled tanks... Each measured 12 feet long and five feet wide, weighed four tons and carried 800 [pounds] of explosive. They were seen moving from a small pocket of dead ground southeast of [the Riley's] position at about 15 miles an hour, clearly visible despite the mottled camouflage and the wisps of straw from the stacks in which they had lain concealed from the view of... Typhoons. For some reason six of them turned back, but the others rumbled on towards our forward company," observed an army after-action report.[31]

At first, Lieutenant Colonel Rocky Rockingham only saw one of the "goddamned things coming across the field." It looked like a large coffee table on tracks. "Good God," Rockingham said. "What's that?" Someone shouted it was a remote-controlled tank. "Shoot it!" Rockingham bellowed.[32]

Bren gunners cut loose, "but the bullets rattled harmlessly off the armour plate."[33] Then the anti-tank guns fired, and the devices started exploding with massive blasts. "We shot at one several times, but missed," Rockingham recalled. "Then it got into a slit trench and blew up and there was nothing left there except a churned up patch of ground." The Canadians inside were vapourized.[34] "Two of these robots did actually penetrate the position and explode, causing some casualties from blast and flying pieces," an intelligence after-action report found. Despite the deaths of the men in the trench, the report continued that the "exciting—if ineffectual—attack was over [by 0930 hours]. Our troops stood to for some hours but the phenomenon did not recur." This unusual assault proved the last German attempt to regain Verrières.[35]

WHILE GERMAN ATTENTION focused on Verrières, the Canadians on July 31 concentrated on Tilly-la-Campagne and Saint-Martin-de-Fontenay's church. To attack the former, the Calgary Highlanders had to march from a rest area at Fleury-sur-Orne across the breadth of the Canadian front. Instead of attacking Tilly from Bourguébus, the Calgaries would start from the water reservoir to the northwest.[36]

Tilly, about a thousand yards distant, consisted of eight stone farmhouses complete with gardens, orchards, farm buildings, and stone-wall enclosures. After reinforcing the cellars of each building and carving out firing slits at ground level, the 1st ss Panzer Division had dynamited the overhead structure to create thick stone-rubble blankets that rendered the bastion underneath impregnable to artillery. Tanks hid in the woods on the village's southern and eastern flanks.[37]

The Calgary officers looked all this over from the reservoir and remained "quite optimistic about the outcome of the battle."[38] Their plan was simple. From Bourguébus, 4th Division's Lincoln and Welland Regiment would launch a small diversionary attack at 0100 hours. Then, at 0230, the Calgaries would advance behind a heavy barrage moving at a rate of one hundred yards every five minutes.[39] Major Bill McQueen's 'B' Company would lead on the right and Captain Del Harrison's 'D' Company the left. 'C' Company, under Major

Wynn Lasher, would trail 'B' Company, and 'A' Company, having just come under command of Major John Bright, would be behind Harrison's men.[40] The troops started the four-mile march to the reservoir at 2315 hours.

At 0100 hours, the diversion began with one platoon under Lieutenant R.F. Dickie advancing from Bourguébus. A thousand feet out, the Lincs were driven to ground by volleys of machine-gun and mortar fire.[41]

At 0230 hours, the Calgaries attacked and "all hell let loose," their war diarist recorded. The "noise was terrific and the Hun improved the din and clamour by laying down a terrific mortar barrage and shelled apparent [defensive fire] tasks."[42]

'B' Company's wireless went off the air, but the other three companies reported passing an assigned checkpoint at 0246 hours. Then the lead companies reported being under friendly artillery fire. A steady stream of wounded carried the same story. Lieutenant Colonel MacLauchlan knew the Germans were dropping fire behind the creeping barrage, but just in case, he ordered the artillery stopped. No let-up in the fire hammering the advancing Calgaries resulted. The shells raised so much dust that visibility was cut to ten or fifteen yards. Then rising ground fog further obscured things.

At 0315 hours, 'D' Company reported crossing the rail line west of Tilly's outskirts. Suddenly, the attack stalled, the two leading companies forced to ground while those following piled into them and everyone became "mixed up and scattered."

MacLauchlan urged Major Lasher to get 'C' Company into Tilly.[43] Lasher managed to lead a few men in, only to be fired upon by multiple machine guns and at least three tanks. Lieutenant Arthur Rice-Jones suffered a debilitating leg wound. In his first fight, Sergeant Ken Crockett and ten men vaulted over a wall and faced five tanks. Everyone ran back the way they had come. "There was one guy in front of me that went down and one guy beside me that went down. We got to the other side and tried to give covering fire. What can you do with a tank?" Crockett later said.

That was it. The Calgaries retreated to the railway and dug in. Rice-Jones and nine others were left behind and taken prisoner. Major Bright was among those killed.

At 0700 hours, 'B' and 'D' Companies tried again with support from three tanks of the British Royal Scots Greys. They were immediately engaged by a superior force of German tanks that sallied from La Hogue to the east. Although 'B' Company PIAT teams knocked out two Mark IVs, 88-millimetre anti-tank guns picked off two of the British tanks, and the third fled. The infantry had no choice but to follow. A third attempt at 1400 hours, supported by Fort Garry Horse tanks, collapsed on the start line. Tilly remained in German hands, and the Calgaries counted thirty-six men dead and another ninety-nine wounded.[44]

MAJOR JACQUES DEXTRAZE had spent three relaxing days in Caen at Les Fusiliers Mont-Royal's 'B' Echelon unit. It was through these units that each battalion's supplies and reinforcements flowed to the front lines, to which casualties were evacuated, and where officers and men were sometimes rotated for a rest period. He was planning to have dinner in Bayeux at the home of a French family that had befriended him. Time to kill, Dextraze attended an Orders Group at 6th Brigade headquarters.[45] Brigadier Hugh Young reported flying that morning over Saint-Martin-de-Fontenay church and the mine shafts and concluding that the former could be taken "by a company of determined troops with ample covering fire."[46]

Finding the planning too simplistic, Dextraze offered a number of refinements. "As usually happens with people who say how a thing should be done, I was finally given the job." At 1930 hours, Dextraze arrived in Saint-Martin. Lieutenant Colonel Guy Gauvreau told him to capture the church, churchyard, and adjacent cemetery. Joining 'D' Company at 2200 hours, Dextraze found it dug in alongside the Saint-Martin–Verrières road with Germans on the other side. A wall bordered the road on the Canadian side.

Gauvreau assured him that the Germans had no more than twenty men in the church, churchyard, and surrounding hedges. The fighting component of Dextraze's company numbered seventy-two. Losses at Troteval Farm left him with only two officers, one sergeant, a corporal, and a lance-corporal to lead the platoons and sections. After studying the church from several angles, Dextraze felt "that we could never take and hold the place." He was still examining an aerial photograph when night fell. Although he would have liked more time with the photograph, Dextraze knew not to risk a flashlight. That would draw sniper fire from the Germans lurking in the nearby orchards.

Because there were so few non-commissioned officers, Dextraze personally briefed each man. He emphasized the need for surprise or the attack was doomed. Rather than shell the church, one field regiment would fire a twenty-minute barrage against the high ground east of it.

No. 16 Platoon would provide fire support from a three-storey house overlooking the churchyard. Dextraze had the platoon position eight Bren guns in the top storey. Two would rake a hedge left of the churchyard. The other six would drench the opposite orchard, the church, and cemetery. The main attack would be made by No. 18 Platoon. No. 17 Platoon was broken up for a variety of tasks. One section was to eliminate a machine gun in the churchyard's northeast corner. The other two sections would follow No. 18 Platoon into the churchyard and then clear the cemetery and church. Dextraze set the assault for 0530 hours.

Every man carried "entrenching tools and a pick or shovel tied to their back." They wore skeleton webbing with fifty rifle rounds, two grenades, one tin of bully beef, a package of hardtack, and a twenty-four-hour emergency ration. Most of this was stuffed into the Bren magazine pouches on their web kits, while the magazines were simply buttoned up inside their uniform tunics.

An hour before the attack, the two assault platoons slipped into the three-storey building's courtyard. The men moved "noiselessly...flat on their bellies with the noses of the leading men almost on the road." The men would have to climb the wall, cross the road, and then pass through existing holes in the churchyard wall.

When the artillery opened fire, one gun dropped its rounds just twenty yards in front of the courtyard wall. It took fifteen minutes for Dextraze to get the gun silenced and all through this time his men had to stay "flat on the ground and absolutely silent in the tiny courtyard." While Dextraze was addressing this issue, No. 17 Platoon had attacked the machine gun in the churchyard corner on schedule. They struck fast, killing the gun crew with grenades.

The moment the rest of the company followed, No. 18 Platoon's commander fell with a bullet through his leg. Dextraze yelled for Corporal Joseph Albert Germain Lambert to take over. "He carried through the job very coolly as if nothing had happened," Dextraze said later. "Having been briefed thoroughly, he found no difficulty in carrying out his orders."[47]

Despite machine-gun fire from the left flank, Lambert led the platoon into the churchyard. Standing in the middle of the yard, bullets snapping around him, Lambert calmly assigned a position to each section. When a machine gun opened up from beside a back wall, Lambert led several men in silencing it. His actions earned him a Distinguished Conduct Medal.[48]

One Bren gunner and a rifleman burst into the church. The Bren gunner sprayed the interior with several magazines. This awoke the only occupants, three panzer grenadiers who had slept through the churchyard fight. There were three unmanned machine guns mounted on window ledges and sited on the three-storey house.

Saint-Martin church—the source of so much trouble for the Canadians—was finally in hand. Men started working with picks and shovels to improve the depth of slit trenches running all through the churchyard. Dextraze counted thirty Germans killed or wounded. The panzer grenadiers counterattacked within thirty minutes, but the move was half-hearted and easily beaten off. Same result for a second attempt fifteen minutes later. After that the Germans resorted to mortaring 'D' Company non-stop for the next thirty-six hours.

Asked what lessons he learned from the attack, Dextraze said, "In the actual attack...yell like hell. This keeps everyone cool and in good temper, in fact men start to laugh. Have a simple plan."[49]

PART THREE

TOTALIZE

17

Sheer Slaughter

DAILY LOSSES DURING the "static battle" that ended July 31 still numbered about a hundred men. "If we were to sit without further offensive action for [twenty] days our casualties would amount to more than would normally be sustained by the corps in a stiff battle," Lieutenant General Guy Simonds warned. Simonds "was determined that our existing situation, however irksome or discouraging, must be exploited, no matter how tired the troops might be. When possible, they were to be rested, but on that he would make no promises. He fully realized how much reorganization was necessary to place the fighting units and formations on a sound footing again, especially in view of the coming offensive, but he made it plain that in the circumstances, the second best must be accepted, and that though wearied by incessant fighting, the troops must be pushed, if need be, to the bitter end."[1]

On the morning of August 1, General Montgomery re-emphasized that the Canadians must "put on further prods to continue to pin" the Germans to their front. Lieutenant General Harry Crerar, 11 Canadian Corps having come under his command the previous day, instructed Simonds to assault Tilly-la-Campagne. Simonds ordered 4th Canadian Armoured Division's Lincoln and Welland Regiment to strike that very night.[2]

During 3rd Infantry Division's hand-off to 4th Division, Major General Rod Keller had told Major General George Kitching to "leave it alone—try somewhere else." But Simonds was insistent, so his division's first battle would be at Tilly.[3]

Lieutenant Colonel J.G. McQueen received his marching orders from 10th Canadian Infantry Brigade's Brigadier Jim Jefferson at 1800 hours. Two field regiments and one medium regiment would provide fire support.[4] The South Alberta Regiment's 'A' Squadron's tanks would form on high ground northwest of Bourguébus in order to join the infantry inside Tilly at dawn. If, however, the attack bogged down, the tanks would "shoot the Lincs into their objective."[5] The attack was set for 2345 hours. McQueen held an O Group at 2000 hours. Twenty-five minutes before the attack, he said, the artillery would hammer Tilly. During this time, 'A' and 'B' Companies would advance two thousand feet from Bourguébus to a road running east from Tilly to La Hogue. The two companies would establish a PIAT gun killing line to stop tanks from reinforcing Tilly, as they had during the Calgary Highlander attack. 'D' Company, meanwhile, would advance about a thousand feet along the road from Bourguébus to Point 63. This was mid-way between the two villages and also where a narrow farm track intersected the road. 'C' Company would then pass through and gain a foothold in Tilly itself. It took two hours to work out the timings for this complex night operation. At 2200 hours, company commanders hurriedly briefed their men and started moving towards the start line in front of Bourguébus.[6]

As these briefings were under way, 15th Field Regiment's intelligence officer, Lieutenant W.K. Thomson, learned of the attack at a divisional meeting. "The plan was simple and of the silent type," Thomson recorded that evening. Everyone, he boasted, was "set to hear that the 4 Div had done what both 3 Div and 2 Div had failed to do. It was a chance for the [Lincs] to get their feet wet."[7]

There had been no time to reconnoitre routes to be used or the lay of ground that must be crossed. But the Lincs were confident. Their inexperience was evident in the loads carried. Regulation small packs, gas respirators, utility pouches, mess tins, water bottles, and copious amounts of ammunition. 'B' Company took along twenty shovels and fifteen picks. The two companies tasked with blocking tanks out of La Hogue carried extra PIATs and bombs. Quiet or quick movement while so overloaded was impossible.

Major Forbes Bell Fisher advanced 'B' Company single file into the wheat field and headed for the roadblock position. Private Ronald Barton was close to the front, the second man in No. 17 Platoon's lead Bren gun team. The three-quarter moon having not yet risen, the night was inky black. Halfway to the objective, someone broke the stillness by shouting, "Let's go, 'B' Company!" Men started running, stumbling under the weight of their gear.

A flare sliced the sky. Machine-gun tracers ripped the wheat. 'B' Company hit the dirt. Private Eugene Joseph Blake landed next to Barton and called for help getting the PIAT strapped across his back off. As Barton started working at the straps, he saw tracers cutting "through the stubble and just drumming into him." Blake died while Barton lay entirely untouched.[8]

'A' Company's Lieutenant Ernest Phair's No. 7 Platoon had advanced well ahead of the rest of the company and was cut off. Despite the mortar, machine-gun, and small-arms fire whipping at them, the Lincs "were hesitant about returning the fire...for fear of shooting one another." When Lieutenant John Martin's No. 8 Platoon tried to reach Phair's men, it was driven back. As several men were killed or wounded, those behind mistakenly thought they were only waiting for orders. These men paused, while others kept crawling forward. The platoon broke into scattered sections, "which lost direction or were too weak to cope with the more experienced enemy."[9] Thirty Lincs, including Private Barton, were taken prisoner.[10]

'B' Company lost all cohesion. Major Fisher was killed, and the company reeled back into the midst of an equally disorganized 'A' Company. Major A.U. "Andy" Gilles led both back to Bourguébus to reorganize. Although this left the main force's left flank unprotected from La Hogue, Brigadier Jefferson interceded at 0030 hours with a direct order for 'C' Company to pass through 'D' Company at Point 63 and attack Tilly.[11] Major R.F. Willson and his men got to within two hundred yards of Tilly before being caught in a carefully laid trap. Medium machine guns opened up from three directions, and mortars saturated the kill zone in which the men were trapped. It was just "a blaze of tracer across there," one of those who managed to escape said.[12]

At 0200 hours, 'A' and 'B' Companies set out again from Bourguébus to establish the roadblock. 'B' Company was now commanded by Lieutenant J.S.W. Burnett. Only two 'A' Company platoons and the headquarters section actually gained any ground, the rest of the force hitting the dirt just past the start line. Major Gilles and the men with him were stopped in the middle of the field by "a wall of machine-gun fire." Gilles crawled to Lieutenant Martin. "Well, we've got to get up that hill," Gilles said. "You be my guest," Martin replied. "There is nothing we can do." Just before dawn, Martin told Gilles he was taking No. 8 Platoon back no matter what Gilles thought. Leaving its dead, including Lieutenant Phair, the force fell back to Bourguébus.

At 0545 hours, McQueen told Jefferson the Lincs were finished. In less than five hours the battalion suffered sixty-four casualties, fifteen fatal. 'A' and 'B' Companies were hardest hit, reduced equally by 30 per cent.[13] On August 3, Jefferson gave the battalion a dressing down. "His principal criticism was that insufficient determination had been shown in attacking what should have been a two-company objective."[14] None of the Lincs bought this. They admitted inexperience had led to many mistakes, but Tilly was clearly so heavily defended, no single battalion could win it.

Belatedly acknowledging this, Simonds had Tilly heavily bombed and then shelled by artillery at 1800 hours on August 2. The Calgary Highlanders' war diarist observed: "Typhoons arrived and Tilly went up and then down in a mess of smoking rubble... Shortly afterwards our arty played terrifically heavy fire into the rubble and many air bursts were fired directly over Tilly as well. It is a seemingly impossible thing for anyone to live under such fire." When the fire eased, the diarist ruefully noted: "Snipers continue to be very active and the seemingly impossible has happened because we are once again receiving MG fire from the slits at Tilly. The Hun is like a rat and comes up for more no matter how hard we pound him."[15]

WHILE THE CANADIANS and Germans stalemated on the Caen front, the breakout on the American front continued to gain momentum. On August 1, not only was First Canadian Army fully operational, but the Americans completed deployment of Lieutenant General George S. Patton's Third Army. With two American armies in Normandy, General Omar Bradley turned over First Army's reins to Lieutenant General Courtenay Hodges and was elevated to command of Twelfth U.S. Army Group.

Taking over the Allied extreme right flank, Patton's mission was to seize the ports of Saint-Malo and Brest in Brittany. In Patton's trademark style, Third Army had two divisions driving forward by the afternoon. Expectation had been that the new army would face a slow, deliberate fight, with *bocage* and stubborn German defences conspiring to prevent rapid movement.

By dawn on August 2, events were developing differently. Struggling more with getting his divisions through the bottleneck by Avranches at the base of the Cotentin Peninsula, Patton realized he had been handed the opportunity "to slash forward and exploit not only the mobility and striking power of his armored divisions but also the German disorganization...There seemed little point in slowly reducing Brittany by carefully planned and thoroughly supervised operations unraveled in successive phases."

Concurring, Bradley ordered Patton to leave only minimum forces to "secure Brittany." The new American mission was to "drive eastward and expand the continental lodgment area." Patton set eyes on the Seine. Although the initiative was American, Montgomery recognized the developing breakout "radically changed the entire conception of how operations would develop." On August 4, he cabled the Chief of Imperial General Staff, General Sir Alan Brooke: "The main business lies to the east." Montgomery, Bradley, Patton, and General Eisenhower all agreed that the Americans should advance towards Paris. This large wheeling turn would force the Germans to retreat to the Seine River. As all bridges there had been destroyed, they might be pinned against the river and crushed.[16]

Against these developments the Germans could do little. Commander in Chief, West Generalfeldmarschall Günther von Kluge had been hamstrung by Hitler, who on July 31 had issued orders that "no withdrawal would be tolerated."[17] Even as these orders were being sent to von Kluge at his headquarters in Le Mans, he was describing Normandy as "a hell of a mess" in a signal to Hitler that warned the American advance was unstoppable.[18] The only recourse was a rapid retreat to the Seine and establishment of a strong blocking position on its northern bank.

Hitler would have none of it. On August 2, he ordered von Kluge to muster his armoured strength and assume the offensive. With remarkable self-delusion, Hitler envisioned stopping the Americans with a breakthrough assault at the point where the two U.S. armies met at Mortain. The German tanks would then charge twenty miles to Avranches on the Atlantic coast. This attack would buy time for the recently deployed v-1 and v-2 rockets to so devastate London that the Allies would agree to negotiations.[19]

Five panzer and panzer-grenadier divisions were to attack on August 7. They would include 116th Panzer, 2nd Panzer, 2nd ss Panzer, and 1st ss Panzer Divisions and remnants of 17th ss Panzer-Grenadier Division. The 1st ss Panzer Division would have to be withdrawn from the Canadian front.

Oberdommando der Wehrmacht's deputy chief of operations, General der Artillerie Walter Warlimont, visited Panzer Group West's headquarters the day after Hitler hatched his plan. General der Panzertruppen Hans Eberbach "described our situation to him with complete candour and frankness. We suggested a retreat to the Seine as the only possible solution. He answered that Hitler would never accept that. He was unable to give us an objective or hope for a positive solution. Those at the top expected everything from the counterthrust of Seventh Army to Avranches which we considered as hopeless."

Warlimont doled out Hitler's tortured reasoning and offered promises of reinforcement and supply both men knew would never materialize. Eberbach obstinately repeated that "ultimately the situation of the two German armies will become untenable."

"But you have been able to hold on until now. If you can do this for another month or two, this summer's fighting will not have been in vain," Warlimont declared. "The British people have been assured that the war will end this year. If this fails to happen, there exists for us one more great opportunity." This allusion to the v-weapons break-ing British morale failed to impress Eberbach. "The situation of Seventh Army makes it necessary to arrive at a big decision," he countered.

Warlimont insisted that Eberbach release four armoured divi-sions for the "thrust to Avranches and to cut off the Americans."

"If the ss divisions are pulled out south of Caen, the enemy will attack there and break through," Eberbach replied. While Eberbach wanted to withdraw these divisions from the immediate front lines, he pleaded with Warlimont to agree that the "ss divisions must be held ready in the rear to support the front. The main question remains how the front can be held in the long run against an enemy so far superior in matériel." Warlimont promised him two ss bri-gades from Denmark and said okw was combing "the homeland and occupied France...for all available matériel."

Eight to ten days to move the brigades from Denmark, Eberbach estimated. Too long—the matter would be decided by then. Moving the ss divisions to the Mortain area would require three to four days. It was impossible to say what Seventh Army's situation would be then. Warlimont promised that a thousand new fighter planes would be deployed in the second half of August and Allied air supremacy broken.

"But there still remains the question whether the situation in the Seventh Army area can ever be restored," Eberbach insisted.[20]

It was a losing battle. Eberbach had to order 1st ss Panzer Divi-sion to prepare for withdrawal from Verrières Ridge. Already this division had been badly weakened by casualties, as well as the need to cover the entire front facing the Canadians when 9th ss Panzer Division moved west of the Orne in an attempt to stem British Sec-ond Army's advance.[21] The 1st ss were scheduled to entirely withdraw on the night of August 5–6, being replaced by the newly arrived 89th Infantry Division. Once this hand-off was complete, the only armoured division east of the Orne would be 12th ss Panzer Division, which had left the front lines on the night of August 3–4. Except for one battle group sent west of the Orne to reinforce the German forces there, the division stood in reserve.

ULTRA INTERCEPTS ALERTED the Allies to the planned German thrust into the twenty-mile-wide corridor leading to Avranches. Bradley, who was privy to Ultra intelligence, presented his knowledge to Patton and Hodges as a hunch. He positioned U.S. VIII Corps's four infantry divisions and elements of two armoured divisions to defend this front. For extra insurance, Bradley also ordered Patton to halt three divisions from XX Corps about fifty miles to the east at Saint-Hilaire-du-Harcouët. If needed, he would turn these divisions about to cut the Germans off from behind. The order disgusted Patton, who thought reining in his divisions based on a hunch was bloody poor tactics.[22]

Unlike their American counterparts, British and Canadian Army commanders were apprised of relevant intelligence gleaned by the Ultra code breakers. Both Crerar and Simonds had been informed. Knowing the Germans intended to attack the American sector on August 7, Crerar had his chief of staff, Brigadier C.C. "Church" Mann, phone II Canadian Corps headquarters on the night of August 4 and ask whether the Canadian offensive could proceed on that date rather than the day following. II Canadian Corps chief of staff Brigadier Elliot Rodger quickly canvassed Simonds and other key staff and then replied that advancing the operation was possible.[23]

By now the Canadians knew that 9th SS Panzer Division had slipped away and 1st SS Panzer Division was thinning its strength to hold everything from La Hogue across to May-sur-Orne. This change prompted Major General Charles Foulkes to order a renewed attempt to eliminate the threat posed by the mine shafts next to Saint-Martin-de-Fontenay. The Cameron Highlanders with a sixteen-man party of sappers from IIth Field Company were directed to raid the mine area on the night of August 4–5 and blow both mine shafts shut with explosives. Brigadier Hugh Young objected to the timing, arguing it would be better to strike just before the major offensive. Anxious to keep the Germans engaged, Foulkes stood firm.

At midnight, Camerons and sappers advanced behind a covering bombardment. Meeting light resistance, they isolated the two mine shafts, and the sappers began setting charges. It was soon apparent they lacked sufficient explosives to seal the shafts at ground level. Thinking they could block the shafts by dropping the sturdy hoist towers onto them, the sappers climbed twenty feet into the rigging and began placing charges. It was a clear, moonlit night, and German snipers in the nearby ruins fired on the exposed men.[24] Seven sappers were killed or wounded before the Camerons' Major A.C. Kavanagh ordered the attempt ended. The raiders retired to Saint-Martin. The Camerons had one officer and eight men missing and another twenty-one other ranks wounded.[25]

On August 5, a new Ultra intelligence alert reported that 1st ss Panzer Division might move to join the forthcoming assault on Avranches. At 1330 hours, Brigadier Mann called Rodger at 11 Canadian Corps with the news. He ordered the two front-line divisions "to push their necks out" to maintain contact and try to stop them.[26]

Hours earlier, 5th Brigade had relieved 6th Brigade on the western flank in order to free the latter to rehearse for the forthcoming offensive. Brigadier Bill Megill had expected to quietly ease the reconstituted Black Watch into a combat role. The battalion was now commanded by a Black Watch veteran, Lieutenant Colonel Frank Mitchell, but only thirteen of its twenty-seven original officers remained.[27]

By Megill's reckoning, a battalion that had suffered as heavy losses as had the Black Watch should have at least a month to absorb and train new men. Now, just eleven days after its virtual destruction, the Black Watch re-entered the line.[28]

Megill had previously considered the Black Watch his best battalion under the "outstanding" leadership of Lieutenant Colonel Stuart Cantlie. Megill had little use for Mitchell, considering him unfit for command, while Mitchell blamed Megill for destroying his regiment. The friction between the two men was palpable.[29]

Mitchell established his headquarters in Saint-André-sur-Orne on the evening of August 4, and the battalion's companies were distributed through Saint-André and Saint-Martin shortly after midnight. At dawn, both towns were subjected to steady artillery and mortar fire, and a number of snipers were active in Saint-Martin. The Black Watch war diarist noted that it was "rather disconcerting to have bullets whistle around one's ears in the odd moments when we are not 'biting the dust' on account of [Jerry] mortar and 88-mm fire."

At mid-day, Megill told Mitchell to ready for an advance on May-sur-Orne. He was joined shortly thereafter at Mitchell's headquarters by Major General Foulkes, who said that the 1st ss was believed to be "withdrawing his depleted forces and we must keep contact with him and hold him where he is so that a larger plan may be successfully accomplished." At 1620 hours, the Black Watch was to "advance until the enemy is contacted."

Major Tom Anyon's 'A' Company led, with 'D' Company under newly promoted Major Ronnie Bennett close behind. 'B' and 'C' Companies were, respectively, on the right and left flanks.[30] Because so many of the men were inexperienced, Mitchell had Anyon take only fifty forward, leaving the rest, who were only likely to get themselves or someone else killed. 'A' Company advanced in two single files up opposite sides of the road. They passed bloated and decaying corpses of Canadians who had fallen in earlier attacks on May.

Supporting artillery shelled May until Anyon's men were within a hundred yards of it.[31] As the artillery lifted, the battalion war diarist recorded, "Jerry started plastering them with [mortar and artillery fire] as fast as he could load." A tank ground out of May and into the midst of 'A' and 'D' Companies, which had taken cover in the roadside ditches. This "tank caused havoc among their numbers." Anyon was killed and most of his men were taken prisoner. Major Ronnie Bennett, who had survived the July 25 debacle, died when a mortar shell landed next to him. The Black Watch fell back to regroup between Saint-André and Saint-Martin. "Some of the new lads whom we have recently received as replacements are taking this action quite hard, for most of them are fresh from Canada," the diarist reported. The Black Watch's casualties were estimated at seventy all ranks.[32] Twenty were fatal, and twenty-one men were lost as prisoners.[33]

At dusk, Megill ordered Le Régiment de Maisonneuve to advance through the Black Watch. He insisted that the "only defences there are a...few dug-in tanks," the Maisonneuve war diarist wrote. The battalion was supported by a medium artillery regiment and a squadron of tanks firing from near Saint-Martin. 'A' Company advanced on the right and 'C' Company the left. So serious were the French-Canadian reinforcement shortages that each company fielded only forty men. The Maisies were trapped exactly as the Black Watch had been, and a confused firefight continued through the night. In the morning, the attack was broken off.[34] Ten men died.[35] The Maisies were twice unlucky on August 6, however, when two 88-millimetre shells struck their kitchen area as the regiment gathered for lunch. Thirteen men were killed and 22 seriously wounded.[36] The regimental historian noted that during the period of July 25 to August 7, the Maisies reported 56 men killed, 116 wounded, and 4 missing.[37]

ON AUGUST 5, 4th Canadian Armoured Division had also tested German defences. In response to intelligence reports that Tilly-la-Campagne had been "evacuated by the enemy," Lieutenant Colonel David Stewart was instructed to check it with a platoon of Argyll and Sutherland Highlanders. As Bourguébus had been subject to small-arms and mortar fire from Tilly throughout the day, Stewart questioned "the authenticity of this report." But Brigadier Jim Jefferson insisted the intelligence was sound.

Sergeant Alexander McLaren led a thirty-man platoon from 'B' Company into the shell-cratered wheat field at 1630 hours. Thirty minutes later, Stewart, from the top of a three-storey building, watched the patrol enter Tilly and immediately come under fire from three sides. It took three field regiments and the battalion's 3-inch mortars firing directly on Tilly to help the platoon break free. But it was really Private Edgar M. Purchase who saved the platoon.[38]

Many Argylls considered Purchase "the world's worst soldier." Yet it was this "dumb, dumb soldier," as one Argyll put it, who "gathered up the hand grenades and ammunition and went in on the town himself." As the others withdrew, Purchase walked forward "firing a Bren gun from the hip." Initially believed killed, he was later confirmed as a prisoner of war. Years later, he told Lance Corporal Harry Ruch: "Harry, I woke up and found myself in the middle of Germans with a machinegun in my hand." He had no memory of "getting up and charging."[39] For bringing back twenty-three of thirty men, McLaren was awarded the Military Medal.[40]

Despite clear proof that Tilly was held in force, Jefferson ordered another attack with two companies. From the three-storey building,

Stewart examined the flat ground between Bourguébus and Tilly. "This is sheer slaughter," Stewart said. "What's the matter with those people back there, telling me to send these guys in?"[41] A dutiful soldier, Stewart sent 'C' and 'D' Companies in at 1900 hours with two troops of the South Alberta Regiment's 'C' Squadron in support. Major Gordon Winfield's 'C' Company went straight up the road towards Tilly with 'D' Company close behind.[42] Two tanks were immobilized by mines, one after advancing only two hundred yards.[43] As 'C' Company and the tanks closed on the village, Major W.K. "Bill" Stockloser swung the tail company out to the left to provide covering fire. Accompanied by four tanks, Lieutenant James G. Sloan's platoon was struck by a maelstrom of fire the instant it entered the village. Anti-tank guns knocked two Shermans out of action, and machine guns ripped point-blank into the Argylls. Sloan was killed while single-handedly taking on an 88-millimetre gun. Agreeing there was no point in throwing more men into the grinder, Winfield and Stockloser ordered a withdrawal. The Argylls suffered twenty-four casualties.[44] Several tankers were wounded but none killed.[45] Montgomery remarked to Simonds that evening, "Congratulations, you've been kicked out of Tilly again."[46]

If the two-company attack on Tilly was poorly conceived, the decision by Jefferson's counterpart at 4th Canadian Armoured Brigade to send two platoons of the Lake Superior Regiment (Motor) into La Hogue was even more so. Brigadier Leslie Booth told Major Robert Keane—the battalion's second-in-command—at 1400 hours that intelligence reports indicated that most ss troops in La Hogue "had departed" and a single platoon should easily take it. The platoon would be supported by artillery and two tank troops of the Canadian Grenadier Guards. Keane had no intention of sending only one platoon. He tasked the job to 'A' Company at 1800 hours, emphasizing that the attack had to begin in ninety minutes to benefit from the artillery. Major E.J.O. Gravelle decided to go in with just two platoons, with No. 1 Platoon coming up once the others gained La Hogue. Because the ground to the right of the field contained a minefield, the Grenadiers concentrated their tanks on the left side.[47]

When the artillery barrage lifted, the small force was caught in the wheat field by heavy machine-gun and mortar fire. No. 3 Platoon, under Lieutenant R.A. Hinton, was so slowed by intense fire from the right flank that Lieutenant Frederick Thomas White's No. 2 Platoon got well ahead. When a sniper shot Gravelle in the leg, the attack foundered, until the second-in-command, Captain P. Malach, arrived to take over. When he tried leading the platoons onward, No. 3 Platoon wavered before the fierce incoming fire. Again, White's men outpaced the other platoon, until White was killed 150 yards short of La Hogue.

Realizing the Superiors would only die if they pushed on, Malach ordered a withdrawal. He called for artillery to smother La Hogue, to screen the men going back. The Grenadiers moved between the exposed infantry and the village, firing their 75-millimetre guns "until the barrels glowed red with heat." This enabled the Superiors to extricate themselves.[48] The Grenadiers continued shooting until the "barrels of the Brownings began to droop" and their "ammunition was almost expended." Then they rumbled back to Bourguébus without suffering any loss.[49]

"This was the first action in which the [Superiors] had taken part in the war," the regiment's official historian wrote, "and it had been—one could not but admit it—a failure. It was small consolation that the Lincoln and Wellands and the Argyll and Sutherland Highlanders could do no better in their successive attacks upon Tilly-la-Campagne."[50]

That night, 1st ss Panzer Division left the front. Many of its men had spent some portion of the past ten days in Tilly. "Tilly was a tiny and, in the context of the war, insignificant town. But none of the men who spent even a few days in that inferno will ever forget the name," one wrote.[51]

The 89th Infantry Division slotted into place. "Quietly and without any fuss, the enemy had been able to withdraw [1st ss Panzer Division]...Allied intelligence had no idea where the ss formation had gone and so assumed it had aligned with the 12th ss to form a mobile reserve in the Bretteville-sur-Laize area. The 89th was considered far inferior to the ss divisions. It had been formed in January 1944, deployed from Germany to Normandy, and had not yet seen combat. Still, its strength was estimated at about 10,000 men possessing a full complement of machineguns, mortars and artillery."[52]

The division's commander, General der Infanterie Konrad Heinrichs, held a Knight's Cross and had served on the Russian front. Its other officers and non-commissioned officers were experienced combat veterans. About 65 per cent of the troops were nineteen or under. Some were over forty, and others were foreign conscripts of dubious loyalty. What the division possessed was something the ss had lacked all along—sufficient men to "cover the ground."

The changeover presented Simonds with a new dilemma. Virtually on the eve of his planned thrust to Falaise, the opposition had changed from one possessing mobile armour to one lacking almost any mobility. This presented new challenges and opportunities that his plan did not take into account. It was also probable that the two ss Panzer divisions would be "used to bar the way to Falaise, or to meet any serious threat to the line."[53]

[18]

Jaws Dropped

ON JULY 18, Lieutenant General Guy Simonds and his aide-de-camp, Captain Marshal Stearns, had crouched in a ditch on a hill west of the Orne River to watch Operation Goodwood unfold. "This was a mid-morning attack and within seconds it seemed as though 20 or 30 British tanks were 'brewing up'...One could not help but be most impressed with the thickness, camouflage and marksmanship of the German gunners whether in tanks or manning anti-tank guns." As the two men walked to their jeep, Simonds told Stearn, "When my turn comes, we will do it at night."[1]

His turn arrived on July 29 when Simonds started planning a breakthrough to Falaise. The opposing forces at the time were 1st and 9th ss Panzer Divisions, so Simonds intended to match them armour for armour. As II Canadian Corps had only 4th Armoured Division, he asked Crerar to secure a second armoured division. He also sought another infantry division, so his 3rd Division could be left out of the initial phases. Crerar was able to accommodate relieving 3rd Division by shuffling 51st (Highland) Infantry Division and 33rd British Armoured Brigade from 1 British Corps to II Canadian Corps command. Then, on August 5, Crerar secured the services of 1st Polish Armoured Division—beginning what would be a long relationship between the Canadians and the Poles.[2]

In an August 5 briefing, Crerar described how First Canadian Army faced "the vital northern hinge, or pivot" of the German line before Caen. Their responsibility was "the breaking off of that pivot, or the smashing of that hinge, and to do this decisively and quickly." A successful thrust to Falaise, he said, could spell "the end of the German Army now assembled in North West Europe."[3]

These were the high stakes around which Operation Totalize was conceived. For Simonds, the stakes were also personal. The only partial success of Operation Atlantic and the failure of Operation Spring had sullied his reputation. He needed Totalize to restore his image as a masterful strategist.[4]

Operation Spring had revealed that the Germans' main resistance line ran across Verrières Ridge from May-sur-Orne to Tilly-la-Campagne. The key to breaking this line was still to punch through to the high ground of Point 122, also known as the Cramesnil Spur. Behind this spur lay the German second line. Believed still under construction, it ran from Bretteville-sur-Laize to Hautmesnil and then east to Saint-Sylvain. At Hautmesnil, the Caen-Falaise highway crossed another commanding knoll. This was where the second line must be broken.[5] From Hautmesnil it was then twelve miles to Falaise.

The Germans held many strong cards, including firmly held, deep defences from which they enjoyed superb fields of fire and observation over the Canadian lines. Simonds planned to trump the Germans by attacking at night. Speed was essential. They must punch deep and at such a pace that the Germans were denied the opportunity to regroup and counterattack. This would inevitably mean outrunning the supporting artillery, while the Germans would fall back on their guns and consequently always have artillery able to range on the Canadians.[6] Simonds planned to overcome this problem by having air support that was "genuinely total" and guaranteed for forty-eight hours.

When Simonds learned that a single infantry division had replaced the ss Panzer divisions, he significantly altered the plan. The first phase would now be conducted by infantry divisions supported by armoured brigades, rather than two armoured divisions.

Using the Caen-Falaise highway as a boundary, 2nd Canadian Infantry Division and 2nd Canadian Armoured Brigade would operate to the right. The 51st Highland Division and 33rd Armoured Brigade would be on the left. To achieve surprise, there would be no preliminary artillery. Instead, heavy bombers would "obliterate the area May-sur-Orne–Fontenay-le-Marmion and the wooded area east of Secqueville-la-Campagne." In the second phase, 3rd Canadian Infantry Division and 4th Canadian Armoured Division would carry the Hautmesnil–Saint-Sylvain line. The third phase would see 4th Armoured Division and the Poles dash to the heights overlooking Falaise from the north.[7]

NEED FOR RAPID movement posed the greatest obstacle. Commonwealth infantry attacked on foot. The only Canadian exception was 4th Armoured Division's Lake Superior Regiment, equipped with M-14 half-tracks. Their armoured protection enabled infantry to advance apace with tanks. While Simonds could borrow some half-tracks, they would not be sufficient to mobilize the required infantry battalions.

Simonds was chewing on this problem one day in late July when he happened upon 3rd Division's M-7 self-propelled guns. Nicknamed "Priests" because of their pulpit-shaped machine-gun mounting, these M-7s were basically tanks from which the turret had been exchanged for an open top to accommodate a 105-millimetre gun. "I was one day watching some of these vehicles and it occurred to me that, if the equipment were stripped, they would be sufficiently roomy and have adequate protection to provide the sort of vehicle I had in mind," Simonds wrote.[8]

Outfitting 3rd Division's field regiments with Priests had been a temporary measure to increase artillery mobility during the initial invasion phase. At the end of July, the three regiments began switching back to the standard 25-pounders. This process was completed over the first two days of August.[9] The gunners did not surrender the Priests willingly. With a "feeling of great regret...all personnel saw the equipment leave," 14th Field Regiment's war diarist recorded. "They had given good service and had proved

258 / BREAKOUT FROM JUNO

very satisfactory in the role of assault artillery."[10] The return to 25-pounders by 13th Field Regiment occurred "amid great arguments among the gunners as to their relative merits. The preponderance of opinion was in favour of the [Priests] and some gunners were as downcast as though they had lost their best friends."[11]

On July 31, Lieutenant Colonel Carl Rice Boehm, assistant director of the Royal Canadian Electrical and Mechanical Engineers, was asked by phone how long it would take to remove the gun from seventy-six M-7s and ready them to carry infantry. "That's a big job," Boehm replied. "What priority are we going to have?" He was promised top priority and told to finish the job in a week. Boehm had been thinking three weeks at a rush.

Boehm "rang the panic button." That evening the army's senior mechanical engineers—Boehm; his superior, Brigadier G.M. Grant; Major George Wiggan of the Advanced Workshop Detachment; and Major Gil Pointer met literally under a table because of a German air raid. The task seemed insurmountable. But as the men considered problems and developed solutions, they agreed it could work. Defrocked Priests, they first called them, but then Pointer suggested Kangaroos "because they carry their young in their belly."[12]

Wiggan assembled the ad hoc group of about 250 engineers— mostly welders and mechanics—from about fourteen British and Canadian units. Deploying in two fields near Bayeux, the men had fourteen Priests stripped by the end of August 2.[13] The following evening, a test model was ready for inspection. Delighted, Simonds gave his blessing to continue.[14]

Former mining engineers, Boehm and Wiggan were used to improvisation in the field. While Wiggan managed the conversions, Boehm sourced required equipment and materials. Both realized there was no point in converting a Priest "unless the engine, transmission and the track equipment were fully serviceable...Ended up that we changed twenty-eight engines with replacement engines."

Welding rod was voraciously consumed. Boehm tracked down a source of "liberated...German welding rod" and confiscated it. When official stores of armour plate were exhausted, Boehm led

teams to scrounge from unofficial sources. Badly damaged Bren carriers and armoured cars were stripped. The steelworks at
Colombelles were plundered. Then Boehm attacked beached landing craft on Juno Beach. Ignoring the complaints of sailors, who had
thought to refloat them, Boehm and his men cut away armoured
sides and ramps. He had a signed document from Crerar giving him
top priority. Nobody could stand in his way.

Boehm subjected one finished Kangaroo to the ultimate test,
hammering it with machine-gun fire. The high-calibre rounds
pierced the armour. To increase its density, the engineers added
another layer of plate with a space between filled with beach sand,
which acted as a shock absorber.[15]

With cranes, recovery vehicles, workbenches, guns, engines, steel,
welding gear, and men working around the clock, the field "soon
resembled a Clyde-side shipyard."[16] August 6 was a Sunday, and at
sunrise that morning the engineers delivered seventy-six Kangaroos.
For his part in providing the "enthusiasm, initiative and driving
force" that enabled completion in "three and one half days of what
appeared to be an impossible task," Wiggan was inducted into the
Order of the British Empire. Boehm, who had received an OBE in
1943, was Mentioned in Despatches.[17]

Simonds had hoped to give the infantry a week to train with the
Kangaroos. Instead they had two days to practise how to board, race
to an "imaginary dispersal area," unload, and attack an objective.[18]

Not all of the Canadian assault battalions received Kangaroos.
The seventy-two were insufficient. Sixty M-14 half-tracks were added
to enable all the troops to be motorized.[19] The Essex Scottish received
half-tracks, while Kangaroos were assigned to the Royal Hamilton
Light Infantry and Royal Regiment. The Rileys were in a foul mood
when they started the process, for they had just lost their popular
commander, Lieutenant Colonel Rocky Rockingham. Summoned to
2nd Division headquarters on August 4, Rockingham had arrived
anxious. Major General Foulkes offered no relief when he told Rockingham to report to Simonds. He found Simonds bent over a large
topographic map in a caravan outside 11 Corps headquarters.
Simonds looked up. "Sorry to take you away from the battalion."

"Oh God, what's coming up?" Rockingham wondered.

"You've done pretty well," Simonds said. "You're going to command 9th Brigade. Report to General Keller." Rockingham was still digesting the news, not sure he had heard right, as he stepped from the caravan. Captain Stearns shook his hand. "What did the general say?" Rockingham asked. Stearns confirmed Rockingham's promotion.

When Rockingham arrived at 9th Brigade headquarters, an aura of gloom surrounded the staff there. Not only had Brigadier Ben Cunningham been sacked but also two brigade battalion commanders. Realizing he had been handed a problem outfit, Rockingham returned to Simonds. "Would you mind explaining why these people have all left?"

"There's no partial commitment in war," Simonds said sharply. "I told them to do something and they said they couldn't because they weren't up to it, so I fired them." Simonds added that the same fate would befall anybody who failed to measure up.

Back at 9th Brigade, the staff officers were all nervously gathered. "I'm going to command this brigade," Rockingham said, "and you're going to do exactly what I tell you or else I'll have you removed, too."

Rockingham had no issue with Simonds. "You knew exactly where you stood," he said later. "You did a superior job, you would get promoted and decorated. If you didn't, you got fired. Oh, I loved Guy Simonds. Got along very well with him. A lot of people didn't. He told me what to do and how to do it. That's what I liked."[20]

AT NOON ON August 5, Simonds held a corps-level O Group under the shade of a grove of tall pine trees. "Gentlemen, we plan to attack in depth with armour in the night," Simonds opened. Brigadier Elliot Rodger saw "jaws dropped" all around. Someone said, "We have never done that before." Simonds crisply replied, "That is why we will do so."[21]

Operation Totalize was now fully developed. To keep the armoured columns on proper course, the corps's chief signal officer, Brigadier S.F. Clark, had improvised a directional wireless beam using a No. 33 set that issued a simple dot-and-dash signal along a

At 1300 hours, 8th Brigade's slowdown had sufficiently frustrated Simonds that he simply bypassed Keller and ordered 7th Brigade's Brigadier Harry Foster to test the enemy strength in Vaucelles.[18] Guided by Raymond Chatelain from the French Resistance, the Regina Rifle's scout platoon crossed the Orne by picking their way over two wrecked bridges. One man was killed by machine guns covering the crossing point. This fire also prevented the platoon from transferring a 24-pound No. 46 wireless set with enough range to report directly to corps headquarters on the west bank. Instead, Lieutenant Lorenzo Bergeron passed messages to Chatelain, who then ran back to the river and crossed perilously through the machine-gun fire to deliver it to the signallers. They then sent the message through to Simonds.[19] Bergeron soon reported Vaucelles lightly held. Simonds instructed Foster to advance all the Reginas across the river at 1630 hours.[20]

In Colombelles, the Chauds had thrown everything they had at the château, while the Glens would clear the area to the east. The division's artillery rained hundreds of shells onto the building at 1440 hours.[21] When the barrage appeared over, Captain Barney Fowler of the Glens stepped through a gap in a brick wall and said over his shoulder, "Okay guys, let's go." A shell slammed down and Fowler was killed.[22] Signaller Lance Corporal Francis R. McDonald was struck by shrapnel. Lieutenant James William Hartley's head was torn off; Company Sergeant Major Frederick Linsey's head remained barely attached. Smoke curled around McDonald as he calmly stripped off his equipment and exposed a body that was riddled with holes gushing blood. These images were seared into Private Mervyn Williams's memory. When someone brought a stretcher, Williams helped carry McDonald to a waiting jeep ambulance; then he ran back to his company.[23]

Eleven men had suffered savage injuries from the medium artillery's terrific blasts and big chunks of shrapnel. The Glens' RAP was soon awash with blood. McDonald died on the stretcher surrounded by a pool of his own blood.[24] In addition to the wounded, four men, including Fowler and Hartley, died on the spot. "These [were] casualties from our own shells," Lieutenant Reg Dixon recorded in the Glens' daily diary.[25]

The barrage set the château ablaze. As soon as the shelling ceased at 1518 hours, the Chauds started clearing those parts not engulfed in flames. Fighting around the château raged until midnight, the Chauds being engaged there for a total of eleven hours. When the final shots were fired, they counted one hundred casualties, twenty-five fatal.[26]

Still reeling from their friendly artillery losses, the Glens came to a field separating them from Colombelles. From the cover of a wall, they repeatedly tried to go forward, only to be driven back by heavy machine-gun fire. Other Germans crept up close to throw potato-mashers. These made a lot of noise but otherwise caused no harm. The Glens stalled here for almost two hours before Brigadier Ben Cunningham insisted they push the attack home regardless of losses. Private Williams's platoon headed along a road that led through the open field. Williams saw several men fall fatally wounded, but by 1700 hours the Glens had gained the eastern edge of Colombelles.[27] Progress was slow, one pocket of resistance after another needing to be eliminated. Christiansen repeatedly appealed to brigade for tanks but was rebuffed.

Continually urged to make haste, Christiansen had Dixon record the reasons for the delay. Gaining the start line had required a bull-dozer's intervention to clear a path through the rubble created by the bombing. Being shelled by their own medium artillery had thrown the battalion into "confusion and concernment." Then there was the refusal to provide tanks. "As it was, much time was lost, and casualties were heavier" than they should have been.[28]

WHILE THE CHAUDS and Glens had been fighting inside Colombelles, the North Shores had advanced behind an artillery barrage at about 1800 hours. The men were in extended lines, 'B' Company forward to the right and 'D' Company left. 'C' Company and 'A' Company followed, respectively. Buell's tactical headquarters was in the middle. Walking ahead of its carrier, he led it into a small minefield. When a mine detonated beneath a track, a large spring narrowly missed Buell. Although dazed, the carrier's three occupants suffered only scratches.

It was soon apparent that the North Shores had caught the Germans off guard. The North Shores hooked into the vast steelworks. "Some of the enemy had been dazed by the [artillery] and showed little fight," Buell later reported. "But others resisted fiercely, concealing themselves in dug-outs, craters and rubble, and had either to be killed or wounded. To clear the place of such opposition NCOs organized small parties to dislodge snipers and machine-gunners... So gradual and so difficult was the mopping-up process that the area was not clear until 0600 hours the next morning... Even then some sniping activity was heard during the day."[29]

"Take the largest steel mill in Hamilton," Captain H.S. MacDonald wrote, "drop thousands of tons of bombs on it and then shell it and pour infantry through it and do a bit of scrapping—and what have you? Well, we have it. It was a big day for us. We gained a lot but had only a few casualties. I am sitting on rubble, my back against an iron vat, have two days' growth as water is at a premium this side of the river Orne. Looking up and over and sideways you see just masses of twisted iron and concrete rubble, with white dust everywhere, all the men looking like ghosts."[30]

Like the North Shores and the Chauds, the Glens had fought through the night to secure their sector of Colombelles. They had advanced "literally yard by yard, unsupported by armour... and the men were weary. Their food had been only one hardtack biscuit and a single slice of Spam." By 0400 hours on July 19, however, they had secured a start line for the rest of 9th Brigade to push into Vaucelles, where the 7th Brigade's Reginas had already established themselves.

At 1700 hours, Lieutenant Bergeron had led his scouts back across the bridges, just as a covering artillery barrage smothered the east bank of the Orne. A short round killed the guide, Raymond Chatelain. Fifteen minutes later, 'A' and 'B' Companies had begun crossing in a few amphibious trucks (DUKWS).[31] When it became apparent this would be a slow process, most of the men opted to wade or swim across.[32]

The two companies met only light resistance from several machine-gun posts and hidden snipers. Extensive bomb and shell damage made Vaucelles a difficult battlefield. It was also a sprawling, built-up area, with every suspicious rubble pile and still-standing house needing to be searched for hidden Germans. Lieutenant Jack Nelles commanded the flame-thrower platoon. As the carriers could not get across the river, he and his men were fighting as riflemen alongside 'B' Company. Nelles had another Free French volunteer along. Coming upon a stone house, the front yard secured by a high wall, Nelles told a couple of men and the Frenchman to cover him. "I'm going to run across the courtyard and look in the front door...and see if there's anything doing." As he dashed past a window, Nelles spotted a German heading out the back door. Nelles ordered one of his men to break down the front door. Then he led the way through with the Frenchman right on his heels. Reaching the backyard in time to see the last Germans escape over the wall, the Frenchman pushed past Nelles. Before Nelles could caution him, the man jumped up onto the wall, silhouetting himself against the sky. A shot rang out. The man fell backward and crashed through the glass roof of a greenhouse adjacent to the wall. Pulling him free, Nelles saw the man had been shot in the groin.

Yanking out the field dressing that each soldier carried tucked into his helmet netting, Nelles cut the man's pants open and stuffed the dressing into the bullet hole. He then used his belt as a tourniquet to force the dressing deeper into the wound. The man was in bad shape, still bleeding profusely, when he was evacuated. Nelles was surprised to learn later that he survived.[33]

Night was falling by the time 'C' and 'D' Companies joined the leading companies. They had been held up by German artillery and mortar fire that destroyed most of the DUKWs. But by the time the Reginas were mostly intact on the east side of the Orne, at 2100 hours, German resistance in Vaucelles was crumbling. Two hours later, Lieutenant Colonel Foster Matheson established his battalion headquarters across the Orne in a "large dirty house" alongside the riverbank. The Reginas had taken sixty to seventy prisoners. Their own casualties numbered eighteen, three fatal. Captain William Sydney Huckvale, the battalion medical officer, had suffered a serious head wound while treating the wounded by the riverbank. For this and many earlier examples of selfless devotion to his duties, he fixed line. As long as the commanders of guide tanks kept the signal strength steady, the column would be on the correct bearing. If the signal weakened, they were drifting off line.

Additional guidance would be provided by Bofors anti-aircraft guns firing tracer rounds once a minute on fixed lines, inside of which the columns were to advance. Artillery would also fire night marker shells that would eject coloured flares over specific objectives. Taken together, Simonds and his staff believed these aids should keep the columns on course.

True to form, the artillery support would be stunning. Although there would be no preliminary bombardment, once the attack began 312 guns would fire for twenty minutes at identified German artillery batteries. Fifteen minutes later, a massive two-mile-wide rolling barrage would advance at a rate of two hundred yards every two minutes to a depth of three and a half miles beyond the German front lines. A total of 720 guns would support Totalize, and they would fire approximately 200,000 rounds in the first phase alone.

RAF Bomber Command would attack known German defensive concentration areas with high-explosive and fragmentation bombs prior to the first phase. Then the U.S. 8th Air Force would deliver a large-scale attack twelve hours after the opening of Totalize to "pave the way for the armour to crack through the next German line of defence."

At first, Air Chief Marshal Sir Arthur Harris had opposed night bombing for fear of inadvertently dropping ordnance on the advancing Canadian and British troops. It was one thing to carpet-bomb a German city, he said, but quite another to do the same against dark countryside through which thousands of our men were moving. In response, Simonds arranged a demonstration on the night of August 6–7 to prove that coloured artillery shells could mark targets for the master bombers guiding the formations. The bombers flying over the test ground reported they could see their targets clearly and then mark them with flares for the bombers behind.

Totalize had originally been conceived as a three-phase operation. Now, in addition to swapping armoured divisions for infantry in phase one, Simonds got rid of the third phase. He removed 3rd

262 / BREAKOUT FROM JUNO

Infantry Division from its second-phase role and combined the last
two phases. Accordingly, 4th Armoured Division and 1st Polish
Armoured Division would now advance side by side to Falaise. In the
first phase, tanks would advance ahead of the mounted infantry. On
either side of the highway boundary, tanks and infantry would
advance in four columns.

On the right side of the highway, the main force consisted of
three columns, each based upon a single 4th Infantry Brigade battalion. The fourth column was anchored on the 14th Canadian
Hussars reconnaissance regiment. Each column would advance with
vehicles four abreast. At the head would be a heavily armoured "gapping force" comprised of two troops of Shermans, two troops of Flail
tanks, and a troop of engineers from the 79th British Assault Squadron. The engineers would mark the route with tape and lights. The
gapping force was followed by the "assault force." First came tanks,
then the infantry in the Kangaroos, half-tracks, and their battalion's
Bren carriers. Each column would be supported by Toronto Scottish
heavy machine-gun teams, anti-tank guns, and engineers driving
bulldozers. At the rear, a "fortress force" of tanks would secure the
start line for all four columns and protect the other infantry battalions when they advanced on foot.[22]

Brigadier Bob Wyman of 2nd Armoured Brigade had overall
command. A tough, no-nonsense tanker, Wyman had commanded
1st Canadian Armoured Brigade in Italy before a short staff appointment at army headquarters. He had led 2nd Armoured Brigade
ashore on D-Day.

Wyman's force formed up south of Ifs. In the advance, the three
4th Brigade columns would roll up Verrières Ridge in one tightly
grouped "lane" to pass west of Verrières village and then also west of
Rocquancourt. Four thousand yards south of the latter village, the
infantry would dismount far behind the German front. The Essex
Scottish, which formed the right-hand column, would hook west into
Caillouet, while the Royal Hamilton Light Infantry marched dead
ahead to gain a spur running northeast from Bretteville-sur-Laize.
On the left, the Royal Regiment of Canada would strike to the east
and take Gaumesnil alongside the Caen-Falaise highway. Advancing

on a separate axis from Ifs, the 14th Canadian Hussars would hug the highway before hooking across to seize Point 122 just back of Gaumesnil.

Advancing on foot, 6th Infantry Brigade's task was to clear May-sur-Orne, Fontenay-le-Marmion, and Rocquancourt. This brigade would be supported by British Crocodile tanks, 4.2-inch mortars from the Toronto Scottish, and limited artillery. Les Fusiliers Mont-Royal would seize May; the Cameron Highlanders, Fontenay; and Rocquancourt would fall to the South Saskatchewan Regiment. The 5th Infantry Brigade would be in reserve.

In the British sector, the assault force consisted of three battalion groups moving in two lanes that would bypass Tilly-la-Campagne on either flank, leaving it to be cleared by foot infantry. The two groups in the westerly lane would seize Cramesnil and Garcelles-Secqueville, while the more easterly column headed for Saint-Aignan-de-Cramesnil.

Once on their objectives, British and Canadian columns would both provide a firm base through which the two armoured divisions would begin the second phase in the early morning.[23]

TOTALIZE WAS NOW the key component in Montgomery's plan to crush the Germans in Normandy. If successful, the operation would see First Canadian Army gain control of Falaise—closing the many roads running through that hub. Second British Army would meanwhile be forcing the Germans out of the *bocage* country west of the Orne River and up against the Canadians. Once these two armies joined hands—having eliminated any Germans caught between—they would advance towards the Seine River, while the Americans carried out their "long envelopment" to the east. When the Allies linked up at the Seine, they would trap the German armies in Normandy and eliminate them.[24]

Ultra's discovery of Hitler's planned thrust through Mortain to Avranches had enabled General Omar Bradley to set a trap intended to smash the Panzer Divisions. Just after midnight on August 7, the Germans attacked. None of their divisions gained even their first objectives. Although the American 30th Infantry Division was surrounded on Hill 317 east of Mortain, it stoutly repelled repeated counterattacks. With the dawn, fighter-bombers from 83 Group RAF and U.S. 9th Air Force swarmed the skies.[25]

In what became known as "the Day of the Typhoon," the German armoured divisions were decimated in "three hours of uninter-rupted hell." Eighty-one tanks were destroyed and twenty-six abandoned by crews who fled rather than be incinerated in their metal coffins. Hundreds of vehicles, artillery pieces, anti-tank guns, and self-propelled assault guns were destroyed.[26]

Although the German offensive would sputter on for six days, it was effectively lost on August 7. Hitler refused to admit this, forcing its continuance.[27] The decision was disastrous. With the German armoured divisions locked in a hopeless battle on a narrow front, General Patton's U.S. Third Army ran virtually unimpeded to the southeast. The vital supply and tactical centre of Le Mans fell on the evening of August 8. "If only the Germans will go on attacking at Mortain for a few more days it seems that they might not (repeat not) be able to get away," an excited Montgomery signalled London.[28]

It had been Ultra intelligence regarding the German offensive that led to Montgomery's advancing Totalize's timetable to the night of August 7–8. Having taken a pummelling during the day at Mor-tain and under great pressure almost everywhere else along their front, the Germans would suddenly see their east flank being smashed open by the battering ram of 11 Canadian Corps. The entire front might well collapse completely.

There appeared to be little standing in the way. Most of the front was held by a badly strung out 89th Infantry Division with elements of 272nd Infantry Division holding east of La Hogue to Frénouville. Behind the front, a much-reduced 12th ss Division formed the only effective reserve, and it had sent a battle group to join the fight against the British west of the Orne. But the Allies were unaware of the formidable nature of the force that Standartenführer Kurt Meyer had assembled at Bretteville-sur-Laize. Here were stationed thirty-nine Mark IVs of 2nd ss Panzer Battalion; eight operational Tigers from 101st Heavy Panzer Battalion; twenty-seven Panthers; a battal-ion of panzer grenadiers; corps and divisional escort companies; the division's artillery regiment comprised of three battalions, a flak battalion, and elements of III Luftwaffe Flak Corps; and the 83rd Nebelwerfer Regiment. Meyer's anti-tank capability was formidable. He had more than a hundred 88-millimetre and 75-millimetre guns and another hundred artillery pieces of varying calibres.

Meyer had not assembled this force in anticipation of fighting the Canadians. He was preparing to meet the British advance.[29] But Meyer was also warily watching the Canadian front in recognition that he possessed the only reserve capable of intervening if an offensive developed there. "In the event of a renewed Allied attack, the eastern flank of the German front would inevitably cave in and open the way to the interior of France," he wrote. Meyer was under no illusions that the 12th SS could stop such an offensive. He "foresaw the collapse of the German eastern flank and prepared [his men] for [their] last fight."[30]

Recognizing that he would need as much notice as possible, Meyer posted SS liaison officers with the 89th Division. The moment one issued an alert, Meyer would roll eastward from Bretteville.[31]

"DURING THE MORNING, the marshalling and movement of our [armoured] column was practiced in a large field to the west of Louvigny. The column was formed up with four vehicles abreast on a [sixteen-yard] front. A squadron of tanks was in the lead followed by the two forward Rifle Coys who divided the frontage between them," the Royal Regiment's war diarist recorded on August 7. "In other words, each Rifle Coy moved with its vehicles two-abreast with another Rifle Coy moving in similar formation alongside. Our own supporting weapons and [anti-tank] guns were distributed through the column, but no soft vehicles were included. The column practiced movement in this formation, and also practiced...dispersal to an imaginary...objective where the troops jumped off the Priests [Kangaroos] and took up their positions. This rehearsal was completed quite satisfactorily, and the troops returned to the [battalion] area for lunch."[32]

At 1700 hours, the Royals boarded the Kangaroos and an hour later joined the other 4th Brigade columns outside Ifs. Between each column was a fifty-yard gap. This great mustering was a spectacular sight. Sergeant C.W. Wilson, a 14th Hussars carrier section leader near the head of that regiment's column, wrote: "When we arrived at our assembly area all that could be seen for miles around were great masses of tanks, equipment and men, all waiting for zero hour."[33]

"From the windows of the château at Cormelles," added 2nd Canadian Armoured Brigade's war diarist, "it was possible to see the vast [formations] of armour and [armoured infantry] drawn up in the final assembly area in preparation for the night break-through. Despite the dust raised...no concentration of German arty [artillery] fire was brought down upon the densely concentrated [formations]."[34] The Canadians alone were jammed into an area covering four square miles.[35]

Although there was an appearance of clockwork precision, 2nd Armoured Brigade staff officers fretted. When the 79th Armoured Division specialized units trickled in haphazardly and off schedule, their anxiety grew. Then an anti-tank battery appeared in the wrong place "just a few hours before the attack." These late arrivals "seriously handicapped" training.[36]

By 2200 hours, the entire force was "awaiting the signal to advance." At 2230 hours—just as the first Bomber Command wave struck—Wyman ordered the gapping force forward. A few minutes later the assault columns rolled. "The weather was warm, dusty and somewhat cloudy but not cloudy enough to prevent the force from seeing the tracer shells fired by the bofors guns. The entire area was lighted somewhat by means of artificial moonlight and after [fifteen] minutes of progress the dust raised by the steel columns was such that it was hardly possible to see the [vehicle] ahead. [Vehicles] accordingly turned on tail lights which made following much easier. At 2340 hours brilliant flashes in the sky to right and left flanks ahead of us indicated that the [heavy] bombing programme was in progress. At 2359 [hours] the [column] had passed the start line," 2nd Brigade's war diarist recorded.[37]

A TOTAL OF 1,019 heavy bombers streamed across the French coast at 2300 hours. Canadian artillery marked the western targets with green flare shells, while the British indicated the eastern ones with red shells. The raid lasted forty minutes. To Simonds the explosions seemed "like the worst thunderstorm" ever seen. As the bombing ended and the 720 artillery pieces began firing at 2345 hours, Simonds realized events were now out of his hands. The columns were advancing. Phase one of Operation Totalize would succeed or fail on the merits of his plan. Appreciating that there would likely be many decisions required come morning, Simonds went to bed.

Bomber Command had hoped winds would clear the smoke and dust raised by the lead bombers so those at the rear could see the marking flares. But there was hardly a breeze, and the master bombers at the tail ordered their squadrons to turn about without dropping any bombs. In all, 642 bombers dropped 3,456 tons of high-explosive and fragmentation bombs.[38] Even as the bombs were falling, Crerar signalled Harris at Bomber Command: "Timing and accuracy of tonight's . . . heavy bombers now in progress reported one hundred per cent. Greatly appreciate outstanding contribution your Command. We shall hope to continue and complete this battle as well as you have commenced it."

Harris signalled back, "Thanks for message. Regret lack of wind and accumulating smoke made it unsafe to put down last third of tonnage on each objective but hope two thirds will do the trick. Don't be shy of asking. Good luck."[39]

Crerar's report was mistaken. Although the bombing in the eastern zone largely fell on target, this was not the case to the west. Most bombs directed at May-sur-Orne exploded harmlessly in adjacent fields. Fontenay-le-Marmion suffered slight damage, while the majority of bombs obliterated the tactically irrelevant little hamlet of La Val about a half-mile westward.[40]

19

The Fullest Success

"**N**O ONE WHO was present that night is likely to forget the eerie sight of the great rumbling columns pushing relentlessly into the darkness," wrote the Royal Regiment's historian. "Overhead anti-aircraft tracers were being fired in lanes on either side of the lumbering vehicles; great red flares burned in the bombed villages on the flanks; green marker shells fell on the high ground at Point 122 to identify the divisional boundary, artificial moonlight gave a weird luminescence to the scene; and on all sides could be seen the innumerable pin-points of ineffective small arms fire from the bewildered enemy. Before long, as the Germans began spasmodically shelling and mortaring, burning tanks were blazing brightly throughout the area, and knocked-out vehicles were passed. The air was filled with clouds of dust churned up from the dry ground, and a low mist, thickened with smoke shells fired by the German guns, further reduced visibility."[1]

Once past the start line, each column increased its speed to five miles per hour. Out front, gapping forces maintained a five-hundred-yard lead to give the engineers time to lay their tape and plant the illuminated guidance markers.[2]

It was "pitch black and the Flails were raising a terrific dust," Sergeant C.W. Wilson of the 14th Hussars' 'B' Squadron wrote. The reconnaissance regiment's troops had swapped their armoured cars for half-tracks and would fight as infantry. "Every 150 yards, a green light was placed on the right of the line and a red light on the left...At midnight we were in the thick of it. The noise was deafening, artillery machine guns and vehicle motors combined into a crescendo of sound. A tank on our right went up in a burst of flame and then another to our front."[3]

The tanks were from Fort Garry Horse's 'C' Squadron, and their losses occurred as the column passed east of Rocquancourt and made for Point 122.[4] Then one of the eighteen half-tracks was blocked by an anti-tank ditch. Backing up a short distance, the driver gunned the accelerator and jumped the vehicle across. Enemy fire soon knocked out five half-tracks, and the advance "bogged down." Major Donald J. Scott, 'B' Squadron's commander, "jumped out of his vehicle and [directed] the troops to dig-in. While doing so he was caught in a burst of machine-gun fire and...killed."[5]

Lieutenant Colonel Bruce Alway thought his column almost on Point 122, but it was barely past Rocquancourt and just north of Lorguichon, a small mining village.[6] Alway's confusion was not unique—every column commander struggled to reconcile ground features and landmarks with those marked on maps. When the men started digging, their shovels and picks chunked into hard chalk. It took the sweat-soaked Hussars until 0600 hours to carve out slit trenches three feet deep.[7]

The wireless directional system proved of mixed worth. In the British sector the signals mostly failed, while the magnetic compasses in the tanks twirled around like tops due to disturbances caused by the bombing and shelling.[8]

Sherbrooke Fusiliers' Captain Merritt Hayes Bateman was guiding the centre Royal Hamilton Light Infantry column. Wounded on June 7, Bateman had drawn this duty the day he returned from hospital in England. Despite his having had only three nights to familiarize himself with the system, the entire column now counted on his navigational skills. As the column crossed over Verrières Ridge and descended the southern slope, the wireless signal weakened and each dot or dash seemed to come later than the last. Yet Bateman thought the column still on course and nearing Rocquancourt after a three-and-a-half-mile advance.[9] When the centre column drove straight into the village rather than skirting it to the west, Bateman realized he had drifted slightly off course.

The Rileys had actually enjoyed a remarkably smooth advance. Despite coming under small-arms fire upon crossing the ridge, they suffered no vehicle losses or casualties until two Kangaroos became stuck in bomb craters. The infantry aboard, however, crammed in with the passengers of other Kangaroos.

When the tanks and Kangaroos clattered onto the cobbled streets and lanes of Rocquancourt, the formation became scattered. They were also fired on by an 88-millimetre gun hidden on the southern outskirts. After a few inaccurate shots, however, the gun switched its attention to the Essex Scottish Regiment column passing to the west.[10]

As the Bren carrier bearing 4th Field Regiment's Captain Len Harvey—the FOO attached to the Rileys—entered the village, its driver turned up a lane and lost touch with the column. Suddenly, both sides of the carrier were scraping against what Harvey thought were buildings. An out-put hand came to rest on cold steel instead of brick. In the faint light, Harvey realized he was "patting a German hash-mark cross on the side of a tank!" But its crew seemed unaware of the carrier's presence as it slunk off "undetected into the swirling dust and smoke of the flashing, roaring night."[11]

The 88-millimetre gun switching its attention to the Essex Scottish was just the latest woe to beset their advance. Smoke, dust, and thickening ground mist had caused the assault column to lose sight of the gapping force. Then 'A' Company, the leading infantry unit, lost touch with the tanks at the head of the assault column. Major Stewart Bull was unable to contact the tanks by wireless. Nor could Lieutenant Colonel Thomas Jones, and by 0130 hours the Essex had no wireless links to any other units in the column.[12]

Blundering forward by fits and starts, the column was subjected during each pause to increasingly accurate mortar and small-arms fire from the flanks. By the time the column reached Rocquancourt, it had split in two. Just before the village, 'A' company reconnected with the leading tanks, and this group passed to the west and made towards the objective of Caillouet. The following group drove into the 88-millimetre gun's sights. Several half-tracks and tanks were knocked out. Attempting to escape its fire, other vehicles and tanks collided. One platoon jumped out of its half-tracks to attack the gun but was driven back by protective machine guns. Then Jones was wounded and went missing. The second-in-command, Major J.W. Burgess, attempted to restore order by dismounting the infantry, while the officers regrouped the vehicles west of the village. Not until 0327 hours could Burgess report to 4th Brigade headquarters that things were under control. Uncertain of his location, Burgess went into the village seeking signage. He found the South Saskatchewan Regiment instead and was informed they had just arrived and were clearing Rocquancourt without difficulty. They were also caring for Jones.[13]

Burgess now knew that his battalion was about three thousand yards west of its objective. Returning to the column, he counted fourteen half-tracks knocked out or missing. All the tanks, save one Flail, had disappeared. Two self-propelled anti-tank guns were destroyed.[14] During his absence, 'A' Company had rejoined the column. During the separation, however, Major Bull had suffered a serious facial wound.[15] Burgess decided to wait for daybreak in the hope that some tanks might be found before then.[16]

The Rileys, meanwhile, had earlier shaken out of Rocquancourt to continue towards their objective—a spur, identified as Point 46, that stood next to a large quarry. When scouts reported German tanks on the hilltop, Lieutenant Colonel Graham Maclachlan—who had replaced Rocky Rockingham—decided against a night attack. Instead, he deployed the infantry in a network of abandoned German trenches two hundred yards north of the quarry and surrounded them with the tanks and other vehicles.[17]

On the main assault group's left flank, the Royal Regiment had also become disoriented during the advance, with 'B' Company ending up tagging along behind the Rileys. Further confusion ensued after a shell killed 'C' Company's Major Thomas John MacArthur.[18] Passing to the east, rather than west of Rocquancourt, the Royals were by 0430 hours "concentrated in the low ground between the railway tracks and Point 122." Hoping to beat the dawn, Lieutenant Colonel Jock Anderson ordered 'A' Company onto the summit with 'D' Company following. Mounted on their Kangaroos, the two companies drove through without incident. By 0600 hours the entire column, less 'B' Company, was firmly ensconced on Point 122.[19]

BEHIND THE MOBILE columns, 6th Infantry Brigade had advanced the traditional way—on foot.[20] Lieutenant General Guy Simonds had confidently assured Brigadier Young that May-sur-Orne and Fontenay-le-Marmion should fall easily to a single battalion once they were "obliterated" by the bombers. Consequently, Simonds offered no tanks or artillery to support attacks on these villages. Nine Crocodile flame-throwers of British 141st Armoured Regiment would be available.[21]

On the brigade's left flank, the Sasks had begun the mile-long descent on Rocquancourt as soon as the 14th Canadian Hussars column had passed them by.[22] Due to the swirling smoke and dust, they advanced almost blindly. Private Charles "Chic" Goodman had joined the battalion after its near destruction during Operation Atlantic. Having lied about his age during enlistment, Goodman had just turned eighteen. He carried a rifle in 'B' Company and found the night attack eerie. The dust was choking. Sometimes artificial moonlight broke through and bathed the ground in a ghostly light. Tracer rounds from the Bofors flicked unexpectedly overhead. The heat was dreadful. And there was the smell. The putrid stench of the rotting flesh of dead soldiers, horses, and cows littering Verrières Ridge was almost overwhelming.[23]

Inside the village, the Sasks found no Germans. Instead, the place was milling with confused Essex Scottish, who told them the Rileys had already come and gone.[24] As Lieutenant Colonel Fred Clift assigned his men to defensive positions, he was struck in the back by shrapnel from a stray German artillery round. Figuring the Germans would counterattack in the morning, Clift refused evacuation.

Because the RAF bombardment barely touched either May or Fontenay, it became quickly evident that both remained formidable bastions. The Fusiliers attacked May with only about forty men in every company. Just beyond the start line they came under heavy artillery fire. Half the men in 'B' Company went to ground, leaving Captain Georges Bregent with only about twenty by the time he reached May. Dividing this force into two groups, Bregent led one up the main street. Fifty yards past the first house a machine gun opened fire, and Bregent, his batman, and the Bren gunner were killed. "The remainder withdrew in disorder." 'B' Company's other section had taken cover in a shell hole twenty yards short of the first house. There it stayed until the lieutenant in command was wounded at 0530 hours and ordered a withdrawal.

Lieutenant Colonel "Guy" Gauvreau decided to try again, using stealth. While 'A' and 'B' Companies would draw German attention by advancing up the road, 'C' and 'D' Companies would sneak into the village from the left flank. 'C' Company led off with just thirty-five men. Creeping silently through the darkness, the men were caught in machine-gun fire from both flanks just outside of May. They were just about to charge when a German officer "was observed going around [and] putting his sleepy men on the alert." With the Germans shouldering weapons, 'C' Company quickly withdrew. The battalion fell back to Saint-André, where it spent the morning of August 8 under heavy mortar and artillery fire.[25]

As the Fusiliers had advanced on May, the Queen's Own Cameron Highlanders had made for Fontenay-le-Marmion. The battalion advanced from west of Saint-André. Fontenay was three thousand yards distant. Between stood Saint-Martin-de-Fontenay and the large mine complex. Again the bombers had mostly missed the village. The Germans were well dug in and alert. The Camerons advanced in a T-formation, with 'C' and 'D' Companies up front and 'B' Company trailing.[26] Each company fielded between sixty and seventy men.[27]

Ten minutes into the advance, several machine guns lashed the leading companies. Although blinded by smoke, dust, and ground mist, the Camerons were able to keep direction by following a poplar-lined road. But the road and its verges were sown with mines and had been registered by German mortar crews and artillery batteries. Casualties mounted, while other men elected to go to ground or became disoriented and lost. The battalion was still short of Fontenay when its new commander, Lieutenant Colonel John Runcie, was wounded.[28]

Wireless communication back to 6th Brigade was spotty, which delayed this news from reaching Young. When he did hear, Young dispatched his brigade major, Major Clarence William Ferguson—a long-standing Cameron officer—to take over.[29]

'B' Company, meanwhile, was under constant fire from Germans bypassed by the leading companies. Halfway to Fontenay, Lieutenant N.J. Burnside's platoon was suddenly confronted by Germans charging out of the darkness. The men met them with rifles, Stens, and Brens blazing. After several attempts to overrun the company, the Germans withdrew. Struggling on, 'B' Company came under a "huge amount of enemy resistance, at least [five] German machine-gun posts and a lot of infantry" anchored on a quarry pit. "It was a running battle for quite some time," Burnside later reported, with a direct attack on the quarry required to quell this opposition.[30]

When No. 11 Platoon's commander was killed just short of Fontenay, Sergeant James Mahon took over. His men pinned down by the machine-gun and small-arms fire, Mahon crawled off alone and outflanked the German position. Chucking two grenades into the machine-gun position, he killed the crew and then led the platoon through to the village. For this action, Mahon was awarded a Military Medal.[31]

Much reduced, 'B' Company pushed into the village, and newly promoted Major J.E.E. McManus was relieved to find remnants of 'D' and 'C' Companies also there.[32] The three companies were so depleted, their commanders agreed they could only hang on to the north end of the village with a defence centred on the church.[33]

Taking advantage of the semi-darkness, still lingering smoke, and mist, Major Ferguson—who had arrived at about 0500 hours—slipped the support company through to Fontenay. This gave the Camerons a full complement of anti-tank guns and 3-inch mortars, plus ten carriers. The carrier crews removed the Bren guns and spread out alongside the infantry. By first light, the Camerons had a strong toehold within Fontenay.[34]

ALTHOUGH THE GERMANS had anticipated an attack east of the Orne River, they had not expected a night attack preceded by an aerial and artillery bombardment.[35] As one German report concluded,

Operation Totalize occurred so suddenly that 89th Infantry Division was "overrun. A few German bases still held, but the [division's troops] stampeded and fled the majority of their bases."

The stampede isolated elements holding at places such as May-sur-Orne, Fontenay-le-Marmion, and Tilly-la-Campagne. (In Tilly, the British engaged in a bloody firefight that sucked in two battalions and an armoured regiment before the defenders were subdued on August 8.) Where the division stood firm, it fought well and inflicted heavy casualties.

And the 12th ss "reacted immediately. It advanced, quickly occupied some hills and villages, and launched short counter attacks."[36] This was in large part due to Standartenführer Kurt Meyer reading the situation rapidly and correctly. The moment he heard bombs and shells exploding, Meyer had rushed from his headquarters and seen that the entire "front was on fire!"

After recalling the 12th ss Kampfgruppe (battle group) from west of the Orne River, Meyer jumped into his *Kubelwagen* and raced forward. At Bretteville-sur-Laize he conferred with the 89th Division's commander, General der Infanterie Konrad Heinrichs, who reported that the bombardment had cut all communication lines to the front. Meyer construed that the division "was as good as destroyed. Only a few individual strongpoints were still intact; they were like islands in the stream of battle, giving the attacking Canadians a hot reception time and again."[37]

Seeking a clearer picture, Meyer headed to a rise just north of Cintheaux and next to the Caen-Falaise highway. "I got out of my car and my knees were trembling, the sweat was pouring down my face, and my clothes were soaked with perspiration. It was not that I was particularly anxious for myself because my experiences of the last five years had inured me against fear of death, but I realized that if I failed now and if I did not deploy my division correctly, the Allies would be through to Falaise and the German armies in the west trapped. I knew how weak my division was and the task which confronted me gave me ... the worst moments I ever had in my life."

Meyer saw groups of 89th Division fleeing down the road below. He ordered his driver to head north towards Caen, the vehicle pushing through the stream of panicked soldiers. Suddenly, artillery struck, killing many men on the road. As the smoke thinned, Meyer got out of his car and stood alone. On either side of the road, men fled southward. Meyer "calmly lit a cigarette, stood in the middle of the road and in a loud voice asked them if they were going to leave [him] alone to cope with the Allied attack." Reorganizing some of this rabble, Meyer ordered Cintheaux held at all costs. He needed to buy time for his 12th Division to arrive.[38]

Meyer next raced to Urville, south of Bretteville, to confer with Obersturmbannführer Wilhelm Mohnke, who commanded 12th Division's 26th Panzer-Grenadier Regiment. Mohnke said the Germans still held Garcelles-Secqueville, but British tanks were reportedly in Saint-Aignan-de-Cramesnil to the south of Garcelles. Who controlled Rocquancourt or May-sur-Orne was unclear.

At Mohnke's headquarters, Meyer, Heinrichs, and General der Panzertruppen Hans Eberbach, commander of 5th Panzer Army (formerly Panzer Group West), decided next moves. Restoring the line was not possible. All Meyer could suggest was blocking the two routes logically leading to Falaise. One of these was directly down the Caen-Falaise highway; the other ran east through open country from Saint-Aignan to Falaise. Meyer proposed that his division block these routes as far to the north as possible.[39] His ss troops would win time to allow the 85th Infantry Division and 9th ss Panzer Division's Panther battalion to come forward and reinforce them.[40] Agreeing, Eberbach ordered the plan put into action.

MEYER'S BELIEF THAT the 89th Division had collapsed was ill founded. Although many troops "stampeded," more stood their ground during the terrifying night. With the morning, those bypassed came to life—either firing from slit trenches and dugouts or counterattacking. Germans driven from positions during the night's fighting attempted to regain lost ground. Little of the 89th's artillery or mortar strength had been destroyed. With daylight, the gun crews could see targets and began firing at the Canadian and British forces at a terrific rate. Later estimates determined that about 50 per cent of the division regrouped into fighting units during the morning. The division's fusiliers battalion also remained fully intact at Bretteville-sur-Laize. These units were supported by tanks and self-propelled guns, including some 12th ss armour that had arrived.[41]

This sudden resistance by a division supposedly swept away by the massive bombardment presented 2nd Division's Major General Charles Foulkes with no end of challenges. All his forward battalions were either being counterattacked or struggling to wrest final objectives from a defiant enemy.

The early morning situation remained confused. Wireless communication was spotty, and commanders were having trouble getting a clear grasp on the situation. Sherbrooke Fusiliers' commander, Lieutenant Colonel Mel Gordon, wanted to form his tanks at Rocquancourt and punch down the highway to Falaise. He was convinced nothing stood in the way.[42] Before Gordon could raise the idea with Brigadier Bob Wyman, however, the 2nd Armoured Brigade commander was shot in the arm by a sniper at 0615. Wyman retained command until Lieutenant Colonel John Bingham arrived at 0730 to take over.[43] Gordon later asserted that he had asked Wyman's permission to charge for Falaise. Wyman refused. Their orders, he said, were to establish a firm base through which 4th Canadian Armoured Division would advance for the second phase of Operation Totalize.

Given the German forces in front of, behind, and on all flanks, Wyman's decision was wise. Besides the fact that none of the tanks had sufficient fuel or ammunition for such a venture, a bold charge would have kicked open a hornet's nest of opposition. Gordon could not even arrange Wyman's evacuation until about 1300 hours because the route back was under such thick German fire.[44]

Winning first-phase objectives remained Wyman's primary concern until he was evacuated. With the Essex Scottish still separated from their supporting tanks, he ordered the 14th Canadian Hussars to cross the front from near Point 122 and seize Caillouet.[45] The reconnaissance troops attempted to comply, but by 0845 hours reported still being a thousand yards northeast of Rocquancourt and reduced to 140 men. They were meeting steady resistance and were stalemated.[46]

Major Burgess, meanwhile, had started the Essex Scottish towards the village. He had two anti-tank guns in support, a self-propelled M-10, and a towed 17-pounder. As the column closed on Caillouet, Burgess "saw four tanks on a crest in front of the objective" and called a halt. The anti-tank gun crews identified a Panther and refused to engage the tanks, "as such action might endanger their weapons." A few minutes later, a 4th Brigade signal warned that eight enemy tanks were about five hundred yards south of his position. Although these tanks were quickly re-identified as British Churchills, the incident made Burgess wary. Even when the four German tanks withdrew, he kept the column in place for the rest of the morning, while brigade sent ever-conflicting reports. "It was variously reported that our own tanks were on the objective, the [14th Hussars] were on the objective, that none of our own troops were on the objective and that nothing was known about the objective," the Essex war diarist wrote.[47]

Finally, an exasperated Foulkes ordered the Essex Scottish to attack without dismounting and sent a squadron of Sherbrooke Fusiliers to support them. At 1300 hours, Burgess advanced. The half-tracks ground forward with the men hunkering behind the armoured sides to escape the heavy rifle and machine-gun fire from Germans hidden in slit trenches along the route. As the Essex Scots entered Caillouet, the Germans retreated out the other side. Burgess thought they had been "frightened off by our half-tracks." By 1330 hours, the village was in their hands. Neither a living nor dead German was found.[48] Despite the travails that had beset the Essex, its casualties were only three men killed and seventeen wounded.[49]

While the Essex had been on the offensive, their sister battalions in 4th Brigade spent the morning of August 9 fending off counter-attacks. Having stopped the Royal Hamilton Light Infantry a couple of hundred yards north of the quarry and Point 46, Lieutenant Colonel Graham Maclachlan had got his men well dug in before daybreak. Mustered around the Rileys were the Shermans of Major Sydney Radley-Walters's 'A' Squadron and several 2nd Canadian Anti-Tank Regiment anti-tank guns. When the ground mist lifted at about 0800 hours, the Germans struck with a force consisting of eight to ten tanks and self-propelled guns (SPGs) followed by infantry. A sharp tank fight ensued. Two enemy tanks and one SPG were quickly destroyed in exchange for a Sherman lost, one damaged, and an M-10 of the anti-tank regiment knocked out. The remaining German armour and infantry hurriedly withdrew.[50]

From their vantage atop Point 122, the Royals had greeted the dawn by looking northward and being "disconcerted to realize the extent of the observation that had been enjoyed by the Germans. From the hazy spires of Caen on the horizon, through Verrières and Rocquancourt, a broad expanse of exposed terrain fell away to the north with all the detail of a sand table or an air photograph. Every move the Royals had made for the past month had been plainly visible to the enemy."

The battalion was counterattacked while still digging in at 0830 hours. Four enemy tanks charged up the highway towards Point 122, while another group approached from Cramesnil, about a half-mile to the east. One Panther broke through the perimeter defence and closed to within yards of battalion headquarters. A Toronto Scottish machine-gun platoon supporting the Royals had its carriers blown to pieces or set ablaze. The Royals' mortar platoon also lost its carriers. Exploding ammunition and mortar bombs aboard the carriers added to the confusion. Only the timely intervention of some nearby Canadian tanks saved the situation. After the tanks reduced two Panthers and two Tigers to flaming wrecks, the Germans broke off the attack.[51]

Thereafter, the Germans subjected the Canadian positions five miles behind their former main resistance line to sporadic artillery and mortar fire. Since the beginning of Totalize, the Royals had lost only three men killed and twenty-five wounded. The Rileys counted just one man dead and fourteen wounded.[52]

As a 2nd Brigade report concluded, the use of mobilized columns had enabled the Allies to advance "more than five miles through strong enemy def[ences]...with the absolute minimum of [casualties]." But the author's enthusiasm for this "novel use" of tanks and infantry in armoured carriers was tempered by the knowledge that operations of "this type can be of the fullest success, but could equally well have been a complete and utter failure either through loss of direction or enemy counter-action. Such a force has little offensive power in the dark and this method of employing [tanks] should be used only with the greatest circumspection."[53]

THE UNORTHODOX OPERATION unquestionably saved Canadian and British lives while breaking a previously impregnable line. Even though the tough ss troops that had defended it during Goodwood and Spring had been replaced by the weaker 89th Infantry Division, standard, infantry-based offensives here would likely have been defeated. The 6th Brigade and British battalions that had assaulted on foot suffered heavier casualties than any of the mobile column units. Only 6th Brigade's Saskatchewan Rifle Regiment fared well, but they had benefited from following the same route as a preceding armoured column.

The other two 6th Brigade battalions faced continuing stubborn resistance. Although the Queen's Own Cameron Highlanders had a solid toehold inside Fontenay-le-Marmion, they spent the day surrounded by German tanks and under machine-gun fire from the southern part of the village. During an Orders Group at about 0900 hours, a shell landed in the farmyard, and Major Ferguson fell mortally wounded. The support company commander, battalion adjutant, and anti-tank platoon commander, as well as the artillery FOO supporting the battalion were all injured by shell splinters. With the wireless sets disabled, the Camerons lost all contact with brigade.[54]

The FOO's assistant, Bombardier Peter Lancelot Pearce, survived unscathed. Snatching up his still-intact wireless, Pearce ran to an adjacent building. From here he directed artillery fire that helped the Camerons stave off ensuing counterattacks. He was also able to establish a link for the Camerons to brigade by passing messages through 6th Field Regiment's headquarters. Pearce alerted Brigadier Young to the fact that the Camerons were hanging on by a thread. Pearce's steadiness would earn a Distinguished Conduct Medal.[55]

As soon as Ferguson fell, Major J.E.E. McManus of 'B' Company took command before also being wounded by a sniper. So many officers were down that 'B' Company was led by Company Sergeant

Major Abram Arbour. When the Germans threatened to overrun 'B' Company's position, Arbour gathered the company headquarters section and No. 10 Platoon to carry out a counterthrust. Finding themselves under attack, the Germans panicked and were either killed or captured. Arbour led the company through the long day's fighting. His skilled leadership was deemed "directly responsible for the battalion holding and consolidating the objective." In a highly unusual gesture, Arbour was awarded a Military Cross—normally reserved for officers.[56]

Young, meanwhile, had sent his new brigade major, Major George Hees, driving forward with instructions to direct the first tanks encountered towards Fontenay. Young also ordered the South Saskatchewans' Lieutenant Colonel Clift to send men to relieve the pressure on the Camerons. Hees happened across Major D'Arcy Marks of the 1st Hussars and led 'C' Squadron to Rocquancourt. Here the tankers married up with two companies of infantry. Still ignoring his shrapnel wound, Clift climbed onto Marks's Sherman while the infantry started marching. Suddenly, Marks spotted a large force of German infantry about six to eight hundred yards distant on the southern skyline. Advancing twenty yards, Marks opened up with his machine guns. As he sprayed the entire field, Germans began popping up to surrender. Leaving the prisoners to the two Saskatchewan companies not joining the march to Fontenay, 'C' Squadron went to the rescue of the Camerons.[57]

The rescue force circled in from the north and cleared the slopes of Verrières Ridge, which broke the siege in Fontenay. By noon, the counterattacks were lessening. With the tanks and Saskatchewan troops ranging the countryside around Fontenay, the Camerons easily secured the village. Both battalions started reeling in prisoners as the 89th Division began losing its fighting spirit. The Camerons had four hundred prisoners by mid-afternoon.

As the crisis in Fontenay passed, Les Fusiliers Mont-Royal formed for another attempt on May-sur-Orne. The Fusiliers, Major J.M.P. Brochu later wrote, were "now seriously depleted." But they had support from four Crocodile flame-throwing tanks and that boosted morale. 'C' and 'D' Companies, with a combined total of sixty men, were to advance down the right side of the road from Saint-André, while the ninety men of 'A' and 'B' Companies would be to the left.

The Fusiliers counted on the Crocodiles to break the Germans. Although fitted with a flame projector, these adapted Churchills still retained 75-millimetre guns and machine guns. This gave them substantial firepower and flexibility. The fuel for the flame-thrower was towed behind in a trailer and piped along the underside of the tank to the projector.

Two infantry sections moved closely behind each Crocodile. "As the tank approached a house it would fire, knock a hole in the house, then squirt the liquid flame into the opening thus created. Immediately the section directly behind...would dash for the doorway and clear the house as quickly as possible," Brochu wrote. "This sounds very dangerous but the fire once ignited is not dangerous. The thing to beware of is getting in the path of the flame thrower itself for everything touched by the liquid is ignited. The tank meanwhile moves [forward] down the line to a second house." In this way, the two sections leapfrogged forward.

The companies on the right soon reached the church in the centre of May and realized the Germans had fled rather than deal with the Crocodiles. To the left, with fewer buildings to clear, the Crocodiles contented themselves with setting fire to the "few trees remaining in the battle-scarred orchards." By the time the Fusiliers and Crocodiles were finished, most of May was on fire, and "the buildings blazed all night and some...continued to burn all the next day," Brochu reported. The Fusiliers were elated by how easily they had won this round. "The infantry were not disturbed by the problem of having to clear houses ablaze, but were very glad to have such effective [support] even at the cost of a lot of extra sweat." Better sweat than blood.[58]

When heads were counted, the Fusiliers were surprised to find that casualties had been relatively light: eight men killed and seventeen wounded. Clearly, a significant number of men had gone to ground—a fact indicative of how worn out 6th Brigade's battalions were. The South Saskatchewans were harder hit, with sixteen men killed and forty-two wounded. Worst off were the Camerons, who lost thirty dead and ninety-six wounded.[59] But 6th Brigade had finally broken the German hold on the fortified villages along the Orne, and this win meant that the second phase of Operation Totalize could begin.

20

Many Anxious Moments

NEITHER MAJOR GENERAL George Kitching nor Major General
Stanislaw Maczek agreed with Lieutenant General Guy
Simonds's plan to combine the final two phases of Operation Totalize. Kitching was particularly concerned about the insistence that
each division attack on a narrow, thousand-yard front. When they
asked for wider frontages, Simonds refused. He envisioned a narrow,
mailed fist punching through to Falaise. Kitching feared that instead
the Germans would be free to concentrate and block their divisions.
Both generals also opposed the long pause between phases. Simonds
held firm.[1]

Ultra decryptions still mistakenly situated 1st ss Panzer Division
holding a line crossing the Caen-Falaise highway at Cintheaux. This
misinformation reinforced Simonds's determination to advance the
armoured divisions side by side.[2] Correctly, Simonds knew that 12th
ss Panzer Division lurked somewhere north of Falaise and that 89th
Infantry Division remained potent—particularly its heavy artillery.
Consequently, the scheduled bomber strike remained essential to
his plan.

The changed plan had presented Kitching with a logistical nightmare that had to be resolved in little more than twenty-four hours.
All objectives were reassigned, brigade centre lines changed and narrowed, assembly areas relocated, and everything carefully woven into
a new design where no operational detail was left unmended.

Maczek, his Polish counterpart, had to not only prepare a new plan but move the Poles across the Orne, then through the congested rear areas of 11 Canadian Corps, and assemble them east of the Caen-Falaise highway behind 51st (Highland) Division. The highway served as the divisional boundary. Both divisions would advance from a road connecting Bretteville-sur-Laize to Saint-Aignan-de-Cramesnil. Running down the centre of the Canadian advance line, a railway paralleled the highway. It ran alternately along fifteen-foot-high embankments and through deep cuttings. Half a mile west of the highway, the ground sloped steeply to the wooded valley bordering the Laize River. The Canadian objectives were a series of hills between the highway and the river, six to seven miles south of the start line.[3] The Poles had two sets of objectives—Point 140 to the south of Estrées-la-Campagne and thereafter Points 170 and 159 overlooking Falaise.[4]

Neither Maczek nor Kitching had previously led an armoured division into battle. But Maczek was more experienced. Born in 1892, he had first seen military service during the 1920–1922 Polish-Bolshevik War. When the Germans invaded Poland, Maczek commanded 10th Armoured Cavalry Brigade. With Poland's defeat, Maczek fled to France and re-formed the brigade from expatriates before fleeing again to Britain in 1940. After two years commanding the armoured brigade, he was promoted to command 1st Polish Armoured Division.[5]

Maczek's English was poor, so he often fell back on French. Kitching served as translator, although he suspected Simonds understood more French than he let on. In Kitching's opinion, Simonds used this ruse to allow him time to muster arguments he could then deploy to dismiss Maczek's concerns and opinions.[6]

Born on September 19, 1910, in Canton, China, Kitching had trained at Sandhurst before being commissioned into the British army. He served through the late 1920s and 1930s in Singapore, Malaya, and India before resigning his commission to move to Canada in 1938. With the war, he joined the Royal Canadian Regiment and went overseas in 1939. A slender man with a handlebar moustache and clipped British accent, Kitching had more experience with staff postings than with line units. He had risen rapidly on the staff track to the post of general staff officer, 1st grade, of 1st Infantry Division and served under Simonds during the Sicily invasion. In October 1943, he was promoted to brigadier and command of 5th Armoured Division's 11th Infantry Brigade. He returned to Britain in March 1944 to take over 4th Armoured Division.[7]

Kitching had brought along a core group of Italian campaign veterans to fill key positions. Brigadier Jim Jefferson, previously commander of the Loyal Edmonton Regiment, headed up 10th Infantry Brigade, while Brigadier Leslie Booth took over the 4th Armoured Brigade. Brigadier J.N. "Herm" Lane controlled the division's artillery. Kitching also leavened through the division a small coterie of tank and infantry majors from Italy.[8] Although this gave 4th Armoured Division some combat-experienced officers, the division still had never fought a battle. The same was true for the Poles.

On the morning of August 8, Kitching and Maczek were again of one mind and opposing Simonds. They wanted the air bombardment scrapped so their divisions could advance the moment they reached the start line. Kitching even invoked Lieutenant General Harry Crerar. "Whatever you do in this attack, don't let the enemy get away, keep pushing, push, keep the mobility. Don't stop," Crerar had earlier insisted. Kitching thought it foolish not to advance until 1400 hours. "Why do we have to wait before going forward?" he asked. Simonds cited his certainty that 1st SS Panzer Division held a strong line that must be broken by bombing. Until the air force struck, there could be no advance.[9]

As it turned out, Kitching and Maczek could not have advanced immediately, because 2nd Canadian Infantry Division and the 51st (Highland) Division were still fighting for final objectives that morning. As a result, 4th Canadian Armoured Brigade made only slow progress through terrific congestion to a position in front of Ifs, while 10th Infantry Brigade similarly moved to a concentration area between Fleury-sur-Orne and Ifs. This put 4th Division about four miles north of its start line.

By mid-morning, the division's artillery reconnaissance teams were working their way forward to scout allocated gun positions between Verrières and Rocquancourt.[10] "After a sleepless night," wrote the 23rd Field Regiment (Self-Propelled) official historian, "the recce parties [headed] for a deployment area south of Rocquancourt. As they inched along the road the first grim scenes of death met their eye—smashed equipment, battered buildings, sunblacked bodies of Germans and British and Canadians who would fight no more and now lay side by side in the silent comradeship of death. No matter how one prepares for that sight, it still comes as a shock.

"The recce party ran into a heap of trouble in the form of an enemy 88-mm gun which had the road well covered. Major [Robert Ernest] Hogarth and Lieutenant [D.A.] Short had to make a fast gallop back to their vehicles after they had gone ahead to look the situation over and the whole column was backed up to a crossing where we turned east and then south to another area. Progress during the night had not been up to expectations so that the original deployment area could not be occupied without ending up dead or a POW.

"Towards noon the regiment finally got deployed near Verrières right in the middle of what seemed to be the main tank paths for the armoured attack."[11]

When 15th Field Regiment's reconnaissance personnel reached Rocquancourt, they huddled behind a stone wall, while the "whole area was being systematically shelled from three sides, snipers were everywhere, and anti-tank guns engaged any vehicle that moved over high ground. Nonetheless, battery and troop areas were allotted, gun platforms were selected, and survey was begun. This work was well under way when it was decided that the area was too exposed, and recce parties were ordered to withdraw north of the town where the regiment had lain for several hours awaiting the order to deploy, still in complete ignorance of what was going on in front and around it." Not until shortly after noon were the regiment's guns deployed in an orchard north of Rocquancourt.[12]

Because armoured divisions had only two inherent field artillery regiments, First Canadian Army's 19th Field Regiment was attached for Totalize. Struggling through intense traffic congestion, these gunners didn't reach their gun area near Rocquancourt until after noon and were not ready to fire until 1300 hours.[13]

Getting the guns positioned was just one problem besetting the division's artillery headquarters staff. At 0930 hours, they suddenly learned it was their responsibility to mark bomb targets with red smoke. They assigned the task to 23rd Field Regiment, only to learn the gunners had insufficient shells of this type. At 1100 hours, a "priority" convoy rolled into divisional headquarters with the requisite shells, and Captain B.S. Saunders guided it to the regiment's gun line. "After many anxious moments, [the regiment began] firing red smoke at correct places at the correct time," the divisional artillery's war diarist recorded.[14]

AT 1255, 680 American B-17 and B-24 bombers arrived. Their assigned targets were Bretteville-sur-Laize on the right, Saint-Sylvain to the left, Hautmesnil astride the Caen-Falaise highway, and the little hamlet of Gouvix immediately south of Bretteville.[15] Approaching on a west-to-east trajectory crossing the Canadian and Polish front, the bombers were also exposed to heavy German flak, which caused considerable disorganization. Ten bombers were shot down and 294 sustained damage. Low cloud, lingering haze, and battlefield smoke hampered the ability to see assigned targets despite the red smoke. Consequently, a number of bombardiers released bombs onto Canadian, Polish, and British troops.[16] Two twelve-plane groups veered far off course, and most of these dropped their payloads between Vaucelles and Cormelles.[17]

A 3rd Infantry Division column was just coming out of Vaucelles. The North Shore (New Brunswick) Regiment was in trucks near its head. Major Robert Robichaud "saw a cloud of dust, smoke and fire rolling toward us." Soldiers piled out of still rolling trucks to seek cover. "The bombing stopped right in front of my company...As soon as the air cleared up a bit I proceeded to the head of the column with [Company Sergeant Major] Roger Tremblay...Fires were burning all over the place and a continuous staccato of bursting shells filled the air, the artillery ammunition dumps had been set on fire. We saw several bodies in flames...This was a severe blow to the unit and we stopped for the night shortly afterward."[18] Twenty-three other ranks were killed, seventy-three other ranks and two officers wounded.[19] This was about the same casualty rate the battalion suffered on D-Day.

On the outskirts of Cormelles, the 1st Hussars 'B' Echelon had eight men killed and ten wounded. A hit on the 2nd Canadian Armoured Brigade's headquarters resulted in several casualties and the destruction of much equipment. The 3rd Division headquarters was also struck. Its signals office took a direct hit that killed or wounded everyone inside and knocked out all communication. Major General Rod Keller was critically wounded.[20]

The Fort Garry Horse's 'B' Echelon was close by. Major Bruce Macdonald had just overseen loading eight Kangaroos with ammunition and fuel to take to the regiment's tanks on the front line when a stick of bombs struck. Several Kangaroos were blown up, and a couple of others started burning. To prevent its ammunition and fuel from exploding in the congested area, Macdonald jumped aboard one burning Kangaroo and raced it out onto the adjacent road and into the midst of a passing Polish column. As the Kangaroo plunged through the column and out the other side, it sheered the rear end off a staff car. Snatching up an extinguisher, Macdonald smothered the flames. He was horrified to see the bodies of two Polish officers hanging out of the wrecked car. "Oh, my God," he cried. A Polish soldier shook his head. "Do not worry," he said. "They were already dead from the bombs."

Macdonald staggered off, sick to his stomach but also dizzy. As he remembered all the inhaled extinguisher fumes, Macdonald passed out. When he awoke, he stared up at a movie camera manned by a Canadian Army cameraman. "What the hell are you doing?" he gasped. "Jesus," the man said, "I thought I was filming one of the dead. Glad to see you're not." The cameraman offered a flask of whisky and Macdonald took a grateful slug.[21] Returning to the regiment's harbour, he learned that ten Fort Garry Horse soldiers had died.[22]

A final casualty toll, including those of the Polish division, was estimated at 65 killed and 250 wounded. In addition, four Canadian medium and heavy guns were damaged and about fifty-five vehicles destroyed or damaged. Large quantities of ammunition and fuel were lost.[23]

"This misadventure in the rear did not affect the advance of [4th Canadian Armoured Division]," an army report later concluded. "Its troops were [instead] held up by the jammed traffic resulting from the difficulties around Rocquancourt."[24] This and other critical delays meant that most benefits accruing from the bombing were lost, as the Germans gained several hours to recover and strengthen defensive lines.

While the targets at Bretteville, Hautmesnil, and Saint-Sylvain were heavily bombed, only one bomber dropped on Gouvix. Unable to identify that target, the other bombers assigned to it returned to base without releasing any bombs. Only 492 bombers in fact dropped their ordnance, for a total of about 1,848 tons.[25]

The bombers had arrived just as Standartenführer Kurt Meyer was launching a 12th ss Panzer Division counterattack. Although his tanks and infantry were rolling through open fields, not a single bomber altered course to engage them.[26] The counterattacking force consisted of seven Tigers, a company of Mark IV Panzers, a mixed group of two companies fielding several anti-tank guns, a company of self-propelled guns, and a thinned-out infantry battalion. It advanced against the right flank of 51st (Highland) Division in front of Saint-Aignan-de-Cramesnil. While German artillery and mortars hammered the British troops, the Tigers led off from Cintheaux. ss Hauptsturmführer Michael Wittmann commanded the Tigers. A Knight's Cross winner and minor German celebrity, Wittmann was the country's top tank ace, having amassed 143 armoured vehicle kills during fighting on both the eastern and western fronts.

Wittmann directed the Tigers, several Mark IVs, some half-tracks carrying panzer grenadiers, and two SPGs straight up the highway on a trajectory passing immediately east of Gaumesnil.[27] From positions south of Saint-Aignan, British tankers prepared to engage the Tigers, while 'A' Squadron of the Sherbrooke Fusiliers also zeroed in from next to Gaumesnil. Major Sidney Radley-Walters had established the squadron in the grounds of a large château, surrounded by a high concrete wall that ran alongside the highway. 'A' Squadron had eight Shermans, two of which mounted 17-pounders. The crews had cut holes in the walls to create firing ports for the main guns.

Seeing a column of five Tigers with the last just ahead of the Mark IVs, half-tracks, and SPGs, Radley-Walters warned his crew commanders to hold fire until he signalled. At a range of only five hundred yards, 'A' Squadron started shooting, and the lead Tiger was instantly knocked out. Radley-Walters scored a killing hit on an SPG as the German column swung off the highway towards a wood south of Saint-Aignan. This exposed the column's rear, and Radley-Walters counted two Mark IVs and a Tiger at the tail as additional kills. While this shootout was under way, the first Tiger exploded, its massive turret somersaulting through the air to land right side up behind the burning hulk. Painted on the turret were the numbers "007"— Wittmann's designation. Although argument raged over whether Canadian, British, possibly Polish, or even a stray Typhoon was responsible for killing the German tank ace, 'A' Squadron's claim proved the most convincing.[28]

'A' Squadron's fire forced the column away from the highway and directly into the British right flank. A fierce tank engagement ensued with both sides suffering heavy losses. When the panzer grenadiers dismounted, they were unable to close with the British tanks because of heavy machine-gun fire tearing into their ranks. At 1500 hours, the counterattack collapsed.[29]

AT 1355 HOURS, the two armoured divisions finally gained their start lines. Kitching's plan envisioned 4th Armoured Brigade advancing on the left and 10th Infantry Brigade the right. The Canadian Grenadier Guards supported by the Lake Superior Regiment's motorized infantry headed the armoured advance. They were accompanied by a Flail squadron and the 96th Anti-Tank Battery of the division's 5th Anti-Tank Regiment. Dubbed "Halpenny Force," after Grenadier commander Lieutenant Colonel Bill Halpenny, this unit was to bypass Cintheaux and Hautmesnil to the east, capture Bretteville-le-Rabet, and then proceed to Points 195 and 206. The infantry brigade—less the Algonquin Regiment, which was under 4th Brigade's command— would clear the bypassed villages through to and including Bretteville-le-Rabet. Armour support was provided by the South Alberta Regiment.[30]

Before 4th Division could advance, however, 2nd Division was to clear Gaumesnil. Due to various communication gaffes within 2nd

Division, 4th Infantry Brigade only received instructions to send the Royal Regiment from Point 122 to take the village at 1300 hours. When Lieutenant Colonel Jock Anderson asked whether Gaumesnil was still in German hands, Brigadier Eddy Ganong had no idea. Proceeding cautiously, Anderson sent the commanders of 'A' and 'D' Companies on a reconnaissance.

About three hundred yards north of Gaumesnil, the two officers found 'A' Squadron in the château grounds. Radley-Walters said he "had been all around Gaumesnil, but no one as yet had attempted to enter the village." Returning to Point 122, the company commanders gathered their men and advanced on Gaumesnil through thick artillery and mortar fire that was lacing the entire 11 Canadian Corps front. It took until 1530 hours for the Royals to reach Gaumesnil. They found "no opposition, although a few stray prisoners were collected." The Royals were well pleased with the village, finding it "considerably more pleasant than any we had had to date as the barns and farm buildings were not too badly wrecked, and there was a plentiful supply of excellent water at the château."[31]

"With this improvement, traffic congestion around Gaumesnil eased, and the tanks...were able to move more freely," stated one army report. "The infantry of 10[th Brigade], moving down the Falaise road, resumed the advance as soon as Gaumesnil fell."[32] But precious hours had been lost.

During the afternoon of August 8, an odd disconnect prevailed between Operation Totalize's phase-two conception and its actual execution, as a rapid armoured breakout was stalled by the slow pace at which 2nd Division was clearing the way. Having crossed their start lines five minutes before the Royals had even received orders to attack Gaumesnil, Halpenny Force and the Argyll and Sutherland Highlanders, which were leading 10th Infantry Brigade's advance, had spent hours waiting on the village's northern outskirts.

Instead of bulling ahead by skirting the village, Lieutenant Colonel Bill Halpenny did nothing. Nor did Brigadier Leslie Booth urge the force to make haste. The movements of 4th Armoured Brigade that afternoon were marked by a curious lethargy. In Italy, Booth had won a Distinguished Service Order and Bar for courage. But

Kitching had noticed lately that Booth was no longer "the keen and cheerful man" he had been. In fact, Kitching worried that Booth had some premonition of impending death, a factor that might explain Booth's increasingly heavy drinking.[33]

Although Kitching had given his operational briefing at 1900 hours on August 6, Booth had waited until 1100 hours the following day to brief his brigade. That left little more than a day to get ready. Lake Superior Regiment's Lieutenant Colonel J.E.V. Murrell and his intelligence officer, Lieutenant D.A. Johnson, left the briefing with only "a rough outline of the operation which was to take place the following day."

Things did not become clearer over the course of the afternoon and several equally uninformative briefings. Finally, at 2230 hours, Lieutenant Colonel Halpenny presented the final briefing to his officers.[34] The Superior's historian later described this as "not...a very auspicious beginning for the action...In any event, the officers of 'Halpenny Force' crowded into the Intelligence room with its smoky, excited atmosphere, its dim light, and its small map tacked to the wall, all eager to learn what they could, and believing that upon their own particular tasks depended the success of the whole battle."

One observer thought "the milling, pressing mob, except for the presence of army uniforms, had all the appearance of a bargain sale counter in a department store." Halpenny started ponderously reading orders, only to be drowned out by the sudden appearance of RAF bombers supporting Totalize's first phase. Someone extinguished the lights. "In the noisy darkness the Orders Group, already large and unwieldy, lost whatever sense of cohesion it might ever have had, and when the lights were finally turned on again, the place was in a state of utmost confusion. And yet it was in this state...that the orders were completed. As he returned to his own lines each officer possessed but the vaguest notion as to what was going to happen on the morrow and what his own role was to be."[35]

Watching with a jaundiced eye was Major Hershell "Snuffy" Smith, who commanded the Grenadiers' No. 3 Squadron. (4th Division armoured regiments used numbers to denote squadrons rather than first letters of the alphabet, as did 2nd Armoured Brigade.) Like

Booth, Smith had fought in Italy. Major Ned Amy, commanding No. 1 Squadron, was also an Italian veteran. Both were highly capable.

Smith found Halpenny "didn't inspire confidence." At somewhere between age thirty-five and forty, Halpenny was "too old for regimental command," he thought. His lack of combat experience seemed to have undermined his self-confidence. Whenever Smith or Amy contradicted an order, Halpenny deferred to him without argument. "Hell, he's the boss," Smith would complain to Amy. Smith liked Halpenny. He just considered him a "round peg in a square hole."

As for Booth, Smith flatly believed that "as a brigade commander, Booth was just no good." He was the brigade's "weak link." If Booth "had been stronger, his regimental commanders would have been stronger."[36]

After the briefing fiasco, Halpenny Force started moving painfully slowly at 0300 hours on August 8. At dawn, they were still short of the forming-up position at Troteval Farm. Wireless sets crackled with Booth alternately pleading with and haranguing everyone to "get cracking." At 0845 hours, Booth instructed Halpenny to pass through 2nd Division and move to the start line. Instead, Halpenny Force lurched along through endless gridlock resulting from vehicles of every division seemingly moving in an absence of traffic control. Five hours later, Major Amy's No. 1 Squadron led the force past Rocquancourt and immediately lost three tanks to mines. Then it was held up before Gaumesnil. Not until sometime between 1530 and 1600 hours did Halpenny Force finally enter enemy country.[37]

THE GAUMESNIL LOGJAM resulted from two critical planning errors. First, lying as it did south of the phase-two bomb line, 2nd Division could not secure the village until the bombers left. Second, Simonds had given 2nd Division too many unprioritized missions to complete after conducting a landmark night advance. Despite the urgency of removing the Gaumesnil roadblock, Simonds attached no more urgency to this than clearing May-sur-Orne, Fontenay-le-Marmion, or even Bretteville-sur-Laize. With a list of equally weighted tasks, Major General Charles Foulkes spread his already-depleted forces ever thinner through the course of the day in an attempt to simultaneously complete them all.

At the same time as the Royal Regiment was clearing Gaumesnil, 5th Brigade advanced its battalions towards Bretteville-sur-Laize about a mile and a quarter to the west. This brigade had concentrated in the early morning just north of Rocquancourt and could easily have dealt with Gaumesnil—certainly a more pressing task than expanding the corps flank westward to the Laize River. Instead, at 1000 hours, sticking to 2nd Division's rote, Brigadier Bill Megill directed the Calgary Highlanders and Régiment de Maisonneuve to attack from Caillouet towards Bretteville at noon.[38] Two squadrons of 1st Hussars supported this attack, 'A' Squadron moving with the Calgaries and 'B' Squadron the Maisies.[39]

At 1400 hours, the Calgaries advanced along the right side of the road leading to Bretteville, while the Maisies were to the left. The hamlet of Quilly and its surrounding woods that overlooked Bretteville were to be taken by the Maisies. They would then cover the Calgaries' descent to Bretteville. It was about a half-mile through smouldering wheat fields to the edge of the valley. At first the descent was gradual, but then the slope fell away steeply.

To the consternation of both battalions—so used to being mauled by artillery and mortar fire during advances—no opposition was met crossing the open ground fringed on all sides by what the Calgary war diarist described as "evil looking" woods. With the tanks on the ridge to provide covering fire, the Calgaries slipped into the valley with two companies forward and two back.

Bretteville "was a complete shambles" due to bombing damage, and the road leading to it had been badly churned up. Inside the village, the Calgaries met only slight resistance and secured it without a single casualty.[40] By 1630 hours, all objectives had been secured without any losses.[41]

As both battalions brought support company, headquarters, and other rear-echelon elements forward, these encountered German fire. Calgary Highlanders' Lieutenant Colonel Donald MacLauchlan's Bren carrier was hit by 88-millimetre fire from the opposite side of the river, and MacLauchlan was blown out of the vehicle. Unhurt, he climbed through the woods to the tanks and pointed out the German gun position. The tank fire silenced and possibly destroyed the gun. A "very beautiful château" standing on the edge of Bretteville was sheltering several machine guns firing on the village. MacLauchlan hated to do it, but he had artillery reduce the fine building to a battered ruin, which 'B' Company swept through without finding any trace of Germans.[42]

When two Nebelwerfers started firing salvoes into Bretteville from a position five hundred yards to the northeast, the Maisies charged it. The crews fled, leaving behind brand-new launchers around which was stacked "a plentiful supply of ammunition."[43]

Bretteville, MacLauchlan observed, lay "in a saucer...commanded by the high ground north of it."[44] It was also surrounded by wooded heights that made MacLauchlan uneasy. Always before, the Germans had counterattacked any objective won. He expected them to do so that night. His companies had little room to manoeuvre. With the roads virtually impassable, reinforcing them would be difficult. MacLauchlan decided to withdraw from the village and up onto the high ground for the night.

The decision meant carrying out "one of the most dangerous manoeuvres in modern warfare," according to one regimental historian—a withdrawal "over a forward slope." The move was made while still light and without covering artillery. Nor did MacLauchlan have either the tanks or his battalion mortars fire a smokescreen.

A hundred men were still climbing the exposed slope when an 88-millimetre gun opened from the ridgeline to the east. Shrapnel cut down rows of men; concussion sent others sprawling. Soldiers wandered blindly in shock or cowered.[45] Captain Ross Ellis scrambled down the slope with a party of stretcher-bearers. He found the acting company commander of 'D' Company severely wounded, hefted the man over his shoulder, and carried him through shellfire 250 yards up the hill.[46] When everyone gained the covering woods, the battalion counted three officers wounded, one in shock, three other ranks killed, thirty-nine wounded, and twenty missing.[47]

The average remaining company strength was twenty-five to thirty men. This "extremely small number of bodies," MacLauchlan said later, "was thickened" by having the tanks stay through the night and the battalion's anti-tank guns, carriers, and mortars deploy with them. During the night, Brigadier Megill reinforced the

Calgaries with a Toronto Scottish heavy-machine-gun platoon and a troop of 2nd Anti-Tank Regiment's 17-pounders.

Megill ordered Bretteville retaken the following morning. The Calgaries went in at noon. MacLauchlan kept 'D' Company back to provide covering fire, while 'A' Company gained the edge of the village to establish a base through which the other two companies passed.[48] Captain R.L. Morgan-Dean's 'A' Company was fifty yards short of the river when a machine gun opened fire and drove the leading platoon to ground. Bren gunner Private William Cook dodged into the open to draw fire and situate the German gun. Alternately crawling and dashing across open ground, he closed in. Then, firing from the hip, he rushed the position and took six prisoners. Cook's rapid elimination of this threat earned him a Military Medal.[49]

Resistance collapsed. Two officers and nineteen soldiers surrendered, mostly Russian or Polish conscripts happy to give up. The Calgaries spent the rest of August 9 "sleeping in shifts" and enjoying "two hot meals." Rumour held they were in for several days of rest, 2nd Division's role in the big offensive over.[50]

21

That'll Be a Tough One

ABOUT THE TIME 2nd Division's 5th Brigade had started the
Bretteville-sur-Laize attack, the Grenadier Guards' No. 1
Squadron had edged around Gaumesnil's eastern flank. Four Ger-
man tanks burned beside the village. Lieutenant Craig Smith's No. 3
Troop came under fire from an anti-tank gun shooting from south
of Saint-Aignan-de-Cramesnil. Two rounds slashed into Smith's
Sherman, killing both the gunner and the loader-operator. Smith,
who was badly burned, and the two drivers bailed out.[1]

No. 2 Squadron was barely past Gaumesnil when the Sherman in
which Guardsman Stuart Johns served as loader-operator plunged
into a narrow drainage ditch. As the tank clawed up the opposite
bank, a shell punched into the engine compartment. Steel shards
spattered into the ventilation fan, causing a hellish racket. The engine
sounded as if it were tearing apart. Fearing the Sherman would burst
into flames, the crew bailed out. The nineteen-year-old Johns watched
the rest of the Grenadiers rumble southward. Johns figured his tank
had the distinction of being first in the regiment to be knocked out.[2]

It was about 1600 hours, and Brigadier Leslie Booth was again
imploring Lieutenant Colonel Bill Halpenny to dash forward. As
No. 1 Squadron had lost a third of its tanks, Halpenny ordered Major
Hershell Smith to lead with No. 3 Squadron. After advancing just
five hundred yards, the squadron came under intense 88-millimetre

gunfire from orchards on either side. Smith's tank was disabled. He and his crew quickly commandeered one of the other tanks to stay in the fight. Troop leader Lieutenant Fred Fisher's tank was also knocked out. He and Lance Corporal Thomas Ryan died.

Smith ordered the squadron to break off. While two troops covered the withdrawal of Fisher's remaining tanks, Smith radioed No. 4 Troop's Lieutenant Ivon Phelan. "The advance on the left is held up. Can you make an end run on the right?"

"Wilco," Phelan replied. It was 1700 hours.

Phelan's four tanks headed for the gap between the railway to the west and Cintheaux to the east. The Argyll and Sutherland Highlanders' 'A' Company was close behind. After pushing into dense woods, which proved impenetrable, and having one tank break down, Phelan moved into the open.[3] Seeing gun flashes from an orchard on Cintheaux's northern edge, he engaged the gun with high-explosive shot that knocked the 88-millimetre out.[4]

The gun's destruction drew an angry response from several anti-tank guns stationed six hundred yards distant among farm buildings on the edge of the orchard. Telling his other two tanks to cover him, Phelan charged through heavy fire to within a hundred yards of the enemy guns. He then destroyed two more 88-millimetres and two 20-millimetre flak guns. No. 4 Troop went on to knock out three self-propelled guns.[5]

Pausing next to the burning SPGs, Phelan realized the orchard was teeming with German infantry. The Argylls had disappeared towards Cintheaux. His wireless had stopped working, so there was no way to get the Argylls to return to the tanks. Standing up, Phelan shouted for the tankers to dismount and attack the infantry with personal weapons.[6]

As the crews jumped out, an SPG exploded. A flaming tree fell on Sergeant Samuel Hurwitz, pinning him. Suffering burns and a minor shrapnel wound, Hurwitz wriggled out from under the tree. Grabbing a Bren gun, he joined Phelan in assaulting the German position.[7] Thirty-one prisoners were captured. A further three 88-millimetre guns and two 2-centimetre guns were taken.[8] Phelan was awarded a Military Cross and Hurwitz a Military Medal.

While the tank action had been under way, the Argylls had quelled Cintheaux. 'A' and 'D' Companies had taken the village in sixteen minutes flat, reporting all clear at 1816 hours. The Germans seemed "too dazed" by the artillery and aerial bombardment "to put up much opposition." Most of the forty-two prisoners had been manning the anti-tank guns knocked out by No. 3 Squadron.[9] Private Bill Jones was killed when one of the crew blew their anti-tank gun and he was caught in the blast.[10]

Lieutenant Colonel David Stewart ordered the remaining two Argyll companies on to Hautmesnil, a scattering of buildings gathered around a large quarry. Hautmesnil was less than a mile away. When they arrived, Stewart sent 'C' Company to clear the buildings and ordered 'B' Company to contain the quarry. This was a huge, open-pit operation. By the time the buildings had been secured, night was falling. Deciding the quarry was too large for one company, Stewart left it and ordered the Argylls to dig in.[11] The Argylls had lost Jones killed and twenty-four others wounded.

WHILE THE ARGYLLS had marched on Hautmesnil, Halpenny Force had stood down despite several hours of light remaining. Halpenny announced that it was necessary to "renet, regroup, and plan."[12] Unable to contact Booth since late in the afternoon, Halpenny reached this decision alone.

Major General George Kitching had also been unable to raise Booth or determine his whereabouts. At the same time, a livid Lieutenant General Guy Simonds was demanding that Kitching get his division moving. At 1830, he ordered an immediate advance through Bretteville-le-Rabet and on to Point 195, even if it meant marching through the night.[13]

Unable to pass on these orders by wireless, Kitching set out by jeep and finally discovered Booth's tactical headquarters two miles behind the battle front. Booth's headquarters staff were sitting about, looking sheepish. Peering into the turret hatch of Booth's command tank, Kitching saw the brigadier apparently asleep.[14] When he climbed inside, Kitching realized Booth was passed out drunk. Shaking him awake, Kitching yanked Booth out of the tank and subjected him to a furious five-minute tongue-lashing. Almost in tears, Booth swore he would pull himself together and do his job.[15]

By the time Kitching sorted out Booth and convened a new Orders Group, it was 2000 hours. Kitching ordered 4th Armoured Brigade to renew the advance. Halpenny Force would capture Bretteville-le-Rabet with two Grenadier squadrons and two Lake Superior Regiment companies riding on the tanks. Point 195 would then be taken by a flying column comprised of the British Columbia Regiment and three Algonquin Regiment companies. This force would be commanded by the BCR's Lieutenant Colonel Don Worthington.[16] Although Kitching was retrieving the situation, nothing could change the fact that Halpenny had, as the Grenadier Guards' regimental historian remarked, "vitiated Simonds' intention 'to push on steadily regardless'" of opposition.[17]

In fact, little had gone right in Totalize's second phase. While 4th Canadian Armoured Division's advance had been fraught with delays and then derailed by Booth and Halpenny, 1st Polish Armoured Division's gains had been even more disappointing.

Major General Stanislaw Maczek's Poles had crossed the start line on schedule at 1355 hours with 10th Armoured Cavalry Brigade's 24th Lancers and 2nd Armoured Regiment advancing to the south of Saint-Aignan-de-Cramesnil. Within thirty minutes, Maczek radioed Simonds that his leading troops had been engaged by twenty Tiger tanks in woods about a mile southeast of Saint-Aignan. Another ten Tigers were firing from a wood about a mile south of the village. Artillery was also hammering them. "We have suffered some losses in tanks," Maczek added. "Appreciate that enemy pushed armour [forward] to gain time to strengthen second defence line with troops reported...coming from south."[18]

The Poles seriously overestimated the Tiger numbers. There were actually only three, those left from Hauptsturmführer Michael Wittmann's command. The other tanks were Mark IVs.[19] But they were well concealed, while the Poles were in the open. In the thick of the battle, the Lancers requested artillery "which neutralized the opposition sufficiently to enable a short advance, though the left flank was consistently...menaced by enemy armour. The terrain, studded with small woods and high hedges," a Polish report stated, "made the position very favourable to the enemy!"[20] The battle raged until dusk with the Poles losing forty tanks—twenty-six from 2nd Armoured Regiment, fourteen from the Lancers.[21]

As night closed in, the 3rd Rifle Brigade pushed ahead against heavy opposition. "The battle continued throughout the night and by 0600 hours 9 Aug[ust] little ground had been gained."[22]

DESPITE ITS FAILINGS, Totalize had panicked the German command. At 0045 hours on August 8, Generalfeldmarschall Günther von Kluge had informed General der Panzertruppen Hans Eberbach that his Fifth Army—as Panzer Group West had been redesignated—must facilitate "a speedy transfer" of 12th ss Panzer Division to Seventh Army. They were to join the unravelling German offensive at Avranches.

Then, at 0545 hours, 1 ss Corps commander Obergruppenführer Josef "Sepp" Dietrich reported 89th Infantry Division under attack and tanks reportedly already in Saint-Aignan. At 1420 hours, Dietrich pleaded for armoured reinforcements, only to learn that "all flying formations are committed in support of the attack on Avranches."

At 1600 hours, Eberbach requested 1st ss Panzer Division's return to the Canadian front. He was considering withdrawing to a line running from Saint-Sylvain through Cintheaux to Grimbosq and "probably even throwing straight into battle the newly arriving elements" of 85th Infantry Division. Von Kluge said 1st ss Division was already committed by Seventh Army to the Avranches offensive. By 1730 hours, Eberbach reported that his just-proposed new line of resistance "will have to be withdrawn during the coming night, as it [can] no longer be held against the severe enemy pressure." The Canadians, he said, had "already pushed...tanks as far as Hautmesnil."

Von Kluge responded at 2000 hours with instructions to send an artillery battalion and Nebelwerfer brigade to Seventh Army. At the end of his tether, Eberbach phoned von Kluge and provided an "exhaustive description" of his army's "difficult position."

Eberbach said 12th ss Panzer Division had been "crushed." Only individual tanks from the counterattacking force were returning. "The enemy pressed...as far as Gaumesnil and is continuing his advance." He doubted the current defensive line at Bretteville-le-Rabet could be held "if the enemy attacks more energetically." The 89th Infantry Division and the 12th ss, Eberbach stated, "are fifty percent knocked out. I shall be lucky if by tonight I am able to round up 20 tanks, including Tigers." The 271st Infantry Division facing 1 British Corps and part of 1st Polish Armoured Division had suffered two thousand casualties and was "very weak. I must confess quite frankly that I am looking forward to tomorrow with anxiety."

"I am unfortunately not in a position to send you anything," von Kluge responded. "That this would all go so quickly, we too did not expect. But I can imagine that it did not happen quite so unexpectedly. I have always anticipated this and have always looked forward to the coming day with a very heavy heart."

Fifteen minutes after von Kluge rang off, Eberbach learned that the 12th ss Panzer Division battle group that was to have returned from west of the Orne was still far away. Leading elements of 85th Infantry Division would also not arrive until some time on the morning of August 9.

Eberbach phoned von Kluge again. He reiterated that the "Hitler Youth Division has been exhausted so much...that 1 ss Panzer Corps was not able even by means of roving staff officers to get together a combat team again. Telecoms, wireless included, are knocked out."

"As a last measure," von Kluge said, "I have set into march this night twenty tanks of 9th ss Panzer Division, but I fear that, with the long approach march, only half of them will arrive tomorrow morning. If you get back one Panzer Division which I had taken away from you, what will you then be short of most?"

"Most of all, tanks are lacking," Eberbach replied.

"Have you a commander who understands how to handle tanks? Where is the commander of the Hitler Youth?"

"The Hitler Youth commander telephoned me this afternoon from Saint-Aignan. He was there to organize the resistance."

"That is Panzer Meyer," von Kluge said. "Have you had news from him since?"

"No news. That was before the area bombing...Since then, I have no further news from him." Unspoken was the fear that Meyer was dead, wounded, or captured.

"If I send you a tank formation, would that help you?"

"Yes."

"Have you then a man who could lead them?"

"Yes, that man Wünsche." Eberbach referred to Obertsturmbann-führer Max Wünsche, the 12th ss Division's 12th Panzer Regiment commander.

"He is still there? Aha! I am considering whether I should still send you a Panzer battalion."

At 2330 hours, the two conferred again. Eberbach expected the morning to bring a "penetration on the Caen road in the direction of Falaise...Enemy has pressed forward from Hautmesnil with very strong elements through to Langannerie. I hope that we succeed in destroying the enemy during this night...and hold the line Saint-Sylvain-Bretteville."

Von Kluge reassured Eberbach that the 9th Panzer Division tanks were marching from Argentan to Falaise, "so that early tomorrow they will be half way on. That is a very weighty decision for me, a major abandonment of an order that has been given to me. I know of no other solution—have no further forces. If it goes on like this tomorrow, there will be no more stopping them at all...I know that, in the long run, the forces will be inadequate," von Kluge said resignedly.

At 2350 hours, the commander of 11 ss Panzer Corps advised Eberbach the tanks to be sent were "built into the main line of resistance, hence he would [instead] send 9th ss Panzer Division's Tiger Battalion with thirteen tanks...ready for action."[23]

SHORTLY AFTER MIDNIGHT on August 9, Brigadier Booth briefed his two force commanders by flashlight on the floor of his tank. Halpenny Force would first take Bretteville-le-Rabet, and then Worthington Force would advance through to Point 195.[24] Halpenny assigned the Lake Superiors' 'B' Company to take the village. Mounted on the Grenadiers' No. 2 Squadron tanks, the small force set off at 0330 hours. Following behind was the Superiors' 'C' Company with No. 1 Squadron, Halpenny's tactical headquarters, and Lieutenant Colonel J.E.V. Murrell's headquarters section.[25]

Advancing alongside the Caen-Falaise highway, the column was about a thousand yards north of Bretteville as dawn broke, and it suddenly came under fire. Guardsman Neil J. Stewart "could faintly hear the shouts and screams of the men clinging to the turret, along with the crackle of bullets hitting the steel castings as the Spandau fire swept the top and sides of the tanks."[26] Spilling into the wheat field beside the road, the Superiors shot back at snipers and machine guns that seemed "everywhere." 'B' Company was driven to ground.[27]

No. 2 Squadron ripped loose with machine guns, "and the tracer bullets were about as thick as snow in a snowstorm," the Grenadier war diarist recorded. "Gradually everyone stopped firing, and it was then possible to observe flashes from an anti-[tank] gun," which was quickly knocked out.[28]

Arriving with the follow-on force, Lieutenant Colonel Murrell heard wounded men crying in the wheat field and yelled to 'C' Company, "Follow me." Ignoring the gunfire snapping through the grain, Murrell and some men dashed forward. They carried the wounded to a ditch on the opposite side of the road.

Realizing 'B' Company was broken, Murrell ordered Major E.G. Styffe to advance 'C' Company.[29] Halpenny sent Major Amy's No. 1 Squadron in support. He then saddled up his tactical headquarters, gathered No. 2 Squadron, and returned to Gaumesnil.[30] Determined to see Bretteville taken, Murrell stayed put.

The attack went in at 0600 hours. While No. 1 Troop swung to the east to enter the village, the rest of the squadron pounded the buildings with high-explosive shells. 'C' Company advanced straight up the road, a move the Superiors' historian acknowledged "was without subtlety or complex manoeuvre." It was "perhaps, for sheer courage, the most heroic action by any company of the battalion during the whole war. The resistance put up by the Germans was hard and determined. They had both cannon and small arms and the advantage of prepared positions and good knowledge of the terrain. Steadily the Lake Superiors edged forward. The sun bore down upon them. They were thirsty and choked with dust. Men fought and died; killed and were killed; but their comrades fought on."[31]

Clearly, if the Germans were so determined to stand at Bretteville, they would equally defend the three villages immediately west of it. Directly astride the Caen-Falaise highway was Langannerie. From this village, Grainville-Langannerie trailed away to the southwest, while Vieille Langannerie stood to the northwest. In the late morning, Kitching ordered 10th Infantry Brigade to advance the Lincoln and Welland Regiment south from Hautmesnil to clear these. The Argylls, who had seized the quarry south of Hautmesnil without difficulty over the course of the morning, would follow the Lincs. Both battalions were supported by the South Alberta Regiment, Major Arnold Lavoie's 'A' Squadron with the Lincs and Major David V. "Dave" Currie's 'C' Squadron, the Argylls.

The Lincs and Lavoie's tanks attacked frontally at 1300 hours.[32] 'A' Company, under Major Andy Gilles, led on the left with Major Merv McCutcheon's 'B' Company to the right. It was a mile from the start line to the villages. Two of Lavoie's tanks were disabled by mines, but the crews escaped unhurt.

The 89th Infantry Division remnants offered a spirited fight, and soon all four companies were entangled in house-to-house battling, with the tanks providing close support. Trooper Bob Henning's tank was firing high-explosive and armour-piercing rounds into buildings the infantry were attacking. An infantryman walked out of one front door "holding a German helmet with the owner's head still in it." Henning scrambled out of the turret and puked into a ditch. "There is no way I can do this," he was thinking, when a German counterattack caught him outside the tank. After the Germans were driven back, he climbed back in. To survive, Henning decided, "I would have to do what I had to do and that was the way it was for the rest of the war."[33]

Elsewhere, Major Jim Swayze's 'D' Company met only slight resistance. "We got into the main street, and I put one platoon on the one side of the street and I was on the other…About fifty yards down, two German soldiers ran across the road with a machinegun. They were just putting it in a better position, and, being the first Germans any of us had ever seen, we just stood there with our mouths open and watched them run across."[34]

When the Argylls arrived at 1600 hours, German resistance began collapsing. Two hours later, the villages were secure. About a hundred prisoners were taken. Canadian casualties were very light. The Lincs, their regimental historian noted, "were beginning to get the feel of things, and they thought of objectives ahead, not with the idea, 'That'll be a tough one!' but instead, 'Wonder how long it'll take us to get Jerry out of there.'"[35]

In Bretteville, where the Superiors won the village in the late afternoon, the prisoners exceeded two hundred. "There had been casualties," the Superiors' historian wrote, "a considerable number of them; but whatever the losses had been, the men of the battalion had won their battle spurs. They had a new sense of dedication and a new consciousness of their strength."[36]

But command responsibility had taken its toll. Lieutenant Colonel Murrell was evacuated by the battalion's medical officer. Major Robert Keene took over and reported that the Superiors would be relieved in Bretteville by 3rd Canadian Infantry Division's North Shore (New Brunswick) Regiment at 0300 hours on August 10.[37]

Come What May

ORTHINGTON FORCE HAD advanced before the battle for
Bretteville and the other villages was concluded. Comprised
of British Columbia Regiment's three tank squadrons and three
Algonquin Regiment companies, with Lieutenant Colonel Don
Worthington commanding, the force had been created by Major
General George Kitching the previous evening. Worthington was
young and competent, considered next in line to Booth for command
of 4th Armoured Brigade.[1]

The "Dukes," as the tankers were nicknamed in reference to the
regiment's relations with the Duke of Connaught, had already been
well positioned for the advance in a field north of Cintheaux. Not so
the Algonquins. They had spent hours advancing in half-tracks
through a traffic jam at Rocquancourt and arrived at the Dukes' harbour purely by chance.[2] 'B' Company's Major Lyle Monk had just
parked opposite Brigadier Booth's tank when Worthington walked
up and announced that "there had been a change of plans. We were
to go under command of the British Columbia Reg[iment] and take
on a job as soon as it could be arranged." Worthington asked Monk
to tell Lieutenant Colonel Don Hay he was to attend an "immediate
O Group."

This was easier said than done, because Hay's headquarters and
'A' Company had missed the harbour area and were almost in

Bretteville when Monk reached Hay by wireless at about 2200 hours. It was midnight before Hay returned and climbed into Booth's tank. Monk and two other Algonquin company commanders, Major Keith Stirling and Major "Wally" MacPherson, "lay on the grass in the dark and talked quietly of what was to come."

An hour later, Hay and Worthington "crawled out of the Brigadier's tank." Worthington started an immediate briefing. Circled around were Hay, his company commanders, and Worthington's squadron commanders. They were to seize Point 195 "and hold this feature until the rest of our troops can reach us." The advance would parallel the Caen-Falaise highway until they came opposite Point 195. They would then turn and assault the hill from the southeast. "The tanks will do the fighting on the way down," Worthington said. "Keep moving. Try to reach the objective before daylight."[3] 'C' Squadron would lead. Worthington's regimental headquarters would be behind. The rest of the force would form in line—'B' Squadron, 'B' Company, 'A' Squadron, 'C' and 'D' Companies, and the light Stuart tanks of the reconnaissance squadron at the tail.[4] Hay would ride in Worthington's tank. Zero hour was thirty minutes away.[5]

While company and squadron commanders worked out details, Hay raced back to 'A' Company and told Captain Clark Robertson there were new orders. His company, along with the support company, was to go under command of the Governor General's Foot Guards. The rest of the battalion, Hay said, would be operating elsewhere.[6]

Monk and his 'B' Squadron counterpart, Major J.H. "Johnny" Carson, walked to the latter's squadron area. "We agreed that, as it would be impossible for me to read my map in the carrier in the dark, he would answer for direction, and I would keep 'B' Company on his tail." Monk went back to his company and found that two detachments of the Algonquins' 3-inch mortars had joined it.

At about 0230 hours, Worthington Force "crawled out...nose to tail, crossed the highway and started south...At first there were frequent halts. We were in waist-high wheat." Going into their first action, the tankers chattered on the wireless. Monk tried "to figure out what was going on ahead...but between the excited voices and considerable static, it was difficult."[7]

After thirty minutes, the column was fired upon by Germans to the east. These were bypassed in accordance with Worthington's admonition to keep moving. As 'C' Squadron passed between Haut-mesnil and Cauvicourt, it came under heavier fire from an anti-aircraft gun in an open field just north of Bretteville.[8] Worthington suddenly faced a dilemma. Ahead, Halpenny Force was still fighting in Bretteville. Should he wait until it was cleared and pass through according to plan? This would ensure that the column followed its mapped course but might mean losing the cover of darkness. Worthington signalled: "Move on anyway, while we still have surprise."[9]

'C' Squadron swung east to hook past the village and then cross to the west side of the highway to head for Point 195. As the column left the highway, it came under increasing fire from Cauvicourt, and the lead tanks replied with high-explosive shells while cutting back to the west to gain some distance from this hamlet. Buildings in Cauvicourt began burning. Fires broke out in the wheat, as the tankers slammed rounds into haystacks that might conceal German tanks or anti-tank guns. In their half-tracks and carriers, the Algonquins felt "very conspicuous. There was much small arms fire which seemed to be coming from all directions, but no heavy shells or 88s," Monk wrote.

"With the tanks firing their machineguns as they moved, we began to move more and more rapidly, getting pretty well spread out and travelling generally south, over rolling country in waist-high wheat. Most of the enemy fire was directed at the tanks. We remained huddled down in our half-tracks, half-hidden in the wheat and moving in fits and starts."[10]

Bearing eastward, the force crossed the Chemin Haussé du duc Guillaume—a dead-straight relic of William the Conqueror's time—that angled to the southeast and away from the Caen-Falaise highway.[11] Worthington Force rolled alongside this route. Pushing through a small wood south of Cauvicourt, the lead tanks "sighted enemy soft skin vehicles, armoured cars, and half-tracks. These were duly shot up as we proceeded and many...enemy were killed."[12]

As the column gathered speed, it lost cohesion. 'C' Squadron, with Worthington's headquarters, emerged from the wood and followed the Chemin Haussé. Dawn was breaking. The tanks were alongside a straight road; ahead high ground was visible. Assuming they were following the Caen-Falaise highway, the lead element dashed on. "The whole area shakes with blast, 88's fire from all angles. The air is streaked with tracer, smoke rises, tanks brew, crews bail out. Orders are shouted over the wireless, crew commanders strain their eyes through binoculars," the Dukes' Captain Douglas Harker wrote.[13]

Through this gauntlet, the leading element gained the slopes ahead. At about 0650 hours, Worthington called a halt and deployed 'C' Squadron's sixteen remaining tanks and his four headquarters tanks in a square formation on high ground that offered a commanding view.[14] Over the wireless, Worthington reported to Booth that he was on Point 195. "No evidence of enemy occupation, but recent signs," he said. "We are holding until our friends come forward to consolidate."[15]

In fact, Worthington was about three miles east of Point 195. A hill to the southwest of where he stood was Point 140, a Polish first objective. Because of this wireless report, 4th Armoured Division assumed Worthington Force was where it should be.

THE ALGONQUINS HAD watched 'B' and 'C' Squadrons disappear "over the crest of a hill" as they had entered a dense wood. Trying to follow the tracks left by the tanks, their vehicles struggled over "stumps and fallen brushwood. Some...got stuck and had to be pulled clear with the carrier using...tow chains." An 88-millimetre gun started sniping at the infantry trying to free the half-tracks. Breaking free of the woods, the Algonquins "sped up the steep slope."

Clear of the crest, 'B' and 'C' Companies raced along, following the track marks left by the tanks. Sporadically, they came under inaccurate small-arms fire, to "which we replied...by firing...Brens from our moving vehicles." As the infantry came to a small village with a prominent stone church, Monk saw 'B' Squadron stopped ahead. The Algonquins also halted, and Monk sent No. 10 Platoon to reconnoitre the village. Then he and Major MacPherson of 'C' Company joined Major Carson, who was studying a map.[16]

Although Monk thought Carson was as disoriented as he was, the tank commander had managed to situate himself. Realizing that the village was Estrées-la-Campagne, Carson knew the force had lost direction. While still trying to establish wireless contact with Worthington, Carson ordered his No. 2 Troop to lead the squadron towards the actual Point 195. The troop was just leaving as the Algonquins arrived. Then Worthington came up on the wireless and ordered everyone to "advance to high ground in front." Not recalling No. 2 Troop, Carson led the rest of the squadron towards Worthington's position with 'C' Company following.[17]

'B' Company remained in place to wait for No. 10 Platoon. Once it reported that Estrées-la-Campagne was clear, Monk rolled his men "into a valley, up the far slope, passing several orderly rows of trees and finally into a rectangular field surrounded by a shoulder-high hedge."[18] Gathered here were now sixteen 'C' Squadron tanks, eleven from 'B' Squadron, four from Worthington's headquarters, and a reconnaissance troop Stuart.[19] 'C' Company was already digging slit trenches along the southern hedge that ran to a finger of woods at the field's southwestern corner. The mortar detachments set up in the northwest corner of the perimeter. Monk's 'B' Company was directed to hold the east flank and about a hundred yards of the northern front. When 'D' Company arrived, Lieutenant Colonel Hay said, it would occupy the rest of the northern flank and the western front.

Monk realized, as he got his men digging, that No. 10 Platoon had gone missing. The platoon had come under fire from two 88-millimetre guns manned by about thirty Germans when it was four hundred yards short of the summit. Lieutenant Claire Dutcher charged the guns with the two half-tracks, and as they closed in, the platoon piled out with bayonets fixed. The five Germans not killed were taken prisoner. Dutcher's men disabled the guns and proceeded to the summit.

Monk surveyed the situation. Because there was little cover, the half-tracks and carriers were positioned at measured intervals tight against the hedges. The tanks were arrayed so their 75-millimetre guns could fire in any direction. 'D' Company was still absent, its portion of the perimeter barely defended.[20]

At 0800 hours, a Tiger tank appeared in the distance. Worthington told 'C' Squadron's Major Tom Baron to command the tanks while he controlled the entire force. By this time, everyone knew Worthington Force was out on a limb and about to fight for its life.

Worthington Force had been discovered by Obersturmführer Bernhard-George Meitzel of 12th ss Division's headquarters. He had ventured east from Quesnay Wood in an armoured car to find the division's Kampfgruppe Waldmüller. Instead, he saw Canadian tanks on a hill. Returning to the wood, Meitzel reported the news to Obertsturmbannführer Max Wünsche. Fearing the Canadian appearance signalled a drive into largely undefended territory, Wünsche decided to attack. Five Tigers would strike from the west, while fifteen Panthers approached from the east.[21] Anti-tank guns and infantry were also dispatched.

WORTHINGTON STILL HELD the forlorn hope that 'A' Squadron and 'D' Company would arrive. But by the time 'A' Squadron reached Estrées-la-Campagne, the approaches to where Worthington was, on Point 111, had been shut by German tanks and anti-tank guns. Lieutenant L.D. Stevens and No. 1 Troop in the lead lost one Sherman to a mechanical breakdown next to the village. Then Stevens saw tanks silhouetted on a nearby summit and recognized them as Shermans. As Stevens and his corporal's tanks moved into the open, a Tiger immediately knocked them out.

About this time, 'A' Squadron was joined by 'B' Squadron's No. 2 Troop. It had gone to within a mile of Point 195 before withdrawing. The two elements linked up just as Tigers inside Estrées opened fire. Three 'A' Squadron tanks and one of No. 2 Troop's blew up.[22] One observer noted that when the Tiger's 88-millimetre shells sliced into a Sherman, there was usually an "immediate explosion and flames roared 20 to 30 feet out of the top of the turret. This was followed by two or three explosions of high octane gas and the high-explosive shells and the ammunition racks exploding."[23]

'A' Squadron's Major Geoffrey "Jeff" Sidenius ordered the surviving tanks to break through to Point 111. The running fight became completely disorganized. Two 'A' Squadron's No. 2 Troop tanks dashed desperately through fire and gained the Worthington Force perimeter. When Sidenius's headquarters section and No. 3 Troop attempted to follow, three tanks "were hit within a few yards of their starting point. Major Sidenius was seen to start out of his turret and then fall back again." The rest of the tanks, now consisting of a single one of 'A' Squadron and three of 'B' Squadron's No. 2 Troop, were pinned down short of Point 111.

Lieutenant Harvey Allen McDiarmid, commanding 'A' Squadron's No. 2 Troop, told Worthington that the "enemy armour and anti-tank guns had completely cut off our approaches and no further reinforcements from the original battle group could reach our position."[24]

When the Tigers opened fire from Estrées, Sidenius had ordered the Algonquins' 'D' Company to wait until the tanks opened a route for them. Standing next to his half-track, Major Keith Stirling then watched Sidenius die. Unable to raise Worthington by wireless, Stirling made for the hill, only to be driven back by anti-tank gun and mortar fire. Realizing 'D' Company could never get through, Stirling linked up with the Lake Superiors in Bretteville, and 'D' Company spent the afternoon fighting alongside them.[25]

Although he had brought it to the wrong place, Worthington was on good ground for a fight. The field was three hundred yards long by one hundred yards wide. It enjoyed good fields of fire. The edge was surrounded by a four-foot hedge. The eastern flank was also bordered by a thin line of tall trees inside the hedge. A thick wood extended from the western flank, and most of the slopes off Point 111 were covered in rough gorse. It was most vulnerable from the north and south, where wheat fields sloped gradually up to the hedge. Worthington had deployed most of his tanks to cover these two approaches. His headquarters tank was inside the cover provided by a few trees next to the northern hedge.[26]

At about 0800, Worthington stood alongside Major Monk and gazed with binoculars at their route of approach. "He was quite calm, but I think concerned over the non-arrival of the rest of our force. He told me we would stay and hold here, come what may."[27] Over the next hour, Worthington sent several signals reporting himself still on

Point 195. At 4th Armoured Division headquarters, Kitching was increasingly uneasy. He ordered red smoke shells fired to the front of Point 195. "Where are you in relation to the red smoke?" Kitching asked. "I can't see it. Where is the red smoke?" Worthington replied.[28]

When Worthington requested artillery against a target, brigade directed the fire against a reference point five hundred yards southeast of Point 195. "Are you getting required support now?" the brigade signaller asked. There was no answer. Worthington Force was off the air.[29]

Kitching suspected Worthington had swung behind the German front and was somewhere near Potigny, about a half-mile southeast of Point 195. Although both divisional and brigade headquarters could hear heavy fighting under way near Point 111, everyone thought this marked the Polish Division advancing to its objectives.

In the mid-morning, 4th Armoured Division's chief artillery officer, Brigadier Herm Lane, went aloft in his small spotting plane. Circling over the battleground, he saw no signs of the lost force.[30] At 4th Armoured Brigade headquarters, Brigadier Leslie Booth was also trying to locate Worthington. He sent Major N.A. Buckingham, the Governor General's Foot Guards liaison officer, looking in a scout car. Buckingham passed Bretteville and made for Point 195. Soon Buckingham, his driver, and his bodyguard were creeping the scout car through open fields. No signs of fighting ahead. No tank tracks visible. "We couldn't find anything or hear anything except noise [of fighting] to the right and left. It became awfully eerie and awfully quiet out in the right direction. I decided we had gone far enough and went back and told [Booth] how far we had gone and that we couldn't find anything out there."[31]

ON POINT 111, Major Tom Baron decided the best defence was an offence and sent Lieutenant William Harrison Bicknell with three tanks, including two 17-pounders, northward to engage the earlier spotted Tiger. He also directed 'B' Squadron to seize a wood to the southwest concealing anti-tank guns. The two tanks remaining in Lieutenant John Stock's No. 4 Troop headed for the woods, while Lieutenant John Scudamore's No. 3 Troop covered the move with fire and smoke shells. Stock's troop reached the edge of the wood and found it "clear of the enemy."[32] Hoping to extend the fortress defences farther, Major Carson headed for the wood with his squadron headquarters. Crew commanders in the other two tanks were Captain Johnny Hope and Sergeant George Wallbank.[33] Suddenly, the tanks that had ventured out from the fortress on either side "began to 'brew up' and none were able to return, even with the smoke provided by the remaining troops."

Almost everyone in Bicknell's troop, including the lieutenant, died.[34] A Tiger round cut through Stock's front right sponson and killed the co-driver. Ammunition and fuel exploded, the resulting blast blowing Stock and the rest of the crew out.[35] In Carson's group, only Captain Hope survived the destruction of his Sherman, emerging from the turret with an arm sheered off.[36] Stock found Wallbank lying next to his burning Sherman "moaning, with one foot completely blown off and the boot lying about four feet from the stump with a long piece of Achilles tendon still attached." A fine athlete, Wallbank pleaded with Stock to shoot him. Stock gave him a morphine injection instead. Suffering severe burns, Stock could do nothing more for Wallbank. Although a half-track reached the tankers, its crew could not recover all the injured. Wallbank and several others crawled painfully back to the perimeter.[37]

In the fortress, the situation kept deteriorating as the morning progressed. Mortar and artillery fire pounded it. Casualties mounted. Then two Typhoon fighter-bombers circled overhead before swooping down to fire rockets and machine guns. Recognition panels were thrown out and yellow smoke fired to signal they were friendly forces. The Typhoons rocked their wings in recognition. Thereafter, Typhoons came over at thirty-minute intervals to rocket and strafe the closing enemy. "They were heartily cheered many times during the day," Monk wrote.[38]

One of the great puzzles in the Worthington Force debacle was why the RAF, which organized repeated support flights, never reported its activities to First Canadian Army. Had it done so, the missing force might have been situated and reinforced.

Air support alone could not drive off the Germans. At 0930 hours, an 88-millimetre shell exploded. Lieutenant Colonel Hay fell with part of one leg severed off—a wound that ultimately claimed his life in 1949. Company Sergeant Major Aldege Primeau fell dead. Major MacPherson's back was riddled with gravel and shrapnel. The wounded commander of the half-track drivers from the Royal Army Service Corps, a Captain Lewis, suggested loading the remaining eleven half-tracks with wounded and breaking out. Worthington agreed.

MacPherson announced he would stay and command the Algonquins. He and Monk knew they were nowhere near Point 195, but had no idea of their true whereabouts. The two officers took Lewis aside. As it was daylight, they said, he should be able to fix their location and report it to 10th Infantry Brigade headquarters. Lewis agreed to try.[39] The half-tracks made a "mad dash to safety."[40] Only one was knocked out.[41] Disoriented during the escape, Lewis reported to brigade headquarters staff at 1030 hours that he thought Worthington Force was correctly on Point 195.[42]

At noon, MacPherson and Monk conferred again. MacPherson said Worthington had "given the same order to hold here come what may. We discussed the situation and although casualties were piling up, we were not unduly concerned. We felt that we could hold for the day and were confident that some of our troops would reach us before long. About seven tanks were still in action and these had been moved to the wooded west edge of our position."

Two hours later, the embattled force watched German infantry forming a thousand yards to the east. The fortress position was suddenly subjected to heavy mortar and 88-millimetre gunfire that "would begin at one end of the field and sweep the length of it and back."[43] Then the infantry advanced through the wheat, but were driven back by small-arms and tank fire. Attacks continued through the afternoon, each "repulsed, due to infantry fire and concentrated fire from our tanks," 'C' Company's No. 15 Platoon commander, Lieutenant Robert Saville, later wrote.[44]

Shortly after the first attack, a force of Sherman tanks, which the Canadians quickly identified as being Polish, appeared about two miles distant and headed towards the hill. As it came within a mile, the Germans shifted artillery and tank fire away from the Canadians and onto the Poles. Ignoring this fire, the Poles continued to close on the Canadian position and began shelling it while on the move, until the Algonquins released yellow smoke that identified the hill as being held by friendly forces.[45]

At about this time, Worthington apparently lost faith in his ability to hold out. "All the tanks that can still run will make a dash for it, return to original [forming-up position]; use fire and movement," he ordered by wireless. Eight tanks busted out of the fortress. Fortuitously covered by the Polish tanks firing smoke, all managed to escape. Left behind were four immobilized Shermans that could still fight.[46]

When the Poles closed to within three hundred yards, they broke up a forming attack with machine-gun fire. But a number of the Polish tanks were burning along their line of advance, and the survivors turned about and withdrew. Within minutes, the German fire "began again on us, if possible, with even more intensity," Monk wrote later.

"By 1730 hours, no Polish tanks were in sight, none of ours were in action. In fact, most of them were burning furiously, many with their dead crews still in them. The exploding ammunition in the burning tanks added to the noise and danger. Our mortar detachments were out of action. The field was a mass of shell holes. The trees and shrubs were cut to pieces from shrapnel. The smell of burning flesh, the odour of exploding enemy H.E. [high-explosive] mingled to make most of us nauseated.

"The continuous crash of exploding shells and mortar bombs began to have its effect, first among the wounded and then the rest of us began to get 'battle wacky.' We had run out of morphine and bandages. Many of the wounded men were delirious, shouting and screaming, jumping out of their slits, having to be pulled forcibly to cover again. Things looked pretty grim."

Another attack formed at 1700 hours. This time infantry were joined by tanks, "monsters, camouflaged, moving very slowly and staying at ranges of over 600 yards." From this range, the Panthers savaged the field with high-explosive rounds.

At 1730 hours, Monk saw Worthington "in the open, walking casually across the field." A mortar bomb whistled in, and the force commander "fell dead into a crater in the northeast corner of the field."[47] Another mortar round killed Major Baron.[48]

MacPherson joined Monk. "We should pull out," he said. Monk agreed to go, but not until night could cover their escape. Increasingly tormented by his back wounds, MacPherson panicked. Taking four men, the major attempted to escape down the northwest slope. A machine gun killed MacPherson and three of the men while badly wounding the other.

Several tanks gained the high ground overlooking the field at 1800 hours and started raking it with machine guns. This fire concentrated on the Algonquins' 'C' Company. After four hours under this withering fire, Lieutenant Robert Saville pulled the survivors back to 'B' Company's lines. Lieutenant Rod Blais and his platoon were left behind, shortly overrun, and taken prisoner.

The Germans closed in with the gathering darkness. A tank rolled into the southwest corner of the field and swept the hedge and gorse with fire. Lieutenant Dutcher sent a message to Monk that his No. 10 Platoon was unengaged at the southeast edge of the field. Monk quickly ordered what remained of Worthington Force to escape through that hole. Dutcher's men led the way, while Monk and his company headquarters section took Brens and lay down a steady fire towards the Germans. The last men out were Lieutenants Ken Gartley, Saville, and Fisher and Major Monk. At the last minute they "ceased fire and crawled through the gorse. The minute our firing stopped, the German infantry stood up, they were about 50 yards away, coming in, talking loudly.

"We left many dead and wounded men on the position and others were pinned down in their slits unable to move and were captured." Those who escaped stumbled blindly through the darkness, until searchlights lit the sky and "made a great guide for direction...In small groups we crawled north through the gorse and wheat and cautiously made our way back to our lines, dodging enemy patrols and posts here and there and eventually reaching the Polish lines at dawn." In Monk's party were forty-two Algonquins and ten tankers. Many were wounded. The Poles gave them hardtack and bottles of Calvados. Then the men marched to 10th Brigade headquarters at

Cintheaux and from there to the Algonquin rear area at Rocquan-court. "We were exhausted, filthy, and covered with dust and grime, aching from minor cuts and bruises. We swam in a river, washed, and fell asleep."[49]

While Monk's group had been the largest to escape, it was not the only one. Lieutenant Harvey McDiarmid and Lieutenant A.E. Biddle-comb commanded the two remaining undestroyed tanks. Biddlecomb's was the reconnaissance Stuart with its light 37-millimetre gun—useless against German armour. It hardly mattered, as neither had ammunition. With a Tiger closing to within a hundred yards, McDiarmid and Biddlecomb ordered their crews to abandon the tanks. Gathering together a dozen tankers, the two officers "told them to split up into groups and make their way back to our own lines." After holding the hill for about fourteen hours, they slipped away at 2100 hours.[50]

Worthington Force's losses were disastrous. In their first battle, the Dukes had 47 tanks—44 Shermans, 2 Stuarts, and 1 Crusader anti-aircraft tank—destroyed. Personnel casualties totalled 112—40 killed, 38 wounded, and 34 taken prisoner. The Algonquins counted 128 casualties—45 fatal, 38 wounded, and 45 taken prisoner.

"Such losses would have been deeply regrettable even had they been the price of success," the army's official historian wrote. "Unfortunately, they were suffered in the course of a tactical reverse which did much to prevent us from seizing a strategical opportunity of the first magnitude."[51] Point 195, which Worthington Force was expected to easily capture during the night advance, remained in German hands, and the road to Falaise was still blocked.

IN THE EVENING, Algonquin Major George Cassidy, who was acting second-in-command, learned he commanded the battalion. Briga-dier Jim Jefferson said "there was only the vaguest of reports of the unit's whereabouts, although it was believed that they were on or near Point 195." This belief was based on Captain Lewis's report. Hoping for more information, Cassidy visited Brigadier Leslie Booth, who confirmed the "situation was very obscure" and there had been no contact with the British Columbia Regiment for hours. Acquiring a scout car, Cassidy followed the Caen-Falaise highway until encountering the Algonquins' 'D' Company at Bretteville. "This was very heartening, as now at least there was a nucleus and the machinery for reorganizing if need be," Cassidy wrote. 'D' Company's Major Keith Stirling told Cassidy he was convinced Captain Lewis was mistaken about Worthington Force being on Point 195. Stirling believed the force had strayed into the Polish sector. Returning to 10th Infantry Brigade headquarters, Cassidy located Captain Lewis. Using a map and avoiding "leading questions," Cassidy had him walk through the route Worthington Force had taken and confirmed it had indeed wandered into the Polish sector.[52]

UPON RECEIVING WORTHINGTON'S initial report, Booth had set about filling the gap between Halpenny Force at Bretteville and Point 195. At 1030, he ordered the Governor General's Foot Guards to get through to Worthington "as quickly as possible." The Algonquins' 'A' Company and its remaining 3-inch mortars were to support the tankers along with a New Brunswick Rangers machine-gun platoon, 5th Anti-Tank Regiment's 96th Anti-Tank Battery, and a troop of Flails. This force "was to by-pass all opposition and make for the objective with all speed."[53]

The assigned support units had to assemble alongside the Foot Guards, and most were not in place until early afternoon. When Booth urged Lieutenant Colonel Murray Scott at 1345 hours to make haste, the tank commander said they would advance at 1430 hours. He "was not about to charge pell-mell along a single narrow axis in full view of the enemy to a likely strongpoint, Bretteville-le-Rabet, and then up a long open slope with only his tanks—all in broad daylight, without any reconnaissance having been done and with no smoke to screen their movement," Scott declared.[54]

At 1430 hours, advancing without having called for any covering smoke, the tankers led with the Algonquins' 'A' Company trailing the third squadron. Passing Bretteville, the column was turning west towards Point 195 when it came under anti-tank gunfire from Quesnay Wood. Three Shermans were knocked out.[55]

"Keep going, don't stop," Scott ordered.[56] The column shrank into an orchard and re-emerged about 1,500 yards distant. But tanks and infantry were now higher than the woods with nothing but open fields between. Realizing the tanks were ducks in a shooting gallery, Scott ordered the Algonquins to assault and clear Quesnay Wood. When Captain Clark Robertson demanded to know what support the Foot Guards were offering, the lead squadron commander, Major Robert Hall Laidlaw, said it would be suicide for the tanks to accompany the infantry, and they had no communication with artillery regiments. Robertson bluntly refused to advance. As the two officers walked back to inform Scott, Laidlaw was killed by a shell.

Robertson understood Scott's "quandary." Damned if he didn't go forward, facing certain slaughter if he did. The infantry officer suggested setting up a defensive position in the orchard.[57] Even then, under constant anti-tank fire, the tankers lost twenty-two tanks.[58]

Those surviving, however, served as mobile artillery supporting an advance by the Lincoln and Welland Regiment towards a spur extending from Point 195. As it was clear Worthington Force had never reached the feature, this move was a prelude to a renewed assault. Not only did the Lincs gain the spur but, when their 'D' Company wandered off course to the west, they wrested the village of Saint-Germain-le-Vasson from the control of what turned out to be only a dozen Germans.[59]

Simonds was deeply dissatisfied with the day's gains, which had created a line running from Vimont east through Saint-Sylvain to Bretteville-le-Rabet and then Saint-Germain on the western flank. There would be no pause, he declared. Point 195 must be secured immediately by 4th Division and the advance continued one and a half miles to Point 206, overlooking Potigny from the west. The Poles were to capture Point 140, west of where Worthington Force had met its end. They would then cross the Laison River and clear the heights by Olendon. In this way, First Canadian Army would end Operation Totalize looking over Falaise.[60]

Despite having committed the entire division during the day, Kitching ordered Point 195 taken in a night attack. With no fresh reserves, he turned to the least worn out infantry battalion—the Argylls.

What a Stupid Place

WHEN TOLD TO take Point 195, Lieutenant Colonel Dave Stewart "mentally wrote the Argylls off." Even if they had heavy artillery and an accompanying tank regiment, Stewart was certain a traditional attack would see the regiment decimated. At 2200 hours, Stewart, looking "cool and confident" held an O Group. "This is what is happening," Stewart said, "and the first company moves...in twenty minutes."[1] No artillery, no tanks. Instead, a single file following a circuitous route that would gain the hill by its northeast flank. Lieutenant Lloyd Johnson's scout platoon would lead, marking the route as it went.[2]

'B' Company's Major Don "Pappy" Coons grinned. "Piece of cake, we'll take it." Coons went up a notch in Stewart's estimation. Major Bill Stockloser of 'D' Company took Stewart aside. "You're sending us to our death." Stewart had thought Stockloser made of sterner stuff. "He let me down," Stewart said later.

Stewart's plan did not rest on bravado. Captain Pete MacKenzie of the support company thought it audacious but well conceived. Stewart "was a pretty independent thinker in the way he went about things, and while he always kept the objective in mind, he went about getting it in his own way. [Stewart] was always very conscious of casualties and did his best to avoid them wherever possible."

"We're going to lead the battalion up this hill single file," Lieutenant Johnson told his scouts, and then simply led them into the pitch-black night just before midnight.

Corporal Gord Boulton helped lay tape to mark the route. If a junction still seemed unclear, a man was left to point out the right way. Although everyone tried to move quietly, Boulton could hear several hundred Argylls "coming single file...behind us...[W]e could hear the shovels hitting the rifles and things like that...and they were supposed to be muffled, but with that many men" it was impossible.

Stewart was at the head of the main body, wearing his trademark tam-o'-shanter. "You can't win battles being behind," he claimed. There was no talking. If they were detected, it would be impossible to shake out into a coordinated battle line before the Germans tore the battalion apart. Private Bruce Johnson, a 'B' Company sniper, passed the "torso of a Canadian officer. Where the rest of his body should have been was tank tracks. Just completely obliterated. I knew he was a Canadian officer by the shoulder pips." The image would haunt Johnson ever after.

Private Mac MacKenzie saw nothing. Since he suffered from night blindness, others had to "lead [him] around by the bloody hand."[3]

At 0430 hours on August 10, the Argylls found Point 195 undefended. Dawn was breaking. Stewart directed the company commanders to the areas where each would position his men. "Dig like hell," he ordered. After six inches of soft loam, the shovels and picks struck chalk. Getting below two feet proved impossible, so the men dug outward—creating rectangles one or two men could lie in.

Not long after the Argylls started digging, they heard the grinding of tracked vehicles. Noisily, the support company arrived with the battalion's 6-pounder anti-tank guns and 3-inch mortars. A 5th Anti-Tank Regiment troop armed with 17-pounders and the New Brunswick Rangers (MG) No. 3 Platoon with its heavy Vickers machine guns also rolled in. Having walked in, Captain Bill Whiteside had already selected positions for the supporting arms.[4]

He placed the 17-pounders overlooking the long, gentle slope to the west. That was the most likely approach for tanks. The 6-pounders, of no use against armour, were spread out among the infantry.

Not worth "a pinch of coon shit," Stewart said of them.[5] The heavy machine guns were arrayed to provide "flanking protection" for the infantry.[6]

Point 195 had no peak. It was a plateau with rows of tall cypress trees bordering wheat fields, small groves, and thickets of brush. Too much ground to occupy, so Stewart positioned each company where it had a reasonable field of fire towards one line of approach. With the Lincoln and Welland Regiment to the northwest on the long spur running from near Saint-Germain to Point 195, that flank was protected. The Argylls still had to defend three other flanks.

Arriving undetected and without losing a single man seemed little short of a miracle. As another blistering hot August day was born, however, "the enemy awakened to the situation and began to react violently. He opened on our position," the Argyll war diarist wrote, "with heavy mortar fire [and] sent out a force to deal with one of our 17-[pounders]. 'A' Company and the scouts were dug in beside this gun. "In the ensuing skirmish the enemy was beaten back and 27 prisoners were taken." Intelligence officer Lieutenant Milton Howard Boyd was interrogating these men when the first 88-millimetre shell struck and killed him.[7]

Point 195 had been lost due to carelessness and lack of manpower. Now the Germans were determined to win it back. Artillery and mortar fire grew constant. Lieutenant Ken Frid "lost a whole section, which is one third of my platoon, as fast as you could bat an eye. They were just dishing out their noon meal when two 88-mm. shells landed right among them. It was an awful mess and sort of took the wind out of our sails. I lost two more men when their nerves went to pieces after seeing this sight...that hill turned out to be another hell-hole. We stayed all that day in our slit trenches while [the enemy] tried to knock us off the hill with shells and mortars."

Whiteside saw German tanks firing from Quesnay Wood. Transformed into a fortress by the 12th ss Division, the wood teemed with infantry, and from here most of the counterattacks emanated. The Germans "would come out of the woods quite broadly spaced... 150 yards from side to side. And [they would] start walking up the hill toward 'A' Company...it became almost like shooting fish in a barrel...the machine guns had a field day."[8]

On the other flanks, German crews pushed and pulled 88-millimetre guns through woods and brush to within five hundred yards. After firing a few rounds, they dragged the guns to a new location before the 17-pounders could range in. It was a deadly game of hide-and-seek the Germans played well.[9]

BY 0800 HOURS, the Governor General's Foot Guards, the Lincs, and part of the South Alberta Regiment had spread out through orchards in front of Grainville-Langannerie and Saint-Hilaire Farm to the north to establish a supportive base for the Argylls on Point 195. The Canadian Grenadier Guards were ordered to advance from here first to Point 195 and then to Point 206, overlooking Potigny.[10] At 0815, Major Pete Williamson's No. 2 Squadron led the way with the rest of the regiment following in line. During the night, Tiger tanks had been reported in the orchards of Saint-Hilaire Farm. Lieutenant Colonel Bill Halpenny was confident, however, that these had withdrawn. This erroneous conclusion was dispelled when a shell cracked through the lingering ground mist and punched a hole in the front of his command tank. Although Halpenny's Sherman remained operational, two other Grenadier tanks were knocked out by the Tiger. This signalled the start of a mile-long race that cost the Grenadiers six tanks before they reached Point 195 at 1130 hours.

Having gained the hill, Halpenny had the three squadron commanders and the artillery officer form their Shermans around his in a box formation in the middle of a cornfield two hundred yards north of Point 195. To their right, a Sherman that had ventured too far beyond the infantry was "ominously brewing."[11]

The squadron commanders and Major R.D. Telford of 23rd Field Regiment stood in a circle around Halpenny to discuss the advance on Point 206. Smith and Amy shrugged at each other. Neither could believe they were actually holding an O Group on an exposed hill with nothing but tank hulls for protection. "What a stupid place to be," Smith thought.[12]

Point 206 stood about 2,500 yards distant and was obviously strongly defended. In the valley between the two hills, the little hamlet of Fontaine-le-Pin was surrounded by artillery, mortars, and infantry stationed in the orchards. More gun positions stood behind the railway embankment passing a mine north of Potigny. As many as fourteen tanks and a large force of infantry were visible in Quesnay Wood. About two miles to the rear and northwest of Point 195, an 88-millimetre battery fired from another wood.[13] All agreed that the Grenadiers would only reach Point 206 with lavish and well-directed artillery and air support. When Halpenny tried to raise 10th Brigade on the wireless, however, he was unable to get through.

It was 1155 hours.[14] Smith was antsy. This crazy meeting had gone on too long. Suddenly 88-millimetre shells tore up great gouts of earth around the Shermans. Shrapnel clattered off armour and sizzled overhead. Halpenny and Telford leapt into their Shermans. Major Williamson bolted off on foot, leaving his tank crew to extricate themselves. Smith and Amy stood in front of their respective tanks, directing the drivers. "Back up," Smith yelled, "straight back. As fast as you can." Amy shouted similar commands. Halpenny's tank roared off. Smith and Amy had just slipped into their turrets when the area erupted with explosions.[15]

Most of the fire came from a line of trees extending from Aisy, a village on the Caen-Falaise highway directly opposite Point 195.[16] Telford smothered the tree line with artillery. His tank had been hit in the turret, knocking the fake wooden gun barrel askew. The 75-millimetre guns had been removed from FOO tanks and a wooden barrel substituted to create room inside for the wireless equipment. The dummy gun drooped "drunkenly," giving the Sherman a wrecked appearance that led the German anti-tank gunners to ignore it. But Telford's direction of the artillery from inside, noted the Grenadiers' regimental historian, made the derelict "indirectly the most effective weapon on the hill."[17]

The intense shelling of Point 195 presaged a major attack from Quesnay Wood. Six tanks and about three hundred infantry headed up the long slope. Scooting along at a rapid fifteen miles per hour ahead of tanks and infantry were three small remote-controlled tanks.

Smith stood on his tank's hull, a long cord threading back from his headset into the turret to the wireless set. Because Halpenny was engaged in discussion on the brigade wireless net over the infeasibility of advancing on Point 206, Smith temporarily controlled the regiment. Seeing the remote-controlled tanks, he rapped on the turret and pointed them out to his gunner.[18]

As the Grenadiers opened fire, each remote tank exploded in turn. It was unclear whether they had been hit or prematurely detonated by their operators. "Their value is problematic," the Grenadiers' war diarist commented, "for the blast, being vertical, caused no material injury to us."[19]

Their real purpose may have been to distract. Eliminating the little tanks left the Grenadiers exposed. Several Shermans were burning by the time Smith resituated the squadrons to meet the attack. Although the German tanks were driven off by artillery, the infantry kept coming.

"For over an hour the battle raged," one Grenadier report stated. The tanks threw out "a veritable hail of machine gun and [high-explosive] fire. Elements of the [Argylls]...ably assisted us. Defensive [artillery] fire was called down...both medium and field. In return the enemy kept up a bitter blanket of mortar, 88, H.E. and machine-gun [fire] and, although the attacking infantry was halted, they gave no sign of retiring."[20]

'B' Company's Private Albert Clare Huffman "thought it was maybe the end of the world." Shells were exploding all around. Men were dying wherever he looked. Huffman manned a Bren gun. "I was stopping some. It was just a job to do because I realized that they were out to get me. If I didn't stop them, well, I guess that's the basics, isn't it, of war? You get the other guy before he gets you...I was never a killer or anything, never wished to kill anyone, but I know I did."

When a tank next to Private Jim Coughlin's slit trench exploded in flame, "only the guy sitting up in the turret managed to get out by doing a perfect back flip into some brush behind the tank." He listened in horror to the screams of the others.[21]

A shell tore into Sergeant John Henry Andrews's Sherman and he ordered the crew out. As Andrews turned to run, he heard Guardsman M. Lutsky crying from inside the tank. Climbing back in, Andrews saw his gunner had both feet blown off. Andrews lifted

Lutsky out, lowering him to the ground. Kneeling beside the flaming wreckage, Andrews wrapped a tourniquet around each stump to stem the gushing blood. Then he carried Lutsky to an improvised aid post on the hill. Andrews stayed there the rest of the day giving medical aid to the wounded. He was awarded a Military Medal.[22]

At 1300 hours the attack crumbled, "but seven or eight shattered tanks were still brewing on the side of the hill under the August sun to warn the regiment of the fury of the German guns that surrounded it on all three sides." Telford estimated there were twenty-four self-propelled 88-millimetre guns firing on Point 195. Halpenny, meanwhile, had been instructed by 4th Armoured Brigade's Brigadier Leslie Booth to stay on the hill with the Argylls. There would be no advance on Point 206 until infantry could "knock out the anti-tank guns."[23]

Booth told Halpenny the Governor General's Foot Guards were en route to reinforce Point 195. Firing smoke to blind the guns in Quesnay Wood, Nos. 2 and 3 Squadrons of the Foot Guards dashed towards Point 195. No. 1 Squadron remained in reserve. Their arrival secured the Canadian grip on Point 195, but the Germans refused to concede. Heavy shelling and repeated counterattacks lasted all day.[24]

LIEUTENANT GENERAL SIMONDS realized that to reach the heights overlooking Falaise, the Quesnay Wood strongpoint had to be first eliminated. Advancing beyond Point 195 was impossible due to the guns in the wood. Left of Quesnay Wood, the Poles had seized Estrées-la-Campagne and Soignolles. Attempting to push on from these villages to Point 140, the Poles "attacked wherever the enemy was found and made every effort to exploit even the smallest success." But all was in vain. At every turn, the Polish right flank "received a ferocious mauling from...Quesnay Wood."[25]

With 4th Armoured Division near the end of operational effectiveness, Simonds decided to bring 3rd Canadian Infantry Division forward. Since Major General Rod Keller's wounding, 8th Brigade's Brigadier Ken Blackader had taken temporary command. Simonds gave him 2nd Armoured Brigade and, in addition to the divisional artillery, that of the Poles and II Canadian Corps. Typhoons would strike before the infantry advanced. Driving the Germans out of Quesnay Wood was the first objective, but Simonds also wanted the infantry to retrieve Operation Totalize's momentum. They were to push southward from Quesnay, gain a crossing over the Laison River, and then advance to a commanding ridge west of Épaney—attaining the prized view over Falaise.[26]

Blackader ordered his brigade, temporarily commanded by Lieutenant Colonel Jock Spragge, to carry out the attack. During his briefing at 1500 hours, Spragge said intelligence on enemy dispositions "was meagre," but the advance must continue. The attack would happen at 2000 hours.[27]

It would be a two-battalion show—the Queen's Own Rifles on the right, and the North Shore (New Brunswick) Regiment on the left. Once the wood was cleared, Le Régiment de la Chaudière would pass through and drive south to the mine north of Potigny. The latter regiment would be supported by the 1st Hussars. Because the woods were thick with anti-tank guns, no tanks would support the other two battalions. They would rely on the artillery and Typhoons.[28]

Stretching about a mile from north to south and approximately the same distance in width, Quesnay Wood was an irregularly shaped cultivated forest. Within were strips and patches of open ground where trees had been harvested. Being completely surrounded by open fields, the wood was impervious to surprise attack. About two hundred panzer grenadiers supported by twenty tanks and numerous 88-millimetre anti-tank guns were inside the wood.[29]

Neither the Queen's Own nor the North Shores welcomed the assignment. It seemed too hurried and ambitious. Major Steve Lett detailed all the Queen's Own objectives, including an advance beyond the wood by Major R.A. Cottrill's 'D' Company to a hill overlooking Falaise. Cottrill growled, "There must be a new boy on the staff, who can't read maps. No one else would expect a single company...to advance five miles through enemy held territory."[30]

The North Shore's Major Robert Robichaud, meanwhile, "had a premonition that something would go wrong." His 'D' Company would be out front on the left with Major Ralph Daughney's 'C' Company alongside.[31]

Keeping as close to the barrage as possible, the Queen's Own headed for the wood. Then the barrage lifted, and "a murderous fire opened from hidden tanks and the German infantry." 'A' and 'B' Companies gained the edge of the wood. But the following 'C' and 'D' Companies strayed into a U-shaped grain field with woods on three flanks bristling with panzer grenadiers and tanks. Nebel-werfers and mortars had zeroed in on the open ground. The two companies were pinned in the shoulder-high grain for four hours. On the edge of the wood, neither of the other two companies could make further progress.[32]

The North Shore attack was similarly stopped cold. Robichaud was struck in the chest by a bullet and temporarily paralyzed. Lieu-tenant Kevin Keirans led one 'D' Company platoon forward and Lieutenant Harry Smith another. As the company crossed a low rise and headed towards the wood, mortar rounds started falling and machine guns fired from the tree line. Smith was killed. Keirans and his men were three hundred yards from the wood when a tank started shooting. As Kierans threw a grenade into a slit trench on the edge of the wood, he felt a twinge in his left hand. Drawing his pistol, Kierans jumped into the trench and found it empty. Unable to move his left hand, Kierans glanced down and saw blood dripping from the wrist. Then he looked back and discovered none of his men were there. Kierans went back and found only four men unwounded. Someone said Robichaud was lying in the field they had crossed and was in a bad way. Kierans crawled to him. Carrying on to the com-pany tactical headquarters, Kierans directed stretcher-bearers to where the company's many wounded men lay.[33]

On the right of 'D' Company, Major Ralph Daughnay's 'C' Com-pany had also met withering fire. Daughnay was killed. Only forty-five men reached the woods. They remained pinned against the edge through the long night and withdrew at daybreak.

Shortly after first light on August 11, both battalions regained Canadian lines. The Queen's Own had lost twenty-two killed and sixty-three wounded. For the North Shores the cost was slightly less, twenty-two killed and fifty-eight wounded.[34] Lieutenant Colonel Buell had been badly wounded by shellfire. The North Shores considered Buell the division's best battalion commander, and his loss was keenly felt.[35]

"WITH THE FAILURE to take Quesnay Wood General Simonds' new plan had fallen to the ground," the official army historian conceded. "We had advanced some nine miles from our start line of 7 August; but the enemy, inferior though his forces were, had successfully sta-bilized the situation. To penetrate to Falaise First Canadian Army would need to mount another large-scale deliberate attack." Simonds cancelled further operations and ordered the Canadian and Polish armoured divisions be relieved by infantry divisions—3rd Canadian Division taking over from the Poles, 2nd Canadian Division reliev-ing 4th Armoured Division.[36]

Pulling back was not easy for those on Point 195. The Grenadier Guards, having suffered numerous tank losses during the morning of August 11, left first. Six Shermans were picked off during the escape.[37]

The Grenadiers reached Langannerie at about 1500 hours. Major Hershell Smith was surprised to see some of the men shedding tears of relief at having escaped the cauldron. "These guys need stiffening up," he thought. Then someone reported a tank with a broken wire-less had missed the order to withdraw. "I'll go back and get them," Smith said. As Smith walked along a hedgerow that led up to Point 195, he saw three Germans in a dugout. Realizing he had left his pis-tol behind, Smith shouted: "God damn it! Get out of there!" Pimply-faced youths crawled out with hands up. Dropped their guns, grenades, everything. "Go down there," Smith barked, pointing towards Langannerie. Dutifully, they filed off. "All they had to do was shoot me. I just scared the hell out of them. It was a spontane-ous thing, not thought out. I was scared mad."

Smith found the wayward tank. The crew commander was "scared and lost." Smith jumped up and grabbed the main-gun barrel. "I'll hang on to the gun and don't shoot it," he cautioned. "Go like hell," he said, and the tankers did. Huge plumes of dust roiled behind them, but they made it to safety. As Smith dropped clear, an officer from Halpenny's headquarters ran up. "Go over and put that officer who raised the cloud of dust under charge," the man said.

"Go back and tell Halpenny to stick it up his ass," Smith bellowed. "I brought the tank and the crew out. All are safe and I'm not concerned." As the man dithered, Smith said to tell Halpenny to press the issue personally. Which, he knew, Halpenny wouldn't do.[38]

Over the course of the night of August 11–12, the Argylls were replaced by the Stormont, Dundas and Glengarry Highlanders. Then the Governor General's Foot Guards left.

Totalize failed to achieve its final objective. As a consequence, the army's official historian deemed it a failure and blamed the troops—particularly the Canadian and Polish armoured divisions. Due to Totalize's failure, he wrote, "the capture of Falaise was long delayed." Had Totalize succeeded, Falaise would have fallen, with the Germans likely encircled and destroyed in Normandy. This would have led to the war's earlier end. "Had our troops been more experienced, the Germans would hardly have been able to escape a worse disaster."[39]

Lieutenant General Harry Crerar pointed his finger at the Poles. Why had they stopped advancing because of the fire from Quesnay Wood? They could have fired smoke to screen the wood and left a small containing force behind while advancing in strength on a wider front farther to the east. The Polish failure to keep abreast of the Canadians allowed the Germans to concentrate on a narrow front that eventually bogged the whole operation down.[40]

Simonds directed his ire at 4th Canadian Armoured Division's commanders, particularly the tankers. During a subsequent meeting of corps senior commanders, Simonds lashed out. Major General George Kitching thought it "a very tough and unpleasant briefing ... Simonds blasted armoured regiments for their lack of support for infantry—he quoted the heavy infantry casualties of the past month compared to armour. He demanded greater initiative from [armoured regiments]—drive on—get amongst the enemy ... Forget about harbouring at night—keep driving on. Arrange your resupply accordingly. Don't rely on the infantry to do everything for you! It was a real blast and it shook everyone up. I was upset because ... I felt our commanders of regiments did not deserve such treatment ... it is important to remember that up to that occasion *none* of our [armoured regiments] had had to operate in the dark—it was policy to harbour and refuel."[41]

At no time did Simonds concede that Totalize had been a large, overly complex operation. The precisely scheduled aerial bombardments had failed to shatter German defences. Masters at regrouping—not only the 12th ss but even the 89th Infantry Division—had offered stout resistance not easily overcome. And did Simonds really think that if the armoured regiments had got "amongst the enemy" their Shermans would have lived long in close-range shootouts with the 12th ss Tigers and Panthers?

Remarkable was what Totalize did achieve. An advance of nine miles over four days was unprecedented in Canadian or British formations in Normandy. Where Operation Goodwood had failed to break the German cordon at Caen, Totalize shattered it. At Totalize's end, the Canadians were more than halfway to Falaise and within grasp of the overlooking heights. During Totalize, the Canadian, Polish, and British divisions had 560 men killed and 1,600 wounded.[42]

PART FOUR

THE GAP

[24]

Without a Hitch

AT 1400 HOURS on August 11, Lieutenant General Harry Crerar and Lieutenant General Guy Simonds met to consider First Canadian Army's next move. Crerar first briefed Simonds on General Montgomery's new orders. On August 8, U.S. Fifth Army Group's General Omar Bradley had realized that the disastrous German counterattack at Avranches presented the Allies with an unforeseen opportunity. Instead of the wide American sweep to the Seine, Bradley proposed sending a corps from General George Patton's Third Army due north from Le Mans through Alençon to Argentan. This would place the Americans twelve and a half miles southeast of Falaise. If the Canadians and Americans then drove towards each other, they could close this narrow gap to "isolate and destroy the German forces on our front."

Montgomery had immediately recognized that "the prospective prize was great." Leaving Bradley to oversee the American drive, he worked up conforming orders on August 8 for Twenty-First Army Group. British Second Army would "advance its left to Falaise" as a "first priority, and a vital one." First Canadian Army would then "capture Falaise. It is vital that it should be done quickly. The army will then operate with strong armoured and mobile forces to secure Argentan."

337

By the time Crerar and Simonds met, Montgomery had adjusted his plan so that First Canadian Army would now "swing to the east around Falaise and then south towards Argentan, at which point it is proposed to link up with the Third U.S. Army." The Canadian advance would take it in a southeasterly direction that would cut the main road out of Falaise at Trun and then south to Argentan.[1]

As Simonds began planning this operation, he ordered an immediate attack west of the Laize River. Over the past few days, the 12th Manitoba Dragoons—II Canadian Corps's reconnaissance regiment—had been patrolling across the river from Bretteville-sur-Laize to test German defences and establish contact with British Second Army. On August 11, the Dragoons reported "large enemy withdrawals" under way.[2]

Simonds decided to advance 2nd Canadian Infantry Division, supported by 2nd Canadian Armoured Brigade, south along the west side of the Laize to come astride a road that ran from Saint-Lô to Falaise. The division would not only deny the Germans use of this road but also dominate the ground to the south and west of Falaise and be well positioned to advance on the town itself.[3]

Major General Charles Foulkes ordered 4th Infantry Brigade to lead the division "on a single thrust line."[4] The Royal Hamilton Light Infantry advanced from Bretteville along a road that led to Barbery. From here, the Rileys would hook to the southeast to Clair-Tison and cut the road. The Royal Regiment would then pass through to Ussy— just five miles west of Falaise.[5] The ambitious plan called for a rapid advance across seven and a half miles, but it was understood that the Germans were running.

As the Rileys marched forward on August 12, it seemed army intelligence staff had been correct for once. Snaking out of Bretteville, the brigade formed one continuous line. Each of its three battalions was accompanied by a squadron of tanks from the Sherbrooke Fusiliers. Certain the road would be mined, the Rileys pushed through chest-high wheat in the adjacent fields with the tanks behind. Twenty-two-year-old Major Joe Pigott's 'C' Company was on point to the left. Tall and hard muscled, Pigott had proven "very cool, almost lackadaisical" in battle.

'B' Company under Major H.A. "Huck" Welch—a thirty-year-old former football player with the Hamilton Tigers—was to the right. Welch's men were followed by Major Jack Halladay's 'A' Company, while 'D' Company, under Major Dunc Kennedy, trailed Pigott.

Barbery, a few houses at a crossroads, proved deserted. An eerie full-scale crucifix stood on the edge of the hamlet. "Quite a sight in the middle of a war," Sergeant Arthur Kelly observed. "I hope the peace that Jesus thought he died for prevails today," replied a man beside him.[6]

Turning towards Clair-Tison, the Rileys moved through fields that "narrowed about a thousand yards beyond Barbery where woods closed in on each side of the road. The men were sodden with sweat and chaff and pollen clung to their trousers as they walked resolutely toward the wood. A breeze rustled the aspen and poplar, their whispers punctuated by the odd clink of equipment and the whine and slap of the Shermans," wrote the regiment's official historian.

Suddenly, tracers streaked out of a copse left of Pigott's 'C' Company, and the hellish shriek of MG42s began. Mortar rounds whistled in, explosions sending men flying. Every rifle company was under fire.[7] Four Tigers hiding in the woods lashed at the Sherbrookes' 'A' Squadron. Five Shermans were soon burning in exchange for one Tiger, and 'A' Squadron retreated.[8]

"There was hand-to-hand fighting as these fellows came running out of their slits, firing rifles and grenades," Pigott said later. "The opposition was so bitter that I determined...that we were going to have to limit our objective." The Rileys fought fiercely. Scout platoon leader Lieutenant Hugh Hinton was killed while charging German positions.

The Tigers raked the Rileys with machine guns while standing well out of PIAT range. Lieutenant Colin Gibson, a 'B' Company platoon commander, led his men in overrunning several German slit trenches.[9]

"That's when the stuff started flying" Gibson said. "I ducked part way under a carrier when an 88-millimetre shell from a German tank exploded near me. The blast broke my leg; I was in pretty bad shape. [Lieutenant] Gordie Holder got out of his trench even while we were under fire. He came over, stuck the shell dressing on me and gave me a jab of morphine. It was one of the bravest acts I can remember. While he was doing that he got hit in the shoulder and I got hit again, this time in my other leg and arm. Right after that I turned my platoon over to the senior NCO."[10]

The fight raged through the day. At 1800 hours, a mortar round struck the slit trench housing Lieutenant Colonel Graham Maclachlan's tactical headquarters. Maclachlan and five others were wounded. Pigott took over until Major Hugh Arrell, the second-in-command, came forward. Towards twilight the Tigers ground in for the kill. Welch thought the "tank commanders had no nerves at all. They stood exposed in their turrets, looking for targets through their binoculars, their guns traversing all the time." Wary of PIATs, they suddenly stopped. After a "last desultory sweep with their machine-guns," the Tigers "left the field of smoking hulks, the dead and wounded." Twenty Rileys were dead and about a hundred wounded.[11]

WITH THE RILEYS heavily engaged, Brigadier Eddy Ganong had ordered the Royal Regiment—waiting near Barbery—to turn the German flank by hooking to the west and regaining the road at Moulines.[12] 'A' Company led on the right, 'B' Company the left, when the battalion moved at 1000 hours. They advanced on either side of a dirt track running through wheat fields. The Sherbrooke squadron followed in single file along the dusty track. Just four hundred yards out, machine guns in a barn and adjacent grove fired on 'A' Company. Captain John Ellis Strothers shouted for everyone to use fire and movement but to keep going.[13]

Then an 88-millimetre gun opened up from the right flank, and the advance crumbled. Some men dived into old slit trenches next to the dirt track, while the rest lay down in the wheat field. The lead Sherman was struck and started burning, prompting the rest of the squadron to withdraw.

At 1730 hours, Ganong ordered the Royals to try again. Surprised to meet no fire, they hurried into Moulines. August 12 cost the Royals ten dead and fifty-seven wounded.[14]

Three thousand yards south of Moulines lay Point 184, towards which Ganong advanced the Essex Scottish as the brigade's last task.

The Essex had a new commander, Lieutenant Colonel Peter W. Bennett, who replaced the badly wounded Lieutenant Colonel Thomas Jones.

Advancing at 2000 hours from midway between Bretteville and Barbery, the Essex swung to the east through a gap between Moulines and the Laize River. Several hours of night marching brought them to the edge of a wood southeast of the village by dawn on August 13. As soon as 'B' Company stepped into the open, it came under heavy fire. Veering west, the company became separated from the battalion and ended up on the outskirts of Tournebu, a village on the opposite side of the Saint-Lô–Falaise road from Point 184. The company's two officers were both wounded by machine-gun fire, and thirty of its ninety men were also either killed or wounded. Sergeant Stuart Kirkland placed "himself at the head of the remaining riflemen." With the Bren gunners and 2-inch mortar crew providing covering fire, "he led a bayonet charge against at least two machine-gun posts in the hedge on the outskirts of the village." Kirkland and his men took thirty prisoners. Another nine prisoners were netted inside Tournebu. Kirkland's actions earned a Distinguished Conduct Medal.[15]

While 'B' Company was so engaged, the rest of the battalion attacked Point 184 with five Sherbrooke tanks supporting. Two Shermans were knocked out by mines. When the Essex spotted five Tigers astride their line of advance, infantry and tanks slipped to one side without being detected. Then they came up against a field completely surrounded by a ditch filled with a dozen machine guns and five Germans armed with Panzerfausts. The carrier section charged the position with machine guns blazing, and seventy-five Germans surrendered.[16]

In the late morning, Major General Charles Foulkes ordered 5th Brigade to take over the advance. Brigadier Bill Megill warned the Calgary Highlanders to prepare for a night march to Clair-Tison. Once the Calgaries seized the village, Le Régiment de Maisonneuve would pass through and capture Point 176 near Ussy. This would place 2nd Division overlooking Fontaine-le-Pin and Potigny alongside the Caen-Falaise highway.[17]

The Calgaries left Bretteville-sur-Laize at 1400 hours and by nightfall gained their start line between Barbery and Moulines. As the road running from Moulines to Clair-Tison passed through open fields overlooked by wooded hills, Lieutenant Colonel Don MacLauchlan decided to instead follow a narrow dirt track that passed through a forest to the east. MacLauchlan realized that it was going to be "incredibly difficult at night" for the battalion to stay on course. And he was unsure whether the carriers would be able to navigate the track.

The battalion set out at 0145 hours on August 13. MacLauchlan found the advance "nerve racking in the extreme." The track proved to be "just that and no more. It was sunken through a large part of the route and throughout...continual checking was necessary as extra trails and tracks throughout the orchards and woods appeared" that were not marked on maps. "The move was made through darkness and in considerable mist." Passing through "deserted woods and empty villages and past quiet orchards," the Calgaries were "all the time uncertain as to where the enemy was and expecting and dreading at any moment a well-informed and sudden thrust...which would split the force into two parts. Progress was slow, but speed was not possible in a night move over such unknown country."

About one and a half miles short of Clair-Tison, the Calgaries came up alongside the road and were soon exchanging shots with snipers firing from all sides. MacLauchlan ordered the men to dig in. A squadron of tanks was to have met the Calgaries at the road, but it was nowhere to be seen. Not until 1400 hours did the Shermans appear, and the advance, in MacLauchlan's words, began "with caution." They pushed through orchards, one company leapfrogging another. The whole way, "men [were] being killed or injured, enemy killed or taken prisoner." The closer they got to Clair-Tison, the hotter the fight. At Clair-Tison a bridge crossed the Laize River. From the opposite bank, 88-millimetre guns and machine guns fired from woods. Two Shermans were knocked out, but the rest stayed and provided vital gun support. Artillery pounded every target the Calgaries identified.

Soon three companies were inside the battered buildings of Clair-Tison. Discovering the bridge still intact, the pioneer platoon crept out under fire to check for mines or wired explosives. They found nothing. The intensity of German fire from the other side kept increasing. By late afternoon the village was engulfed in flames, and any movement drew immediate response from 88-millimetres or machine guns. At 1732, MacLauchlan signalled Megill that the bridgehead at Clair-Tison was intact. He had 'A' and 'B' Companies across the river and everyone dug in. The way was open for Le Régiment de Maisonneuve.[18]

MacLauchlan's leadership this day earned a Distinguished Service Order medal.[19] Casualties proved extremely low—three killed and three wounded.[20]

By this time the French-Canadian regiment's dire manpower situation had reduced it to just 231 men.[21] At 1900 hours, 'A' Company, under Major Alexandre Dugas, made to cross the bridge and establish a firm base through which 'C' Company would then advance on the heights. As 'A' Company closed on the bridge, the Germans opened with heavy artillery, 88-millimetre guns, and mortars that "sent all their hellish cargoes on our heads," the battalion war diarist wrote. As Dugas tried to reorganize the panicking men, he was killed by a shell. The Maisies' attack stopped in its tracks.[22] Thirteen men were dead, another forty-one wounded.[23]

THROUGH THE COURSE of August 13, Lieutenant General Simonds and his staff had finalized plans for Operation Tractable—the next major 11 Canadian Corps offensive. Tractable had earlier been focused on winning Falaise, but General Montgomery now gave this task to Second British Army because 2nd Division's advance through Clair-Tison had paved the way for a British advance eastward. The Canadians would now gain the heights overlooking Falaise "in order that no enemy may escape by the roads which pass through, or near, it." Once the heights and Falaise fell, 11 Canadian Corps would advance southeastward to Trun, five and a half miles from Falaise. This would effectively close a gap German forces might use to escape between the Americans advancing from Argentan and the Canadians from the north.[24]

Simonds faced the same "gun screen" that had halted Totalize. As artillery bombardments "only warned [the] enemy of impending attack and [gave] him time to get down defensive fire and move reserves," Simonds decided to use smoke screens to "blind enemy guns, tanks, and flanks." Other than that, the operation was largely Totalize reborn. The 3rd Infantry Division with 2nd Armoured Brigade—less the Sherbrookes—would be on the right. Left would be 4th Armoured Division, bolstered in infantry by 3rd Division's 8th Brigade. Tractable's start line ran between Estrées-la-Campagne and Soignelles. The leading infantry would again use Kangaroos and half-tracks.

The attack would start at noon on August 14 with the armoured brigades going "straight through to their final objectives." Leading armoured infantry "would bail out" at the Laison River, "clear it and then push on to the high ground to the south." The 7th and 10th Brigades of infantry would then advance to the heights overlooking Falaise.

Simonds wanted the flanking smoke screens to "be impenetrable," while the smoke ahead would simulate the "density of thick mist." Although artillery would pound known German gun positions, Simonds again turned to the air force for extra punch.[25] RAF fighter-bombers would strike the Laison area fifteen minutes after the advance began. Medium bombers of No. 2 Group, 2nd Tactical Air Force (RAF) would attack the wooded Laison River valley through which both columns must pass to gain the heights beyond. Then, two hours into the operation, Bomber Command would unleash 811 Lancaster and Halifax heavy bombers to smash the Germans with a total of 3,627 tons of ordnance.[26]

Concerned about Simonds's request, Bomber Command warned that attacking the specified targets "involved serious risk to our troops. This risk was accentuated by the fact that the time table laid down by the Army involved bombing of up-wind targets first, with the result that drifting smoke would obscure the later targets. In spite of the risk, it was agreed that the expected gains from the proposed bombing outweighed the disadvantages."[27]

Quesnay Wood, Fontaine-le-Pin, and Potigny were to be saturated. The intent was to either destroy the Germans blocking the Caen-Falaise highway or prevent them from moving eastward to block the Canadian advance.

Considerable regrouping was required on August 13 to "pull this out without a hitch." By first light on August 14, however, both divisions were ready. The 3rd Division column stretched across a wide front from Bretteville-le-Rabet through to a point north of Soignelles, with 4th Division alongside to the east.[28]

DURING THE EVENING of August 13, Major Alec Blachi, second-in-command of 2nd Division's 14th Canadian Hussars reconnaissance regiment, had inadvertently strayed into the German lines while returning from a divisional briefing. He was killed and his driver taken prisoner. Documents he carried provided a complete description of Operation Tractable.[29] This intelligence, though late in coming, gave the German formations facing the Canadian front some warning. Extra anti-tank guns were moved to the high ground overlooking the Laison River.[30]

However, the German situation was too chaotic for the intelligence to have far-reaching consequence. Standartenführer Kurt Meyer never saw it. But instinctively suspecting what was coming, he had by the morning of August 14 split most of 12th SS Panzer Division into "penny packets" across a front stretching from Quesnay Wood east to the Dives River.[31]

The main German force facing the Canadians was the 85th Infantry Division supported by what was left of the 89th, 271st, and 272nd Divisions.[32] Commanded by Generalleutnant Kurt Chill, the 85th was responsible for five miles of line running from Quesnay Wood west to Mazières. Chill had deployed two infantry regiments north of the Laison and supported them with numerous 88-millimetre guns provided by III Flak Corps. The division's artillery, a number of anti-tank guns, and its Fusilier battalion stood south of the river.[33] In the ground between the Caen-Falaise highway and Mazières, at least ninety 88-millimetre guns were deployed.[34]

Born in 1895, Chill had served through the Great War. With the German army's disbandment after the armistice, he became a policeman before returning to military service in 1935. He had risen to divisional command in September 1942.[35] In February 1944, Chill raised the 85th Division from a cadre of Eastern Front veterans. By August, the division was a cohesive unit. In the words of one

analyst, it "was as good an infantry division as the Germans possessed at this stage of the war."[36]

The mustering German forces were looking anxiously over their
shoulders. Meyer knew their position "had become untenable."[37]
Generalfeldmarschall Günther von Kluge advocated withdrawal of
German forces west of the Orne and a retreat to the Seine. All the
high commanders in Normandy recognized the danger faced. The
Americans were closing on Argentan, the Canadians at any moment
likely to come down on Falaise. As von Kluge explained to OKW on
August 13, "the enemy is attempting to achieve an encirclement by
all means." He sought a "new directive."

Hitler responded with an opening diatribe about "the bungled
initial attack against Avranches." He demanded that General der
Panzertruppen Hans Eberbach attack the Americans in the Alençon
sector. Hitler envisioned Eberbach destroying "a large portion of
xv U.S. Corps" with this attack.

Eberbach received Hitler's order early on the morning of August
14. He immediately sent his "last special missions staff officer" to von
Kluge with a report. On paper his assigned force was impressive—
1st ss Panzer, 2nd Panzer, 9th Panzer, and 116th Panzer Divisions.
But each was in tatters, dangerously short of fuel and ammunition.
Lack of fuel had caused 1st ss Division to "blow up a number of tanks"
to prevent their capture. Eberbach urged "a quick withdrawal from
encirclement of Seventh Army [as] imperative to avoid catastrophe."
Unless his panzers were resupplied with fuel or ammunition, they
could not fight. Even with such supply, he could not strike the Americans at Alençon before August 16. "Success improbable," Eberbach
said in closing.[38]

Meyer knew the Canadians "were the northern claw of the encircling pincer; the southern claw was formed by the Americans at
Argentan. The death struggle of the two German armies would
begin as soon as the two claws met." Meyer did not expect to keep
these pincers prized apart for long.[39]

AT 2300 HOURS on August 13, Major General Charles Foulkes held
an Orders Group in a farmhouse to the east of Barbery. Tractable's
impending launch heightened the urgency of 2nd Division's drive to

the high ground overlooking Falaise from the west. It now fell to Brigadier Hugh Young's 6th Infantry Brigade to complete the task by pushing through the narrow bridgehead the Calgary Highlanders had won at Claire-Tison.

Reconnaissance parties reported the bridgehead "was a very weak one and covered a front of some 200 yards." Because of heavy casualties the brigade had suffered to date, Young worried about having so many "untrained" troops passing through the Calgaries in the dark. He figured the odds of soldiers getting muddled and scattered were high. There was also potential for a friendly-fire incident. "As this was a night attack it was necessary that the plan be very simple," he decided. Instead of worrying about the Calgary bridgehead, the battalions would line up on the river's western bank opposite their respective objectives. Patrols would then cross and establish small bridgeheads through which the attacking companies would advance.

The Cameron Highlanders would be on the right and bound for the village of La Cressonnière. In the centre, South Saskatchewan Regiment's objective was Point 176, about a half-mile from the river and next to the Saint-Lô–Falaise road. On the left flank, Fusiliers Mont-Royal would win a "small wood and orchard directly north" of the Sasks.[40] The Fusiliers were so reduced by casualties they were organized into two small companies. Zero hour was 0400 hours. Support from the Sherbrookes would be available only after dawn and depended on tanks being able to cross the Clair-Tison bridge. Young had also teed up substantial artillery.

When the barrage started, the Sasks advanced, Lieutenant Colonel Fred Clift and the company commanders guiding by compass. The men waded the shallow stream and then ran "to try and keep up with the barrage."[41] Moving unerringly through orchards, the battalion gained its objective despite "stiff resistance."[42] By the time the mist lifted around 0800 hours, the battalion was dug in. After some difficulty finding a navigable path through Clair-Tison, the supporting tanks, 2nd Anti-Tank Regiment's 17-pounders, and battalion support company carriers and anti-tank guns arrived.

On the right, the Camerons had a new battalion commander, Lieutenant Colonel A.S. Gregory, formerly of the Regina Rifles. Their attack progressed smoothly, and by dawn the village was secure.[43]

The Fusiliers met stiff resistance as they emerged from the low brush bordering the river and entered an open field. Heavy fire drove them back. After Major Georges White reorganized the two companies, they made another crossing at 0700. Despite heavy fire from both flanks, they gained a foothold in the orchard and occupied a small farm building. White counted only sixty-nine "fighting men" left. These hung on until German infantry counterattacked with two tanks in support at 1430 hours. Having nothing to match the tanks, the Fusiliers withdrew. Men crawled through ditches in the field and then dashed across the three-foot-deep Laize.[44] Some were taken prisoner. Lieutenant Pierre Bazin and twenty-six men were killed. About sixty men were evacuated with wounds.[45]

As the mist had lifted that morning, both the Saskatchewan and Cameron positions were counterattacked behind a screen of heavy 88-millimetre and mortar fire. At one point the Cameron anti-tank platoon manhandled one 6-pounder to where it could engage a tank from two hundred yards. Two shots set the tank on fire and killed two of its crew.[46] During lulls between counterattacks, the shell and mortar fire increased in intensity. Yet neither regiment suffered many casualties.

With these two battalions well dug in on excellent fighting positions, there was consternation when Young ordered a limited withdrawal by the most forward companies to ensure that they were not exposed to the heavy bombing attack supporting Tractable. This withdrawal was to occur at 1400 hours.[47]

The Mad Charge

LIEUTENANT GENERAL HARRY Crerar's rallying cry on August 14 was: "Hit him first, hit him hard and keep on hitting him. We can contribute in major degree to speedy Allied victory by our action today."[1]

Sitting in a Sherman to the east of Soignelles, Captain Jim Tedlie, the newly arrived battle captain of British Columbia Regiment's 'C' Squadron, had never seen so many tanks. "Visualize a mass of tanks, sponson to sponson, just a phalanx of armour. It was a beautiful sunny day. No clouds in the sky."[2] Tedlie's squadron commander was Major Jack Worthington, Lieutenant Colonel Don Worthington's younger brother. He and Major Jack Toogood of 'B' Squadron were the regiment's last original senior commanders. Lieutenant Colonel C.E. "Chuck" Parish was new, as was 'A' Squadron's Major Jack Austin. A lot of new men had been required to fill the Dukes' diminished ranks after Worthington Force's destruction.[3]

"Each column resembled a solid block of steel," wrote Algonquin Regiment's Major P.A. Mayer. "First were the Flails...whose task it was to clear the mines in the path of the advance." Next in 4th Division's sector were the Governor General's Foot Guards and Canadian Grenadier Guards "formed...in four lines with...tanks track to track." Behind the Guards were the Dukes' Shermans and then the Lake Superior Regiment's armoured cars. Then came 8th Infantry

Brigade's regiments loaded into Kangaroos and half-tracks. The column was "an immaculate formation...presenting a formidable sight."[4]

"Seemed to be tanks as far as one could see," newly promoted 1st Hussars Major Brandy Conron observed. To his left were the tanks of 4th Division. On his right, the Fort Garry Horse stood in line alongside the Hussars at the head of 3rd Division's column.[5] Behind the tankers, Stormont, Dundas and Glengarry Highlander Sergeant Doug Conklin sat uncomfortably in a Kangaroo. Unprotected from the searing sun, the dozen men were sweat-drenched. Conklin and most of the others also suffered from dysentery, due to poor sanitary conditions, which attained epidemic proportions in the ranks shortly after the new divisions advanced into the hot, dusty country south of Caen.[6]

At 1137 hours, artillery fired shells to identify targets for the medium bombers. Three minutes later, Brigadier Leslie Booth of 4th Armoured Brigade "broke the suspense and stillness of the wireless silence with the words, 'Move now.'" The tanks rolled forward "to begin the most daring and spectacular advance in Canadian military history."[7]

"All hell broke loose," the Grenadiers' historian wrote. "The whole earth trembled with the rattle of a thousand vehicles and the shock of gun recoil and discharge. The acrid air throbbed with the hum of engines and the explosion of all manner of screaming missiles. An incomprehensible range of reverberating vibrations struck upon the senses with confused and bewildering beat. The eyes were dimmed by dust and smoke until only the sights of the gun and the red disc of the sun could be seen through the quivering misty veil.

"For the first two minutes the original formation was maintained, but before the first half mile a concertina movement developed on account of minor bottlenecks caused by bomb craters, a sunken road, and other irregularities of the terrain. Then all were running blindly forward with pedals to the floor, in mixed groups of Grenadiers, Foot Guards and Churchills [79th British Armoured Division support tanks]. In five minutes we were through the outposts and in an area where Mark iv tanks, S.P. [self-propelled] guns, mortars and German infantry were thick on the ground awaiting our attack."[8]

"This is perhaps the only time in the war on the western front in Europe," Conron wrote, "where eight squadrons in the van, followed by four more squadrons, went roaring across country to overwhelm an impregnable anti-tank screen by sheer weight of numbers. As the tanks went crashing through obstacles at top speed they were continually confronted by...anti-tank guns behind each hedge. Invariably one or more tanks became casualties, but most of the guns were run down as the advance pushed on...For three to five miles the path was marked with burning tanks. Tanks crossed the start-line in line abreast—160 tanks in the first wave followed closely by a second wave of 90 tanks."[9]

"As soon as we crossed the start line, we churned up the most amazing clouds of dust," Tedlie said, "and that, coupled with the smoke that had been laid on our flanks to screen us...made the fog of battle...very real." Tedlie directed two 'C' Squadron troops to fire on earlier-identified German gun positions while the tanks were moving. Dozens of Germans spilled from them with arms raised. Tedlie stood in the turret, pointing an arm imperiously towards the rear as the Shermans churned past.[10]

On the far right, the Fort Garry Horse enjoyed "a great run over open country."[11] Blinded by smoke and billowing dust, the 1st Hussars' 'A' Squadron strayed to the left, almost mixing into 4th Division's column. "The speed of the attack over rough, uneven ground, which kept ammunition continually falling out of its racks, made it impossible to read a map," Conron noted.

Suddenly, two Tiger tanks fired on the straying squadron. Sergeant Arthur Boyle knocked one out with a shot from his 17-pounder tank, but the second Tiger hit Lieutenant Curtis Cole's Sherman. Cole and Trooper Gordon Linstead were killed. Another 1st Hussar Firefly fired back and silenced the Tiger.

All four tanks of 'A' Squadron's No. 3 Troop mired in an anti-tank ditch. Firing from these "stationary positions," they knocked out several German half-tracks, a small car, and six anti-tank guns before running out of targets.

Opposite 'A' Squadron, 'C' Squadron "swept" into an anti-tank screen. Squadron commander Captain Hugh Stanley Brydges was passing a hedge when an infantryman chucked a grenade into his turret hatch. When Brydges grabbed the grenade to throw it clear, it exploded and killed him. His body absorbed the blast, which likely saved his crew.

When a 75-millimetre shell penetrated Sergeant Roy Graham Lilley's turret, he was mortally wounded. The dying man traversed the gun from where it blocked the front hatch, enabling his crew to escape.

Because the two leading squadrons had strayed off course, 'B' Squadron reached the Laison River at Rouvres ahead of them. This squadron had destroyed a battery containing eight 105-millimetre field guns and six 88-millimetre anti-tank guns. It also bagged a huge haul of prisoners. Sergeant Leo Gariépy, his gun disabled, escorted 342 Germans to the rear.[12]

"To an enemy already deafened by shell and bomb blast and mystified by the dense smoke, the situation presented by the appearance of massed armour left no alternative but surrender, and this they did in large bewildered numbers as the advance continued," one Canadian report commented.[13]

"The first four hundred yards out," Major Hershell Smith of the Grenadiers' No. 3 Squadron recalled, "lots of casualties happened. We pushed through...a wheat field. There were copses of trees and open areas. Anti-tank guns in the copses and you're going through the hole between but there are so many [tanks] coming. And there was just a hail of bullets being thrown at them. Knock out one or five, but there's 250 more [German infantry]. Germans running across the field and it's middle of summer and they've got their great coats on...I'm on the left-hand boundary of the whole thing. I'm over the boundary line and lost...There was confusion. There was dust. The sun, you couldn't see the sun. It was a ball up there in the dust...It was wild. We were just running. Tanks were on fire. And people were firing every direction." Smith's squadron descended into the valley, off course, and came to Ernes about one and a half miles east of the objective of Maizières. Smith spotted a battery of 88-millimetre guns on the edge of the village. "It was mayhem for a while" as the tankers destroyed the guns.

Then Smith saw three Germans push another anti-tank gun

from behind trees. Two of the men ran back to the wood while the third stared over the sight, barrel pointed directly at Smith's tank. He shouted at his gunner, slewed the turret around, and tried to lay the 75-millimetre onto the anti-tank gun before it could fire. Smith was in a race already lost. The gun on the tank next to his flashed, and the anti-tank gun disappeared in an explosion. Smith looked over at the corporal commanding the Sherman, waved his thanks.[14]

"IN LESS THAN an hour, the splendid ceremonial array of the forenoon had degenerated into a heterogeneous mass pouring down the smoke-filled valley against a current of prisoners streaming to the rear."[15] The steep, heavily wooded valley caused further disorganization as drivers struggled to control plunging vehicles and avoid striking trees. At 1330 hours, the first tanks reached the river.[16]

The Laison was six feet wide and about two feet deep. Assuming bridges would be blown, the plan relied on special 79th Armoured Division tanks called Fascines creating crude crossings by dumping the great bundles of brushwood they carried into the river. Slower and clumsier, however, the Fascines were a full hour behind the columns' heads.[17] In the meantime, tankers and reconnaissance regiments "raced up and down the banks...to find suitable crossing places."

At Ernes, the Grenadiers' Major Smith discovered "the somewhat crumbling remnants of a small bridge," and No. 3 Squadron began crossing.[18] Over the wireless, No. 1 Squadron's Major Ned Amy reported being hopelessly lost. Smith fired a flare to guide Amy's squadron to Ernes. "You can't read a map worth a damn," Smith teased. Soon both squadrons were across the river.

This left the Grenadiers split—one part at Ernes, the other, consisting of No. 2 Squadron and acting regimental commander Major Doug Hamilton's headquarters troop, stuck at Maizières. Lieutenant Colonel Bill Halpenny had been ordered LOB, so Hamilton was in charge. Tanks and infantry carriers were piling into the village, and Hamilton saw no sign of anyone with authority to assign crossing priority. He was unable to raise Brigadier Leslie Booth on the wireless. The Tractable plan had the Grenadiers crossing the river and advancing to Point 159, "the highest point overlooking Falaise." Instead of unleashing Smith and Amy, Hamilton ordered them to wait for him "on the rising ground a mile southeast of Rouvres."[19]

Once again Booth's tactical headquarters was off the air, but not due to his being drunk. Instead, it had strayed from the column and been ambushed by several 88-millimetres. Booth's command tank suffered a direct hit. From another Sherman, Brigade Major Gerry Chubb saw the artillery officer pile out of the turret, followed by Booth, "who fell behind the tank and sort of half sat up on the ground." Chubb ran over. "They have got me," Booth said. "Balls," Chubb replied, before seeing that Booth's "foot had been shot off." Chubb applied a tourniquet and then "called up...a tank...threw Booth's body on the back deck and told the [artillery officer] to get him the hell out of there which he did...At this point we were out of all wireless communication with the rear of the brigade."

A jeep ambulance happened by, and Booth was transferred into the care of its stretcher-bearers. Bleeding heavily despite the tourniquet, Booth soon died, and his body was unloaded by the roadside to make room for two other wounded men. Wearing black tanker coveralls lacking a brigadier's red tabs, the body went undiscovered until the following day, fuelling rumours that Booth was somewhere in the medical evacuation chain.[20]

Word of Booth's loss spread haphazardly through the brigade. Lieutenant Colonel Murray Scott of the Foot Guards heard the news upon reaching the riverbank. Scott's command tank had been wrecked during the charge by an anti-tank shell. Despite having his leg broken, Scott had commandeered another tank and carried on. The senior surviving officer, Scott assumed brigade command and ordered the advance continued. As all brigade communications equipment had been destroyed in Booth's tank, Scott was incapable of communicating beyond his own regimental net because signals to the other regiments or to division would have been routed through the fallen brigadier's network.[21] This left Major General George Kitching and Lieutenant General Guy Simonds in the dark as to the status of 4th Armoured Brigade.

Lacking direction from above, the other two tank regiments and Lake Superiors went their own way. As the Grenadier Guards' Major

Jim Munro described it, the Superiors had shown "all sorts of battle courage." They "were an efficient, fast-striking force of skilled infantrymen. They were heavily tracked—their carriers looked like battleships—and they had every weapon they could get on them. They were over-sized, over-strength and very tough guys—just great to work with."

Lieutenant Colonel Robert Keane displayed this kind of courage when some Superiors stalled before a trench held by German infantry. Jumping from his command vehicle, Keane strode up and shot two dead. That produced the desired surrender.[22]

By the time Keane arrived at Rouvres, the Fascines were in place, but both the group of Grenadiers and the entire Foot Guard regiment were jockeying before them. With the column stalled in the village, German artillery and mortar fire was picking off growing numbers of men and vehicles. Get moving or be shot to pieces, Keane decided. Ordering the men out of the carriers, Keane led them in chucking rubble from ruined buildings into the river. Over this "rubble crossing," they gained the south bank.[23]

At Montboint on the western flank, the Fort Garry Horse also found only destroyed bridges. With 88-millimetre shells "cutting down good sized trees by the road," the tankers were frantic to keep moving. 'C' Squadron dismounted and used logs to brace and create decking on one wrecked bridge. Lieutenant Colonel Ronald Morton, meanwhile, struck out eastward. At a burning château, Morton discovered a little bridge completely intact. "All was quiet here and the beautiful summer day seemed almost sinister in its stillness." Realizing there were no Germans across the river, he summoned the regiment and then notified 2nd Brigade of the bridge. As 'A' and 'B' Squadrons funnelled across it, 'C' Squadron passed over their log-improved bridge. It was 1630 hours, the way clear for mounted infantry.[24]

IN THE CONFUSION, few upfront had noticed Bomber Command's arrival at 1400 hours. Guided by 42 Mosquitoes, 417 Lancasters and 352 Halifaxes came "straight from the coast line" in "a carefully timed run...over our own troops." While most of the hundreds of bombers dropped accurately, over the ensuing two hours, seventy-seven bombers—forty-four of them Royal Canadian Air Force—"by ill hap" dropped payloads short. Most of the errant bombs fell in the area of Saint-Aignan and around the huge Hautmesnil quarry, both important hubs.

The sight of open bomb-bay doors sparked a general panic in the rear areas. Yellow smoke sprouted all over, yellow recognition panels were thrown out, and yellow flares were fired to indicate friendly positions. But Bomber Command knew nothing about yellow indicators marking friendly forces. Incredibly, its Pathfinders used yellow flares and smoke bombs to situate assigned targets.[25]

The 12th Field Regiment's guns were deployed at Hautmesnil. The gunners enjoyed a "grandstand seat" as bombers released on Quesnay Wood. "It really looked impressive and one wondered how the Jerries could live through it," Captain Thomas Bell wrote.

Then the next wave came over at less than a thousand feet altitude. As "they approached we could see the bomb doors open and bombs come tumbling out. It was a horrifying sight and the result was a terrible nightmare. In a steady, stately procession the heavies came over, wave after wave, unendingly. The first bombs dropped on us at 1430 hours and at 1540 hours we had our last."

Yellow smoke canisters were ignited, and men waved large yellow flags. Bell could see the pilots and co-pilots in the cockpits. "How can they mistake us!" he yelled. Then more bombs fell. "The agony of suspense was terrifying and escape impossible. The air after each stick was dropped would be filled with flying debris, and between waves the ammunition from dumps and blazing vehicles was exploding in every direction. The whole area of the quarry was a raging inferno."[26]

When it ended, 12th Field counted its losses—twenty-one dead and forty-six wounded.[27] No. 16 Battery was hardest hit and then No. 11, while No. 43 Battery escaped any damage. All of No. 16 Battery's vehicles and trailers were destroyed and most guns damaged.[28]

During the morning, 2nd Division's 6th Infantry Brigade had ordered its leading battalions back of the bomb targets around Fontaine-le-Pin, west of the Caen-Falaise highway. The Queen's Own Cameron Highlanders duly complied. South Saskatchewan

Regiment's Lieutenant Colonel Fred Clift disagreed. Pulling back the forward companies would reveal their positions to the Germans. And the distance authorized for withdrawal "would leave [them] still very close to the bombing without being dug in."[29]

Both Camerons and Sasks were bombed with equal ferocity despite opposite responses. The densest bomb concentration landed precisely where Clift had been instructed to situate 'B' Company, leaving twenty-four "huge craters."

Not that 'B' Company got off unscathed. It still suffered heavy casualties. Private Chic Goodman was in a slit trench near that of company commander Captain Henry Maxwell Inglis. When the bombs fell, Inglis was checking on his men. In a bombing lull, Goodman saw Inglis and his batman running towards their slit trench. Then another bomb exploded. The twenty-year-old officer and his batman "just disappeared," and their slit trench was replaced by a huge bomb crater.[30] South Saskatchewan casualties tallied twenty-eight killed and forty-one wounded.[31]

For saving some lives, much credit was given at the time and subsequently to pilots of Auster spotting planes used by artillery officers to direct fire. These pilots bravely flew into the midst of the bombers, firing red flares to guide them away.[32] At 9th Infantry Brigade headquarters, near Cintheaux, the intelligence officer spotted an Auster "signalling to the heavy aircraft in what seemed…a successful attempt to direct them on the proper target."[33]

However, in a detailed investigation of the August 14 bombing errors, Air Chief Marshal Sir Arthur Harris dismissed any possibility that the Auster pilots had a positive effect. "My comment on this is that in the first place the rest of the bombing was under way, firmly controlled by the Master Bombers and achieving excellent results on the correct aiming points. In the second place red Verey lights fired into smoke or seen through smoke burning on the ground are likely to and did in fact, give a misleading imitation of target indicators." Whether the Auster pilots influenced events in any form remains a matter of debate.

Harris was furious with his bomber crews. "I regard the errors of the few who erred as being in this particular case inexcusable solely on the grounds that no matter what misleading conditions and indications existed any adequate effort to maintain the check on a timed run from the coast line to the target area could and would have prevented those errors."[34]

The two Pathfinder crews involved were dismissed and reposted to "ordinary crew duties." Squadron and flight commanders "relinquished their commands." They and their crews were returned to ordinary duties. Harris pointed out that despite "the regrettable errors during the action, more than 90% of the Bomber Force attacked, accurately and heavily, the correct targets."[35]

Nothing could undo the damage. Sixty-five Canadians were confirmed killed, 241 wounded, another 91 declared missing and later presumed dead. The Poles counted 42 dead and 51 missing.[36]

WHILE THE BOMBS were falling, Tractable had become increasingly confused. In the middle of 3rd Division's column, the Glens' Sergeant Doug Conklin had found riding in the Kangaroo a strange experience. "If you dared peek over the side, you could see us going by Germans...And it was scary! You wondered what was going to happen...Then they just stopped...and everybody jumped out and after a bit of confusion, they got us together and we were pretty well behind the Germans, though there were some there."[37]

The Glens dismounted to seize Montboint and the adjacent château. Thick woods surrounded both, and a tough fight was expected. Instead, the Germans, who "occupied the area in considerable strength, surrendered after brief engagements, and an enormous quantity of equipment was taken," Lieutenant Colonel Roger Rowley reported. The Glens rounded up 220 prisoners.

'B' Company met stout resistance around the château from four machine guns, which a Tiger tank protected from being flanked. Just before Tractable, the Canadians had been supplied with Wasps—Bren carriers mounting flame-throwers—and Rowley sent for some. They quickly wiped out three machine guns, flaming one "at the extraordinary range of 120 yards." The Germans manning the fourth gun fled, rather than suffer a fiery death.

The Tiger was not so easily quelled. Three Crocodiles attempted to engage it and were promptly knocked out. Finally, the Glens pushed a 6-pounder anti-tank gun through woods to gain a side-on angle. A round of newly issued Sabot ammunition put the Tiger out of action.[38]

For Rowley, the day had been a test. Since replacing Lieutenant Colonel G.H. Christiansen, he had been treated icily by the regiment. Rowley had no connection to the Glens. He had come from the Cameron Highlanders of Ottawa. And this day, Rowley had led well—he had been aggressive, but not careless of lives.

In the 4th Division column, 8th Infantry Brigade had dismounted upon reaching the Laison and forded it on foot. The Queen's Own Rifles secured Maizières. Le Régiment de la Chaudière passed through and advanced up the wooded slope to look down upon the valley beyond. The North Shore (New Brunswick) Regiment then marched southeastward to Sassy. They entered the village at 2200 hours, finding it "clear of enemy."[39]

Out front, the tankers had continued advancing. The Foot Guards punched through to Olenden. "Everywhere were knocked out and burning tanks, our own and the enemy's, while the air was choked with dust, cordite fumes and smoke and laced with machine-gun tracers. Olenden was very strongly held and here all squadrons engaged in a violent battle. Tank and personnel casualties were very high. The area was soon littered with burning tanks and dead Germans, while as each enemy position was destroyed, prisoners came forth in large numbers."[40]

With South Alberta Regiment in support, 10th Infantry Brigade closed on Olenden shortly after the Foot Guards left to continue southward. The Argyll and Sutherland Highlanders attacked cautiously, finding nothing but dead bodies, burning tanks, and shattered houses. Pressing on, they occupied an equally undefended Perrières before nightfall.[41]

After the Superiors had crossed their "rubble bridge," the British Columbia Regiment followed suit. Together, Superiors and Dukes had advanced to high ground four miles south of the Laison. En route, they overran a large German infantry force evacuating Sassy and tore into them with machine guns. In a matter of minutes, 250 Germans surrendered and "as many more" were killed.[42]

Gaining the high ground, Lieutenant Colonel Keane and

360 / BREAKOUT FROM JUNO

Lieutenant Colonel Parish studied their maps, confirming that the contour lines accorded with the surrounding terrain. "It was quiet, the sun was getting low. Tanks glided into position, crews dismounted, stretched their stiff muscles, lit cigarettes, cracked open a package of hardtack or wrestled with a tin of sardines or bully beef and looked around...to count the losses. We had lost 15 tanks," Captain Douglas Harker wrote.[43] The Dukes and Superiors had gained the most ground this day—close to six miles. For those who participated in it, Tractable's first day would forever be known as "the Mad Charge."

AS NIGHT FELL, General Montgomery modified his orders. Instead of just winning the heights overlooking Falaise, the Canadians would now also take the town. Second British Army would concentrate on eliminating elements of Fifth Panzer and Seventh Armies attempting to escape eastward from the developing pocket. Falaise was to be taken quickly, so as not to delay the primary Canadian task of advancing southeastward to Trun and then turning south to meet U.S. Third Army and close the gap that existed between.

On August 5, Montgomery had set a boundary between the 12th U.S. Army Group and Twenty-First Army Group of eight miles south of Argentan. The xv U.S. Corps of Third Army reached this boundary on the evening of August 12, crossed it, and advanced to within two and a half miles of Argentan. Major General Wade H. Haislip then ordered the corps to halt while he sought instruction from General George Patton. Early on August 13, Patton told Haislip to take Argentan and "push on slowly in the direction of Falaise." Patton's emphasis on "slowly" was to prevent a potential friendly-fire clash.

That afternoon, with Haislip just fifteen miles south of Falaise, Patton ordered a halt in response to Bradley's fear that the Germans "now stampeding to escape the trap" would trample xv Corps in their path. He also fretted that when Canadians and Americans met, there would be "a disastrous error in recognition." Bradley discussed none of this with General Montgomery.[44] Meeting with Montgomery and Second Army's General Myles Dempsey earlier in the day, Bradley left them with the impression that "there was apparently no restraint placed on further northward movement by xv Corps."

Having added to First Canadian Army's tasks, Montgomery did nothing to strengthen it. Montgomery had been highly flexible—shifting divisions and corps from one army to another as required. Yet at a time when reinforcing First Canadian Army with divisions from the bloated British Second Army would have hastened closing the gap, he did nothing.

Hence, Bradley and Montgomery—each in his own way and for differing reasons—critically delayed encircling the Germans. Both generals, it seemed, were casting eyes towards the Seine and the original long encirclement strategy for destroying German forces in Normandy.[45]

The Germans were not stampeding. But Commander in Chief, West Generalfeldmarschall Günther von Kluge recognized the time for flight fast approached. On the night of August 14–15, he reported that First Canadian Army had launched a "big attack on both sides of the Caen-Falaise highway. It had been halted for the moment but would be continued." 1 ss Panzer Corps could "only stand fast if additional forces were moved in."

He also reported that the attack by General der Panzertruppen Hans Eberbach "could not be carried out." Eberbach, in fact, "had gone over to the defensive." If the attack did not occur, von Kluge said, "the only remaining possibility was to break out with all forces from the pocket towards the Northeast."[46]

26

A Molten Fire Bath

LIEUTENANT GENERAL GUY Simonds had wanted to continue the drive to the heights overlooking Falaise through the night, but 3rd Infantry Division and 4th Armoured Division were in too much "disorder." The night was instead spent "collecting stragglers and in getting wireless sets back on their proper nets." There was also the need to alter the operation to include capturing Falaise.[1] The 3rd Division plan remained unchanged. Having outflanked Quesnay Wood, the division would hook westward to the Caen-Falaise highway and then advance to Point 159 and Versainville, from where they could continue straight into Falaise from the north.

Slight modifications were required for 4th Armoured Division. Major General George Kitching proposed "to clean up the triangle between Olendon, [É]pan[e]y and Perrières by first light, then get the armour on to its original objectives and pass a battalion through to Falaise."[2] The loss of 4th Armoured Brigade's commander and essential communications equipment stalled implementation of this plan till morning, as Kitching needed the night to build a new brigade headquarters and have it rendezvous with Lieutenant Colonel Murray Scott, who temporarily commanded the brigade.

Kitching had not wanted Scott. He had asked for Lieutenant Colonel Bob Moncel, currently a staff officer at corps headquarters.

Simonds and Kitching were agreed that he was the best candidate to command the brigade following Leslie Booth's death. Without explanation, Simonds deferred making the appointment. That left Kitching with Scott, a competent commander of the Governor General's Foot Guards but not suitable for brigade. Kitching was also unaware that Scott had broken his leg the previous day and was trying to carry on despite this painful injury.

"The combination of so many casualties amongst my senior officers," he later wrote, "the frequent changes of command of regiments, squadrons and troops; the loss of so many tanks and crews; the breakdown of communications and our inexperience of battle were factors that greatly affected our ability to function as a division...I do not think these factors were appreciated sufficiently by General Simonds whose vision was focussed on the horizon and whose thoughts were often a day or two ahead of us."[3]

In the early morning, 4th Armoured Brigade renewed its southward advance. While the tank regiments passed west of Épaney, the Lake Superior Regiment supported by a Canadian Grenadier Guards squadron approached the village from the east, and 10th Infantry Brigade's Algonquin Regiment assaulted it from the north.[4]

Having assumed command of the Algonquin Regiment the previous day, Lieutenant Colonel Robert Bradburn advanced 'D' Company at first light. Major P.A. Mayer directed No. 16 Platoon to capture some farms on Épaney's outskirts to set up a firm base. The other two platoons would then enter the village with No. 17 Platoon and seize the church in the central square. All went well until No. 17 Platoon "stirred the hornet's nest," and a hail of sniper fire drove both platoons to ground. Withdrawing the company, Bradburn threw the rest of the battalion into a full-scale attack that raged through the day. By the time the Germans withdrew, the division's "time schedule was breaking down."[5] To the east, the Superiors never reached Épaney. They met one resistance pocket after another and finally dug in on the village's outskirts for the evening.[6]

For the tankers, August 15 was a day of muddling disappointment. The Foot Guards, under command of Major E.M. Smith, advanced west of Épaney and encountered a strong gun line in woods south of the village that engaged the tanks from head on and both flanks. After losing several tanks, the Foot Guards pulled back.[7]

By initially screening their advance with smoke shells, the Grenadier Guards avoided tank losses until Major Doug Hamilton directed them towards a ridge between Épaney and Point 159. Coming within range of the gun line in the trees, one tank was hit and brewed, its crew so badly burned that one man died.

By 1300 hours, 4th Division's advance was stalled before the German guns in the woods. The Grenadiers, British Columbia Regiment, and elements of South Alberta Regiment were all gridlocked. "In the absence of guidance from above," the Grenadiers' war diarist wrote, regimental commanders were left to their own devices. During this entire time, 4th Armoured Brigade relayed no orders. The Dukes' Major Chuck Parish and Hamilton dismounted to confer. "Observation showed the high ground to be open and flat without cover and it was felt by both the BCR and ourselves that an [advance] across this ground without [infantry] and proper [artillery support] would prove disastrous." Artillery was called for, but not delivered. At 1500 hours, an erroneous report placed the Foot Guards on Point 159. They were actually well behind the other regiments. "All together the whole day proved very much wasted," the Grenadiers' war diarist complained.[8]

During the afternoon, Lieutenant Colonel Scott—virtually incapacitated by pain—agreed to evacuation. With Simonds still refusing to send Moncel and refusing to explain his reasons, Kitching proposed personally leading the brigade while also commanding the division. Simonds scotched that notion immediately. When he continued to withhold Moncel, Kitching had no recourse but to appoint the overly cautious Lieutenant Colonel Bill Halpenny temporary commander.[9]

RIGHT OF 4TH Armoured Division, 3rd Infantry Division had met fierce resistance during its advance on the heights overlooking Falaise. With its 8th Brigade having fought in 4th Division's ranks the previous day, 3rd Division was badly overextended. Its 9th Brigade was still engaged in mopping up German resistance in the Laison Valley. To take over the divisional advance, 7th Infantry Brigade's

Canadian Scottish and Royal Winnipeg Rifles had spent the night on a forced march to reach the front by dawn.

The Winnipegs ended their march in woods midway between Olenden and Tassily, while the Can Scots pushed on a mile to Point 175. Reveille was sounded by German machine guns hidden in nearby farm buildings "strewing lead all through our lines," Lieutenant T.A. Burge reported. Assisted by supporting tanks, the Can Scots soon drove the Germans off.[10]

At 1000 hours, Major R.M. Lendrum, temporarily commanding because Lieutenant Colonel Fred Cabeldu had been sidelined by enteritis, received a coded summons to an O Group. Unable to decrypt the code, Lendrum requested the meeting location sent in the clear. That informed him that the Can Scots had been placed under 2nd Armoured Brigade command, its headquarters at Montboint.[11]

Lendrum and Burge arrived there to find the brigade also under a temporary commander—the 1st Hussars' Lieutenant Colonel Ray Colwell. Brigadier John Bingham, who had taken over after Brigadier Bob Wyman was wounded, had been sent to the rear for a rest by the brigade's medical officer.[12] Colwell said the Can Scots were to lead 3rd Division's advance by seizing Point 168 at 1130 hours. This would bring it parallel with 4th Division at Épaney.

Point 168 lay a mile south of the battalion's present position and held a commanding view of Falaise. While emphasizing speed, Colwell could offer no information on enemy defences. The battalion was out of range of any possible supporting artillery, but Colwell assured Lendrum the hill was believed only lightly defended.[13]

Persuading Colwell to set the attack back to 1230, Lendrum sent Burge to brief the battalion while he worked out armoured support details with 1st Hussars' Major Brandy Conron. The 1st Hussars had ended the August 14 "Mad Charge" with 'A' Squadron mustering seven tanks, 'B' Squadron thirteen, and 'C' Squadron only four. The two weakest squadrons were merged into one in order to support the Can Scots.[14]

Just before Lendrum returned to Point 175, Colwell reported that medium artillery could range on Point 168 and would provide a pre-assault bombardment. Lendrum arrived at the battalion just two minutes before the attack was to begin. He was still briefing company commanders when the bombardment fell.[15] The Can Scots crossed the start line thirty minutes late.[16]

They advanced in box formation, 'D' Company leading on the left, 'B' Company the right, followed respectively by 'A' and 'C' Companies and with Lendrum's tactical headquarters in the middle. They advanced into a checkerboard of small fields surrounded by dense hedgerows, so that each company ended up isolated and fighting its own battle.[17]

A battle began the instant the Can Scots crossed the start line and, in Burge's words, "stepped into a molten fire bath."[18] Captain Harvey Bailey, 'D' Company's second-in-command, "watched tracer bullets go between my legs." Pressing on despite the intense fire, 'D' Company advanced through a hedgerow and came up against a Tiger tank stationed behind the facing hedgerow. Major Larry Henderson summoned the Hussars to engage it.

With no time to resupply, the Hussars were fighting with little ammunition and even less fuel. Not that it mattered. As the eleven tanks emerged from the first hedgerow, several fell prey to hidden anti-tank guns and burst into flame. The survivors reversed into the hedgerow's cover, ignoring the Can Scots' pleas for help.

Henderson sent one of 'D' Company's PIAT teams crawling towards the hedge to range in on the Tiger. Their first round exploded harmlessly inside the hedge, and the Tiger's machine gun killed the two men. After raking the field and firing 88-millimetre rounds into 'D' Company's position, the Tiger prowled off.[19]

'D' Company advanced again, only to be pinned on the edge of the next field. This time two Tigers were firing downslope from the cover of an orchard about four hundred yards distant. Knowing his remaining PIAT team would never get within range, and with casualties mounting, Henderson had no idea what to do next.[20]

Unbeknown to Henderson, one 1st Hussar tanker had recognized 'D' Company's plight. In a move that earned a Military Medal, Sergeant Arthur Boyle advanced in a wide arc to get within range of the Tigers undetected. Although one Tiger spotted the Sherman and disabled it before Boyle's gunner could fire, the sergeant ordered the men to stay on board. Their first shot sent one Tiger up in flames, convincing the other to retreat.[21]

In the smoke and dust, the Can Scots knew nothing of Boyle's heroic intervention. They believed, mostly correctly, that the battalion fought alone. Again they faced the young 12th ss Division fanatics. "More than once," Burge wrote, someone "would see a tank through a hedgerow and conclude it was one of ours come to assist us. He would dash through the intertwined brambles and thorns to pound on the side of the tank thus attracting the attention of the occupants. Too late realizing he was pounding on a large black swastika!"

The ss "fought...bitterly but could not stop the momentum of our advance. Few prisoners were taken—the enemy preferring to die rather than give in. Snipers were posted in hedgerows covering each tiny field with rifle and [light machine guns]. Heavier MGs were dismounted from tanks to cover positions until they were almost overrun. Then they would mount the tanks and retire to another hedgerow. More enemy tanks plowed back and forth spitting both heavy and light calibre ammunition into our advancing formations."

Advancing to the right of 'D' Company, 'B' Company "slugged its way through all opposition to be the first...to consolidate on its objective, where they were counterattacked."[22] After the counterattack was repulsed, Captain David Pugh crouched in a ditch and called for support on the wireless. Due to some atmospheric anomaly, a BBC announcer introduced a musical program called "Music While You Work." No matter how Pugh twisted the dial, the wireless remained jammed with lively music.

By 1530 hours, the Can Scots had won Point 168 and were digging in on the forward slope. 'D' Company's Company Sergeant Major John Stanley Grimmond was consolidating the headquarters section in an orchard when the 12th ss counterattacked with two tanks and infantry. Gathering a small force armed with Brens, rifles, and PIATS, Grimmond led such a fierce charge that the tanks withdrew, leaving their infantry to be killed or taken prisoner. Grimmond was awarded a Distinguished Conduct Medal.[23]

A lull ensued that the Can Scots used to dig as deeply as possible into the rocky soil. Sergeant Ron Bland and two other men of

'D' Company looked into a large valley "with no cover but grass." He, Sergeant George Lorimer, and Private Peter Smolkoski dug individual slit trenches. Bland had just dropped his web gear and was turning to pick up a shovel when he was suddenly flat on the ground, unable to move. He called to Lorimer and Smolkoski, but neither responded. Then Corporal Leo Netzel appeared and reported that Smolkoski was dead, Lorimer unconscious—apparently both severely concussed by a shell explosion. Bland was bleeding from eleven penetrating wounds. All three men were loaded on a carrier and evacuated to the RAP. Lorimer died en route. The twenty-six-year-old Lorimer was the younger brother of Lieutenant Duncan Lorimer, who had been wounded on July 8 at Cussy.[24] "Slaughter Hill," as the survivors called Point 168, cost thirty-seven dead and ninety-three wounded, the heaviest casualty rate the Can Scots suffered in a single day.[25]

Despite their hesitance to join the fray, the Hussars lost six tanks. "The morale of the unit that night was low," Conron noted. "The men were dog-tired and it seemed as if a very determined effort was being made to beat the [2nd Armoured Brigade] right into the ground. All the regiments in the brigade had terrific casualties in both tanks and men."[26]

Lieutenant Colonel Colwell next ordered the Winnipeg Rifles to assault Soulangy, a village astride the Caen-Falaise highway and roughly parallel to Point 168. Only the 17th Duke of York's Hussars' armoured cars were available, but again minimal resistance was promised. Instead, more 12th ss infantry and Tiger tanks waited. Only 'A' Company managed to gain the village, immediately being set upon by two Tigers. After half its men were killed or wounded, the company retired at 2100 hours. The Yorks wisely opted to steer well clear of the Tigers, staying out of the fight entirely. Dismissed by Corps intelligence as shattered, the 12th ss ended the day holding the field.[27]

Under pressure to keep moving, Colwell sent the Regina Rifles from behind the Can Scots towards Aubigny-sur-Nère—another village beside the Caen-Falaise highway.[28] Unable to contact the supporting Fort Garry Horse, however, Lieutenant Colonel Foster Matheson stood his men down. The Garrys, meanwhile, had four tanks immediately knocked out upon arriving at what they mistakenly thought was the start line. Seeing no infantry, Lieutenant Colonel Ronald Morton ordered the squadron back to harbour.[29]

RECOGNIZING BY LATE morning that the two divisions advancing on Falaise from the north were being checked, Simonds ordered 2nd Division to carry the town from the west. The order caught Major General Charles Foulkes in the midst of relieving the 1st Polish Armoured Division, which had seized Fontaine-le-Pin and Potigny during the night. Foulkes was acting on a previous instruction from Simonds to take over the Polish sector to free them for a move across the corps front to come up alongside 4th Division's left flank.

This move required the Poles to shift about eighteen thousand men and their vehicles, tanks, and equipment. However, "during this crossing the Division passed through the formation of the whole Corps...without any difficulty," Lieutenant Colonel L. Stankiewicz wrote. "This definitely proves that the Division had, by this time, become an efficient piece of machinery, in which the work of the staffs and the accomplishments of the units were performed smoothly."[30]

As the Poles departed, 2nd Division's 4th and 5th Brigades had taken their positions. This left the division's two freshest brigades misplaced for an advance on Falaise.

Suddenly handed a new priority, Foulkes could only turn to 6th Brigade, despite its having won the Clair-Tison river crossing the day before, on August 14. At 1100 hours, Brigadier Hugh Young briefed his tired battalion commanders. As patrols had detected a "withdrawal of the enemy" in progress from west of Falaise, Young expected weak opposition. However, having been fooled in the past, Young arranged artillery support and a squadron of Sherbrooke Fusiliers for each battalion. The advance would follow the road from Clair-Tison to Falaise. South Saskatchewan Regiment would be on the left, the Queen's Own Cameron Highlanders the right. First objective was the village of Ussy. If no fight developed, the two battalions would then continue to Villers-Canivet, about four miles northwest of Falaise.

About noon, both battalions moved with companies strung out in single file alongside the road. By 1400 hours, Ussy was secure.[31] The push to Villers-Canivet proceeded well. Then, as the Sasks entered it at 1800 hours, they came under fire from Germans dug into farm fields and adjacent farmhouses.[32] 'B' Company became entangled with an MG-42 position situated behind a stone fence. Attempting to close on the gun, Private Chic Goodman's section reached a gap in the wall where a gate had been. When Goodman's section leader stepped into the gap, an MG-42 burst killed him. That left the survivors with a choice. They could run past the gap, together, surely drawing fire but also ensuring that some men got through. Or they could stagger things—two men duck across, then someone crawls past, then maybe three dash through—each variation forcing the German gunners to try to anticipate the next move. The section did this, and Goodman decided to crawl—the slowest option, but hugging the ground meant possibly getting past unseen. Cradling his rifle across his arms, Goodman worked elbows and knees frantically and made the crossing in seconds.[33] Clearing Villers-Canivet took two hours and yielded fourteen prisoners.[34]

By the time 6th Brigade secured Villers-Canivet, the Polish division had already gained the corps's left flank and gone straight into battle. Attacking at two separate crossing points, 10th Regiment of Motorized Riflemen and First Armoured Regiment surprised the Germans defending the opposite shore of the Dives River. Jort, a village on the south bank that was also astride a main road running from Falaise north through Saint-Pierre-sur-Dives and on to Lisieux, was captured. The Poles had cut one possible German escape route from the pocket.

During the night, the 3rd Brigade of Riflemen expanded the bridgehead. "Sappers built a bridge and cleared the mined terrain. The artillery...was brought up [and] set in readiness to defend the bridgehead." The brigade was also well positioned to begin closing the gap between Falaise and Argentan.[35]

By evening, Simonds decided that events had outpaced the plan to advance 4th Armoured Division towards Falaise. The town should fall easily enough to 2nd and 3rd Divisions, so 4th Division would join the Poles in a southeastward advance to cut the most direct route out of the pocket—a road running due east from Falaise through Trun and on to Chambois.[36]

Arriving at Kitching's headquarters in Bretteville-le-Rabet at 1000 hours on August 16, Simonds ordered him to first take the wooded Monts d'Eraines Ridge north of Damblainville, which looked down upon the Falaise–Saint-Pierre-sur-Dives road. It was from this ridge that German anti-tank guns and tanks had significantly contributed to blocking the division's advance from Épaney. Once the ridge was clear, the division would cross the Ante and Train Rivers south of Damblainville and cut the highway connecting Falaise and Trun. Here it would turn east to capture Trun and then, finally, close the gap between First Canadian Army and Third U.S. Army.

Kitching was in no position to swing the division about so rapidly. With Halpenny commanding the armoured brigade, a turtle's haste was more likely. Kitching again asked for Bob Moncel and again Simonds demurred. Kitching's armoured brigade desperately needed a firm hand on the tiller. Every regiment had a new commander, most with little experience. They were also in contact with the Germans around Épaney, so extracting the regiments and routing them to a new axis of advance was going to take time. This move would not be completed until the early morning hours of August 17.[37]

WHILE 4TH ARMOURED Division was reorganizing, 2nd and 3rd Infantry Divisions spent August 16 closing on Falaise. The Royal Winnipeg Rifles and Regina Rifles led 3rd Division's advance. Supported by 17th Duke of York's armoured cars, the Winnipegs bypassed Soulangy and headed for Aubigny, gaining its outskirts within thirty minutes. By 1355 hours, Aubigny was clear, the one prisoner captured from 85th Infantry Division.

From here on, "it was a very subdued enemy they met, and an enemy who withdrew with far more alacrity than on 15 August," one Canadian officer noted. At 1900 hours, the Winnipegs and Yorks reached the crossroads running out of Falaise to Saint Pierre-sur-Dives and were looking down on the town.[38]

When the Reginas passed through the Can Scots on Point 168 en route to Point 159 and Versainville beyond, they met "a little more determined" German opposition than the Winnipegs had encountered.[39] What was left of the 1st Hussars were in support, Major Brandy Conron's composite force on the left and 'B' Squadron, under Major G.W. Gordon, on the right.[40]

A screen of 88-millimetre guns firing from woods northeast of Épaney "were so well situated that whenever one of our tanks so much as showed itself on the crest line it was either knocked out or the near miss took the tank crew's breath away," reported 7th Brigade's war diarist.[41] The Reginas, with 'A' and 'B' Companies leading, hid behind tank-fired smoke shells and their own mortars during the advance to Point 159 and suffered few casualties. As they descended the long slope leading to the road and Versainville beyond, however, heavy machine-gun fire stalled their advance. It took the 3-inch mortar platoon's laying down a concentration of fire to silence the enemy positions. Fighting remained stiff all the way to the road. Here the Reginas dug in for the night. Another costly day—eighty-five casualties, including seven officers.[42]

When the Reginas halted, the 1st Hussars withdrew. "At the termination of this day's operation the Regiment could hardly field one complete [squadron] and many of these tanks were not battle worthy," their war diarist reported.[43]

Prisoners were a mixed bag, including personnel from 1st ss Panzer, 89th Infantry, and 85th Infantry Divisions. The 7th Brigade intelligence officer thought this "confirmed what we already knew, that the enemy was grabbing troops from anywhere and forming them into battle groups in a desperate last effort to hold up our advance."[44]

Falaise, however, was defended by 12th ss Division's Kampf-gruppe Krause. Sturmbannführer Bernhard Krause had 150 Hitler Youth infantry, two Tiger tanks, and two 75-millimetre anti-tank guns inside Falaise. There was also a small 12th ss force of two Tigers and infantry armed with heavy machine guns near the crossroads that the Winnipegs were approaching when 2nd Division assaulted the town.[45]

Falaise was the birthplace of William the Conqueror, whose castle stood on a high crag overlooking the Ante River and ancient market town below. On the night of August 12–13, Bomber

Command had struck with 144 aircraft in an attempt to block the German escape route through the town with rubble. About two-thirds of Falaise was destroyed. Fortunately, the inhabitants had earlier evacuated. Since the bombing, First Canadian Army's medium artillery had further battered Falaise. The castle miraculously escaped significant damage throughout.[46]

After a series of delays, 6th Brigade's South Saskatchewan and Queen's Own Cameron Highlander Regiments attacked from the northwest. Les Fusiliers Mont-Royal was in close support, and both leading regiments were backed by squadrons of Sherbrooke Fusiliers. Tank losses had resulted in its three squadrons being collapsed into two.[47]

The South Saskatchewan Regiment on the left came under fire from the Tigers and machine guns dug in near the crossroads. While the infantry ducked for cover, two of Major Sydney Radley-Walters's 'A' Squadron tanks were knocked out. But a concentration of heavy artillery forced the Tigers and their supporting infantry to withdraw into Falaise.

Soon both battalions reached the outskirts. Two bridges crossed the steep Ante River valley. The 12th ss had heavily barricaded each with girders and rocks. An anti-tank gun and machine guns covered the one the Sasks approached, while machine guns defended the one assigned to the Camerons. Ten Shermans supported the Camerons, but as these closed in, they became mired in the soft wet ground or stuck in huge craters created by the earlier bombing. An armoured bulldozer attempted to reach the tanks to drag them free with chains, but so much traffic had built up on the road behind the leading troops that the route became gridlocked. Without supporting tanks, the Camerons were unable to silence the machine guns, and their attack stalled.[48]

The Sasks were also lashed by mortar and machine-gun fire short of the bridge, and Radley-Walters lost another two tanks to anti-tank guns. "The infantry went to ground; the tanks went into firing positions; and everything came to a standstill," he recalled.

Lieutenant Colonel Fred Clift grabbed a rifle from a nearby man. Radley-Walters saw Clift and intelligence officer Captain N.H. Hadley run to the head of the column. Clift "was a great marksman and he ran forward to where the first platoon was and began firing."[49] After Clift shot three of the gun crew, the survivors blew up the gun and fled.

The Sasks spilled down the slope, splashed over the river, and scaled the opposite bank, while the tankers busted through the bridge's barricade.[50] Clearing houses and rooting out the still fanatically resisting Hitler Youth began. It was slow, dangerous work. The Germans were spread out, fighting in small groups or even singly. Every sniper had to be cornered and killed. Few surrendered. Night fell and the battle raged on.

Radley-Walters recalled: "It was dark and we had to move through Falaise, which was burning; the whole bloody town was on fire; the streets were blocked. The city had been bombed and as we came in on the right hand side, we saw the castle...and close to it, the big Gothic church where I believe [William the Conqueror] was baptized. Everywhere we went there were obstacles—buildings burning and those that had burned had fallen down into the street and the rubble slowed us down.

"We were taking a long time to get through the city and Freddie Clift was forcing us, saying, 'Come on, let's go.' I was trying to get my people to move faster but it was tough going. I tried two or three different approaches on streets running parallel to the main drag but didn't have too much luck. I got behind Lieutenant Charlie Williams and as I did, I noticed he was moving very slowly, but the attack got going."[51]

The fires silhouetted the infantry. Private Goodman felt spotlighted when his company passed the burning cathedral. He expected the Germans to rake them with machine guns, but they slipped past untouched and started clearing towards the railroad on the eastern side of town.[52] By midnight, the Sasks controlled most of their assigned area and by 0300 hours had established a firm base alongside the rail line. "Although the men were tired they had carried out their work efficiently," Brigadier Young observed. "On the other hand the Camerons...continued to make slow progress." By 0500 hours, a perturbed Young discovered they were only about five hundred yards from the river with another fifteen hundred yards

top · A Canadian convoy heads across the wide, flat terrain near Caen en route to the front lines on July 31. The photo was taken from an Auster aircraft, which took off from the Allied-built airstrip in the background. Donald I. Grant photo. LAC PA-129123.

bottom · Soldiers of 4th Infantry Brigade are mounted in Kangaroos and lined up in columns just before the kick-off of Operation Totalize on August 7. H.A. Barnett photo. LAC PA-129174.

above · Canadian troops advance near Ifs on July 25 as part of Operation Spring. Ken Bell photo. LAC PA-116528.

top right · Flames and smoke boil up from ammunition and fuel dumps next to the Caen-Falaise highway on August 8. The fire was the result of misdirected bombs dropped by U.S. B-17 bombers. Photographer unknown. LAC PA-154826.

bottom right · Lieutenant General Guy Simonds, General Bernard Montgomery, and Lieutenant General Harry Crerar determined how, where, and when First Canadian Army fought. Possession of author.

top · A Fascine and a Petard tank assemble near Bretteville-le-Rabet in advance of Operation Tractable, August 14. Donald I. Grant photo. LAC PA-116523.

bottom · Armour forms up for Operation Tractable near Bretteville-le-Rabet on August 14. The nearest vehicle is a 17-pounder self-propelled anti-tank gun. Immediately behind is a Crocodile flame-thrower tank with attached fuel trailer. Donald I. Grant photo. LAC PA-116525.

top · A Fusiliers Mont-Royal patrol supported by a Sherman tank searches for snipers in Falaise on August 17. Donald I. Grant photo. LAC PA-115568.

bottom · A Canadian soldier uses a fountain for cover in the badly bomb-damaged central square of Falaise. Donald I. Grant photo. LAC PA-116503.

Canadian soldiers examine damage to the inside of the Falaise cathedral.
Possession of author.

German prisoners caught in the Falaise Gap stream towards the Canadian rear lines on August 19. Many look quite content to be out of the war. Possession of author.

top · Major Dave Currie speaks with a French Resistance fighter (left), while a member of the Argyll and Sutherland Highlanders takes the surrender of an officer. The man had led his convoy directly into Saint-Lambert, resulting in its complete capture. Donald I. Grant photo. LAC PA-111565.

bottom · Major Dave Currie (left, with pistol in hand) of the South Alberta Regiment directs captured German troops towards the Canadian rear at Saint-Lambert-sur-Dives on August 19. Donald I. Grant photo. LAC PA-116586.

required to reach the other side of Falaise. "They were pressed for more hurried action."

It was about 1000 hours when the Camerons gained the eastern outskirts and were sent on to the tiny village of Saint-Clair about a mile beyond. Here they and the supporting tanks were to dig in and fend off counterattacks. Behind them, Les Fusiliers Mont-Royal had entered Falaise and begun painstakingly searching it for bypassed resistance. The Fusiliers learned from one of the few remaining civilians that a large four-storey stone building surrounded by a heavy stone wall held fifty to sixty Hitler Youth sworn to fight to the last. At 1800 hours, tanks punched a hole through the outer wall. Ten Fusiliers slipped in only to be driven back by the young fanatics. At 0200 hours on August 18, the Fusiliers assaulted with anti-tank guns, Bren guns and mortars covering. As the attack began, German fighter-bombers unexpectedly flew over, dropping bombs and flares. The large building was set on fire. Inside, the French Canadians and Hitler Youth shot it out. Only a few Germans surrendered; a handful of others were picked up trying to escape through the Saskatchewan lines.[53]

A 12th ss officer attempted to escape through Major Jacques Dextraze's 'D' Company. Armed with a Schmeisser, he wounded several men before dashing for the cover of a nearby shed. A Fusilier killed him with a grenade.[54]

By 0500 hours, there "were several piles of German dead around the [building] and burnt bodies within."[55]

Seizing Falaise largely concluded 2nd Division's role in closing what had become known as the Falaise Gap. Its remaining duties over the next few days included establishing a perimeter running northeast from Falaise to the Dives River in order to prevent any German attempt to break out of the pocket via this route.

27

Guns Chattering

THE PAST TWO days had been disastrous for the Germans. On August 15, Generalfeldmarschall Günther von Kluge's car was shot up by Allied aircraft. Although he survived, all wireless sets were destroyed, and the small command party only reached General der Panzertruppen Hans Eberbach's headquarters after nightfall. His unexplained absence fuelled Hitler's suspicion that von Kluge was negotiating a ceasefire with the Allies.

Hitler was demanding a renewed counterattack by Eberbach's hopelessly weak five armoured divisions. "To cling to a hope that cannot be fulfilled by any power in the world...is a disastrous error. That is the situation!" von Kluge shouted upon hearing this order. Finally, Hitler acceded to a withdrawal east of the Orne and then the Dives, with Falaise held "as a corner post." Von Kluge ordered the withdrawal begun that very night. Fifth Panzer Army and Seventh Army would "withdraw without delay to the sector of the Dives and the line Morteaux-Trun-Gacé-Laigle [L'Aigle]." This was von Kluge's last instruction. On August 17, Generalfeldmarschall Walter Model arrived with a letter from Hitler relieving von Kluge and appointing Model in his place. En route by plane to his rear headquarters at Metz, von Kluge took poison. He was dead when the plane landed. Von Kluge left a letter declaring unwavering loyalty to Hitler, National Socialism, and Germany. Model came to Normandy with no intention of returning to the offensive. Even Hitler seemed to belatedly recognize the time for that was past. The priority was to keep Falaise Gap prized open and to extricate as many as possible of the approximately 100,000 Germans inside the pocket.[1]

At 1530 hours, meanwhile, General Bernard Montgomery called Lieutenant General Harry Crerar and instructed First Canadian Army to immediately capture Trun, in the centre of the gap and midway between Falaise and Argentan. Crerar immediately phoned Simonds with Montgomery's new directive. No real adjustment to Simonds's current plan was required, for he was already pushing towards Trun.[2] At 2200 hours on August 16, the Argyll and Sutherland Highlanders with 'C' Squadron of the South Alberta Regiment had started this effort by advancing from Olenden five miles southeast to Damblainville. Lieutenant Colonel Dave Stewart had wanted to gain the village by first light. Because of the distance involved, Stewart mounted 'B' Company into Kangaroos and sent it ahead with the South Albertas' tanks. The rest of the Argylls had followed on foot.[3]

In one tank, Trooper John Neff believed the nighttime move offered a first taste of France unscarred by war. The column moved through "grand rolling country, all young pine forests [and] cider apple orchards. Moving through the orchards, the crew commanders hunched in the turrets to avoid being hit by overhead branches. Ripe apples plopped through open hatches and soon the tank floors were covered in a pulpy, sweet smelling mess of fruit crushed underfoot."[4]

Shortly after midnight, the tankers and 'B' Company reached a large hill overlooking Damblainville. As the night wore on, the rest of the Argylls arrived. Stewart sent the scout platoon into the village. They found no Germans, "with the exception of enemy tanks moving through the town from time to time."[5]

At first light, the Argylls advanced 'A' and 'C' Companies. The move proved to be "a matter of walking in and taking over," recorded the regiment's historian. "It all seemed unbelievable. The other companies soon followed and the town was occupied completely."[6] The village and a bridge over the Ante River were secured by 0830 hours.[7] There was one moment of anxiety when the Argylls spotted a Tiger squatting in a narrow street.[8] Before anyone could react, however, the crew blew it up and surrendered. "While getting into position, 'A' Company saw a good many Germans in the woods in front of their position, and these seemed of two minds what to do. Our men made signs to these people, some of whom surrendered, while the rest ran into the woods."[9]

The previous night, two Algonquin Regiment 'A' Company platoons under Lieutenant R.H. Scott had also advanced aboard carriers left of the Argylls in an attempt to seize a Dives River bridge crossing at Couliboeuf. The aim, as Algonquin Major George Cassidy put it, "was in the nature of coppering our bets, because our main effort was to be closer in, through...Damblainville and over the Ante and Traine Rivers. As it turned out, it was a master stroke. Their effort was successful in seizing a bridge before the enemy could destroy it."

By noon, the Algonquin Regiment—less Scott's two platoons—arrived at Damblainville. The Algonquins were the lead element in a long column of 10th Infantry Brigade and other 4th Armoured Division formations expecting to push across the Ante River bridge and advance on Trun. At the column's head was the remaining platoon and headquarters section of 'A' Company. Lieutenant Colonel Robert Bradburn had instructed Captain Clark Robertson to cross the river and proceed to Point 77, which dominated the Traine River.

Crossing the Ante, Robertson came to an east-west-running rail line close to Point 77. Seeing the line led to a small railway bridge immediately west of Point 77, Robertson ordered one section to seize it. The moment the section crossed the railroad, a "hail of small arms fire carpeted the entire area of the bridge, and not another man could get over the rail line." Robertson spotted two gun positions covering the bridge and requested artillery. Bradburn instead ordered him to pull back, so he could tee up a heavier artillery program. Extracting the section across the tracks proved no easy matter, but the men escaped under covering fire from the rest of the company. When it was discovered that a seriously wounded man had been left behind, 'A' Company's stretcher-bearer, Private A.J. Cote, went to get him. As everyone else threw out fire, Cote dashed forward, found the man, quickly tended his wounds, and carried him to safety. "Quite the bravest act I saw during the entire war," Robertson said later, even though Cote's gallantry went officially unrecognized.

Behind 'A' Company, the situation had completely unravelled. Expecting a hasty passage, "the brigade column had been oozing over and down the hill...coming into perfect view of the German force only 1,800 yards away. Plastered against the forward slope of the hill, and jammed together in a nose-to-tail column, they made a dream target for the enemy artillery, and it wasn't long in coming down." Confusion reigned for three hours. There were so many vehicles, tanks, and infantry in Damblainville that nobody could move, and German artillery and Tiger tanks pounded it from the high ground south of the Ante.[10]

Major General George Kitching had just started breakfast at his tactical headquarters about two thousand yards from Damblainville when the German shelling began. With rounds landing nearby, Kitching and his staff finished eating in a ditch. Then Kitching went to see what was happening. Appreciating that forcing crossings over the two rivers at Damblainville was going to be a costly and time-consuming affair, Kitching remembered the bridge at Couliboeuf. By this time, the small Algonquin force had actually secured two bridges, the single-lane one at Couliboeuf and a wider, stronger bridge in the adjacent town of Morteaux-Couliboeuf. When he informed Lieutenant General Guy Simonds of this, Kitching was ordered to switch the division's axis of advance to the bridges at Couliboeuf and Morteaux across the Dives and then to drive east cross-country to Trun.

A fair battle was by now under way at Damblainville. The Lake Superior (Motor) Regiment supported by British Columbia Regiment tanks had gained the rail line. Unable to go farther, infantry and tanks were caught in the narrow ground between the Ante and Trains Rivers. The Argylls and Algonquins were mired inside Damblainville. It would take hours to extricate these battalions. So Kitching ordered Lieutenant Colonel Bill Halpenny to send his remaining two armoured regiments eastwards, "head for the bridge at Couliboeuf and, once across, go as fast as possible to Trun." As soon as feasible, the infantry brigade would hand over to 3rd Infantry Division and follow.[11]

THE DECISION TO strike east through Couliboeuf "across the rolling country and attack Trun from the northwest involved a colossal manoeuvre in the shortest possible time," Algonquin's Major P.A. Mayer wrote. "But the already weary troops responded to the call for speed with the result that by 1600 hours after a miracle of traffic control supervised by [the division's divisional staff officer 11] Major M.R. Dare...the greater part of the armoured brigade had crossed the Dives River through the Morteaux bridge and the single track Couliboeuf bridge."[12]

Neither the Canadian Grenadier Guards nor the Governor General's Foot Guards were close to full strength. The Foot Guards were organized into two squadrons. Captain George Taylor Baylay headed No. 1 Squadron, and Captain G.G. Froats had No. 2 Squadron. Major H.F. Baker was the regiment's acting commander. It was early afternoon when the Foot Guards crossed the Dives at Morteaux, which was being heavily shelled.[13] Once clear of Morteaux, the Foot Guards advanced alongside the river.[14]

The Grenadiers headed for Couliboeuf bridge. As the leading tank rolled up, its crew found a Sherman "set squarely in the roadway to cover the exit." A Polish officer strode up and declared he was "under orders to fire on anyone attempting to cross." Major Doug Hamilton tried unsuccessfully to contact brigade. So "to avoid international complications," he went back to 4th Armoured Brigade's headquarters at Perrières. Hamilton was told that, Poles notwithstanding, the Grenadiers were to get cracking and cut all routes leading from Trun "at any cost, by last light."

Hamilton hurried back, explained things to the Polish officer, and got moving. He set a course that kept the Grenadiers to the north and parallel to the German front line. In this way they motored along Les Moutiers-en-Auge "unchallenged and with all speed" until the lead tank was fired on from the left flank. "I think it is the Poles," the crew commander said. "They are damned bad shots."

A thousand yards north of Louvières-en-Auge they met two German trucks, shot them up, and took the surviving infantry aboard prisoner. Soon thereafter two signals trucks were discovered concealed in haystacks. Both were destroyed and the signallers killed. This was later revealed to have been a 1st SS Panzer Division signals-exchange unit, and its loss severed a vital link in the main German communication network. A thousand yards east of Lou-vières, the Grenadiers halted at dusk on the spur of Point 118. They had come eight miles from Couliboeuf.[15]

While the Grenadiers had enjoyed a brisk canter across Norman countryside, the Foot Guards brushed the German front soon after crossing the Morteaux bridge. Major Baker's tank was struck by an anti-tank gun. Lance Corporal Richard Steele died, but the others aboard escaped. Baker and Lieutenant S.G. Checkland, however, were then wounded by sniper fire and evacuated. Captain Baylay assumed temporary regimental command.

Unable to raise brigade on the wireless, Baylay ordered the Foot Guards onward. On the edge of woods west of Les Moutieres-en-Auge, Baylay halted at nightfall. Everyone was told to maintain a high state of alert. Baylay believed they were in the blue, no friendly forces on either flank.[16]

Because 4th Armoured Brigade's communications net was broken, the Foot Guards were unaware that the British Columbia Regiment and Lake Superior Regiment were close by. These had pushed out of Damblainville at about 1700 hours. With orders to pass through the Grenadiers at Point 118, they eventually found it "too dark...to read maps, so rather than proceed into enemy territory we stopped for the night near Les Moutiers-en-Auge," reported the BCR war diarist. During the advance, tanks and Superiors had lost each other.[17]

When the tanks stopped, Captain Jim Tedlie and his crew, like everyone else, were exhausted. Tedlie thought they would be okay in a fight, but staying alert posed a challenge. He was nodding off when there was a loud crash, and a shell screeched overhead. Seconds later a 17-pounder gunner came up on the regimental net and confessed that, as he was falling asleep, his foot had depressed the firing button. "That woke us up," Tedlie muttered.[18]

The Superiors' 'B' and 'C' Companies had in fact lost contact with each other, in addition to the tanks. Unable to establish wireless contact with the Dukes, both companies "spent the night independently in 'No man's land.'"[19]

Left of 4th Canadian Armoured Division, 1st Polish Armoured Division had enjoyed a deep and fast advance on August 17. In two formations, the 10th Regiment of Motorized Riflemen, 10th Dragoon Regiment, and 10th Uhlan Regiment had swept forward. By evening, one formation had reached Hill 259, a short distance north of where the Grenadiers were bedded down.[20] The other, more southerly formation gained the hamlet of Neauphe-sur-Dives, directly east of Trun and about three miles short of Chambois.[21]

As night fell on August 17, 11 Canadian Corps was poised to begin closing the Falaise Gap. Although 4th Armoured Division had a long extended open flank to its right, Simonds was unconcerned. Behind it, 3rd Infantry Division maintained a firm base on the hills above the Ante River, and 2nd Infantry Division was arrayed around Falaise. Simonds considered the Poles "well on the way to Chambois," which Montgomery had emphasized should be taken quickly. His 4th Canadian Armoured Division was ready to capture Trun. To provide the tanks with infantry strength, 10th Infantry Brigade was to be relieved that night from its positions around Damblainville and Morteaux-Couliboeuf.[22]

On the opposite side of the gap, the Americans had idled August 17 away. Generals Omar Bradley and George Patton, independently of each other, had attempted to get an advance on Trun going in accordance with Montgomery's instructions. Acting at cross purposes, their orders left the divisional commanders uncertain about who actually commanded them. Finally, Bradley declared them under First U.S. Army's v Corps, commanded by Major General L.T. Gerow. The following morning, Gerow deployed his divisions accordingly. Between Ecouché and Argentan, 2nd French Armored Division held the American left flank. In the centre, 80th U.S. Infantry Division would isolate Argentan from the left, while 90th U.S. Infantry Division would close the gap to the right of this division by advancing through Le Bourg-Saint-Léonard to Chambois.[23]

As the Americans sluggishly began stirring, increasing numbers of Germans were escaping. Generalfeldmarschall Walter Model arrived at the Fifth Panzer Army's battle headquarters at 0900 hours on August 18 to impress upon everyone that a "coherent front" must be re-established and that Seventh Army and General der Panzertruppen Eberbach's Panzer Group had to be "extricated as quickly as possible" from the gap. "Shoring up the walls of the escape corridor" required 11 ss Panzer Corps, just having come through the gap, to turn about and attack the Canadians and Poles.[24] The corps was to do this with 2nd and 9th ss Panzer Divisions. Still inside the pocket, 12th and 21st Panzer Divisions would shore up the gap's northern wall.[25] The 2nd and 116th Panzer Divisions would do the same to the south. August 18 marked the point where the German withdrawal through the gap reached "full flood."[26]

THE GRENADIER GUARDS spent an eerie night on Point 118. It seemed extraordinary that the Germans were ignorant of their presence. They expected a counterattack or at least testing probes, but the night passed quietly. An ominous silence prevailed. There were no signs of fighting to the north, where the Poles supposedly pushed for Chambois. Behind them, everything was equally quiet. Yet to the southeast "towards Chambois, to the south beyond Trun, and all down the valley towards Falaise the lights of a hundred fires—blazing vehicles, ammunition dumps and buildings—made it very evident that the Regiment was out in front, the spearhead in the gut of the gap."[27]

At first light, Major Ned Amy's No. 1 Squadron and Major Hershell Smith's No. 3 Squadron advanced to a road running north from Trun to Vimoutiers. German infantry on foot, vehicles, and many horse-drawn wagons clogged the road, and the tankers ground through these with "their guns chattering." Gaining the heights to the east, the Grenadiers proceeded to shoot up anything coming along the road.

This was good work, but not their day's purpose. That was to take Trun. Although the Lake Superior Regiment had been scheduled to appear during the night, there was still no sign of it. So the tankers kept the road to Vimoutiers closed and waited impatiently.[28]

At 0530 hours, the British Columbia Regiment's squadron commanders had briefed their troop leaders while everyone ate cold rations and sipped tea. Major Jack Worthington and Captain Jim Tedlie held opposite ends of a large topographic map so 'A' Squadron's troop leaders could see their route. The objective was to cut the

Trun-Vimoutiers road by seizing Hordouseaux, three miles north of Trun. Suddenly, an American P-47 Thunderbolt fighter-bomber shrieked down with machine guns blazing, and a 50-calibre round "caught Jack...right in his throat and blood spurted just like a fountain from him," Tedlie said later. "I hit the ground and I'm holding the other end of the map, so that pilot missed me by inches. Then I jumped up after they passed and we threw out smoke showing we were friendly and hoped they would recognize it this time. I put a field dressing, with the idea of staunching the flow of blood, on his neck. He couldn't speak because his vocal chords were...shot away. And he finished the O Group [by] writing with a chinagraph [grease] pencil on the top of the map to finish his orders. I had given him a shot of morphine to ease the pain and you could see his writing trail away. We were close to the Poles and a first-aid team from the Poles picked him up and took him back. He subsequently died. That was a very brave thing to do, because most wounded people think of themselves. But he thought of the well being of the squadron to make sure that I had everything he had received from higher headquarters. I'm very proud of him."[29] The regiment's two Worthington brothers had been killed within the space of nine days. Trooper Albert Hallmark was also fatally wounded by the friendly fire.[30]

For the British Columbia Regiment, the tragedy of Worthington's death during the briefing was the only difficulty faced that day. The squadrons carved a path through the retreating Germans. Hundreds of prisoners were taken. The roads to Hordouseaux were "littered with enemy dead, equipment, and horses, knocked out by our Typhoons."[31]

The regiment reached the village to find it abandoned an hour earlier. "We parked right up on top of a hill in an orchard and if there had been fewer trees we could have commanded a view of the whole countryside for miles," Captain Douglas Harker wrote. "So we just spent a quiet night with the usual guards amidst a cloudburst that lasted all night."[32]

Prior to August 17, the Germans had avoided daylight movement because it inevitably attracted Allied fighter-bombers. That day, however, thousands moved in long columns towards the gap. Allied Expeditionary Air Force flew 2,029 sorties and claimed to have destroyed or damaged hundreds of vehicles. At 1030 hours on August 18, fighter-bombers again swarmed over the pocket to attack the thousands of panicked Germans. More than 3,000 sorties were made this day, with 2nd Tactical Air Force alone claiming 124 tanks destroyed and 96 damaged; 1,159 transport vehicles wrecked and 1,724 damaged.

Given the fluid battlefront, inevitably some fighter-bombers strafed or bombed Allied forces. Deeper into the German lines than anybody else, the Poles suffered most. Between the 16th and 18th they had 72 men killed and another 191 wounded.[33]

The Governor General's Foot Guards kept as wary an eye on the skies as they did the ground during their August 18 advance. With only twenty-two Shermans and three Stuarts operational, the regiment's fighting ability was greatly limited. But they met only light opposition en route to Point 118, which lay a short distance east of Louvières-en-Auge and provided a firing point onto the Falaise-Trun and Trun-Vimoutiers roads.[34]

All 4th Armoured Brigade's regiments were severely reduced. At 1300 hours, when the Superiors' 'A' Company joined the Grenadiers, Major Smith's No. 3 Squadron had only seven tanks. It and the Superiors moved at 1400 hours to cut off Trun. Crossing the highway between Trun and Saint-Lambert-sur-Dives, they came under fire from 88-millimetre anti-tank guns and several multi-barrelled 20-millimetre guns mounted on half-tracks from the high ground southwest of Trun.[35] The Superiors went to ground and Smith advanced to Trun alone, finding the Superiors' 'C' Company had already taken the village.[36]

By late afternoon, 10th Infantry Brigade was firming up around Trun. The village had been badly shot up by Allied fighter-bombers, and much of it was still burning when the Lincoln and Welland Regiment's 'A' Company and a troop of South Alberta Regiment tanks relieved the Superiors at 1500. "Trun continued to burn all night."[37] The Lincs expected a counterattack, but instead gathered in five hundred prisoners who had entered the village to surrender.[38]

East of Trun, the Argyll and Sutherland Highlanders considered the battle over and that "it had become a pursuit, a rout." Less 'B' and 'C' Companies, which were under South Alberta Regiment command and directed towards Saint-Lambert-sur-Dives, the battalion's role for the next three days entailed taking surrenders and gathering great quantities of loot. As the Argyll's regimental historian wrote, "Any soldier who had a 'small smitchin' of enterprise sported the coveted Luger or P-38. One could find any number of cameras, watches and binoculars and of a variety extensive enough to please the most particular taste. Germans looking for places to give themselves up were everywhere, in our lines, in the woods and on the roads. Few ever showed arrogance or fight, for they were beaten. Sometimes our men herded them together and sent them back towards the rear, where they could find their own way to the prisoner of war cages. The whole thing failed to make sense, but it was a fantastic sort of heaven for the average Canadian infantryman, who had seen only the seamy side of war."[39]

BY EVENING ON August 18, Falaise Gap had narrowed to less than three miles. The Germans still fleeing funnelled into the ground separating Trun and Chambois to the north and the large, dense Forêt de Gouffern to the south. This forest stretching from immediately north of Argentan across to Le Bourg-Saint-Léonard was largely impassable to transport.[40]

For 1st Polish Armoured Division, the day's advance had been confused and bloody. The Poles "were already exhausted in fighting alone, without support, and so bearing the brunt of engaging enemy forces to the east of River Dives." Despite this, Major General Stanislaw Maczek had dispatched an armoured column at 0200 hours to break through to Chambois. Comprised of 2nd Armoured Regiment, 8th Infantry Battalion, and an anti-tank battery, it had advanced through an "extremely dark night and most difficult, roadless terrain, lost its direction and arrived in the early hours at the locality of Les Champeaux [on the Trun-Vimoutiers road], where it took the Germans by surprise, it is true, but at the same time became engaged with the infantry and anti-tank units, regardless of the terrain being difficult for the maneuvering of tanks. The stories about the Germans being taken by surprise, running around in the woods in their pyjamas and trying to board our tanks, thinking they were their own, circulated for a long time among our soldiers," Lieutenant Colonel L. Stankiewicz wrote.

When Maczek realized the formation had become lost, he ordered the 10th Armoured Brigade commander to dispatch a rescue force. Its attempts to locate the column proved fruitless. The column, however, managed to extricate itself from the Germans and withdrew southward.

Abandoning hope that this column would ever reach Chambois, Maczek assembled two other formations in the early morning. One, dubbed the western formation, comprised of the 24th Uhlan (Lancers) Regiment, 10th Dragoon Regiment, and an anti-tank battery preceded by the division's reconnaissance unit, the 10th Regiment of Mounted Infantry, was to advance from near Louvières-en-Auge to Hill 137 and then on to Chambois. The second or eastern column, made up of 1st Armoured Regiment, the Highland Infantry Battalion, and elements of the anti-tank battalion, would advance on a more northeasterly axis, using Hills 259 and 240 as intermediary objectives, with Hill 262 its final goal.

Hill 262 was really two hills separated by a narrow valley. The northerly hill was sometimes referred to as Mont Ormel, after a nearby hamlet, or as Hill 262 (North) with the southerly hill being Hill 262 (South). During a wireless discussion, Maczek mentioned that the map contour lines made the northerly hill resemble the pommel and the southerly one the shaft of a mace. The Poles consequently designated the north hill "Maczuga," Polish for mace.

Meeting stiff resistance, the two columns were short of their objectives by nightfall. The western column stopped on Hill 137, a little more than a mile north of Chambois, while the western column was on Hill 240 and about two miles short of Maczuga. Ahead of the western column, a 10th Mounted Infantry squadron and an anti-tank battery reached the northern outskirts of Chambois by late evening, but found it heavily defended.[41]

The Germans fully understood the threat the Poles posed. So critical was the situation that Fifth Panzer Army reported that the Allies had succeeded "in advancing past Trun and past Argentan with strong forces and in completing a still loose encirclement of

Seventh Army Group and Panzer Group Eberbach." Generalfeld-marschall Model believed the Canadians had advanced "past Trun to St. Lambert, where he established contact with the enemy forces from the south which had broken through at the edge of the wooded area [Forêt de Gouffern] east of Argentan (about 2 kms south of Chambois). Thus he has closed the bottleneck, though for the moment presumably only with light forces."[42] The Americans and First Canadian Army had in fact not yet met, but clearly time was running out.

Inside the pocket, Seventh Army pulled away from the Orne River during the night of August 18. Nipping at its heels were three British Second Army divisions and two American divisions. Despite severely depleted numbers and critical shortages of fuel and ammu-nition, the army's rearguard prevented it from being overwhelmed. Overall, the German divisions moved in a disciplined and orderly manner towards the gap throughout the night of August 18–19. In the morning, however, rearguard forces were pushed across the Falaise-Argentan road on the north flank by the British 53rd (Welsh) Infantry Division. With Allied bombing increasingly augmented by shelling from artillery regiments coming within range, a "wholesale abandonment of destroyed and damaged vehicles and guns" began, and the cohesion "was largely lost."[43]

Maintaining cohesion also proved increasingly problematic for First Canadian Army. Around Falaise, 2nd Infantry Division had established a stout, well-organized barrier through which escape was impossible. To the east, 3rd Infantry Division controlled the north bank of the Dives River from Morteaux-Couliboeuf to Trun. In principle, this enabled 4th Armoured Division to push on from Trun to Chambois with 1st Polish Armoured Division descending from the north on the same objective.[44] In fact, the situation facing these two divisions on the evening of August 18–19 was decidedly less tidy. Regiments were scattered.

The Grenadier Guards, for example, moved during the early morning hours of August 19 to Point 259, about three miles north of Trun, to overlook the Trun-Vimoutiers road.[45] No. 2 Squadron then advanced a mile closer to the road, with orders to close it to

German traffic. The squadron numbered only eight Shermans. Guardsman Stuart Johns thought they were terribly vulnerable in the dark with no covering infantry. The commander of Johns's tank deployed his crew, save the driver, to provide an infantry screen. They dug a slit trench and settled in. As the night wore on, they heard a couple of small convoys grinding past. When the men prepared to open fire with their Stens, the crew commander stopped them. "It'd be suicide. You fire and they dismount and attack us, the whole regiment's done for because we don't have any infantry," he said. Johns listened morosely to the German convoys roll by, knowing they were escaping.[46]

28

A Little Wild

AT 1800 HOURS on August 18, the South Alberta Regiment's 'C' Squadron had left Trun for Saint-Lambert-sur-Dives and then Chambois. Fifty-five men of 'B' Company, Argyll and Sutherland Highlanders, rode on the tanks. Quickly reaching Saint-Lambert, Major Dave Currie sent one tank troop into the village with the infantry following on foot. Passing the first house, the lead tank was knocked out by an anti-tank gun, its crew bailing out safely.

Contacting Lieutenant Colonel Swatty Wotherspoon by wireless, Currie proposed dismounting all but three tank crews to serve alongside the Argylls as infantry in order to clear the Germans out of the village. Wotherspoon instead ordered a thousand-yard withdrawal westward to Point 117 for the night rather than step into a potential hornet's nest in the dark. Here Wotherspoon rendezvoused with Currie's force, bringing up his headquarters troop, the reconnaissance squadron, 'B' Squadron, and a troop of 5th Anti-Tank Regiment's 17-pounders.[1] "It began to look as if a big show were coming off," the South Alberta war diarist wrote. "Infantry and everybody stood...awaiting...some movement which would start things flying."[2]

Growing up in Saskatchewan, Currie had experienced the typical hardships wrought by the Great Depression. Unable to afford university, he attended technical school instead, subsequently earning a living as an auto mechanic and welder during the "Dirty Thirties." When war broke out, he was married and a father but immediately joined the militia. Two years later, he enlisted in the regular army. He "wasn't a brilliant tactician, but he was very stubborn," Wotherspoon said. "If you gave him an order to do something that was within his capabilities, he would do it—period."[3]

At 0500 hours on August 19, Currie set his stubborn sights on Saint-Lambert. The night's light rain had stopped at dawn.[4] Grey mist clung to the ground as 'C' Squadron and the Argylls' 'B' Company descended through open fields towards the village. Major Ivan Martin commanded the Argylls. Technically a lieutenant, Martin had been raised to the rank of acting major due to severe officer casualty rates during the past two weeks.[5]

The western end of the village consisted of two rows of opposing houses bordering the highway until coming to a square anchored on the mayor's office. Another cluster of houses on the eastern side encircled a church next to a narrow stone bridge over the Dives River. The riverbank was bordered by trees and dense brush.

The three surviving Shermans of the troop that had tested Saint-Lambert the previous evening led, with the infantry following on foot. Currie walked alongside Martin. Three hundred yards into the village, the lead tank was hit by an armour-piercing round. The three men in the turret bailed out fast, but the driver and co-driver suffered serious burns before escaping.[6]

On foot, Currie lacked any wireless to report the positions of the Mark IV and Tiger tanks that had fired. Realizing Currie needed communications fast, Captain John Redden, 'C' Squadron's rear-link officer, jumped into the major's tank and ordered it forward. Spotting the Mark IV, Redden pointed it out to Trooper Roy Campbell, who fired a high-explosive round into the tank's tracks and then sent it up in flames with six armour-piercing shells. This was the South Albertas' first confirmed tank kill.[7]

With a Tiger still lurking, Martin and Currie agreed that the Argylls would continue alone. Lieutenant Gil Armour's No. 10 Platoon on point, 'B' Company advanced. The few German infantry encountered were methodically killed. Closing on a lane that ran south to the bridge, Armour spotted a Panther tank pressed against the side of a building. When he called for volunteers, Corporal S.N. Hannivan and Privates Jimmy LaForrest and H.W. Code stepped forward.[8] More reluctantly, Private W.F. Cooper also volunteered. Armour had a reputation for being "a little wild, but the guys wouldn't hesitate to follow him," Cooper said later.[9]

Closing on the tank, Armour silently crept up onto it, intending to drop a Type 36 grenade through the open turret hatch. He was just starting to pull the pin when the crew commander's head popped into the open. Armour dropped the grenade, grabbed the man, and yanked him out. The German drew an automatic pistol and the two men grappled until Armour threw the commander off the tank. Flailing for balance, Armour was helpless to defend himself as the German raised the pistol. Before he could shoot, Private LaForrest fired his rifle. The German fell seriously wounded.

Turret hatches slammed shut, the Panther's engine fired up, and the tank lurched back about twenty-five feet. Here it stopped, 75-millimetre and machine guns aimed to protectively cover the fallen crew commander. Hidden in some nearby brush, Armour's men waited until the small hatch left of the main gun opened and a man's head appeared. Hannivan fired a Sten-gun burst that hit him in the forehead. Before anyone could close the hatch, Armour ran over and dropped in a fragmentation grenade.[10]

By mid-morning, the village was cleared. Currie disposed the infantry and tanks so that Armour's platoon held the crossroads with three supporting tanks. The rest of the tanks and 'B' Company set up in the western part of Saint-Lambert. They numbered fifty infantry and twelve Shermans.[11]

AT 1100 HOURS, Lieutenant General Guy Simonds conferred with his four divisional commanders. Just arrived from Italy, Major General Dan Spry now led 3rd Infantry Division, Brigadier Ken Blackader returning to 8th Infantry Brigade. Simonds had belatedly acquiesced to Major General George Kitching by promoting Bob Moncel to command 4th Armoured Brigade. Simonds's orders were straightforward. The encirclement was to be completed and "no Germans were to escape."[12]

As 11 Canadian Corps had focused on closing the gap, Simonds reported, Lieutenant General Harry Crerar had started 1 British Corps eastward on August 17. Within two days, meeting only slight resistance, 51st (Highland) Infantry and 49th Infantry Divisions had established bridgeheads across the Vie River, while 6th Airborne Division (including 1st Canadian Parachute Battalion) gained the outskirts of Cabourg and Dozule. A snaking front now stretched from Cabourg on the coast southward to a point about five miles east of Saint-Pierre-sur-Dives. These advances were the first step in First Canadian Army's joining the developing Allied drive to the Seine.[13] Montgomery had already announced his intention to complete "destruction of the enemy forces in north-west France. Then to advance northwards, with a view to the eventual destruction of all enemy forces in north-east France."[14] First, however, the pocket had to be eliminated.

Inside the pocket, "the German agony continued." By mid-morning of August 19 the skies had cleared, the mist dissipated, and fighter-bombers returned in earnest. Long columns straggled along the remaining byroads and narrow lanes running towards the gap. Allied Expeditionary Air Force flew 2,535 sorties that returned "enormous claims...against military transport and tanks." British 2nd Tactical Air Force sortied 1,321 times, claiming 52 tanks destroyed and 92 damaged, with 617 other vehicles wrecked and 981 damaged.[15]

In addition to fighter-bombers, the Germans were now within range of First Canadian Army's artillery and that of the Americans to the south. "The pocket is...being drawn closer on what is now known as the Falaise trap," wrote 15th Canadian Field Artillery's war diarist. "It is as if the Americans and British were huge brooms sweeping the Germans into the dustpan that at the moment is the [Canadian Army]." From the heights north of the Dives, FOOs from every regiment, looking down on "the slaughterhouse," were "having a field day."[16]

Every gun in 11 Canadian Corps roared unceasingly, responding to targets provided by observers on the ground and orbiting overhead in planes.[17] The 19th Field Regiment's historian wrote that "by walking a few hundred yards ahead of the guns one could look down into 'the pocket' and see the targets... It was breath-taking to watch the scenes of destruction. The guns would roar, shells would whistle overhead, then far in the distance little orange spurts of flame would blossom out. A few seconds later clouds of smoke would start to rise followed by raging fires."[18]

Inside the cauldron, Seventh Army commander ss Obergruppen-führer Paul Hausser decided to attempt a mass breakout past Chambois at dawn on August 20. Sitting on the edge of a ditch a mile south of Trun, Hausser issued his orders to Standartenführer Kurt Meyer and other senior commanders. Hausser, who had lost an eye at Moscow, gravely bid the others farewell. None expected to reunite.

"The misery around us screamed to high heaven," Meyer wrote. "Refugees and soldiers from the defeated German armies looked helplessly at the bombers flying continuously overhead. It was use-less to take cover from the bursting shells and bombs. Concentrated in such a confined space, we offered once-in-a-lifetime targets to the enemy air power. The wooded areas were full of wounded soldiers and the sundered bodies of horses. Death shadowed us at every step. We stood out like targets on a range. The guns of the Canadian 4th Armoured and Polish 1st Armoured Division could take us under open sights. It was impossible to miss."

Meyer was out of touch with most of 12th Division, but his Hitler Youth continued to fight in isolated, uncoordinated groups around Trun, Saint-Lambert, and Chambois. Chaos reigned.[19]

Beyond the gap, the situation was little different. General der Panzertruppen Hans Eberbach—who had emerged from the gap a couple of days earlier—was ordered to coordinate a II ss Panzer Corps assault back into the pocket to open an escape route for Sev-enth Army. Eberbach had reached II Panzer Corps headquarters on the evening of August 18 after dodging fighter-bombers and having his car "pierced by bullets." Obergruppenführer Wilhelm "Willi" Bittrich reported the corps "torn asunder in consequence of the night marches and air attacks. Until now he could not contact any of his division staffs, but he knew that his troops had neither fuel, ammunition, food, nor signal equipment. He could not tell when the corps would again be ready for action." Eberbach told Bittrich he must attack no later than the evening of August 19–20 with 2nd and 9th ss Panzer divisions advancing southeast towards Trun.

Returning on the afternoon of August 19, Eberbach learned that Bittrich "still had no fuel and had received very insufficient quantities of ammunition," but still hoped to attack that night.[20]

THE GERMANS BEGAN fleeing pell-mell into the gap on the morning of August 19. About three miles north of Trun, on Point 259, the Grenadier Guards covered a road running towards Vimoutiers. Guardsman Stuart Johns and three comrades had been ordered to a hill a quarter-mile distant in hopes of linking up with the Americans reportedly nearby. Finding the mission fruitless, the men were walking back when a German convoy appeared on the road between them and Point 259. As the tanks opened fire, "suddenly Germans popped up all over the place. They had been walking through at night and hiding during the daytime. There was a very low hedge in front of us. The other three guys ran around it and I thought, 'I'm not going to run around it.' I tried to jump over it. Just as I jumped over and was coming down a German in a camouflage uniform stood up and we collided." As Johns rolled clear, he realized the individual wearing a camouflage smock was ss. Gaining his feet, Johns levelled his Sten gun. Suffering a bad leg wound and using two tree branches for crutches, the young ss trooper glared back at him.

Johns gestured to two nearby surrendered Germans to carry the wounded man. But when they approached, the man waved one of the branches threateningly. "What's going on?" Trooper McDonald shouted. "I'm trying to take this guy prisoner and he doesn't want to be taken," Johns answered. McDonald strode over and punched the German in the mouth, knocking him flat. The other Germans picked the stunned man up, and everyone ran for Point 259. By the time they gained the summit, the convoy was burning.[21]

The area around the Grenadiers quieted down after that. "It is wonderful to stop for a bit of a rest," the war diarist said, "and get a chance to eat and sleep."[22] The Grenadiers were not alone in an unexpected quiet day. Both the Governor General's Foot Guards and

British Columbia Regiment found themselves in areas of little action. Brigadier Moncel spent the day reorganizing 4th Armoured Brigade's headquarters and visiting the regiments. It was evening before he ordered the brigade to "advance to a position on high ground overlooking Vimoutiers."[23]

While not engaged themselves, the tankers were constantly aware that a great battle raged nearby. The Foot Guards could see the Poles to the southeast, and at one point several of their tanks "burst into flames and for an hour or more the crews—as spectators of a drama in a great amphitheatre—watched while tank after tank of the Poles was destroyed in a bitter battle... Close at hand, green hills slumbered in the sunlight and the birds sang."[24]

August 19 saw the beginning of almost seventy-two hours of hellish fighting for the Poles. Their 1st Armoured Regiment with two companies of the Highland Battalion fought through heavy opposition to win Maczuga—Hill 262 (North). The combat group comprised of 2nd Armoured Regiment and 8th Infantry Battalion, which had wandered astray the previous day to near Les Champeaux, arrived in the evening to strengthen this position. Meanwhile, the 10th Dragoon Regiment—likely the one watched by the Foot Guards—fought fiercely for Chambois. The town fell at 1930 hours.[25] Roads leading into Chambois and its streets were "jammed with German armour already alight or smouldering, enemy corpses and a host of wounded soldiers," one Polish officer wrote.[26] The Poles rooted hundred of prisoners out of orchards, ditches, and battered buildings. "Shortly afterwards, this group established contact with American infantry which moved up to Chambois from the south," Lieutenant Colonel L. Stankiewicz recorded.[27]

The actual link-up was made by Captain Michael Gutowski's 10th Mounted Rifles squadron and Major Leonard Dull of 2nd Battalion, 359th Infantry Regiment, 90th U.S. Infantry Division. Dull's men advanced past burning houses, German corpses, and dead horses.

Suddenly, Poles and Americans spotted each other. Guns rose momentarily before recognition came. An American captain ran to one Polish officer "and lifted me in the air as if I had been a child." Major H. Zgorzelski, commanding 10th Polish Dragoons, arrived.

Captain Laughlin Waters, commanding 'G' Company, 359th Regiment, represented the Americans. Zgorzelski spoke English, but when asked his name said, "Here, give me a book and pencil. You'll never be able to pronounce it anyway so I'll write it down." A scrap of paper was ripped from a notebook and he scrawled his name. Waters reciprocated. A bottle of Polish vodka appeared and toasts were drunk.

Then Gutowski got down to business. "Our position is very flimsy," he told the Americans. "We are out of food. We have no water, no gasoline and no ammunition. Some tanks have no more than five or ten shells left. For machine guns there is maybe ten minutes' firing." After interminable negotiations up the American command chain, Dull secured 4,000 gallons of fuel, 140,000 rounds of machine-gun ammunition, and 189 75-millimetre rounds.[28]

These supplies were welcome, but they only served the Poles in Chambois. Those on Maczuga remained cut off and under relentless artillery fire. Their situation by nightfall looked increasingly grim.[29]

SIMONDS HAD PLANNED for 4th Canadian Armoured Division to reach Chambois coincident with the Poles. As the mist burned off in the early morning of August 19, however, the South Albertas' 'C' Squadron and the Argylls' 'B' Company became deadlocked in Saint-Lambert. Hundreds of Germans streamed into surrounding orchards or advanced on the village. Most wanted to surrender, and soon the volume of prisoners posed a logistical nightmare. Others, however, came looking for a brawl. With so many prisoners, it was easy for the brawlers to infiltrate alongside them. Captain John Redden was wounded trying to take the surrender of a fighting convoy that had driven into the village under a white flag.

Lieutenant Colonel Wotherspoon maintained his regimental headquarters on Point 117 to provide a firm supportive base while advancing 'B' Squadron, under Major T.B. "Darby" Nash, to Point 124. To protect Currie's rear, he moved 'A' Squadron to where the Trun-Chambois road crossed a small stream called the Foulbec. The tanks also blocked any German attempt to cross the Dives between

Trun and Saint-Lambert. 'B' Squadron spent the day shooting up German vehicles on the roads running towards Vimoutiers immediately east of Saint-Lambert.

At noon, another German convoy entered the village, preceded by an officer in a motorcycle's sidecar. Surprised by Argylls, the officer surrendered. Present were photographers from No. 1 Canadian Army Film and Photographic Unit, hoping to capture the Canadian link-up with the Americans. Instead, cameraman Donald I. Grant shot the German officer's surrender to Major Currie—possibly the most famous Canadian photograph of the war.

Soon after the film unit departed for safer climes at 1300 hours, the entire village erupted in a wild, disorganized firefight. Germans swarmed Saint-Lambert with guns blazing. 'C' Squadron tanks whirled frantically to engage them with machine guns and main guns. Currie asked Wotherspoon to fire artillery on his positions and warned everyone to take cover. Expecting 25-pounder fire, he was horrified when 4.5- and 5.5-inch medium shells exploded. These could easily knock out his tanks. "Is [the artillery] killing more Germans or more of your people?" Wotherspoon asked. Currie conceded the Germans were doing the dying. His men suffered no casualties.[30]

Wotherspoon asked Brigadier Jim Jefferson of 10th Infantry Brigade for infantry reinforcement. Jefferson, whose three battalions were stretched thin around Trun, could only round up the Argylls' understrength 'C' Company, along with 'C' Company of the Lincoln and Welland Regiment. They marched for Saint-Lambert in the late afternoon.[31]

From Trun to Saint-Lambert the Germans, in complete confusion, were "attempting to break out *en masse*," as one army report put it. Throughout the day the Lincs at Trun, along with medium machine guns of 4th Division's New Brunswick Rangers, had "held off continuous attacks as column after column of madly shouting, grey-clad men tried to force their way through only to be cut down at point-blank range by the medium machineguns... It was fantastic to watch so dreadful a slaughter, then to see the remnants reforming and attack again only to fall as the sustained machine-gun fire smashed through them.

"The whole battlefield by sundown [was] an unholy panorama of burnt-out vehicles and unburied dead."[32]

The two companies sent to reinforce Saint-Lambert arrived at dusk. The Lincs were commanded by Major R.F. Willson, while the Argylls were under Major Gordon Winfield. Willson blended his platoons with the Argylls of 'B' Company.[33] For some unexplained reason, Major Winfield marched his Argyll company through Saint-Lambert and out the other side.

Private Arthur Bridge of No. 14 Platoon thought they were headed for Chambois. "By now it was quite dark. The glare from burning houses and vehicles that had been knocked out along the road provided us with some visibility." Everyone was "having a ball scrounging through the trucks along the way." At Moissy, a hamlet halfway to Chambois, the pleasant night stroll ended with the screech of an MG-42. "We were spread out single file, and the company commander and two or three others were hit by this burst. As the firing continued and we couldn't tell where it came from, we took to the shelter of the ditch, and started shooting back at the unseen enemy, who were obviously close by as they began throwing hand grenades at us. One grenade fell among several of us in the ditch and exploded, making a lot of noise but causing little damage."

With Winfield wounded, Lieutenant Phil Whitehead and Company Sergeant Major George Mitchell tried establishing a fighting position in an orchard next to a farmyard, only to realize they were surrounded by Germans. Finally, the company snuck back to Saint-Lambert along a narrow side lane that was lined with German tanks. "It was an eerie feeling to be slinking by them in the darkness." Bridge thought the tankers must have believed they were Germans, for nobody issued a challenge or opened fire. Regaining the village, 'C' Company settled down for an uneasy night.[34]

THE GERMANS WERE well experienced in escaping encirclements on the Eastern Front. They did so by attacking the weakest point from within and without. In this case, the weak spot was the area between Saint-Lambert and Chambois, where only elements of 1st Polish Armoured Division atop Maczuga stood in opposition.

The Poles had about fifteen hundred infantry, more than eighty tanks, and roughly twenty anti-tank guns dug in on an approximately one-square-mile perimeter. From Maczuga they could see the entire pocket. But Hill 262 (South) and the lower foothills about it blocked observation to the southeast. The steep ground nearby was also scattered with hedges and woods that denied the Poles clear fields of fire. Preventing passage through the ground immediately to the west and southwest during the day was difficult. At night, it was hopeless.[35]

Seventh Army's breakout began in the early morning hours of August 20 with 3rd Parachute Division advancing under command of 11 Parachute Corps commander Generalleutnant Eugen Meindl. Two thousand strong, the paratroopers were disciplined, hard fighters. They were to cross the Dives and attack Maczuga at first light. Together with 11 Panzer Corps, expected to arrive from the east, the paratroopers would maintain a breach through which Seventh Army would pass. At the same time, 353rd Infantry Division—less seasoned and well trained—would seize Hill 262 (South). Close behind the paratroopers and this division would be the remaining armoured divisions. Then—almost entirely on foot—the rest of the army would follow. Everybody was to travel lightly. Only a few non-self-propelled anti-tank guns were taken. After firing off their ammunition, the artillerymen destroyed their guns. Surplus stores, vehicles, and other equipment were either burned or blown up. It was "do or die." If the breakout failed, Seventh Army could no longer fight.[36] For the tanks to escape, the Germans required bridges over the Dives. There were only two possible. One was at Saint-Lambert, the other at Chambois. At 2230 hours on August 19, Meindl's paratroopers formed in woods by the Dives. "Our crossing stands or falls at St. Lambert," a 1st Panzer reconnaissance officer signalled his divisional headquarters.[37]

"The night was rather hectic with considerable infiltration," the South Albertas' war diarist reported. "Small parties of infantry were shot up all night and the bag of prisoners considerably augmented."[38]

While some were stragglers, the paratroopers were deliberately probing Saint-Lambert's strength. By early morning, Meindl knew what he faced. Saint-Lambert and Point 117 appeared strongly held, but the tanks at the Foulbec lacked infantry protection. Meindl had no intention of tangling with Major Arnold Lavoie's 'A' Squadron. He wanted to filter quietly through. Although at times fired on, Meindl slipped most of his paratroopers past the South Albertas' screen.

Towards dawn, the paratroopers—partially concealed by a hot, damp ground mist and light rain—closed on Maczuga. By 0730 hours, the leading elements were engaging the Poles. Meindl happened upon Seventh Army's Obergruppenführer Hausser, who had also crept past the South Alberta positions. The two men hunkered in a crater and agreed that the paratroopers should circle around the hill and attack it from the north.[39]

As dawn broke in Saint-Lambert, the Argylls' Private Arthur Bridge "realized we were in for a time of it, as enemy activity was apparent wherever we looked." At 0800, the village came "under constant attack by masses of the enemy."[40]

"It could hardly be called an attack as there was no covering fire plan, simply a mass movement of riflemen," the South Alberta war diarist wrote. On Point 117, Wotherspoon moved the headquarters tanks to "better fire positions and [they] began to mow down the advancing infantry. Similar activity occurred on 'B' and 'C' [Squadrons'] sectors."[41]

The attacks still threatened to overwhelm Saint-Lambert. A Tiger ground over the bridge and gained the square by the mayor's office. Firing armour-piercing rounds, it drove the infantry out of nearby buildings. The tank also set two Shermans ablaze. German infantry waded the river in waves and surrounded the infantry holding the northwest part of Saint-Lambert. Only the fact that most Germans were more interested in fleeing than fighting prevented the Canadians from being overrun.[42]

Private Bridge was near a Sherman brewed by the Tiger. The shell had penetrated the turret next to the gun. When the crew bailed out, he realized the gunner "was still inside and the tank was starting to burn." With the main gun blocking the gunner's hatch, the man could not escape. Suddenly, 'C' Company's Company Sergeant Major George Mitchell "showed us what a true hero he was. He climbed up on the burning tank in full view of the enemy, aided by

Corporal J.R. Holmes, and traversed the turret of the tank so the gun no longer blocked the hatch. A couple more of us climbed up when the hatch had been opened and we pulled the poor driver out. His face and hands were literally cooked from the heat, and the flesh was hanging off him. Although he was still alive, he was unconscious."[43]

With Wotherspoon on Point 117 was 15th Field Regiment FOO Captain Harold Clerkson, who "had never seen anything like it." Everywhere, Germans marched. "It seemed almost a kind of a dream in a way...all those men down there. My God, what ever brought me to this and what do I do now?" But Clerkson knew. It was a job he did for the next two days and which earned a Military Cross. "I called for a Mike Target [all the regiment's guns] and that was approved." After the shells struck, hundreds of Germans emerged from the smoke to surrender. "I sent word back that for every Mike Target we were getting about 500 to 1,000 prisoners."

Currie was in regular contact with Clerkson, feeding targets. Major Ivan Martin, commanding the Argylls' 'C' Company, also passed along targets. Fired upon by two 88-millimetre self-propelled guns when there were no Shermans nearby to help, Martin had Clerkson engage them. But the shell fell wide. Unable to accurately situate the SPGS, Martin took the wireless set and, according to his subsequent citation, "went forward alone on foot...to a position from which he could...direct the artillery and neutralize the enemy guns."[44] On Point 117, Clerkson also spent "a fair amount of time running about, exposing myself to fire, in order to effectively direct the fire." Point 117 was increasingly under threat of being overrun.[45] Realizing the danger, Wotherspoon ordered 'A' Squadron to return to the hill. When Lavoie's tanks arrived, "the enemy broke and fled."[46]

By 1000 hours, thousands of Germans swarmed around Saint-Lambert. Wotherspoon warned Jefferson that unless he was reinforced with more infantry, Saint-Lambert might be lost. Jefferson had been promised reinforcement by 3rd Infantry Division's 9th Brigade at Trun, so he could shift men eastward to Wotherspoon. Delayed by the arrival of their relief, however, 9th Brigade only began moving in the late morning of August 20. Wotherspoon's force would continue its lone fight.[47]

A Hellhole

THE BREAKOUT ON August 20 had caught 4th Canadian
Armoured Division wrong footed. As ordered by Lieutenant
General Guy Simonds, 4th Canadian Armoured Brigade had begun
moving that morning northeast towards Vimoutiers. The brigade
was to secure a crossing over the Vie River to facilitate the expected
advance to the Seine.[1] The Governor General's Foot Guards had
already reached Camembert when Major General George Kitching
instructed Brigadier Bob Moncel to turn the brigade about.[2] Moncel
ordered the Foot Guards back to Point 258 in order to close the Trun-
Vimoutiers road.[3] With the brigade so far north, Moncel realized his
best option was to send the British Columbia Regiment and Grenadier Guards due east to the Poles on Maczuga. Driving into the midst
of the gap, they met bitter resistance while at the same time having
to deal with hundreds of surrendering Germans. By 1600 hours,
they were halfway to Maczuga, "but the battlefield now presented a
confusing picture, fighting was taking place on all sides." At nightfall, the tanks halted.[4]

On Maczuga, the situation worsened throughout the day. Surrounded by 3rd Parachute Division—supported by tanks and
self-propelled guns that had escaped the pocket—the Poles clung
tenaciously to the summit. "It reminded one of medieval days, when
the defence of the battlefield was organized by placing camps in a

tight quadrangle," Polish Lieutenant Colonel L. Stankiewicz wrote. "The densely wooded hills were extremely difficult for observation, as a result of which…German tanks would approach unnoticed, almost up to our positions." When a shootout between one Panther and Sherman ended, they faced "one another barrel to barrel at a distance of a few metres, both burn[ing]."[5]

The Germans kept looking northeastward for 11 Panzer Corps, but Obergruppenführer Willi Bittrich had only received his fuel at dawn, and so it was not until 1000 hours that 2nd ss and 9th ss Panzer Divisions advanced. The 9th ss moved through Camembert, while the 2nd ss followed the Chambois-Vimoutiers road. Each division had only about twenty tanks. The 9th ss fielded a single infantry regiment, 2nd ss two infantry regiments. Each regiment numbered no more than a hundred men. General der Panzertruppen Hans Eberbach believed the advance possible "only because of the bad weather which hindered the operations of the enemy air force." The warm drizzle made the roads greasy. The way "was packed with burned out vehicles to such an extent that tanks had to clear an alley before it was passable."[6]

At 1500 hours, 2nd ss Division joined the battle against the Poles. From a nearby hill, a Panther picked off five Shermans in the same number of minutes.[7] At 1700 hours, "German tanks penetrated to within a few paces of the defence positions. After a heavy battle they were, however, forced to withdraw with losses."[8] Three Mark ivs burned inside the Polish perimeter.[9]

Maczuga remained cut off and heavily embattled as the sun set. On every side, Germans streamed through the gap held open by those fighting the Poles. Standartenführer Kurt Meyer escaped this way. Meyer was soon joined by Obersturmbannführer Max Wünsche, who had brazenly driven a German car right through Saint-Lambert. The two began gathering the badly scattered Hitler Youth and readying them for the next battle. Although seriously wounded by a mortar round, Obergruppenführer Paul Hausser also escaped.[10]

The Germans tried to break out across a front that stretched from Trun to Chambois, but those coming up against these two villages were rebuffed, sustaining heavy losses. At Trun, the New Brunswick Rangers "continued firing throughout the morning and into the late afternoon, [when] the battle of annihilation reached its climax," stated their war diarist. "So great was the slaughter that blood was actually flowing in the gutters." No. 4 Platoon alone fired fifty thousand rounds.[11]

At Saint-Lambert, the South Alberta Regiment and two Argyll and Sutherland Highlander and one Lincoln and Welland Regiment companies fought on in isolation through the afternoon. Major Dave Currie withdrew the entire force to the western half of the village, as the leading elements of 2nd ss and 9th ss Panzer Divisions threatened to overwhelm it. Gruppenführer Heinrich von Lüttwitz, commanding 2nd ss Division, was deeply worried by the Canadian presence. Although Currie's force was just trying to survive with only five remaining Shermans and an ever-shrinking number of infantrymen, von Lüttwitz believed they were attacking *him*.

Currie and Martin were as worried as Lüttwitz. Both moved about ceaselessly, encouraging the men. When a German machine gun started blazing away, Martin asked a private in a slit trench to help him eliminate it. "You're kidding, of course," the man replied. Martin headed out with a Sten gun. After a long burst of gunfire, he returned with a shouldered MG-42.[12] Moments later, Martin and fellow Argyll Lieutenant Albini Dalpe were killed by an 88-millimetre round. Because he did not receive the only posthumous Commonwealth award, the Victoria Cross, Martin's heroism went unrecognized until the United States bestowed on him a Distinguished Service Cross.[13]

After Martin fell, Currie—with only two other officers remaining—asked permission to pull out. Lieutenant Colonel Swatty Wotherspoon told him to stay put, as 3rd Infantry Division's 9th Brigade should soon break through to Saint-Lambert. It was a vain hope. This brigade's closest battalion was the Highland Light Infantry, supported by the 1st Hussars Regiment. They had advanced to about a mile and a half west of Saint-Lambert and immediately south of Neauphe-sur-Dives by late afternoon. Coming under machine-gun fire "from all points of the compass...supplemented by the occasional solid shot and mortar shells...both [regimental commanders] appreciated that it was impossible to move under these circumstances and the move...was postponed till first light."[14]

Inside Saint-Lambert, Currie told the men they had to stick it out. Standing alongside Trooper Jimmy Eastman's tank, Currie said, "Dig out everything you've got, all the shells—everything you've got, this is it." Because it was Currie speaking, nobody questioned the order. Even the Argylls and Lincs, who had never met Currie before, now trusted him. Sergeant John Gunderson, commanding a 'C' Squadron troop, felt that "just to go up and talk to him was enough to give us confidence...without his example I do not believe we could have held out. He didn't give a damn how close the Jerries were, and he always had the same every-day expression, just as if we were on a scheme. He was wonderful."[15]

At 1500 hours, the Canadians in Saint-Lambert were unexpectedly reinforced by two troops of 6th Anti-Tank Regiment. Taking a wrong turn, 'J' and 'L' Troops had driven into the village by accident. One troop towed 17-pounders; the other rode in 105-millimetre self-propelled M-10s. Both went into "crash action" along the road and "soon had their guns...deployed so as to lend all possible aid." Once the guns were firing, the two troop commanders set off to find the column from which they had become separated—the one comprised of the 1st Hussars and Highland Light Infantry—and were captured by the Germans.[16] With fifteen of the sixteen guns aimed towards the German-occupied end of the village, the anti-tank guns ripped into every vehicle they saw. When a Tiger rolled by at a range of eight hundred yards, one gun punched a hole in it with an armour-piercing shell, then widened this to about a two-foot diameter with high-explosive shells.

Soon thereafter the gunners stripped their .50-calibre machine guns off the M-10s and deployed them about the perimeter. The machine guns and anti-tank guns greatly strengthened the Canadian position. It was soon estimated that about two hundred German infantry had been either killed or wounded.[17] The numbers surrendering grew exponentially, as it became clear that Saint-Lambert no longer provided a safe escape route.

AS NIGHT FELL, Lieutenant General Guy Simonds personally intervened to close the gap. At 1500 hours, he visited 4th Armoured Division's headquarters and learned from Kitching that Trun and

Saint-Lambert were in Canadian hands. Wanting a closer look, Simonds headed for Saint-Lambert in his Staghound armoured car. About a mile east of Trun, Simonds stopped on a hill and was fired on by a German machine gun. Storming back, Simonds berated Kitching for giving him inaccurate information, brushing aside the general's explanation that he had never said the ground *between* Trun and Saint-Lambert was secure.

After a whirlwind tour of Canadian and Polish headquarters, Simonds directed 4th Armoured Brigade's Moncel to send his tank regiments and the Lake Superior Regiment immediately to rescue the Poles on Maczuga.[18] It was 2000 hours.[19] The Foot Guards moved eastward one and a half miles from Point 258 to Point 239 to "dominate the roads radiating from both St. Lambert and...Chambois." They were supported by a Superior company and a 5th Anti-Tank Regiment self-propelled gun troop. Reaching the hill unopposed, the force spent a "tense night in a high state of alert, with flares constantly dropping on the flanks." Twice Germans tried to attack the tanks with Panzerfausts but were driven off.[20]

The Grenadier Guards had advanced on Point 240, about a mile due west of Point 239. Major Hershell Smith's No. 3 Squadron led. Heavy rain was falling, and the tanks clawed their way through mud to the summit. No. 2 Squadron advanced a half-mile farther to Point 147 and blocked a narrow road passing through the draw between Point 239 and Point 240.[21]

Understanding that Point 240 was unoccupied, the tankers were surprised to find the Algonquin Regiment had arrived there at 1600 hours and been "having a swell time shooting up German staff cars at long range from the top of the hill." 'B' Company's Major Lyle Monk had his men "out on the bald slope overlooking a deep valley with a road at the bottom. Across the valley, about two miles away, was another high slope where the [Poles] had been established for almost three days."[22]

Nightfall found the Polish situation on Maczuga dire. Fighting raged on unceasingly. The Poles in Chambois fought off a "furious mechanized attack supported by tanks" that pierced the first line of defence before the force was "almost completely annihilated."

Neither at Chambois nor Maczuga were the Poles able to evacuate wounded. These "had to remain amongst our fighting soldiers, and were exposed to the enemy's heavy artillery and mortar fire" while "the combat lasted [through] the night and the morning of August 21st. Our detachments were using up literally their last ammunition. The suffering of the wounded became almost intolerable. Tortured by lack of sleep and long hours of battle, which lasted without cessation for two days, the soldiers made their utmost efforts," Lieutenant Colonel L. Stankiewicz recorded.[23]

Compared to the Polish situation, the night was comparatively quiet in Saint-Lambert. At 2000 hours, responding to what turned out to be false reports of great masses of German tanks approaching the whole Canadian front, the two anti-tank troops from 6th Anti-Tank Regiment were ordered to join a massive gun screen erected to meet the threat. They went reluctantly, having already accounted for a half-track, an armoured car, one Tiger, one Panther, three Mark IVs, a self-propelled gun, and a large number of infantry.[24]

When Wotherspoon protested losing the anti-tank gunners, he was offered empty assurances that 9th Brigade would arrive imminently. Instead, this brigade's regiments and supporting tankers advanced at a snail's pace. The first North Nova Scotia Highlanders finally arrived at Point 117 at about 2100 hours, and over the next two hours the battalion deployed so that it had one company in Neauphe-sur-Dives, one on Point 117, another in Saint-Lambert, and the fourth in a farm east of the village.

During this time, 2nd ss Panzer Division's von Lüttwitz, after nine hours conducting operations at Saint-Lambert, left the town after a remnant of tanks, self-propelled guns, and vehicles of 116th Panzer Division passed through.[25] This was the last organized motorized column to escape the pocket.

As the sun rose on Monday, August 21, the Argyll's Private Arthur Bridge observed that the "Germans able to escape had already gotten by us; those who couldn't were either prisoners or dead, and eventually the shooting and shelling stopped."[26]

Currie had not slept for almost three days. He was discussing the handover of Saint-Lambert to the North Novas during the late morning when Sergeant John Gunderson saw him "actually...fall asleep on his feet while he was talking...one of the boys caught him before he could fall to the ground." All the courageous defenders of Saint-Lambert were in similar condition. One delay following another, 9th Brigade's relief dragged on interminably. Not until late afternoon were the infantry units released, and it was the morning of August 22 before the South Albertas left. "When we had come to St. Lambert," Currie recalled, "it was a neat, small, quiet French village." By the time they left, "it was a fantastic mess," the "clutter of equipment, dead horses, wounded, dying and dead Germans, had turned it into a hell-hole."[27] Currie was unaware that his bravery at Saint-Lambert had been noticed. He would be the first Canadian in the Northwest Europe campaign awarded a Victoria Cross.

NORTHEAST OF SAINT-LAMBERT, fighting continued through the morning of August 21. But the Germans were increasingly desperate and disorganized. On Point 239, the Foot Guards and Superiors had awakened to an utterly quiet morning. Not a sign of Germans anywhere. Consequently, at 0815, the tankers dismounted and began cooking breakfast. That was precisely when a German mobile column rolled up the narrow road in the valley bottom. The German tanks and self-propelled guns opened fire, while infantry manning heavy machine guns mounted on half-tracks also blazed away. Foot Guards commander Major E.M. Smith's Sherman was hit and burned. Jumping clear, Smith directed the regiment's fire from the ground despite having a bullet graze his scalp.

The fight proved no real contest. Confined to the narrow road, the Germans could only try to shoot their way through. But the Foot Guards, as their regimental historian noted, "and their friends from the Lake Superior Regiment and the anti-tank gunners were able to enjoy the most frequently encountered German method of doing battle—that of sitting back on a good defensive position and picking off the attackers as they advanced."[28]

One 75-millimetre SPG quickly "brewed up," another was damaged, and two more were abandoned. A dozen half-tracks and trucks were destroyed. Thirty Germans surrendered and another fifty were killed or wounded. Besides Smith's minor wound, the Foot Guards had only one other casualty. Only Smith's tank was lost.[29]

The Foot Guards on Point 239 were not only keeping the road

below closed, they backstopped the advance of the two other 4th Armoured Brigade regiments. At 0800 hours, the Grenadier Guards with the Lake Superiors' 'B' Company had set off on a two-phase move that first passed Point 239 and then proceeded for a 2,200-yard push through to Maczuga.[30] The British Columbia Regiment followed them into the valley between Maczuga and Point 240—held by the Algonquin Regiment—and then veered southward to Hill 262 (South).[31]

For the first half-mile, the Grenadier advance was hindered only by wrecked German vehicles. Then, as the tankers reached the valley floor, two SPGs opened up and knocked out three Shermans of No. 1 Squadron's No. 3 Troop. Troop commander Lieutenant Leonard Manning Hobday and Corporal James Reginald Leney were killed. Sergeant Henry Watters Macdonald, commanding the only No. 3 tank remaining, deliberately drove into open ground to pinpoint the German position. Although his Sherman was hit, he was able to accurately direct fire that destroyed the two SPGs. Major Ned Amy's No. 1 Squadron was now reduced to just three serviceable tanks. So Lieutenant Colonel Bill Halpenny ordered Major Hershell Smith to join Amy with his nine tanks. No. 2 Squadron remained behind to "guard the line of communication."

Firing smoke to supplement the cover offered by the rain and low clouds, the Grenadiers and Lake Superiors "sped down the valley." Coming into Coudehard, immediately south of Maczuga, the column lost one tank to enemy fire. Machine-gun fire from virtually every house forced the Superiors to dismount and begin clearing buildings. "With all guns blazing," the Grenadiers "beat down the infantry" they could see and set buildings on fire with high-explosive shells. Captain Bernard Ghewy took on a Mark IV and a Panther. It should have been an uneven shootout for one Sherman, but Ghewy emerged victorious. Two more Panthers were eliminated by the Grenadiers. By battle's end, virtually every building and even the gardens between were ablaze.[32]

It was about noon, and the Grenadiers and Superiors paused to regroup for the charge to the summit of Maczuga. The Poles, unaware that deliverance was close at hand, had detected a slackening in the ferocity of attempts to overrun their position. But they were unaware that the Germans were leaving. Throughout the morning they had repelled continual "bloody and stubborn battles" that gave them no cause to believe the siege was ending. "By this time shortage of ammunition, water and food supplies became exceedingly acute. A great many of our injured men died," wrote Lieutenant Colonel L. Stankiewicz.[33]

Around the same time, a small battle group of 10th ss Panzer Division had reached Generalleutnant Eugen Meindl's headquarters near the base of Maczuga. Its commander informed Meindl that his would be the last men out of the pocket. Meindl started readying his paratroopers and the remnants of 11 Panzer Corps to pull out. At 1600 hours, the Germans began leaving.[34]

The Grenadiers had finally managed to reach the Poles about two and a half hours earlier. Advancing up a narrow track through dense woods, the leading Grenadier tank found the way blocked by a burning Mark IV. "Turning off to avoid it, our leading tanks, crashing their way through the bordering trees, were suddenly confronted with two advancing Stuarts. Recognition was immediate: these were the last remaining Polish tanks making a final dash for help, and here we were. The delight on both sides was a sight for jaded eyes. Almost the first question the Poles asked was: 'Have you a cigarette?' Everything, even snipers, was forgotten in the relief of the moment."

On the summit, "the scene was...the grimmest. Scores of corpses were scattered all about. The road was blocked with derelict vehicles. Several hundred wounded and some seven hundred loosely guarded prisoners were lying in an open field. The Poles, isolated for three days, cried with relief." Soon a convoy of five Priests under command of the Grenadiers' Captain George Sherwood arrived. Each vehicle was full of food, medical supplies, ammunition, and fuel. The regiment's medical officer, Captain S.A. MacDonald, was also aboard. He began preparing Polish wounded for evacuation. Through the rest of the day and ensuing night, Sherwood's Priests made a total of ten round trips that greatly relieved the Polish situation on Maczuga.[35]

Late in the day, the Highland Light Infantry and 1st Hussars linked up with the Poles in Chambois after advancing out of Saint-Lambert. Total Polish casualties during the three-day battle numbered 325 killed, 1,002 wounded, and 114 missing. This contrasts starkly with 1st Polish Armoured Division's losses during the rest of the August fighting, which totalled 656 killed, wounded, and missing.[36]

Northeast of Chambois, the Dukes put in the last Canadian attack to close the Falaise Gap. Hill 262 (South) overlooked a deep valley in which lay a small collection of houses. The tankers were to seize these buildings and then the summit. After pasting the buildings with a heavy main-gun bombardment, the tanks rolled in to find only Germans dead, wounded, or wanting to surrender. Hill 262 was equally seized without a fight.

Captain Douglas Harker looked upon the scene. "The little cluster of houses had taken an awful beating. Besides the pounding our guns had given it, a squadron of RAF Typhoons had...strafed and bombed it into dust. Gargantuan pieces of field equipment lay in twisted masses on the road. Blasted mobile 88's, shattered cannons and overturned tanks, self-propelled guns, assault vehicles, trucks and staff cars mingled with the bloody ripped carcasses of rotting horses and men. Bodies floated face downwards in the muddy ditches and water-filled shell craters. Ammunition, food, and quartermasters' supplies littered the roads and fields and in the midst of it all, pale, feeble wounded Germans weakly waved white cloths and pointed to the lacerated stump of a leg or arm, or to an oozing red smear. There were no houses left in that 'village,' just dust and charred wood and at the crossroads, where the market square had been, stood a Crucifix."[37]

BY MID-AFTERNOON OF August 21, Falaise Gap was closed. This concluded the great battle in Normandy. Another two days passed before the last Germans trapped inside the pocket were disarmed and sent to prisoner-of-war cages or medical facilities. First Canadian Army reported that, during the period August 18–23, it took 208 officers and 13,475 other ranks prisoner. Many more were taken by the other Allied armies.

Just how many Germans managed to escape from the pocket would never be accurately determined. German reports were widely contradictory. One claimed that 40–50 per cent got away.[38] Yet on

August 25, Fifth Panzer Army—which had Seventh Army under command—reported combined total fighting strength at 17,980 men, 314 artillery pieces, and only 42 tanks and assault guns. One report stated 12th ss Panzer Division's total strength on August 23 at 300 men, 10 tanks, and no artillery.[39] These figures were roundly refuted by the division's chief of staff Sturmbannführer Hubert Meyer (no relation of Kurt Meyer). He reported on August 22 that the division was 12,500 men strong, of which about 2,500 were men in supply units. Because the division had no combat-ready tanks, spgs, or armoured personnel carriers and barely any artillery, Meyer conceded it was no longer "ready for action as a divisional fighting unit."[40]

There were approximately 100,000 Germans in the pocket, and of these about 10,000 were killed and 40,000 to 50,000 either taken prisoner or listed as missing. Certainly fewer than 50,000 escaped, and a high percentage of these were supply and service personnel rather than front-line fighting troops. But the disaster that befell the Germans during the Normandy Campaign must take into account not just the numbers who did or did not escape through the Falaise Gap. That was merely the endgame in a long, bloody campaign that raged from June 6 to August 21.

Again, no clear tally for German casualties exists. But most reports roughly agree with General Dwight D. Eisenhower's conclusion that by August 25, the Germans had "lost, in round numbers, 400,000 killed, wounded, or captured, of which total 200,000 were prisoners of war." Of the prisoners, he believed, 135,000 were taken in the period between July 25 and the closing of the gap.

German losses in equipment, particularly within the pocket, were terrific. Overall, Eisenhower reported the Germans losing 1,300 tanks, 500 assault guns, 1,500 field and heavier artillery, and 20,000 vehicles. Within the Falaise Gap area alone, Britain's No. 2 Operational Research Section found 187 tanks and self-propelled guns, 157 lightly armoured vehicles, 1,778 lorries, 669 cars, and 252 guns—a total of 3,043 guns and vehicles.

Allied losses in the Normandy Campaign were also high. By the end of August, total casualties had reached 206,703—124,394 of those American and 82,309 British and Canadian. The numbers of

Canadians killed, wounded, or missing was high relative to overall committed strength. Most casualties were suffered by the troops in the three divisions and single armoured brigade. Together, these had a strength of about 52,500 men. From the storming of Juno Beach through the breakout and closing of the Falaise Gap, there were 18,444 Canadian casualties, of whom 5,021 were fatal. Within Twenty-First Army Group, the divisions that suffered the highest casualty rates were 3rd Canadian Infantry Division followed by 2nd Canadian Infantry Division.[41]

A campaign as vast, long, and costly as Normandy inevitably becomes a source of endless debate on the comparative strategies, tactics, leadership abilities, and fighting quality of the various forces involved. These debates began even before the guns ceased firing. No question that the Canadian soldier fought as well or better than any other. The Germans would insist that they were always outnumbered and outgunned—this being the real reason they were defeated. The truth is that Canadian infantry, reduced to half or less their normal number, repeatedly attacked heavily defended positions held by forces of equal or superior strength and won. The same was true for Canadian tankers. Strategists generally argue that three-to-one force superiority is required for an attacker to overcome a prepared defence. The Canadians seldom enjoyed a ratio greater than one to one. Yet they prevailed.

Simonds emerged with a solid reputation. No Allied operation had gone even close to plan, but Totalize and Tractable were both considered at the time to have contributed significantly to the Allied breakout in Normandy.

Battle casualties among senior officers were shocking—Major General Rod Keller critically wounded, one brigadier killed, three others wounded; two out of eleven armoured regiment commanders killed or wounded; fourteen infantry commanders from twenty-four battalions lost due to wounds or illness.[42]

On August 18, the three Canadian divisional commanders had enjoyed a brief drink together. Dan Spry, Charles Foulkes, and George Kitching had all served in the Royal Canadian Regiment and were toasting that coincidence. Foulkes was down at the mouth, though, "quite sure...that he was going to be relieved...because he...felt that Simonds was 'on the warpath' and was going to fire someone!" Kitching felt Foulkes was safe, a hero even. Spry joked that having just arrived, he, at least, could hardly be fired. All agreed that Kitching was secure.

Yet on the afternoon of August 21, with the Falaise Gap safely closed, Simonds informed Kitching he was replacing him with 7th Canadian Infantry Brigade's Harry Foster that very evening. Foster's first words were, "What the hell's gone wrong, George—you and Guy Simonds were so close?"[43]

"Shortly afterwards General Simonds told me what he had done," his aide-de-camp Captain Marshal Stearns later said, "and that it was the most difficult thing he had ever had to do; that he had tremendous confidence in [Kitching] because of their close association in Sicily and Italy and almost loved him as he would a brother, and admired his great courage and personal ability; that he found it impossible to understand how things in the 4th Armoured had got so out of control. He felt he had no other choice than to replace him; that lives were at stake and he could take no more chances."[44]

Lives were at stake. For even as the Normandy Campaign was brought to a successful finish, First Canadian Army began marching. Normandy was but the beginning. As August 21 closed, Algonquin Major George Cassidy looked from Point 240 out over the Falaise Gap. "As far as the eye could see lay the Valley of Desolation, palled in smoke from a thousand fires, alive with the stench of dead and burning flesh. Through the valley and beyond it, back along the battered road to Caen, the eye of the imagination could see once more the dust-laden air, shimmering in the August sun, and in that dust, swimming up to face us again, the shapes of those we had had to leave behind. Was it imagination that their fingers all pointed east, urging us on to the end for which they had died?"[45]

The Normandy Campaign in Memory

IT'S A WARM sunny day in late May, and the surf rolls gently onto the sand of Juno Beach in front of the resort hotels of Courseulles-sur-Mer. Across the bustling little harbour, the modernistic Juno Beach Centre—its shiny steel exterior and sharp, jutting angular roofline looking slightly menacing—is crowded with French school groups and busloads of Canadian and British tourists visiting the Normandy invasion beaches. Since its opening on June 6, 2003, the centre has become a must-visit attraction for the thousands of Canadians who come here each year. Some have relatives who were involved in the landing or the long summer of fire that followed in Normandy. But this is not true for most. In recent years, Canadian tourist visits to the invasion beaches has risen dramatically and show no sign of tapering or even levelling off.

Inside the centre, I meet a couple in their sixties from Halifax. The man's father came ashore as a reinforcement nine days after the invasion and saw the war through to its end. There is also a middle-aged man and his elderly father from Regina. The elderly man is not a veteran, a little too young for that. But his brother was. He served in Italy and then the Netherlands as an artilleryman in a 1st Division regiment. Neither the father nor his son have been to Italy or the Netherlands and have no plans to go. Normandy is the draw, particularly the beaches. Juno Beach is the Canadian star of World War II remembrance.

Later, on the beachside promenade at Saint-Aubin-sur-Mer—where the North Shore (New Brunswick) Regiment landed—I stand near a restored German 50-millimetre gun battery. Not so covertly I overhear a conversation between a young family from Vancouver and their privately hired French tour guide. He describes the problems this gun gave the North Shores and Fort Garry Horse tankers that momentous day, until three tanks silenced it with a joint attack. Even the youngest daughter about age ten listens with rapt attention to the guide's vivid retelling.

There are a lot of tour guides in Normandy, mostly helping Canadian, British, and American tourists visit the beach areas and understand the experiences of the soldiers who landed on June 6. A French friend of mine, whose family farm was near Carpiquet, often volunteers to show Canadian visitors around the beaches, sharing his great knowledge of the battle for no charge. He tells me that likely no more than one in a hundred visitors to the Normandy battlefield ever venture inland more than a mile. Carpiquet, the Abbaye d'Ardenne, Verrières Ridge, Point 111 where Worthington Force met disaster, Falaise, and Saint-Lambert-sur-Dives are seldom visited. Even the Canadian War Cemetery at Bretteville-sur-Laize draws fewer visitors than the closer-to-the-coast Bény-sur-Mer Canadian Cemetery.

Yet all these sites are within a couple of hours' drive of the beaches and readily accessible with the help of the many guidebooks published in recent years. At each site there are monuments, commemorative plaques, and interpretive panels that explain the course of battle. To see the ground, surprisingly little changed over the course of time in many places, is to better appreciate what the soldiers faced.

Verrières Ridge is a case in point. Standing on its summit, looking north to the route that the Black Watch took during their ascent on July 25, it is impossible not to see how that attack was doomed to fail. Verrières is not a ridge in the way most Canadians imagine. Its northern slope rises only 121 feet over a distance of 3,280 feet. So, contrary to what Brian McKenna claimed in a November 11, 2002, *Maclean's* article, the problem was not that the Black Watch had to scale this great height. Instead, they faced a long, futile hike into the face of German fire from well-sited positions along the ridge's crest. Heroism here, to be sure, but also fatal errors of judgement from the corps commander, Lieutenant General Guy Simonds, down to the acting battalion commander, Major Philip Griffin.

Verrières Ridge is a grim place for Canadians—a place of tears, for so many of the nation's youth perished here during the series of attacks. Each line of approach is as poor as any other. The Germans on the crest held all the advantages. Yet Canadians did ultimately prevail. The ridge fell, and the way was opened for Totalize, Tractable, and the closing of the Falaise Gap.

Today, at points along the ridge there are various monuments recognizing the battalions that seized or attempted to seize that particular section of it. All are worth visiting. This is also true for the many other monuments and battle sites scattered from Carpiquet to Chambois.

One, however, is unique. In Verrières village there is a small, dark chapel—really all that is left of the village. Facing it, a monument honours the Royal Hamilton Light Infantry for being the only fighting unit in the battle for the ridge to win its objective on July 25. Having visited several times, I've invariably found the chapel's door unlocked. Unheated, thick walled, it is chilly inside. Where once there was likely a small window, today there is inset a wooden-framed glass case. Within the case is a photograph of a young Canadian soldier, wearing a beret and standing in a snowy field that is probably in Quebec. He is a smiling, handsome lad. Beneath the photo is a newspaper clipping in French.

On July 23, 1944, Gérard Doré was just fifteen years and nine months old. He was a soldier in Les Fusiliers Mont-Royal, and he died at nearby Beauvoir Farm. Doré came from the small village of Roberval. He used falsified documents to enlist. According to the newspaper report, he joined the regiment in England in 1943 and was inspired to fight for the liberation of France. This small shrine to Doré's memory is touching, but not just because of its presence in this chapel. Each time I have visited, set on the ledge before his picture has been a bouquet of fresh flowers in a brass vase. A Royal Canadian Legion poppy is pinned to the right-hand side of the wooden frame, a small Canadian flag leans against the left. Someone nearby ensures that the memory of this young man is lovingly preserved. I wonder who?

During my visits to Normandy and travels across the battlefields where Canadians, like Gérard Doré, fought and died for the freedom of others, I am repeatedly struck by the care and attention local people give to the maintenance of the many monuments recognizing this sacrifice. There are skeptics who say that it is only the old French people, those alive when the liberation came, who remember, and that the time of remembrance in Normandy will pass with their deaths. I am optimistic, however, that this will not be the case. During my journeys I encounter many younger French people, who do care and do remember. The schoolchildren coming in and out of the Juno Beach Centre seem genuinely interested and moved by the experience of their visit.

And it is children who are the hope of remembrance. Not just in France or the other parts of Europe that the war rolled through with such destructive force, but also here in Canada. It is heartening to see school tours being organized that take young people to Europe to visit the battle sites. It is heartening to see, in conjunction with Remembrance Day, schools inviting veterans in to talk of their experiences—to see other activities designed to make the nation's children aware of the sacrifices that one generation made to ensure the freedom of those to come. Ultimately, though, children only remember if adults ensure that they are given the opportunity to do so. It falls on our shoulders to keep the stories and the history alive, to pass it on down.

APPENDIX A:
PRINCIPAL COMMANDERS IN THE NORMANDY CAMPAIGN

AMERICAN

Supreme Headquarters, Allied Expeditionary Force (SHAEF),
    Gen. Dwight D. Eisenhower
Twelfth U.S. Army Group, Gen. Omar Bradley
First Army, Gen. Bradley, then Lt. Gen. Courtenay Hodges
Third Army, Gen. George S. Patton

BRITISH

Chief of Imperial General Staff, Gen. Sir Alan Brooke
Commander Allied Ground Forces and Twenty-First Army Group,
    Gen. Bernard Law Montgomery
Second Army, Lt. Gen. Miles Dempsey
I Corps, Lt. Gen. John Crocker
VIII Corps, Lt. Gen. Richard N. O'Connor

CANADIAN

First Army, Lt. Gen. Harry Crerar
First Army Chief of Staff, Brig. Church Mann
II Corps, Lt. Gen. Guy Simonds
II Corps, General Chief of Staff, Brig. Elliot Rodger
II Corps, Corps Royal Artillery, Brig. Bruce Matthews
2nd Division, Maj. Gen. Charles Foulkes
3rd Division, Maj. Gen. Rod Keller (WIA Aug. 8),
    then Brig. Ken Blackader, then Maj. Gen. Dan Spry
4th Division, Maj. Gen. George Kitching, then
    Maj. Gen. Harry Foster

2nd Brigade, Brig. Ron Wyman (WIA Aug. 8), then
    Brig. John Bingham
4th Armoured Brigade, Brig. Leslie Booth (KIA Aug. 14), then
    Lt. Col. Bill Halpenny, then Brig. Robert Moncel
4th Brigade, Brig. Sherwood Lett (WIA July 18), then
    Brig. Eddy Ganong
5th Brigade, Brig. W.J. "Bill" Megill
6th Brigade, Brig. Hugh Young
7th Brigade, Brig. Harry Foster
8th Brigade, Brig. Ken Blackader
9th Brigade, Brig. Ben Cunningham, then
    Brig. J.M. "Rocky" Rockingham
10th Brigade, Brig. Jim Jefferson

GERMAN
Commander in Chief, West, Gen. Gerd von Rundstedt, then
    Gen. Günther von Kluge, then Gen. Walter Model
Army Group B, Gen. Erwin Rommel, then Gen. von Kluge
Panzer Group West, Gen. Leo Freiherr Geyr von Schweppenburg,
    then Gen. Hans Eberbach
Fifth Panzer Army, Gen. Hans Eberbach
Seventh Army, Oberg. Paul Hausser
1 ss Corps, Oberg. Josef "Sepp" Dietrich
2nd ss Panzer Division, Grupp. Heinrich von Lüttwitz
12th ss Panzer Division, Stand. Kurt Meyer
85th Infantry Division, Gen. Kurt Chill
89th Infantry Division, Gen. Konrad Heinrichs

POLISH
4th Polish Armoured Division Commander,
    Maj. Gen. Stanislaw Maczek

APPENDIX B:
THE CANADIAN ARMY IN THE
NORMANDY CAMPAIGN
(COMBAT UNITS ONLY)

FIRST CANADIAN ARMY TROOPS

2nd Army Group, Royal Canadian Artillery:
19th Field Regiment
3rd Medium Regiment
4th Medium Regiment
7th Medium Regiment

Corps of Royal Canadian Engineers:
10th Field Park Company
5th Field Company
20th Field Company
23rd Field Company

II CANADIAN CORPS TROOPS
18th Armoured Car Regiment (12th Manitoba Dragoons)
6th Anti-Tank Regiment
2nd Survey Regiment
6th Light Anti-Aircraft Regiment

Corps of Royal Canadian Engineers:
8th Field Park Company
29th Field Company
30th Field Company
31st Field Company

2ND CANADIAN INFANTRY DIVISION
8th Reconnaissance Regiment (14th Canadian Hussars)
Toronto Scottish Regiment (MG)

Royal Canadian Artillery:
4th Field Regiment
5th Field Regiment
6th Field Regiment
2nd Anti-Tank Regiment
3rd Light Anti-Aircraft Regiment

Corps of Royal Canadian Engineers:
1st Field Park Company
2nd Field Company
7th Field Company
11th Field Company

4th Canadian Infantry Brigade:
Royal Regiment of Canada
Royal Hamilton Light Infantry
Essex Scottish Regiment

5th Canadian Infantry Brigade:
Black Watch (Royal Highland Regiment) of Canada
Le Régiment de Maisonneuve
Calgary Highlanders

6th Canadian Infantry Brigade:
Les Fusiliers Mont-Royal
Queen's Own Cameron Highlanders
South Saskatchewan Regiment

3RD CANADIAN INFANTRY DIVISION
7th Reconnaissance Regiment
     (17th Duke of York's Royal Canadian Hussars)
Cameron Highlanders of Ottawa (MG Battalion)

Royal Canadian Artillery:
12th Field Regiment
13th Field Regiment
14th Field Regiment
3rd Anti-Tank Regiment
4th Light Anti-Aircraft Regiment

Corps of Royal Canadian Engineers:
3rd Field Park Company
6th Field Company
16th Field Company
18th Field Company

7th Canadian Infantry Brigade:
Royal Winnipeg Rifles
Regina Rifle Regiment
1st Battalion, Canadian Scottish Regiment

8th Canadian Infantry Brigade:
Queen's Own Rifles of Canada
Le Régiment de la Chaudière
North Shore (New Brunswick) Regiment

9th Canadian Infantry Brigade:
Highland Light Infantry of Canada
Stormont, Dundas and Glengarry Highlanders
North Nova Scotia Highlanders

4TH CANADIAN ARMOURED DIVISION
29th Armoured Reconnaissance Regiment
    (South Alberta Regiment)
10th Canadian Independent MG Company
    (New Brunswick Rangers)
Lake Superior Regiment (Motor)

Royal Canadian Artillery:
15th Field Regiment
23rd Field Regiment (Self-Propelled)
5th Anti-Tank Regiment
4th Light Anti-Aircraft Regiment

Royal Canadian Corps of Engineers:
6th Field Park Squadron
8th Field Squadron
9th Field Squadron

4th Canadian Armoured Brigade:
21st Armoured Regiment (Governor General's Foot Guards)
22nd Armoured Regiment (Canadian Grenadier Guards)
28th Armoured Regiment (British Columbia Regiment)

10th Canadian Armoured Brigade:
Lincoln and Welland Regiment
Algonquin Regiment
Argyll and Sutherland Highlanders of Canada

2ND CANADIAN ARMOURED BRIGADE
6th Armoured Regiment (1st Hussars)
10th Armoured Regiment (Fort Garry Horse)
27th Armoured Regiment (Sherbrooke Fusiliers Regiment)

APPENDIX C:
CANADIAN INFANTRY BATTALION
(TYPICAL ORGANIZATION)

HQ COMPANY
No. 1: Signals Platoon
No. 2: Administrative Platoon

SUPPORT COMPANY
No. 3: Mortar Platoon (3-inch)
No. 4: Bren Carrier Platoon
No. 5: Assault Pioneer Platoon
No. 6: Anti-Tank Platoon (6-pounder)

'A' COMPANY
No. 7 Platoon
No. 8 Platoon
No. 9 Platoon

'B' COMPANY
No. 10 Platoon
No. 11 Platoon
No. 12 Platoon

'C' COMPANY
No. 13 Platoon
No. 14 Platoon
No. 15 Platoon

'D' COMPANY
No. 16 Platoon
No. 17 Platoon
No. 18 Platoon

APPENDIX D:
CANADIAN ARMY, GERMAN ARMY, AND WAFFEN-SS ORDER OF RANKS
(LOWEST TO HIGHEST)

Like most Commonwealth armies, the Canadian Army used the British ranking system. Except for the lower ranks, this system differed little from one service arm to another. The German Army system, however, tended to identify service and rank throughout most of its command chain, and the ss ranking system was further complicated by the fact that many of its ranks harked back to the organization's clandestine paramilitary roots. The translations are roughly based on the Canadian ranking system, although many German ranks have no Canadian equivalent, and there is some differentiation in the responsibility each rank bestowed on its holder.

CANADIAN ARMY	GERMAN ARMY	SS
Private, infantry	Schütze	Schütze
Rifleman, rifle regiments	Schütze	Schütze
Private	Grenadier	Grenadier
Gunner (artillery equivalent of private)	Kanonier	Kanonier
Trooper (armoured equivalent of private)	Panzerschütze	Panzerschütze
Sapper (engineer equivalent of private)	Pionier	Pionier
Signaller (signals equivalent of private)	Funker	Funker
Lance Corporal	Gefreiter	Sturmmann

Corporal	Obergefreiter	Rottenführer
Lance Sergeant	Unteroffizier	Unterscharführer
Sergeant	Unterfeldwebel	Scharführer
Company Sergeant Major	Feldwebel	Oberscharführer
Battalion Sergeant Major	Oberfeldwebel	Hauptscharführer
Regimental Sergeant Major	Stabsfeldwebel	Sturmscharführer
Second Lieutenant	Leutnant	Untersturmführer
Lieutenant	Oberleutnant	Obersturmführer
Captain	Hauptmann	Hauptsturmführer
Major	Major	Sturmbannführer
Lieutenant Colonel	Oberstleutnant	Obersturmbannführer
Colonel	Oberst	Standartenführer
Brigadier	Generalmajor	Brigadeführer
Major General	Generalleutnant	Gruppenführer
Lieutenant General	General der (service arm)	Obergruppenführer
(No differentiation)	General der Artillerie	(No differentiation)
	General der Infanterie	
	General der Kavallerie	

	General der Pioniere	
	General der Panzertruppen	
General	Generaloberst	Oberstgruppenführer
Field Marshal	Generalfeldmarschall	(No differentiation)
Commander-in-Chief	Oberbefehlshaber	(No differentiation)

APPENDIX E:
ARMY DECORATIONS

The decoration system that Canada used in World War II, like most other aspects of its military organization and tradition, derived from Britain. Under this class-based system, most military decorations can be awarded either to officers or to "other ranks" but not to both. The Canadian army, navy, and air force also have distinct decorations. Only the Victoria Cross—the nation's highest award—can be won by personnel from any arm of the service or of any rank. The decorations and qualifying ranks are as follows.

VICTORIA CROSS (VC): Awarded for gallantry in the presence of the enemy. Instituted in 1856. Open to all ranks. The only award that can be granted for action in which the recipient was killed, other than Mentioned in Despatches—a less formal honour whereby an act of bravery was given specific credit in a formal report.

DISTINGUISHED SERVICE ORDER (DSO): Army officers of all ranks, but more commonly awarded to officers with ranks of major or higher.

MILITARY CROSS (MC): Army officers with a rank normally below major and, rarely, warrant officers.

DISTINGUISHED CONDUCT MEDAL (DCM): Army warrant officers and all lower ranks.

MILITARY MEDAL (MM): Army warrant officers and all lower ranks.

NOTES

PREFACE

1 Louis "Studs" Terkel, *"The Good War": An Oral History of World War Two* (New York: Pantheon, 1984).

INTRODUCTION: A FORMIDABLE ARRAY

1 Jean E. Portugal, *We Were There: The Navy, the Army and the RCA—A Record for Canada*, vol. 6 (Shelburne, ON: Battered Silicon Dispatch Box, 1998), 2923.

2 J.L. Granatstein and Desmond Morton, *Bloody Victory: Canadians and the D-Day Campaign, 1944* (Toronto: Lester & Orpen Dennys, 1984), 70–71.

3 David Clark, *Angels Eight: Normandy Air War Diary* (Bloomington, IN: 1st Books Library, 2003), 70.

4 "Report No. 58, Canadian Participation in the Operations in North-West Europe, 1944, Part II: Canadian Operations in July," Historical Section (G.S.) Army Headquarters, DHH, DND, para. 21.

5 Ralph Bennett, *Ultra in the West: The Normandy Campaign of 1944–45* (New York: Charles Scribner's Sons, 1979), 82–83.

6 Robin Neillands, *The Battle of Normandy, 1944* (London: Cassell, 2002), 163.

7 Samuel W. Mitcham Jr., *Panzers in Normandy: General Hans Eberbach and the German Defense of France, 1944* (Mechanicsburg, PA: Stackpole Books, 2009), 70–71.

8 David Patterson, "Outside the Box: A New Perspective on Operation Windsor—The Rationale behind the Attack on Carpiquet, 4 July 1944," *Canadian Military History*, vol. 17, no. 2 (Spring 2008), 70–73.

9 "Report No. 58," paras. 12–13.

10 Paul Douglas Dickson, *A Thoroughly Canadian General: A Biography of General H.D.G. Crerar* (Toronto: University of Toronto Press, 2007), 270.

I LITTLE SHORT OF HELL

1 Michael Reynolds, *Steel Inferno: 1 ss Panzer Corps in Normandy* (New York: Dell, 1997), 23.

2 Kurt Meyer, *Grenadier: The Story of Waffen ss General Kurt "Panzer" Meyer* (Mechanicsburg, PA: Stackpole Books, 2005), 253–54.

3 Hubert Meyer, *The History of 12. ss-Panzerdivision "Hitlerjugend."* (Winnipeg: J.J. Fedorowicz, 1994), 134.

4 Howard Margolian, *Conduct Unbecoming: The Story of the Murder of Canadian Prisoners of War in Normandy* (Toronto: University of Toronto Press, 1998), 187.

5 Reginald H. Roy, *1944: The Canadians in Normandy* (Toronto: Macmillan, 1984), 47–48.

6 "Report No. 58, Canadian Participation in the Operations in North-West Europe, 1944, Part II: Canadian Operations in July," Historical Section (G.S.) Army Headquarters, DHH, DND, para. 27.

7 David O'Keefe, "Notes on Kenneth Gault Blackader," Black Watch Regimental Museum and Archives.

8 "Report on Ops 3 Cdn Inf Div 1/31 Jul 44: Windsor Appendix," 235C3.013(D10), vol. 10908, RG24, LAC, 1–2.

9 Will Bird, *North Shore (New Brunswick) Regiment* (Fredericton: Brunswick Press, 1963), 273.

10 Jean E. Portugal, *We Were There: The Navy, the Army and the RCAF—A Record for Canada*, vol. 6 (Shelburne, ON: Battered Silicon Dispatch Box, 1998), 2922–23.

11 *Vanguard: The Fort Garry Horse in the Second World War* (Doetinchem, NL: Uitgevers-Maatschappij 'C. Nisset, 1945), 31.

12 "Report No. 58," para 32.

13 Bird, *North Shore (New Brunswick) Regiment*, 266.

14 Ibid., 269.

15 "Report No. 58," para. 30.

16 Kurt Meyer, 255–56.

17 Hubert Meyer, 136.

18 Portugal, vol. 6, 3099–3100.

19 Ibid., 2923.

20 Ibid., 2881.

21 Jean Portugal, *We Were There: The Navy, the Army and the RCAF—A Record for Canada*, vol. 5 (Shelburne, ON: Battered Silicon Dispatch Box, 1998), 2325.

22 Charles P. Stacey, *The Victory Campaign: The Operations in North-West Europe, 1944–1945*, vol. 3 (Ottawa: Queen's Printer, 1960), 154.

23 Portugal, vol. 5, 1690.

24 R.M. Hickey, *The Scarlet Dawn* (Campbelltown, NB: Tribune, 1949), 219.

25 Bird, *North Shore (New Brunswick) Regiment*, 269.

26 Ibid., 270.

27 Hubert Meyer, 136.

28 Marc Milner, *D-Day to Carpiquet: The North Shore Regiment and the Liberation of Europe* (Fredericton: Goose Lane Editions, 2007), 100.

29 Stacey, 154.

30 Milner, 102.

31 Jacques Castonguay and Armand Ross, *Le Régiment de la Chaudière* (Lévis, QC: n.p., 1983), 271–72.

32 8th Canadian Infantry Brigade War Diary, July 1944, RG24, LAC, 3.

33 Portugal, vol. 5, 2325.

34 Portugal, vol. 6, 2923–24.

35 Royal Winnipeg Rifles War Diary, July 1944, RG24, LAC, 2.

36 8th Canadian Infantry Brigade War Diary, 3.

37 Portugal, vol. 6, 2924.

38 Royal Winnipeg Rifles War Diary, 2.

39 *Vanguard*, 32.

40 Portugal, vol. 6, 2924.

41 Stacey, 154.

42 Portugal, vol. 6, 2924.

43 Ibid., 3072.

44 Ibid., 3050–51.

45 *Vanguard*, 33–38.

46 8th Canadian Infantry Brigade War Diary, 3.

47 Portugal, vol. 6, 2924.

48 Jean Portugal, *We Were There: The Navy, the Army and the RCAF—A Record for Canada*, vol. 2 (Shelburne, ON: Battered Silicon Dispatch Box, 1998), 700–01.

49 Roy Whitsed, *Canadians: A Battalion at War* (Mississauga, ON: Burlington Books, 1996), 48–49.

50 "Memorandum of Interview with Maj. S.M. Lett, 2IC, QOR of C by Historical Officer, 15 Jul. 44," 145.2Q2011(D3), DHH, DND, I.

51 Whitsed, 49–50.

52 "Interview with Maj. Lett," I.

53 Whitsed, 50–51.

54 "Interview with Maj. Lett," 1–2.

55 "Report No. 58," para. 35.

56 Stacey, 155.

57 Hickey, 219.

2 A MURDEROUS BEATING

 1 "Report No. 50, The Campaign in North-West Europe—Information from German Sources, Part II: Invasion and Battle of Normandy (6 Jun–22 Aug 44)," Historical Section (G.S.) Army Headquarters, DHH, DND, appendix A.

 2 "Report No. 162, Canadian Participation in the Operations in North-West Europe, 1944, Part II: Canadian Operations in July," Canadian Military Headquarters, DHH, DND, para. 22.

 3 Carlo D'Este, *Decision in Normandy: The Unwritten Story of Montgomery and the Allied Campaign* (London: Penguin, 1983), 327.

 4 Hubert Meyer, *The History of 12. SS-Panzerdivision "Hitlerjugend."* (Winnipeg: J.J. Fedorowicz, 1994), 139.

5 Charles P. Stacey, *The Victory Campaign: The Operations in North-West Europe, 1944–1945*, vol. 3 (Ottawa: Queen's Printer, 1960), 155.

6 *Vanguard: The Fort Garry Horse in the Second World War* (Doetinchem, NL: Uitgevers-Maatschappij 'C. Nisset, 1945), 33.

7 Stan Medland, "Confrontation in Normandy: The 3rd Canadian Anti-Tank Regiment on D-Day" *Canadian Military History*, vol. 3, no. 1 (1994), 55.

8 Richard M. Ross, *The History of the 1st Battalion Cameron Highlanders of Ottawa (MG)* (n.p., n.d.), 50.

9 Will Bird, *North Shore (New Brunswick) Regiment* (Fredericton: Brunswick Press, 1963), 282.

10 Roy Whitsed, *Canadians: A Battalion at War* (Mississauga, ON: Burlington Books, 1996), 65–66.

11 Marc Milner, *D-Day to Carpiquet: The North Shore Regiment and the Liberation of Europe* (Fredericton: Goose Lane Editions, 2007), 107–09.

12 Hubert Meyer, 139.

13 North Shore (New Brunswick) War Diary, July 1944, RG24, LAC, 2.

14 Bird, *North Shore (New Brunswick) Regiment*, 286–88.

15 North Shore War Diary, 3.

16 Ross, 50.

17 Milner, 112.

18 Ross, 50.

19 *History of the 3rd Canadian Anti-Tank Regiment Royal Canadian Artillery: October 1st 1940–May 8th 1945* (n.p., 1945), 36.

20 Ross, 50.

21 Hubert Meyer, 139.

22 Milner, 113–14.

23 "Report No. 50," para. 137.

24 Jacques Castonguay and Armand Ross, *Le Régiment de la Chaudière* (Lévis, QC: n.p., 1983), 272.

25 Jean Portugal, *We Were There: The Navy, the Army and the RCAF—A Record for Canada*, vol. 4 (Shelburne, ON: Battered Silicon Dispatch Box, 1998), 1747–48.

26 Bird, *North Shore (New Brunswick) Regiment*, 273.

27 Ibid., 285–86.

28 Ibid., 293–94.

29 Queen's Own Rifles War Diary, July 1944, RG24, LAC, 2.

30 "Report on Ops 3 Cdn Inf Div 1/31 Jul 44: Windsor Appendix," 235C3.013(DIO), vol. 10908, RG24, LAC, 4.

31 Stacey, 157.

32 David A. Wilson, "The Canadian Role in Operation 'Charnwood,' 8 July 1944: A Case Study in Tank/Infantry Doctrine and Practice," *Canadian Military History*, vol. 8, no. 3 (1999), 12–13.

33 Stacey, 157.

34 Wilson, 13.

35 Samuel W. Mitcham Jr., *Panzers in Normandy: General Hans Eberbach and the German Defense of France, 1944* (Mechanicsburg, PA: Stackpole Books, 2009), 67–68.

36 "Report No. 50," para. 137.

37 Mitcham, 67.

38 Kurt Meyer, *Grenadier: The Story of Waffen ss General Kurt "Panzer" Meyer* (Mechanicsburg, PA: Stackpole Books, 2005), 260.

39 L.F. Ellis, *The Battle of Normandy,* vol. 1 of *Victory in the West* (London: Her Majesty's Stationery Office, 1962), 311.

40 G.W.L. Nicholson, *The Gunners of Canada,* vol. 2 (Toronto: McClelland & Stewart, 1972), 288.

41 "Report No. 58," para. 52.

42 Stacey, 157–58.

43 "Report No. 162," para. 46.

44 Robin Neillands, *The Battle of Normandy, 1944* (London: Cassell, 2002), 205–06.

45 "Report No. 162," para. 46.

46 Paul Douglas Dickson, *A Thoroughly Canadian General: A Biography of General H.D.G. Crerar* (Toronto, University of Toronto Press, 2007), 273.

47 Terry Copp, *Fields of Fire: The Canadians in Normandy* (Toronto: University of Toronto Press, 2003), 112.

48 Dickson, 274.

49 Ibid., 274.

3 HOPELESS SITUATION

1 *Bomber Command, Campaign Diary, July 1944,* July 7, 1944, www.raf.mod.uk/bomber-command/Jul44.html (accessed October 5, 2010).

2 Harvey Bailey, interview by Tom Torrie, August 19, 1987, UVICSC.

3 J. Duncan Lorimer, interview by Cameron Falconer, March 6, 1983, UVICSC.

4 "Report 162, Canadian Participation in the Operations in North-West Europe, 1944, Part II: Canadian Operations in July," Canadian Military Headquarters DHH, DND, para. 48.

5 *Bomber Command, Campaign Diary.*

6 "Report 162," para. 39.

7 *Damage and Civilian Casualties: Battle for Caen,* www.servinghistory.com/topics/Battle_for_Caen::sub::Damage_And_Civilian_Casualties (accessed October 5, 2010).

8 Samuel W. Mitcham Jr., *Panzers in Normandy: General Hans Eberbach and the German Defense of France, 1944* (Mechanicsburg, PA: Stackpole Books, 2009), 68–69.

9 Charles P. Stacey, *The Victory Campaign: The Operations in North-West Europe, 1944–1945,* vol. 3 (Ottawa: Queen's Printer, 1960), 158.

10 Hubert Meyer, *The History of 12. ss-Panzerdivision "Hitlerjugend."* (Winnipeg: J.J. Fedorowicz, 1994), 143.

11 Michael Reynolds, *Steel Inferno: 1 ss Panzer Corps in Normandy* (New York: Dell, 1997), 188.

12 Kurt Meyer, *Grenadier: The Story of Waffen ss General Kurt "Panzer" Meyer* (Mechanicsburg, PA: Stackpole Books, 2005), 259.

13 Reynolds, 187–89.

14 Kurt Meyer, 259.

15 Reginald H. Roy, *1944: The Canadians in Normandy* (Toronto: Macmillan, 1984), 53.

16 Stormont, Dundas and Glengarry Highlanders War Diary, July 1944, RG24, LAC, 7.

17 Roy, *1944*, 53.

18 "Report on Ops 3 Cdn Inf Div 1/31 Jul 44: Charnwood Appendix," 235C3.013(DIO), vol. 10908, RG24, LAC, 2.

19 G.W.L. Nicholson, *The Gunners of Canada*, vol. 2 (Toronto: McClelland & Stewart, 1972), 289.

20 T.J. Bell, *Into Action with the 12th Field* (Utrecht: J. van Boekhoven, 1945), 64.

21 12th Field Regiment, RCA War Diary, July 1944, RG24, LAC, 2–3.

22 Bell, 59.

23 Kurt Meyer, 259–60.

24 "27 CDN ARMD REGT (SHER FUS) CAC: OP 'Charnwood,' The Fall of Caen–8/9 Jul 44," 17 Jul 44, 141.4A27013(D2), DHH, DND, 11.

25 *1st Battalion, The Highland Light Infantry of Canada: 1940–1945* (Galt, ON: Highland Light Infantry of Canada Assoc., 1951), 28.

26 Ibid., 28.

27 "27 CDN ARMD REGT," 11.

28 David A. Wilson, "The Canadian Role in Operation 'Charnwood,' 8 July 1944: A Case Study in Tank/Infantry Doctrine and Practice," *Canadian Military History*, vol. 8, no. 3 (1999), 15.

29 Jean Portugal, *We Were There: The Navy, the Army and the RCAF—A Record for Canada*, vol. 5 (Shelburne, ON: Battered Silicon Dispatch Box, 1998), 2380–81.

30 J. Allan Snowie, *Bloody Buron: the Battle of Buron, Normandy 08 July 1944* (Erin, ON: Boston Mills Press, 1984), 65.

31 "27 CDN ARMD REGT," 11.

32 Snowie, 65.

33 Portugal, vol. 5, 2401.

34 Ibid., 2386–87.

35 "Memorandum of Interview with Lt-Col F.M. Griffiths, at H.Q. C.R.U. on 24 May 46, concerning attack on Buron by H.L.I. of C. on 8 Jul 44," 145.2H2011(D3), DHH, DND, 1.

36 Portugal, vol. 5, 2401–02.

37 Stormont, Dundas and Glengarry Highlanders War Diary, July 1944, RG24, LAC, 7–8.

38 Walter G. Pavey, *An Historical Account of the 7th Canadian Reconnaissance Regiment in the World War, 1939–1945* (Gardenvale, QC: Harpell's Press, 1948), 47–48.

39 "27 CDN ARMD REGT," 13–14.

40 William Boss, *Up the Glens: Stormont, Dundas and Glengarry Highlanders, 1783–1994*, 2nd ed. (Cornwall, ON: Old Book Store, 1995), 108.

41 Jean Portugal, *We Were There: The Navy, the Army and the RCAF—A Record for Canada*, vol. 3 (Shelburne, ON: Battered Silicon Dispatch Box, 1998), 1320.

42 "27 CDN ARMD REGT," 14.

43 Ibid.

44 Stormont, Dundas War Diary, 8.

45 Wilson, 18.

46 "27 CDN ARMD REGT," 12.

47 Portugal, vol. 5, 2379–82.

48 Ibid., 2391.

49 *1st Battalion*, 30.

50 Portugal, vol. 5, 2402.

51 Snowie, 72–73.

52 Portugal, vol. 5, 2384.

53 *1st Battalion*, 30.

54 "Report No. 162," para. 54.

55 "Memorandum of Interview with Maj. F.A. Sparks, Comd, HQ Coy HLI of C by Historical Offr, 12 Jul 44: Lessons learned in the battle of Buron 8 Jul 44," 145.2H2011(D1), DHH, DND, 1.

56 "Report No. 162," para. 54.

57 Wilson, 15.

58 "Interview with Maj. Sparks," 1.

59 "Interview with Lt-Col Griffiths," 1.

60 "Report No. 162," para. 56.

61 Stacey, 161.

62 "27 CDN ARMD REGT," 12.

4 DAY OF REVENGE

1 Charles P. Stacey, *The Victory Campaign: The Operations in North-West Europe, 1944–1945*, vol. 3 (Ottawa: Queen's Printer, 1960), 161.

2 "Report on Ops 3 Cdn Inf Div 1/31 Jul 44: Charnwood Appendix," 235C3.013(D10), vol. 10908, RG24, LAC, 3.

3 "Report No. 50, The Campaign in North-West Europe—Information from German Sources, Part II: Invasion and Battle of Normandy (6 Jun–22 Aug 44)," Historical Section (G.S.) Army Headquarters, DHH, DND, para. 142.

4 "Report No. 50," paras. 142–44.

5 "Memorandum of Interview with Lt-Col F.M. Griffiths, at H.Q. C.R.U. on 24 May 46, concerning attack on Buron by H.L.I. of C. on 8 Jul 44," 145.2H2011(D3), DHH, DND, 2.

6 Will R. Bird, *No Retreating Footsteps: The Story of the North Nova Scotia Highlanders* (Hantsport, NS: Lancelot Press, 1983), 122.

7 "Interview with Lt-Col Griffiths," 2.

8 "Report No. 58, Canadian Participation in the Operations in North-West Europe, 1944, Part II: Canadian Operations in July," Historical Section (G.S.) Army Headquarters, DHH, DND, para. 62.

9 North Nova Scotia Highlanders War Diary, July 1944, RG24, LAC, 5.

10 Bird, *No Retreating Footsteps*, 125.

11 "27 CDN ARMD REGT (SHER FUS) CAC: OP 'Charnwood,' The Fall of Caen—8/9 Jul 44," 17 Jul 44, 141.4A27013(D2), DHH, DND, 19.

12 Bird, *No Retreating Footsteps*, 125–29.

13 North Nova Scotia War Diary, 5.

14 Bird, *No Retreating Footsteps*, 129–31.

15 North Nova Scotia War Diary, 5.

16 Jean Portugal, *We Were There: The Navy, the Army and the RCAF—A Record for Canada*, vol. 3 (Shelburne, ON: Battered Silicon Dispatch Box, 1998), 1378.

17 William Boss, *Up the Glens: Stormont, Dundas and Glengarry Highlanders, 1783–1994*, 2nd ed. (Cornwall, ON: Old Book Store, 1995), 108.

18 "Report No. 58," para. 64.

19 North Nova Scotia War Diary, 5–6.

20 Bird, *No Retreating Footsteps*, 131.

21 Kurt Meyer, *Grenadier: The Story of Waffen SS General Kurt "Panzer" Meyer* (Mechanicsburg, PA: Stackpole Books, 2005), 264–65.

22 Stewart A.G. Mein, *Up the Johns! The Story of the Royal Regina Rifles* (North Battleford, SK: Turner-Warwick, 1992), 116.

23 Jean E. Portugal, *We Were There: The Navy, the Army and the RCAF—A Record for Canada*, vol. 6 (Shelburne, ON: Battered Silicon Dispatch Box, 1998), 925.

24 Gordon Brown and Terry Copp, *Look to Your Front... Regina Rifles: A Regiment at War, 1944–45* (Waterloo, ON: Laurier Centre Military Strategic Disarmament Studies, 2001), 96.

25 Portugal, vol. 3, 925.

26 Reginald H. Roy, *Ready for the Fray: The History of the Canadian Scottish Regiment (Princess Mary's), 1920 to 1955* (Vancouver: Evergreen Press, 1958), 255–57.

27 Geoffrey Corry, interview by Tom Torrie, August 12, 1987, UVICSC.

28 Roy, *Ready for the Fray*, 258.

29 "Report on Ops 3 Cdn Inf Div 1/31 Jul 44: Charnwood Appendix," 235C3.013(DIO), vol. 10908, RG24, LAC, 3.

30 Brown and Copp, 97.

31 *The Regina Rifles in WW II*, "War Diaries, Intelligence Logs," 1st Battalion, Regina Rifle Regiment, July 1944, www.reginarifles.ca/ (accessed April 18, 2011), 15.

32 Jean E. Portugal, *We Were There: The Navy, the Army and the RCAF—A Record for Canada*, vol. 2 (Shelburne, ON: Battered Silicon Dispatch Box, 1998), 926–27.

33 Michael R. McNorgan, *The Gallant Hussar: A History of the 1st Hussars Regiment* (Aylmer, ON: 1st Hussars Cavalry Fund, 2004), 161.

34 1st Hussars War Diary, July 1944, RG24, LAC, 2.

35 Portugal, vol. 2, 927.

36 12th Field Regiment War Diary, July 1944, RG24, LAC, 4.

5 A TERRIBLE DREAM

1 'A' Company–Cussy, 1 Bn, Canadian Scottish Regiment, Personal Accounts of Battle Cdn Scottish Jun 44–May 45," 145.2C4009(DII), DHH, DND, 1.

2 Jean E. Portugal, *We Were There: The Navy, the Army and the RCAF—A Record for Canada*, vol. 4 (Shelburne, ON: Battered Silicon Dispatch Box, 1998), 2047.

3 J. Duncan Lorimer, interview by Cameron Falconer, March 6, 1983, UVICSC.

4 Reginald H. Roy, *Ready for the Fray: The History of the Canadian Scottish Regiment (Princess Mary's), 1920 to 1955* (Vancouver: Evergreen Press, 1958), 259.

5 Portugal, vol. 4, 2048.

6   "A Company—Cussy," 1.

7   Portugal, vol. 4, 2048.

8   Lorimer interview.

9   "A Company—Cussy," 1.

10 Lorimer interview.

11 *Canadian Army Overseas Honours and Awards Citation Details*, DHH, DND, www.cmp-cpm.forces.gc.ca/dhh-dhp/gal/cao-aco/details-eng.asp?firstname= George&lastname=Kawiuk&rec=id345 (accessed October 19, 2010).

12 "A Company–Cussy," 1.

13 Gordon Brown, "The Capture of the Abbaye D'Ardenne by the Regina Rifles, 8 July 1944," *Canadian Military History*, vol. 4, no. 1 (1995), 92.

14 Regina Rifle Regiment War Diary, July 1944, RG24, LAC, 4.

15 *Canadian Army Overseas Honours and Awards Citation Details*, DHH, DND, www.cmp-cpm.forces.gc.ca/dhh-dhp/gal/cao-aco/details-eng.asp?firstname= John Clealand&lastname=Treleaven&rec=id3783 (accessed October 20, 2010).

16 Regina Rifle Regiment War Diary, 4.

17 Jean E. Portugal, *We Were There: The Navy, the Army and the RCAF—A Record for Canada*, vol. 2 (Shelburne, ON: Battered Silicon Dispatch Box, 1998), 920–21.

18 Regina Rifle Regiment War Diary, 5.

19 Portugal, vol. 2, 921.

20 Regina Rifle Regiment War Diary, 5.

21 Portugal, vol. 2, 928–30.

22 "Correspondence with J. Walter Keith based on his interviews of Jack Mooney," possession of the author.

23 Portugal, vol. 2, 931.

24 Roy, *Ready for the Fray*, 260.

25 Michael R. McNorgan, *The Gallant Hussars: A History of the 1st Hussars Regiment* (Aylmer, ON: 1st Hussars Cavalry Fund, 2004), 161.

26 Roy, *Ready for the Fray*, 261–62.

27 'C' Company–Cussy, 1 Bn, Canadian Scottish Regiment, Personal Accounts of Battle Cdn Scottish Jun 44–May 45," 145.2C4009(DII), DHH, DND, 1.

28 Geoffrey Corry, interview by Tom Torrie, August 12, 1987, UVICSC.

29 "C Company–Cussy," 1.

30 Canadian Scottish Regiment War Diary, July 1944, RG24, LAC, 10.

31 Corry interview.

32 Portugal, vol. 2, 931.

33 Brown, 96–97.

34 Portugal, vol. 2, 931–32.

35 Eric Luxton, ed., *1st Battalion, The Regina Rifles Regiment, 1939–1946* (Regina: The Regt., 1946), 117.

36 "Report No. 50, The Campaign in North-West Europe—Information from German Sources, Part II: Invasion and Battle of Normandy (6 Jun–22 Aug 44)," Historical Section (G.S.) Army Headquarters, DHH, DND, para. 143.

37 Kurt Meyer, *Grenadier: The Story of Waffen SS General Kurt "Panzer" Meyer* (Mechanicsburg, PA: Stackpole Books, 2005), 265–66.

38 Charles P. Stacey, *The Victory Campaign: The Operations in North-West Europe, 1944–1945*, vol. 3 (Ottawa: Queen's Printer, 1960), 162.
39 Stacey, 162.
40 Reginald H. Roy, *1944: The Canadians in Normandy* (Toronto: Macmillan, 1984), 61.
41 Stormont, Dundas and Glengarry Highlanders War Diary, July 1944, RG24, LAC, 6.

6 MOST SUCCESSFUL OPERATION
1 Jean E. Portugal, *We Were There: The Navy, the Army and the RCAF—A Record for Canada*, vol. 6 (Shelburne, ON: Battered Silicon Dispatch Box, 1998), 934–37.
2 Terry Copp, *Fields of Fire: The Canadians in Normandy* (Toronto: University of Toronto Press, 2003), 115.
3 Portugal, vol. 6, 934–37.
4 W.T. Barnard, *The Queen's Own Rifles of Canada, 1860–1960: One Hundred Years of Canada* (Don Mills, ON: Ontario Publishing Company, 1960), 209.
5 Le Régiment de la Chaudière War Diary, July 1944, RG24, LAC, 4.
6 "Report No. 162, Canadian Participation in the Operations in North-West Europe, 1944, Part II: Canadian Operations in July," Canadian Military Headquarters, DHH, DND, para. 64.
7 North Shore (New Brunswick) Regiment War Diary, July 1944, RG24, LAC, 5.
8 Will Bird, *North Shore (New Brunswick) Regiment* (Fredericton: Brunswick Press, 1963), 306.
9 North Shore Regiment War Diary, 5.
10 Bird, *North Shore (New Brunswick) Regiment*, 299–303.
11 North Shore Regiment War Diary, 5.
12 Bird, *North Shore (New Brunswick) Regiment*, 300–01.
13 "Memorandum of Interview with Lt. Col. G.H. Christiansen, OC, SD&G Highlanders, by Historical Officer, 1 Aug 44," 145.258011(D2), DHH, DND, 1.
14 Stormont, Dundas and Glengarry Highlanders War Diary, July 1944, RG24, LAC, 10.
15 H.M. Jackson, *The Sherbrooke Regiment (12th Armoured Regiment)* (n.p., 1958), 133.
16 Charles P. Stacey, *The Victory Campaign: The Operations in North-West Europe, 1944–1945*, vol. 3 (Ottawa: Queen's Printer, 1960), 162.
17 "Interview with Lt. Col. Christiansen," 1.
18 Jean E. Portugal, *We Were There: The Navy, the Army and the RCAF—A Record for Canada*, vol. 3 (Shelburne, ON: Battered Silicon Dispatch Box, 1998), 1239.
19 "Interview with Lt. Col. Christiansen," 1.
20 Portugal, vol. 3, 1239.
21 "27 CDN ARMD REGT (SHER FUS) CAC: OP 'Charnwood,' The Fall of Caen— 8/9 Jul 44," 17 Jul 44, 141.4A27013(D2), DHH, DND, 12–14.
22 "Interview with Lt. Col. Christiansen," 2.
23 Stormont, Dundas War Diary, 10.
24 "Interview with Lt. Col. Christiansen," 2–3.
25 Walter G. Pavey, *An Historical Account of the 7th Canadian Reconnaissance Regiment in the World War, 1939–1945* (Gardenvale, QC: Harpell's Press, 1948), 48.
26 Stacey, 162.

27 "Memorandum of Interview with Lt. Col. T.C. Lewis, OC 7 CDN RECCE REGT (17 DYRCH) by Historical Officer, 24 Jul. 44." 141.4A7011(D1), DHH, DND, 2.

28 Stacey, 162–63.

29 Stormont, Dundas War Diary, 10.

30 William Boss, *Up the Glens: Stormont, Dundas and Glengarry Highlanders, 1783–1994*, 2nd ed. (Cornwall, ON: Old Book Store, 1995), 109.

31 Jean E. Portugal, *We Were There: The Navy, the Army and the RCAF—A Record for Canada*, vol. 2 (Shelburne, ON: Battered Silicon Dispatch Box, 1998), 937.

32 Regina Rifle Regiment War Diary, July 1944, RG24, LAC, 7.

33 Thomas William Lowell Butters, interview by Tom Torrie, August 19, 1978, UVICSC.

34 "Report on Ops 3 Cdn Inf Div 1/31 Jul 44: Charnwood Appendix," 235C3.013(D10), vol. 10908, RG24, LAC, 4.

35 Stacey, 163.

36 "Report No. 58, Canadian Participation in the Operations in North-West Europe, 1944, Part II: Canadian Operations in July," Historical Section (G.S.) Army Headquarters, DHH, DND, para. 76.

37 9th Canadian Infantry Brigade War Diary, July 1944, RG24, LAC, 4.

38 Boss, 110–11.

39 Copp, *Fields of Fire*, 115.

40 John A. English, *Failure in High Command: The Canadian Army and the Normandy Campaign* (Ottawa: Golden Dog Press, 1995), 226–27.

41 English, 226.

42 J.L. Granatstein, *The Generals: The Canadian Army's Senior Commanders in the Second World War* (Toronto: Stoddart, 1993), 166.

43 Copp, *Fields of Fire*, 115.

44 Stephen Ashley Hart, *Montgomery and 'Colossal Cracks': The 21st Army Group in Northwest Europe, 1944–45* (London: Praeger, 2000), 175.

45 Copp, *Fields of Fire*, 115.

46 Granatstein, *The Generals*, 109–10.

47 Paul Douglas Dickson, *A Thoroughly Canadian General: A Biography of General H.D.G. Crerar* (Toronto, University of Toronto Press, 2007), 280.

48 Granatstein, *The Generals*, 109–10.

49 Crerar Papers, MG30 #157, vol. 7, 985C.001(D180), LAC.

7 LITTLE EXCUSE FOR IT

1 J.L. Granatstein, *The Generals: The Canadian Army's Senior Commanders in the Second World War* (Toronto: Stoddart, 1993), 163.

2 "Lessons learned from Ops during War, by Lt-Gen GG Simonds, 1 Jul 44," 225C2.012(D8), vol. 10799, box 215, RG24, LAC.

3 "Personal Diary of Brig N.E. Rodger, C of S 2 Cdn Corps," 225C2.011(D2), vol. 10798, box 214, RG24, LAC, 13.

4 Terry Copp, *Fields of Fire: The Canadians in Normandy* (Toronto: University of Toronto Press, 2003), 117.

5 "Report No. 162, Canadian Participation in the Operations in North-West Europe,

1944, Part II: Canadian Operations in July," Canadian Military Headquarters, DHH, DND, para. 77.

6 Carlo D'Este, *Decision in Normandy: The Unwritten Story of Montgomery and the Allied Campaign* (London: Penguin, 1983), 321.

7 "Report No. 58, Canadian Participation in the Operations in North-West Europe, 1944, Part II: Canadian Operations in July," Historical Section (G.S.) Army Headquarters, DHH, DND, para. 100.

8 D'Este, 325–32.

9 Ibid., 333.

10 Robin Neillands, *The Battle of Normandy, 1944* (London: Cassell, 2002), 216–18.

11 "Report No. 162," para. 80.

12 Ibid., para. 82.

13 "Report No. 50, The Campaign in North-West Europe—Information from German Sources, Part II: Invasion and Battle of Normandy (6 Jun–22 Aug 44)," Historical Section (G.S.) Army Headquarters, DHH, DND, para. 144.

14 Michael Reynolds, *Steel Inferno: I SS Panzer Corps in Normandy* (New York: Dell, 1997), 205.

15 Kurt Meyer, *Grenadier: The Story of Waffen SS General Kurt "Panzer" Meyer* (Mechanicsburg, PA: Stackpole Books, 2005), 267–68.

16 "Report No. 58," paras. 97–100.

17 Ken M. Hossack, *Mike Target* (Ottawa: n.p., 1945), 3.

18 George G. Blackburn, *The Guns of Normandy: A Soldier's Eye View, France 1944* (Toronto: McClelland & Stewart, 1997), 62.

19 Hossack, 3.

20 George Blackburn, *The History of the 4th Field Regiment* (n.p., 1945), 81.

21 James Douglas Baird, interview by William S. Thackray, June 17 and 27, July 18, 1980, UVICSC.

22 Blackburn, *Guns of Normandy*, 69–71.

23 Ibid., 79.

24 Blackburn, *History of 4th Field Regiment*, 82.

25 5th Field Regiment, RCA War Diary, July 1944, RG24, LAC, 2.

26 6th Field Regiment, RCA War Diary, July 1944, RG24, LAC, 2.

27 D.J. Goodspeed, *Battle Royal: A History of the Royal Regiment of Canada, 1862–1962* (Toronto: The Royal Regiment of Canada Assoc., 1962), 416–18.

28 Royal Hamilton Light Infantry War Diary, July 1944, RG24, LAC, 6.

29 Arthur K. Kembar, *The Six Years of 6 Canadian Field Regiment, Royal Canadian Artillery* (Amsterdam: Town Printing, 1945), 52.

30 Denis Whitaker, Shelgah Whitaker, and Terry Copp, *The Soldiers' Story: Victory at Falaise* (Toronto: Harper Collins, 2000), 43.

31 Hossack, 3–4.

8 OFFENSIVE SPIRIT

1 Dominick Graham, *The Price of Command: A Biography of General Guy Simonds* (Toronto: Stoddart, 1993), 145.

2   J.L. Granatstein, *The Generals: The Canadian Army's Senior Commanders in the Second World War* (Toronto: Stoddart, 1993), 166–67.

3   Maj. A.T. Sesia, "General Simonds Speaks: Canadian Battle Doctrine in Normandy," *Canadian Military History*, vol. 8, no. 2 (Spring 1999), 70–76.

4   Canadian Scottish Regiment War Diary, July 1944, RG24, LAC, 17.

5   Harvey Bailey, interview by Tom Torrie, August 19, 1987, UVICSC.

6   Canadian Scottish War Diary, 13.

7   Bailey interview.

8   Reginald H. Roy, *Ready for the Fray: The History of the Canadian Scottish Regiment (Princess Mary's), 1920 to 1955* (Vancouver: Evergreen Press, 1958), 269.

9   Canadian Scottish War Diary, 19.

10 L.F. Ellis, *The Battle of Normandy*, vol. 1 of *Victory in the West* (London: Her Majesty's Stationery Office, 1962), 334–38.

11 "Report No. 58, Canadian Participation in the Operations in North-West Europe, 1944, Part II: Canadian Operations in July," Historical Section (G.S.) Army Headquarters, DHH, DND, para. 145.

12 Ibid., para. 137.

13 Ellis, 336.

14 "3rd Canadian Infantry Report on Operation 'Atlantic,'" 235C3.013(D14), vol. 10908, RG24, LAC, 1–2.

15 Charles P. Stacey, *The Victory Campaign: The Operations in North-West Europe, 1944–1945*, vol. 3 (Ottawa: Queen's Printer, 1960), 171.

16 "Report No. 50, The Campaign in North-West Europe—Information from German Sources, Part II: Invasion and Battle of Normandy (6 Jun–22 Aug 44)," Historical Section (G.S.) Army Headquarters, DHH, DND, para.154.

17 Samuel W. Mitcham Jr., *Panzers in Normandy: General Hans Eberbach and the German Defense of France, 1944* (Mechanicsburg, PA: Stackpole Books, 2009), 76–79.

18 Robin Neillands, *The Battle of Normandy, 1944* (London: Cassell, 2002), 256–57.

19 *Honorary Colonel Charley Fox: Canadian Wartime Fighter Pilot*, November 11, 2008, www.timesonline.co.uk/tol/comment/obituaries/article5126145.ece (accessed November 17, 2010).

20 "Report No. 50," paras. 157–164.

21 "Report No. 58," para. 137.

22 George G. Blackburn, *The Guns of Normandy: A Soldier's Eye View, France 1944* (Toronto: McClelland & Stewart, 1997), 156.

23 "Report No. 58," para. 146.

24 G.W.L. Nicholson, *The Gunners of Canada*, vol. 2 (Toronto: McClelland & Stewart, 1972), 295.

25 Blackburn, *Guns of Normandy*, 158.

26 "Report No. 58," para. 146.

27 Ibid., para. 147.

28 Mitcham, 77–78.

29 Reynolds, 215.

9 EXPENSIVE VICTORIES

1 "Report No. 58, Canadian Participation in the Operations in North-West Europe, 1944, Part II: Canadian Operations in July," Historical Section (G.S.) Army Headquarters, DHH, DND, paras. 149–50.

2 Jacques Castonguay and Armand Ross, *Le Régiment de la Chaudière* (Lévis, QC: n.p., 1983), 276.

3 Roy Whitsed, *Canadians: A Battalion at War* (Mississauga, ON: Burlington Books, 1996), 85–87.

4 Charles Cromwell Martin, *Battle Diary: From D-Day and Normandy to the Zuider Zee* (Toronto, Dundurn, 1994), 48–49.

5 Whitsed, 87.

6 W.T. Barnard, *The Queen's Own Rifles of Canada, 1860–1960: One Hundred Years of Canada* (Don Mills, ON: Ontario Publishing Company, 1960), 211.

7 Whitsed, 87–92.

8 Martin, 48–49.

9 Barnard, 211.

10 Whitsed, 91–92.

11 "Memorandum of Interview with Lt. J.A.C. Auld, Comd 13 PL, QOR of C by Historical Officer, 22 Jul 44," 145.2Q2011(D1), DHH, DND, 2.

12 Queen's Own Rifles of Canada War Diary, July 1944, RG24, LAC, 5.

13 Whitsed, 89.

14 "Report No. 162, Canadian Participation in the Operations in North-West Europe, 1944, Part II: Canadian Operations in July," Canadian Military Headquarters, DHH, DND, para. 95.

15 "Memorandum of Interview with Lt. Col. D.B. Buell, OC, and Lt. H.L. Day, 10, N Shore R by Historical Officer, 27 Jul 44," 145.2N3011(D2), DHH, 1.

16 "3rd Canadian Infantry Report on Operation 'Atlantic,'" 235C3.013(D14), vol. 10908, RG24, LAC, 3.

17 "Interview with Lt. Col. Buell," 1.

18 "Report No. 58," para. 155.

19 Eric Luxton, ed., *1st Battalion, the Regina Rifles Regiment, 1939–1946* (Regina: The Regt., 1946), 45.

20 "Report No. 58," para. 155.

21 Ibid., para. 153.

22 Jean E. Portugal, *We Were There: The Navy, the Army and the RCAF—A Record for Canada*, vol. 6 (Shelburne, ON: Battered Silicon Dispatch Box, 1998), 2839.

23 Jean E. Portugal, *We Were There: The Navy, the Army and the RCAF—A Record for Canada*, vol. 3 (Shelburne, ON: Battered Silicon Dispatch Box, 1998), 1314.

24 Portugal, vol. 6, 2839–40.

25 Stormont, Dundas and Glengarry Highlanders War Diary, July–Aug 1944, RG24, LAC, 15.

26 Castonguay and Ross, 276.

27 Portugal, vol. 6, 1314–15.

28 Stormont, Dundas War Diary, 15.

29 "Interview with Lt. Col. Buell," 1–2.

30 Will Bird, *North Shore (New Brunswick) Regiment* (Fredericton: Brunswick Press, 1963), 343–44.

31 Regina Rifle Regiment War Diary, July 1944, RG24, LAC, 10.

32 7th Canadian Infantry Brigade War Diary, July 1944, RG24, LAC, 9.

33 Gordon Brown and Terry Copp, *Look to Your Front... Regina Rifles: A Regiment at War, 1944–45* (Waterloo, ON: Laurier Centre Military Strategic Disarmament Studies, 2001), 117–18.

34 Stewart A.G. Mein, *Up the Johns! The Story of the Royal Regina Rifles* (North Battleford, SK: Turner-Warwick, 1992), 119.

35 Regina Rifle Regiment War Diary, 11.

36 Will R. Bird, *No Retreating Footsteps: The Story of the North Nova Scotia Highlanders* (Hantsport, NS: Lancelot Press, 1983), 143.

37 Charles P. Stacey, *The Victory Campaign: The Operations in North-West Europe, 1944–1945*, vol. 3 (Ottawa: Queen's Printer, 1960), 172.

10 GREENHORNERS

1 2nd Canadian Infantry Division (General Staff) War Diary, July 1944, RG24, LAC, 135.

2 J.L. Granatstein, *The Generals: The Canadian Army's Senior Commanders in the Second World War* (Toronto: Stoddart, 1993), 174–75.

3 Royal Regiment of Canada War Diary, July 1944, RG24, LAC, 9.

4 "Account of the attack on Louvigny night 18–19 Jul given by Maj. T.F. Whitley, R Regt C, as told to Capt. Engler at Venoix, 20 Jul 44," 145.2R17011(D4), DHH, DND, 1.

5 *Canadian Army Overseas Honours and Awards Citation Details*, DHH, DND, www.cmp-cpm.forces.gc.ca/dhh-dhp/gal/cao-aco/details-eng.asp?firstname=Oliver Clifford&lastname=Tryon&rec=id1171 (accessed November 20, 2010).

6 "Account by Whitley," 1–2.

7 *Canadian Army Overseas Honours and Awards Citation Details*, DHH, DND, www.cmp-cpm.forces.gc.ca/dhh-dhp/gal/cao-aco/details-eng.asp?firstname=James Robert &lastname=Corbett&rec=id4601 (accessed November 20, 2010).

8 Terry Copp, *The Brigade: Fifth Canadian Infantry Brigade, 1939–1945* (Stoney Creek, ON: Fortress Publications, 1992), 54.

9 Black Watch War Diary, July 1944, possession of the author, 5.

10. Copp, *The Brigade*, 55.

11 A.J. Kerry and W.A. McDill, *History of the Corps of Royal Canadian Engineers*, vol. 2 (Ottawa: Military Engineers Assoc. of Canada), 277–78.

12 D.J. Goodspeed, *Battle Royal: A History of the Royal Regiment of Canada, 1862–1962* (Toronto: Royal Regt. of Canada Assoc., 1962), 423–24.

13 "Account by Whitley," 2.

14 "War Diaries 2 Cdn Corps, Jul/Dec 44 in details of Op 'Atlantic,' 'Totalize,' 'Tractable,' etc by Brig. NE Rodger, C of S, Atlantic," 225C2.008(D9), vol. 10798, box 214, RG24, LAC, 5.

15 John Keegan, *Six Armies in Normandy: From D-Day to the Liberation of Paris* (London: Pimlico, 2004), 216.

16 Max Hastings, *Overlord: D-Day and the Battle for Normandy* (London: Pan Books, 1985), 277.

17 Alexander McKee, *Caen: Anvil of Victory* (London: Souvenir Press, 1964), 278.

18 Simon Trew and Stephen Badsey, *Battle For Caen* (Phoenix Mill, UK: Sutton, 2004), 89–94.

19 "Report No. 58, Canadian Participation in the Operations in North-West Europe, 1944, Part II: Canadian Operations in July," Historical Section (G.S.) Army Headquarters, DHH, DND, paras. 169–71.

20 Ibid., para. 173.

21 Regina Rifle Regiment War Diary, July 1944, RG24, LAC, 11.

22 Gérard Marchand, *Le Régiment de Maisonneuve vers la Victoire, 1944–1945* (Montreal: Les Presses Libres, 1980), 64.

23 Le Régiment de Maisonneuve War Diary, July 1944, RG24, LAC, 4.

24 Copp, *The Brigade*, 56.

25 Le Régiment War Diary, 4.

26 Calgary Highlanders War Diary, July 1944, RG24, LAC, 20.

27 David Bercuson, *Battalion of Heroes: The Calgary Highlanders in World War II* (Calgary: Calgary Highlanders Regimental Funds Fdn., 1994), 62–63.

28 Roy Farron, *History of the Calgary Highlanders, 1921–54* (Calgary: Bryant Press, 1954), 147.

29 Bercuson, 62–63.

30 Paul P. Hutchinson, *Canada's Black Watch: The First Hundred Years, 1862–1962* (Montreal: Black Watch [RHR] of Canada, 1962), 222.

31 *Canadian Army Overseas Honours and Awards Citation Details*, DHH, DND, www.cmp-cpm.forces.gc.ca/dhh-dhp/gal/cao-aco/details-eng.asp?firstname= William Francis&lastname=Clements&rec=id4556 (accessed November 15, 2010).

32 L.F. Ellis, *The Battle of Normandy*, vol. 1 of *Victory in the West* (London: Her Majesty's Stationery Office, 1962), 348.

33 Ross Munro, *Gauntlet to Overlord: The Story of the Canadian Army* (Toronto: Macmillan, 1945), 159.

34 Hastings, 278.

35 Ellis, 348–49.

36 Reginald H. Roy, *1944: The Canadians in Normandy* (Toronto: Macmillan, 1984), 78–79.

37 Charles P. Stacey, *The Victory Campaign: The Operations in North-West Europe, 1944–1945*, vol. 3 (Ottawa: Queen's Printer, 1960), 174.

38 Roy, *1944*, 79–80.

39 Queen's Own Cameron Highlanders War Diary, July 1944, RG24, LAC, appendix 6, 1.

40 Terry Copp, *Fields of Fire: The Canadians in Normandy* (Toronto: University of Toronto Press, 2003), 148.

41 "War Diaries 2 Cdn Corps, Atlantic," 8.

42 "Report 162, Canadian Participation in the Operations in North-West Europe, 1944, Part II: Canadian Operations in July," Canadian Military Headquarters, DHH, DND, para. 111.

43 South Saskatchewan Regiment War Diary, July 1944, RG24, LAC, 11.

44 *Cent ans d'histoire d'un regiment canadien-français: les Fusiliers Mont-Royal, 1869–1969* (Montreal: Éditions Du Jour, 1971), 195.

45 Jean E. Portugal, *We Were There: The Navy, the Army and the RCAF—A Record for Canada,* vol. 5 (Shelburne, ON: Battered Silicon Dispatch Box, 1998), 2477.

46 Roy, *1944,* 80.

47 Essex Scottish Regiment War Diary, July 1944, RG24, LAC, 12.

48 Roy, *1944,* 80.

49 Ibid., 81.

50 "Report No. 58," para. 196.

51 G.W.L. Nicholson, *The Gunners of Canada,* vol. 2 (Toronto: McClelland & Stewart, 1972), 297.

52 "Report No. 58," para. 194.

53 Roy, *1944,* 82.

54 Doug Nash, "History of the 272nd at Caen, July 1944," *Der Este Zug* (2005), www.dererstezug.com/272ndCaen.htm (accessed November 24, 2010).

55 Michael Reynolds, *Steel Inferno: 1 ss Panzer Corps in Normandy* (New York: Dell, 1997), 229.

II WE NEED HELP

1   Queen's Own Cameron Highlanders War Diary, July 1944, RG24, LAC, appendix 6, 1.

2   Norman H. Ross, interview by William S. Thackray, May 27, June 16, and July 4, 1980, UVICSC.

3   R.W. Queen-Hughes, *Whatever Men Dare: A History of the Queen's Own Cameron Highlanders of Canada, 1935–1960* (Winnipeg: Bluman Bros., 1960), 103.

4   Queen's Own War Diary, appendix 6, 1.

5   *Canadian Army Overseas Honours and Awards Citation Details,* DHH, DND, www.cmp-cpm.forces.gc.ca/dhh-dhp/gal/cao-aco/details-eng.asp?firstname=Robert Edward&lastname=Lucy&rec=id2796 (accessed November 25, 2010).

6   Ross interview.

7   Queen's Own War Diary, appendix 6, 3.

8   Ross interview.

9   Queen's Own War Diary, appendix 6, 4.

10 Jean E. Portugal, *We Were There: The Navy, the Army and the RCAF—A Record for Canada,* vol. 5 (Shelburne, ON: Battered Silicon Dispatch Box, 1998), 2477.

11 Ross interview.

12 John Edmondson, interview by Ryan Hill, November 3 and 20, 2009, UVICSC.

13 John S. Edmondson and R.D. Edmondson, "The Pawns of War: A Personal Account of the Attack on Verrières Ridge by The South Saskatchewan Regiment, 20 July 1944," *Canadian Military History,* vol. 14, no. 4 (Autumn 2005), 50.

14 "Account of the Attack by s Sask R on the High Ground 0459 in the Afternoon of 20 Jul 44 Given by Maj L.L. Dicken 'D' Coy, s Sask R, at La Villeneuve, 23 Jul 44," 145.2S7011(D5), DHH, DND, 2.

15 "Report No. 162, Canadian Military Headquarters—Canadian Participation in the Operations in North-West Europe, 1944, Part II: Canadian Operations in July," DHH, DND, para. 111.

16 Edmondson and Edmondson, 51–52.

17 "Account by Dickin," 1–3.

18 John Edmondson, interview by Chris Bell, June 6, August 4 and 12, 1982, UVICSC.

19 Edmondson and Edmondson, 53.

20 "Account of the Attack by S Sask R on the High Ground 0459 in the Afternoon of 20 Jul 44 Given by Lt. F. Mathers of 'A' Coy, S Sask Regt, at Villeneuve, 23 Jul 44," 145.2S7011(D4), DHH, DND, 1.

21 Edmondson and Edmondson, 53.

22 "Account by Dickin," 2.

23 "Account by Mathers," 1.

24 Edmondson, interview by Bell.

25 Edmondson and Edmondson, 54.

26 "Account by Dickin," 1.

27 "Account of the Actions of the Fus MR 19–25 Jul 44 as Given by Lt-Col Gauvreau, OC," 145.2R1011(D2), DHH, DND, 1.

28 A. Britton Smith, "A FOO at Troteval Farm, 20–21 July 1944," *Canadian Military History*, vol. 14, no. 4 (Autumn 2005), 67.

29 "27 CDN ARMD REGT (SHER FUS) CAC, OP 'Atlantic,' Overture to the Breakthrough," Gordon Fonds, MG30-E367, LAC, 15.

30 "Account by Gauvreau," 1.

31 "27 CDN ARMD REGT (SHER FUS) CAC, OP 'Atlantic,'" 15–20.

32 "Account by Gauvreau," 1.

33 Smith, 69–70.

34 "Attack on Beauvoir and Troteval Farms by FUS MR, 20 Jul 44 As Given By Capt Maurice Gravel, 10 FUS MR, to Capt Engler at Etavaux, 28 Jul 44," 145.2F1011(D1), DHH, DND, 1.

35 "Account by Gauvreau," 1.

36 Edmondson and Edmondson, 54.

37 Edmondson, interview by Bell.

38 Edmondson and Edmondson, 54–55.

39 "Account by Dickin," 1–2.

40 Edmondson, interview by Bell.

41 John Maker, "The Essex Scottish Regiment in Operation Atlantic: What Went Wrong?" *Canadian Military History*, vol. 18, no. 1 (Winter 2009), 11.

42 Edmondson and Edmondson, 57.

43 Maker, 11–12.

44 "Account by Dickin," 2.

45 Sandy Antal and Kevin R. Shackleton, *Duty Nobly Done: The Official History of the Essex and Kent Scottish Regiment* (Windsor, ON: Walkerville, 2006), 451–54.

46 Maker, 13.

47 1 Battalion, The Essex Scottish Regiment, 1940–1945: A Brief Narrative (Aldershot, UK: Gale and Polden, 1946), 34.

48 Edmondson and Edmondson, 57.

49 Edmondson, interview by Hill.

50 Edmondson and Edmondson, 57–58.

51 South Saskatchewan Regiment War Diary, July 1944, RG24, LAC, 13.

52 2nd Canadian Anti-Tank Regiment War Diary, July 1944, RG24, LAC, 12.

53 Maker, 13–14.

12 NOT A PLEASANT PICTURE

1 "War Diaries 2 Cdn Corps, Jul/Dec 44 in details of Op 'Atlantic,' 'Totalize,' 'Tractable,' etc by Brig NE Rodger, C of S, Atlantic," 225C2.008(D9), vol. 10798, box 214, RG24, LAC, 8.

2 "Report No. 162, Canadian Participation in the Operations in North-West Europe, 1944, Part II: Canadian Operations in July," Canadian Military Headquarters, DHH, DND, paras. 115–17.

3 Essex Scottish Regiment War Diary, July 1944, RG24, LAC, 12.

4 John Maker, "The Essex Scottish Regiment in Operation Atlantic: What Went Wrong?" *Canadian Military History,* vol. 18, no. 1 (Winter 2009), 71.

5 Queen's Own Cameron Highlanders War Diary, July 1944, RG24, LAC, appendix 6, 1–2.

6 Norman H. Ross, interview by William S. Thackray, May 27, June 16, and July 4, 1980, UVICSC.

7 Queen's Own Highlanders War Diary, appendix 6, 1–5.

8 Ross interview.

9 Queen's Own Highlanders War Diary, appendix 6, 1–2.

10 A. Britton Smith, "A FOO at Troteval Farm, 20–21 July 1944," *Canadian Military History,* vol. 14, no. 4 (Autumn 2005), 72.

11 Essex Scottish War Diary, 12–13.

12 Maker, 14–15

13 "Report No. 162," para. 117.

14 Queen's Own Highlanders War Diary, appendix 6, 1–2.

15 "27 CDN ARMD REGT (SHER FUS) CAC, OP 'Atlantic,' Overture to the Breakthrough, Gordon Fonds, MG30-E367, LAC, 11.

16 Charles P. Stacey, *The Victory Campaign: The Operations in North-West Europe, 1944–1945,* vol. 3 (Ottawa: Queen's Printer, 1960), 176.

17 Smith, 72–74.

18 Reginald H. Roy, *1944: The Canadians in Normandy* (Toronto: Macmillan, 1984), 95.

19 "Notes on the Diary by Pte. W.T. Booth (D-83056)," *The Black Watch (Royal Highland Regiment of Canada) Regimental Archives,* www3.ns.sympatico.ca/laird.niven /public_html/booth.htm (accessed December 2, 2010).

20 Brandon Conron, *A History of the First Hussars Regiment, 1856–1980* (n.p., 1981), 83–84.

21 Paul P. Hutchison, *Canada's Black Watch: The First Hundred Years, 1862–1962* (Montreal: Black Watch (RHR) of Canada, 1962), 222.

22 Stacey, 176.

23 "Report No. 58, Canadian Participation in the Operations in North-West Europe, 1944, Part II: Canadian Operations in July," Historical Section (G.S.) Army Headquarters, DHH, DND, February 15, 1953, para. 203.

24 "Report No. 162," para. 120.

25 John Edmondson, interview by Ryan Hill, November 3 and 20, 2009, UVICSC.

26 John A. English, *Failure in High Command: The Canadian Army and the Normandy Campaign* (Ottawa: Golden Dog Press, 1995), 239.

27 South Saskatchewan Regiment War Diary, July 1944, RG24, LAC, 13.

28 John S. Edmondson and R.D. Edmondson, "The Pawns of War: A Personal Account of the Attack on Verrières Ridge by the South Saskatchewan Regiment, 20 July 1944," *Canadian Military History*, vol. 14, no. 4 (Autumn 2005), 60–61.

29 John Maker, "The Essex Scottish Regiment in Operation Atlantic: What Went Wrong?" *Canadian Military History*, vol. 18, no. 1 (Winter 2009), 18.

30 Sandy Antal and Kevin R. Shackleton, *Duty Nobly Done: The Official History of the Essex and Kent Scottish Regiment* (Windsor, ON: Walkerville, 2006), 456.

31 Maker, 7.

32 Essex Scottish War Diary, 13.

33 Maker, 15.

34 Ibid., 16.

35 Stacey, 177.

36 Roy, *1944*, 97–100.

37 Le Régiment de Maisonneuve War Diary, July 1944, RG24, LAC, 5.

38 *Canadian Army Overseas Honours and Awards Citation Details*, DHH, DND, www.cmp-cpm.forces.gc.ca/dhh-dhp/gal/cao-aco/details-eng.asp?firstname=Benoit&lastname=Lacourse&rec=id4193 (accessed December 5, 2010).

39 *Canadian Army Overseas Honours and Awards Citation Details*, DHH, DND, www.cmp-cpm.forces.gc.ca/dhh-dhp/gal/cao-aco/details-eng.asp?firstname=Joseph Paul Emile Wilson&lastname=Ostiguy&rec=id3207 (accessed December 5, 2010).

40 "Report No. 162," para. 130.

41 Terry Copp, *The Brigade: Fifteenth Canadian Infantry Brigade, 1939–1945* (Stoney Creek, ON: Fortress, 1992), 62.

42 "Report No. 162," para. 131.

43 Jean E. Portugal, *We Were There: The Navy, the Army and the RCAF—A Record for Canada*, vol. 5 (Shelburne, ON: Battered Silicon Dispatch Box, 1998), 2478.

44 Ross interview.

13 DESPERATE MOVE IN THE DARK

1 Charles P. Stacey, *The Victory Campaign: The Operations in North-West Europe, 1944–1945*, vol. 3 (Ottawa: Queen's Printer, 1960), 187.

2 "Report No. 162, Canadian Military Headquarters—Canadian Participation in the Operations in North-West Europe, 1944, Part II: Canadian Operations in July," DHH, DND, paras. 133–36.

3 "Operation Spring: 25 Jul 1944, Factors in Assessing Results," 112H1.003(D43), DHH, DND, 1.

4 Samuel W. Mitcham Jr., *Panzers in Normandy: General Hans Eberbach and the German Defense of France, 1944* (Mechanicsburg, PA: Stackpole Books, 2009), 81.

5 "Operation Spring: Assessing Results," 1.

6   L.F. Ellis, *The Battle of Normandy*, vol. I of *Victory in the West* (London: Her Majesty's Stationery Office, 1962), 378.

7   "Operation Spring: 25 Jul 1944, Relative Strengths," 112H1.003(D43), DHH, DND, 3–6.

8   "II Canadian Corps Intelligence Summary No. 15, 25 Jul 44," 225C2.023(D39), vol. 10812, box 221, RG24, LAC, I.

9   Lt. Gen. G.G. Simonds, "Operation Spring, *Canadian Military History*, vol. I, nos. 1–2 (1992), 66.

10 Reginald H. Roy, *1944: The Canadians in Normandy* (Toronto: Macmillan, 1984), 100.

11 Stacey, 187.

12 7th Canadian Infantry Brigade War Diary, July 1944, RG24, LAC, 10.

13 George Kitching, *Mud and Green Fields: The Memoirs of Major General George Kitching* (Langley, BC: Battleline Books, 1985), 205–06.

14 John A. English, *Failure in High Command: The Canadian Army and the Normandy Campaign* (Ottawa: Golden Dog Press, 1995), 250.

15 *Army Cadet History*, www.armycadethistory.com/Vernon%20photo%20gallery /biography_Brig_Megill.htm (accessed December 7, 2010).

16 Queen's Own Cameron Highlanders War Diary, July 1944, RG24, LAC, appendix 6, 2–6.

17 *Cent ans d'histoire d'un régiment canadien-français: les Fusiliers Mont-Royal, 1869–1969* (Montreal: Éditions Du Jour, 1971), 203.

18 "Account of A Coy Attack on Troteval Farm by Fus MRS on 23 Jul 44 Given to Capt Engler by Maj Dextraze at Caen, 30 Jul 44," 145.2F1011(D5), DHH, DND, 1–3.

19 Royal Hamilton Light Infantry War Diary, July 1944, RG24, LAC, appendix I, I.

20 "Account by Dextraze," 1–3.

21 *Canadian Army Overseas Honours and Awards Citation Details*, DHH, DND, www.cmp-cpm.forces.gc.ca/dhh-dhp/gal/cao-aco/details-eng.asp?firstname=Amedee Joseph Philippe&lastname=Thibault&rec=id1128 (accessed December 7, 2010).

22 *Canadian Army Overseas Honours and Awards Citation Details*, DHH, DND, www.cmp-cpm.forces.gc.ca/dhh-dhp/gal/cao-aco/details-eng.asp?firstname= Paul&lastname=Lebrun&rec=id4244 (accessed December 8, 2010).

23 George G. Blackburn, *The Guns of Normandy: A Soldier's Eye View, France 1944* (Toronto: McClelland & Stewart, 1997), 247–50.

24 "Account by Dextraze," 2.

25 "Attack on Beauvoir and Troteval Farms by Fus MR 20 Jul 44 as Given by Capt Maurice Gravel, 10 FUS MR, to Capt Engler at Etavaux 28 Jul 44," 145.2F1011(DI), DHH, DND, I.

26 "Account of the Actions of the Scout PL RHLI in the Attack and Holding of Verrieres, 25 Jul 44, as Given by Lt Hinton, Scout PL, to Capt Engler at Louvigny, 5 Aug 44," 145.2R14.011(D2), DHH, DND, 1–2.

27 "Operation Spring: 25 Jul 1944, The Royal Hamilton Light Infantry," 112H1.003(D43), DHH, DND, I.

28 Kingsley Brown Sr., Kingsley Brown Jr., and Brereton Greenhous, *Semper Paratus: The History of the Royal Hamilton Light Infantry (Wentworth Regiment), 1862–1977* (Hamilton: RHLI Historical Assoc., 1977), 245–46.

29 "Account of the Attack and Holding of Verrieres by RHLI on 25 Jul 44, as Told by Capt. J. Williamson, 2IC, 'C' Coy, RHLI, to Capt. Engler, at Louvigny, 5 Aug 44," 145.2R14.011(D2), DHH, DND, I.

30 Calgary Highlanders War Diary, July 1944, RG24, LAC, 26.

31 "Operation Spring, 25 Jul 1944, The Calgary Highlanders," 112H1.003(D43), DHH, DND, I.

32 Ibid., 13–15.

33 Will R. Bird, *No Retreating Footsteps: The Story of the North Nova Scotia Highlanders* (Hantsport, NS: Lancelot Press, 1983), 154.

34 Stacey, 189.

35 Bird, *No Retreating Footsteps*, 154.

14 VIOLENCE OF BATTLE

1 Will R. Bird, *No Retreating Footsteps: The Story of the North Nova Scotia Highlanders* (Hantsport, NS: Lancelot Press, 1983), 155–61.

2 North Nova Scotia Highlanders War Diary, July 1944, RG24, LAC, 18.

3 Bird, *No Retreating Footsteps*, 161–63.

4 North Nova Scotia War Diary, 18.

5 Roman Johann Jarymowycz, "Der Gegenangriff vor Verrières: German Counterattacks during Operation 'Spring,' 25–26 July 1944," *Canadian Military History*, vol. 2, no. 1 (1993), 78.

6 North Nova Scotia War Diary, 18–19.

7 Charles P. Stacey, *The Victory Campaign: The Operations in North-West Europe, 1944–1945*, vol. 3 (Ottawa: Queen's Printer, 1960), 187.

8 Reginald H. Roy, *1944: The Canadians in Normandy* (Toronto: Macmillan, 1984), 109.

9 *Vanguard: The Fort Garry Horse in the Second World War* (Doetinchem, NL: Uitgevers-Maatschappij 'C. Nisset, 1945), 46.

10 Stormont, Dundas and Glengarry Highlanders War Diary, July 1944, RG24, LAC, 19.

11 Terry Copp, *Fields of Fire: The Canadians in Normandy* (Toronto: University of Toronto Press, 2003), 178.

12 "Account of 'A' Coy RHLI in the Attack on Verrieres 25 Jul 44, Given by Maj Halladay to Capt Engler at Louvigny, 4 Aug 44," 145.2R14.011(D2), DHH, DND, I.

13 Kingsley Brown Sr., Kingsley Brown Jr., and Brereton Greenhous, *Semper Paratus: The History of the Royal Hamilton Light Infantry (Wentworth Regiment), 1862–1977* (Hamilton: RHLI Historical Assoc., 1977), 248.

14 John Meredith Rockingham, interview by Reginald H. Roy, July 11, 1979, UVICSC.

15 Brown, Brown, and Greenhous, 247.

16 Royal Hamilton Light Infantry War Diary, July 1944, RG24, LAC, appendix 2, 3.

17 Ibid., 10.

18 "Account by Halladay," I.

19 2nd Anti-Tank Regiment War Diary, July 1944, RG24, LAC, 16.

20 "Account of the Actions of the RHLI in the Battle of Verrieres as Given by Lt.-Col. Rockingham," 145.2R14011(D3), DHH, DND, 2.

21 Brown, Brown, and Greenhous, 248.

22 Rockingham interview.

23 Royal Hamilton War Diary, appendix 2, 2.

24 David Bercuson, *Battalion of Heroes: The Calgary Highlanders in World War II* (Calgary: Calgary Highlanders Regimental Funds Fdn., 1994), 72.

25 "Operation Spring: 25 Jul 1944, The Calgary Highlanders," 112H1.003(D43), DHH, DND, 13.

26 Roy Farron, *History of the Calgary Highlanders, 1921–54* (Calgary: Bryant Press, 1954), 152.

27. Bercuson, 74.

28 "5 Cdn Inf Bde report on use of artificial moonlight by Calgary Highrs 25 Jul 44," 260C5.009(D8), vol. 10978, box 304, RG24, LAC, 1.

29 Terry Copp, "Operation Spring: An Historian's View," *Canadian Military History,* vol. 12, nos. 1–2 (Winter–Spring 2003), 65.

30 Bercuson, 72–76.

15 A STONE WALL

1 Terry Copp, *The Brigade: Fifth Canadian Infantry Brigade, 1939–1945* (Stoney Creek, ON: Fortress, 1992), 84–85.

2 "Report on Ops 3 Cdn Inf Div 1/31 Jul 44: Spring Appendix," 235C3.013(D10), vol. 10908, RG24, LAC, 3.

3 *1st Battalion, The Highland Light Infantry of Canada: 1940–1945* (Galt, ON: Highland Light Infantry of Canada Assoc., 1951), 40.

4 4th Canadian Infantry Brigade War Diary, July 1944, RG24, LAC, 8.

5 T. Robert Fowler, *Courage Rewarded: The Valour of Canadian Soldiers Under Fire, 1900 to 2007* (Victoria: Trafford, 2009), 201.

6 "Account by Maj. Bennett, 'D' Coy, RHC, of the Attack by the Black Watch on May-sur-Orne, 25 Jul 44, as given to Capt. Engler at Basse, 1 Aug 44," 145.2R15.011(D7), DHH, DND, 1.

7 "Notes on the Movements of R.H.C. at May-sur-Orne, France, 25 Jul 44," 145.2B1(D1), DHH, DND, 5–6.

8 "Account by Maj. Bennett," 1.

9 Ibid., 2.

10 "Notes on the Movements of R.H.C.," 6–7.

11 "Memorandum of an Interview with Major W.E. Harris, MP, Formerly OC 'B' Squadron 6 Cdn. Armd. Regt., at Historical Section (GS), Department of National Defence, 24 Jan. 46, The Attack on Fontenay-Le-Marmion, 25 Jul 44," appended document to "Notes on the Movements of R.H.C.," 2.

12 "Account by Maj. Bennett," 2.

13 "Notes on the Movements of R.H.C.," 11.

14 "Operation Spring: 25 Jul 1944, 1st Battalion, The Royal Regiment of Canada," 112H1.003(D43), DHH, DND, 5–6.

15 "Notes on the Movements of R.H.C.," 2.

16 D.J. Goodspeed, *Battle Royal: A History of the Royal Regiment of Canada, 1862–1962* (Toronto: Royal Regiment of Canada Assoc., 1962), 428.

17 Brandon Conron, *A History of the First Hussars Regiment, 1856–1980* (n.p., 1981), 85.

18 Goodspeed, 429.

19 John Marteinson and Michael R. McNorgan, *The Royal Canadian Armoured Corps: An Illustrated History* (Toronto: Robin Brass Studio, 2000), 257.

20 Michael R. McNorgan, *The Gallant Hussars: A History of the 1st Hussars Regiment* (Aylmer, ON: The 1st Hussars Cavalry Fund, 2004), 167.

21 Conron, 86.

22 Goodspeed, 429.

23 Royal Regiment of Canada War Diary, July 1944, RG24, LAC, 15.

24 "Operation Spring, Royal Regiment," 7–8.

25. Reginald H. Roy, *1944: The Canadians in Normandy* (Toronto: Macmillan, 1984), 117.

26 "Account by Sgt. Benson, Scout PL, RHC of the Attack by the Black Watch on May-sur-Orne 25 Jul 44. Given to Capt. Engler at Basse, 2 Aug. 44," 145.2R15.011(D6), DHH, DND, 1.

27 "Interview with Maj. Harris," app. doc., 2.

28 Copp, *The Brigade*, 79.

29 "Notes on the Movements of R.H.C.," 10.

30 Copp, *The Brigade*, 79.

31 Fowler, 201.

32 "Action by RHC, Fontenay le Marmion–25 Jul 44," 145.2R15.011(D12), DHH, DND, 2.

33 "Notes on the Movements of R.H.C.," 13–14.

34 Charles P. Stacey, *The Victory Campaign: The Operations in North-West Europe, 1944–1945*, vol. 3 (Ottawa: Queen's Printer, 1960), 192.

35 "Memorandum of Interview with D.81360 Pte. Williams, A.R., RHC, at Canadian Military Headquarters, 4 Jan 46," 145.2R15.011(D13), DHH, DND, 1.

36 "Account by Sergeant Benson," 2.

37 "Notes on the Movements of R.H.C.," 13.

38 "Interview with Maj. Harris," app. doc., 3.

39 "Notes on the Movements of R.H.C.," 16.

40 Paul P. Hutchinson, *Canada's Black Watch: The First Hundred Years, 1862–1962* (Montreal: The Black Watch (RHR) of Canada, 1962), 223.

41 Roy, *1944*, 128.

42 "Interview with Pte. Williams," 1.

43 Hutchinson, 223.

44 "Interview with Maj. Harris," app. doc., 3.

45 "Interview with Pte. Williams," 1.

46 Roy, *1944*, 127–28.

47 Hutchinson, 223.

48 "Black Watch Fontenay," 145.2R15.0111(D12), DHH, DND, 1.

49 Copp, *The Brigade*, 80.

50 "Interview with Pte. Williams," 2.

51 Stacey, 194.

52 Hutchinson, 223–24.

53 Stacey, 194.

54 Roman Johann Jarymowycz, "Der Gegenangriff vor Verrières: German Counterattacks during Operation 'Spring,' 25–26 July 1944," *Canadian Military History*, vol. 2, 1993, no. 1, 83.

55 John Meredith Rockingham, interview by Reginald H. Roy, July 11, 1979, UVICSC.
56 Kingsley Brown Sr., Kingsley Brown Jr., and Brereton Greenhous, *Semper Paratus: The History of the Royal Hamilton Light Infantry (Wentworth Regiment), 1862–1977* (Hamilton: RHLI Historical Assoc., 1977), 249–50.
57 Jarymowycz, 84.
58 Roy, *1944*, 114.
59 Royal Hamilton Light Infantry War Diary, July 1944, RG24, LAC, 15.
60 Stacey, 193.
61 Roy, *1944*, 129.
62 Le Régiment de Maisonneuve War Diary, July 1944, RG24, LAC, 6.
63 Roy, *1944*, 129–30.
64 Copp, *The Brigade*, 83.
65 Roy, *1944*, 130–31.
66 Terry Copp, *Fields of Fire: The Canadians in Normandy* (Toronto: University of Toronto Press, 2003), 307.
67 Stacey, 193.
68 Ibid., 194.

16 SIMPLE PLANS
1 Reginald H. Roy, *1944: The Canadians in Normandy* (Toronto: Macmillan, 1984), 139.
2 "Operation Spring: 25 Jul 1944, Factors in Assessing Results," 112H1.003(D43), DHH, DND, 1–2.
3 Lt. Gen. G.G. Simonds, "Operation Spring," *Canadian Military History*, vol. 1, nos. 1–2 (1992), 66–68.
4 Stormont, Dundas and Glengarry Highlanders War Diary, July 1944, RG24, LAC, 24.
5 North Nova Scotia Highlanders War Diary, August 1944, RG24, LAC, 1.
6 John A. English, *Failure in High Command: The Canadian Army and the Normandy Campaign* (Ottawa: Golden Dog Press, 1995), 251.
7 Stormont, Dundas and Glengarry Highlanders War Diary, August 1944, RG24, LAC, 2.
8 English, 251.
9 Simonds, 65.
10 Samuel W. Mitcham Jr., *Panzers in Normandy: General Hans Eberbach and the German Defense of France, 1944* (Mechanicsburg, PA: Stackpole Books, 2009), 87–88.
11 Dan Hartigan, *A Rising of Courage: Canada's Paratroops in the Liberation of Normandy* (Calgary: Drop Zone, 2000), 244.
12 Charles P. Stacey, *The Victory Campaign: The Operations in North-West Europe, 1944–1945*, vol. 3 (Ottawa: Queen's Printer, 1960), 196.
13 Paul Douglas Dickson, *A Thoroughly Canadian General: A Biography of General H.D.G. Crerar* (Toronto, University of Toronto Press, 2007), 284.
14 Stacey, 196–97.
15 English, 192–93.
16 Ibid., 194.
17 Stacey, 198–99.
18 L.F. Ellis, *The Battle of Normandy*, vol. 1 of *Victory in the West* (London: Her Majesty's Stationery Office, 1962), 386–87.

19 "Report No. 58, Canadian Participation in the Operations in North-West Europe, 1944, Part II: Canadian Operations in July, Historical Section (G.S.) Army Headquarters," DHH, DND, para. 321.

20 Ibid., para. 305.

21 Stacey, 201.

22 "Report No. 58," para. 320.

23 Ibid., paras. 321–23.

24 Ibid., para. 320.

25 Essex Scottish Regiment War Diary, July 1944, RG24, LAC, 19.

26 Sandy Antal and Kevin R. Shackleton, *Duty Nobly Done: the Official History of the Essex and Kent Scottish Regiment* (Windsor, ON: Walkerville, 2006), 459–60.

27 Essex Scottish War Diary, 20.

28 Le Régiment de Maisonneuve War Diary, July 1944, RG24, LAC, 7–8.

29 W.R. Freasby, ed., *Organization and Campaigns*, vol. 1 of *Official History of the Canadian Medical Services, 1939–1945* (Ottawa: Queen's Printer, 1956), 234.

30 Stacey, 204.

31 "Report No. 58," para. 334.

32 John Meredith Rockingham, interview by Reginald H. Roy, July 11, 1979, UVICSC.

33 "Report No. 58," para. 334.

34 Rockingham interview.

35 "Report No. 58," para. 334.

36 Calgary Highlanders War Diary, July 1944, RG24, LAC, 34.

37 David Bercuson, *Battalion of Heroes: The Calgary Highlanders in World War II* (Calgary: Calgary Highlanders Regimental Funds Fdn., 1994), 82.

38 "Account of Attack by the Calg Highrs on Tilly-La-Campagne Night 31 Jul/1 Aug 44 as told to Capt. Engler by Lt. R. Porter, LO 5 BDE, at Basse, 2 Aug 44," 145.2CI.011(DI), DHH, DND, I.

39 Calgary Highlanders War Diary, August 1944, RG24, LAC, I.

40 Bercuson, 82.

41 Lincoln and Welland Regiment War Diary, August 1944, RG24, LAC, I.

42 Calgary Highlanders War Diary, August 1944, I.

43 "Account by Porter," 1–2.

44 Bercuson, 83–84.

45 "Account of the Attack on the Church in Saint-Martin-de-Fontenay by 'D' Coy, FUS MR, 31 Jul/1 Aug as Told by Maj. Dextraze to Capt. Engler at Saint-Martin-de-Fontenay, 3 Aug 44," 145.2FI.011(D6), DHH, DND, I.

46 Roy, *1944*, 141.

47 "Account by Dextraze," 1–3.

48 *Canadian Army Overseas Honours and Awards Citation Details*, DHH, DND, www.cmp-cpm.forces.gc.ca/dhh-dhp/gal/cao-aco/details-eng.asp?firstname=Joseph Alfred Germain&lastname=Lambert&rec=id4208 (accessed December 24, 2010).

49 "Account by Dextraze," 4.

17 SHEER SLAUGHTER

1 "Report No. 58, Canadian Participation in the Operations in North-West Europe, 1944, Part II: Canadian Operations in July," Historical Section (G.S.) Army Headquarters, DHH, DND, para. 325.

2 Charles P. Stacey, *The Victory Campaign: The Operations in North-West Europe, 1944–1945*, vol. 3 (Ottawa: Queen's Printer, 1960), 206.

3 George Kitching, *Mud and Green Fields: The Memoirs of Major General George Kitching* (Langley, BC: Battleline Books, 1985), 209.

4 Lincoln and Welland Regiment War Diary, August 1944, RG24, LAC, I.

5 South Alberta Regiment War Diary, August 1944, RG24, LAC, I.

6 Lincoln and Welland War Diary, I.

7 15th Field Regiment War Diary, August 1944, RG24, LAC, I.

8 Geoffrey Hayes, *The Lincs: A History of the Lincoln and Welland Regiment at War* (Alma, ON: Maple Leaf Route, 1986), 26–28.

9 R.L. Rogers, *History of the Lincoln and Welland Regiment* (Montreal: Industrial Shops for the Deaf, 1954), 136.

10 Hayes, 26.

11 Lincoln and Welland War Diary, I–2.

12 Hayes, 26.

13 Ibid., 27.

14 Lincoln and Welland War Diary, 2.

15 Calgary Highlanders War Diary, August 1944, RG24, LAC, 4.

16 Carlo D'Este, *Decision in Normandy: The Unwritten Story of Montgomery and the Allied Campaign* (London: Penguin, 1983), 408–10.

17 L.F. Ellis, *The Battle of Normandy*, vol. I of *Victory in the West* (London: Her Majesty's Stationery Office, 1962), 397–98.

18 Robin Neillands, *The Battle of Normandy, 1944* (London: Cassell, 2002), 323.

19 Ibid., 335.

20 "Report No. 50, The Campaign in North-West Europe–Information from German Sources, Part II: Invasion and Battle of Normandy (6 Jun–22 Aug 44)," Historical Section (G.S.) Army Headquarters, DHH, DND, paras. 207–08.

21 Michael Reynolds, *Steel Inferno: I SS Panzer Corps in Normandy* (New York: Dell, 1997), 249.

22 Samuel W. Mitcham Jr., *Panzers in Normandy: General Hans Eberbach and the German Defense of France, 1944* (Mechanicsburg, PA: Stackpole Books, 2009), 97.

23 "Personal Diary of Brig N.E. Rodger, C of S 2 Cdn Corps," 225C2.011(D2), vol. 10798, box 214, RG24, LAC, 15.

24 Reginald H. Roy, *1944: The Canadians in Normandy* (Toronto: Macmillan, 1984), 140–41.

25 Queen's Own Cameron Highlanders War Diary, August 1944, RG24, LAC, I.

26 "Personal Diary of Brig N.E. Rodger," 15.

27 Terry Copp, *The Brigade: Fifth Canadian Infantry Brigade, 1939–1945* (Stoney Creek, ON: Fortress, 1992), 90.

28 David R. O'Keefe, " 'Pushing Their Necks Out': Ultra, The Black Watch, and Command Relations, May-sur-Orne, Normandy, 5 August 1944," *Canadian Military History* vol. 15, no. I (Winter 2006), 34.

29 Copp, *The Brigade*, 91.

30 Black Watch War Diary, August 1944, possession of the author, 2.

31 O'Keefe, 37.

32 Black Watch War Diary, 2.

33 Stacey, 207.

34 Le Régiment de Maisonneuve War Diary, August 1944, RG24, LAC, 4–5.

35 Gérard Marchand, *Le Régiment de Maisonneuve vers la Victoire, 1944–1945* (Montreal: Les Presses Libres, 1980), 88.

36 Le Régiment War Diary, 5.

37 Marchand, 88.

38 Argyll and Sutherland Highlanders War Diary, August 1944, RG24, LAC, 2.

39 Robert L. Fraser, *Black Yesterdays: The Argyll's War* (Hamilton: Argyll Fdn. 1996), 217.

40 *Canadian Army Overseas Honours and Awards Citation Details*, DHH, DND, www.cmp-cpm.forces.gc.ca/dhh-dhp/gal/cao-aco/details-eng.asp?firstname= Alexander&lastname=McLaren&rec=id400 (accessed December 30, 2010).

41 Fraser, 217.

42 H.M. Jackson, *The Argyll and Sutherland Highlanders of Canada (Princess Louise's), 1928–1953* (Montreal: Industrial Shops for the Deaf, 1953), 78–79.

43 10th Canadian Infantry Brigade War Diary, August 1944, RG24, LAC, 4.

44 Jackson, 78–79.

45 Donald Graves, *South Albertas: A Canadian Regiment at War* (Toronto: Robin Brass Studio, 1998), 108.

46 William Ernest John Hutchinson, "Test of a Corps Commander, Lieutenant-General Guy Granville Simonds: Normandy, 1944," unpublished master's thesis, Victoria: University of Victoria, 1982), 188.

47 Lake Superior Regiment (Motor) War Diary, August 1944, RG24, LAC, 3.

48 George F.G. Stanley, *In the Face of Danger: The History of the Lake Superior Regiment* (Port Arthur, ON: Lake Superior Scottish Regt., 1960), 149–50.

49 A. Fortescue Duguid, *History of the Canadian Grenadier Guards, 1760–1964* (Montreal: Gazette Printing, 1965), 260.

50 Stanley, 149–50.

51 Reynolds, 250.

52 "Report No. 65, Canadian Participation in the Operations in North-West Europe, 1944, Part III: Canadian Operations, 1–23 August," Historical Section (G.S.) Army Headquarters, DHH, DND, para. 35.

53 Ibid., para. 35.

18 JAWS DROPPED

1 Reginald H. Roy, *1944: The Canadians in Normandy* (Toronto: Macmillan, 1984), 149.

2 Charles P. Stacey, *The Victory Campaign: The Operations in North-West Europe, 1944–1945*, vol. 3 (Ottawa: Queen's Printer, 1960), 208.

3 "Report No. 65, Canadian Participation in the Operations in North-West Europe, 1944, Part III: Canadian Operations, 1–23 August," Historical Section (G.S.) Army Headquarters, DHH, DND, para. 13.

4 William Ernest John Hutchinson, "Test of a Corps Commander, Lieutenant-General Guy Granville Simonds: Normandy, 1944," unpublished master's thesis, Victoria: University of Victoria, 1982), 189.

5 Stacey, 208.

6 Roy, *1944: The Canadians in Normandy*, 148–49.

7 Stacey, 208–09.

8 Hutchinson, 194.

9 T.J. Bell, *Into Action with the 12th Field* (Utrecht: J. van Boekhoven, 1945), 68.

10 14th Field Regiment (RCA) War Diary, August 1944, RG24, LAC, 2.

11 13th Field Regiment (RCA) War Diary, August 1944, RG24, LAC, 1.

12 Carl Rice Boehm, interview by Chris D. Main, May 30 and June 8, 1978, UVICSC.

13 John R. Grodzinski, " 'Kangaroos at War': The History of the 1st Canadian Armoured Personnel Carrier Regiment," *Canadian Military History*, vol. 4. no. 2 (Autumn, 1995), 43–44.

14 Roy, 1944, 152.

15 Boehm interview.

16 Roy, 1944, 151.

17 *Canadian Army Overseas Honours and Awards Citation Details*, DHH, DND, www.cmp-cpm.forces.gc.ca/dhh-dhp/gal/cao-aco/details-eng.asp?firstname=George Alfred&lastname=Wiggan&rec=id3932 (accessed January 3, 2011).

18 Roy, 1944, 152.

19 "Immediate Report on Op 'Totalize' 7/9 Aug 44 by 2 Cdn Corps (Col. Massy)," 25C2.013(D15), vol. 10800, box 215, RG24, LAC, 6.

20 John Meredith Rockingham, interview by Reginald H. Roy, July 11, 1979, UVICSC.

21 "Personal Diary of Brig. N.E. Rodger, C of S. 2 CDN CORPS," Canadian War Museum, Arch Docs, Manu 58A 1 114.1, handwritten notes by Rodger entered below August 5, 1944, entry.

22 Roy, 1944, 153–58.

23 Stacey, 217–18.

24 Carlo D'Este, *Decision in Normandy: The Unwritten Story of Montgomery and the Allied Campaign* (London: Penguin, 1983), 422.

25 Ralph Bennett, *Ultra in the West: The Normandy Campaign of 1944–45* (New York: Charles Scribner's Sons, 1979), 114–15.

26 Samuel W. Mitcham Jr., *Panzers in Normandy: General Hans Eberbach and the German Defense of France, 1944* (Mechanicsburg, PA: Stackpole Books, 2009), 97–98.

27 Robin Neillands, *The Battle of Normandy, 1944* (London: Cassell, 2002), 342–46.

28 L.F. Ellis, *The Battle of Normandy*, vol. 1 of *Victory in the West* (London: Her Majesty's Stationery Office, 1962), 415–16.

29 Michael Reynolds, *Steel Inferno: 1 SS Panzer Corps in Normandy* (New York: Dell, 1997), 283–85.

30 Kurt Meyer, *Grenadier: The Story of Waffen SS General Kurt "Panzer" Meyer* (Mechanicsburg, PA: Stackpole Books, 2005), 274.

31 Stacey, 221.

32 Royal Regiment of Canada War Diary, August 1944, RG24, LAC, 6.

33 VIII CDN *Recce Rgt 14 CH: Battle History of the Regt* (Victoria: 8th Cdn Recce Association, 1993), 7.
34 2nd Canadian Armoured Brigade War Diary, August 1944, RG24, LAC, 9.
35 Roy, *1944*, 163.
36 "Operation Totalize: An Account of Ops by 2 CDN ARMD BDE in France 5 to 8 Aug 44," 275C2.013(D4), vol. 10992, box 313, RG24, LAC, 4–5.
37 2nd Canadian Armoured War Diary, 9–10.
38 Brian A. Reid, *No Holding Back: Operation Totalize, Normandy, August 1944* (Toronto: Robin Brass Studio, 2005), 172–74.
39 Stacey, 218.
40 Reid, 175.

19 THE FULLEST SUCCESS
1 D.J. Goodspeed, *Battle Royal: A History of the Royal Regiment of Canada, 1862–1962* (Toronto: Royal Regt. of Canada Assoc., 1962), 440.
2 Brian A. Reid, *No Holding Back: Operation Totalize, Normandy, August 1944* (Toronto: Robin Brass Studio, 2005), 176.
3 VIII CDN *Recce Rgt 14 CH: Battle History of the Regt* (Victoria: 8th Cdn Recce Assoc., 1993), 6–8.
4 Reginald H. Roy, *1944: The Canadians in Normandy* (Toronto: Macmillan, 1984), 166.
5 VIII CDN *Recce Rgt*, 6–8.
6 Reid, 196.
7 VIII CDN *Recce Rgt*, 8.
8 Reid, 179.
9 Merritt Hayes Bateman, interview by Tom Torrie, May 28, 1987, UVICSC.
10 Royal Hamilton Light Infantry War Diary, August 1944, , RG24, LAC, appendix 1, 1.
11 George G. Blackburn, *The Guns of Normandy: A Soldier's Eye View, France 1944* (Toronto: McClelland & Stewart, 1997), 331.
12 Essex Scottish Regiment War Diary, August 1944, RG24, LAC, 3.
13 "Report No. 65, Canadian Participation in the Operations in North-West Europe, 1944, Part III: Canadian Operations, 1–23 August," Historical Section (G.S.) Army Headquarters, DHH, DND, para. 61.
14 Essex Scottish War Diary, 4.
15 Sandy Antal and Kevin R. Shackleton, *Duty Nobly Done: The Official History of the Essex and Kent Scottish Regiment* (Windsor, ON: Walkerville, 2006), 463–64.
16 Essex Scottish War Diary, 4.
17 Kingsley Brown Sr., Kingsley Brown Jr., and Brereton Greenhous, *Semper Paratus: The History of the Royal Hamilton Light Infantry (Wentworth Regiment), 1862–1977* (Hamilton: RHLI Historical Assoc., 1977), 257–58.
18 Goodspeed, 440.
19 Royal Regiment of Canada War Diary, August 1944, RG24, LAC, 9.
20 6th Canadian Infantry Brigade War Diary, August 1944, RG24, LAC, 7.
21 Reginald H. Roy, *1944: The Canadians in Normandy* (Toronto: Macmillan, 1984), 174.
22. South Saskatchewan Regiment War Diary, August 1944, RG24, LAC, 4.
23 Charles Goodman, phone interview by author, January 7, 2011.

24 South Saskatchewan War Diary, 4.

25 "Account of the Attáck and Capture of May-sur-Orne by FUS MR, Night of 7/8 Aug 44, Given by Maj. Brochu and Capt. Lamothe to Capt. Engler at Etavaux and May-sur-Orne, 12 Aug 44," 145.2FI011(D4), DHH, DND, 1–2.

26 R.W. Queen-Hughes, *Whatever Men Dare: A History of the Queen's Own Cameron Highlanders of Canada, 1935–1960* (Winnipeg: Bluman Bros., 1960), 111.

27 Reid, 205.

28 Roy, *1944*, 176.

29 Queen-Hughes, 111.

30 Queen's Own Cameron Highlanders War Diary, August 1944, RG24, LAC– appendix 2.

31 *Canadian Army Overseas Honours and Awards Citation Details*, DHH, DND, www.cmp-cpm.forces.gc.ca/dhh-dhp/gal/cao-aco/details-eng.asp?firstname= James&lastname=Mahon&rec=id4386 (accessed January 9, 2011).

32 Queen-Hughes, 111.

33 Reid, 206.

34 Roy, *1944*, 178.

35 "Report No. 50, The Campaign in North-West Europe–Information from German Sources, Part II: Invasion and Battle of Normandy (6 Jun–22 Aug 44)," Historical Section (G.S.) Army Headquarters, DHH, DND, para. 222.

36 "German Report on Operation Totalize (Translation)," 112.3M1.009(DI53), DHH, DND, 5.

37 Kurt Meyer, *Grenadier: The Story of Waffen SS General Kurt "Panzer" Meyer* (Mechanicsburg, PA: Stackpole Books, 2005), 277–78.

38 Roy, 186.

39 Reid, 217–18.

40 Charles P. Stacey, *The Victory Campaign: The Operations in North-West Europe, 1944–1945*, vol. 3 (Ottawa: Queen's Printer, 1960), 208.

41 Reid, 224–25.

42 Ibid., 220–21.

43 "Operation Totalize: An Account of Ops by 2 CDN ARMD BDE in France 5 to 8 Aug 44," 275C2.013(D4), vol. 10992, box 313, RG24, LAC, 7.

44 Reid, 221.

45 Roy, *1944*, 173.

46 Reid, 228.

47 Essex Scottish War Diary, 4–5.

48 "Account of the Attack by Essex Scottish on Caillouet, 0555, Night 7/8 Aug 44 Given by Maj. Burgess to Capt. Engler at Caillouet, on 10 Aug 44," 145.2E3011(D5), DHH, DND, 2.

49 Stacey, 220.

50 Royal Hamilton War Diary, August 1944, appendix I, 1.

51 Goodspeed, 442–43.

52 Stacey, 220.

53 "Operation Totalize: An Account of Ops by 2 CDN ARMD BDE in France 5 to 8 Aug 44," 7.

54 Roy, 1944, 178.
55 *Canadian Army Overseas Honours and Awards Citation Details*, DHH, DND, www.cmp-cpm.forces.gc.ca/dhh-dhp/gal/cao-aco/details-eng.asp?firstname=Peter Lancelot&lastname=Pearce&rec=id669 (accessed January 10, 2011).
56 *Canadian Army Overseas Honours and Awards Citation Details*, DHH, DND, www.cmp-cpm.forces.gc.ca/dhh-dhp/gal/cao-aco/details-eng.asp?firstname=Abram&lastname=Arbour&rec=id41 (accessed January 9, 2011).
57 Reid, 230.
58 "Account of the Attack and Capture" 2–3.
59 Stacey, 220.

20 MANY ANXIOUS MOMENTS

1 George Kitching, *Mud and Green Fields: The Memoirs of Major General George Kitching* (Langley, BC: Battleline Books, 1985), 210.
2 Roman Johann Jarymowycz, "Canadian Armour in Normandy: Operation 'Totalize' and the Quest for Operational Maneuver," *Canadian Military History*, vol. 7, no. 2 (Spring 1998), 19.
3 Reginald H. Roy, *1944: The Canadians in Normandy* (Toronto: Macmillan, 1984), 192–93.
4 "1 Polish Armoured Division: Order for the Attack No. 1 on 8 Aug 44," 245P1.016(D1), vol. 10942, box 287, RG24, LAC, 1.
5 *Permanent Delegation of the Republic of Poland to NATO*, First Polish Armored Division, www.brukselanato.polemb.net/index.php?document=78 (accessed January 11, 2011).
6 George Kitching, interview by Ken MacLeod, March 16 and 18, 1998.
7 "Major-General George Kitching, CBE, DSO, CD," *The Army Doctrine and Training Bulletin*, www.army.forces.gc.ca/caj/documents/vol_02/iss_3/CAJ_vol2.3_01_e.pdf (accessed January 11, 2011), 1.
8 Kitching, 196.
9 Kitching, MacLeod interview.
10 "Report No. 65, Canadian Participation in the Operations in North-West Europe, 1944, Part III: Canadian Operations, 1–23 August," Historical Section (G.S.) Army Headquarters, DHH, DND, para. 69.
11 Lawrence N. Smith, *The History of the 23rd Field Regiment (S.P.) RCA, World War II* (St. Catharines, ON: St. Catharines Standard, 1945), 44.
12 Robert A. Spencer, *A History of the Fifteenth Canadian Field Regiment, Royal Canadian Artillery: 1941 to 1945* (New York: Elsevier, 1945), 100–01.
13 19th Field Regiment War Diary, August 1944, RG24, LAC, 2.
14 4th Canadian Armoured Division Headquarters, RCA, August 1944, RG24, LAC, 3.
15 Charles P. Stacey, *The Victory Campaign: The Operations in North-West Europe, 1944–1945*, vol. 3 (Ottawa: Queen's Printer, 1960), 223.
16 Brian A. Reid, *No Holding Back: Operation Totalize, Normandy, August 1944*. Toronto: Robert Brass Studio, 2005, 265–67.
17 Stacey, 223.
18 Will Bird, *North Shore (New Brunswick) Regiment* (Fredericton: Brunswick Press, 1963), 360–61.

19 North Shore (New Brunswick) Regiment War Diary, August 1944, RG24, LAC, 2.

20 Roy, *1944*, 195–96.

21 Bruce F. Macdonald, interview by Reginald H. Roy, September 4, 1980, UVICSC.

22 Fort Garry Horse Regiment War Diary, August 1944, RG24, LAC, 4.

23 "Report No. 65," para. 72.

24 Ibid., para. 74.

25 Stacey, 223.

26 Kurt Meyer, *Grenadier: The Story of Waffen SS General Kurt "Panzer" Meyer* (Mechanicsburg, PA: Stackpole Books, 2005), 281.

27 Reid, 239–42.

28 Ibid., 410–30.

29 Ibid., 245–47.

30 Stacey, 222.

31 Royal Regiment of Canada War Diary, August 1944, RG24, LAC, 10.

32 "Report No. 65," para. 74.

33 Kitching, 213.

34 Lake Superior Regiment (Motor) War Diary, August 1944, RG24, LAC, 5.

35 George F.G. Stanley, *In the Face of Danger: The History of the Lake Superior Regiment* (Port Arthur, ON: Lake Superior Scottish Regt., 1960), 159–60.

36 Hershell Smith, interview by Reginald H. Roy, July 7, 1981, UVICSC.

37 A. Fortescue Duguid, *History of the Canadian Grenadier Guards, 1760–1964* (Montreal: Gazette Printing, 1965), 262–63.

38 Calgary Highlanders War Diary, August 1944, RG24, LAC, 9.

39 1st Hussars War Diary, August 1944, RG24, LAC, 2.

40 Calgary Highlanders War Diary, 9.

41 Le Régiment de Maisonneuve War Diary, August 1944, RG24, LAC, 4.

42 "Account of the Seizure of Bretteville-sur-Laize 0552 by the Calg Highrs, 8 Aug 44 as Given by Lt.-Col. MacLauchlan to Capt. Engler at Bretteville-sur-Laize, 11 Aug 44," 145.2C1011(D2), DHH, DND, 1.

43 Roy Farron, *History of the Calgary Highlanders, 1921–54* (Calgary: Bryant Press, 1954), 158.

44 "Account by MacLauchlan," 1.

45 David Bercuson, *Battalion of Heroes: The Calgary Highlanders in World War II* (Calgary: Calgary Highlanders Regimental Funds Fdn., 1994), 96.

46 Farron, 159.

47 Calgary Highlanders War Diary, 9.

48 "Account by MacLauchlan," 2.

49 *Canadian Army Overseas Honours and Awards Citation Details*, DHH, DND, www.cmp-cpm.forces.gc.ca/dhh-dhp/gal/cao-aco/details-eng.asp?firstname=William Matthew Bruce&lastname=Cook&rec=id4595 (accessed January 14, 2011).

50 Calgary Highlander War Diary, 10.

21 THAT'LL BE A TOUGH ONE

1 Brian A. Reid, *No Holding Back: Operation Totalize, Normandy, August 1944* (Toronto: Robin Brass Studio, 2005), 271–72.

2 Stuart Johns, phone interview by author, June 3, 2009.

3 A. Fortescue Duguid, *History of the Canadian Grenadier Guards, 1760–1964* (Montreal: Gazette Printing, 1965), 263.

4 Canadian Grenadier Guards War Diary, August 1944, RG24, LAC, 5.

5 *Canadian Army Overseas Honours and Awards Citation Details*, DHH, DND, www.cmp-cpm.forces.gc.ca/dhh-dhp/gal/cao-aco/details-eng.asp?firstname=Ivon Patrick&lastname=Phelan&rec=id3286 (accessed January 13, 2011).

6 Duguid, 264.

7 *Canadian Army Overseas Honours and Awards Citation Details*, DHH, DND, www.cmp-cpm.forces.gc.ca/dhh-dhp/gal/cao-aco/details-eng.asp?firstname=Ivon Patrick&lastname=Phelan&rec=id3286 (accessed January 13, 2011).

8 Reid, 280–81.

9 Argyll and Sutherland Highlanders War Diary, August 1944, RG24, LAC, 4.

10 Robert L. Fraser, *Black Yesterdays: The Argyll's War* (Hamilton: Argyll Fdn., 1996), 224.

11 H.M. Jackson, *The Argyll and Sutherland Highlanders of Canada (Princess Louise's), 1928–1953* (Montreal: Industrial Shops for the Deaf, 1953), 86.

12 Duguid, 264.

13 Reginald H. Roy, *1944: The Canadians in Normandy* (Toronto: Macmillan, 1984), 203.

14 George Kitching, *Mud and Green Fields: The Memoirs of Major General George Kitching* (Langley, BC: Battleline Books, 1985), 213.

15 Reid, 301–02.

16 Ibid., 203–04.

17 Duguid, 264.

18 "Seven miscellaneous messages 1 Polish Armoured Division Aug., Sep and Dec 44," 245P1.045(D1), vol. 10942, box 287, RG24, LAC, 4.

19 Roman Johann Jarymowycz, "Canadian Armour in Normandy: Operation 'Totalize' and the Quest for Operational Maneuver," *Canadian Military History*, vol. 7, no. 2 (Spring 1998), 27.

20 "Polish Armoured Division in Op 'Totalize,' 7–13 Aug," 245P1.013(D7), vol. 10942, box 287, RG24, LAC, 2.

21 "Polish Armoured Division History," DHH, DND, 23–24.

22 "Polish Armoured Division in Op 'Totalize,' 7–13 Aug," 2–3.

23 "Report No. 50, The Campaign in North-West Europe—Information from German Sources, Part II: Invasion and Battle of Normandy (6 Jun–22 Aug 44)," Historical Section (G.S.) Army Headquarters, DHH, DND, para. 222.

24 Roy, *1944*, 209.

25 Canadian Grenadier Guards War Diary, August 1944, 5.

26 Neil J. Stewart, *Steel My Soldier's Heart* (Victoria: Trafford, 2000), 105.

27 Lake Superior Regiment (Motor) War Diary, August 1944, RG24, LAC, 6.

28 Canadian Grenadier War Diary, 5.

29 Lake Superior (Motor) War Diary, 6.

30 Canadian Grenadier War Diary, 5.

31 George F.G. Stanley, *In the Face of Danger: The History of the Lake Superior Regiment* (Port Arthur, ON: Lake Superior Scottish Regt., 1960), 163.

32 Lincoln and Welland Regiment War Diary, August 1944, RG24, LAC, 4–5.

33 Donald Graves, *South Albertas: A Canadian Regiment at War* (Toronto: Robin Brass
     Studio, 1998), 114.

34 Geoffrey Hayes, *The Lincs: A History of the Lincoln and Welland Regiment at War* (Alma,
     ON: Maple Leaf Route, 1986), 31.

35 H.M. Jackson, *The Argyll and Sutherland Highlanders of Canada (Princess Louise's),
     1928–1953* (Montreal: Industrial Shops for the Deaf, 1953), 87.

36 Stanley, 163.

37 Lake Superior (Motor) War Diary, 7.

22 COME WHAT MAY

 1 Roy, *1944: The Canadians in Normandy* (Toronto: Macmillan, 1984), 209–10.

 2 "An Account of the Battle Experience of 'A' Coy, Algonquin Regiment, August 8 to 11,
     1944 by Capt. (Now Major) C. Robertson O/C 'A' Coy," 145.2A1013(D1), DHH, DND, 1.

 3 "An Account of the Battle Participation of the Algonquin Regiment Between August 6
     and August 11, 1944, Prepared by Major L.C. Monk," 145.2A1013(D1), DHH, DND, 2–3.

 4 Douglas E. Harker, *The Dukes: The Story of the Men Who Have Served in Peace and War
     with the British Columbia Regiment (D.C.O.), 1883–1973* (British Columbia Regt., 1974),
     n.p.

 5 "Account by Monk," 3.

 6 "Account by Robertson," 1.

 7 "Account by Monk, 3–4.

 8 Mike Bechtold, "Lost in Normandy: The Odyssey of Worthington Force, 9 August
     1944," *Canadian Military History,* vol. 19, no. 2 (Spring 2010), 8.

 9 British Columbia Regiment War Diary, August 1944, RG24, LAC, 6.

10 "Account by Monk," 4.

11 Bechtold, 9.

12 British Columbia War Diary, 6.

13 Harker, n.p.

14 British Columbia War Diary, 6.

15 Charles P. Stacey, *The Victory Campaign: The Operations in North-West Europe,
     1944–1945,* vol. 3 (Ottawa: Queen's Printer, 1960), 226.

16 "Account by Monk," 4.

17 British Columbia War Diary, 7.

18 "Account by Monk," 4.

19 British Columbia War Diary, 6.

20 "Account by Monk," 5.

21 Stacey, 227.

22 British Columbia War Diary, 8.

23 Bechtold, 14.

24 British Columbia War Diary, 7–8.

25 "An Account of the Battle Experience of 'D' Coy, Algonquin Regiment, Aug. 8, 9, 10,
     11, 12, 1944 by Major Keith Stirling, O.C. 'D' Coy, Algonquin Regiment,"
     145.2A1013(D1), DHH, DND, 1.

26 "Sketch of Position, Diagrammatic Only," 145.2A1013(D1), DHH, DND, 1.

27 "Account by Monk," 5.

28 George Kitching, interview by Ken MacLeod, March 16 and 18, 1998.

29 Stacey, 227.

30 George Kitching, *Mud and Green Fields: The Memoirs of Major General George Kitching* (Langley, BC: Battleline Books, 1985), 214.

31 N.A. Buckingham, interview by Reginald H. Roy, June 16, 1981, UVICSC.

32 British Columbia Regiment War Diary, 7.

33 Bechtold, 15.

34 British Columbia War Diary, 7.

35 Bechtold, 15.

36 Brian A. Reid, *No Holding Back: Operation Totalize, Normandy, August 1944* (Toronto: Robin Brass Studio, 2005), 313.

37 Bechtold, 16.

38 "Account by Monk," 6.

39 Ibid., 6.

40 "The Algonquins First Battle Inoculation by Lt. Ken Gartley, O.C. 11 Pl. 'B' Coy, Alg. R.," 145.2A1013(D1), DHH, DND, 2.

41 "Account by Monk," 6.

42 Reid, 316.

43 "Account by Monk," 6.

44 "Outline of Events ('C' Coy) Algonquin Regiment, Aug. 8, 9, 10, 1944, by Lt. Robert Saville, O.C. 15 Pl, 'C' Coy, Alg. R.," 145.2A1013(D1), DHH, DND, 1.

45 "Account by Monk," 7.

46 British Columbia War Diary, 9.

47 "Account by Monk," 7.

48 British Columbia War Diary, 9.

49 "Account by Monk," 7–8.

50 British Columbia War Diary, 9–10.

51 Stacey, 228.

52 "Outline of Events (A, D, HQ and Sp. Coys) Algonquin Regiment, Aug. 9–12, 1944, Major G.L. Cassidy," 145.2A1013(D1), DHH, DND, 1–2.

53 Governor General's Foot Guards War Diary, August 1944, RG24, LAC, 7.

54 Robert M. Foster, et al., *Steady the Buttons Two by Two: Governor General's Foot Guards Regimental History, 125th Anniversary: 1872–1997* (Ottawa: Governor General's Foot Guards, 1999), 184.

55 "Account by Robertson," 1.

56 Foster, 184.

57 "Account by Robertson," 1.

58 Foster, 185.

59 R.L. Rogers, *History of the Lincoln and Welland Regiment* (Montreal: Industrial Shops for the Deaf, 1954), 142.

60 "Report No. 65, Canadian Participation in the Operations in North-West Europe, 1944, Part III: Canadian Operations, 1–23 August," Historical Section (G.S.) Army Headquarters, DHH, DND, para. 98.

23 WHAT A STUPID PLACE

1 Robert L. Fraser, *Black Yesterdays: The Argyll's War* (Hamilton: Argyll Fdn., 1996), 227.

2 Argyll and Sutherland Highlanders War Diary, August 1944, RG24, LAC, 5.

3 Fraser, 227–28.

4 Argyll and Sutherland War Diary, 5.

5 Fraser, 230.

6 New Brunswick Rangers (MG) War Diary, August 1944, RG24, LAC, 10.

7 Argyll and Sutherland War Diary, 5.

8 Fraser, 231.

9 H.M. Jackson, *The Argyll and Sutherland Highlanders of Canada (Princess Louise's), 1928–1953* (Montreal: Industrial Shops for the Deaf, 1953), 90.

10 Reginald H. Roy, *1944: The Canadians in Normandy* (Toronto: Macmillan, 1984), 223–24.

11 Canadian Grenadier Guards War Diary, August 1944, RG24, LAC, 7.

12 Hershell Smith, interview by Reginald H. Roy, July 7, 1981, UVICSC.

13 A. Fortescue Duguid, *History of the Canadian Grenadier Guards, 1760–1964* (Montreal: Gazette Printing, 1965), 267.

14 "Report No. 65, Canadian Participation in the Operations in North-West Europe, 1944, Part III: Canadian Operations, 1–23 August," Historical Section (G.S.) Army Headquarters, DHH, DND, paras. 102–03.

15 Smith interview.

16 "Report No. 65," para. 103.

17 Duguid, 268.

18 Roy, *1944*, 224–25.

19 Canadian Grenadier War Diary, 8.

20 Roy, *1944*, 225.

21 Fraser, 230–32.

22 Duguid, 268–69.

23 "Report No. 65," para. 103.

24 Governor General's Foot Guards War Diary, August 1944, RG24, LAC, 8.

25 "Polish Armoured Division in Op 'Totalize,' 7–13 Aug," 245P1.013(D7), vol. 10942, box 287, RG24, LAC, 4.

26 Charles P. Stacey, *The Victory Campaign: The Operations in North-West Europe, 1944–1945*, vol. 3 (Ottawa: Queen's Printer, 1960), 230.

27 8th Canadian Infantry Brigade War Diary, August 1944, RG24, LAC, 4.

28 "Report No. 65," para. 106.

29 Roy, *1944*, 226–27.

30 W.T. Barnard, *The Queen's Own Rifles of Canada, 1860–1960: One Hundred Years of Canada* (Don Mills, ON: Ontario Publishing Company, 1960), 215.

31 Will Bird, *North Shore (New Brunswick) Regiment* (Fredericton: Brunswick Press, 1963), 365.

32 Barnard, 215–17.

33 Bird, *North Shore Regiment*, 366–67.

34 Stacey, 231.

35 Bird, *North Shore Regiment*, 377.

36 Stacey, 231.

37 "Report No. 65," para. 112.

38 Smith interview.

39 Stacey, 275–76.

40 John A. English, *Failure in High Command: The Canadian Army and the Normandy Campaign* (Ottawa: Golden Dog Press, 1995), 290.

41 Dominick Graham, *The Price of Command: A Biography of General Guy Simonds* (Toronto: Stoddart, 1993), 153–54.

42 Terry Copp, "Reassessing Operation Totalize: Army, Part 27," *Legion Magazine*, www.legionmagazine.com/en/?s=Reassessing+Operation+Totalize (accessed September 1, 1999).

24 WITHOUT A HITCH

1 Charles P. Stacey, *The Victory Campaign: The Operations in North-West Europe, 1944–1945*, vol. 3 (Ottawa: Queen's Printer, 1960), 235–36.

2 C.E. Henry, *Regimental History of the 18th Armoured Car Regiment (XII Manitoba Dragoons)* (Deventer, NL: Nederlandsche Diepdruk Inrichting, 1945), 20.

3 "Report No. 65, Canadian Participation in the Operations in North-West Europe, 1944, Part III: Canadian Operations, 1–23 August," Historical Section (G.S.) Army Headquarters, DHH, DND, paras. 116–17.

4 Royal Regiment of Canada War Diary, August 1944, RG24, LAC, 12.

5 Royal Hamilton Light Infantry War Diary, August 1944, RG24, LAC, 5.

6 Denis Whitaker, Shelgah Whitaker, and Terry Copp, *The Soldiers' Story: Victory at Falaise* (Toronto: Harper Collins, 2000), 153–54.

7 Kingsley Brown Sr., Kingsley Brown Jr., and Brereton Greenhous, *Semper Paratus: The History of the Royal Hamilton Light Infantry (Wentworth Regiment), 1862–1977* (Hamilton: RHLI Historical Assoc., 1977), 259.

8 Michael Reynolds, *Steel Inferno: I SS Panzer Corps in Normandy* (New York: Dell, 1997), 306–07.

9 Brown , Brown, and Greenhous, 260.

10 Whitaker, Whitaker, and Copp, 155.

11 Brown, Brown, and Greenhous, 260–61.

12 4th Canadian Infantry War Diary, August 1944, RG24, LAC, 9.

13 Royal Regiment of Canada War Diary, appendix 7, 1.

14 D.J. Goodspeed, *Battle Royal: A History of the Royal Regiment of Canada, 1862–1962* (Toronto: Royal Regiment of Canada Assoc., 1962), 447–48.

15 *Canadian Army Overseas Honours and Awards Citation Details*, DHH, DND, www.cmp-cpm.forces.gc.ca/dhh-dhp/gal/cao-aco/details-eng.asp?firstname=Stuart Bennett&lastname=Kirkland&rec=id4165 (accessed January 25, 2011).

16 Essex Scottish Regiment War Diary, August 1944, RG24, LAC, 6.

17 Terry Copp, *The Brigade: Fifth Canadian Infantry Brigade, 1939–1945* (Stoney Creek, ON: Fortress, 1992), 102–03.

18 "Account of the Seizure of the Bridgehead over the River Laize at Clair Tizon 0643, 13 Aug 44, by Calg Highrs as Given by Lt. Col. MacLauchlan to Capt. Engler at Bretteville sur Laize, 15 Aug 44," 145.2C1011(D3), DHH, DND, 1–4.

19 Copp, *The Brigade*, 103.

20 Roy Farron, *History of the Calgary Highlanders, 1921–54* (Calgary: Bryant Press, 1954), 160.

21 Copp, *The Brigade*, 103.

22 Le Régiment de Maisonneuve War Diary, August 1944, RG24, 5–6.

23 Copp, *The Brigade*, 104.

24 Stacey, 237.

25 "2 Cdn Corps, Immediate Report on Op 'Tractable' (capture of Falaise) 14/16 Aug 44, by Col R. Massy-Westropp, GSO 1 (Liaison) d/22 Aug 44," vol. 10800, box 215, RG24, LAC, 2.

26 Stacey, 243.

27 "Operation 'Tractable,' Bombing errors in close support operation of August 14, 1944," 181.0003(D450), DHH, DND, 1.

28 "2 Cdn Corps, Immediate Report," 3.

29 Whitaker, Whitaker, and Copp, 159–62.

30 Reginald H. Roy, *1944: The Canadians in Normandy* (Toronto: Macmillan, 1984), 237–38.

31 Terry Copp, *Fields of Fire: The Canadians in Normandy* (Toronto: University of Toronto Press, 2003), 225.

32 "Report No. 65," para. 155.

33 Copp, *Fields of Fire*, 225.

34 "Op 'Tractable:' An Account of Ops by 2 CDN ARMD BDE in France 14 to 16 Aug 44," 275C2.013(D1), vol. 10992, box 313, RG24, LAC, 1.

35 "Biography of Generalleutnant Kurt Chill," *Axis Biographical Research*, www.reocities.com/Pentagon/Bunker/7729/WEHRMACHT/HEER/Generalleutnant /CHILL_KURT.html (accessed January 25, 2011).

36 Copp, *Fields of Fire*, 225.

37 Kurt Meyer, *Grenadier: The Story of Waffen SS General Kurt "Panzer" Meyer* (Mechanicsburg, PA: Stackpole Books, 2005), 291.

38 "Report No. 50, The Campaign in North-West Europe—Information from German Sources, Part II: Invasion and Battle of Normandy (6 Jun–22 Aug 44)," Historical Section (G.S.) Army Headquarters, DHH, DND, paras. 242–46.

39 Kurt Meyer, 291.

40 6th Canadian Infantry Brigade War Diary, August 1944, RG24, LAC, 13–14.

41 "Account of the S Sask R in the Attack on Le Chesnaie from Clair Tizon and the Attack on Falaise Given by Capt. N.H. Hadley, 10, S Sask R, to Capt. Engler at Falaise, 19 Aug 44," 145.2S7011(D1), DHH, DND, 1.

42 George B. Buchanan, *March of the Prairie Men: A Story of the South Saskatchewan Regiment* (Weyburn, SK: S. Sask. R. Olderly Room, 1958), 29.

43 R.W. Queen-Hughes, *Whatever Men Dare: A History of the Queen's Own Cameron Highlanders of Canada, 1935–1960* (Winnipeg: Bluman Bros., 1960), 114–15.

44 "Account of the Attack on La Commaderie 0644 14 Aug 44 by Fus Mr as Given by Maj. White to Capt. Engler at Ussy, 15 Aug 44," 145.2FI011(D8), DHH, DND, 1–2.

45 *Cent ans d'histoire d'un régiment canadien-français: les Fusiliers Mont-Royal, 1869–1969* (Montreal: Éditions Du Jour, 1971), 219.

46 Queen's Own Cameron Highlanders War Diary, August 1944, RG24, LAC, 5.

47 6th Canadian Infantry War Diary, 15.

25 THE MAD CHARGE

1 Charles P. Stacey, *The Victory Campaign: The Operations in North-West Europe, 1944–1945*, vol. 3 (Ottawa: Queen's Printer, 1960), 240.

2 Alfred James Tedlie, interview by Chris D. Main, June 28 and July 9, 16, and 23 1979, UVICSC.

3 Douglas E. Harker, *The Dukes: The Story of the Men Who Have Served in Peace and War with the British Columbia Regiment (D.C.O.), 1883–1973* (British Columbia Regt., 1974), n.p.

4 "Op 'Tallulah,' later changed to 'Tractable,' by Capt. P.A. Mayer," 215C1.013(D26), vol. 10638, box 126, RG24, LAC, 3.

5 Brandon Conron, *A History of the First Hussars Regiment, 1856–1980* (n.p., 1981), 92.

6 Jean E. Portugal, *We Were There: The Navy, the Army and the RCAF—A Record for Canada*, vol. 3 (Shelburne, ON: Battered Silicon Dispatch Box, 1998), 1240.

7 "Op 'Tallulah,'" 3.

8 A. Fortescue Duguid, *History of the Canadian Grenadier Guards, 1760–1964* (Montreal: Gazette Printing, 1965), 271.

9 Conron, 92.

10 Tedlie interview.

11 *Vanguard: The Fort Garry Horse in the Second World War* (Doetinchem, NL: Uitgevers-Maatschappij 'C. Nisset, 1945), 56.

12 Conron, 92–94.

13 "Op 'Tallulah,'" 3–4.

14. Hershell Smith, interview by Reginald H. Roy, July 7, 1981, UVICSC.

15 "3 Cdn Inf Div in Op 'Tractable,' 10–17 Aug 44 by Capt. P.A. Mayer," 235C3.013(D23), vol. 10909, box 270, RG24, LAC, 5.

16 8th Canadian Infantry Brigade War Diary, August 1944, RG24, LAC, 5.

17 Stacey, 241.

18 "Op 'Tallulah,'" 4.

19 Duguid, 272–73.

20 Reginald H. Roy, *1944: The Canadians in Normandy* (Toronto: Macmillan, 1984), 255–56.

21 *The Regimental History of the Governor General's Foot Guards* (Ottawa: Mortimer, 1948), 114.

22 Denis Whitaker, Shelgah Whitaker, and Terry Copp, *The Soldiers' Story: Victory at Falaise* (Toronto: Harper Collins, 2000), 164–65.

23 Lake Superior Regiment (Motor) War Diary, August 1944, RG24, LAC, 10.

24 *Vanguard: The Fort Garry Horse,* 56.

25 "Report of the Bombing of Our Own Troops During Operation 'Tractable,'" 181.003(D2972), DHH, DND, 4–8.

26 T.J. Bell, *Into Action with the 12th Field* (Utrecht: J. van Boekhoven, 1945), 73–74.

27 Stacey, 243.

28 12th Field Regiment War Diary, August 1944, RG24, LAC, 4.

29 "Account of the S Sask R in the Attack on Le Chesnaie from Clair Tizon and the Attack on Falaise Given by Capt. N.H. Hadley, 10, S Sask R, to Capt. Engler at Falaise, 19 Aug 44," 145.2S7011(D1), DHH, DND, 2.

30 Charles Goodman, phone interview by author, January 7, 2011.

31 "Report No. 65, Canadian Participation in the Operations in North-West Europe, 1944, Part III: Canadian Operations, 1–23 August," Historical Section (G.S.) Army Headquarters, DHH, DND, para. 177.

32 "Report of the Bombing," 5–9.

33 9th Canadian Infantry Brigade War Diary, August 1944, RG24, LAC, 4.

34 "Report of the Bombing," 10–11.

35 "Operation 'Tractable,' Bombing errors in close support operation of August 14, 1944," 181.0003(D450), DHH, DND, 3–4.

36 Stacey, 243.

37 Portugal, vol. 3, 1240.

38 "Memorandum of Interview with Lt. Col. R. Rowley OC, SD&G Highrs by Historical Officer, 17 Aug 44," 145.258011(D3), DHH, DND, 1.

39 North Shore (New Brunswick) Regiment War Diary, August 1944, RG24, LAC, 6.

40 Regimental History, 114.

41 H.M. Jackson, The Argyll and Sutherland Highlanders of Canada (Princess Louise's), 1928–1953 (Montreal: Industrial Shops for the Deaf, 1953), 94.

42 Lake Superior (Motor) War Diary, 10.

43 Harker, n.p.

44 Stacey, 245–46.

45 Carlo D'Este, Decision in Normandy: The Unwritten Story of Montgomery and the Allied Campaign (London: Penguin, 1983), 444–52.

46 "Report No. 50, Historical Section (G.S.) Army Headquarters: The Campaign in North-West Europe–Information from German Sources, Part II: Invasion and Battle of Normandy (6 Jun–22 Aug 44)," Historical Section (G.S.) Army Headquarters, DHH, DND, paras. 246–47.

26 A MOLTEN FIRE BATH

1 "3 Cdn Inf Div in Op 'Tractable,' 10–17 Aug 44 by Capt. P.A. Mayer," 235C3.013(D23), vol. 10909, box 270, RG24, LAC, 9.

2 "Report No. 65, Canadian Participation in the Operations in North-West Europe, 1944, Part III: Canadian Operations, 1–23 August," Historical Section (G.S.) Army Headquarters, DHH, DND, paras. 178–79.

3 George Kitching, Mud and Green Fields: The Memoirs of Major General George Kitching (Langley, BC: Battleline Books, 1985), 213–19.

4 "Op 'Tallulah,' later changed to 'Tractable,' by Capt. P.A. Mayer," 215C1.013(D26), vol. 10638, box 126, RG24, LAC, 6.

5 George L. Cassidy, Warpath: The Story of the Algonquin Regiment, 1939–1945 (Markham, ON: Paperjacks, 1980), 127–28.

6 George F.G. Stanley, In the Face of Danger: The History of the Lake Superior Regiment (Port Arthur, ON: Lake Superior Scottish Regt., 1960), 173–74.

7 Governor General's Foot Guards War Diary, August 1944, RG24, LAC, 12.

8 Canadian Grenadier Guards War Diary, August 1944, RG24, LAC, 12.

9 Kitching, 220–21.

10 Canadian Scottish Regiment War Diary, August 1944, RG24, LAC, 16.

11 Reginald H. Roy, *Ready for the Fray: The History of the Canadian Scottish Regiment (Princess Mary's), 1920 to 1955* (Vancouver: Evergreen Press, 1958), 286.

12 2nd Canadian Armoured Brigade War Diary, August 1944, RG24, LAC, 20.

13 Canadian Scottish War Diary, 16.

14 Michael R. McNorgan, *The Gallant Hussars: A History of the 1st Hussars Regiment* (Aylmer, ON: The 1st Hussars Cavalry Fund, 2004), 181–82.

15 Roy, *Ready for the Fray*, 287.

16 Canadian Scottish War Diary, 16.

17 Roy, *Ready for the Fray*, 287.

18 Canadian Scottish War Diary, 17.

19 Roy, *Ready for the Fray*, 288.

20 Ibid.

21 McNorgan, 182.

22 Canadian Scottish War Diary, 17.

23 Roy, *Ready for the Fray*, 292.

24 Jean E. Portugal, *We Were There: The Navy, the Army and the RCAF—A Record for Canada*, vol. 4 (Shelburne, ON: Battered Silicon Dispatch Box, 1998), 2051–52.

25 Stacey, 249.

26 Brandon Conron, *A History of the First Hussars Regiment, 1856–1980* (n.p., 1981), 97.

27 Royal Winnipeg Rifles War Diary, August 1944, RG24, LAC, 4.

28 "Report No. 65," para. 180.

29 Fort Garry Horse Regiment War Diary, August 1944, RG24, LAC, 5.

30 "Polish Armoured Division History," DHH, DND, 8.

31 6th Canadian Infantry Brigade War Diary, August 1944, RG24, LAC, 15.

32 "Account of the S Sask R in the Attack on Le Chesnaie from Clair Tizon and the Attack on Falaise Given by Capt. N.H. Hadley, 10, S Sask R, to Capt. Engler at Falaise, 19 Aug 44," 145.2S7011(D1), DHH, DND, 2.

33 Charles Goodman, phone interview by author, January 7, 2011.

34 "Account by Hadley," 2.

35 "Polish Armoured Division," 8–9.

36 "Report No. 65," para. 184.

37 William Ernest John Hutchinson, "Test of a Corps Commander, Lieutenant-General Guy Granville Simonds: Normandy, 1944," unpublished master's thesis, Victoria: University of Victoria, 1982, 229.

38 "3 Cdn Inf Div in Op 'Tractable,' 10–17 Aug 44 by Capt. P.A. Mayer," 10.

39 7th Canadian Infantry Brigade War Diary, August 1944, RG24, LAC, 13.

40 Conron, 96.

41 7th Canadian Infantry Brigade War Diary, August 1944, 13.

42 Eric Luxton, ed., *1st Battalion, The Regina Rifles Regiment, 1939–1946* (Regina: The Regiment, 1946), 47.

43 1st Hussars Regiment War Diary, August 1944, RG24, LAC, 5.

44 7th Canadian Infantry War Diary, RG24, LAC, 13.

45 Hubert Meyer, *The History of 12. SS-Panzerdivision "Hitlerjugend"* (Winnipeg: J.J. Fedorowicz Publishing, 1994), 189.

46 Stacey, 250.

47 Reginald H. Roy, *1944: The Canadians in Normandy* (Toronto: Macmillan, 1984), 285.
48 6th Canadian Infantry War Diary, 17–18.
49 Jean E. Portugal, *We Were There: The Navy, the Army and the RCAF—A Record for Canada*, vol. 5 (Shelburne, ON: Battered Silicon Dispatch Box, 1998), 2485.
50 6th Canadian Infantry War Diary, 18.
51 Portugal, vol. 5, 2485–86.
52 Goodman interview.
53 6th Canadian Infantry War Diary, 19–20.
54 "Account of the Capture of the Monastery 144358 in Falaise by FUS MRS, Night 17/18 Aug 44, as Given by Maj. Brochu to Capt. Engler Near Dieppe, 4 Sep 44," 145.2FI011(D3), DHH, DND, 2–3.
55 6th Canadian Infantry War Diary, 20.

27 GUNS CHATTERING

1 Charles P. Stacey, *The Victory Campaign: The Operations in North-West Europe, 1944–1945*, vol. 3 (Ottawa: Queen's Printer, 1960), 254–55.
2 Ibid., 250–51.
3 H.M. Jackson, *The Argyll and Sutherland Highlanders of Canada (Princess Louise's), 1928–1953* (Montreal: Industrial Shops for the Deaf, 1953), 95.
4 Donald Graves, *South Albertas: A Canadian Regiment at War* (Toronto: Robin Brass Studio, 1998), 133.
5 Argyll and Sutherland Highlanders War Diary, August 1944, RG24, LAC, 7.
6 Jackson, *Argyll and Sutherland*, 96.
7 "Op 'Tallulah,' later changed to 'Tractable,' by Capt. P.A. Mayer," 215C1.013(D26), vol. 10638, box 126, RG24, LAC, 8.
8 Argyll and Sutherland War Diary, 7.
9 Jackson, *Argyll and Sutherland*, 96.
10 George L. Cassidy, *Warpath: The Story of the Algonquin Regiment, 1939–1945* (Markham, ON: Paperjacks, 1980), 130–31.
11 George Kitching, *Mud and Green Fields: The Memoirs of Major General George Kitching* (Langley, BC: Battleline Books, 1985), 222.
12 "Op 'Tallulah,'" 9.
13 Governor General's Foot Guards War Diary, August 1944, RG24, LAC, 15.
14 *The Regimental History of the Governor General's Foot Guards* (Ottawa: Mortimer, 1948), 118.
15 A. Fortescue Duguid, *History of the Canadian Grenadier Guards, 1760–1964* (Montreal: Gazette Printing, 1965), 276–77.
16 *Regimental History*, 118–19.
17 British Columbia Regiment War Diary, August 1944, RG24, LAC, 16.
18 Alfred James Tedlie, interview by Chris D. Main, June 28 and July 9, 16, and 23, 1979, UVICSC.
19 Lake Superior Regiment (Motor) War Diary, August 1944, RG24, LAC, 13.
20 "Polish Armoured Division History," DHH, DND, 31.
21 Stacey, 252.
22 "Report No. 65, Canadian Participation in the Operations in North-West Europe, 1944,

Part III: Canadian Operations, 1–23 August," Historical Section (G.S.) Army Headquarters, DHH, DND, para. 202.

23 Stacey, 251–52.

24 "Report No. 50, The Campaign in North-West Europe—Information from German Sources, Part II: Invasion and Battle of Normandy (6 Jun–22 Aug 44)," Historical Section (G.S.) Army Headquarters, DHH, DND, para. 267.

25 Michael Reynolds, *Steel Inferno: I SS Panzer Corps in Normandy* (New York: Dell Publishing, 1997), 327.

26 Stacey, 255.

27 Duguid, 278.

28 Canadian Grenadier Guards War Diary, August 1944, RG24, LAC, 13–14.

29 Tedlie interview.

30 Douglas E. Harker, *The Dukes: The Story of the Men Who Have Served in Peace and War with the British Columbia Regiment (D.C.O.), 1883–1973* (British Columbia Regt., 1974), n.p.

31 British Columbia Regiment War Diary, August 1944, RG24, LAC, 16B.

32 Harker, n.p.

33 Stacey, 256–57.

34 Robert M. Foster, et al., *Steady the Buttons Two by Two: Governor General's Foot Guards Regimental History, 125th Anniversary: 1872–1997* (Ottawa: Governor General's Foot Guards, 1999), 193.

35 Duguid, 279.

36 Lake Superior (Motor) War Diary, 14.

37 R.L. Rogers, *History of the Lincoln and Welland Regiment* (Montreal: Industrial Shops for the Deaf, 1954), 156.

38 Geoffrey Hayes, *The Lincs: A History of the Lincoln and Welland Regiment at War* (Alma, ON: Maple Leaf Route, 1986), 36.

39 H.M. Jackson, *The Argyll and Sutherland Highlanders of Canada (Princess Louise's), 1928–1953* (Montreal: Industrial Shops for the Deaf, 1953), 97.

40 "Operations of First Canadian Army, 7–23 Aug 44," 215C1.012(D11), vol. 10635, box 125, RG24, LAC, 5.

41 "Polish Armoured Division History," DHH, DND, 11–13.

42 "Report No. 50," para. 269.

43 L.F. Ellis, *The Battle of Normandy*, vol. 1 of *Victory in the West* (London: Her Majesty's Stationery Office, 1962), 444–45.

44 Stacey, 259.

45 Canadian Grenadier Guards War Diary, August 1944, RG24, LAC, 14.

46 Stuart Johns, phone interview by author, June 3, 2009.

28 A LITTLE WILD

1 Donald Graves, *Century of Service: The History of the South Alberta Light Horse* (Toronto: Robin Brass Studio, 2005), 275–76.

2 South Alberta Regiment War Diary, August 1944, RG24, LAC, 15.

3 Denis Whitaker, Shelagh Whitaker, and Terry Copp, *The Soldiers' Story: Victory at Falaise* (Toronto: Harper Collins, 2000), 222.

4 Donald Graves, *South Albertas: A Canadian Regiment at War* (Toronto: Robin Brass Studio, 1998), 141.

5 *Canadian Army Overseas Honours and Awards Citation Details*, DHH, DND, www.cmp-cpm.forces.gc.ca/dhh-dhp/gal/cao-aco/details-eng.asp?firstname=Ivan H&lastname=Martin&rec=id2910 (accessed February 3, 2011).

6 Whitaker, Whitaker, and Copp, 231.

7 Graves, *South Albertas*, 142.

8 Argyll and Sutherland Highlanders War Diary, August 1944, RG24, LAC, 8.

9 Whitaker, Whitaker, and Copp, 232.

10 Argyll and Sutherland War Diary, 8.

11 Graves, *South Albertas*, 142.

12 Charles P. Stacey, *The Victory Campaign: The Operations in North-West Europe, 1944–1945*, vol. 3 (Ottawa: Queen's Printer, 1960), 259.

13 "First CDN Army Ops to Capture Falaise and to seal gap Trun–Chambois area," 215C1.0129(D10), vol 10635, box 125, RG24, LAC, 10.

14 L.F. Ellis, *The Battle of Normandy*, vol. 1 of *Victory in the West* (London: Her Majesty's Stationery Office, 1962), 450.

15 Stacey, 259.

16 15th Canadian Field Regiment War Diary, August 1944, RG24, LAC, 7.

17 G.W.L. Nicholson, *The Gunners of Canada*, vol. 2 (Toronto: McClelland & Stewart, 1972), 327.

18 *19 Canadian Army Field Regiment, RCA: Regimental History, September 1941–July 1945* (Deventer, NL: Nederlandsche Diepdruk Ihrichting, 1945), 55.

19 Kurt Meyer, *Grenadier: The Story of Waffen SS General Kurt "Panzer" Meyer* (Mechanicsburg, PA: Stackpole Books, 2005), 296–97.

20 Samuel W. Mitcham Jr., *Panzers in Normandy: General Hans Eberbach and the German Defense of France, 1944* (Mechanicsburg, PA: Stackpole Books, 2009), 157–58.

21 Stuart Johns, phone interview by author, June 3, 2009.

22 Canadian Grenadier Guards War Diary, August 1944, RG24, LAC, 14.

23 10th Canadian Armoured Brigade War Diary, August 1944, RG24, LAC, 11.

24 *The Regimental History of the Governor General's Foot Guards* (Ottawa: Mortimer, 1948), 121.

25 "Polish Armoured Division History," DHH, DND, 33–34.

26 Whitaker, Whitaker, and Copp, 243–46.

27 "Polish Armoured Division," 33–34.

28 Whitaker, Whitaker, and Copp, 243–46.

29 Zygmunt Nagórski Jr., *Falaise Gap Has Been Closed* (London: C. Tinling & Co., 1944), 18–19.

30 Graves, *South Albertas*, 143–49.

31 10th Canadian Infantry Brigade War Diary, August 1944, RG24, LAC, 10.

32 "Report No. 65, Canadian Participation in the Operations in North-West Europe, 1944, Part III: Canadian Operations, 1–23 August," Historical Section (G.S.) Army Headquarters," DHH, DND, paras. 208–09.

33 R.L. Rogers, *History of the Lincoln and Welland Regiment* (Montreal: Industrial Shops for the Deaf, 1954), 157.

34 Arthur Bridge, " 'In the Eye of the Storm': A Recollection of Three Days in the Falaise
    Gap, 19–21 August 1944," *Canadian Military History*, vol. 9, no. 3 (Summer 2000),
    62–64.
35 Michael Reynolds, *Steel Inferno: 1 ss Panzer Corps in Normandy* (New York: Dell
    Publishing, 1997), 337.
36 "Report No. 50, The Campaign in North-West Europe–Information from German
    Sources, Part 11: Invasion and Battle of Normandy (6 Jun–22 Aug 44)," Historical
    Section (G.S.) Army Headquarters, DHH, DND, para. 273.
37 Graves, *South Albertas*, 152.
38 South Alberta War Diary, 17.
39 Graves, *South Albertas*, 153.
40 Bridge, 64.
41 South Alberta War Diary, 17.
42 Graves, *A Century of Service*, 285.
43 Bridge, 64–65.
44 *Canadian Army Overseas Honours and Awards Citation Details*, DHH, DND,
    www.cmp-cpm.forces.gc.ca/dhh-dhp/gal/cao-aco/details-eng.asp?firstname=
    Ivan H&lastname=Martin&rec=id2910 (accessed February 6, 2011).
45 Harold Clerkson, interview by William S. Thackray, August 19, 1980, UVICSC.
46 South Alberta War Diary, 17.
47 "Report No. 65," para. 217.

29 A HELLHOLE

 1 "Report No. 65, Canadian Participation in the Operations in North-West Europe, 1944,
    Part 111: Canadian Operations, 1–23 August," Historical Section (G.S.) Army
    Headquarters, DHH, DND, December 23, 1953, para. 216.
 2 "Op 'Tallulah,' later changed to 'Tractable,' by Capt. P.A. Mayer," 215C1.013(D26),
    vol. 10638, box 126, RG24, LAC, 15.
 3 Governor General's Foot Guards War Diary, August 1944, RG24, LAC, 17.
 4 "Op 'Tallulah,'" 15.
 5 "Polish Armoured Division History," DHH, DND, 18.
 6 "Report No. 50, The Campaign in North-West Europe–Information from German
    Sources, Part 11: Invasion and Battle of Normandy (6 Jun–22 Aug 44)," Historical
    Section (G.S.) Army Headquarters, DHH, DND, para. 277.
 7 Michael Reynolds, *Steel Inferno: 1 ss Panzer Corps in Normandy* (New York: Dell
    Publishing, 1997), 344.
 8 "Polish Armoured Division," 18–19.
 9 Reynolds, 344.
10 Ibid., 340–45.
11 New Brunswick Rangers (M.G.) Regiment War Diary, August 1944, RG24, LAC, 16.
12 Arthur Bridge, " 'In the Eye of the Storm': A Recollection of Three Days in the Falaise
    Gap, 19–21 August 1944," *Canadian Military History*, vol. 9, no. 3 (Summer 2000),
    66.
13 H.M. Jackson, *The Argyll and Sutherland Highlanders of Canada (Princess Louise's),
    1928–1953* (Montreal: Industrial Shops for the Deaf, 1953), 99.

14 1st Hussars Regiment War Diary, August 1944, RG24, LAC, 7.

15 Donald Graves, *South Albertas: A Canadian Regiment at War* (Toronto: Robin Brass Studio, 1998), 163.

16 G.T. Heintzman, W.A. Hand, E.H. Heeney, eds., *History of the Sixth Anti-Tank* (Toronto: 6th Canadian Anti-Tank Regt., Royal Canadian Artillery, 1989), 23.

17 Donald Graves, *Century of Service: The History of the South Alberta Light Horse* (Toronto: Robin Brass Studio, 2005), 287.

18 William Ernest John Hutchinson, "Test of a Corps Commander, Lieutenant-General Guy Granville Simonds: Normandy, 1944," unpublished master's thesis, Victoria: University of Victoria, 1982, 241.

19 "Op 'Tallulah,'" 15.

20 *The Regimental History of the Governor General's Foot Guards* (Ottawa: Mortimer, 1948), 124–25.

21 A. Fortescue Duguid, *History of the Canadian Grenadier Guards, 1760–1964* (Montreal: Gazette Printing, 1965), 280–81.

22 George L. Cassidy, *Warpath: The Story of the Algonquin Regiment, 1939–1945* (Markham, ON: Paperjacks, 1980), 137–38.

23 "Polish Armoured Division," 18–20.

24 Heintzman, Hand, and Heeney, 23.

25 Graves, *South Albertas*, 166–67.

26 Bridge, 68.

27 Graves, *Century of Service*, 172–73.

28 *The Regimental History of the Governor General's Foot Guards*, 125.

29 Governor General's Foot Guards War Diary, August 1944, 18.

30 Duguid, 281.

31 Douglas E. Harker, *The Dukes: The Story of the Men Who Have Served in Peace and War with the British Columbia Regiment (D.C.O.), 1883–1973* (British Columbia Regt., 1974), n.p.

32 Duguid, 281–82.

33 "Polish Armoured Division history," 36.

34 Graves, *South Albertas*, 172.

35 Duguid, 282.

36 Zygmunt Nagórski Jr., *Falaise Gap Has Been Closed* (London: C. Tinling & Co., 1944), 20–21.

37 Harker, n.p.

38 Stacey, 262–65.

39 Ibid., 270–71.

40 Hubert Meyer, *The History of 12. SS-Panzerdivision "Hitlerjugend."* (Winnipeg: J.J. Fedorowicz Publishing, 1994), 204.

41 Stacey, 270–71.

42 Ibid., 275.

43 George Kitching, *Mud and Green Fields: The Memoirs of Major General George Kitching* (Langley, BC: Battleline Books, 1985), 226–27.

44 Reginald H. Roy, *1944: The Canadians in Normandy* (Toronto: Macmillan, 1984), 318.

45 Cassidy, 140.

Abbreviations: DND–Department of National Defence, DHH–Directorate of Heritage and History, LAC–Library and Archives Canada, UVICSC–University of Victoria Special Collections.

BOOKS

Antal, Sandy, and Kevin R. Shackleton. *Duty Nobly Done: The Official History of the Essex and Kent Scottish Regiment.* Windsor, ON: Walkerville, 2006.

Barnard, W.T. *The Queen's Own Rifles of Canada, 1860–1960: One Hundred Years of Canada.* Don Mills, ON: Ontario Publishing Company, 1960.

Bell, T.J. *Into Action with the 12th Field.* Utrecht: J. van Boekhoven, 1945.

Bennett, Ralph. *Ultra in the West: The Normandy Campaign, 1944–45.* New York: Charles Scribner's Sons, 1979.

Bercuson, David. *Battalion of Heroes: The Calgary Highlanders in World War II.* Calgary: Calgary Highlanders Regimental Funds Fdn., 1994.

Bird, Will R. *North Shore (New Brunswick) Regiment.* Fredericton: Brunswick Press, 1963.

———. *No Retreating Footsteps: The Story of the North Nova Scotia Highlanders.* Hantsport, NS: Lancelot Press, 1983.

Blackburn, George. *The Guns of Normandy: A Soldier's Eye View, France 1944.* Toronto: McClelland & Stewart, 1997.

Boss, William. *Up the Glens: Stormont, Dundas and Glengarry Highlanders, 1783–1994,* 2nd ed. Cornwall, ON: Old Book Store, 1995.

Brown, Gordon, and Terry Copp. *Look to Your Front... Regina Rifles: A Regiment at War, 1944–45.* Waterloo, ON: Laurier Centre Military Strategic Disarmament Studies, 2001.

Brown, Kingsley Sr., Kingsley Brown Jr., and Brereton Greenhous. *Semper Paratus: The History of the Royal Hamilton Light Infantry (Wentworth Regiment), 1862–1977.* Hamilton: RHLI Historical Assoc., 1977.

Buchanan, George B. *The March of the Prairie Men: A Story of the South Saskatchewan Regiment.* Weyburn, SK: S. Sask. R. Olderly Room, 1958.

Cassidy, George L. *Warpath: The Story of the Algonquin Regiment, 1939–1945.* Markham, ON: PaperJacks, 1980.

Castonguay, Jacques, and Armand Ross. *Le Régiment de la Chaudière*. Lévis, QC: n.p., 1983.

Cent ans d'histoire d'un régiment canadien-français: les Fusiliers Mont-Royal, 1869–1969. Montreal: Éditions Du Jour, 1971.

Clark, David. *Angels Eight: Normandy Air War Diary*. Bloomington, IN: 1st Books Library, 2003.

Conron, Brandon. *A History of the First Hussars Regiment, 1856–1980*. N.p., 1981.

Copp, Terry. *The Brigade: The Fifth Canadian Infantry Brigade, 1939–1945*. Stoney Creek, ON: Fortress, 1992.

———. *Fields of Fire: The Canadians in Normandy*. Toronto: University of Toronto Press, 2003.

D'Este, Carlo. *Decision in Normandy: The Unwritten Story of Montgomery and the Allied Campaign*. London: Penguin, 1983.

Dickson, Paul Douglas. *A Thoroughly Canadian General: A Biography of General H.D.G. Crerar*. Toronto: University of Toronto Press, 2007.

Duguid, A. Fortescue. *History of the Canadian Grenadier Guards, 1760–1964*. Montreal: Gazette Printing, 1965.

VIII CDN Recce Rgt 14 CH: Battle History of the Regt. Victoria: 8th Cdn Recce Assoc., 1993.

Ellis, L.F. *The Battle of Normandy*. Vol. 1 of *Victory in the West*. London: Her Majesty's Stationery Office, 1962.

English, John A. *Failure in Command: The Canadian Army and the Normandy Campaign*. Ottawa: Golden Dog Press, 1995.

Farran, Roy. *The History of the Calgary Highlanders, 1921–54*. Calgary: Bryant Press, 1954.

1 Battalion, the Essex Scottish Regiment, 1940–1945: A Brief Narrative. Aldershot, UK: Gale and Polden, 1946.

1st Battalion, the Highland Light Infantry of Canada: 1940–1945. Galt, ON: Highland Light Infantry of Canada Assoc., 1951.

Foster, Robert M., et al. *Steady the Buttons Two by Two: Governor General's Foot Guards Regimental History, 125th Anniversary—1872–1997*. Ottawa: Governor General's Foot Guards, 1999.

Fowler, Robert T. *Courage Rewarded: The Valour of Canadian Soldiers Under Fire, 1900 to 2007*. Victoria: Trafford, 2009.

Fraser, Robert L. *Black Yesterdays: The Argyll's War*. Hamilton: Argyll Fdn., 1996.

Freasby, W.R., ed. *Organization and Campaigns*. Vol. 1 of *Official History of the Canadian Medical Services, 1939–1945*. Ottawa: Queen's Printer, 1956.

Goodspeed, D.J. *Battle Royal: A History of the Royal Regiment of Canada, 1862–1962*. Toronto: Royal Regt. of Canada Assoc., 1962.

Graham, Dominick. *The Price of Command: A Biography of General Guy Simonds*. Toronto: Stoddart, 1993.

Granatstein, J.L. *The Generals: The Canadian Army's Senior Commanders in the Second World War*. Toronto: Stoddart, 1993.

Granatstein, J.L., and Desmond Morton. *Bloody Victory: Canadians and the D-Day Campaign, 1944* (Toronto: Lester & Orpen Dennys, 1984).

Graves, Donald. *Century of Service: The History of the South Alberta Light Horse.* Toronto: Robin Brass Studio, 2005.

———. *South Albertas: A Canadian Regiment at War.* Toronto: Robin Brass Studio, 1998.

Harker, Douglas E. *The Dukes: The Story of the Men Who Have Served in Peace and War with the British Columbia Regiment (D.C.O.), 1883–1973.* Vancouver: British Columbia Regt., 1974.

Hartigan, Dan. *A Rising of Courage: Canada's Paratroops in the Liberation of Normandy.* Calgary: Drop Zone, 2000.

Hart, Stephen Ashley. *Montgomery and 'Colossal Cracks': The 21st Army Group in Northwest Europe, 1944–45.* London: Praeger, 2000.

Hastings, Max. *Overlord: D-Day and the Battle for Normandy.* London: Pan Books, 1985.

Hayes, Geoffrey. *The Lincs: A History of the Lincoln and Welland Regiment at War.* Alma, ON: Maple Leaf Route, 1986.

Heintzman, G.T., W.A. Hand, and E.H. Heeney, eds. *History of the Sixth Anti-Tank.* Toronto: 6th Canadian Anti-Tank Regt., Royal Canadian Artillery, 1989.

Henry, C.E. *Regimental History of the 18th Armoured Car Regiment (XII Manitoba Dragoons).* Deventer, NL: Nederlandsche Diepdruk Inrichting, 1945.

Hickey, R.M. *The Scarlet Dawn.* Campbelltown, NB: Tribune, 1949.

History of the 3rd Canadian Anti-Tank Regiment Royal Canadian Artillery: October 1st 1940–May 8th 1945. Canada, 1945.

Hossack, Ken M. *Mike Target.* Ottawa: n.p., 1945.

Hutchison, Paul P. *Canada's Black Watch: The First Hundred Years, 1862–1962.* Montreal: Black Watch (RHR) of Canada, 1962.

Jackson, H.M. *The Argyll and Sutherland Highlanders of Canada (Princess Louise's), 1928–1953.* N.p., 1953.

———. *The Sherbrooke Regiment (12th Armoured Regiment).* N.p., 1958.

Keegan, John. *Six Armies in Normandy: From D-Day to the Liberation of Paris.* London: Pimlico, 2004.

Kembar, Arthur K. *The Six Years of 6 Canadian Field Regiment Royal Canadian Artillery: September 1939–September 1945.* Amsterdam: Town Printing, 1945.

Kerry, A.J., and W.A. McDill. *History of the Corps of Royal Canadian Engineers.* Vol. 2. Ottawa: Military Engineers Assoc. of Canada, 1966.

Kitching, George. *Mud and Green Fields: The Memoirs of Major General George Kitching.* Langley, BC: Battleline Books, 1985.

Luxton, Eric, ed. *1st Battalion, the Regina Rifles Regiment, 1939–1946.* Regina: The Regt., 1946.

Marchand, Gérard. *Le Régiment de Maisonneuve vers la victoire, 1944–1945.* Montreal: Les Presses Libres, 1980.

Margolian, Howard. *Conduct Unbecoming: The Story of the Murder of Canadian Prisoners of War in Normandy.* Toronto: University of Toronto Press, 1998.

Marteinson, John, and Michael R. McNorgan. *The Royal Canadian Armoured Corps: An Illustrated History.* Toronto: Robin Brass Studio, 2000.

Martin, Charles Cromwell. *Battle Diary: From D-Day and Normandy to the Zuider Zee.*
    Toronto: Dundurn, 1994.
McKee, Alexander. *Caen: Anvil of Victory.* London, UK: Souvenir Press, 1964.
McNorgan, Michael R. *The Gallant Hussars: A History of the 1st Hussars Regiment.*
    Aylmer, ON: 1st Hussars Cavalry Fund, 2004.
Mein, Stewart A.G. *Up the Johns! The Story of the Royal Regina Rifles.* North Battleford,
    SK: Turner-Warwick, 1992.
Meyer, Hubert. *The History of 12. SS-Panzerdivision "Hitlerjugend."* Winnipeg:
    J.J. Fedorowicz, 1994.
Meyer, Kurt. *Grenadier: The Story of Waffen SS General Kurt "Panzer" Meyer.*
    Mechanicsburg, PA: Stackpole Books, 2005.
Milner, Marc. *D-Day to Carpiquet: The North Shore Regiment and the Liberation of Europe.*
    Fredericton: Goose Lane Editions, 2007.
Mitcham, Samuel W., Jr. *Panzers in Normandy: General Hans Eberbach and the German
    Defense of France, 1944.* Mechanicsburg, PA: Stackpole Books, 2009.
Munro, Ross. *Gauntlet to Overlord: The Story of the Canadian Army.* Toronto:
    Macmillan, 1944.
Nagórski, Zygmunt, Jr. *Falaise Gap Has Been Closed.* London: C. Tinling, 1944.
Neillands, Robin. *The Battle of Normandy, 1944.* London: Cassell, 2002.
Nicholson, G.W.L. *The Gunners of Canada.* Vol. 2. Toronto: McClelland & Stewart,
    1972.
19 Canadian Field Regiment, RCA: Regimental History, September 1941–July 1945.
    Deventer, NL: Nederlandsche Diepdruk Ihrichting, 1945.
Pavey, Walter G. *An Historical Account of the 7th Canadian Reconnaissance Regiment
    (17th Duke of York's Royal Canadian Hussars).* Gardenvale, QC: Harpell's Press,
    1948.
Portugal, Jean E. *We Were There: The Navy, the Army and the RCAF—A Record for
    Canada.* 7 vols. Shelburne, ON: Battered Silicon Dispatch Box, 1998.
Queen-Hughes, R.W. *Whatever Men Dare: A History of the Queen's Own Cameron
    Highlanders of Canada, 1935–1960.* Winnipeg: Bulman Bros., 1960.
The Regimental History of the Governor General's Foot Guards. Ottawa: Mortimer, 1948.
Reid, Brian A. *No Holding Back: Operation Totalize, Normandy, August 1944.* Toronto:
    Robin Brass Studio, 2005.
Reynolds, Michael. *Steel Inferno: 1 SS Panzer Corps in Normandy.* New York: Dell, 1997.
Rogers, R.L. *History of the Lincoln and Welland Regiment.* Montreal: Industrial Shops for
    the Deaf, 1954.
Ross, Richard M. *The History of the 1st Battalion Cameron Highlanders of Ottawa (MG).*
    N.p., n.d.
Roy, Reginald H. *1944: The Canadians in Normandy.* Toronto: Macmillan, 1984.
———. *Ready for the Fray: The History of the Canadian Scottish Regiment (Princess
    Mary's), 1920 to 1955.* Vancouver: Evergreen Press, 1958.
Smith, Lawrence N. *The History of the 23rd Field Regiment (S.P.) RCA, World War II.*
    St. Catharines, ON: St. Catharines Standard, 1945.
Snowie, J. Allan. *Bloody Buron: The Battle of Buron, Normandy 08 July 1944.* Erin, ON:
    Boston Mills Press, 1984.

Spencer, Robert A. *History of the Fifteenth Canadian Field Regiment, Royal Canadian Artillery: 1941 to 1944.* New York: Elsevier, 1944.

Stacey, Charles P. *The Victory Campaign: The Operations in North-West Europe, 1944–1945.* Vol. 3. Ottawa: Queen's Printer, 1960.

Stanley, George F.G. *In the Face of Danger: The History of the Lake Superior Regiment.* Port Arthur, ON: Lake Superior Scottish Regt., 1960.

Stewart, Neil J. *Steel My Soldier's Heart.* Victoria: Trafford, 2000.

Tascona, Bruce, and Eric Wells. *Little Black Devils: A History of the Royal Winnipeg Rifles.* Winnipeg: Frye, 1983.

Terkel, Louis "Studs." *"The Good War": An Oral History of World War Two.* New York: Pantheon, 1984.

Trew, Simon, and Stephen Badsey. *Battle for Caen.* Phoenix Mill, UK: Sutton, 2004.

Vanguard: The Fort Garry Horse in the Second World War. Doetinchem, NL: Uitgevers-Maatschappij, 'C. Misset, 1945.

Whitaker, W. Denis, Shelagh Whitaker, and Terry Copp. *The Soldiers' Story: Victory at Falaise.* Toronto: Harper Collins, 2000.

Whitsed, Roy. *Canadians: A Battalion at War.* Mississauga, ON: Burlington Books, 1996.

JOURNAL ARTICLES

Bechtold, Mike. "Lost in Normandy: The Odyssey of Worthington Force, 9 August 1944." *Canadian Military History.* Vol. 19, no. 2 (Spring 2010), 5–23.

Bridge, Arthur. "'In the Eye of the Storm': A Recollection of Three Days in the Falaise Gap, 19–21 August 1944." *Canadian Military History.* Vol. 9, no. 3 (Summer 2000), 61–68.

Brown, Gordon. "The Capture of the Abbaye D'Ardenne by the Regina Rifles, 8 July 1944." *Canadian Military History.* Vol. 4, no. 1 (1995), 91–99.

Copp, Terry. "Operation Spring: An Historian's View." *Canadian Military History.* Vol. 12, nos. 1–2 (Winter–Spring 2003), 63–70.

Edmondson, John S., and R.D. Edmondson. "The Pawns of War: A Personal Account of the Attack on Verrières Ridge by the South Saskatchewan Regiment, 20 July 1944." *Canadian Military History.* Vol. 14, no. 4 (Autumn 2005), 49–66.

Grodzinski, John R. "'Kangaroos at War': The History of the 1st Canadian Armoured Personnel Carrier Regiment." *Canadian Military History.* Vol. 4, no. 2 (Autumn 1995), 43–50.

Jarymowycz, Roman Johann. "Canadian Armour in Normandy: Operation 'Totalize' and the Quest for Operational Maneuver." *Canadian Military History.* Vol. 7, no. 2 (Spring 1998), 19–40.

———. "Der Gegenangriff vor Verrières: German Counterattacks during 'Operation Spring,' 25–26 July 1944." *Canadian Military History.* Vol. 2, no. 1 (1993), 74–89.

Maker, John. "The Essex Scottish Regiment in Operation Atlantic: What Went Wrong?" *Canadian Military History.* Vol. 18, no. 1 (Winter 2009), 7–19.

Medland, Stan. "Confrontation in Normandy: The 3rd Canadian Anti-Tank Regiment on D-Day." *Canadian Military History.* Vol. 3, no. 1 (1994), 54–60.

O'Keefe, David R. "'Pushing Their Necks Out': Ultra, the Black Watch and Command Relations, May-sur-Orne, Normandy, 5 August 1944." *Canadian Military History.* Vol. 15, no. 1 (Winter 2006), 33–44.

Patterson, David. "Outside the Box: A New Perspective on Operation Windsor—the Rationale behind the Attack on Carpiquet, 4 July 1944." *Canadian Military History*. Vol. 17, no. 2 (Spring 2008), 66–74.

Sesia, Maj. A.T. "General Simonds Speaks: Canadian Battle Doctrine in Normandy." *Canadian Military History*. Vol. 8, no. 2 (Spring 1999), 69–80.

Simonds, Lt. Gen. G.G., "Operation Spring." *Canadian Military History*. Vol. 1, nos. 1–2 (1992), 65–68.

Smith, A. Britton. "A FOO at Troteval Farm, 20–21 July 1944." *Canadian Military History*. Vol. 14, no. 4 (Autumn 2005), 67–74.

Wilson, David A. "The Canadian Role in Operation 'Charnwood,' 8 July 1944: A Case Study in Tank/Infantry Doctrine and Practice. *Canadian Military History*. Vol. 8, no. 3 (1999), 7–21.

WEBSITES

Army Cadet History. www.armycadethistory.com/Vernon%20photo%20gallery /biography_Brig_Megill.htm (accessed December 7, 2010).

"Biography of Generalleutnant Kurt Chill." *Axis Biographical Research*. www.reocities .com/Pentagon/Bunker/7729/WEHRMACHT/HEER/Generalleutnant/CHILL _ KURT.html (accessed January 25, 2011).

Bomber Command, Campaign Diary, July 1944. July 7, 1944. www.raf.mod.uk/bomber command/Jul44.html (accessed October 5, 2010).

Canadian Army Overseas Honours and Awards Citation Details. DHH, DND. www.cmp-cpm.forces.gc.ca/dhh-dhp/gal/cao-aco/index-eng.asp (various citations and accession dates given in notes).

Copp, Terry. "Reassessing Operation Totalize: Army, Part 27." *Legion Magazine*. September 1, 1999. www.legionmagazine.com/en/?s=Reassessing+Operation+ Totalize (accessed January 5, 2011).

Damage and Civilian Casualties: Battle for Caen. www.servinghistory.com/topics/Battle forCaen::sub::Damage_and_Civilian_Casualties (accessed October 5, 2010).

Honorary Colonel Charley Fox: Canadian Wartime Fighter Pilot. November 11, 2008. www.timesonline.co.uk/tol/comment/obituaries/article5126145.ece (accessed November 17, 2010).

"Major-General George Kitching, CBE, DSO, CD." *The Army Doctrine and Training Bulletin*. www.army.forces.gc.ca/caj/documents/vol_02/iss_3/CAJ_vol2.3_01_ e.pdf (accessed January 11, 2011).

Nash, Doug. "History of the 272nd at Caen." *Der Erste Zug*. www.dererstezug .com/272ndCaen.htm (accessed November 24, 2010).

"Notes on the Diary by Pte. W.T. Booth (D-83056)." *The Black Watch (Royal Highland Regiment of Canada) Regimental Archives*. www3.ns.sympatico.ca/laird.niven /public_html/booth.htm (accessed December 2, 2010).

Permanent Delegation of the Republic of Poland to NATO. First Polish Armored Division. www.brukselanato.polemb.net/index.php?document=78 (accessed January 11, 2011).

The Regina Rifles in WW II. "War Diaries, Intelligence Logs," Jul–Aug 1944. www.reginarifles.ca (all accessed July 15, 2009).

UNPUBLISHED MATERIALS

"Account by Maj. Bennett, 'D' Coy, RHC, of the Attack by the Black Watch on May-sur-Orne, 25 Jul 44, as given to Capt. Engler at Basse, 1 Aug 44." 145.2R15.011(D7), DHH, DND.

"Account by Sgt. Benson, Scout PL, RHC of the Attack by the Black Watch on May-sur-Orne 25 Jul 44. Given to Capt. Engler at Basse, 2 Aug. 44." 145.2R15.011(D6), DHH, DND.

"Account of A Coy Attack on Troteval Farm by Fus MRS on 23 Jul 44 Given to Capt Engler by Maj Dextraze at Caen, 30 Jul 44." 145.2FI011(D5), DHH, DND.

"Account of 'A' Coy RHLI in the Attack on Verrieres 25 Jul 44, Given by Maj Halladay to Capt Engler at Louvigny, 4 Aug 44." 145.2R14.011(D2), DHH, DND.

"Account of the Actions of the Fus MR 19–25 Jul 44 as Given by Lt-Col Gauvreau, OC." 145.2RI011(D2), DHH, DND.

"Account of the Actions of the RHLI in the Battle of Verrieres as Given by Lt.-Col. Rockingham." 145.2R14011(D3), DHH, DND.

"Account of the Actions of the Scout PL RHLI in the Attack and Holding of Verrieres, 25 Jul 44, as Given by Lt Hinton, Scout PL, to Capt Engler at Louvigny, 5 Aug 44." 145.2R14.011(D2), DHH, DND.

"Account of the Attack and Capture of May-Sur Orne by FUS MR, Night of 7/8 Aug 44, Given by Maj. Brochu and Capt. Lamothe to Capt. Engler at Etavaux and May-sur-Orne, 12 Aug 44." 145.2FI011(D4), DHH, DND.

"Account of the Attack and Holding of Verrieres by RHLI on 25 Jul 44, as Told by Capt. J. Williamson, 2IC, 'C' Coy, RHLI, to Capt. Engler, at Louvigny, 5 Aug 44." 145.2R14.011(D2), DHH, DND.

"Account of the Attack by Essex Scottish on Caillouet, 0555, Night 7/8 Aug 44 Given by Maj. Burgess to Capt. Engler at Caillouet, on 10 Aug 44." 145.2E3011(D5), DHH, DND.

"Account of the Attack by s Sask R on the High Ground in the Afternoon of 20 Jul 44 Given by Lt F. Mathers of 'A' Coy, s Sask Regt, at Villeneuve, 23 Jul 44." 145.2S7011(D4), DHH, DND.

"Account of the Attack by s Sask R on the High Ground 0459 in the Afternoon of 20 Jul 44 Given by Maj L.L. Dickin 'D' Coy, s Sask R, at La Villeneuve, 23 Jul 44." 145.2S7011(D5), DHH, DND.

"Account of the Attack by the Calg Highrs on Tilly-La-Campagne Night 31 Jul/1 Aug 44 as told to Capt. Engler by Lt. R. Porter, LO 5 BDE, at Basse, 2 Aug 44." 145.2CI.011(DI), DHH, DND.

"Account of the Attack on La Commaderie 0644 14 Aug 44 by Fus Mr as Given by Maj. White to Capt. Engler at Ussy, 15 Aug 44." 1452FI011(D8), DHH, DND.

"Account of the attack on Louvigny night 18–19 Jul given by Maj T.F. Whitley, R Regt C, as told to Capt Engler at Venoix, 20 Jul 44." 145.2R17011(D4), DHH, DND.

"Account of the Attack on the Church in St. Martin-de-Fontenay by 'D' Coy, FUS MR, 31 Jul/1 Aug as Told by Maj. Dextraze to Capt. Engler at St. Martin-de-Fontenay, 3 Aug 44." 145.2FI.011(D6), DHH, DND.

"An Account of the Battle Experience of 'A' Coy, Algonquin Regiment, August 8 to 11 by Capt. (Now Major) C. Robertson O/C 'A' Coy." 145.2A1013(DI), DHH, DND.

"An Account of the Battle Experience of 'D' Coy, Algonquin Regiment, Aug. 8, 9, 10, 11, 12, 1944 by Major Keith Stirling, O.C. 'D' Coy, Algonquin Regiment." 145.2A1013(D1), DHH, DND.

"An Account of the Battle Participation of the Algonquin Regiment Between August 6 and August 11, 1944, Prepared by Major L.C. Monk." 145.2A1013(D1), DHH, DND.

"Account of the Capture of the Monastery 144358 in Falaise by FUS MRS, Night 17/18 Aug 44, as Given by Maj. Brochu to Capt. Engler Near Dieppe, 4 Sep 44." 1452FI011(D3), DHH, DND.

"Account of the Seizure of Bretteville-sur-Laize 0552 by the Calg Highrs, 8 Aug 44 by Lt.-Col. MacLauchlan to Capt. Engler at Bretteville-sur-Laize, 11 Aug 44." 145.2C1011(D2), DHH, DND.

"Account of the Seizure of the Bridgehead over the River Laize at Claire Tizon 0643, 13 Aug 44, by Calg Highrs as Given by Lt. Col. MacLauchlan to Capt. Engler at Bretteville sur Laize 15 Aug 44." 145.2C1011(D3), DHH, DND.

"Account of the S Sask R in the Attack on Le Chesnaie from Clair Tizon and the Attack on Falaise Given by Capt. N.H. Hadley, 10, S Sask R, to Capt. Engler at Falaise, 19 Aug 44." 145.2S7011(D1), DHH, DND.

"Action by RHC, Fontenay le Marmion–25 Jul 44." 145.2R15.011(D12), DHH, DND.

Algonquin Regiment War Diary, Jul–Aug 1944. RG24, LAC.

"The Algonquins First Battle Inoculation by Lt. Ken Gartley, O.C. 11 Pl. 'B' Coy, Alg. R." 1452A1013(D1), DHH, DND.

Argyll and Sutherland Highlanders War Diary, Jul–Aug 1944. RG24, LAC.

"Attack on Beauvoir and Troteval Farms by FUS MR, 20 Jul 44 As Given by Capt. Maurice Gravel, 10 FUS MR, to Capt. Engler at Etavaux, 28 Jul 44." 145.2FI011(D1), DHH, DND.

Blackburn, George. *The History of the 4th Field Regiment*. N.p., 1944.

Black Watch of Canada War Diary, Jul–Aug 1944. Possession of author.

British Columbia Regiment War Diary, Aug 1944. RG24, LAC.

Calgary Highlanders War Diary, Jul–Aug 1944. RG24, LAC.

Canadian Grenadier Guards War Diary, Jul–Aug 1944. RG24, LAC.

Canadian Scottish Regiment War Diary, Jul–Aug 1944. RG24, LAC.

"Correspondence with J. Walter Keith based on his interviews of Jack Mooney," Possession of the author.

Crerar, Gen. H.D.G. "Reports by Gen H.D.G. Crerar, C.B., D.S.O., on Operations 1st Cdn Army to McNaughton: 7.11 Mar to 5 May 45." RG24, vol. 10636, LAC.

"Crerar Papers." MG30 #157, vol. 7, 985C.001, LAC.

8th Canadian Infantry Brigade War Diary, Jul–Aug 1944. RG24, LAC.

8th Canadian Reconnaissance Regiment (14th Canadian Hussars) War Diary, Jul–Aug 1944. RG24, LAC.

Essex Scottish Regiment War Diary, Jul–Aug 1944. RG24, LAC.

"Extracts Polish Armoured Division History." RG24, vol. 10538, LAC.

"5 Cdn Inf Bde report on use of artificial moonlight by Calgary Highrs-25 Jul 44." RG24, 260C5.009(D8), vol. 10978, box 304, LAC.

5th Field Regiment, RCA War Diary, Jul–Aug 1944. RG24, LAC.

15th Field Regiment, RCA War Diary, Jul–Aug 1944. RG24, LAC.

1st Battalion, the Black Watch (RHR) of Canada War Diary, Mar–May 1944. RG24, LAC.

"1 Bn, Canadian Scottish Regiment, Personal Accounts of Battle Cdn Scottish Jun 44–May 45." 145.2C4009 (DII), DHH, DND.

"First CDN Army Ops to Capture Falaise and to seal gap Trun–Chambois area." RG24, 215CI.0129 (DIO), vol. 10635, box 125, LAC.

1st Hussars Regiment War Diary, Jul–Aug 1944. RG24, LAC.

"1 Polish Armoured Division: Order for the Attack No. 1 on 8 Aug 44." RG24, 245PI.016 (DI), vol. 10942, box 287, LAC.

Fort Garry Horse War Diary, Jul–Aug 1944. RG24, LAC.

14th Field Regiment, RCA War Diary, Jul–Aug 1944. RG24, LAC.

4th Canadian Armoured Brigade War Diary, Jul–Aug 1944. RG24, LAC.

4th Canadian Armoured Division Headquarters, RCA, Aug 1944. RG24, LAC.

"German Report on Operation Totalize (Translation). 112.3MI.009 (DI53), DHH, DND.

Governor General's Foot Guards War Diary, Jul–Aug 1944. RG24, LAC.

Highland Light Infantry War Diary, Jul–Aug 1944. RG24, LAC.

Hutchinson, William Ernest John. "Test of a Corps Commander, Lieutenant General Guy Granville Simonds: Normandy, 1944." Master's thesis. Victoria: University of Victoria, 1982.

"Immediate Report on Op 'Totalize' 7/9 Aug 44 by 2 Cdn Corps (Col. Massy)," RG24, 25C2.013 (DI5), vol. 10800, box 215, LAC.

Lake Superior Regiment (Motor) War Diary, Jul–Aug 1944. RG24, LAC.

Le Régiment de la Chaudière War Diary, Jul–Aug 1944. RG24, LAC.

Les Fusiliers Mont-Royal War Diary, Jul–Aug 1944. RG24, LAC.

"Lessons learned from Ops during War, by Lt-Gen GG Simonds, 1 Jul 44." RG24, 225C2.012 (D8), vol. 10799, box 215, LAC.

Lincoln and Welland Regiment War Diary, Jul–Aug 1944. RG24, LAC.

"Memorandum of Interview with D.81360 Pte. Williams, A.R., RHC, at Canadian Military Headquarters, 4 Jan 46." 145.2R15.011 (DI3), DHH, DND.

"Memorandum of Interview with Lt. J.A.C. Auld, Commd 13 PL, QOR of C by Historical Officer, 22 Jul 44." 145.2Q2011 (DII), DHH, DND.

"Memorandum of Interview with Lt. Col. D.B. Buell, OC and Lt. H.L. Day, IO, N Shore R by Historical Officer, 27 Jul 44." 145.2N3011 (D2), DHH, DND.

"Memorandum of Interview with Lt. Col. F.M. Griffiths at H.Q. C.R.U. on 24 May 46, concerning attack on Buron by H.L.I. of C. on 8 Jul 44." 145.2H2011 (D3), DHH, DND.

"Memorandum of Interview with Lt. Col. G.H. Christiansen, OC, SD&G Highlanders, by Historical Officer, 1 Aug 44." 145.2S8011 (D2), DHH, DND.

"Memorandum of Interview with Lt. Col. R. Rowley OC, SD&G Highrs by Historical Officer, 17 Aug 44." 145.2S8011 (D3), DHH, DND.

"Memorandum of Interview with Lt. Col. T.C. Lewis OC 7 CDN RECCE REGT (17 DYRCH) by Historical Officer, 24 Jul. 44." 141.4A7011 (DI), DHH, DND.

"Memorandum of Interview with Maj. F.A. Sparks, Commd, HQ Coy HLI of C by Historical Offr, 12 Jul 44: Lessons learned in the battle of Buron 8 Jul 44." 145.2H2011 (DI), DHH, DND.

"Memorandum of an Interview with Major W.E. Harris, MP, formerly OC 'B' Squadron

6 Cdn. Armd. Regt., at Historical Section (GS), Department of National Defence, 24 Jan. 46, The Attack on Fontenay-Le-Marmion, 25 Jul 44." Appended document to "Notes on the Movements of R.H.C." 145.2B1(D1), DHH, DND.

"Memorandum of Interview with Maj. S.M. Lett, 21C, QOR of C by Historical Officer, 15 Jul. 44." 145.2Q2011(D3), DHH, DND.

New Brunswick Rangers (MG) War Diary, Aug 1944. RG24, LAC.

9th Canadian Infantry Brigade War Diary, Jul–Aug 1944. RG24, LAC.

19th Field Regiment, RCA War Diary, Jul–Aug 1944. RG24, LAC.

North Nova Scotia Highlanders War Diary, Jul–Aug 1944. RG24, LAC.

North Shore (New Brunswick) Regiment War Diary, Jul–Aug 1944. RG24, LAC.

"Notes on the Movements of R.H.C. at May-sur-Orne, France, 25 Jul 44." 145.2B1(D1), DHH, DND.

O'Keefe, David. "Notes on Kenneth Gault Blackader." Black Watch Regimental Museum and Archives.

"Operation Spring: 25 Jul 1944, The Calgary Highlanders." 112H1.003(D43), DHH, DND.

"Operation Spring: 25 Jul 1944, Factors in Assessing Results." 112H1.003(D43), DHH, DND.

"Operation Spring: 25 Jul 1944, Relative Strengths." 112H1.003(D43), DHH, DND.

"Operation Spring: 25 Jul 1944, The Royal Hamilton Light Infantry." 112H1.003(D43), DHH, DND.

"Operation Spring: 25 Jul 1944, 1st Battalion, The Royal Regiment of Canada." 112H1.003(D43), DHH, DND.

"Operations of First Canadian Army, 7–23 Aug 44." RG24, 215C1.012(D11), vol. 10635, box 125, LAC.

"Operation Totalize: An Account of Ops by 2 CDN ARMD BDE in France 5 to 8 Aug 44." RG24, 275C2.013(D4), vol. 10992, box 313, LAC.

"Operation 'Tractable,' An Account of Ops by 2 CDN ARMD BDE in France 14 to 16 Aug 44." RG24, 275C2.013(D1), vol. 10992, box 313, LAC.

"Operation 'Tractable,' Bombing errors in close support operation of August 14, 1944." 181.0003(D450), DHH, DND.

"Op 'Tallulah,' later changed to 'Tractable,' by Capt. P.A. Mayer." RG24, 215C1.013(D26), vol. 10638, box 126, LAC.

"Outline of Events (A.D, HQ and Sp. Coys) Algonquin Regiment, Aug. 9–12, 1944, Major G.L. Cassidy." 1452A1013(D1), DHH, DND.

"Outline of Events ('C' Coy) Algonquin Regiment, Aug. 8, 9, 10, 1944, by Lt. Robert Saville, O.C. 15 Pl, 'C' Coy, Alg. R." 145.2A1013(D1), DHH, DND.

"Personal Diary of Brig N.E. Rodger, C of S 2 Cdn Corps." RG24, 225C2.011 (D2), vol. 10798, box 214, LAC. Also photocopy in Canadian War Museum, Arch Docs, Manu 58A1114.1. Includes handwritten notes by Rodger entered below August 5, 1944, entry.

"Polish Armoured Division History." DHH, DND.

"Polish Armoured Division in Op 'Totalize,' 7–13 Aug." RG24, 245P1.013(D7), vol. 10942, box 287, LAC.

Queen's Own Cameron Highlanders of Canada War Diary, Jul–Aug 1944. RG24, LAC.

Queen's Own Rifles of Canada War Diary, Jul–Aug 1944. RG24, LAC.

Régiment de Maisonneuve War Diary, Jul–Aug 1944. RG24, LAC.

Regina Rifle Regiment War Diary, Jul–Aug 1944. RG24, LAC.

"Report No. 50, The Campaign in North-West Europe—Information from German Sources, Part II: Invasion and Battle of Normandy (6 Jun–22 Aug 44)." Historical Section (G.S.) Army Headquarters. DHH, DND.

"Report No. 58, Canadian Participation in the Operations in North-West Europe, 1944, Part II: Canadian Operations in July." Historical Section (G.S.) Army Headquarters. DHH, DND.

"Report No. 65, Canadian Participation in the Operations in North-West Europe, 1944, Part III: Canadian Operations, 1–23 August." Historical Section (G.S.) Army Headquarters. DHH, DND.

"Report No. 162, Canadian Participation in the Operations in North-West Europe, 1944, Part II: Canadian Operations in July." Canadian Military Headquarters. DHH, DND.

"Report of the Bombing of Our Own Troops During Operation 'Tractable.'" 181.003(D2972), DHH, DND.

"Report on Ops 3 Cdn Inf Div 1/31 Jul 44: Charnwood Appendix." RG24, 235C3.013(D10), vol. 10908, LAC.

"Report on Ops 3 Cdn Inf Div 1/31 Jul 44: Spring Appendix." RG24, 235C3.013(D10), vol. 10908, LAC.

"Report on Ops 3 Cdn Inf Div 1/31 Jul 44: Windsor Appendix." RG24, 235C3.013(D10), vol. 10908, LAC.

Royal Hamilton Light Infantry War Diary, Jul–Aug 1944. RG24, LAC.

Royal Regiment of Canada War Diary, Jul–Aug 1944. RG24, LAC.

Royal Winnipeg Rifles War Diary, Jul–Aug 1944. RG24, LAC.

2nd Canadian Anti-Tank Regiment War Diary, July–Aug 1944. RG24, LAC.

2nd Canadian Armoured Brigade War Diary, Jul–Aug 1944. RG24, LAC.

"11 Canadian Corps Intelligence Summary No. 15, 25 Jul 44." RG24, 225C2.023(D39), vol. 10812, box 221, LAC.

"2 Cdn Corps, Immediate Report on Op 'Tractable' (Capture of Falaise) 14/16 Aug 44, by Col R. Massy-Westropp, GSO 1 (Liaison) d/22 Aug 44." RG24, vol. 10800, box 215, LAC.

2nd Canadian Infantry Division (General Staff) War Diary, Jul 1944. RG24, LAC.

"Seven miscellaneous messages 1 Polish Armoured Division Aug., Sep. and Dec. 44." RG24, 245P1.045(D1), vol. 10942, box 287.

7th Canadian Infantry Brigade War Diary, Jul–Aug 1944. RG24, LAC.

7th Canadian Reconnaissance Regiment (17th Duke of York's Royal Canadian Hussars) War Diary, Jul–Aug 1944. RG24, LAC.

6th Canadian Infantry Brigade War Diary, Jul–Aug 1944. RG24, LAC.

6th Field Regiment, RCA War Diary, Jul–Aug 1944. RG24, LAC.

Sherbrooke Fusiliers Regiment War Diary, Jul–Aug 1944. RG24, LAC.

"Sketch of Position, Diagrammatic Only." 145.2A1013(D1), DHH, DND.

South Alberta Regiment War Diary, Jul–Aug 1944. RG24, LAC.

South Saskatchewan Regiment War Diary, Jul–Aug 1944. RG24, LAC.

Stormont, Dundas and Glengarry Highlanders War Diary, Jul–Aug 1944. RG24, LAC.

"The Recollections of the Regina Rifles: N.W. Europe World War 2, June 6, 1944– May 8, 1945." Looseleaf folder in possession of author.

10th Canadian Independent Machinegun Company (New Brunswick Rangers) War Diary, Jul–Aug 1944. RG24, LAC.

10th Canadian Infantry Brigade War Diary, Jul–Aug 1944. RG24, LAC.

"3rd Canadian Infantry Report on Operation 'Atlantic.'" RG24, 235C3.013(D14), vol. 10908, LAC.

"3 Cdn Inf Div in Op 'Tractable,' 10–17 Aug 44 by Capt. P.A. Mayer." RG24, 235C3.013(D23), vol. 10909, box 270, LAC.

13th Canadian Field Regiment, RCA War Diary, Jul–Aug 1944. RG24, LAC.

12th Canadian Field Regiment, RCA War Diary, Jul–Aug 1944. RG24, LAC.

"27 CDN ARMD REGT (SHER FUS) CAC, OP 'Atlantic,' Overture to the Breakthrough." Gordon Fonds, MG30-E367, LAC.

"27 CDN ARMD REGT (SHER FUS) CAC: OP 'Charnwood.'" 141.4A27013(D2), DHH, DND.

"War Diaries 2 Cdn Corps, Jul/Dec 44 in details of Op 'Atlantic,' 'Totalize,' 'Tractable,' etc by Brig NE Rodger, C of S, Atlantic." 225C2.008(D9), vol. 10798, box 214, RG24, LAC.

INTERVIEWS AND CORRESPONDENCE

Bailey, Harvey. Interview by Tom Torrie. Victoria, August 19, 1987. UVICSC.

Baird, James Douglas. Interview by William S. Thackray. Victoria, June 17 and 27, July 18, 1980. UVICSC.

Bateman, Merritt Hayes. Interview by Tom Torrie. Victoria, May 28, 1987. UVICSC.

Boehm, Carl Rice. Interview by Chris D. Main. Victoria, May 30 and June 8, 1978. UVICSC.

Buckingham, N.A. Interview by Reginald H. Roy, Ottawa, June 16, 1981. UVICSC.

Butters, Thomas William Lovell. Interview by Tom Torrie. Victoria, August 19, 1987. UVICSC.

Clerkson, Harold. Interview by William S. Thackray. Victoria, August 19, 1980. UVICSC.

Corry, Geoffrey. Interview by Tom Torrie. Victoria, August 12, 1987. UVICSC.

Edmondson, John. Interview by Chris Bell. Victoria, June 6, August 4 and 12, 1982. UVICSC.

Edmondson, John. Interview by Ryan Hill. Victoria, November 3 and 20, 2009. UVICSC.

Goodman, Charles. Interview by author. Saanichton, BC, January 27, 2009.

———. Phone interview by author. January 7, 2011.

Johns, Stuart Louis. Interview by author. Windsor, ON, June 3, 2009.

Kitching, George. Interview by Ken MacLeod. Victoria, March 16 and 18, 1998.

Lorimer, Duncan. Interview by Cameron Falconer. Victoria, March 6, 1983. UVICSC.

Rockingham, John Meredith. Interview by Reginald H. Roy. Qualicum Beach, BC, July 11, 1979. UVICSC.

Ross, Norman H. Interview by William S. Thackray. Victoria, May 27, June 16, and July 4, 1980. UVICSC.

Smith, Hershell. Interview by Reginald H. Roy. Victoria, July 7, 1981. UVICSC.

Tedlie, Alfred James. Interview by Chris D. Main. Victoria, June 28 and July 9, 16, and 23, 1979. UVICSC.

INDEX OF FORMATIONS, UNITS, AND CORPS

New Brunswick Rangers, 321,
324, 398, 404, 424, 467,
476, 487, 489
Toronto Scottish (MG), 139,
151, 262–63, 279, 297

BRITISH

Air Force
2nd Tactical Air Force, 21, 344,
385, 393
Bomber Command, 5, 49–50,
53, 121, 126, 261, 266–67,
344, 355–56
83 Group, 122, 264
84 Group, 122

Army
3rd Army Group (RA), 49
4th Army Group (RA), 49
8th Army Group (RA), 150
21st Army Group, 105, 148,
228, 337, 360, 414
Second Army, 21–23, 50, 98–99,
106–08, 112, 127, 148, 175,
178–79, 226, 228–29, 247,
337–38, 360–61, 388
I Corps, 48, 91, 99, 104, 148,
226, 228, 255, 303, 393
VIII Corps, 22, 122–24, 144,
148, 228–29, 248
XII Corps, 148, 229
XXX Corps, 148, 185, 228–29

DIVISIONS
3rd Infantry, 47–48, 57, 68, 89,
98, 108, 119, 121, 226
6th Airborne, 226, 229, 393
7th Armoured, 148, 179, 204, 216, 224
11th Armoured, 125, 144, 148–49
43rd Infantry (Wessex), 22, 92, 98, 106,
108, 138–39, 149, 154, 180
49th Infantry (West Riding), 148, 226,
229, 393
51st Infantry (Highland), 226, 255, 257,
285–86, 290, 393

53rd Infantry (Welsh), 388
59th Infantry (Staffordshire),
48–49, 57, 68, 75, 89
79th Armoured, 28, 56, 151,
266, 350, 353
Guards Armoured, 144

BRIGADES
33rd Armoured, 148, 257
4th Infantry, 149

BATTALIONS/REGIMENTS/SQUADRONS
1st Royal Tank Regiment, 204
4th County of London Yeomanry, 151
79th Assault Squadron, 262
141st Armoured Regiment, 272
Royal Scots Greys Regiment, 235

OTHER
No. 2 Operational Research Section, 413

FRENCH
2nd Armoured Division, 382

POLISH
1st Polish Armoured Division,
255, 262, 285, 289, 301,
303, 315, 369, 381, 386, 388,
394, 399, 412
3rd Rifle Brigade, 302
10th Armoured Cavalry
Brigade, 285, 301
1st Armoured Regiment, 387, 396
2nd Armoured Regiment,
301–02, 386, 396
8th Infantry Battalion, 386, 396
10th Dragoon Regiment, 382,
387, 396
10th Regiment of Mounted
Infantry, 387
10th Regiment of Motorized
Riflemen, 370, 382
10th Uhlan (Lancers) Regiment, 382
24th Uhlan (Lancers) Regiment, 387
Highland Infantry Battalion, 387, 396

BATTALIONS
2nd ss Panzer, 264
2nd ss Panzer-Grenadier, 152
101st Heavy Panzer, 264

OTHER
Kampfgruppe Krause, 372
Kampfgruppe Waldmüller, 313
Panzer Group Eberbach, 388

ABOUT THE AUTHOR

MARK ZUEHLKE's Canadian Battle Series, of which this is the ninth volume, is the most extensive published account of the combat experiences of Canada's Army in World War II. These best-selling books continue to confirm his reputation as the nation's leading writer of popular military history. In 2006, *Holding Juno: Canada's Heroic Defence of the D-Day Beaches, June 7–12, 1944*, won the City of Victoria's Butler Book Prize. *Breakout from Juno* concludes the story of First Canadian Army during the Normandy Campaign, while *Juno Beach* detailed the Canadian experience on the first day of the invasion.

Besides this series, Zuehlke has written five other historical works, including *For Honour's Sake: The War of 1812 and the Brokering of an Uneasy Peace*, which won the 2007 Canadian Authors Association Lela Common Award for Canadian History. Also a novelist, he is the author of the popular Elias McCann crime series. The first in the series, *Hands Like Clouds*, won the Crime Writers of Canada Arthur Ellis Award for Best First Novel in 2000, and the later *Sweep Lotus* was a finalist for the 2004 Arthur Ellis Award for Best Novel.

Zuehlke lives in Victoria, British Columbia, and is currently at work on his next Canadian Battle book, which turns to the August 1942 Dieppe raid. He can be found on the web at www.zuehlke.ca and Mark Zuehlke's Canadian Battle Series Facebook site.